T4-AKX-877

12.95

Sociology:
A Critical Approach to Power, Conflict, and Change

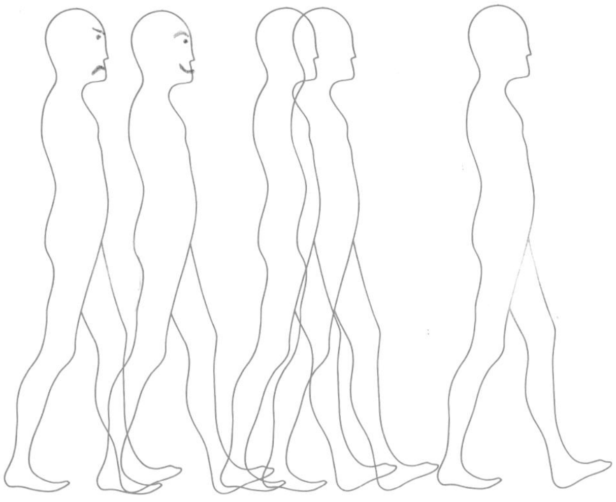

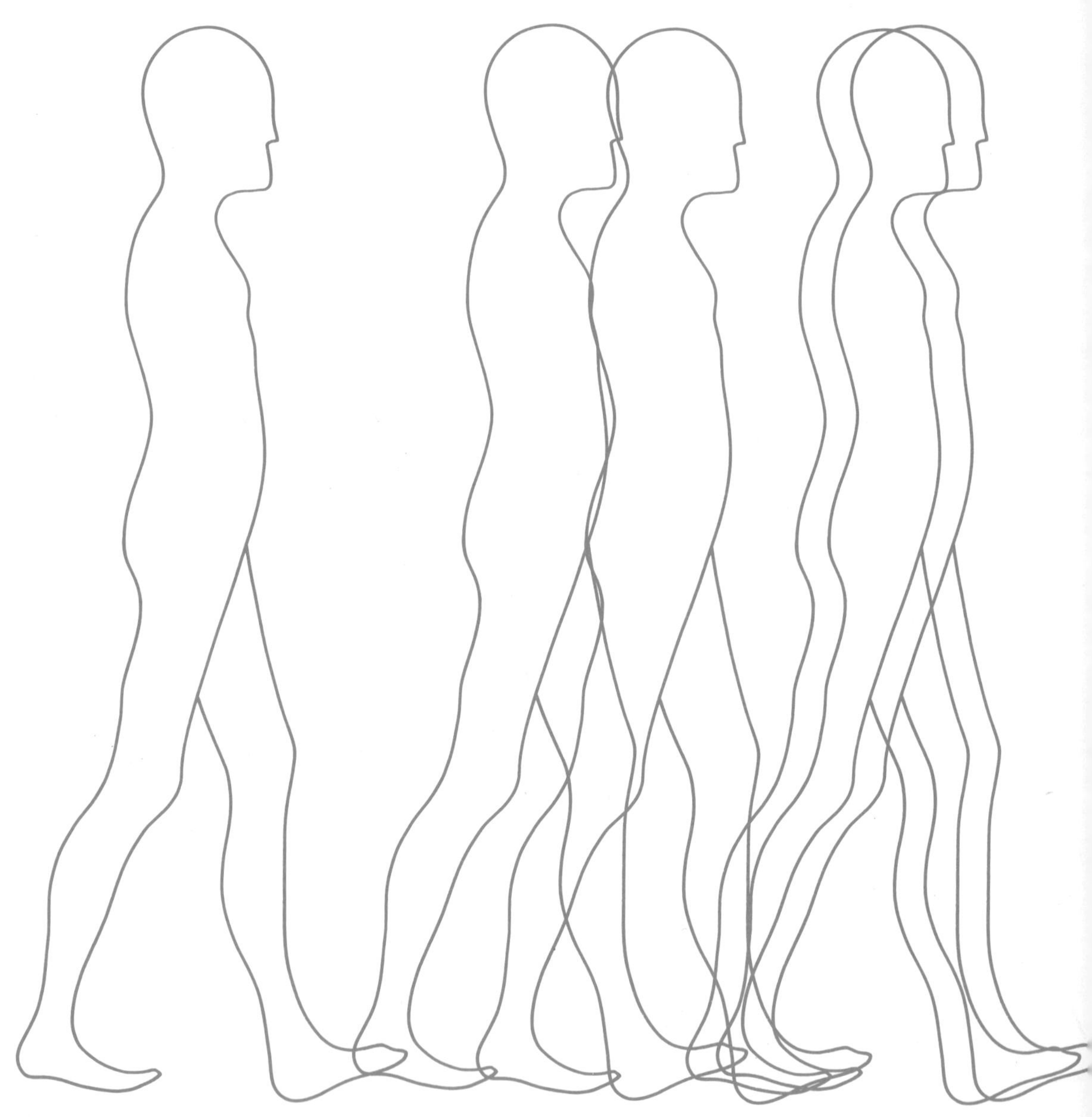

Sociology: A Critical Approach to Power, Conflict, and Change

J. VICTOR BALDRIDGE
STANFORD UNIVERSITY

JOHN WILEY & SONS, INC.
NEW YORK LONDON SYDNEY TORONTO

Copyright © 1975, by John Wiley & Sons, Inc.

All rights reserved. Published simultaneously in Canada.

No part of this book may be reproduced by any means, nor transmitted, nor translated into a machine language without the written permission of the publisher.

Library of Congress Cataloging in Publication Data

Baldridge, J Victor.
Sociology: a critical approach to power, conflict, and change.

Includes bibliographies.
1. Sociology. 2. Social history—20th century.

I. Title.
HM51.B18 301 74-19065
ISBN 0-471-04573-X

Printed in the United States of America

10 9 8 7 6 5

PERMISSIONS

p. 3 Excerpt from *Nature and Types of Social Theory*, by Donald Martindale. Copyright © 1960 by Houghton Mifflin Company.

p. 15 Martin Nicolaus, "Remarks at ASA Convention," *TAS, 4* (2), May 1969, pp. 154–156. Reprinted by permission of the author and the American Sociological Association.

p. 17 Excerpt from *The Coming Crisis of Western Sociology*, by Alvin W. Gouldner, copyright © 1970 by Alvin W. Gouldner. Published by Basic Books Inc., Publishers, New York.

p. 41 American Sociological Association, "Code of Ethics," Preamble, 1971; Gerald Marwell, "Introducing Sociology:The Social Awareness Test," *TAS*, November 1966, pp. 253–254. Reprinted by permission of the authors and the American Sociological Association.

p. 43 Excerpts from "Sociological Snoopers and Journalistic Moralizers," from *Transaction*, Vol. 7, May 1970, by Nicholas Von Hoffman, Irving Horowitz, and Lee Rainwater, pp. 4–9.

p. 74 Excerpts from "Body Ritual Among the Nacirema," by Horace M. Miner, Reproduced by permission of the American Anthropological Association from *American Anthropologist, 58* (3), 1956.

p. 85 Excerpt from the book *For Fear We Shall Perish* by Joseph Pigney. Copyright © 1961 by Joseph Pigney. Published by E. P. Dutton & Co., Inc. and used with their permission.

p. 116 Excerpt from "Feral Children and Autistic Children," by Bruno Bettelheim, from the *American Journal of Sociology*, March 1959. Copyright © 1959 by the University of Chicago. Reprinted by permission.

p. 124 Excerpt from *Social Psychology*, by Roger Brown. Copyright © 1965 by Macmillan Publishing Company, Inc. Reprinted by permission.

p. 130 Excerpt from "Case Study of a non-Conscious Ideology: Training Woman to Know Her Place," by S. L. Bem and D. J. Bem in *Beliefs, Attitudes, and Human Affairs*, 1970, Brooks/Cole Publishing Company.

permissions continued on pg. 490.

TO HOWARD, JEANNE, MIKE, AND JENNIFER,
THE FAMILY WHO BROUGHT ME
TO THIS WORLD AND
NOURISHED ME IN IT

PREFACE

A Critical Sociology. This is a critical sociology text that takes a strong reformist approach to the analysis of contemporary social phenomena. In the past decade, sociology has advanced significantly in its theoretical and methodological sophistication and, along with the rest of society, has been buffeted with change and criticism. Out of that period of trial a new sociology emerged that demands scholarly and scientific excellence, but that is willing and anxious to try its hand with real social issues—issues of power, inequality, racial injustice, social movements, and social conflict. This book is in that new tradition; it is a critical sociology that has its roots firmly planted in the scientific analysis of modern sociology, but it has its conscience firmly rooted in the new yet very traditional concerns of reformism and social concern.

Critical Analysis and Macrosociology The book has a strong interest in *macrosociology,* with most of its emphasis on large-scale social institutions and their role in contemporary society. Power and inequality, conflict and social movements, racial injustice and social policy decisions, political analysis and the economic underpinnings of discrimination—these are some of the book's major thrusts. This does not mean that microsociology is ignored; the text contains major sections on culture, socialization, and the family. However, the overall direction is toward the institutional, conflict, and power dimensions of society that shape and determine the quality of human life.

Social Problems and Social Policy A critical sociology gives special attention to the social problems that are wracking modern society. Of course, most textbooks deal with social problems but, for a critical textbook, issues such as racial discrimination, the lack of social mobility, sex bias, poverty, economic inequities, and educational opportunity are vitally important. This book examines a variety of social issues, especially in the economic, political, and public-policy sectors. Without question, it places more emphasis on sex discrimination than any text presently available in the field and, continuing the concern of most texts, it expresses an interest in racial equality. There is a special chapter on one of the most persistent and important social problems of the last two decades: the quest for educational opportunity.

Advisory Panel A great deal of credit for the content, tone, and direction of the book must be given to an advisory panel of sociologists who spent considerable energy planning, reading, reviewing, and criticizing—mostly criticizing! The panel was selected from many sociological specializations; they represented different kinds of educational institutions, including large private universities, public colleges, community colleges, public universities, and small liberal arts colleges. The panel consisted of:

Pat Allen—Los Angeles Valley College.
Richard Braungart—Syracuse University.
Fred Bunte—Franklin College.
Glen Gaviglio—Solano Community College.
Dan Gilbertson—Johnston College, University of Redlands.
Jim Hanson—West Valley Community College.
Stephen M. Ngin—DeAnza College.
Paige Porter—Stanford University.

These people left varying marks on the pages of this book, even to the extent of reshaping entire conceptual thrusts and content sections. If there are errors, they are mine, of course, but often the strengths should be credited to the others. I especially thank Pat Allen who helped to write the chapter, "Socialization and Family."

A Coordinated Package of Sociological Materials Although a textbook is the backbone of a publisher's offerings, this project was designed from the very beginning as a coordinated package of materials. Teaching styles differ considerably, and it is important to allow maximum flexibility. In addition to this text, the package includes:

ACTION: An Experimental Approach to Sociology. This is an experimental student manual that incorporates simulation games, experience teams, media resources, study aids, and a host of other teaching materials. I believe that it is a truly unusual learning-teaching tool, unique in the sociological field. A panel of about 20 sociologists and educational specialists worked for 3 years designing, testing, and producing this handbook. It deserves serious consideration because it is not the average student manual!

ACTION: Instructor's Manual. An instructor's manual to accompany the student *ACTION* handbook.

Length and Readability The day of the massive textbook that covered everything in the field has passed. Instructors now want a variety of options and seldom wish to be tied down to a huge text. Although this book covers a variety of critical sociological issues, it does not pretend to cover everything. The 13 chapters easily accommodate either a semester or a quarter system, and little effort is necessary to schedule various optional sequences. The accompanying *ACTION* manual provides an assortment of supplementary material to fill out longer periods or to provide options to the text material.

Of course, the very best text is useless if it is not well written and easy for the student to comprehend. From the beginning we worked to produce a book that is lively, that contains interesting material, and that can be readily understood by the average student. The use of color, inserted materials, pictures, and graphics carries out a format that I hope will be attractive and exciting for students. A special Wiley staff depth-edited the manuscript and demanded, at all times, that it be to the point, lively, and readable.

J. Victor Baldridge

ACKNOWLEDGMENTS

Making acknowledgments is a happy task—with the exception that somebody in the long list might be forgotten. Many hands and minds made the task lighter, and genuine concern was shown by a host of people. The project took many years. Ernest Havemann, writer and friend, interested me in the effort and helped me in developing the writing style. Ron St. John, Gary Brahms, and Jack Burton, Wiley editors, helped to give birth to the project and to get it off to a good start.

The advisory panel, listed in the preface, was invaluable; the members reformulated thought, gave suggestions, and constantly prodded me to produce the best material. Many graduate students and friends helped to plan and test the accompanying student manual with its "experiential" approach to teaching sociology. If I mentioned one name, it would invite a whole page of names—so a single vote of thanks must go to all of them!

The number of research assistants who helped is almost beyond remembrance, but several of them made outstanding contributions: Priscilla Gilbertson, Paige Porter, Steve Beaver, and Ken Fulmer, for instance. Often they made the fine difference between sanity and madness for me, and contributed far more than they realized.

As the book finally came to fruition, other helping hands joined in. Carolyn Jenkins devoted untold hours to a superb editing job. Her keen wit is apparent. Tom Gay, Wiley's sociology editor, was a lively critic and a helpful advisor who greatly facilitated the effort in its closing days. Marjorie Graham worked hard at the task of picture editing and significantly enlivened the pages of the book. A great deal of credit must be given to Helen Leamy, Janice Scott, Mary Kugland, Valerie Familant, and Jeanette Wheeler whose splendid secretarial skills, editorial assistance, and friendly help "put it all together." Many anonymous reviewers contributed toward making this a better book and toward helping to interpret sociology to future students. Stan Redferm made a major contribution as the book went into the production phase. Finally, much love and appreciation goes to Pat Miller, who helped in so many ways.

To these and scores of other people who contributed their help, encouragement, and friendship so faithfully, I give a great hearty "thanks!"

J.V.B.

CONTENTS

ONE
A CHANGING SOCIETY AND A CRITICAL SOCIOLOGY

REFLECTIONS ON YEARS PAST

They were wild years, the ones just passed. The nation has almost seemed in some kind of wild fit. It seems like only yesterday that we sat in terrified silence as the minutes of the Cuban missile crisis ticked off relentlessly. We were facing the end, and we knew what death looked like. When we could breathe again the years seemed to crash by us. It was a time when we had few heroes, and the few we had were snuffed out like weak, helpless candles—John Kennedy, Martin Luther King, and Bobby Kennedy all went down. It was the decade when the "civil rights" movement became "black power," when the push for school desegregation charged ahead and then faltered in the busing mess, when the police and the Black Panthers declared open war, when the cities exploded and burned with hate-filled summer riots, when the ghettos smoldered and the suburbs quaked in fear. It was a wild time of war—Vietnam ate at the soul of the nation, the bombs scarred the Asian landscape, a powerful president stepped aside in defeat, and the drive for a democratic South Vietnam turned sour in a one-man election. To many stricken Americans the war was meaningless, or evil or hopeless—or all these things at once. Back home the "beatnik" movement was long dead and the "hippie" movement was moving in, only to be taken over so much by the popular media that its uniqueness was soon lost. The Beatles thrilled the world, but even they fell apart. The campus revolutions swept from Berkeley to Stanford to Kent State and then burned out along with the thrashing death-throes of the New Left. The constant loser, Richard Nixon, became a big winner, twice! China was taken into the United Nations. After a heart-breaking decade the last U. S. combat troops left Vietnam. The Watergate scandal then shook the whole political structure. Oh well, what's left to say? It was a Really Big Show.

SOCIOLOGY: A TOOL FOR UNDERSTANDING THE CHANGING SOCIETY

The opening quotation tells a great deal about the complex society we live in. To understand this dynamic, changing society it is necessary to have some tools, some concepts and theories that can help us make better sense out of social events. This is where sociology comes in, for it is one of the social sciences that studies society and tries to interpret it.

One of the best ways to understand sociology is to look at its subject matter, the issues it covers. Of course, sociologists study many kinds of social events, and it is often difficult to separate sociology from the other social sciences. For example, sociologists study population and urban growth patterns—but so do geographers, demographers, and ecologists; sociologists study small group processes, but so do psychologists and social psychologists; sociologists analyze social institutions such as the family and government and economic systems, but so do political scientists, economists, and anthropologists. In fact, with the enormous overlap among the social sciences, it is difficult to separate the fields of study. Don Martindale makes an interesting analogy between social science and gold mining.

> [*It is often said that*] *the primary differences between the various social sciences lie in their content or subject matter. This is a rather poor way of distinguishing a science which in the nature of the case is more like a mining operation than a set of property claims. Just as a vein of metal may cross property lines, so a problem is no respecter of the niceties of academic departmental distinctions. Precisely for this reason the lines between the social sciences are extraordinarily fluid and at any given time their most exciting developments are likely to occur in the transitional zones. (Martindale, 1960, p. 44)*

Although the lines among the various social sciences are certainly not distinct, there are nevertheless some general differences in what they emphasize. Social behavior may be divided into five general "levels": *physical and biological* aspects of man's life, *individual behavior, group processes, social systems,* and *culture.* Figure 1.1 outlines the various levels, shows how sociologists are concerned with each level, and indicates what other social sciences concentrate on each.

LEVEL I: BIOLOGICAL AND PHYSICAL INFLUENCES ON BEHAVIOR

Human beings are animals and, as such, we all respond to physical stimuli: light, heat, pain, sound, and touch. In the past social scientists largely neglected these physical factors, but lately they have been reevaluating the effects of physical influences on people. Psychologists, for example, are very interested in the human nervous system, the brain, sensory or-

Figure 1.1

Levels of social analysis. Although sociologists study human behavior at all five levels, special emphasis is placed on group processes (Level III) and social systems (Level IV)

Level	Sociologist's Interests at Each Level	Other Social Sciences that Study this Level
I Biological and physical bases of behavior	The biology of race and reproduction, geographical distribution of population	Psychology Ecology
II Individual behavior	The effect of society on individual personality, the influence of the individual on groups and social systems	Psychology Social psychology
III Group processes	Small groups and their influence on individual members and the larger social systems	Social psychology
IV Social systems	Society and social institutions (the family, education, religion, the economy, government)	Anthropology Economics Political science
V Culture	Knowledge, belief systems; values, standards of conduct	Anthropology

gans, and habit patterns, all of which influence people's learning behavior. Sociologists have paid increasing attention to the physical structure of human settlements—to slums, suburbs, traffic patterns, and housing—factors that greatly influence human behavior. And since the early 1970s all the social sciences have been concerned with human ecology. Human ecologists study the interrelationships between man and the physical environment. As pollution of both air and water, urban blight, and overpopulation have gradually wrecked human living space, social scientists have been awakened to the enormous impact that these physical and biological factors have on human social life. Thus several sciences—psychology, sociology, biology, and human ecology—are involved at this level.

LEVEL II: THE INDIVIDUAL

The individual person is the basic building block of society, and all the social sciences are concerned in one way or another with individual behavior. Psychologists, for instance, study a wide range of individual action, including perceptions, motives, learning, and personality. A branch of psychology, social psychology, is largely concerned with individuals in social groups. Sociology, too, includes the study of individuals, both as they influence group behavior and as the group influences them.

LEVEL III: GROUP PROCESSES

People in groups—the family group, the work group, the group that meets to play bridge, run a Parent-Teacher Association, or start a riot—are a special concern of social psychology, but group processes are also a vital part of the field of sociology. Sociologists have devoted considerable study to the processes by which groups are formed and operate and to the influence of the group on its individual members and on the larger institutions of society.

LEVEL IV: SOCIAL SYSTEMS

At the level of social systems the prime concerns are the five major *institutions* of society: *family, religion, education, government,* and the *economy.* Several social sciences have keen interest in these institutions. Economics and political science are primarily involved with the economic and governmental institutions, while sociology has focused on religion, education, and the family as well. Cultural anthropology also deals extensively with these social institutions and with cross-cultural comparisons of them. Other issues included in the social systems level are social processes such as stratification and social classes, social deviance, and race relations. These are all basic to the study of sociology.

LEVEL V: CULTURE

As the sociologist uses the term, "culture" is more than the popular notion of high-brow operas or table manners. Basically culture is a *knowledge system* that includes ideas, values, beliefs, and standards of conduct that regulate the life of a group or society. The social sciences most concerned with the study of culture are cultural anthropology and sociology.

INTERACTION BETWEEN THE VARIOUS LEVELS

Although sociology can hardly claim exclusive rights over any one aspect of human behavior, it is probably more concerned with the *relationships* among the various levels than any other social science. For example, whereas psychologists may study the individual, sociologists try to connect individual behavior with group processes and with behavior in bureaucratic organizations; whereas cultural anthropologists are concerned with cultural symbols, sociologists try to link symbol systems to social situations and institutional patterns in a society; whereas human ecologists study urban growth, sociologists struggle to show

Human culture has invented symbols to capture life. How many symbols can you find in these pictures and what do they mean?

how urban blight and slum development affect the family and political systems. Human behavior does not fall neatly within each of these categories of behavior, and social scientists must constantly show the links between different arenas of social life.

THE HISTORICAL ROOTS OF SOCIOLOGY

One way of defining sociology is to look at some of its *subject matter,* which we just did. But understanding a discipline's *historical background* also reveals much about its current shape. Most of the social sciences—economics, anthropology, political science, and sociology—were founded in the nineteenth and twentieth centuries.

SOCIAL CURRENTS OF THE NINETEENTH CENTURY

The physical sciences had been around for many years, but a unique set of historical circumstances combined to promote the development of the social sciences. Several of these social currents should be mentioned.

Massive Social Change. In the nineteenth century change was occurring more rapidly than at any other time in history. The industrial revolution caused a drastic upheaval in the technological system, while urbanization loosened the traditional roots of the culture. Political upheavals—set in motion by the French and American revolutions of the late eighteenth century—rocked society. In the midst of this change it was only reasonable that people should begin to study their social environment with new urgency.

Exposure to Different Cultures. In the nineteenth century great colonial empires were in full flourish, and the conquering Europeans were constantly amazed by the different social practices in Asia and Africa. Anthropology in particular began to develop at this time, especially under the impetus of the expanding British Empire. Wherever the British Lion went the anthropologists followed behind, exploring the complex social patterns that contrasted so sharply with European ways of life. Faced with the fact that man had developed many different societies, with widely divergent types of religious practices, family structures, and types of communities, scholars began to take a critical look at their own social arrangements.

Secularization. The *sacred* point of view that dominated Western thinking for many centuries held that many phases of human life, such as the divine right of kings to govern and the general makeup of society, were determined by God and were therefore beyond question. The *se-*

cular viewpoint, which was beginning to dominate by the middle of the nineteenth century, removed most of the religious taboos against the study of society.

The Growth of the Physical Sciences. The development of the physical sciences in the nineteenth century gave man a greater understanding of his physical environment and new means of managing it. In a society shaken by rapid change, exposure to alien cultures, and the growth of secular viewpoints, it was inevitable that scholars would apply the same scientific method to social problems.

Social Problems and Social Reform Movements. Social conditions in the nineteenth century were particularly difficult, for the industrial revolution and rapid urbanization had generated appalling conditions. Child labor, sweat shops, labor disputes, terrible housing conditions, and the ravages of centuries of war were all part of the social scene. At this time a number of social reform movements began. The "social gospel" and the Salvation Army were religious movements that worked for social reform; major labor unions and political parties emerged; the political ideology of communism developed.

Rapid social change, the growth of the secular viewpoint, contact with non-Western civilizations, the drive for social reform—these were the social currents that converged in the nineteenth century. Political systems were undermined, family patterns were disrupted, villages gave way to noisy cities, and social problems spread like wildfire. It was one of those breakpoints in history where the order of life was threatened, where the whole fabric of social relationships that had been stable for centuries was called into question. With all this turmoil and confusion it is no wonder that the scientific perspectives that were influencing the physical sciences should be turned to social issues.

TWO TRENDS IN SOCIOLOGY: SCIENTIFIC AND REFORMIST

As sociology grew it developed along two different lines. One trend maintained an aloof, scientific perspective; the other was politically liberal and struggled to change, to reform the society. That tension between scientific social theory and reformist social activism has persisted to the present, and it is important to understand the two perspectives.

There were those who wanted simply to study society, not to change it. With society in turmoil in the nineteenth century it is no wonder that many of the early sociologists were concerned with questions of *social order,* with the conditions of society that might promote stability and reaffirm traditional values. They believed that a scientific discipline should not get involved with social reform movements because they would undermine scientific objectivity. Four men represented the early European sociologists who adopted this point of view: Auguste Comte and Émile Durkheim in France; Herbert Spencer in England; and Max Weber in Germany. The basic concerns of these men led them to develop a "value-free" sociology that was concerned more with scientific investigation than with social reform.

Although most of the early writers in sociology adopted a nonactivist stance, there were some sociologists represented by the German Karl Marx and the American Lester Ward who were interested in social change, social reformism, and social dynamics. Marx was primarily concerned with the plight of the workers in society, social class divisions, and social conflict that emerged from the oppression of the working class in capitalist society. Ward, on the other hand, was directly involved with social reform movements in America and was interested in developing a sociological discipline that would promote social progress. The main theses of the reformists were that since social change is progressive, it should be fostered by deliberate social-reform efforts, and although developing a scientific sociology is important, it is just as important to get involved with social-reform movement.

The two perspectives were very different: on the one hand, neutral scientific investigation was stressed but, on the other, change and active reformism were valued. Sometimes a sociologist would hold both views simultaneously, since it was entirely possible to be *both* scientific and reformist. More often, however, sociologists tended to emphasize one approach more than the other. The tension between scientific sociology and reformist sociology, which began in the nineteenth century, still continues in modern sociology.

MAJOR THEMES IN MODERN SOCIOLOGY

By 1920 sociology had been established as a major social science. Sociology departments had been set up in most of the major universities in the United States, the nation where modern sociology received its greatest impetus. The University of Chicago had started a department in 1893; Brown, Columbia, Dartmouth, Pennsylvania, and Yale had all introduced courses by 1905, at which time the American Sociology Association was formed by a splinter group from the Economic Association. State colleges and universities across the nation gradually adopted sociology courses throughout the first half of the twentieth century, but only since World War II have most colleges had sociology departments. Sociology is presently one of the largest social sciences, and tends to be among the largest undergraduate majors at many schools. Sociologists usually work for universities or colleges, but they are called on more and more often to apply their skills for the government, private industry, and social welfare systems.

The dual emphases on social reformism and scientific, nonreformist sociology has continued to be important in the history of sociology in America. In the early years of the twentieth century the University of Chicago was the preeminent department of sociology in the nation, and its major thrust was the study of social problems and social reformism. The eager students in the Chicago department combed the slums, ghettos, and poverty pockets of the city, studying deviant behavior, poverty, and a wide

Major early sociologists

Auguste Comte (1798–1857) This French philosopher, the "father" of sociology, sought to establish sociology as a combination of history and philosophy. He criticized traditional philosophy on the grounds that it was essentially metaphysical and nonempirical. By contrast, he felt that the new "positive philosophy," which he only later referred to as "sociology," would establish regularities of social events from the study of history. Thus history would provide the raw data from which social theory could be constructed. He tended to believe that all societies move through certain stages in the direction of increasing perfection—his ideas are often classified as an "evolutionary" theory because of the obvious relation to biological evolution.

Karl Marx (1818–1883) As a student, Marx was greatly influenced by the philosophy of Georg Hegel, although he also studied economics in both Paris and Rome. Throughout his life Marx suffered persecution because of his militant atheism and his opposition to capitalism. Like Comte, Marx believed that human society is evolving toward a more perfect state. Unlike Comte, he thought that this process is caused by a complex series of conflicts, which are manifest in the class struggles in a capitalist society such as England. He also believed that the next stage of development would be a classless communist society, a society in which everyone would be equal and where the capitalist economic system would be overthrown.

Major early sociologists (continued)

Émile Durkheim (1855–1917) This French philosopher, son of a rabbi; taught the first university course in social science in France. Durkheim believed that a key element in social behavior is social cohesion, or "solidarity," the force that makes human beings cooperate in a social situation. He distinguished two bases for solidarity: *mechanical,* based on shared norms, values, and beliefs; and *organic,* based on mutual interdependence, or division of labor. He thought that as societies become larger physically, they tend to develop greater division of labor, more specialization, and more complexity. This more complex society has to depend on cooperation among many different specialists in order to operate. This was, of course, precisely what was happening in Europe during the nineteenth century. Durkheim was interpreting these events in light of the sociological thinking of his time while adding some very crucial ideas of his own.

Max Weber (1864–1920) Initially an economist, Weber combined his sociological career with his life as an active liberal German politician. Some feel that he might have been able to deflect Germany from its disastrous foreign policy had he not suffered a nervous breakdown in 1900; he did not recover for many years. Weber was concerned with understanding the social changes in Europe that led to the establishment of modern industrial society. Weber believed that religious attitudes toward work and worldly success could have been fundamental causes of capitalism. In attempting to establish his ideas, Weber conducted a comparative study of world religions. In addition, he analyzed the rise of bureaucracy as an organizational system for getting work done.

Herbert Spencer (1820–1903) Spencer was an English intellectual who lived during one of his nation's most optimistic and tolerant times. He was also imbued with evolutionary ideas, and he combined these with a very conservative point of view. Spencer thought of society as an organism, and thus suggested that the institutions of any society are systematically related and form a functioning whole. Furthermore, he believed that as society progresses, its institutions become more specialized and the overall organization becomes more complex. These ideas were compatible with a conservative political ideology that asserts that people should not self-consciously "tamper" with society in the hope of changing it overnight. Spencer's greatest contribution to sociology probably lies in making society itself and its subunits the relevant objects of analysis and in defining the appropriate interests of sociologists precisely.

Lester Ward (1841–1913) Ward was the first major American sociologist. He essentially synthesized the ideas of Spencer and Comte. He often compared society to a biological organism, just as Spencer and Comte had done, but this analogy led him to different conclusions. Comte and Spencer concluded that society, like an animal, cannot be improved and should be allowed to "evolve" on its own. Ward believed that, like a better hybrid plant, society can be improved. Thus Ward was a liberal social reformist who advocated the use of scientific knowledge to guide the restructuring of society. American sociology was profoundly influenced by these beginnings, and it had strong reform tendencies.

range of social problems. Social reformism and social change were critical concerns that permeated the sociology of the period. In fact, many minister's sons went into sociology because they felt it was one of the best ways to make an impact on society.

During the 1940s and 1950s, however, sociological reformism gradually faded into the background. The rise of statistical methods, the development of survey research, and the widespread use of experiments focused attention on the "scientific" nature of sociology and decreased interest in social reform. In addition, a new set of theoretical concerns came to the forefront under the name of "functionalism." Essentially, functionalism was a perspective that studied the function of various social behaviors in maintaining a stable society and, as such, functionalism was rarely concerned about social change or reform. During that period there were many sociologists still concerned with social problems and reform, but sociologists generally followed the overall trend of the 1950s, a period when the nation was searching for normalcy, not for social change or reform, after World War II.

During the stormy 1960s, however, the nation became involved with the civil rights movement, student revolts, and the controversy over the Vietnam war. Under these social pressures sociologists again began to examine their social-reformist role. Groups of graduate students and young professors formed "radical sociology" movements, and many sociologists joined in the battle for social change. More and more social scientists were drawn into policy-making roles with the government, and individual reform efforts in civil rights, antiwar, and student movements were widespread. On the theoretical front conservative functionalism was being widely challenged, and social-conflict theorists—following Marxist perspectives—again began to assert the need for dynamic, change-oriented theories.

In addition, the tension between "scientific" sociology and "reformist" sociology has been tightly drawn on a political level, for many younger sociologists accuse the more scientifically-oriented sociologists of compromising their social concerns in the service of greater scientific precision or for better consultant fees from the government! In 1968 at the Boston meetings of the American Sociological Association Martin Nicholaus spoke for a radical group called The New University Conference. In that speech he accused the Secretary of Health, Education, and Welfare, Wilbur Cohen, of being a tool of "domestic oppression," and accused the assembled sociologists of being willing dupes who assisted in that oppression. An excerpt from Nicholaus' speech, entitled "Fat-Cat Sociologists," is included in Insert 1.I, along with a brief reply by Alvin Gouldner, a sociologist very much concerned with reforming contemporary sociology.

Even now in the latter half of the 1970s when the heat of the late 1960s has cooled, the debate goes on: reformism versus scientism, conflict theory versus functionalism. To be sure, these two camps are not neatly divided; there are many sociologists who emphasize both

INSERT **1.1**

FAT-CAT SOCIOLOGY

MARTIN NICHOLAUS

At the 1968 meetings of the American Sociological Association the Secretary of Health, Education, and Welfare, Wilbur Cohen, was to address the conference. Martin Nicholaus, representing a radical group called the New University Conference, got up and delivered a stinging rebuke to the Secretary and to the assembled sociologists. The following is an abridged version of his comments.

These remarks are not addressed to the Secretary of Health, Education, and Welfare. This man has agreed voluntarily to serve as a member of a government establishment which is presently fighting a war for survival on two fronts. Imperial wars such as the one against Vietnam are usually two-front wars—one against the foreign subject population, one against the domestic subject population. The Secretary of HEW is a military officer in the domestic front of the war against people. . . .

I do address myself to the Secretary's audience. There is some hope—even though the hour is very late—that among the members and sympathizers of the sociological profession gathered here there will be some whose life is not so sold and compromised as to be out of their own control to change or amend it.

The ruling elite within your profession is in charge of what is called Health, Education, and Welfare. . . . Yet among you are many, including the hard researchers, who do know better or should know better. The department of which the man is head is more accurately described as the agency which watches over the inequitable distribution of preventable disease, over the funding of domestic propaganda and indoctrination, and over the preservation of a cheap and docile reserve labor force to keep everybody else's wages down. He is Secretary of disease, propaganda, and scabbing.

That is to say that this assembly here tonight is a kind of lie. It is not a coming-together of those who study and know—or promote study and knowledge of social reality. It is a conclave of high and low priests, scribes, intellectual valets, and their innocent victims, engaged in the mutual affirmation of a falsehood, in common consecration of a myth.

Sociology is not now and never has been any kind of objective seeking-out of social truth or reality. Historically, the profession is an outgrowth of nineteenth century European traditionalism and conservatism, wedded to twentieth century American corporation liberalism. The eyes of the sociologists, with few but honorable (or honorable but few) exceptions, have been turned downward, and their palms upward. Eyes down, to study the activities of the lower classes of the subject population. . . . The profession has moved beyond the tear-jerking stage today: "social problems" is no longer the preferred term; but the underlying perspective is the same. . . .

Sociologists stand guard in the garrison and report to its masters on the movements of the occupied populace. The more adventurous sociologists don the disguise of the people and go out to mix with the peasants in the "field," returning with books and articles that make it more accessible to manipulation and control. The sociologist as a researcher in the employ of his employers is precisely a kind of spy. . . .

As sociologists you owe your jobs to the union organizers who got beat up, to the voters who got fed up, to the black people who got shot up. Sociology has risen to its present prosperity and eminence on the blood and bones of the poor and oppressed; it owes its prestige in this society to its putative ability to give information and advice to the ruling class of this society about ways and means to keep the people down.

The professional eyes of the sociologist are on the down people, and the professional palm of the sociologist is stretched toward the up people. It is no secret and no original discovery that the major and dominant sectors of sociology today are sold—computers, codes, and questionnaires—to the people who have enough money to afford this ornament, and who see a useful purpose being served by keeping hundreds of intelligent men and women occupied in the pursuit of harmless trivia—and off the streets. . . . The honored sociologist, the big-status sociologist, the jet-set sociologist, the fat-contract sociologist, the book-a-year sociologist, the sociologist who always wears the livery—the suit and tie—of his masters: this is the type of sociologist who sets the tone and the ethic of the profession, and it is this type of sociologist who is nothing more or less than a house-servant in the corporate establishment, a white intellectual Uncle Tom not only for this government and ruling class—which explains to my mind why Soviet sociologists and American sociologists are finding after so many years of isolation that, after all, they have something in common.

Unlike knowledge about trees and stones, knowledge about

people directly affects what we are, what we do, what we may hope for. The corporate rulers of this society would not be spending as much money as they do for knowledge, if knowledge did not confer power. So far, sociologists have been schlepping this knowledge that confers power along a one-way chain, taking knowledge from the people, giving knowledge to the rulers.

It is late; very late; too late to say once again what Robert S. Lynd and C. Wright Mills and hundreds of others have long said: that the profession must reform itself. In view of the forces and the money that stand behind sociology as an exercise in intellectual servility, it is unrealistic to expect the body of the profession to make an about-face.

If the barbed wire goes up around the ASA Convention in a future year, most of its members will still not know why.

SOCIOLOGY AND THE NEW LEFT: A PARADOX

ALVIN GOULDNER

Alvin Gouldner, a sociologist who is very concerned about the direction of modern sociology, basically agrees with Martin Nicholaus's critiques of sociology, but in his book, *The Coming Crisis of Western Sociology* (New York: Equinox Books, 1970), Gouldner argues that sociology may contain the seeds of reform.

There is a deepgoing paradox here, and the young radical himself has already begun to confront it. Some, for example, have noticed that in the past decade or so an Academic Sociology akin to that in the United States has also emerged in the Soviet Union. . . . For clearly the conservative character of American sociology cannot be attributed to its subservience to corporate capitalism if an essentially similar sociology has emerged where, as in the Soviet Union, there is no corporate capitalism.

But this is only one of the paradoxes generated by a blanket critique that views all of sociology as the conservative instrument of a repressive society. For example, many of the most visible leaders of student rebellions throughout the world, from Nanterre to Columbia Universities, have been students of sociology. France's Cohn-Bendit is just one of the most obvious cases in point. Leslie Fiedler has more generally observed that "at the root of any (student) demonstration there is a character who is . . . a student of sociology . . . (and) a Jew . . . (and) an outsider," or who possesses at least two of these characteristics. Without endorsing the validity of all of Mr. Fiedler's designations, I do believe that there is considerable merit in his observation of the prominent role of young sociologists in current student rebellions. Yet, if this is so, how can sociology be an unmitigated expression of political conservatism?

Another version of this paradox was evidenced at the Boston meetings of the American Sociological Association in August 1968. . . . The key dissenting talk was made by a young sociologist, Martin Nicholaus, then from Canada's Simon Fraser University and one of the contributing editors of the New Left journal, *Viet Report*. . . . (His) harsh words were applauded vigorously by the caucus and its sympathizers, hissed by a few of the older ex-radicals, and met by a larger group with shocked, stony forebearance. Now, even those who concur, as I do, in many of Mr. Nicholaus' acerbic judgments, must also acknowledge that their sheer utterance implies a dilemma. It is not so much that he was allowed to speak . . . but, rather, that he wanted to speak. . . . For Nicholaus' very utterances, as well as the vigor and activity of the radical caucus at this same convention, themselves demonstrate that not all sociologists are "intellectual valets" and that not all are "Uncle Toms" of the ruling class.

There is a problem here: How can one account for the very radicalism of those sociologists who accuse sociology of being conservative? . . . The fact that it is often sociologists themselves who criticize sociology for being conservative implies that sociology may produce radicals as well as conservatives. My point then is that sociology may produce, not merely recruit, radicals; that it may generate, not merely tolerate, radicalization. . . . Not all the young socialists of the 1930's who became sociologists also became pillars of the status quo, and neither will all those of the New Left of today. . . . I believe that there are aspects of the character of and outlook intrinsic to Academic Sociology itself that sustain rather than tame the radical impulse. I believe that, in the normal course of working as a sociologist, there are things that happen that may radicalize a man and have a liberating rather than repressive effect upon him. . . . Sociology has a dialectical character and contains both repressive and liberative dimensions. . . .

Just as the sharpest critics of Marxism have usually been Marxists, the keenest critics of sociology today have usually been sociologists and students of sociology. They have commonly been men who regard themselves as sociologists and who have critically evaluated sociology from a sociological perspective. Their prototype, of course, is C. Wright Mills. Thus even the most polemical of their criticisms have an ambiguous implication. At one and the same time, they testify both to the profound flaws and to the continuing value, to the painful predicaments and to the enduring potentialities, of the sociological perspective.

trends, trying to create serious social reform through serious scientific research. In fact, some of the most gifted sociologists are able to be serious social scientists and serious social reformers at the same time. Nevertheless, in spite of many overlaps, the differences in relative emphasis are real and you, a new student of sociology, should be aware of the different trends in the discipline.

MAJOR CONCERNS OF A CRITICAL SOCIOLOGY

An understanding of the tension between reformism and scientific sociology is important for this textbook because it will constantly tend to stress a reformist, critical perspective. But, although social reformism and social conflict are critical themes for this text, the "scientific" side of sociology cannot be ignored. It is entirely possible for a sociologist to be concerned with science and with social problems at the same time; in fact, reformism must be based on the accumulated scientific knowledge that sociology is now able to produce. The goal is to achieve a balance between reformism and science, putting more stress on social reform than a text normally does, but also maintaining serious sociological scholarship. A dynamic synthesis from these two perspectives will hopefully allow the growth of a *critical* sociology.

If this critical synthesis can be achieved it will have some unique concerns, four of which are particularly important: power, conflict, change, and social problems. There are severe inequities in the *distribution of power and wealth* in contemporary society: some people are rich and powerful; others are poor and powerless. Because of these monumental problems of social inequality we are plagued with many *social problems:* poverty, economic stagnation and unemployment, the oppression of minority groups, decaying slums, collapsing family structure, and unresponsive government. Moreover, the maldistribution of power and the spread of social problems is accompanied by massive *social conflict.* To complicate matters, *social change* wracks the society and tears it apart. The world seems to be a wildly turning stage on which the story and actors continually change. The fortunes of political parties shift from one election or one scandal to another; the traditional family values are eroded; the physical shape of cities changes.

We will examine sociology through the prisms of these four issues—power, social problems, conflict, and change. These glasses will help us see every issue more clearly; over and over again we will look at these same problems, first one way, then another. In the process you will understand more about the discipline of modern sociology and about the critical perspective that governs this text. Let us look more closely at these four themes in the next few sections. In effect, the rest of this chapter introduces you to the major thrusts of a critical sociology, while giving you an overview of contemporary society and a preview of issues in the remainder of the book.

POWER AND INEQUALITY

Every theory about modern society must deal with the huge inequalities of wealth and power that exist in most nations. Modern societies are rigidly stratified: people are divided into the poor and the rich, the powerless and the powerful, the victims and the victimizers. Power tends to be concentrated in a few hands, and those that hold the power also gain most of the other benefits in the society—wealth, prestige, health, education, political control. Power is translated into authority systems so that the law and the state help those at the top of the social pyramid to write their advantages into the very structure of the social system. This maldistribution of power and wealth is a major factor in promoting the social conflict and social problems that face us today. The topic of power and inequality will be discussed all through the book, but for a preview let us look at a few examples of how badly power and wealth are distributed (see Gans, 1972, for details).

Income Distribution. The poorest fifth of the population receives only 4 percent of the nation's annual income; the richest fifth gets 45 percent. The gap between the rich and poor is not decreasing.

Wealth Distribution. Income is the money people have coming in, but wealth is the amount that they have accumulated over the years. Here the advantage of privilege is even clearer, for inherited wealth is compounded with normal income. Only 1 percent of the people control about 35 percent of the wealth in the nation! The other 99 percent must divide the leftovers, but the general rule holds: the richer you are, the more you get from the economic system.

Concentration of Business Control. The giant corporations have more and more control over the nation's wealth, and only a handful of companies hold the lion's share. Inequality in corporate holdings is even more unequal than personal income or wealth. Of the 2 million corporations in America, one tenth of 1 percent controls 55 percent of the total corporate assets. At the other end of the spectrum, 94 percent of the corporations together own only 9 percent of the assets.

Unequal Taxes. In theory the tax structure is supposed to tax the rich more heavily, but in practice tax loopholes and highly paid tax lawyers see to it that the rich maintain their advantages. In fact, the poor pay almost 50 percent of their income in direct and hidden taxes, while the rich pay only about 45 percent.

Unequal Subsidies. There is much complaint in the public press that many poor people are living off welfare, soaking up all the honest taxpayers' money and living a lazy life. However, as we will show later, the vast bulk of government subsidies go to support people who are already rich—tax write-offs, subsidies to industry, oil-depletion allowances, and crop supports. When the money goes to the poor it is called the negative term "welfare;" when the money goes to the rich it is called by the perfumed title "subsidy." The effect is the same except for one small detail—the rich get a lot, but the poor get little. In fact, it has been estimated that annual government subsidies come to $720,000 per family for people with million dollar incomes, $650 per family for the $10,000 to 15,000 bracket, and only $16 for a family with an income of less than $3000.

Political Control. These advantages are constantly reinforced by the rich's control of political power. By lobbying, big campaign contributions to conservative legislators, control of the mass media and their grip on the political officeholders, the superrich maintain their advantages and write them into the law.

SOCIAL PROBLEMS

Normally sociology textbooks discuss a wide variety of issues they call "social problems"—urban decay, racial relations, crime and delinquency, divorce rates, problems of the aged, riots and violence. Modern society is certainly plagued by all these dramatic issues, as any glance at the evening news will confirm. Even in this society with its superabundance of material things the social cleavages and conflicts continue to undermine life, making it less humane and less livable.

The important thing to understand is

that social problems do not simply grow up on their own; a set of interconnected factors produce them. Population increases, automobile and factory-produced smog, decaying physical facilities, poor social planning, and racial discrimination are all tied into the fabric of social problems. *However, it is critical to understand that social problems and conflict are most closely linked to the unequal distribution of power and wealth in the society.* The basic problem of inequality is at the root of most social ills.

Social Myths To Explain Problems. Society has invented many myths to explain its social problems, but usually these are rationalizations to keep us from seeing the connections between power and wealth on one side and social problems on the other. The myth says that the poor are lazy; the fact is that the present economic system keeps them that way in spite of everything they try to do. The myth says that black radicalism and "outside agitators" produce race riots; the fact is that racism in the dominant majority breeds the conditions that produce violence (slumlords prefer to blame the rioters rather than look at their own behavior). The myth says "forced busing" is a critical social problem; the fact is that the poor education offered to minorities is a weapon used by the majority to insure their own dominance. The myth said that campus protest was generated by some kind of left-wing conspiracy; the fact is that disillusioned and war-weary youth were crying out against inhumane conditions.

Blaming the Victim. Unfortunately, many people usually identify a social problem with the *victims of society*—the poor, the minorities, the undereducated, the helpless—instead of with the *social forces and conditions that cause the problem.* This tactic has been termed "blaming the victim." Instead of criticizing the economic systems that cause or allow unemployment and poverty, the poor are accused of being lazy. Instead of recognizing white racism, the victim-blaming strategy zeroes in on the malcontent blacks. Instead of attacking miserable school conditions, the slum child is scorned for being inadequately prepared and coming from a "culturally deprived" family. Instead of scrutinizing the scandalously inadequate health services in this nation, the poor who cannot pay the expensive doctor bills for their children are labeled irresponsible.

William Ryan, author of *Blaming the Victim* (1971), tells the story of lead-paint poisoning in New Haven, Connecticut. In New Haven and other cities many small children suffer brain damage and death because they eat lead paint that has peeled off the walls of slum apartments. To use lead paint is illegal; to permit lead paint to be exposed in a residence is illegal; to allow other people to put lead paint into a building you own is illegal, and the law calls for criminal penalties for anyone who uses or allows the use of lead paint. But because lead paint is cheaper and because it had been widely used in older slum houses, landlords continued using the outlawed paint or failed to cover it from previous years' use.

When the problem was publicly recognized, instead of arresting the negligent landlords, the blame was shifted to the poverty-ridden parents. A paint company in New Haven conducted an advertising campaign in which posters warned mothers that it would be their fault if they allowed their children to eat lead paint. Thus, the paint companies shifted the blame from the landlord's illegal action to the mothers—the victims of slumlord neglect. Ryan notes:

The general problem of lead poisoning, then, is more accurately analyzed as the result of a systematic program of lawbreaking by one interest group in the community, with the toleration and encouragement of the public authority charged with enforcing the law. To ignore these continued and repeated law violations, to ignore the fact that the supposed law enforcer actually cooperates in lawbreaking, and then to load a burden of guilt on the mother of the dead or dangerously-ill child is a terrible distortion of reality. . . . But this is how Blaming the Victim works. (Ryan, 1971, p. 23)

The strategy of blaming the victim is widespread in our society. David Tyack, Professor of History at Stanford University, reports that until very recently most libraries in the United States listed information about Negroes under the general heading of "Social Problems." That is, the white majority had defined blacks—victims of discrimination—as a class of social ills and had simply labelled them a "social problem." This is a clear case of Blaming the Victim, for those in power had decided that those who were without power were a problem.

Link Between Power and Social Problems. To repeat the critical point, the distribution of power and wealth in the society is directly linked to what we call "social problems." A "problem" is generally defined by the powerful in such a way that the victims are blamed. It is because of this negative connotation of "social problems" that many sociologists now prefer to focus on the *social conditions that produce problems instead of on the victims of the problem.* This book adopts that strategy. For that reason this book has no special chapters on specific social problems such as urban decay, poverty, and race relations. Instead of looking at urban decay we will look at the power structure that produces that urban decay; instead of looking at minorities as a problem we will look at the attitudes of the white majority that produce racial strife; instead of looking at poverty as a social problem we will examine the economic system that keeps so many people poor. We will look at social problems from the perspective of the victim instead of from the perspective of the establishment, from the bottom up instead of from the top down. The study of social problems, then, will be one of the major thrusts of this book, but it will be a somewhat different perspective than that commonly used.

SOCIAL CONFLICT

Because modern society is plagued by radical inequalities in power and wealth, it is also faced with massive problems of social conflict, conflict that largely results from power inequalities and social problems. There has always been social conflict, of course. Wars, violence, and social upheaval have been a constant factor in mankind's development. It is difficult to say whether there is more or less social conflict in the contemporary society. Certainly the mass media provide instant news about social conflicts: the Vietnam war was the first full-color, flesh-and-blood war to come to the American people in vivid detail with their evening meal; the Senate Watergate hearings brought the political crisis of confidence to a head before the eyes of a watching world.

During the 1960s there was violence in the ghettos and on the campuses, street demonstrations, and a series of political assassinations. During the calmer 1970s more subtle kinds of conflict have continued—between the nation's officials and investigators uncovering scandal, between labor and wage-control boards, between the ecologists and the energy industries. Some social observers are worried that the social cohesion that forms the glue of a stable society is coming unstuck, with resultant instability and disharmony. Such gloomy predictions will probably prove to be false in the long run, but it is nevertheless true that contemporary society is experiencing a great surge of social conflict.

Much of the social conflict in the 1960s focused on five major crusades: (1) the civil rights movements, which included women's liberation, (2) the antiwar movement, (3) the ecology movement, (4) the so-called "war against poverty," and (5) the student revolution, for the campuses took up all the other crusades and made them part of their rebellion. In the 1970s the issues have changed and the conflict has become more subtle, but the strains are still just as real. Of course, it is difficult to be as clear about current issues—hindsight always makes for more accurate sociology—but there seem to be a number of serious conflicts that continue: (1) the ecology movement and its conflict with the industries facing an energy crisis, (2) the women's liberation efforts and civil rights for minorities, (3) the crisis of confidence in the national leaders, (4) the continued struggle over economic conditions and the division of wealth among the rich and poor.

THE BASIC STORY OF MODERN SOCIETY: CHANGE

The three major themes—power, social problems, and conflict—are enormously complicated by the swift pace of social change in modern societies. Alvin Toffler vividly describes what is happening to Western society.

In the three short decades between now and the Twenty-First Century, millions of ordinary, psychologically normal people will face an abrupt collision with the future.

Western society for the past 300 years has been caught up in a fire storm of change. This storm, far from abating, now appears to be gathering force. Change sweeps through the highly industrialized countries with waves of ever accelerating speed and unprecedented impact. It spawns in its wake all sorts of curious social flora—from psychedelic churches and "free universities" to science cities in the Arctic and wife-swap clubs in California.

It breeds odd personalities, too: children who at twelve are no longer childlike; adults who at fifty are children of twelve. There are rich men who playact poverty, computer programmers who turn on with LSD. There are anarchists who, beneath their dirty denim shirts, are outrageous conformists, and conformists who, beneath their button-down collars, are outrageous anarchists. There are married priests and atheist ministers and Jewish Zen Buddhists. We have pop . . . and op . . . and art cinetique. . . . *There are Playboy Clubs and homosexual movie theaters . . . amphetamines and tranquilizers . . . anger, affluence and oblivion. Much oblivion. . . .*

Much that now strikes us as incomprehensible would be far less so if we took a fresh look at the racing rate of change that makes reality seem, sometimes, like a kaleidoscope run wild. For the acceleration of change . . . is a concrete force that reaches deep into our personal lives, compels us to act our new roles, and confronts us with the danger of a new and powerful upsetting psychological disease. This new disease can be called "future shock." . . . Future shock is the dizzying disorientation brought on by the premature arrival of the future. . . .

Now imagine not merely an individual but an entire society, an entire generation . . . suddenly transported into this new world. The result is mass disorientation, future shock on a grand scale.

This is the prospect that man now faces. Change is avalanching upon our heads and most people are grotesquely unprepared to cope with it. (Toffler, Future Shock, *1970, selected from pp. 9–12)*

If change is so much a part of modern society, then we should learn how to study it. That is a tough problem, however, because most people are used to studying how the social system looks at a given moment instead of how it is changing. We are much more accustomed to seeing the snapshot instead of the movie, the still life instead of the moving life. In fact, throughout most of man's history—and to a surprising degree even today—change was viewed with suspicion and distrust. Stability was good, normal, and comfortable; change was abnormal, threatening, and destructive. However, to think about society today is to think about changes, some of which will be mentioned in the next few sections.

THE TECHNOLOGY EXPLOSION

Much of what you use every day—telephones, televisions, cars, electric lights, stereos, refrigerators—have been invented since 1900. In fact, if you took a count of all the inventions in mankind's history, more of them would have been invented in the last two generations than in all the generations of mankind before. Imagine that we took the last 10,000 years of man's existence and compressed them into one hour. The startling conclusion, illustrated in Figure 1.2, is that most of the technological inventions have been made in the last minute. The same rate of technological innovation may be seen in the rapid increase in patents for inventions issued in the United States: in 1790

Social norms are changing rapidly.

there were three inventions patented; in 1835 there were 752; in 1900 there were 24,644; by 1973 the figure was over 65,000. Technology is reshaping our whole social life by its fantastic growth.

THE POPULATION EXPLOSION

There are more people alive at this very second than there have been in all time before 1900, *combined.* Everything about modern social life is influenced by the sheer numbers of people—over 3.5 billion—who are living now and who are reproducing at a staggering rate. The quality of government, the possibility of war, the fear of mass starvation, the hope of modernizing underdeveloped nations, the dream of world cooperation—all of these precious dreams and nightmarish fears hinge precariously on the tick-tock of the population bomb.

The world population increased very slowly throughout the last 500,000 years, but all of a sudden, in the last few years, the population leaped upward at a staggering pace. Think for a moment about the social consequences of this swelling population. Will wars and conflict increase as people fight for living space? Will mass starvation afflict most of the world? Will the rich nations be overthrown by the starving countries? How will the world provide housing, education, food, sanitation, and health services for the teeming masses that will be clamoring for a toehold on this overcrowded planet?

THE KNOWLEDGE EXPLOSION

In addition to the technology explosion and the population explosion, the contemporary world is experiencing a knowledge explosion. Take a few examples.

Ninety percent of all the scientists who ever lived are alive right now.

There are presently more books written in the world each *day* than were written in most *centuries* up until 1600.

There are probably more students in colleges and universities at this moment than there have been in all history up to 1950.

The computer, which has only been in existence for about 30 years, has already revolutionized science.

The United States now spends about $7^1/_2$ percent of its Gross National Product (value all goods and services) on education, a staggering $75 to $80 billion a year.

Government, industry, and universities now spend huge sums of money on "Research and Development," on deliberately planning future change. Once change came accidentally at its own pace; now the society plans for it.

This knowledge explosion feeds the technology explosion, which in turn promotes social change. Francis Bacon once said "Knowledge is Power;" Alvin Toffler speaks more to our age: "Knowledge is Change."

THE URBAN EXPLOSION

Three out of four Americans now live in an urban area. Although this statement may not seem strange to you—after all, you were born into an urban society and probably lived most of your life in or near a city—this is actually the first century in man's long history where over half the population of any nation has lived in cities. Before 1850 no society had a

Figure 1.2
The invention clock: 12,000 years of inventions compressed into one hour

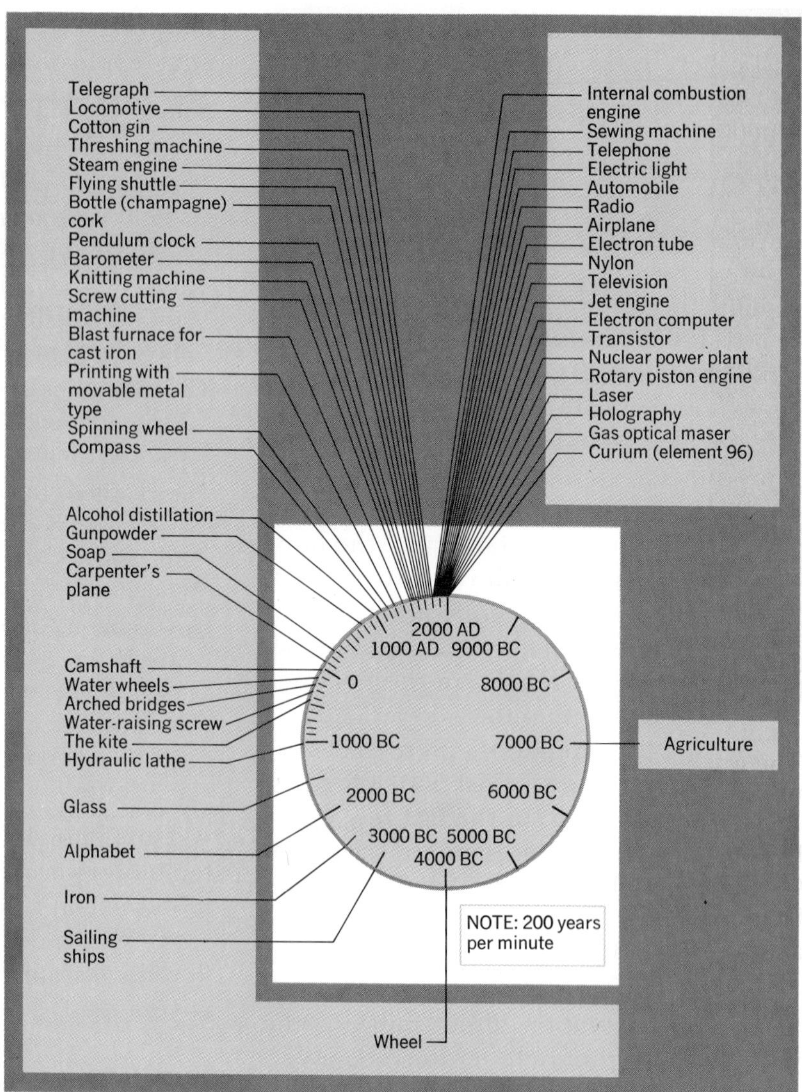

majority of its population living in urban areas, and by 1900 only Great Britain was an urban society. Today, however, almost all industrialized nations are highly urbanized. While nonindustrial societies are still predominately rural, even they are rapidly becoming urban.

Figure 1.3 shows the pace of urbanization in the United States for about the last two centuries. In 1790 only 5.1 percent of the people lived in urban areas; by 1974 the figure was up to about 78 percent. Cities are growing quickly, but the suburban areas around the city are mushrooming even faster. All over the world the growth of cities is much faster than the growth of the general world population. It is estimated that more than 20

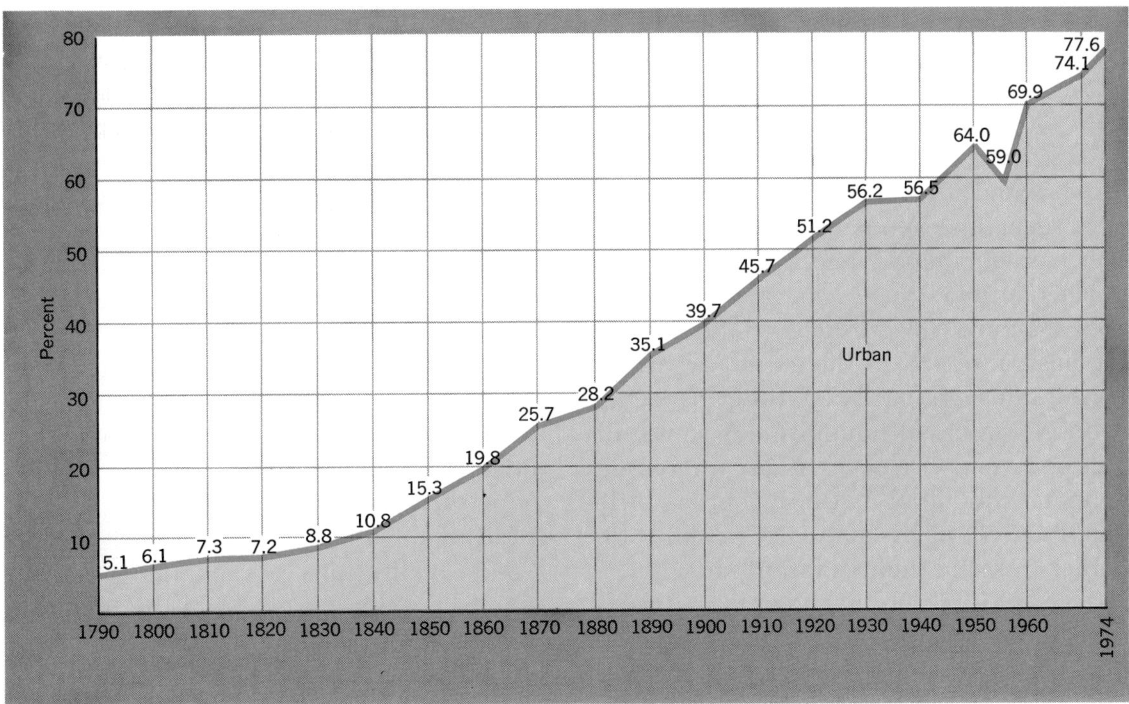

Figure 1.3
The urban explosion: percentage of the U.S. population classified urban 1790–1970

percent of the world's people now live in cities of 100,000 people or more, and the trend is toward increasing urbanization as more countries industrialize.

Urban society is considerably different from the rural society man has known so long. In addition to the obvious physical differences (large concentrations of people, high-rise buildings, tangled highway networks), there are important *social* consequences of urban living. Some of these consequences are negative: poverty, racial segregation, pollution and ecological destruction, crowding, intense social conflict. Other results of urbanization improve the human situation: better economic efficiency, a concentration of manpower and brainpower, expanded opportunities for many people in health care, occupation, recreation, and the arts. In short, urbanization has many important consequences for social life and is a subject to be studied closely by any serious student of modern society.

STRAINED SOCIAL INSTITUTIONS

What difference does all this change make for *social life*—the real point of concern for sociologists? For one thing, our social systems are becoming outmoded, inefficient, and unresponsive. The *government* is a prime example. At the local level most municipalities, towns, and counties were established years ago when transportation was slow, communication difficult, the population small, and problems essentially local. Now that network is falling apart, totally unable to cope with massive regional problems of pollution, population shifts, organized crime, and a withering tax base. At the national level the monster bureaucracies seem unresponsive to the needs of the people, isolated, and hopelessly slow to act. The Watergate scandal of the early 1970s shook the public's confidence in the basic integrity of the nation's leaders. At the international level, the prospect is even gloomier. Although the existence of atomic weapons necessitates increased cooperation among nations, there is little evidence of major countries working together to settle their differences.

The *family* is another social institution that feels the brunt of change. Children rebel against their parents; parents find that their mate choices are not satisfactory under changing situations, and the divorce rate shoots out of sight; aged grandfathers with the wisdom of old age are shuffled out to "senior citizens' homes" instead of receiving the honor and dignity of their position. Young people live together instead of marrying, middle-aged people get married but feel a vacuum of meaningless partnerships, and old people watch their painfully built dreams shattered by social change.

Educational institutions are also changing as the society demands more from them than ever before. Not only must the schools do their traditional job of teaching the three R's—reading, 'riting, and 'rithmetic—but they must also train a labor force for a technological society, instill values, and increase the world's knowledge through research. Moreover, many of the social crises of the past decades—race relations, antiwar sentiment, the ecology and poverty campaigns—have had their roots in the campus, for university students have often been at the vanguard of the nation's basic social changes. The student unrest that swept across the nation in the 1960s was symbolic of the larger society's social ills. Racial problems focused on the schools with a vengeance. School integration, busing, and community control of education are social crises of major significance that have continued on through the 1970s.

As the society changes many of the traditional values and processes of *economic* institutions are challenged. The society is asking more from the business and economic world than merely more goods, cars, and gadgets. The nation is demanding more social responsibility about pollution and ecology, more satisfying work conditions, more human concern, and solutions to unemployment and underemployment. Critics are concerned about the concentration of wealth in the hands of a few giant corporations and the irresponsibility of economic firms that exploit the environment. Some social scientists suggest that traditional work values—work hard, save, and be frugal—are collapsing among the generation of the youth "counterculture." Instead, new work values may be arising that emphasize personal development, work satisfaction, and the creative use of leisure.

THE CAUSES OF SOCIAL CHANGE

Not only must we describe the changes sweeping the society, but we must also explain why society is changing so much. At least five major theories have been offered to explain the origins of social change.

Economic and Technological Impetuses for Change. Change is caused by improvements in technology and shifts in the economic structure. This theory is often called "technological determinism," since it argues that changes in the social system are produced by developments in technology.

Population and Demographic Changes. Major social upheaval is caused by shifts in the amount of population or in its physical distribution within society (such as urbanization).

Social Movements and Revolution. Social change is caused when active subgroups form social movements and try to overthrow the established order. Revolutions, political upheavals, and social reforms have nearly always depended on the deliberate efforts of social movements.

Deliberate Social Planning and Political Modernization. Change is caused when society, acting through its government, decides to manipulate deliberately the processes of social transformation. One critical case is the process of "modernization" by which underdeveloped nations try to build modern industrial systems.

Value Changes. Social change happens when major shifts occur in the values, beliefs, ideologies, and religions that support the culture of a society.

From this list it is obvious that there are many different explanations of change, and no single one has ever completely dominated sociological thought. Unfortunately, theorists have usually seized on one explanation and pushed it to the extreme. Karl Marx, for example, picked the economic theory of change, and other "technological determinists" have followed in his footsteps. Max Weber, on the other hand, believed that "cultural factors" influenced social change more than the "technical factors." Political scientists have usually concentrated on the social change caused by deliberate governmental planning. In most cases, then, a theorist has focused on *one* factor to the exclusion of the others. However, this is a mistake, for social change is usually caused by the interaction of *many* factors, and it is very difficult to assign primacy to any one. For this reason we will discuss all five theories of change at various places in the text.

SUMMARY

Sociologists attempt to understand and to interpret the changing social situation. They study, along with other social scientists, the physical bases of social life, the individual, social groups, social institutions, and culture. The major focus of sociology, however, is on groups and social institutions.

Another way to understand sociology is to examine its historical roots, for knowing the origin of any discipline helps to understand its present shape. Sociology developed in the nineteenth century, a period upset by social change, the rise of secular viewpoints, the discovery of foreign cultures, the growth of social reform movements, and the flowering of the physical sciences. All of these forces helped to promote the growth of the social sciences.

As it developed, sociology seemed to go in two directions. Part of the time sociologists stressed social stability and scientific objectivity. At other times, however, sociologists stressed social reform and practical problem solving, developing theories of conflict that concentrated on the need for social change and reform. That dual focus on "scientific" sociology and "reformist" sociology was present in the early stages, and it continues to this very day. During the 1940s and 1950s the scientific emphasis generally held sway over sociology. However, during the 1960s and 1970s there has been a sharp resurgence of sociology dedicated to social reform, a movement that has not pushed aside the scientific concern, but has paralleled it.

This book stresses the reformist, "critical" perspective, but it tries to balance that concern with serious sociological scholarship. Four master themes are critical for a critical sociology: power and inequality, social problems, social conflict, and social change. The latter half of this chapter has provided an introduction to the major themes of a critical sociology, an overview of some of the main themes in modern society, and a preview of issues that will be explored in the rest of the book.

REFERENCES

Gans, Herbert J. "The New Egalitarianism," *Sociological Research,* May 6, 1972, pp. 43–46.

Gouldner, Alvin. *The Coming Crisis in Western Sociology* (New York: Equinox, 1970).

Martindale, Don. *The Nature and Types of Sociological Theory* (Boston: Houghton Mifflin, 1960).

Ryan, William. *Blaming the Victim* (New York: Pantheon Books, 1971).

Toffler, Alvin. *Future Shock* (New York: Random House, 1970).

TWO
SOCIOLOGY AS A SCIENCE: MYTH AND METHOD

A PARABLE FROM ANCIENT INDIA

There once were several blind men in India who were traveling down a dusty road, led by a kindly old gentleman who still had good eyes. Everywhere the men went the old gentleman would tell them about the wonderful sights and activities that were going on around them, acting as their tour guide and their spare eyes. Here he would explain a temple's beauty; there he would have them feel a statue's face. Sometimes the blind men would cry out with joy, for never before had they experienced so many interesting things.

One day the old man announced that he had a special treat. "On the road ahead," he said, "there is an elephant, one of the most wonderful beasts. You shall have the rare opportunity to feel it." Gleefully the blind men ran forward, and under the old man's guidance they carefully walked up to the huge animal and touched it. After a moment the irritated elephant charged away, leaving the blind men standing in the road. Excited by their new experience, the men outdid each other exclaiming about the wonderful monster they had touched for the first time.

One man, who felt the elephant's leg, cried, "My, the elephant is a marvelous beast, shaped like a tree trunk and steady as a rock."

SOCIOLOGY AND THE SCIENTIFIC METHOD

Several characteristics of the scientific method recommend it as a research procedure. The scientific approach for gathering knowledge is empirical, objective, and theoretical; that is, it seeks concrete data to prove its assertions, it works to minimize biases, and it places its facts into explanatory frameworks. Sociologists and other social scientists use this

"No," exclaimed the second who had grasped the trunk, "an elephant is like a great snake that slowly moves back and forth."

"Impossible," shouted another who had rubbed the beast's ear, "both of you are crazy, for an elephant is like a huge leaf from a tree—broad and thin."

A fourth man, remembering the elephant's tail, chattered about the strange thing, "A twig-shaped animal it was, long and slender."

The fifth man, disgusted at the nonsense he was hearing from the others, explained that "The animal was really like a huge wall." He had touched the elephant's side.

The five men, once good friends, fell into violent arguing over the true nature of the elephant. Finally, in disgust and dismay at the ignorance of the others, the men stalked away in different directions.

MORAL: Everything depends on how you feel the elephant!

Modern society is very much like the elephant in this old parable, for everyone feels and sees social life from a different perspective. In fact, it is extremely difficult to get people even to agree on what is going on, much less on how to interpret the events meaningfully. Because of the difficulty inherent in the study of complex social phenomena, sociology and the other social sciences try to use the scientific method as they "feel the social elephant."

approach, just as do physicists, chemists, and other physical scientists.

However, although sociology uses the scientific method, no science—physical or social—lives up to the ideal of scientific purity. Unfortunately, most scientists give an idealized version of science when they describe their efforts, and they rarely talk about the guesswork, the hunch following, the sheer luck factors in their research. Thus, the following discussion of the scientific nature of sociology will include the shortcomings of scientific enterprises as well as its unique advantages. The task here is not to discredit the scientific method; on the contrary, its shortcomings are presented honestly so you can see the very strong

STANFORD PROJECT ON ACADEMIC GOVERNANCE

STANFORD ACADEMIC GOVERNANCE PROJECT
BACKGROUND INFORMATION

1. Your present academic rank: (Check *one*) (10)
   - Vocational Technical instructor (2-yr. College) ______ 1
   - Academic instructor (2-yr. College) ______ 2
   - Professor ______ 3
   - Associate professor ______ 4
   - Assistant professor ______ 5
   - Instructor ______ 6
   - Lecturer ______ 7
   - My position has no faculty rank ______ 8
2. Administration: (Check *one*) (11)
   - I do not hold any administrative position ______ 1
   - I hold a post in the central administration ______ 2
   - I hold a post in a college or school administration ______ 3
   - I hold a post in a department (chairman, head) ______ 4
   - Other administrative post ______ 5
3. How many years has it been since you received your highest degree? (Check *one*) (12)
   - 1-3 years ______ 1
   - 4-10 years ______ 2
   - 11-20 years ______ 3
   - 21-40 years ______ 4
4. What is your subject-matter area? (Check *one*) (13)
   - Humanities (including history) ______ 1
   - Natural Sciences ______ 2
   - Social Science (including psychology) ______ 3
   - Professional (law, medicine, education, engineering, etc.) ______ 4
   - Vocational education, technical education ______ 5
   - Other ______ 6
5. How long have you been on the staff here? (Check *one*) (14)
   - 1-3 years ______ 1
   - 4-8 years ______ 2
   - 9-15 years ______ 3
   - More than 15 years ______ 4
6. Employment status: (Check *one*) (15)

   In my school there *is* a tenure system, and I am:
   - a) Full-time, tenured ______ 1
   - b) Full-time, nontenured ______ 2
   - c) Part-time ______ 3

   In my school there is *no* tenure system and I am:
   - d) Full-time ______ 4
   - e) Part-time ______ 5
7. Sex: (16)
   - Male ______ 1
   - Female ______ 2
8. What is your age? (17)
   - Under 30 ______ 1
   - 30-40 ______ 2
   - 41-50 ______ 3
   - 51-60 ______ 4
   - Over 60 ______ 5
9. Highest degree earned: (Check *one*) (18)
   - High school diploma ______ 1
   - Associate (or equivalent) ______ 2
   - Bachelors ______ 3
   - Masters ______ 4
   - Professional, other than masters(e.g., M.D., (LLB) ______ 5
   - Ph.D.,Ed.D., or equivalent ______ 6
10. Your identification with the institution as related to employment possibilities elsewhere: (Check *one*): (19)
    - a) My identification with this institution is very *strong*. I probably would not leave except under very unusual circumstances ______ 1
    - b) My identification with this institution is *moderate*. I probably would leave for a better job ______ 2
    - c) My identification with this institution is fairly *weak*. I probably would leave for a better job and perhaps even for a comparable job ______ 3
11. Which of the following statements best characterizes your institutional involvement: (Check *one*): (20)
    - a) My position is one of the most important aspects of my life. It is my prime job and consumes most of my [illegible] time ______ 1
    - b) Although my position is important, it is only one of several important career activities. Other activities, such as practicing a profession or consulting, are of similar importance ______ 2
    - c) My relation to the institution is fairly modest. I have other career activities which are more important, such as finishing a degree, practicing a profession, or working in business ______ 3

LELAND STANFORD UNIVERSITY

THE STANFORD CENTER FOR RESEARCH AND DEVELOPMENT IN TEACHING

STANFORD UNIVERSITY

Source: J. Victor Baldridge, *Questionnaire for the Stanford Project on Academic Governance,* the Stanford Center for Research and Development in Teaching, 1971.

Research methods. "Shooting the bull" on a streetcorner, conducting interviews, submitting questionnaires and analyzing them by computer are all part of the research tradition of sociology.

potentials that outweigh the weaknesses. Before you read further it would be helpful to study Figure 2.1, which previews the topics discussed in the next section.

SCIENTIFIC OBJECTIVITY: MYTH AND REALITY

Scientists are supposedly completely *objective;* that is, impartial, unprejudiced, and able to examine the evidence with an open mind. Although sociologists in their private lives usually have strong opinions, as social scientists they try to put aside their own feelings and look at the evidence as dispassionately as possible, guarding against letting those opinions influence their findings. This does not mean that a sociologist has no feelings, emotions, or prejudices. It only means that he is very self-conscious about them. In short, to be objective is simply to be as fair as possible. Like an umpire sociologists try to "call the facts as they see them," regardless of whose toes are stepped on.

Individual Lapses in Objectivity. The ideal goal of complete objectivity must, however, be balanced against the fact that in real life scientists do have their own pet concerns, their own personal biases, and their own preconceived notions. Surely the choice of a research topic is not a purely objective thing; sociologists study race relations, educational problems, or street gangs because they are concerned about those particular issues. For example, James S. Coleman, a sociologist at the University of Chicago, conducted a huge research project on racial segregation in schools, a study you will read about later in the text. He was passionately concerned that minority children should have equal opportunities for good education and, in dealing with that value question, he was not the cool-headed, objective scientist who never gets involved with his subject. Of course, Professor Coleman tried to keep his biases out of his research, but his feelings and emotions were deeply involved with the topic.

It is important to stress that social scientists themselves are not immune to their own personal concerns. Often scientific objectivity is overshadowed by a desire to please one's financial sponsors, to produce uncontroversial findings, to reflect one's own political persuasions. This is not to imply that social scientists or their sponsors are basically dishonest, or that they do not try to remain as objective as possible. On both accounts most people are trying very hard to do the right thing. The point is that subtle biases, self-interest, and political interests do affect the social sciences. This is the reason the scholarly community tries to be so critical, publishing its findings and subjecting every researcher to the scrutiny of other professional scientists.

The Research Network and Objectivity. *Individual* deviations from the ideal of complete objectivity are important: a scientist's passion to help someone, his desire to prove a pet theoretical point, his attempt to teach political lessons. However, just as important in today's world of large-scale, expensive social science research are breakdowns in objectivity because of the *social network* in which

Figure 2.1
The basic characteristics of science.

social scientists are entangled, a network of financial sponsors, potential users of results, government agencies, and affected interest groups. That is, lapses of objectivity and biases creep into the research as it is being *used,* not while the research was going on. A researcher may be scrupulously objective in doing the research, but to his dismay finds other people in the social network distorting his findings to suit their own interests. This raises a difficult question: Does the scientist have an obligation to insure a responsible, objective use of his findings after they are collected?

TV Violence and Social Research. A classic case of this dilemma occurred in the early 1970s. The Surgeon General of the United States commissioned a panel of social scientists to conduct research to answer this question: "Does violence on television cause children to be more violent?" After two years of work *The New York Times* ran the following headline: TV VIOLENCE HELD UNHARMFUL TO YOUTH. Evidently the social scientists had found that TV violence was not a cause of violence in children, right? Wrong! This was an amazing case where a group of social scientists found their research being completely distorted and misused by policymakers and sponsors.

The facts of the case go like this. First, 40 psychologists, sociologists, and other social scientists carried out 43 separate pieces of research. The results, reported in a series of research papers, suggested that there were some positive links between violence on television and children's actions. In studies of 7500 youngsters ranging from 3 to 19 years of age it was found that (1) over half the children in many of the studies tended to be more violent when they watched TV violence, (2) the children believed the violence was real and did not treat it merely as fantasy, and (3) the long-term relation seemed strong—the more violence they watched the more violently they acted.

The Surgeon General then set up a panel to review the findings and make a summary report. But the television networks, *who were anxious to show that TV violence was acceptable,* were given the right to veto any panel member they might distrust. NBC and ABC vetoed seven members of the panel as "too biased"—meaning they might oppose the television power groups. The panel's 260-page summary report toned down the findings to indicate that there is *not* a clear link between violence on television and violence among children. Moreover, in an 18-page summary of the longer document, almost all doubt was excluded. Violence, the short report claimed, could not be linked to television excesses. Finally, *The New York Times* greatly influenced the media accounts of the research by running an article based only on the shortest report, proclaiming to the world that TV was not involved in the trend to violence in America, even though this statement was in many ways the opposite of the scientists' conclusions.

This series of events is simply amazing. The social scientists said that at least part of their evidence linked TV violence and childhood violence; a stacked advisory panel then toned down the findings; a shorter version went even farther and strongly stated that there was no connection; finally the national press proclaimed to the world the *opposite* of what the scientists had found! This case demonstrates the difficulty of remaining objective in social research, for so many values and prejudices are at stake that the drive for objectivity is sometimes overwhelmed by profit motives, interest group concerns, and power politics. Although each *individual* social scientist surely tried to be objective, a complex web of social politics swept them up into a complicated power play between the scientists and the television industry. The final outcome was anything but a fair, objective piece of social research.

Fortunately, in this instance the scientists themselves raised such a storm of protest that the media revealed some of the behind-the-stage pressures and distortions—although the corrections never received as much coverage as the original distorted reports. It would be interesting to know, however, how many other similar distorted research projects were never revealed by social scientists who kept quiet in order to protect their findings or to help sponsors.

The examples of failures in objectivity given above—both those resulting from individual concerns and those emerging from the social network surrounding research—illustrate the difficulty of achieving unbiased scientific information. This is not to say scientific findings cannot ever be trusted, but only that they have to be carefully evaluated. Most social scientists are honest, scrupulous in their objectivity, and concerned about how policy makers and sponsors use their research. The failures, however, are numerous enough to require constant criticism and evaluation.

SCIENCE IS GUIDED BY A STRICT CODE OF ETHICS

The search for truth is the first goal of the scientist, and over the years a general code of ethics has developed to guide that search. Some of the ethical responsibilities are obvious: scientists must not cheat on their data to prove a point. For example, other, more refined principles have grown up in response to specific sociological problems. The following statements are from the preamble to the *Code of Ethics* of the American Sociological Association.

Sociological inquiry is often disturbing to many persons and groups. Its results may challenge long established beliefs and lead to change in old taboos. In consequence such findings may create demands for the suppression or control of this inquiry or for a dilution of the findings. . . . For these reasons, we affirm the autonomy of sociological inquiry. The sociologist must be responsive, first and foremost, to the truth of his investigation. Sociology must not be an instrument of any person or group who seeks to suppress or misuse knowledge. . . . At the same time this search for social truths must itself operate within constraints. Its limits arise when inquiry infringes on the rights of individuals to be treated as persons, to be considered . . . as ends and not as means. Just as sociologists must not distort or manipulate truth to serve untruthful ends, so too they must not manipulate persons to serve their quest for truth. The study of society, being the study of human beings, imposes the responsibility of respect-

ing the integrity, promoting the dignity, and maintaining the autonomy of these persons.

To achieve these goals the American Sociological Association offers eight principles to guide research.

1. *Objectivity.* Sociologists must maintain scientific objectivity.
2. *Integrity.* Sociologists must recognize their own limitations and must not misrepresent their abilities.
3. *Privacy of subjects.* Sociologists must respect the privacy and dignity of people being studied.
4. *Protection of subjects.* Subjects of research must never be personally harmed.
5. *Preservation of confidentiality.* When requested by the subjects, identities or personal information should not be revealed.
6. *Distortion of findings.* Sociologists must present data and findings fully and without distortion: sponsors must not be allowed to distort findings.
7. *Collaboration must be acknowledged.* People who help with research must be acknowledged.
8. *Research arrangements.* Financial support must be public knowledge, unethical support must be rejected.

One of the most famous controversies about sociological ethics concerned Laud Humphreys' research on homosexual behavior. Posing as a homosexual, Humphreys studied "tearooms" (public restrooms frequented by homosexuals) in order to understand "gay" life. The study touched off a fury of ethical concern. Should disguises be used in research? Should people who are engaging in illegal acts be endangered by sociologists studying them? Should the men involved be given the right to challenge the findings? Is it ethical to misrepresent your role? All these are important ethical questions that have never been satisfactorily resolved. (See Insert 2.I, which discusses this controversial case.) In any event, ethical questions are a part of any social science and are under constant debate.

SCIENTISTS LOOK FOR COMPLEX ANSWERS

Scientific explanations, unlike most commonsense explanations, do not give simple answers to complex questions. Commonsense explanations are often *monocausal;* that is, they give only *one* cause for events. For example, after the 1968 race riots in Detroit many news commentators and government officials said that the riots were caused by high unemployment rates among black teenagers. However, social scientists who studied the same event uncovered literally dozens of interlocked, overlapping causes, including housing shortages, leadership by militants, unemployment, bullying by white policemen, and constant rumors. In short, there were a multitude of causes behind the riots. In fact, almost all explanations that depend on a single cause are at least incomplete if not actually incorrect. Science always looks for complex, *multicausal* answers. They are harder to understand, but they are also much closer to the truth.

Unfortunately social scientists themselves sometimes fall into the trap of monocausal explanations, for they frequently focus on only one cause of complex behavior. Sigmund Freud, for example, overstressed psychological guilt in

INSERT **2.1**

SOCIOLOGICAL ETHICS: THE GREAT TEAROOM DEBATE

Laud Humphreys' famous research on homosexual behavior became the subject of intense ethical debate. In the following material you will find the statement of Nicholas von Hoffman, a columnist for the *Washington Post,* who considered the research unethical, and the defense by Irving Louis Horowitz and Lee Rainwater, two sociologists.

SOCIOLOGICAL SNOOPERS AND . . .
Nicholas von Hoffman

We're so preoccupied with defending our privacy against insurance investigators, dope sleuths, counterespionage men, divorce detectives and credit checkers, that we overlook the social scientists behind the hunting blinds who're also peeping into what we thought were our most private and secret lives . . . . If there was any doubt about there being somebody who wants to know about anything any other human being might be doing it is cancelled out in the latest issue of *Trans-action,* a popular but respected sociological monthly. The lead article, entitled "Impersonal Sex in Public Places," is a resume of a study done about the nature and pattern of homosexual activities in men's rooms. Laud Humphreys, the author, is an Episcopal priest, a duly pee-aich-deed sociologist, holding the rank of assistant professor at Southern Illinois University. . . .

Tearoom is the homosexual slang for men's rooms that are used for purposes other than those for which they were designed. However, if a straight male were to hang around a tearoom he wouldn't see anything out of the ordinary so that if you're going to find out what's happening you must give the impression that you're one of the gang. . . .

Humphreys writes in explaining his methodology, "Fortunately, the very fear or suspicion of tearoom participants produces a mechanism that makes such observation possible; a third man—generally one who obtains voyeuristic pleasure from his duties—serves as a lookout, moving back and forth from door to windows. Such a "watchqueen," as he is labeled in the homosexual jargon coughs when a police car stops nearby or when a stranger approaches. . . . I played that part faithfully while observing hundreds of acts of fellatio."

. . . Of all the men he studied only a dozen were ever told what his real purpose was, yet as a sociologist he had to learn about the backgrounds and vital facts of the other tearoom visitors he'd seen. To do this Humphreys noted their license numbers and by tracing their cars learned their identities. He then allowed time to pass, disguised himself and visited these men under the color of doing a different, more innocuous door-to-door survey. . .

Humphreys said that he did everything possible to make sure the names of the men whose secrets he knew would never get out: "I kept only one copy of the master list of names and that was in a safe deposit box. I did all the transcribing of taped interviews myself and changed all identifying marks and signs. In one instance, I allowed myself to be arrested rather than let the police know what I was doing and the kind of information I had."

Even so, it remains true that he collected information that could be used for blackmail, extortion, and the worst kind of mischief without the knowledge of the people involved. . . . Everybody who goes snooping around and spying on people can be said to have good motives. The people whom Sen. Sam Ervin is fighting, the ones who want to give the police the right to smash down your door without announcing who they are if they think you have pot in your house, believe they are well-motivated. . . .

To this Laud Humphreys replies: "You do walk a really perilous tightrope in regard to ethical matters in studies like this, but, unless someone will walk it, the only source of information will be the police department, and that's dangerous for a society." . . .

Some people may answer that by saying a study on such a topic constitutes deviant sociological behavior, a giving-in to the discipline's sometimes peculiar taste for nosing around oddballs. But . . . Humphreys has evidence and arguments to show that, far from being a rare and nutty aberration, tearoom activity is quite common. . . . He has another study in Mansfield, Ohio . . . saying that police operating with a camera behind a one-way mirror caught 65 men in the course of only two weeks. FBI national crime figures don't have a special category for tearoom arrests, but Humphreys has enough indicative evidence to allow him to say it's a big problem. Even if it weren't, so many parents are worried about their sons being approached by homosexuals that we believe it's a big problem. . . .

Incontestably such information is useful to parents, teenagers themselves, to policemen, legislators and many others, but it was done by invading some people's privacy. . . . No information is valuable enough to obtain by nipping away at personal liberty, and that is true no matter who's doing the gnawing, John Mitchell and the conservatives over at the Justice Department or Laud Humphreys and the liberals over at the Sociology Department.

. . . JOURNALISTIC MORALIZERS
Irving Louis Horowitz and Lee Rainwater

Columnist Nicholas Von Hoffman's quarrel with Laud Humphreys' "Impersonal Sex in Public Places" starkly raises an issue that has grown almost imperceptibly over the last few years, and now threatens to create in the next decade a tame sociology to replace the fairly robust one that developed during the sixties. . . . Somehow, during the 1960's . . . people suddenly began to look to sociologists and social psychologists for explanations of what was going on, of why the society was plagued with so many problems. . . . What sociologists had to say about international relations, or race problems, or deviant behavior, or health care or the crisis of the city became standard parts of the ways Americans explained themselves to themselves.

. . . As the sociological enterprise grew, there also grew up a reaction against it, especially among those who are also in the business of interpreting the society itself. For, as sociologists know . . . any statement, even of "fact," about a society is also a political assertion in that, whatever the motivation of the speaker, his views can have an impact on the political processes of the society. But there are other kinds of occupations that have traditionally had the right to make these kinds of statements. Foremost among them have been journalists, clergymen, politicians and intellectuals generally. When his perspectives and findings began to gain wider currency, the sociologist became willy-nilly a competitor in the effort to establish an interpretation of what we are all about. . . .

"They are there, studying us, taking notes, getting to know us, as indifferent as everybody else to the feeling that to be a complete human involves having an aspect of ourselves that's unknown." Von Hoffman seems to mean this to be a statement about the right to privacy in a legal sense, but it really represents a denial of the ability of people to understand themselves and each other in an existential sense. This denial masks a fear, not that intimate details of our lives will be revealed to *others,* but rather that we may get to know *ourselves* better and have to confront what up to now we did not know about ourselves. . . .

But von Hoffman recognizes that his most appealing charge has to do with privacy, and so he makes much of the fact that Humphreys collected information that could be used for "blackmail, extortion, and the worst kind of mischief without the knowledge of the people involved."

Here his double standard is most glaringly apparent. Journalists routinely, day in, day out, collect information that could be used for "blackmail, extortion, and the worst kind of mischief without the knowledge of the people involved." But von Hoffman knows that the purpose of their work is none of those things, and so long as their information is collected from public sources, I assume he wouldn't attack them. Yet he nowhere compares the things sociologists do with the things his fellow journalists do. Instead, he couples Humphreys' "snooping around," "spying on people" with similarly "well-motivated" invaders of privacy as J. Edgar Hoover and John Mitchell. . . .

The question of the invasion of privacy has several dimensions. We have already noted the public rather than the private nature of park restrooms. It further has to be appreciated that all participants in sexual activities in restrooms run the constant risk that they have among them people who have ulterior purposes. . . . The fact that in this instance there was a scientific rather than a sexual or criminal "ulterior motive" does not necessarily make it more hideous or more subject to criticism, but perhaps less so.

We have called von Hoffman a moralizer, and his moralizing consists precisely in his imputing a moral equivalence to police action, under probably unconstitutional law, and the work of a scholar. Of course the road to hell is paved with good intentions, but good intentions sometimes lead to other places as well. . . .

The only interesting issue raised by von Hoffman is one that he cannot, being a moralizer, do justice to. It is whether the work one does is good, and whether the good it does outweighs the bad. "No information," he writes, "is valuable enough to obtain by nipping away at personal liberty. . . ." It remains to be proven that Humphreys did in fact nip away at anyone's liberty. . . . No amount of self-righteous dogmatizing can still the uneasy and troublesome thought that what we have here is not a conflict between nasty snoopers and the right to privacy, but a conflict between two goods: the right to privacy and the right to know. . . .

Laud Humphreys has gone beyond the existing literature in sexual behavior and has proven once again . . . that ethnographic research is a powerful tool for social understanding and policymaking. And these are the criteria by which the research should finally be evaluated professionally. If the nonprofessional has other measurements of this type of research, let him present these objections in legal brief and do so explicitly. No such attempt to intimidate Humphreys for wrongdoing in any legal sense has been made. . . . The only indictment seems to be among those who are less concerned with the right to know than they are with the sublime desire to remain in ignorance.

Source: Condensed from "Sociological Snoopers and Journalistic Moralizers," *Trans-Action, 7* (7), May 1970, pp. 4–9.

explaining religion; Karl Marx relied too heavily on economic interpretations of human behavior; Max Weber argued too exclusively for religious influence on the growth of modern society. Although all three of these men contributed much to the social sciences, it must be borne in mind that their theories are not complete.

SCIENCE IS THEORETICAL

"Raw empiricism," the gathering of facts without adequate explanatory theories, is not really science. In order to be truly scientific, researchers must go beyond the gathering of raw facts and must integrate those findings into a coherent *theory* that explains the observed behavior. A theory is a statement of general principles that provides a logical explanation for events observed in the past and that, if accurate, will be borne out by events of the future.

Although there are very few well-developed theories in the social sciences, the facts collected by various people are gradually being combined into meaningful theories. For example, there is now a fairly well-developed theory of riots and mass movements (the theory of collective behavior), of stresses experienced by a person who finds himself in two social classes at once (status inconsistency theory), and of interpersonal relations between people of different social rank (status interaction disability).

It is important to stress the theoretical nature of science because the general public often thinks that it is enough to "get the facts, and let them speak for themselves." But, just getting the facts rarely answers the important questions, for the facts rarely speak for themselves; they must be interpreted, clarified, and integrated into a theory that ties together otherwise unconnected events before they have meaning. Theory building is at least as important as field research and data gathering, for the two aspects of science work together.

SCIENCE IS EMPIRICAL

Up to this point the discussion has listed several of the basic characteristics of the scientific method: objectivity, ethics, multicausal explanations, and theoretical frameworks. In addition, the last characteristic of science has proved to be its special strength: *empirical research methods.* Scientists have developed very elaborate research techniques—for example, experiments, surveys, and observation techniques—to assemble data. Scientists are not content simply to argue their positions logically; they must be able to prove their ideas and theories in the real world where evidence can be marshalled for or against them. While philosophy, religion, common sense, poetic vision, and other explanations of human behavior are willing to stop with logic and insight, science must gather empirical information to test its assertions. Whenever possible social scientists state their theories in the form of *hypotheses,* statements that can be tested against empirical events and proven right or wrong with the data. The empirical aspect of science is so important that the entire next section is devoted to explaining it.

RESEARCH METHODS

INTERVIEWER: Well, Professor Johnson, I see you have finished your research project. How did you compile that data about job patterns of male high-school graduates?

PROFESSOR JOHNSON: After I received a $200,000 grant from the Office of Education, I hired four research assistants and two consultants. Working together we constructed a 15-page questionnaire that was sent to a random sample of all the males in the United States. After receiving 52 percent of the questionnaires back, we used a computer to run statistical tests. By analyzing those printouts we arrived at our conclusions.

INTERVIEWER: My, that's very interesting. Oh, I see your friend Professor Thompson. Professor Thompson, you just finished a study of juvenile gangs. How did you go about your research?

PROFESSOR THOMPSON: I'm not exactly sure how to describe it. I played a lot of pool down at Tommy's Joint and ate lots of greasy hamburgers with the Cut-Throat Gang. Besides, I learned how to shoot craps and curse in Italian and steal from the A&P and not get caught. Oh yes, I'm one of the best guys around on that tough Norton 650 cc motorcycle. Of course, I had to do a lot of careful thinking about the facts I gathered this way. I tried to integrate all the bits and pieces I learned into a meaningful theory of group behavior.

Which of these two sociologists was using scientific methodology in his research? Was it the computerized wizard with thousands of questionnaires, or was it the greasy hamburger eater? The answer is simple: both. Both were using legitimate sociological methods to learn about human behavior. How does sociology go about its research? What is the methodology of sociological investigation? By the end of the chapter you will be able to see what the computerized wizard and the greasy hamburger eater had in common.

SOCIAL FACTS ARE NOT OBVIOUS

Before discussing what these two research methods have in common, perhaps we should examine why research is necessary. After all, one of the constant charges against sociology is that it spends a lot of time and money finding out what everybody already knows. In fact, one man once commented that a sociologist is someone who spends $35,000 studying the social patterns in the local whorehouse—social patterns that most of the men in the community already knew quite well. Another wit suggested the following joke against sociologists. "What does a sociologist have in common with Christopher Columbus?" Answer: "When he sets out he doesn't know where he's going; when he gets there he doesn't know where he is; and he does it all at the government's expense."

Nevertheless, the facts discovered by sociologists are not really as obvious as most people think. Of course, they are obvious *after* research has been done, but they really are not so simple *before* the facts are in. Stop reading for a moment to take the test in Insert 2.II (the answers are given on the following page) and to look at the proverbs listed in Insert 2.III. Do not read any further until you have had a chance to look at those inserts.

How well did you do on the test? Most of the answers are obvious when you think about it, but the vast majority of beginning students and the general public miss most of them. And if proverbs are such obvious social facts, why are there so many contradictions? Let us take one more example. During World War II an extensive program of social research was conducted to enhance the effectiveness of the armed forces by discovering ways to keep morale high (Stauffer et al., 1949). Some of the findings were:

1. Southern soldiers are better able to adjust to the hot South Pacific climate than Northerners.
2. White enlisted men are more eager to become noncommissioned officers than blacks.
3. Combat soldiers about ready to be "rotated" home on furlough are more relaxed and happier than those who have just begun a tour of duty.
4. Black soldiers stationed in the United States will be happier in the North than in the South.
5. Better educated soldiers show more psychologically disturbed behavior than less educated men, who tend to be more stable and dependable.
6. Men raised on farms adjust better to the army because they are familiar with many of the hardships that must be endured.
7. Soldiers will be satisfied with the promotion system to the extent that there is a high opportunity for promotion based on individual merit.

Now, none of these results are particularly startling. Why did the government spend a great deal of money to reach these conclusions that common sense would tell you anyway? Well, the answer is rather interesting—the real results were the *exact opposite* of the findings listed above. In order to increase morale on these issues the policies had to contradict common sense. Over and over social science evidence contradicts "Brother Sociology"—social facts that everybody and his brother knows, but that are simply wrong! In short, there really are no obvious answers to most complex social problems, and it takes painstaking, expensive research to discover reasonable scientific answers.

Understanding that research process is the goal of this section, first, we will look at several different kinds of *data-gathering techniques*—interviews, questionnaires, documents, and observation. Next, we will discuss three particularly important *research designs*—surveys, experiments, and case studies. Finally, we will put the various methods together in an idealized *research cycle* that combines the various methods.

INSERT **2.II**

A SELF-TEST OF HOW ACCURATELY THE STUDENT HAS OBSERVED HIS SOCIETY

These true-false questions are on a number of social topics prominent in American society today. None of them is a trick question. After you have taken the test, score yourself according to the answers at the top of p. 52.

	True	False
1. Because of discrimination and deprived living conditions, there are proportionately more suicides among blacks than among whites.	☐	☐
2. Of women divorced from their husbands, more than two-thirds marry again within five years.	☐	☐
3. One of the major reasons the United States has not had revolutions is that the proportion of Americans who rise from the lower social class to the upper classes has been increasing steadily.	☐	☐
4. Because of the increasing complexity of modern life, the amount of psychosis (severe mental disturbance) has been rising.	☐	☐
5. More than half of all known drug addicts are blacks.	☐	☐
6. Even if all drug addicts could be cured, this would probably cause no significant drop in the number of serious crimes.	☐	☐
7. By and large, juvenile delinquents commit the same kinds of crimes as adult criminals.	☐	☐
8. Crime rates have been increasing faster in rural areas than in cities.	☐	☐
9. On the average, Southerners drink less than people in the midwest or the northeast.	☐	☐
10. The American Communist Party has more than 100,000 members, but only a minority supports the platform of violent overthrow of the government.	☐	☐

ANSWERS TO QUESTIONS IN INSERT 2.II

The following answers to the Self-Test are correct according to the best available evidence. The numbers in parentheses show the percentages of students who gave the *correct* answer when the test was tried on a group that had never taken a college sociology course.

1. F (90%)	4. F (15%)	7. F (27%)	9. T (25%)
2. T (86%)	5. T (17%)	8. T (23%)	10. F (26%)
3. F (26%)	6. T (35%)		

Note that only two questions (number 1 and 2) were answered correctly by a majority. On the other eight questions the correct answers ranged from a high of only 35 percent all the way down to a low of 15 percent. Social facts are not nearly as obvious as they seem.

Source: Gerald Marwell, "Introducing Sociology: The Social Awareness Test," *American Sociologist. I* (1) , November 1966, pp. 253–254.

INSERT **2.III**

DOES COMMON SENSE EXPLAIN SOCIAL BEHAVIOR? IF SO, WHY DO COMMON SENSE PROVERBS DISAGREE?

People often claim that social facts are obvious. "Why, even simple proverbs explain social facts, don't they?" But common sense usually has very contradictory explanations—just like these proverbs. And it is not at all obvious which ones really contain the most truth.

1. Honesty is the best policy.	1. Never give a sucker an even break.
2. Absence makes the heart grow fonder.	2. Out of sight, out of mind.
3. It's never too late to learn.	3. You can't teach an old dog new tricks.

4. There's no place like home.	4. The grass is always greener on the other side of the fence.
5. Birds of a feather flock together.	5. Opposites attract.
6. Work today for the night is coming.	6. Eat, drink, and be merry for tomorrow you may die.
7. Two heads are better than one.	7. If you want a thing done well, do it yourself.
8. A penny saved is a penny earned.	8. Easy come, easy go.
9. Look before you leap.	9. He who hesitates is lost.
10. Without wisdom, wealth is worthless.	10. Ignorance is bliss.
11. Haste makes waste.	11. Strike while the iron is hot.
12. It matters not whether you win or lose, but how you play the game.	12. In all games, it is good to leave off a winner.

DATA-GATHERING TECHNIQUES

There are four major data gathering techniques used by sociologists.

INTERVIEWS

In an interview the researcher asks a series of questions in a direct face-to-face meeting. This is a very important way to find something out—as one of my professors once said, "If you want to know how a man thinks, what he feels, or what he wants, the best thing to do is ask him." The interview is a prime tool of sociologists, and they use it with great care, often spending more time designing the interview than giving it. To ask the right questions and to know how to approach a topic, researchers must try to take the perspective of the person being interviewed, to "get inside his skin." Interviewers must also guard against revealing their own attitude toward the questions lest those biases color the answers. In a "structured" interview there is a definite set of questions prepared in advance. The interviewer does not deviate from these questions, and the respondent must select from prepared answers. In an "unstructured" interview only the general topic of the interview is set. The exact questions are left open so the interviewer can feel out the situation; open-ended questions are asked, and the respondent is allowed to discuss his answers without restrictions.

QUESTIONNAIRES

Questionnaires are similar to structured interviews; the questions are written out in advance, and the respondent is given a limited choice of answers. The major difference is that the respondent fills out the questionnaire himself, and can usually return it by mail. This technique is much less expensive than the interview, and it can be completely anonymous, since the respondent can fill out the questionnaire in private and return it without identification. Usually more open responses to controversial topics can be obtained by the anonymous questionnaire. Both the questionnaire and the structured interview have one serious limitation in comparison with the unstructured interview; they do not allow the researcher to probe answers, to rephrase questions, and to explore other topics. Still, all three techniques are widely used for gathering data, often in conjunction with each other.

DOCUMENTS

A third source of information is *personal* and *official records.* Many kinds of official records of potential value to sociologists are kept by the federal, state, and local governments, and by schools, churches, industries, and other organizations. Among the richest sources of data are the official censuses conducted in advanced nations at regular intervals. Personal documents are also valuable sources of knowledge. For example, a sociologist attempting to reconstruct human relations as they must have been in the 1770s might find more information in the diary or letters of a housewife of that day than in the official records of an army general who helped win the Revolutionary War. Sociologists also give due weight to art and literature, for artists and writers often have important insights into their societies. Documents are a critical, although often overlooked, source of data. With increased emphasis on historical studies in sociology, documents are looming ever larger as information sources.

OBSERVATION

The final data-gathering procedure is *participant observation.* Researchers using this method attempt to become active members of the social unit they are examining. They try to cast aside their own values and perspectives, suspend judgment, and enter into the life of the unit. They try to become as much like the actual members in perspective, attitudes, interests, and activities as possible. Some classic sociological studies, including research into street gangs, executive decision-making teams, mental hospital patients, and army units, were made through participant observation. In each case the observer worked and lived among the people being studied, constantly observing their behavior.

RESEARCH DESIGNS

Interviews, questionnaires, documents, and observation are the four major data-gathering tools in the sociologist's workshop. Each method has some strengths and some weaknesses, but together they provide extensive information about human behavior in a wide variety of settings. The overall framework of a research project, the master plan within which the various data-gathering tools are used, is called the *research design.* There are three major research designs: experiments, case studies, and sample surveys. Researchers choose a design based on their *purposes,* and no one design is always best, for each is appropriate to a different kind of question. If you have one kind of research problem you choose one type of method; if you have another problem another method may be best. Remember these two rules: (1) there are many different kinds of research designs—no *one* method is always right; (2) the nature of the research *problem* determines which method will be most useful. The following sections show how the nature of the problem and the selection of a design are interrelated.

EXPERIMENTS

Problem: As more and more schools around the nation have been integrated a serious problem has emerged. Teachers, researchers, and parents have all noticed that while the school may be technically integrated, children of different races are often not really interacting with each other. Part of the problem seems to be that minority children feel overwhelmed by the verbal ability of majority children, and they retreat from interaction situations where they might appear to know less or where they might feel outtalked by middle-class, white children. Some social scientists have labeled this fear "interaction disability."

Suppose we wanted to aid more effective integration in schools by helping minority children overcome this interaction disability. How would we go about doing it?

Under the direction of Elizabeth Cohen, a sociologist at the Stanford School of Education, a team of social scientists undertook a series of experiments dealing with this problem. For years it had been reported in the sociological literature that certain status characteristics—occupation, sex, race, military rank—would affect the social interaction between people who had different prestige rankings. In general, when two people interact, the one with the highest occupational prestige talks much more, has more influence over joint decisions and, in general, dominates the interaction. The same held true for other statuses: men over women, majority races over minority, and higher military rank over lower. The phenomenon was so common, and the research had verified it so often, that a theory called "status characteristics theory" was constructed to explain this type of social behavior.

Professor Cohen's research team believed that the interference of status issues in social situations (which they called "status interaction disability") was one of the root causes of poor interaction among children in integrated schools. Racial characteristics are some of the most powerful status blocks in interaction, and Professor Cohen wondered if minority children could be trained to overcome their interaction disabilities so that they could confront the white children on a more equal basis. She set up series of laboratory experiments in which minority children were coached by adult members of their own race to be more aggressive, to stop giving in to white children so much, and to speak up for their own ideas. This "assertion training" seemed to make a major difference; by the end of the experiments black children were interacting on a much more equal basis with white children.

But Professor Cohen and her colleagues were not content to test their ideas in the artificial laboratory situation. Instead they went to the Oakland public schools with a plan for running a special integrated summer school where the experimental ideas would be tried in a real-life setting. The Oakland schools agreed, the federal government underwrote the cost, and the Stanford team proceeded to run a full-scale high school in the summer of 1972. Their experimental ideas were translated into action in the following steps:

1. Integrated classes were set up, balanced by sex and race.
2. *Pretest.* At the beginning of the summer all classes were tested for signs of racial interaction problems, using an ingenious game called Kill the Bull. In this game students were divided into four-person teams, with two whites and two blacks on each team. The game had clear decision points, and it was possible to easily tell (*a*) who talked the most, and (*b*) who had the most influence over decisions in the game. The pretest showed serious problems of racial interaction disability—the white students clearly dominated the interaction.
3. *Experimental Group.* Classes in the school consisted of a number of special activities such as photography, crystal radio building, and Malaysian language—all activities that were not in the normal school curriculum, so that past experiences would not affect the experiment. Half the classes (the experimental group) were given "assertion training." In those classes black college students were brought in to teach the subjects (providing high-prestige role models) and black students in the class were used as teachers' aides, teaching the white students (upsetting the normal status situation).
4. *Control Group.* The control classes learned the same subjects, but were *not* given assertion training; classes were taught randomly by both blacks and whites, and teachers' aides were randomly either black or white. In this situation the blacks had little if any help in overcoming the normal status interaction patterns.
5. *Posttest.* At the end of summer school all classes played Kill the Bull again to test whether assertion training had helped the black students when they had a competetive situation.

The results were encouraging. By the end of the summer black children who had received assertion training were about equal to whites in verbal interaction and influence over decisions. The training proved especially helpful for black girls who started even farther behind than the boys. Moreover, observers reported that in the experimental classes the daily interaction seemed more equal and harmonious. On the other hand, in the control classes where assertion training was *not* used, blacks were still far behind whites in interaction and influence, and daily interaction was not so equalized. Although this research could hardly provide an immediate solution to major problems of racial interaction in schools, it is, nevertheless, encouraging that some reforms in school policy might help—for example, more black teachers, more minority teacher aides, more chances for minority students to have successes in daily activities especially designed to enhance their self-esteem.

There are many different kinds of experiments, some of them much more complicated than Cohen's. Some are run in the laboratory, others are run in field settings (Cohen did both). However, they all essentially share the same basic logic. First, we must determine what *variable,* or factor, is influencing behavior. In Cohen's case she believed that status differences were hurting the children's social interaction. Next we must select two groups that are basically alike in every significant characteristic, such as race, age, sex, and social background. One group (the "experimental" group) has the critical variable manipulated—as the "assertion training" manipulated the status situation in Cohen's classes. The other group (the "control") does not experience any change in the critical variable; the control did *not* receive assertion training so their status differences were not influenced. After a reasonable period of time the critical question is asked. Does the experimental group act differently from the control group? If so, the difference must be related to the manipulation of the critical variable (the assertion training), since this was the only factor that was different in the two groups. The steps in experimental logic are illustrated in Figure 2.2. Of course, experiments can be more or less complicated than this illustration, but the logic is still essentially the same. Regardless of design and complexity, however, experiments are becoming more important in the social sciences.

CASE STUDIES

Problem: Life in prisons, mental hospitals, and concentration camps has similar characteristics; people are forced into these institutions against their will, lose their identities in a huge mass of inmates, and are subjected to extreme conditions. The world is divided into "inmates," who wear numbers and "staff," who wear badges; the staff is always boss.

Suppose you were interested in life inside such an organization, and you wanted to know how people were treated and how people lived. How would you do research on the topic?

Sociologist Erving Goffman wrote *Asylums,* in which life in "total institutions," such as prisons, mental hospitals, and concentration camps, is described. Goff-

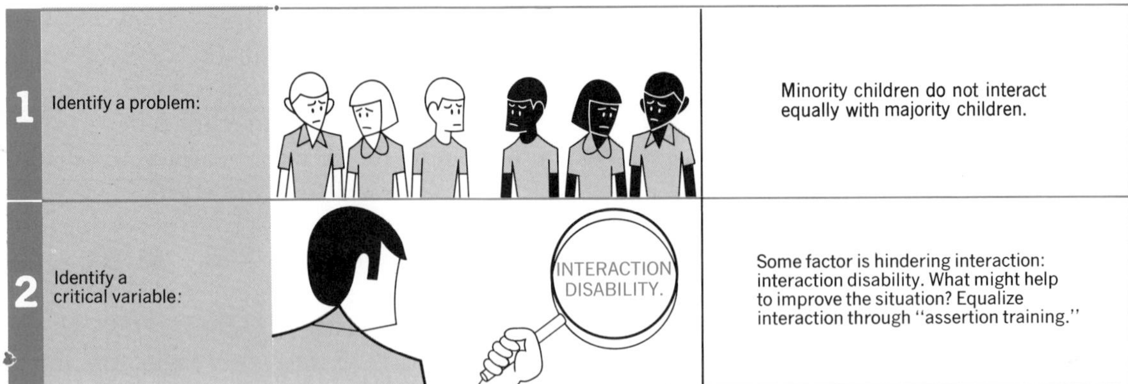

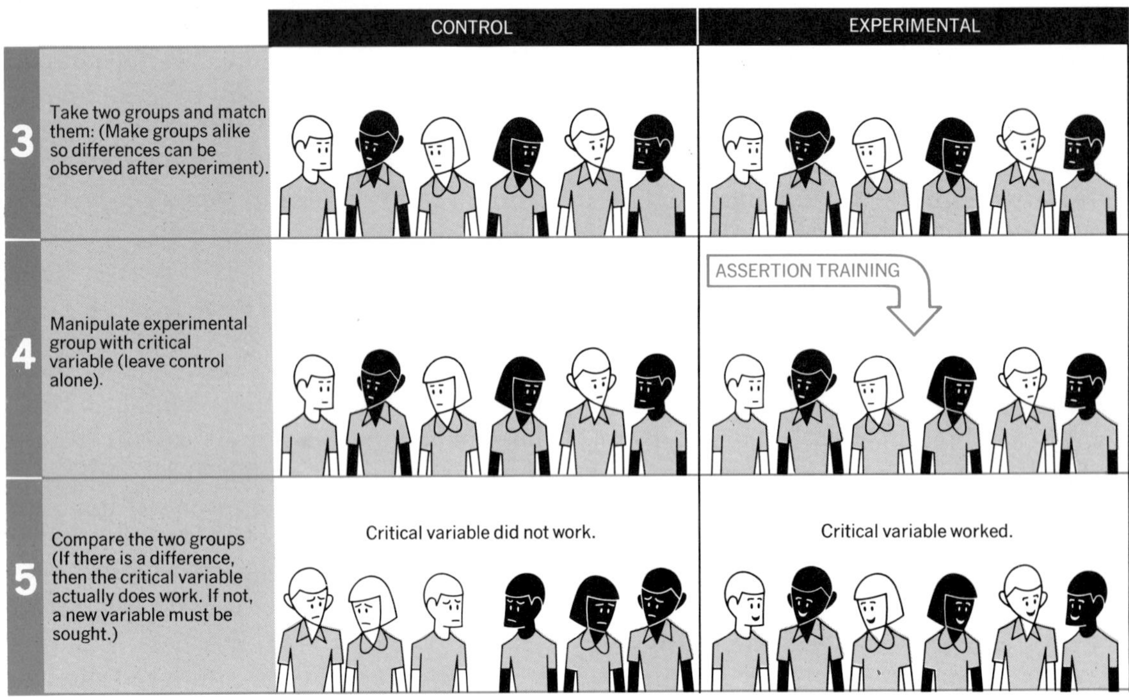

Figure 2.2
The logic of an experiment

man was interested in the whole picture of institutions. For his purposes an experiment would have been too restricting and a questionnaire too superficial. Instead, Goffman designed his research as a *case study.*

A case study is used in a field setting instead of a laboratory. The prime goal of the experiment is to test a rigid hypothesis on a limited topic; the case study, on the other hand, is much looser and explores a wide variety of topics.

Basically the case study is an intensive observation of the whole spectrum of a group's behavior. Sociologists undertaking case studies base their conclusions on intuition and thoughtful mulling over of the facts instead of on statistical analysis. Case studies are usually richer in insight, broader in scope, and more interesting to the average reader than experiments.

The history of Goffman's case study is as follows. From 1954 to 1957 Goffman worked at the National Institute of Mental Health in Bethesda, Maryland. During those years he studied many mental hospital wards, and in 1955–1956 he did a field-work project at St. Elizabeth's Hospital in Washington, D. C., a federal institution of about 7000 patients. With the aid of the hospital administrators Goffman worked under the guise of athletic director, leading various recreational programs for the patients. He lived among the patients, avoided contact with the staff, and immersed himself in patient life. Although he did not sleep in the wards, he tried to get as close to the patients and their situation as possible. Goffman believed that through intense involvement over a long period of time he could get better information about patient life than by using questionnaires, interviews, or experiments. Thus, *observation* was the chief tool in this case study of patient life.

Goffman's book, *Asylums,* is fascinating reading because the texture and fabric of life in a total institution come alive in his vivid portrayal. On entry the patients are *stripped,* of both their clothes and their personal identities. In the hospital they are *resocialized,* that is, they give up their habits and values from the outside world and take on those of the institution. While institutionalized they are *treated as a group;* their individuality is engulfed by the institution's need for mass production. Moreover, the inmates are *controlled;* the staff runs their lives and dictates every move, from meals to toilet to treatment to recreation. We could go into much more detail, but total institutions are examined more thoroughly in Chapter 4.

Many important pieces of sociological research have used the case-study approach. For example, William F. Whyte's observations of street gangs in Boston (*Street Corner Society,* 1943), Burton R. Clark's study of college administration (*The Open Door College,* 1960), and Robert Dahl's study of politics in New Haven, Connecticut (*Who Governs?,* 1961) were all researched through the case-study method. In one of the more interesting studies Julian Roebuck and S. Lee Spray (1967) studied people's behavior in cocktail lounges by visiting the lounges and drinking with the people for a two-year period. Roebuck and Spray enlisted the support of bartenders and lounge managers to collect information about customers, their married lives, and their sex lives with the people they picked up in the bar. Among other things, they found out that the men were older (average age 39), better educated (majority college educated), and married (70 percent). The women, on the other hand, were younger (average 24), had less education (majority high-school educated), and unmarried (100 percent). The main

Case studies are often used by sociologists. The researchers pictured here, in studying native Americans, depend on observation and intuition instead of surveys or experiments.

objectives of cocktail lounge behavior, they report, was sexual contact.

Popular myth has it that the cocktail lounge is a place where strangers pick up sexual partners. The major role of the high-class cocktail lounge studied was to facilitate casual sexual affairs in the context of respectability, but not among strangers. (p. 389)

The case study, then, has served as the methodological tool for many different kinds of sociological research, and it gathers intimate, in-depth information that other methods often miss.

SAMPLE SURVEYS

Problem: According to opinion there is a higher incidence of mental illness in the upper classes than in the lower classes. After all, the corporation executive, the doctor, the lawyer all live very hurried lives, die of heart attacks, have more ulcers, and "crack up" under the strain, don't they?

If somebody asked you to study this problem, how would you do it?

Two Yale professors, A. B. Hollingshead (then Chairman of the Sociology Department) and F. C. Redlich (then Chairman of the Psychiatry Department), decided to try to answer this vexing question. At that time there were many contradictory opinions; some experts claimed that the upper classes had more mental problems, some argued that the lower classes had more, and reliable data was not available. What methods do you suppose they used? A case study of a mental hospital might have helped, but how would they be sure that the hospital studied was typical of all the rest, or that the patients really represented an adequate cross section of typical patients? Hollingshead and Redlich rejected that plan. An experiment seemed out of the question, for they wanted to know about the characteristics of thousands of mental patients, far too many to include in an experiment. They finally decided on the technique known as the *sample survey.*

In the sample survey method sociologists take a small group of people (a "sample") out of a larger group they want to understand (the "universe"). Instead of spending enormous amounts of energy studying everybody, the researchers find out about the characteristics of the sample; they use the sample to judge what the rest of the group is like. The most famous type of sample survey is the public-opinion poll, such as the Gallup or Harris polls.

In order to trust the sample, however, it must be "representative" of the whole population, that is, it must be a fair, typical subset of the population. One of the major roles of statistics is to evaluate how representative a sample really is, how well we can estimate from the sample to the whole group we are interested in. In practice it is very difficult to get such a representative subset, and sociologists and statisticians have developed elaborate procedures for getting samples that really represent the whole population. The most important of these is the "simple random sample," a carefully planned sample that allows every person in the population an equal chance of getting into the sample. The easiest way to think of such a sample is to imagine a

How do social scientists study mental illness? Two studies of mental illness and patient life used very different research techniques. Erving Goffman did a *case study* of life in one mental hospital, whereas A. B. Hollingshead and F. C. Redlich used a *sample survey* to determine that lower classes had more mental illness than upper classes. Thus, different methods can be used to study the same topic, the choice of methods depending on the purposes of the research.

giant barrel into which all the names of people in the defined universe are placed, then stirred up, then certain names selected out at random. In practice the procedure is more complex, but the logic is essentially the same. There are many other kinds of samples, however, and the whole problem of sampling is too involved to go into further at this point.

The sample for the Hollingshead-Redlich research was the area around Yale, including New Haven, Connecticut, and adjoining areas. The study presented some staggering difficulties. To test their hypothesis that lower-class people have more mental illness than upper-class people, Hollingshead and Redlich had to do three things. First, they had to determine how many people in the New Haven area were being treated for mental disturbance, in public hospitals, clinics, private hospitals, or by private practitioners. Second, they had to determine the social class of each patient and compute the percentage of patients from each class. Third, in order to know whether the percentage of each social class being treated for mental illness was relatively large or small they had to determine what percentage each class represented in the whole population. For example, if the lower classes had 50 percent of the mental patients but also 50 percent of the total population, the distribution would be normal. If they had 75 percent of the patients but only 50 percent of the total population, it would be obvious that more lower-class people had mental illness. (This is about what they found.) It actually took two years just to plan how to find the number of patients, determine their social class, and compare the *patient group* to the *whole population.*

The results of the study confirmed the hypothesis: the Hollingshead-Redlich data showed that substantially more lower-class people were being treated for mental disturbance (see Figure 2.3). Among patients being treated for psychosis (the most serious form of disturbance) the differences were even greater. Note that the proportion of patients treated for all kinds of mental disturbance is about three times higher in the lowest class (V) to upper classes (I–II), and that the proportion of psychotic patients is more than seven times higher.

The Hollingshead-Redlich research added a new dimension to the growing picture of the effects of social-class structures on human behavior. Before they began their survey it was known that different social classes have different life expectancies, different educational attainments, different value patterns, and different crime rates. Now it was apparent that the different classes also have different levels of mental illness. In addition, this research gave support to the "stress" theory of mental illness. Environmental factors such as ghetto residence, poor physical health, and lack of job opportunities, commonly associated with lower-class life, could now be seen as intimately related to the problem of mental illness. Thus, the individual piece of research contributed to a growing body of theory. It was only when the theory and the research were coupled that the project was finished.

Figure 2.3
The lower classes have more mental illness: Findings from the Hollingshead-Redlich survey

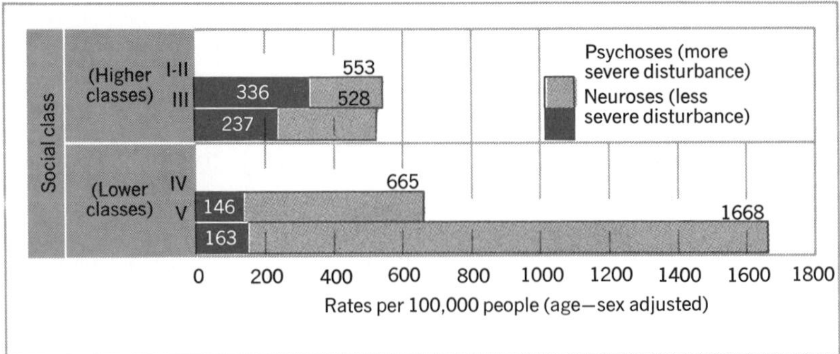

Source: Adapted from A. B. Hollingshead and Frederick C. Redlich, *Social Class and Mental Illness* (New York: Wiley, 1958).

FIVE STEPS IN THE "RESEARCH CYCLE"

There are, then, many different kinds of sociological research. Some research, such as the Hollingshead-Redlich study, requires expensive surveys with thousands of people being interviewed and thousands of dollars being spent on computer analysis. Some research, such as Goffman's work, involves months and years of living among and working with the group under investigation, but almost no money. Other research requires a laboratory in which small group experiments are run or on-the-spot experiments, such as those by Cohen, are conducted. All these research designs have been used successfully by sociologists and have added rich information to our store of knowledge. Figure 2.4 compares some of these different approaches.

Now that we have examined the different research designs, it will be useful to put all the different procedures together in an idealized version of the *research cycle.* Whatever the method, sociologists use the same basic *logic.* In general, researchers (1) get an idea (an hypothesis) about how they can solve practical or theoretical problems, (2) choose a design to get proper information, (3) gather the data in the field, (4) analyze their facts, and (5) try to explain their findings. In actual practice researchers rarely follow the stages in order, nor do they always think every detail out in advance. In fact, the logical, well-thought-out research cycle is one of the "myths" that surrounds scientific sociology. However, with this warning it is still valuable to look briefly at the idealized research cycle as it is presented in Figure 2.5. Please examine this figure carefully as we discuss the five steps.

1. *Step One: Developing a working hypothesis.* Research begins with an idea or a theory, usually arising from the findings of earlier studies, or from the researcher's own

Figure 2.4
Three research designs: a comparison. In planning his research a sociologist picks the method that best suits his particular needs. There is no one "right" method

	Experiment	Case Study	Survey Sample
Site of research	Usually in a laboratory, but sometimes in field	Field setting	Field setting
Purpose	Rigorously establish effect of critical variables by manipulating in an experimental group and comparing to a control group	Probe a single case in great depth	Gather information about "population" by using a representative "sample." Usually by use of interviews or questionnaires with the same sample
Advantages	Great precision about effect of variables	Gives much richer, deeper knowledge of "natural" setting	Allows systematic collection of information about many people
Disadvantages	Laboratory setting is artificial. In real world usually more than one variable affecting events; experiments cannot deal with very many variables at once	Data not very systematic or precise. Very impressionistic. The selected case may be atypical and therefore findings cannot be generalizes to other settings	Gives rather superficial view of sample at one point in time. Does not analyze change over time
Example:	Cohen's study of interaction disability between black and white children	Goffman's analysis of life in mental hospitals and other "total institutions"	Hollingshead and Redlich's research on the relation between mental illness and social class

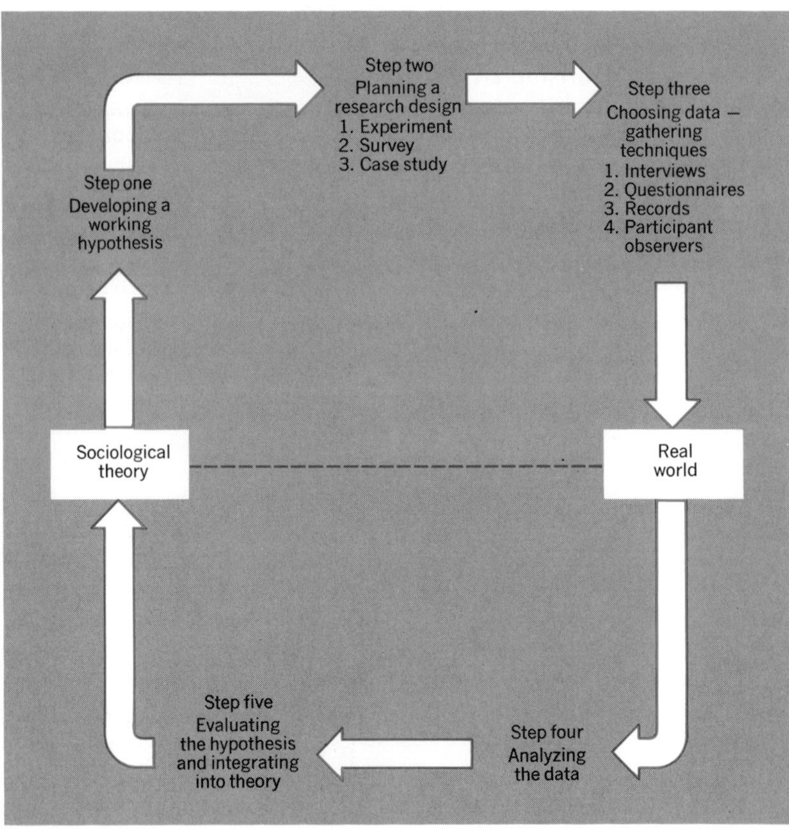

Figure 2.5
The ideal research cycle: A process of linking theory to the real world. Most sociological studies start from previous theories that lead to a new working hypothesis about some aspect of human relations. Then the study proceeds until the working hypothesis is proved, disproved, or revised. The new findings are then integrated into the growing body of sociological knowledge. *WARNING:* While this idealized research cycle is useful as a teaching device, often hypotheses are discarded, methods are switched in midstream, and the data are forced to fit preconceived ideas.

observations of society. Starting with this basic idea the researcher usually proposes a *working hypothesis.* Hollingshead and Redlich, for example, used all the background information they knew to formulate their hypothesis that the lower classes have more mental illness. All hypotheses must be capable of *empirical testing,* that is, they must be subject to proof or disproof by the facts. Occasionally, however, a researcher may not have a formal hypothesis but only a general set of ideas to guide his thought, as Goffman did when he examined mental hospital life.

2. *Step Two: Planning a research design.* After developing a working hypothesis the researcher settles on a method for gathering the information that will prove or disprove his idea. The three overall designs that sociologists use are the experiment, the sample survey, and the case study.

3. *Step Three: Choosing data-gathering techniques.* Once the overall design is planned, a specific instrument for gathering information is selected according to the needs of the research. Interviews, questionnaires, document analysis, or observation procedures may be used individually or in combination.

4. *Step Four: Analyzing the data.* It is often said that "the facts speak for themselves," but this is simply not true, for once gathered, the data must be subjected to careful analysis and comparison to other known facts before their

meaning becomes clear. In the Hollingshead and Redlich study, for example, the raw figures seemed to indicate differences in the proportion of mental patients from class to class. But it was not clear at first whether these differences could actually be attributed to social class or had some other cause. Perhaps some classes contain an unusual proportion of men to women, and mental disturbance is related to sex. Perhaps some classes have a different composition in terms of age, race, or religion, and these are the factors that influence mental illness. Only after analyzing the figures through elaborate statistical procedures to take into account such possibilities—a task that took several years—could Hollingshead and Redlich be confident of the findings.

5. *Step Five: Evaluating the hypothesis and integrating it into theory.* Once the data have been analyzed and their meaning is known, their relationship to the working hypothesis is studied. In some cases, they may clearly disprove the hypothesis, although this in itself may constitute an important contribution to knowledge. In other cases, as in the Cohen and Hollingshead-Redlich studies, they may indicate that the hypothesis is correct. The last step is to integrate the empirical findings into the theory where the research started. Thus, *research begins and ends with theory;* it begins with an hypothesis that emerged from previous research, and it ends with a revision of the theoretical ideas. "Raw facts" never mean anything; they must be coupled with serious intellectual frameworks. One research project never stands by itself; it is only one piece in an overall puzzle. Only when the whole picture is pieced together do the individual pieces have any meaning. Nothing is worse than "raw empiricism," that is, the gathering of bits and pieces of information without having a theory into which the individual facts can be integrated. Sociology has only lately begun to formulate complex theories that unite the various facts accumulated by sociologists, but as the science matures, it will gradually build more meaningful frameworks.

Thus, research ends where it begins—with good ideas and good theories. The most sophisticated research techniques and the most elaborate computer processing can never make up for the fact that a researcher's ideas and theories are weak. Empirical facts must be integrated into a theory; theory must be tested with empirical facts, that is, the real essence of scientific investigation.

PROBLEMS WITH THE IDEAL MODEL

Although the idealized research cycle is helpful as an orientation to the different activities in a research effort, it can be a harmful concept if taken too literally. In actual practice social scientists deviate from that ideal in many situations; the ideal research project with its well-thought-out hypothesis, its careful selection of techniques, its perfectly representative sample of respondents, and its faultless analysis is nothing more than a myth.

THE IDEAL FACES REALITY

In reality hypotheses are often ill-conceived, half-defined, and revised as the data come in. When research gets under way compromises are often made because of time and money limitations. Sampling, too, is often inexact. A totally "representative" sample is so rare that even the most sophisticated pollsters, who have millions of dollars to spend on their research, still include a substantial allowance for error. A selected street address turns out to be a vacant lot; people are not at home; questionnaires are partially completed; questionnaires get mislaid; people make errors in counting; an incorrect number gets punched onto an IBM card; and so on. The real deviation from the ideal consists mostly of such trivia.

Finally, data analysis is supposedly done so that the results cannot be questioned. In the real world of research, however, there is a great deal of juggling facts to prove a researcher's pet point. Although the old saying that "you can prove anything with statistics" is not completely true, it is true that statistics by themselves can be very misleading. In short, the ideal is not always achieved, and it would be the worst kind of deceit to pretend that it is.

This warning should *not,* however, lead you to the decision that sociological research is no good. Good social scientists are well aware of the shortcomings of their research, but they also realize that a well-trained social scientist can gather fairly reliable information in spite of all the compromises, shortcuts, and problems. Sophisticated scientists know that they often have to live with less than ideal findings, and they adjust their evaluation of various findings in view of this imperfection of sociological research. But unsophisticated observers have usually been so misguided by the myth of scientific purity that they reject out of hand anything that is not perfect, thus discounting much valuable information.

THE KINSEY REPORT: FLAWED BUT VALUABLE

One of the most important studies ever done on human sexual behavior, the world-famous work by Alfred C. Kinsey and his associates (*Sexual Behavior in the Human Male,* 1948, and *Sexual Behavior in the Human Female,* 1953) illustrates this point. Up until the Kinsey reports there had been very little research on sexual behavior, which was a taboo subject. The scientific community greeted the research with enthusiasm and excitement, for now the great taboo had been lifted. The impact of the research was enormous: its findings became household truths almost overnight. Among other things Kinsey and his associates found:

1. Masturbation, instead of being a rare practice, was almost universal among males and nearly so among females.
2. Different social classes engaged in different kinds of sex behavior, with the upper classes starting sex later, enjoying it more as mature adults, and experimenting more with a variety of sexual activities than the lower classes.
3. Devoutly religious people engaged in somewhat less sexual behavior than nonreligious people.
4. Nearly 90 percent of all males had sexual intercourse before marriage, but only about two thirds of the college-educated men did.

5. About 50 percent of all females had intercourse before marriage but about 60 percent of college-educated women did.

(Note that whereas premarital intercourse decreases for college men as compared to all men, it increases for college women.)

In spite of its enormous impact the Kinsey study did have very serious methodological problems. The most serious was his sample; it did not come close to being "representative" of any population. In fact, the sample seemed to be a motley collection of subjects picked up in college classes, off the streets, at speaking engagements, and from hired subjects—prostitutes, mental-hospital inmates, and prisoners. Although Kinsey later asserted that his sample represented the entire population of the United States, many social scientists have disagreed strongly with that claim. In addition, Kinsey often used face-to-face interviews, but many critics argue that on such a touchy subject as sex people are very likely to lie about their actions, much more so face-to-face than on an anonymous questionnaire. Moreover, much of the information about childhood sex behavior was culled from the subject's memory, which subsequent analyses have shown to be rather poor. A number of other problems could be cited; many people wonder, for example, why mental and prison inmates comprise so much of the sample, but the point is made: even so important and influential a study as the monumental work of Kinsey had serious methodological shortcomings.

People who have accepted the myth of scientific purity might reject Kinsey's results. But to do so would be to reject a valuable source of information. Instead, we must evaluate these findings carefully in light of everything else we know about sex behavior, plan additional studies on the same topic, and use this new information to correct and extend Kinsey's work. In this way social scientists accumulate important, meaningful facts that help us interpret the world around us.

SUMMARY

Sociologists use scientific procedures just as other scientists do. They strive to be *objective,* observe a *code of ethics,* look for *complex, multicausal* explanations, formulate *theories,* and test their ideas by *empirical* data. Scientific purity is, however, a myth, since science never quite lives up to its ideal vision. But, although research findings should be examined critically, the imperfection of scientific procedures does not negate their findings altogether.

Sociologists have developed a whole battery of research methods to help them uncover social facts. There is no *one* method that sociologists use all the time; the choice of which one to use depends on the research purpose. Questionnaires, interviews, document studies, and observation procedures —all of which may be used individually or in combination —offer different strengths and weaknesses. The specific techniques are used within an overall *research design:* experiment, case study, or sample survey. Again, the choice of research design is based on the objectives of the research.

But methods and techniques are only part of scientific investigation. Every research enterprise starts with a theory or hypothesis. No amount of sophistication about methods can replace the fundamentally important process of theory building, an appropriate *design,* and specific data-gathering *techniques* selected to prove or disprove the hypothesis. After the data are collected there is a phase of *analysis* (where statistics often play a major role) and finally a *reintegration* of the facts into theory.

REFERENCES

Becker, Howard, and Irving Louis Horowitz. "Radical Politics and Sociological Research: Observations on Methodology and Ideology," *American Journal of Sociology,* July 1972, pp. 48–66.

Berger, Joseph, Morris Zelditch, Jr., and Bo Anderson. *Sociological Theories in Progress* (New York: Houghton Mifflin, 1966).

Clark, Burton R. *The Open Door College* (New York: McGraw-Hill, 1960).

Clark, Kenneth B., and Mamie P. Clark. "Racial Identification and Preference in Negro Children," in Eleanor Maccoby, Theodore M. Newcomb, and E. L. Hartley (eds.), *Readings in Social Psychology,* 3rd ed. (New York: Holt, 1958), p. 608.

Cohen, Elizabeth G. "Modifying the Effects of Social Structure," *American Behavioral Scientist,* July/August 1973, *16* (6), pp. 861–878.

Dahl, Robert. *Who Governs?* (New Haven: Yale Press, 1961).

Goffman, Erving. *Asylums* (Garden City, N. Y.: Anchor Books, 1961).

Hollingshead, A. B., and Frederich Redlich. *Social Class and Mental Illness* (New York: Wiley, 1958).

Kinsey, A. C., W. B. Pomeroy, C. E. Martin, and P. H. Gebhard. *Sexual Behavior in the Human Female* (Philadelphia: Saunders, 1953).

Kinsey, A. C., W. B. Pomeroy, and C. E. Martin. *Sexual Behavior in the Human Male* (Philadelphia: Saunders, 1948).

Martindale, Don. *The Nature and Types of Sociological Theory* (Boston: Houghton Mifflin, 1960).

Maxwell, Gerald. "Introducing Sociology: The Social Awareness Test," *American Sociologist 1* (1), November 1966, pp. 253–254.

Riley, Matilda White. "Sources and Types of Sociological Data," in Robert E. Faris, *Handbook of Modern Sociology* (Chicago: Rand McNally, 1964).

Roebuck, Julian, and S. Lee Spray. "The Cocktail Lounge: A Study of Heterosexual Relations in a Public Organization." *Amer-*

ican Journal of Sociology, January 1967, *72* (4), pp. 388–398.

Selltiz, Claire, Marie Jahoda, M. Deutsch, and S. W. Cook. *Research Methods in Social Relations* (New York: Holt, 1959).

Stouffer, Samuel A., et al. *The American Soldier: Adjustment During Army Life* and *The American Soldier: Combat and Its Aftermath* (Princeton: Princeton University Press, 1949).

Von Hoffman, Nicholas, Irving Louis Horowitz, and Lee Rainwater. "Sociological Snoopers and Journalistic Moralizers," *Trans-Action, 7* (7), May 1970, pp. 4–9.

Whyte, William F. *Street Corner Society* (Chicago: University of Chicago Press, 1943).

THREE
CULTURE

NACIREMA

Professor Linton first brought the ritual of the Nacirema to the attention of anthropologists 20 years ago, but the culture of this group is still very poorly understood.

They are a North American group living in the territory between the Canadian Cree, the Yaqui and Tarahumare of Mexico, and the Carib and Arawak of the Antilles. Little is known of their origin, although tradition states that they came from the east. According to Nacirema mythology, their nation was originated by a culture hero, Notgnihsaw, who is otherwise known for two great feats of strength—the throwing of a piece of wampum across the river Pa-To-Mac and the chopping down of a cherry tree in which the Spirit of Truth resides. . . .

While much of the people's time is devoted to economic pursuits, a large part of the fruits of these labors and a considerable portion of the day are spent in ritual activity. The focus of this activity is the human body, the appearance and health of which loom as a dominant concern in the ethos of the people. . . . The fundamental belief underlying the whole system appears to be that the human body is ugly and that its natural tendency is to debility and disease. Incarcerated in such a body, man's only hope is to avert these characteristics through the use of the powerful influences of ritual and ceremony. Every household has one or more shrines devoted to this purpose. The more powerful individuals in the society have several shrines in their

Culture influences almost everything we do, in fact, culture actually defines our world for us. Part of culture's heavy impact can be understood by contrast, because by inspecting strange, alien cultures we can better understand our own. Anthropologists' studies of strange societies have been one of the most important sources of information about the influence of culture. The opening quotation, for example, is a fascinating account of the culture of the Nacirema of North America. Reading of the strange beliefs and elaborate rituals of this North American tribe will perhaps help you to realize how cultural values sneak up on us, how they appear perfectly natural until viewed from the perspective of a stranger. By now you have probably spelled Nacirema backward.

houses and, in fact, the opulence of a house is often referred to in terms of the number of such ritual centers it possesses. . . .

The focal point of the shrine is a box or chest which is built into the wall. In this chest are kept the many charms and magical potions without which no native believes he could live. . . .

Beneath the charm-box is a small font. Each day every member of the family, in succession, enters the shrine room, bows his head before the charm-box, mingles different sorts of holy water in the font, and proceeds with a brief rite of ablution. . . .

The Nacirema have an almost pathological horror of and fascination with the mouth, the condition of which is believed to have a supernatural influence on all social relationships. Were it not for the rituals of the mouth, they believe that their teeth would fall out, their gums bleed, their jaws shrink, their friends desert them, and their lovers reject them. . . .

The daily body ritual performed by everyone includes a mouth-rite. Despite the fact that these people are so punctilious about care of the mouth, this rite involves a practice which strikes the uninitiated stranger as revolting. It was reported to me that the ritual consists of inserting a small bundle of hog hairs into the mouth, along with certain magical powders, and then moving the bundle in a highly formalized series of gestures. . . .

Our review of the ritual life of the Nacirema has certainly shown them to be a magic-ridden people. It is hard to understand how they have managed to exist so long under the burdens which they have imposed upon themselves. . . . (Miner, 1956, pp. 503–507)

WHAT IS CULTURE

The term "culture" has several different meanings in popular usage, one of which is *culture-as-good-taste.* "Cultured" people are those who know good art, attend the opera, and drink expensive French wines. A good education and plenty of money to spend on luxurious, expensive habits are part of the popular image of the "cultured" person. A second popular use of the word culture refers to an entire society and all that is associated with it, for example, "French culture" or "Western culture." Used in this fashion the term becomes a superword, the *culture-as-everything* approach. When used in that broad sense the term is practically meaningless, and this certainly is not what sociologists have in mind.

A SOCIOLOGICAL DEFINITION OF CULTURE

When sociologists refer to culture they are not thinking about the narrow definition of culture-as-good-taste, nor the broad definition of culture-as-everything. Instead, they are thinking about *culture-as-knowledge-and-belief-systems.*

What fundamentally separates human social life from that of other animals is that people can create knowledge and pass it on to future generations through education. Moreover, people acquire beliefs, establish laws and customs, and create art and music. The total of these elements is what sociologists mean by culture. The most famous definition was stated by E. B. Tyler in 1871:

Culture . . . is that complex whole which includes knowledge, belief, art, morals, law, custom, and any other capabilities and habits acquired by man as a member of society. (Tyler, 1871)

Culture is, then, a very broad concept, since it includes all the various kinds of knowledge that people create: art, music, skills, and political and family organization. In addition, it refers to beliefs and values: religious doctrines, norms of behavior, morality, and legal concepts. Earlier, sociologists and anthropologists included *physical things,* such as the wheel, cave painting, or pyramids, in their definition of culture. Today, however, sociologists generally reject the material definition of culture and stress the nonmaterial knowledge. Tools, money, mechanical devices, and other objects are not culture, but *knowledge about* these things is culture. Fundamentally, culture is a *knowledge system.* Herbert Spencer called culture the *superorganic* system, that is, a system of knowledge that exists apart from and above ("super") man's biological nature ("organic"). Culture does not come from instincts or biology; it comes from the knowledge created in man's social life. Since culture is a knowledge system, it is expressed in *symbols.* Knowledge is not a physical thing, and it must therefore be represented by symbols that human beings have created. For example, language, both written and oral, is the most important system of symbols, but road signs, blueprints, and musical and mathematical notations are other examples of cultural symbols.

CULTURE AFFECTS ALL OF LIFE

Most of the time people do not realize that their lives are affected every day by cultural ideas. In fact, culture's impact is so overwhelming and yet so subtle that most people within a given culture think that their way of acting is simply the "natural" way, the way "nature wanted it." An American man is married to one woman at a time and thinks that monogamy is "natural" for all people, but a Moslem may believe equally sincerely that it is "natural" to have several wives. To both men it is obvious that his own way is correct; both may be unaware that it is the culture, not the law of nature, that is determining what is proper.

All human beings must eat, but culture determines what, when, where, and under what conditions they will eat. People have sex drives, but culture determines who the sex partner will be, when sexual relations may be engaged in, and what kind of marriage system will be honored. In most areas of the world people must wear clothes for protection, but culture determines what kind of clothes should be worn, under what circumstances, and over what parts of the body. People are sometimes aggressive, but culture dictates when aggression will be called cruel and unwarranted and when it will be called honorable and just.

Someone once said a fish would be the last animal to discover water. Surrounded by water, the fish does not even notice it until he is pulled out into the air and suddenly misses it. In the same way, cultural values and norms permeate our world so completely that we do not even know they exist until we run head-on into a different culture. It was the early anthropologists who first really dealt with the concept of culture, because they were amazed at the variations in human behavior all over the world. Since this enormous variation could not be explained by biological differences, the anthropologists realized that the different cultural systems were responsible for the diversity. Culture defines the world in which each person lives. It constructs the "social reality" regardless of what the physical reality may be. Even such perfectly natural physical gestures as nodding the head for "yes" and shaking it sidewise for "no" are influenced by culture. Insert 3.I indicates some of the many cultural conventions for gestures.

CONTENT OF CULTURE: THE "IS," THE "BEAUTIFUL," AND THE "RIGHT"

Since culture has such a powerful effect on human behavior, it must be examined very closely. In the next sections we will look at the *content* of cultural systems, which sociologists generally divide into three parts.

1. The *empirical* culture includes technical knowledge, such as how to drive a car or how to construct a spaceship, and the society's definition of reality (what "is").
2. The *aesthetic* culture consists of the values and ideals that determine standards of taste—the "beautiful"—for every society.
3. The *normative* culture specifies how people should and should not behave, outlining what is "right and wrong" in a particular society.

EMPIRICAL CULTURE

Empirical knowledge, techniques for handling the natural environment, is one of the most important aspects of culture. A major element of empirical culture is technology, a knowledge system that deals with physical problems such as housing, agriculture, machinery, and in-

INSERT **3.1**

CULTURE DEFINES SIMPLE GESTURES

We often assume that the meanings of common gestures are "instinctive" or universal, yet they vary greatly among different cultures. This is only one more indication of the pervasive impact of culture on our lives. As illustrated below, a person who takes his own definitions of gestures for granted would run into problems communicating with someone from a different society. Try to make these gestures as you read and you will get a strong sense of the difference between cultures.

	GESTURE	CULTURE
To Say Yes:	1. Rock head forward and backward.	Western
	2. Bring both hands up to the chest and gracefully wave downward.	Ainu—north Japan
	3. Rock head in arc from shoulder to shoulder about four times.	Bengali—India
	4. Thrust head sharply forward.	Semang pygmy—Malaysia
	5. Bend head diagonally forward to the right, gracefully turning chin, and simultaneously curtsey (cross-legged) with arms partly crossed and palms upward.	Singhalese—India
To Say No:	1. Rock head from side to side.	Western
	2. Pass right hand from right to left and then back in front of the chest.	Ainu—north Japan
	3. Jerk head to the right shoulder.	Abyssinian—Ethiopia

	GESTURE	CULTURE
	4. Cast eyes down.	Semang pygmy—Malaysia
	5. Raise head and chin.	Sicilian
To Point:	1. Extend forefinger only with end of finger nearest object.	Western
	2. Extend lips in direction of object.	American Indian
To Greet:	1. Clasp right hand of other person with own right hand and shake up and down.	Western
	2. Lightly hit other's head or shoulders with the fist.	Copper Eskimo
	3. Slap the other on his back while allowing him to do the same to you.	Northwest Amazonian
	4. Embrace and rub the other's back.	Polynesian
	5. Grasp right hand of other with own right hand, raise both hands together to kiss the other's hand and subsequently let him kiss your own.	Kurd—Middle East
To Show Respect:	1. Rise and remain standing.	Western
	2. Sit down.	Fijian and Tongan
	3. Hiss.	Japan
	4. Raise open right hand to the face and place the thumb on the bridge of one's nose ("thumb your nose").	Todan—South India

dustrial production. This knowledge that enables people to deal with their physical world is part of the cultural heritage passed down from generation to generation. Food technology, for example, is a very important aspect of a society's knowledge. In addition, knowledge about building houses, splitting atoms, breeding cattle, and flying kites are all included in our society's store of empirical knowledge.

But culture does more than hand down empirical knowledge; it also specifies *how to find new knowledge.* In previous ages there have been different paths to knowledge, including religion, mysticism, philosophy, tea-leaf reading, magic, and astrology. Now, however, the dominant mode of uncovering new knowledge is through science and the technique of empirical investigation. In fact, human beings and the very culture that defines science in the first place have become objects of scientific investigation in the social sciences. And as new discoveries are made, the definitions of reality furnished by culture are challenged, renewed, and sometimes changed.

Reality is Not Fixed: Culture Defines It for Us. Although it is obvious that trees and rocks and houses and oceans exist, what about demons, germs, gods, or atoms? Let us examine a specific case: Do witches exist? Stop for a moment and read Insert 3.II, "Witchcraft in Geneva."

What was going on in Geneva? First, let us discount the theory the people of Geneva themselves believed, that witches were in fact causing the plague. It is understandable that the people of Geneva would react with fear to the terrible plague that was ravaging the city, and that they would seek the cause of this mass death. But why did they blame nonexistent witches? Because the culture of the time defined witches as the appropriate agency to blame, just as an earlier culture would have blamed the plague on "devils" or "gods," and just as we would blame it on "germs." But, the germs are real, and devils, gods, and witches are not. Or, at least *according to our culture* that is the appropriate way to define the problem.

The Definition of the Situation. This example is a perfect illustration of an important point. *Regardless of what "actually" exists, people act on the basis of what they believe exists.* W. I. Thomas, a sociologist of the early twentieth century, stated that the *"definition of the situation"* determines what men will do. If men define situations as real, they *are* real in their consequences for human action, even if they are not "real" by scientific standards. And it is the *culture* that furnishes the appropriate definition of what exists at any given time, whether it is witches, germs, or atomic particles. Witches may not exist, but they were real for the people of Europe from the fifteenth to eighteenth centuries. People acted on the belief in witches regardless of whether they did or did not exist.

People of the West, rational and scientific, have lulled themselves into feeling that they know "reality" when they see it; reality can be seen, touched, measured, weighed. Industrial societies are not "superstitious" like those before the

INSERT **3.II**

WITCHCRAFT IN GENEVA

It was January 22, 1545. The city was Geneva, Switzerland. Bernard Dallinges, a small and slender local laborer was arrested by the police on charges of participating in a plot to kill the people of the city. Plots to kill city dwellers are not that rare, of course, but the plot that Dallinges was involved in did have a strange twist—the plotters were going to get a special ointment from the Devil and smear it on the doors of Geneva's houses, thus causing a plague.

Today we would only scoff at the raving of such a maniac and pack him off to the nearest insane asylum. But the officials of Geneva acted differently. They rounded up everyone connected with the plot, tortured them all, and then burned them to death. The leader of the plot, a man named Lentille, was killed and his body dragged through the city streets and burned in a special ceremony. Without doubt the city officials did believe in the plot by these "witches" to help the Devil bring a plague to Geneva. And on top of it all, there was really a plague raging through the frightened city! Even such an upstanding citizen as John Calvin, the Protestant reformer and religious leader of the city, swore as a witness against certain witches. Some forty or fifty witches were caught. Most were promptly killed by burning, but several committed suicide.

A panic seized the city of Geneva. The plague was raging, and people were dying like flies. All the witches had to be found before it was too late. Squads of witch-hunters spread out over the city, breaking down doors in the middle of the night to catch witches asleep and arresting scores of suspects. The panic reached new proportions when many of the suspects confessed that they were in fact witches in league with the Devil. They wanted everyone to know it; they were proud of it. The word spread like wildfire, and people all over Switzerland began to arrest any citizen from Geneva for fear that the plot would be exported to the rest of the nation. Hundreds of people were rounded up, tortured, burned, and decapitated. Meanwhile the plague raged on.

twentieth century. But two modern sociologists, Peter L. Berger and Thomas Luckmann, have looked at the behavior patterns of modern man and have concluded that people of the twentieth century, like their ancestors, are trapped by the culture's definition of reality. Their book, *The Social Construction of Reality* (1967), argues that our everyday life is not "real" in any absolute sense of the word, but instead is defined for us by our social situation and culture. Modern science has indeed taken most of the myths, witches, and demons out of the physical aspects of existence. Nevertheless, most of the important areas of life—work, play, marriage, government—are defined by the social system and the culture. Life as we live it seems so concretely "real" that we seldom stop to think that most of it is defined by our particular culture at a particular point in time. Think for a minute about the following questions. Is racial integration desirable? Do atoms exist? Do ghosts stalk the night? Is there a communist conspiracy to take over the world? Do germs cause disease? Is democracy a good form of government?

For every question you answered "Yes" there are plenty of people, in different cultural situations, who would say "No." People see the world differently because the social definition of reality is determined by culture.

Culture Influences How We See the World. Look at the picture on page 83 for a moment. This photograph is important, so be sure to examine it carefully before you read any farther. What do you see? Are you having trouble with it? Try writing down a few of the things it might be. It could be many things, couldn't it? Social reality is very similar; the world of social events is unclear until culture tells us the "correct" way to see things. Let us see if you can "see" the picture better with a little instruction.

The picture is of a cow. Look at the dark spot slightly to the right of center—that is the cow's ear. To the left of the ear is the face and to the right is the cow's body. Now that you see the cow, look at the picture again. Can you see anything *other* than a cow?

Most people, once they see the cow, have a hard time seeing anything else

There are several things to be learned about the nature of culture from this example.

1. Like the ambiguous cow picture, social values, attitudes, and realities are very unclear; they can be interpreted in many different ways.

2. Every society's culture teaches its citizens what to see; it defines their reality.

3. This social definition of reality has to be taught, just as you had to be "taught" to see the cow.

4. Once people see their social world in a particular way, it is then difficult for them to see it in any other way, just as you will now have a hard time seeing anything other than the cow.

THE AESTHETIC CULTURE

Now let us turn from the utilitarian to the aesthetic, to definitions of beauty. There are many forms of artistic expression around the world; music, dance, sculpture, literature, poetry, and painting are found in almost every society. Some beautiful objects are also useful. A spear, for instance, is a useful object, but it may also be elaborately carved and painted. Other beautiful things—the poetry of Poe, Michelangelo's statue of David, the music of Beethoven—have no direct practical use. These are all examples of man's strange habit of creating art that has no direct utilitarian purpose. Man everywhere is Man-the-Artist. But it is the culture that defines what is beautiful.

Because the definition of "beautiful" is not absolute, art forms change and differ from one society to another. Modern Western art is strikingly different from the stone carvings of the Easter Islands, the cave paintings of prehistoric men, and the elaborate Baroque art of the Middle Ages. Modern dance differs considerably from traditional ballet and the various dances of American Indian tribes. In modern America we define "art" as oil paintings by Picasso, music by Bach, or poetry by Frost. In other societies, however, the Eskimos draw on ivory, Bushmen paint on rocks, Fijian Islanders print on bark cloth, and New Guinea natives decorate skulls of their ancestors. Although there is tremendous variation in the art of different cultures, each form is appropriate to and considered beautiful by its culture.

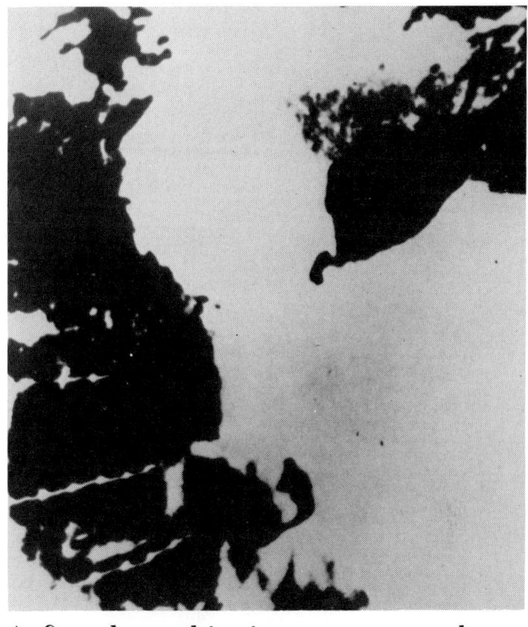

At first glance this picture may seem abstract. But it is an actual photograph of a familiar subject. Can you make it out? Turn page for answer.

NORMATIVE CULTURE: THE "RIGHT" AND THE "WRONG"

Culture defines empirical reality and aesthetic standards in every society. Its third function is to establish what is *right* and *wrong,* the modes of conduct that are expected of a person. And the impact of culture is particularly strong in this area. Read Insert 3.III about the ill-fated Donner Party that tried to cross the snow-covered Sierra mountains, in 1846. The idea of cannibalism strikes us as totally unthinkable, beyond the pale of civilized man. Yet it is obvious that eating human

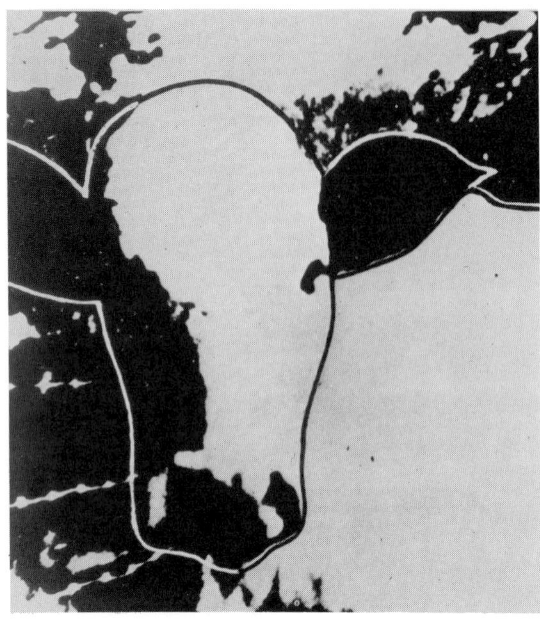

flesh was the "rational" thing for these starving people to do. And that is the point: it is impossible to be calmly rational about such a wildly emotional issue; our culture will not allow it.

NORMS

Culture establishes what is right and wrong by defining rules of conduct called *norms.* All societies have norms, but the norms differ considerably from one society to another. In one society a man may marry his daughter, whereas in others he may marry *no* female relative; in one society food is eaten with chopsticks, in another with forks and knives; in one society cannibalism is unthinkable, in another it may sometimes be a source of food.

William Graham Sumner, an early sociologist at Yale, made the study of social norms, which he usually called "mores" or "folkways," one of his lifetime concerns. In his book *Folkways* (1907) Sumner entitled one of his chapters "The Mores Can Make Anything Right and Prevent Condemnation of Anything." He was stating one of the most important characteristics of cultural norms; they are able to define almost anything as right or wrong.

Legitimation of Norms. Social norms are supported by some form of *legitimation,* that is, an explanation of why the rule should be obeyed. In some cases the legitimation is fairly obvious; there is little need to justify the rules against murder, robbery, and physical attack. In other cases, however, there is little rational reason for the rule; there is no known biological reason why adultery should be outlawed, why gentlemen should shake hands, or why people should not smoke marijuana. In these cases the legitimation is usually based on appeals to gods ("Adultery is wrong because the Ten Commandments forbid it"), or tradition ("Well, we've always greeted others with a handshake"), or the good of the society ("What if everybody decided to smoke pot—nobody would work!"). Often the legitimation makes no sense to the outsider, but to the people of the culture it provides adequate justification for the norm.

Sanctions. In addition to legitimations, norms are backed up by *sanctions,* either

INSERT **3.III**

CANNIBALISM AND THE DONNER PARTY

Every society sets up elaborate systems of taboos to keep the fabric of the society intact. Taboos, a form of cultural norm, cut across many lines, limiting a person's choice of clothing, foods, and sexual partners. For example, Westerners view few acts as more repugnant than murder and cannibalism. But Westerners also believe that "self-preservation is the first law of nature." What happens when these two norms conflict? The Donner Party is a case in point.

For over a century California and its lure has called settlers to its dark black soil and rich mountains. One of the most famous of the emigrant parties to California was the Donner Party, which left Little Sandy Creek, Wyoming, with 23 ox-drawn wagons on July 19, 1846. Shortly thereafter they became separated from the main body of the migration, and by October 31 had already reached the snows in the Sierras near what is now Donner Lake. Fearful that they could never cross the windy, snow-covered mountains, they built their camp for the winter beside the icy lake.

Eighty-seven people—29 men, 15 women, and 43 children—settled down to a nightmare. The food supply quickly ran out, the snows grew heavier, and no help came. As the normal rations were exhausted the starving band was forced to live off of the hides and lean meat of half-starved work oxen. Finally on December 15, 1846, the first death occurred. On the next day 15 desperate men and women set out on snowshoes to cross the mountain. On the way eight men of this scouting party died. Only two men and five women reached the Sacramento Valley. When they arrived they frantically told of the desperate plight of the trapped party.

Back at Donner Lake things had taken a turn for the worse. After the dogs, ox hides, and tree roots were exhausted the starving, ragged survivors began to turn to human flesh from the dead immigrants.

The Irishman rallied and found a knife among the packs broken open and scattered when Peggy had pushed them into the pit. He climbed the sloping tree and cut apart the thin, wasted bodies of the two little boys. Peggy watched him come back, her mouth agape at the sight of the limbs tucked under his arm and his ragged pockets stuffed with the things he had put into them. Later in the day, Breen returned to the surface and tugged Mrs. Graves' body to the edge. He called a warning to those below, and shoved it over.

The Breens' demented state spared them revulsion. The flesh was roasted over the coals and for the children too weak to eat solids Mrs. Breen boiled meat in snow water and fed them a thin soup.

A spark of energy awakened in the pit on Friday morning and grew stronger beneath the sunshine. The thing having been done once, was less difficult to do again. Without emotion, the Breens pulled the rags from Mrs. Graves' body and butchered it with the objectivity they would have shown toward the carcass of an ox. The breasts were removed and the flesh sliced from the arms and legs. While the stew pot simmered the trunk was opened and the heart and liver were taken out. The task exhausted the Breens, and they wrapped themselves in blankets to nap by the fire. The warmth from the flames and the high-riding sun was pleasant, and those in the hideous camp drifted into a stupor.[1]

It wasn't until January 31, 1847, that a relief party could leave Fort Sutter in Sacramento. On February 18, seven men reached the Donners. They took out with them 23 of the starving emigrants, including 17 children. Unfortunately, there were several deaths along the way back to the settlement. There were other relief parties, but it was impossible to move everyone back due to illnesses and injuries.

One of the people left behind, Lewis Keseberg, became the last survivor. Keseberg was forced to live in one of the cabins, gathering fuel as well as he could in his weakness, eating what was at hand, existing in solitude except for the wolves. It wasn't

[1]Joseph Pigney, *For Fear We Shall Perish,* (New York: Dutton, 1961), pp. 209–210.

until just before Keseberg was rescued that Mrs. Tamsen Donner had died. She had come to Keseberg in the middle of one bitter night, sobbing that her husband, the leader of the party, had just died. She seemed a little crazed to Keseberg, who had to put her to bed himself. The next morning she, too, was dead.

The widow's death plunged Keseberg deeper into desolation. Flesh went into the pot to provide an insipid, disgusting diet almost entirely lacking in nourishment. As the slowly melting snow released more frozen victims, the cost of prolonging life became a daily horror. To touch a corpse revolted him, and the stark and ghastly faces pursued him, asleep or awake. . . .

Keseberg was as much a slave to the fire as he was to the flesh; without either he would have perished. He shuffled into the snow every day, hacking and chopping until exhaustion sent him reeling to his blankets.[2]

Keseberg finally staggered out of the bloody camp on April 21, 1847—the last surviving man of the ill-fated Donner Party. Of the original 87 who left Sandy Creek, only 47 survived. Five died before reaching the mountain camp, 34 at the camp or on the mountains, and 1 just after reaching Sacramento. In addition, two rescuers who joined the party at the lake also perished.

The story of the Donner Party shows two very strong cultural values in conflict: the taboo against cannibalism running head-on against the norm of self-preservation. Can it be taken as a general rule that under the compulsion of necessity the strongest of laws and taboos can be overridden? In the case of Keseberg, who later flaunted his acts of cannibalism, people judged him harshly, driving him from town to town, beating him, harassing him until he finally collapsed, almost totally insane. But who can say which social norms should dominate, and which cultural values should control behavior? In this case the individuals in the Donner Party were helplessly trapped between their personal needs and society's rule, a position all men face—even when the situation is everyday life instead of starving desperation.

[2]Ibid., p. 228.

punishments or rewards, that literally "force" people to obey them. Sanctions for some norms are very minor: using the wrong spoon or belching in public draws only frowns of disapproval at worst. Sanctions for major norms, however, are quite severe and include fines, imprisonment, and even exile or death. Although jails and electric chairs are available for the worst violators, social disapproval, a weapon in almost all known societies, is the usual punishment. The Amish, a sect of the Mennonite movement, practice a punishment called "shunning" in which violators are systematically excluded from the activities of the community and avoided like the plague; in New England the Puritans placed sinners in the stocks, not so much for physical punishment but for public ridicule and harassment; Eskimo tribes often act as if a moral violator does not even exist, and they have been known to set up a separate home in which the offender lives in exile; in 1973 a cadet finally graduated from West Point who, because of his supposed cheating, was subjected to four years of "The Silence," a punishment in which no classmate at West Point ever spoke to him. In general, societies depend more on this kind of informal ridicule than on formal punishments dealt out by courts.

Not all sanctions are punishments, however; in many cases a person obeys the norm because of rewards—social prestige, money, power. Usually the carrot is more effective than the stick. In effect, people are rewarded if they obey the norms and punished if they disobey them. Rewards and punishments are two sides of the same sanction coin.

Internalization. The final reason people obey the norms is that they are so constantly exposed to these cultural rules that they simply accept them as the natural way to act. After prolonged exposure people literally take the cultural rules and make them a part of themselves—they *internalize* them. People seldom have to be rewarded or punished for their behavior; they are so socially brainwashed that they rarely think of doing anything to violate the norms. In most cases people literally do not realize that it is possible to violate the norms. The few obvious violations, such as murder and other crimes, cover up the fact that most of the time people simply cannot violate the norms because they do not know of alternatives. They obey the norms simply because they have been culturally taught that no civilized human would act otherwise (Figure 3.1).

FOLKWAYS

Not all norms have the same seriousness; committing murder and violating etiquette are hardly on the same level. The most usual and least serious types of norms are the customary patterns of behavior that Sumner called *folkways.*

Take an example. On Saturday Bob and Jennifer attended an open-air rock concert. They spent most of the sunny afternoon lying on the grass, Bob with his shirt off, Jennifer in her bikini. They kept a bottle of cheap wine and some marijuana at their side, and both of them, together or singly, jumped up to dance whenever the mood struck them. On the following day Bob, dressed in suit and tie and accompanied by Jennifer in a prim,

Figure 3.1
The normative system

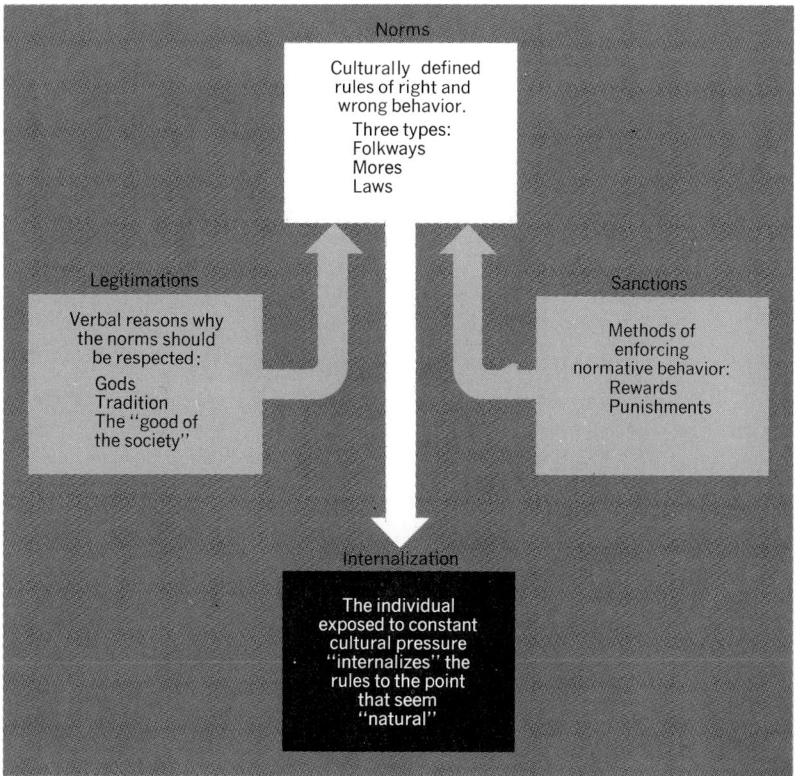

proper dress, met his parents at the door of the church. They went to church as a group and after the service went out to Sunday dinner. At the meal when Bob spilled iced tea onto his lap, he exclaimed "Oh, darn," carefully avoiding the language he would have used at the rock concert.

This incident illustrates the major points about folkways, the *minor rules* of behavior that people observe: (1) they differ depending on what is considered "proper" for a *specific occasion* (behavior acceptable at a rock concert is different from that required at church); (2) the *legitimation* for these minor rules is generally based on tradition (that is the way it has always been done), not on appeals to the good of society or to religion; (3) the *sanctions* accompanying violation of the folkways would be very minor (had Bob exclaimed "Oh, dammit!" his mother probably would have frowned, but surely would not have packed him off to jail).

There are many other examples of folkways, in fact, everything in our daily lives is affected by minor folkways. How many times one eats each day, which side of the street one drives on, whether or not one belches at the table (it is rude *not* to belch in some societies), fads and fashions in dress, table manners, and the appropriate behavior for any particular occasion are all integrated in the folkway system.

MORES

Whereas folkways are relatively minor regulations for social conduct, *mores* are serious social rules; people believe that if the mores are violated the society may actually fall apart. Examples of American mores include protection of young, helpless children, patriotism to the nation, monogomy and sexual fidelity to one's mate, male leadership in dating, respect for elderly people, and reverence in church. The legitimation for mores comes from people's sincere belief that if they are violated, reasonable social life would be impossible. Of course this legitimation is not necessarily valid. Bigamy might very well alter the present family structure, but would it destroy the society? Would female leadership in dating cause society to crumble? The objective facts do not justify people's fears about violating mores, but since people firmly *believe* them, they obey them. Sanctions for violating mores can be severe.

LAWS

Some norms, considered so important that their enforcement cannot be left to chance, are made into *law.* Laws are norms with several special characteristics.

1. Laws are formally enacted by the state. The *legitimation* for law is in this official enactment.

2. Laws are not left open to informal public understanding; they are *codified* into written documents that are precise and subject to legal interpretation.

3. Laws have special *enforcement agents:* police, judges, district attorneys, lawyers, and so forth.

4. Laws have definite, specified *sanctions.* Whereas the penalty or reward for less serious norms may vary considerably, the penalty for disobeying a specific law is clearly stated in the law itself. If you rob a bank, you get 20 years in jail; if you murder your landlord, you get life in prison or death.

Laws and mores usually coincide; for example, both rule out murder, adultery, and robbery. *But there are laws that are not backed up by common mores.* Nobody, for example, believes that society would collapse if we drove on the left side of the street. But this and other "laws of convenience" are generally obeyed just the same. Other laws, however, are widely violated because they are not supported by the common mores; the Prohibition laws of the 1920s were systematically broken, as are current laws against smoking marijuana or prohibiting school segregation. Many people simply did not believe in these laws, and they violated them.

On the other hand, *there are many common mores that have never been made into law.*

- According to the mores a man who gets an unmarried woman pregnant should marry her, but law does not make this mandatory.
- The common mores say that males should take the lead in dating, but there is no law that denies women the right to ask a man out.

INSERT **3.IV**

ANACHRONISTIC LAWS

Laws do not always coincide with what many, or even most, people believe to be "right" or what they actually do. Many laws, for example, have simply become obsolete. They may reflect the norms of the past, but they have not been altered or repealed as society has changed. Generally such laws are ignored. Or the law may be inapplicable—since people rarely ride horses in cities, there is no point in prohibiting them from riding their horses into buildings. Some examples of the many archaic laws still existent are given below.

North Dakota—It is illegal to serve pretzels with beer.

Tulsa, Oklahoma—It is against the law to open a pop bottle in a restaurant or bar unless a licensed bartender is present.

Prescott, Arizona; San Francisco, California; and **Ellensburg, Washington**—A person is forbidden to ride a horse in a public building.

Denver, Colorado—As in most localities it is illegal to be a "vagrant" but here a "vagrant" is defined as follows: ". . . any person who shall be found frequenting or remaining at any place where intoxicating liquors are sold, or tippling houses, ninepin or tenpin alleys, or billiard rooms." The usual test of vagrancy ("no visible means of support") is not mentioned.

Topeka, Kansas—It is against the law to serve wine in a teacup (this is probably a holdover from Prohibition days).

Sources: San Francisco Chronicle, February 14, 1971, "Those Crazy Laws"; *Life, 60,* p. 4, March 4, 1966; *Harper, 230,* pp. 35–40, January 1965; *Time, 76,* p. 17, August 22, 1965.

In general, then, laws and common mores often overlap, but there are many laws that are not supported by mores, and there are many mores that are not backed by law. Laws are more effective when supported by mores, and common mores receive additional force when strengthened by law. But, as indicated in Figure 3.2, when laws and mores are contradictory, social tension results. Figure 3.3 compares the three types of norms that we have been discussing: folkways, mores, and laws.

Wyoming—Women may not drink at or within five feet of a tavern's bar; they may, however, sit at tables and drink.

Florida—It is unlawful to buy or sell ice cream on Sunday.

Ocean City, New Jersey—It is illegal to drive a car on Sunday.

Nebraska—Persons drinking in saloons are prohibited from buying drinks for each other.

Newark, New Jersey—It is illegal to buy or sell ice cream after 6 P.M. without a doctor's prescription.

Nebraska—It is against the law for a tavern to serve beer unless a kettle of soup is brewing at the time.

Arkansas—Waiters may not receive tips, directly or indirectly.

Evansville, Indiana—It is unlawful to sell hamburgers on Sunday.

Maryland—It is criminal to purchase contraceptives from a vending machine, *except* on premises where liquor is sold.

Connecticut—It is illegal for an unwed mother to give "secret delivery of a bastard."

Various states—Almost any sex act besides face-to-face intercourse between married couples is likely to be illegal in one or more states. Anal intercourse and oral-genital relations are often outlawed even within marriage. Adultery and fornication are quite commonly classed as crimes and often carry heavy penalties (in theory). Kinsey has estimated that 90% of American adults are sex criminals in the eyes of these outdated laws.

Laws are not inevitably prohibitive, however. A British Columbia statute requires that debtor prisoners be given beer on request. Neither are all laws unenforced. Relatively recently (1966) a Virginia man was arrested for painting lines on a parking lot on Sunday—the only day it was not in use.

UNIFORMITY AND DIVERSITY IN CULTURE

If we examine cultural systems throughout the world, it seems that everywhere there are *common* patterns and at the same time great *differences* built on that common base. In this section we will examine both the *universal* features of human culture and the *diversity* that makes every culture unique.

Figure 3.2
Mores and laws may or may not overlap

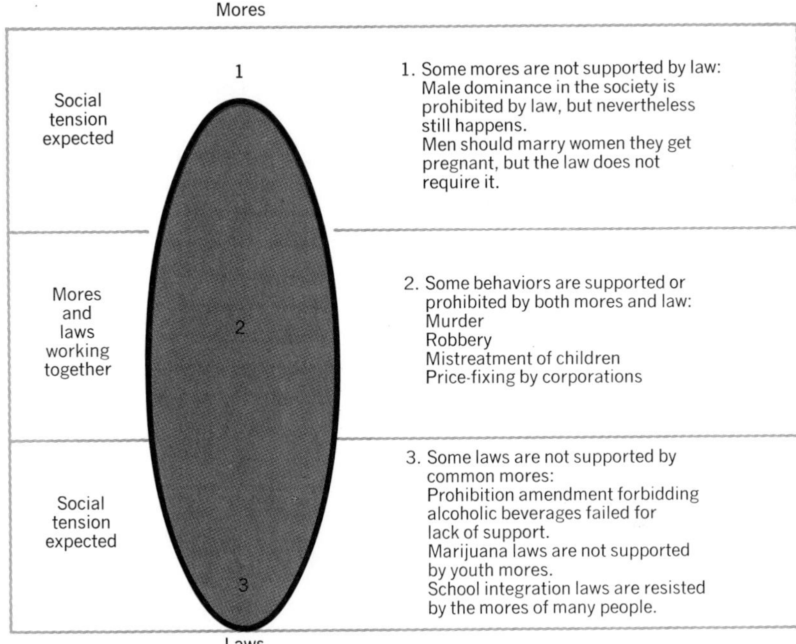

CULTURAL "UNIVERSALS"

Human beings, whether they live in the jungles of South America or the jungles of a New York slum, face many of the same problems. They all have to get food, provide for their children, control violence, and work out a system of government. Although there are many differences among cultures, it is remarkable that societies have so many features in common. Many social scientists are convinced that there are basic patterns that all cultures share called cultural "universals."

As an example, all societies have cultural knowledge that helps them cope with the physical environment. Jungle rains, desert heat, Arctic cold, and mountain winds; tornadoes, hurricanes, ice storms, droughts, and floods; disease-carrying insects, man-eating insects and animals, poisonous plants; are all part of life on this planet. Everywhere people must adapt to their environment, and they have developed elaborate systems of knowledge to help conquer the elements. Knowledge about housing, bridges, clothes, agriculture, tools, flood control, and road construction are all part of the cultural heritage that has been built up to deal with the physical environment.

There has been considerable debate about exactly what the universal aspects of culture are, but control of social violence and war, the rearing and education of children, communication systems, political arrangements, and economic systems are problems that confront every society, and every society has constructed

Figure 3.3
Comparison of three kinds of norms

	Folkways	Mores	Laws
Definition	Minor rules about social conduct	Major rules of conduct deemed essential by society	Formally enacted norms, enforced by police power, codified into documents, and sanctioned by specific penalties
Examples	Dress patterns Dating habits Table manners	Adultery rules Incest taboo Patriotism Religious observances	Laws against murder, stealing, using drugs, or fixing prices
Legitimation	Tradition: "That's just the way we have always done it"	Good of the society or religion: "Society will break down if violated," or "God commanded it"	Official enactment by the state "for the good of the people"
Negative Sanctions	Minor social gossip and ridicule	Severe ridicule, shunning, break in social relations physical attack	Enforcement by police and courts: fines, imprisonment, death

INSERT **3.V**

CULTURAL UNIVERSALS: WHEREVER HE IS, MAN SHARES MANY CULTURAL UNIVERSALS

1. *Relations to the Environment*
Man must somehow adjust to his physical surroundings—the climate, terrain, and natural resources. If he cannot accomplish this, he must move or face extinction. A culture always had knowledge about housing, agriculture (including food production and storage), clothing, and protection from weather.

2. *Relations between the Sexes and Population Control*
Man must always have a pattern for heterosexual relationships to insure opportunities and motivation for a sufficient rate of reproduction. Every society needs enough adult members to insure adequate reproduction and to occupy essential status positions. A society always has knowledge about marriage, dating rituals, incest taboos, limitation of marriage, and practices such as infanticide, geronticide, and birth control.

3. *Role Differentiation and Role Assignment*
There are activities that must be regularly performed in any society if it is to persist. Man and his society must always have a systematic and stable division of these activities. These role systems include: caste and class (and other stratifications), sex roles, age roles, child-rearing activities, occupational roles, distribution of wealth.

4. *Relations with Others—Communication*
No society can exist without shared, learned, symbolic modes of

Source: Adapted from D. F. Aberle, et al. "The Functional Prerequisites of a Society," *Ethics, 60,* 1950, pp. 100–111.

a large body of cultural knowledge to deal with these problems. See Insert 3.V for some of the more important cultural universals.

CULTURAL DIVERSITY: CROSS-CULTURAL DIFFERENCES

The cultural universals mentioned above reveal some of the *similarities* in human cultures. But on these common bases wildly variant cultural systems have been built. It is probably true that for every attitude or behavior valued by any society, there is another society in which that attitude or behavior is considered absolutely inhuman and unthinkable. For example, modern Americans hold the value of private profit and material goods very highly, yet the Indians of the northwest coasts of British Columbia and Alas-

communication. Without them it cannot maintain the common-value structure or the protective sanctions that hold back total chaos. This necessitates a language, gestures and facial expressions, tones of voice, and symbols, especially some form of written communication.

5. *A Common Set of Goals*
Every society has the goal of avoiding extinction. There are, however, many goals that each society may be striving after. Because there is role differentiation, there may be sets rather than one specific goal. It is this range of goals, however narrow, which provides alternatives for individuals and thus reduces one serious source of conflict. This set of goals becomes articulated in a form of government and a type of economic structure.

6. *A Set of Controls for Both Means and Violence*
Man must somehow have a set of controls that both positively defines the means (most noncoercive) to the society's goals and includes pre- and proscriptions regarding the use of force and fraud. These two sets of controls complement each other to keep the society functioning. Man always has a knowledge concerning the rituals and initiatory procedures of his society as well as a knowledge of police and the army.

7. *A Socialization Process*
Man and his society cannot exist unless he has a knowledge of a self-sufficient system of action—whether in changed or traditional form—for the socialization of the society's new members, drawn at least in part from the maturing generation. Socialization includes both the development of new adult members from infancy and the induction of an individual of any age into his role in the society or its subsystems. This includes child-rearing and further education.

ka had an elaborate ceremony called "potlatch," in which they gained social status by giving away as much material wealth as possible. For most modern societies the value of human life is extremely high and, except in time of war, the society spends huge amounts of time, energy, and money protecting even the smallest, weakest individuals. Yet this supreme value of human life has not by any means been a universal trait of man. Witness the slavery that prevailed over most of the world until lately; witness the human sacrifice customs of many ancient civilizations; witness the practice of killing female infants and old people among some Eskimo groups when the population was growing above the starvation level. Figure 3.4 gives many more examples of the different practices and values held by the societies of man. Without doubt, there are amazing cultural differences that give mankind an exciting diversity. Man is *one* human creature, yet he is *many* in his cultural variations.

CULTURAL DIVERSITY WITHIN A SINGLE SOCIETY: SUBCULTURES

We have been discussing the enormous cultural differences between societies throughout the world, but even within a single society there are significant variations on the common culture. There are, to be sure, many norms that everyone obeys; these "universals" govern much of our lives. However, there are many options open to individuals. Some "alternative" norms are matters of personal taste (shall I wear my hair long or short, dress wildly or conservatively, marry an older person or younger?), while others called "specialties" are optional values that apply only to certain occupational groups, for example, medical or legal codes of ethics. These specialty norms control only ranges of occupational life, not a person's entire existence. In addition to these cultural variations that are open to *individuals,* there are cultural differences that are somewhat unique to different *groups,* groups called *subcultures.*

SUBCULTURES

Any group that has a value system different in some respect from the dominant values of the society is called a *subculture.* There are many reasons why subcultures arise. People in different occupations form occupational subgroups; different racial groups have strong subcultural identifications; separate social classes often form a subworld of their own; religious groups sometimes share value systems that are at variance with the dominant culture; youth subcultures frequently exist alongside adult subcultures. In a sense each of these groups have values that "fall in the cracks" between dominant cultural beliefs. They do not challenge the dominant culture; they just ignore certain parts of it and add their own variations. Subcultures, then, provide *options* within the dominant culture.

Subcultures usually develop special life-styles, languages, and value systems. In the United States, for example, immigrant groups have retained many of their old-world values. Speaking the native language, upholding rigid dating patterns in the face of liberal American practices, clinging to the old religion, and stressing the solidarity of the old-world family life are all part of the immigrant subculture. Youth subcultures also flourish, building up special identities, heroes, styles of dress, and personal habits. Patched jeans, long hair, rock festivals, radical political views, and widespread use of marijuana were all part of the youth subculture in the middle of the 1960s and early 1970s, and although the particular styles are changing quickly, the uniqueness of the youth subculture continues to the present.

There are many other examples of subcultures that do not directly challenge the dominant culture. Religious bodies that

Figure 3.4 Cultural variation.

	Cheyenne Indian	Nyakyusa (Tanganyika)	Mentawei (West Malaysia)	Bantu (South Africa)	Anglo-American
Religious Practices	...Two symbolic arrows to control enemies ...Two more to control buffalo ...Worship Great Spirit and Sweet Medicine	...Belief in many spirits of the dead ...Funeral rites used to "drive away" the ghost	...Pantheistic ...Souls attributed to men, animals, objects ...Ghosts and nature spirits also believed to exist	...Ancestor worship ...Sacrifices made to dead ancestors ...Skins of sacrificed sheep are sacred garments	...Monotheistic Christianity ...Religion not emphasized ...Magic has little religious significance

	Hindu (India)	Tokugawa Japan	Maori (New Zealand)	Ruanda (Ruanda-Urundi)	Anglo-American
Class and Caste	...Rigid caste system ...Intricate labor division based on caste ...Now breaking down	...Rigid hereditary classes ...Emperor and nobles on top ...Among commoners farmers highest, merchants last	...Three castes: slaves, commoners, nobles ...Noble loses rank if life saved by another ...Slaves are war captives	...Three racial castes ..."Middle" caste (85%) farms for upper (10%) ...Lowest caste (5%) hunts and makes pottery	...Semiopen classes ...Achievement orientation ...Opportunity depends on family status ...Remnants of castes

live in cohesive groups, such as the Mormons or Mennonites, form enclaves within a highly secularized society. People in some groups find that they form a subculture because they have so few contacts with the outside world. Career military people, clerics in monasteries, students in boarding schools and colleges, and inmates in prisons and mental hospitals often form subcultures with their own values, special languages, and life-styles. Different racial groups and social classes also can develop subcultures. Subcultures are so widespread that it may be reasonable to suggest that a complex modern society is a collection of subcultures that share enough common features—especially political and economic similarities—to bind them together.

Some subcultures do not exist side by

	Eskimo (Sub-Arctic)	Marquesans (Polynesia)	Manus (New Guinea)	Chaga (East Africa)	Anglo-American
Sexual Behavior	...Wives loaned to house guests ...Wives swapped ...Refusal of another man's wife insult	...Polyandry *and* polygymy both used ...Each spouse may have other mates ...A household may include "lovers"	...Puritanical ...Sex shameful, done only at night ...Homosexuality tolerated	...Sex accepted as pleasure ...Premarital sex tolerated if contraception-abortion used	...Puritanical norms breaking down ...Premarital sex now more common ...Fidelity desirable in relationships

	Cheyenne Indian	Ifugao (Philippines)	Ibo (Nigeria)	Yoruba (Nigeria)	Anglo-American
Systems of Justice	...Guilt judged by leaders on basis of evidence ...Driving a person to suicide is murder ...Murder punished by banishment	...Guilt judged by duels or ordeals ...Adultery not a serious offense ...In adultery cases husbands fight a duel with eggs	...Guilt decided by leaders ...If in doubt an oath of innocence is proof ...Bad luck is considered proof of false oath	...Judges decide cases with evidence ...A debtor may have to "pawn" a wife or child ...Well-defined legal principles	...Elaborate system of judges, juries, and attorneys ...Cases often take years to settle ...There are separate criminal and civil laws

side with the dominant culture, but instead actively and aggressively fight against it. Such subcultural variations are sometimes called *countercultures.* Sociological literature abounds with vivid descriptions of all kinds of countercultures: junkies and dope peddlers, criminal countercultures, the hippie movement, women's liberation groups, religious sects, and homosexual freedom leagues. Juvenile gangs have been of particular interest. Their culture includes a vocabulary unintelligible to outsiders, a cult of physical violence, a cycle of narcotics and petty crime, and a hatred of police. All these values help form a tight little world, shut off from the larger society and turned in on itself.

The youth counterculture, the "Flower Child" movement of the 1960s, has gradually expanded until now in the 1970s many Americans share the countercultural values. Charles Reich, in *The Greening of America* (1970), argued that a

Cultural variations in family structures. Although every society provides for stable relationships between partners and for the rearing of children, the family systems vary considerably.

fear of bureaucracy, a drive toward pacificism, a rejection of crass materialism, and a search for individual meaning in a complex society are some of the overriding concerns of the youth counterculture. Without a doubt, this movement has had enormous impact on the values and beliefs of American society. Figure 3.5 shows the contrast between these counterculture values and more traditional American values.

THE SOCIAL FLEXIBILITY GIVEN BY SUBCULTURES

Subcultures and countercultures increase the flexibility in a society by providing options. As societies grow more complex more possibilities open up and more subcultures form. Of course, this diversification can go too far and lead to complete fragmentation and disintegration of the society, but most modern societies are able to handle an enormous variety of subcultures and alternatives without undue strain.

With the rise of the black consciousness movement, women's and gay (homosexual) liberation groups, and the youth countercultures, the ideal of an homogeneous society is being replaced by a greater acceptance of differences. Members of various subcultures are affirming their unique features, their special gifts, and their singular heritages. Black people are insisting that "black is beautiful;" gay men and women are standing up for their rights and coming out of the closets; Spanish-speaking Americans are interjecting alternative life-styles. These subcultures are enriching the society's alternatives, providing the impetus for a diverse, culturally pluralistic society.

INCREASING OPTIONS IN A COMPLEX SOCIETY

Universal values provide a common base for every society, insuring that at least a core of activities will be alike for all people so that the society can function smoothly. On the other hand, alternative norms, occupationally specific values, and the growth of subcultures provide options, choices, and new possibilities, so that each individual within the society has some choice about what he will do, think, and believe. Most sociologists believe that the options and choices in a modern, complex society are richer and more open than in premodern societies. In earlier societies the universal norms, the commonly held values, dominated. Although there was *some* choice, by and large the major differences broke along the lines of sex and age. People came much closer to being carbon copies of one another, and the society was more culturally *homogeneous.*

As societies have grown more complex the array of choices has multiplied, and in the process social systems have grown more culturally *heterogeneous.* New occupations have created more specialties; atomic scientist, newspaper reporter, astronaut, X-ray technician, and submarine captain are all occupations available to us, but not to our distant forefathers. At the same time, as more distinct subcultures are generated in a modern society, the alternatives in behavior, beliefs, and

Figure 3.5
Counterculture values and traditional values

Consciousness I and II (Older Value Systems)	Consciousness III (Counterculture Values)
Industry, hard work	A combination of work and leisure; a "live-life" philosophy
Efficiency (job done best, cheapest), meritocracy.	There are several ways of doing a job, all acceptable
Continued increased production	Only what we need
Bureaucracy is beneficial	Antibureaucratic
System is working and can work (American dream).	System is not working or is working too slowly
Occupational success.	Personal success (individuality)
Complex society	Simpler, more human society
Public-private man split	One man with social concern
Conservative	Liberal, radical
Judeo-Christian ethic	Pantheistic, ecological
Stability	Change, adaptability
Law, order	Antiauthoritarian
Cold war mentality	Pacifistic

24TH
UNUSUAL

Cultural options are greater in a complex society. The alternative life-styles available in a complex society shown here and on the following page are much greater than in simple societies.

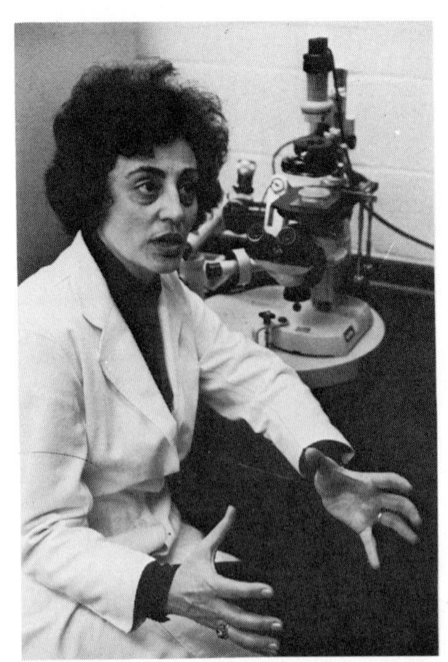

values are greater. Although it may seem at times that the society is rigid ("cut your hair," "join the army," "be a conformist") the rigidity of modern, complex society is probably not as great as it was in premodern societies. In other words, common values dominated premodern societies, but alternative values, occupational specialties, and subcultures all give more options in a complex modern society.

ETHNOCENTRISM AND CULTURAL IMPERIALISM

In considering the issue of cultural diversity it is important to understand some of the *psychological attitudes* that members of one culture hold toward the members and values of a different culture.

ETHNOCENTRISM

People in every society think that *their* way of doing things is right; other ways of doing things are unthinkable, barbarian, uncouth, crude, uncivilized, unreasonable, savage, or superstitious. Every society has a sort of social nearsightedness that allows it to see only its own behavior as reasonable and most others "inhuman" and "unnatural." This kind of social prejudice for one's own group is *ethnocentrism.* It may refer to prejudices between various societies (e.g., Israeli against Arab), or it may refer to prejudices between groups within the same society (e.g., white against black in the United States).

Ethnocentrism affects everybody in every society to a greater or lesser degree. The ancient Chinese viewed Westerners as uncouth savages who could barely read, would never understand Confucius, and had worse manners than any well-bred pig. The Westerners, on the other hand, sent Christian missionaries to "spread the light" to the eternally damned heathens in the Orient. Each group felt that the other was somehow uncivilized and greatly in need of some help if they were to become really human (Figure 3.6).

Ethnocentrism is trained into people as is every other value. From the cradle to the grave social belief systems define the ingroup as good and the outgroup as bad. College fraternities each claim that they are better than the other; college songs insist that good old Podunk U is head and shoulders above the rest; national flags, anthems, and Fourth of July speeches constantly drum into our heads the superiority of the United States. Even Superman displays blatant ethnocentrism when he says he fights for "Truth, Justice, and the American Way!"

In mild forms this kind of ethnocentrism is normal and reasonable. The normal feelings of group self-identity and self-worth are strengthened by ethnocentrism, as the growing self-identity of blacks, Spanish-speaking Americans, and other minority groups illustrates. The strong self-identity of Jewish people has been an ethnocentrism that served the

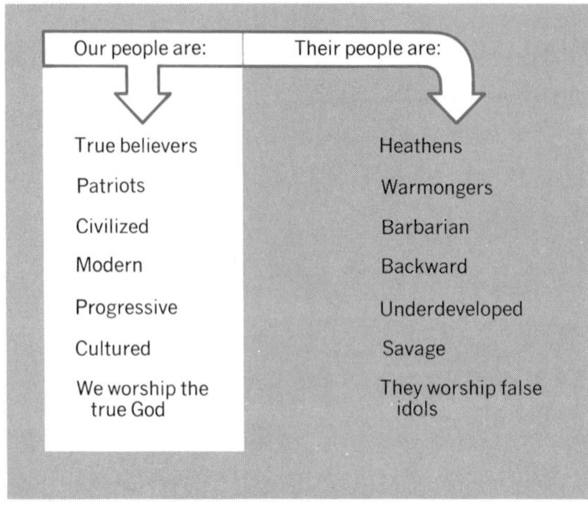

Figure 3.6
Ethnocentrism at work

valuable function of building morale and group cohesion under widespread persecution. In some respects, then, ethnocentrism can serve a positive function.

Negative Effects of Ethnocentrism. Nevertheless, ethnocentrism can be vicious and ugly when carried to the extreme. War-time propaganda posters provide horrible examples of man's ability to think of the enemy as inhuman, cruel, and ruthless. Our side is always "carrying out interrogation," but their side is "using torture and committing bloody atrocities." Ethnocentrism can also tear a society apart internally, for it is at the root of racial hatreds and class conflicts. Extreme ethnocentrism coins ugly epithets to hurl at the outgroup: "nigger," "honkie," "male chauvinist pig," "wop," "dirty Jew." These are the words of hate, hate that grows like a cancer out of the normal ethnocentrism that every person feels. This is ethnocentrism gone wild, ethnocentrism that tears the fabric of the society. Normally we call this kind of attitude *prejudice,* and the negative actions flowing from it *discrimination.* Prejudice, then, is a negative *attitude* toward another group, whereas discrimination is a negative *action.*

Cultural Relativity. Every person is blinded by ethnocentrism to a greater or lesser degree. We are often unable to see the unique values of other societies or other subcultures. However, social scientists usually take a position of "cultural relativity." That is, they believe that a social practice or value can be assessed only *in the context of the particular society at a particular point in history.* The idea of cultural relativity implies that there are few universally true absolutes about what men should do, think, or believe. Instead, there are historically and socially bound customs that are relative to a particular situation. We cannot completely escape our ethnocentrism, but we can appreciate and respect the differences among peoples and enrich our own and other cultures through mutual respectful exchange. This does not mean that all values will be abandoned or that each society will drop its own values. It only means that healthy respect and appreciation may replace blind prejudice.

THE PROBLEM OF CULTURAL IMPERIALISM

Different cultures and subcultures hold different values and support their own beliefs while attacking other groups' values. In its extreme form this attack process can develop into cultural imperialism, an attempt by one group to force its values on another. There are many examples of such cultural attack throughout history. The Greeks and Romans, through the power of their army, were able to conquer a vast expanse of territory. And everywhere they went they imposed their own governments, religious ideas, and economic systems.

Cultural imperialism, however, is not just a thing of the distant past; it has continued up to the present day. The great colonial drives that occupied Europe from the fifteenth century until World War II were accompanied by cultural impositions from the "mother country" onto the colonies—whether the colonies liked it or not. Elaborate rationalizations were developed to cover up the guilt that the imperialists would have otherwise felt; "the white man's burden" was to bring "civilization" to the rest of the world. Sometimes these motives and rationalizations were in fact naively positive, as in the drive to "Christianize the heathens." Unfortunately very often these naively altruistic imperialists succeeded only in disrupting the culture. The utter destruction of the native way of life in Hawaii is one of the worst examples of this disruption. At other times, however, there was nothing more involved than sheer economic exploitation; the conquering of India, Africa, and Southeast Asia by the European empires may have been masked by lofty sounding motives, but in reality they were largely economic rape in the crudest form.

Many critics of the Vietnam war, for example, distrusted the proclamations of both France and the United States that their purpose was "to save the Vietnamese from communism." Instead many people suspected that the motive was really "to save them for Western businessmen." From this perspective the importation of American democracy and American economic values was a classical case of cultural imperialism; the subjected nation and the helpless civilians had new cultural values imposed on them by strong international powers that had self-serving motives for promoting the changes. This kind of international cultural imperialism is as old as history—but no more respectable because of its age.

Internal Imperialism. Cultural imperialism, however, is not a phenomenon that occurs only when one *society* imposes its values on another; it can also happen when one *subculture* has enough social and political power to force its life-styles and values onto other subgroups. In the United States today there are many unhappy signs of internal cultural imperialism. The values of the dominant middle and upper classes are imposed constantly on the lower social classes; the values of the dominant whites are forced on minority groups; the values of dominant

Ethnocentrism in war posters: "Their" side and "our" side.

TELL THAT TO THE MARINES!
HUNS KILL WOMEN AND CHILDREN!
JAMES MONTGOMERY FLAGG

males are pressed on females. In many instances the powerful groups demand that their values be accepted, their beliefs be written into law, and their attitudes be imposed as the "right" way of life.

There are many examples of this "internal colonialization." Blacks and other minorities have for years argued that schools impose on them middle-class, white values through the use of biased textbooks, white middle-class teachers, and a pervasive "institutional racism" that defines them as second-class citizens. In another problem area, homosexuals are now organizing to demand that the dominant cultural heterosexuality not be imposed on them in daily attitudes and in law; they demand the right to be left alone with their private lives. The list of internal cultural imperialism could be extended for pages, but the point is clear. In every society many subcultures find that their own values are attacked while the values of other powerful groups are imposed on them through the media, daily confrontations, and the law.

Assimilation and Pluralism. For years in the United States there was a dominant social belief that everyone should adopt similar values and beliefs, a position called the "melting-pot" theory. The idea was simple; immigrants from other nations, lower social classes, and minority groups were expected to abandon their unique values and "melt" into the dominant middle-class, white, Protestant ethic. In short, there was a widespread expectation that all groups would eventually assume the characteristics of WASPS (white, Anglo-Saxon Protestants) in values and beliefs if not in race and religion. The schools were to implement this policy deliberately, taking the immigrants and minorities and remaking them into imitations of the dominant classes. The mass media reinforced this pressure by holding up the middle-class, white family as the ideal. The melting-pot of American society was supposed to produce assimilation, as all subcultures gradually assimilated, or mixed, with the larger dominant culture.

Over the past few decades many groups have rejected the melting-pot theory and have demanded that their cultural uniqueness be respected, that they be allowed to develop their own life-styles in subcultural enclaves, in small subcultural islands that could coexist peacefully with the dominant culture. In contrast to the melting-pot doctrine of assimilation the idea of separate subcultures is a type of *pluralism* in which a variety of cultural values could exist simultaneously.

In the United States today there are strong demands by minority groups that they be allowed to develop their own subcultures to the fullest, that their unique customs, languages, and social heritages be preserved. The critical demand has been for a serious pluralism that would allow each group its own heritage and would protect them from cultural impositions from the dominant society. The movement in the United States for community-controlled schools is a specific instance of people striving toward a pluralist society.

Before ending this discussion, it is important to note that *power* relations shape much of the social dynamics in a society;

the problem of cultural imperialism demonstrates this fact vividly. In every case it is the powerful, the strong, and the rich who force their values on the powerless, the weak, and the poor—whether they are conquered colonial peoples or subjected, oppressed minority groups within the home country. Ideas and values are intimately tied to power and force, for the winners are generally the ones who determine social values and attitudes. Like so much of the rest of social life, culture is closely linked to social power, conflict, and change.

SUMMARY

Culture is a knowledge system, the complex whole of values, technical knowledge, and aesthetic standards that people create in the interactions of society and pass down from generation to generation through socialization. Every society has its own unique cultural system, consisting of *empirical* facts, *aesthetic* definitions of the "beautiful," and *normative* values that define what is right and wrong. There are enormous variations in normative behavior all over the world, but for a person in any particular society his behavior is "natural" to him; he assumes that the very laws of nature invented the behavior.

All these norms have some form of *legitimation* because they are usually based on religion, custom, and tradition or on appeals to the good of society. But legitimations are not relied on exclusively; societies also use *sanctions*—either rewards or punishments—to force proper behavior. In addition to legitimations and the imposition of sanctions a society depends on the *internalization* process so that people are carefully taught the values of the society.

There are three major types of norms. *Folkways* are minor social rules of behavior; *mores* are behavioral values that are considered very serious; *laws* are either folkways or mores that have been formally passed by the government, have police to enforce them, and have specific sanction processes (courts, judges, prisons, etc.). Laws generally reflect the contemporary mores and folkways of a society, but can become obsolete when the norms changed by the laws are not revised accordingly.

Some of the cultural values are *universals,* norms that are supported by the vast majority of the people in a society. There are, however, many diversities in normative systems—*cross-societal differences*—but also differences between occupational groups, racial groups, and social classes within a single society. All of these various patterns of differences form *subcultures.* These optional patterns of life give a complex society more flexibility.

Although cultural diversity promotes freedom and enlarges options, cultural diversity can also produce intense social conflict because of the attitude known as *ethnocentrism.* In its worst forms ethnocentrism leads to destructive social prejudice and discrimination against other groups and can result in *cultural imperialism.* Cultural imperialism happens on the international scale when a conquering nation forces its values on the subjected nation; it happens internally when one powerful subgroup forces its beliefs on less powerful subcultures. This is also called "forced assimilation," for the powerful group demands that the less powerful mix with the dominant values and drop their own uniqueness. In a pluralistic society subgroups would be given the option to assimilate or to remain.

REFERENCES

Aberle, D. F., et al. "The Functional Prerequisites of a Society," *Ethics, 60,* 1950, pp. 100–111.

Allport, Gordon W. *The Nature of Prejudice* (Cambridge: Addison-Wesley, 1954).

Benedict, Ruth. *Patterns of Culture* (Boston: Houghton Mifflin, 1961).

Berger, Peter L., and Thomas Luckmann. *The Social Constructions of Reality* (Garden City, N. Y.: Anchor Books, 1967).

Blake, Judith, and K. Davis. "On Norms and Values," in R. L. Faris (ed.), *Handbook of Modern Sociology* (Chicago: Rand McNally, 1964).

Hall, Edward T. *The Hidden Dimension* (Garden City, N.Y.: Anchor Books, 1966).

Hall, Edward T. *The Silent Language* (New York: Doubleday, 1959).

Lenski, Gerhard. *Human Societies* (New York: McGraw-Hill, 1970).

Miner, Horace. "Body Ritual Among the Nacirema," *American Anthropologist, LVIII,* June 1956, pp. 503–507.

Parsons, Talcott. "Evolutionary Universals in Society," *American Sociological Review, 29,* June 1964, pp. 339–357.

Parsons, Talcott. *Societies: Evolutionary and Comparative Perspectives* (Englewood Cliffs, N.J.: Prentice-Hall, 1966).

Pigney, Joseph. *For Fear We Shall Perish* (New York: Dutton, 1961), pp. 209-210.

Reich, Charles. *The Greening of America* (New York: Holt, 1970).

Sumner, William Graham. *Folkways* (New York: New American Library, 1969); First published in 1907.

Tyler, E. B. *Primitive Culture* (New York: Holt, 1971).

FOUR SOCIALIZATION AND THE FAMILY

ANNA

What would happen if a child had no social interaction? Would the child grow up like other children, or would he be unusual in some respects? There have been several known cases of children who were raised in virtual social isolation—*feral* children, as they are called. If man's personality were largely determined by biology, these children should have assumed normal human characteristics. But in all actual cases of feral children—children, for instance, who were shut away in attics and fed by hostile mothers—the children did *not* grow up to be normal. In fact, they had all the characteristics that we usually attribute to animals. They could not talk; they walked on all fours; they were afraid and hostile; they bit like wild dogs. One of the most famous cases was that of Anna, a young girl who had been shut away for many years. When she was finally freed, she was brought to the University of Chicago where she was treated along with other socially isolated children, most of whom acted like wild beasts.

During one year a single staff member had to have medical help more than a dozen times for bites she suffered from Anna, and the children regularly bare their teeth when annoyed or angry. Different, and again reminiscent of animals is their prowling around at night. . . . Then there is their great preference for raw food, particularly for raw vegetables. . . . Some of these children on seeing animals, respond as though they had found a dear, long-lost friend. One girl, for example, became extremely excited on seeing a dog; she showed a strong desire to run toward it and cried or howled like an animal. She fell on all fours, jumped like a dog with her head down and made biting gestures. (Bettelheim, 1959, p. 458)

Although Anna had the physiology and genetic inheritance of other humans, she did not have any of the *social* characteristics that people need to function as normal members of society.

1. She did not have a set of *cultural values*—morals, norms, or beliefs.
2. She could not deal with cultural *symbols*—especially language, the tool of human interaction.
3. She had no ability to function in social *roles*—the basic social behavior patterns.
4. She could not link into the *institutional processes* of the larger society—work, education, politics, and religion.

These important skills, skills that connect the individual person to the larger social world, are not inherited but are learned through social interaction. Anna was not fully human because she had not been *taught* to be human; her family had neglected its critical socialization tasks, the process of passing on the culture to children and preparing them to link into the institutions of the larger society.

Examine Figure 4.1 closely. Anna, like all other humans, is linked to the outside world through a complex social process. On one hand, she must be taught the cultural values, knowledge, and belief patterns that people use to govern their social life, and that are expressed in symbols. On the other hand, she must be tied into the institutional structure of society through roles that she learns to play in the world of work, politics, and education. The previous chapter talked about cultural values; future chapters will deal with institutional systems; this chapter shows how the two social systems intersect on the individual, the person who—like Anna—must be taught to be "human." This teaching process is called *socialization,* and the *family* is the critical socializing agent for the society. As the dotted arrows in Figure 4.1 indicate, however, there are other socialization agents besides the family, including the school, peer groups, and on-the-job training.

In this chapter we will explore how all these socialization processes are tied together by examining a number of issues: (1) the socialization *processes* (i.e., how people are taught), (2) the *content* of the socialization process (i.e., what people are taught), and (3) the effect of *cultural* and *institutional* change on the family's socialization role.

THE FAMILY AND THE SOCIALIZATION PROCESS

Human beings are basically social creatures created by society, primarily through the family's influence. Society creates the individual, the individual does not create society. Of course, a society is a collection of individuals, but the individuals have little power to change their society. The society, however, has great power over individuals; it shapes, molds, and creates their personal-

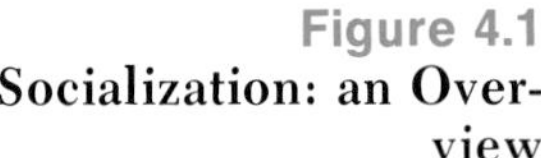

Figure 4.1
Socialization: an Overview

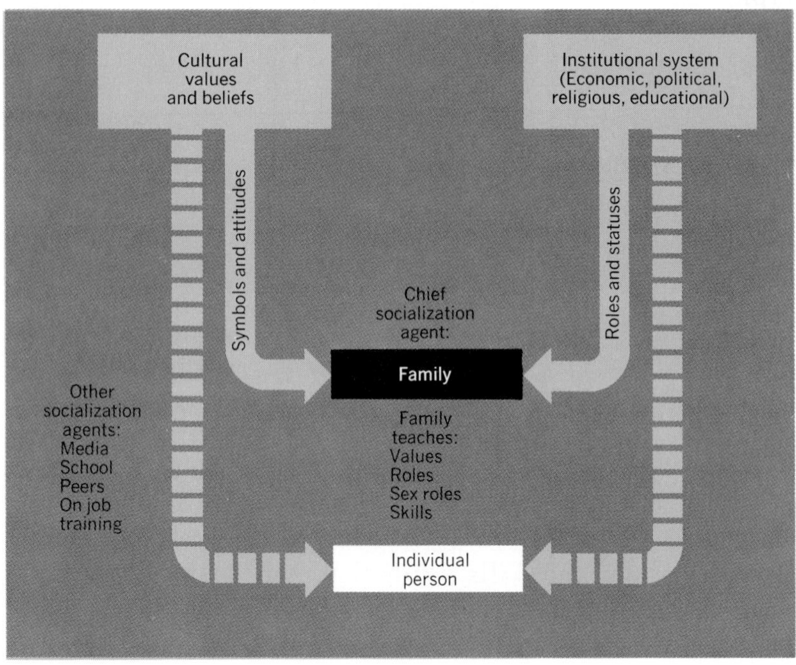

ities. Acting primarily through the family, society stamps its impressions on people, and creates them from the soft wax of their biological inheritances. In this sense, then, the "self" is as much *social* as it is biological. The importance of biology is not denied but the importance of society in remaking, remolding, and shaping the biological being to create a social "person" must be stressed. In short, *personality, the systematic set of values, beliefs, and traits held by any individual, is a by-product of social life.* Let us examine some of the research on this topic.

THE NEED FOR SOCIAL INTERACTION

The opening quotation showed the deprivation that comes from lack of social interaction and family support. But the study of social isolation and incomplete attention during childhood does not depend on the bizarre cases of feral children. There have also been several studies of life in orphanages where children received very little individual attention. René A. Spitz has done several such studies, and his results suggest that children in orphanages have great difficulty learning normal behavior, even though they are physically sound. In one study Spitz administered a Development Quotient Test (1964) to four groups of children, three in normal social settings and one in an orphanage. At the first testing all four groups were similar in ability but, as time passed, the orphanage children fell far behind—so far behind, in fact, that they could easily be mistaken as mentally retarded. At an age when other children were walking and talking, the orphanage children—who started out on approximately equal terms with these other children—could not stand alone or speak a single sentence. In other studies Spitz (1949) and Goldfarb (1945) analyzed mothering behavior of normal infants. Some groups had mothering that included fondling and talking as well as physical care, whereas other groups received only strict physical care with very little emotional involvement. It is important to note that researchers did not contrive such situations. Spitz and Goldfarb were studying variations in behavior among mothers and children in natural settings. The children who had emotional involvement grew up normally, but the socially deprived children had a higher death rate, lower emotional responsiveness, and a general lack of social ability. The evidence from studies of feral children, children in orphanages, and children who experienced different mothering all points to the same conclusion: *children only become "human" when they have continual, rich social interaction, usually in a close family environment.*

CREATING THE SELF: THEORIES OF PERSONALITY DEVELOPMENT

Three highly perceptive men of the early twentieth century—Charles H. Cooley (1864-1929), George Herbert Mead (1863-1931), and Sigmund Freud (1856-1939)—have been extremely influential in explaining the process by which social interaction affects the development of the individual's personality.

Cooley. Cooley's great contribution to our understanding of the socialization process was his idea of the *looking-glass self;* every person understands himself through the eyes of others; every person learns to judge himself based on how he thinks others judge him. How do children come to have a self-concept, an idea of their value, their strong points, and their weak points? By seeing themselves through others' eyes and by understanding how others judge them. If my mother always says I am a bad boy, I learn to view myself as a bad boy. If I think my friends value me highly, I learn to value myself highly. You surely have had this experience of judging yourself by other's opinions, for example, when you failed to live up to your parents' expectations or when you pleased your friends. In those circumstances your own sense of self-worth was shaped according to others' judgments. Suppose you had been told from early childhood that you were superior in every way. How do you think you would feel about yourself? What if people consistently shunned and avoided you? How do you think your self-concept would be affected? Cooley's looking-glass-self concept takes into account what we think others think about us.

Mead. George H. Mead's theory of self development is closely related to and partly built on Cooley's arguments. In his masterpiece, *Mind, Self, and Society* (1934), Mead deals with the creation of the self and the mind and with the social-training process that produces them both. Mead's theory can be summed up in several brief statements.

1. There is no self until the society—

through parents and peers—creates one in the child.

2. Children are not conscious of their own existence or their own minds except through social interaction with the parents who teach them about themselves. At first the infant does not even realize he is a distinct being; later he develops the concept of "other" as he recognizes that he is separate from those outside him. Parents become *significant others* who shape his mind and self-concept.

3. *Language* is the prime tool of social interaction and is therefore extremely critical in developing the social self. In fact, symbols and language are so crucial to Mead's theory that he is known as the father of the "symbolic interactionist" school of thought, which stresses the importance of language as a technique fundamental to social relations.

4. When the growing child begins to develop a general conscience, a general conception of "right" and "wrong," he is using as his reference some *generalized other;* that is, he is beginning to understand how his whole society wants him to act. He is finally becoming socialized into the culture of the society.

5. The social self is not entirely a *passive "me,"* however, that accepts anything the society pours into it, since the person also has an *active, self-directing "I"* that partially controls his destiny. Thus, every individual is a "me" that is shaped by society and an independent "I" that is self-controlling. It is the interaction of these sides of a person's personality that truly makes him human.

6. Most of the impact of socialization occurs in childhood, since the personality is largely shaped by childhood experiences—especially by experiences within the family.

Freud. Whereas Cooley and Mead stressed social interaction as the source of human personality, Sigmund Freud added a biological approach to personality development. He suggested there is a primitive biological force, the *id,* that serves as a wellspring for human personhood. The id, a primitive power driven by sexual urges and violent impulses, is the force behind man's growth. But, in the course of socialization, people also develop an *ego,* a rational, thinking, calculating element that controls and channels the id's basic drives. In addition, a *superego* regulates both the id and the ego, acting as a conscience and defining "right" and "wrong" behavior. Freud held that the superego is a social product because norms of right and wrong behavior come from the social setting instead of from biology. He elaborated on the concept of superego in *Civilization and its Discontents* (1930), arguing that the superego's social conscience is a repressive, hostile imposition that makes people incapable of acting freely.

Since the early 1900s when Cooley, Mead, and Freud wrote, there have been literally thousands of studies on the socialization process. It is impossible even to begin reviewing all of them, but two major thrusts should be mentioned.

Behaviorist Theories. The *behaviorist* approach stresses the role of direct rewards and punishments in the socialization process. The basic thesis is that when children find their behaviors rewarded, they will continue them, but when they are punished, the behavior will be "extinguished." Thus, behavior can be "conditioned" by the application of rewards and punishments so that the child learns, usually from his parents, what is "proper" and "right." (See Skinner, 1938, and Hilgard and Marquis, 1940 for two important classic works on the behaviorist theme; and Brown, 1966 for a review of current research.)

Modeling Theories. The second new approach is the *modeling* interpretation of the learning process. Bandura and Ross (1963) have argued that much successful socialization results from children imitating (modeling) the behavior of adults, and this process is at least as important as rewards and punishments. For example, a boy without a father could be rewarded by his mother whenever he displayed appropriate "masculine" behavior, but without a father to imitate the boy may have trouble learning the proper behavior. Thus the modeling theory stresses the need for appropriate *role models* in the socialization process.

All of these various theories—interactionist (Cooley and Mead), Freudian, behaviorist, and modeling—have important things to say about the socialization process, each adding a slightly different interpretation. However, they all share certain basic sociological points: (1) *human social interaction* helps to create the personality; it is not a biological inheritance; (2) the *family* is a critical link in the socialization process; and (3) social *roles* are key links between the individual and society. The next section further explores the issue of social roles.

THE CONTENT OF SOCIALIZATION

Up to this point we have been discussing the *process* of socialization, the question of how people are taught. Now we turn to the second major issue, the *content* of socialization, a discussion of what is taught.

SOCIALIZATION FOR STATUSES AND ROLES

As noted in Figure 4.1, the family teaches the child how to relate to larger social institutions, especially by developing "statuses and roles." A *social status* is a specific social position with attached privileges and duties, such as the status of being a father, a president, or a soldier. A *social role* is the behavior that goes with the status, the behavior of a father, a president, or a soldier. Thus status is the social position, whereas role is the behavior expected in that position. These statuses and roles are the key link between the individual and the larger society's institutions.

Sociologists have borrowed the concept of role from the drama world, for on stage in life is very much like on stage in the theater. Proper lines and behaviors must be learned and connected to roles. Statuses and roles are the fundamental building blocks for social behavior because they connect individuals' activities with the social network around them, thus tying people to the social system. If, for example, a man has status of "father," this social position implies that he will

Children often learn by "modeling" parents' behavior.

take certain roles of behavior, such as providing financial support for the family. Any social position is a status: mother, university president, gas station attendant, woman, student, minority-group member. And every status has a set of role behaviors associated with it. A student, for instance, occupies a certain status within the school, and with that status role behaviors are expected: handing in papers, reading books, taking exams.

The socialization process teaches people their "proper" statuses in society and the "appropriate" behavior that accompanies that status. Little children are taught that "mommies" (a status) take care of children (a role behavior) and that "daddies" (another status) go out to make money (another type of role activity). Society teaches minority children that their status is lower than that of other children and that their "proper" role is to have low ambitions and low expectations in life. The family, peer groups, and the school all work to instill appropriate role behavior. Often people feel trapped by the many roles society tells them they must play—like the young man in the cartoon on p. 125. Statuses and roles are, then, key factors in social life.

SOCIALIZATION INTO SEX ROLES

Another of the most important kinds of role socialization deals with behavior appropriate to men and women:

We have all heard it said in praise of some little boy, "He's all boy!" or in a praise of some little girl, "She's a real little girl!" How can a boy be less than all boy or a girl other than a real girl? It is the roles *built around the biological distinction of sex that makes maleness and femaleness matters of degree.*

In the United States a real *boy climbs trees, disdains girls, dirties his knees, plays with soldiers, and takes blue for his favorite color. A real girl dresses dolls, jumps rope, plays hopscotch, and takes pink for her favorite color. When they go to school, real girls like English and music and "auditorium;" real boys prefer manual training, gym, and arithmetic. In college the boys smoke pipes, drink beer, and major in engineering or physics; the girls chew Juicy Fruit gum, drink cherry Cokes, and major in fine arts. The real boy matures into a "man's man" who plays poker, goes hunting, drinks brandy, and dies in the war; the real girl becomes a "feminine" woman who loves children, embroiders handkerchiefs, drinks weak tea, and "succumbs" to consumption. (Brown, 1965, p. 161)*

We all know the stereotypes: men are aggressive, tough, independent, and intellectual, whereas women are passive, weak, dependent, and intuitive. Are the stereotypes true? If so, are these differences innate? Current research indicates that both statements are false and that sex roles are taught just like any other role. Indeed, the majority of behavioral traits we associate with males and females are cultural effects; men and women were not *born* that way—they are *trained* that way.

We normally link differences between men and women to biological factors and, there are, in fact, biological differences between the sexes. For instance, men are about 20 percent heavier at maturity and about 30 to 50 percent stronger depending on the measure (Terman and Tyler, 1954). Women, bear and nurse the chil-

© 1971 Jules Feiffer, Courtesy Publishers-Hall Syndicate

dren, and in addition, seem to be more resistant to some kinds of diseases and certainly live longer (about three to four years)—although this latter statistic may not be a biological difference as much as a difference in working conditions and daily habits (men smoke more, for example). There are differences between males and females, but in general the biological variations are relatively small—certainly not large enough to account for the huge divergence we find in the roles of men and women.

If biology does not determine the differences between sexes, the most likely explanation is that cultural training produces them. One examination of this hypothesis was undertaken by anthropologist Margaret Mead. In her classic book *Sex and Temperament* (1935) she asks: Is culture critical in determining sex roles? If so, she reasoned, different cultures should have different definitions of appropriate behavior for the two sexes. But, if biology alone defines the critical differences, men and women would always play the same roles, regardless of the culture. Thus, if sex roles were everywhere the *same, biology* makes the difference; if sex roles were *different* in various societies, *culture* makes much of the difference.

Mead's research indicated that different societies do have widely divergent definitions of sex roles, thus reinforcing the idea that culture and socialization are major influences on them. In the United States she found that males were aggressive and independent, whereas females were gentle and passive. But among the

Tchambuli people in New Guinea the females were dominant and aggressive, and the males were passive, artistic, and dependent. Between the two extremes she found one group, the Arapesh, who thought both males and females should be gentle and passive, and another, the Mundugumor, who defined both males and females as aggressive. The scale of variation is shown in Figure 4.2. As a result of this study Mead concluded that *sex differences on the social and psychological levels (attitudes, behaviors, aggressiveness, etc.) are primarily a result of cultural socialization, not biological differences.* Although there have been some criticisms of Mead's study (e.g., Scott, 1958), most social scientists now largely accept her basic thesis.

VICTIM SOCIALIZATION

The young child is taught many different statuses and roles; his social self, his fundamental status, and his sex roles are creations of the social environment around him. But not all children are treated the same by the society. One of sociology's critical roles is to study power relationships, inequality, and social stratification. This task is just as relevant to the socialization process as it is to other areas.

The phrase *victim socialization* describes the process by which society socializes some children into lower statuses and disadvantageous roles. From very early in their lives some children—lower-class and minority children in particular—are taught that they are not as good as other people, that they must be satisfied with fewer of life's pleasures, and that they must be humble. If Cooley's idea that people learn their self-concepts from other people's feedback to them is correct, then victim socialization constitutes a relentless cultural attack on the very personhood of many people in our society. "Black man, Mexican-American man, lower-class man, woman of whatever background" the message cries, "you must be second-class citizens—and you damn well better get used to it! Internalize it, believe it, feel it, because we are going to see that it's your life!"

The message is relayed through the subtle snub of a lower-class man at the country club, the violent beating of a black man when he "gets out of line," the never-ending tyranny of school textbooks that display a middle-class bias, the stone wall of indifference or outright hostility that greets a woman who tries to succeed in the occupational world. From the cradle on, the socialization process sends different messages to different people. And the poor child begins to believe the message, to act on it, to absorb it.

Let us take an example. The black psychologists Kenneth B. Clark and Mamie P. Clark decided to study the problem of the self-identity of black children. The Clarks studied 253 black children, about half from segregated schools and half from integrated schools (Clark and Clark, 1958, p. 608 ff.). Their procedure was simple. They showed each child a dark-colored doll and a light-colored doll and then asked a series of questions

Figure 4.2

Sex and temperament: Mead's study of sex differences in different cultures. Since sex-related behavior varied considerably from one society to another, Mead concluded that most differences between male and female behavior resulted from culture and *socialization*, not from biological differences.

	Behavior: Aggressive Dominant Independent	Behavior: Gentle Passive Dependent
Western Europe, America	Males	Females
Tchambuli of New Guinea	Females	Males
Mudugumor of New Guinea	Males and Females	
Arapesh of New Guinea		Males and Females

Source: Margaret Mead, *Sex and Temperament* (New York: Morrow, 1935).

about them: "Which doll is nice to play with, looks bad, has a nice color, is a nice doll?" The startling conclusion was that most of the black children preferred the *white* doll, indicating that they had internalized a value system that made them victims, that made them second-class citizens. The responses of black children were as follows:

	Dark doll	White doll	Do not know
Give me the doll that you would like to play with	32%	67%	1%
Give me the doll that is a nice doll	38	59	3
Give me the doll that looks bad	59	17	24
Give me the doll that is a nice color	38	60	2

From these results the Clarks concluded that black children were subject to an intense brainwashing by the larger society, to the point that their own self-respect was very low. They had indeed experienced "victim socialization." Two additional facts should be mentioned. First, the older children favored the black dolls somewhat more than the younger children. This might mean that they were regaining their self-respect, or it could mean the opposite, that they were so self-conscious they had learned to hide their self-hatred. Second, this experiment was done in the late 1950s and, since that time, there has been a major campaign among blacks to break the stereotypes and the traditional prejudices; thus, it would be unlikely that black children today would exhibit the same high degree of victim socialization.

As will be seen in Chapter Nine one of the first tasks of any revolutionary social movement is to resocialize its members, to stamp out the oppressive aspects of socialization that its members have internalized. The "Black is Beautiful" slogan is a resocialization campaign that has had significant success. The resocialization process, however, is not easy to accomplish, for years of repressive mind-tinkering have gone into the warping of the victims' minds. It takes strong action to begin tearing out the roots of a victimized self-concept.

THE SOCIALIZATION OF WOMEN

The socialization of women will serve as an extended example of victim socialization: What *cultural values* are being taught to boys and girls? What are the *processes* by which these values are instilled? What are the major *roles* that males and females learn? In what manner is *victim socialization* taking place?

The *socialization patterns* of young girls relegate them to second-class citizenship roles in the society, secondary to men. Social scientists have only recently begun studying this question, but their conclusions seem to show that the socialization process almost uniformly channels women into housewife roles or into low-paying, low-responsibility jobs. From the crib to the grave women are told to keep in their place, to tend the home, to be passive, and to accept the dominance of men. The Germans summarize it in a neat little phrase: *"Kinder, Kuche, Kirche"*—children, kitchen, and church, the traditional concerns of women. The power of this channeling process is suggested by the Stanford psychologists Bem and Bem (1970).

> *Consider the following "predictability test." When a boy is born, it is difficult to predict what he will be doing 25 years later. We cannot say whether he will be an artist, a doctor, or a college professor because he will be permitted to develop and to fulfill his own unique potential, particularly if he is white and middle-class. But if the newborn child is a girl, we can usually predict with confidence how she will be spending her time 25 years later. Her individuality doesn't have to be considered; it is irrelevant. (Bem and Bem, 1970, p. 11.)*

According to Bem and Bem the social system does not leave women as many options as men. Women frequently forego careers to become housewives not because of conscious choice, but because they were never given role models of women outside the home during the socialization process. The socialization process is a "channeling" system; it molds the minds of children so that they almost inevitably "want" to do whatever the society defines as appropriate. How is this socialization process carried out? How does the society train its little girls to play the *Kinder, Kuche, Kirche* roles?

The Young Girl and Infant Socialization. At birth girls and boys are likely to get different receptions because many parents have a preference in terms of sex. And, especially if it is a first child, chances are pretty high the parents want a boy. A number of sociological studies (Mead, 1950; Bell, 1967; Etzioni, 1968; and Westoff, 1959) indicate that there is a preference for male children in most nations, including the United States. Etzioni suggests that for every couple who wants a female child there are probably two who want a male, and he fears that if science develops a method to control the sex of unborn children, there may be a serious imbalance toward males. The parental desire for male children probably colors children's training and early life experiences.

Training children in behavior appropriate to their sex begins very early. During infancy and childhood boys and girls are treated radically differently. A number of social-psychological studies show that boys are encouraged to be aggressive, independent, adventurous, and tough-minded, whereas girls are more protected, kept closer to their mothers, and rewarded for being passive and quiet (Barry, Bacon, and Child, 1957; Bem and Bem, 1970; Sears, Maccoby, and Levin, 1957). Bem and Bem report:

In one study, six-month-old infant girls were already being touched and spoken to more by their mothers while they were playing than were infant boys. When they were thirteen months old, these same girls were more reluctant than the boys to leave their mothers; they returned more quickly and more frequently to them, and they remained closer to them throughout the entire play period. When a physical barrier was placed between mother and child, the girls tended to cry and motion for help; the boys made more active attempts to get around the barrier. (Bem and Bem, 1970, p. 2)

Toys, Picture Books, and Play. As children grow, most of their activities are channeled. Take their play, for example. Parents give little boys fire trucks, baseball bats, toy guns, chemistry sets, building blocks, and tool sets; they give little girls dolls, doll houses, little ironing boards, and nurse's kits. And the message gets across. Smith (1933) reports that as early as nursery school age, boys are actively asking questions about how things work, how machines function, and how life occurs outside the home. Girls, on the other hand, are much more passive, ask fewer questions, and talk less about things outside the home. By the third grade boys can do better at improving toys, even if they are girl's toys (Torrance, 1962).

Children are taught their "proper" sex roles in a number of different ways. In addition to carefully selected sex-linked toys, parental encouragement of "appropriate" play activity and early school experiences unite to present a different view of a woman's world from a man's. Books, both preschool picture books and early school texts, are a dramatic example of the socialization process. What do the children learn from books about their future sex roles in adult life? Weitzman and associates studied hundreds of children's books that had won various outstanding awards. Their findings were startling. First, *the books did not show many women:*

It would be impossible to discuss the image of females in children's books without first noting that, in fact, women are simply invisible. We found that females were underrepresented in the titles, central roles, pictures and stories of every sample we examined. Most children's books are about boys, men, and male animals, and most deal exclusively with male adventures. . . . Even when women can be found in the books, they often play insignificant roles, remaining both inconspicuous and nameless. . . . In our sample . . . we found 261 pictures of males compared to 23 pictures of females. This is a ratio of 11 pictures of males for every one picture of a female. (Weitzman, et al., 1971, p.5)

Second, the stories were almost always about men and boys. Boys were adventurers, hunters, dragon slayers, sailors, soldiers, doctors, workers—active, busy, lively. Girls were passive and quiet—creatures to make homes for the boys, to be rescued from dragons by the boys, to play back up roles to boy heroes. Boys were rugged, tough, and dressed for action; girls were frilly, neat, clean, and primly dressed for sitting quietly and passively. When the books showed the grown-up future it was clear that little girls would grow up to be housewives, in spite of the reality that most women work outside the home for part of their lives. In fact, in their sample Weitzman and associates could not find even one woman in the story books who had a profession or a job outside the home! Many other studies have shown the same stereotyped version of sex roles in children's books (see Heyn, 1969).

Image of Women in School Textbooks. The same pattern seems to persist in school; textbooks portray men and women in stereotypical, traditional roles. Many studies have been done on the images projected in textbooks. Paige Porter (1971) found that social studies textbooks pictured men three times as often as women, and the women portrayed were in minor roles. See Figure 4.3 for Porter's analysis of textbook versions of women's and men's activities. Child, Potter, and Levine (1946) examined third-grade readers and found that they showed traditional, home-oriented roles for women. In addition, there were a number of instances where women were depicted as lazy and selfish in comparison to energetic, altruistic men. Betty Miles (1971) reported that in a study of every major child's reader in the United States boys were always the main characters; girls were usually passive and indecisive, and the role models offered for girls were traditional housewife roles. Jamie Kelen Frisof (1969) suggests that social studies textbooks invariably imply that "Mothers are (apparently) not capable of doing anything worthwhile, or at least not worth reading about in school."

Image of Women in the Mass Media. With the kind of indoctrination they receive from children's books and textbooks it is no wonder that girls adopt traditional values and often feel that their options in life are limited. But the process does not stop in school. The myth is reiterated to adult women through the media. Television, films, books, magazines, and advertisements all tell people what they should do, be, love, hate, and value. How do the media view women?

In *The Feminine Mystique* (1963) Betty Friedan reported that the stories in popular women's magazines were usually about the personal frustrations and family problems of housewives, rarely ever about major social issues or life outside the family. The few working women who managed to sneak into the stories were almost always unhappy and frustrated until they found the right man, settled down in the suburbs, and had pink-faced, happy children. Or look at television soap operas. They project two basic images of women: the house-bound mother whose only concern is personal problems and the consumer who must buy the sponsor's products. Alice Embree put it well.

The nine-to-five television schedule is geared particularly to women. From Captain Kangaroo to several comedies, . . . and then an afternoon predominated by soap operas and a few game shows. The media provide trivia and comedy for diversion from serious matters, while constantly pounding in the message of consumption. Stay slim, don't have bad breath or underarm odor, have long eyelashes, buy an endless assortment of products for the home, become a blonde, become a more beautiful brunette, smoke a woman's cigarette, smoke a man's cigarette. If you do all these things, you can capture a boyfriend, get married, stay happily married, and be a good hostess to boot. . . .

The soap operas themselves—the kitchenette version of the "adult" horse opera—deserve a special study. Aside from simply diverting energy to a fantasy family's worries, they reinforce the image of male-dominated women. Like all TV programs, they are safely middle class. Women are almost always pictured as housewives and mothers . . . there is rarely any mention of a woman who has work outside the home. The formula for the shows are infinite interpersonal conflicts. Collective struggles are taboo. The realities of urban riots, the draft for the war in Vietnam, labor-union struggles, insurgent political groupings, etc., don't intrude upon the fantasy. The question of a new and collective identity for women can't be raised, for it would completely destroy the soap opera's formula. (Embree, 1970, pp. 181-182)

The television soap operas, novels, motion pictures, magazine articles, and commercials all send out the same dreary message: women are homebodies and women are consumers. If a woman tries to be anything else, she will be miserable and lonely. Of course, the stereotype is unrealistic. The statistics on women's employment and women in the labor force indicate that many women work outside the home in their lifetime. But the mass media ignore reality, and the myth goes on. From the Miss America Pageant to the ads in women's magazines, society outlines the limited, second-class role of women. Their options are limited be-

Figure 4.3
Men and women's activities in social studies textbooks

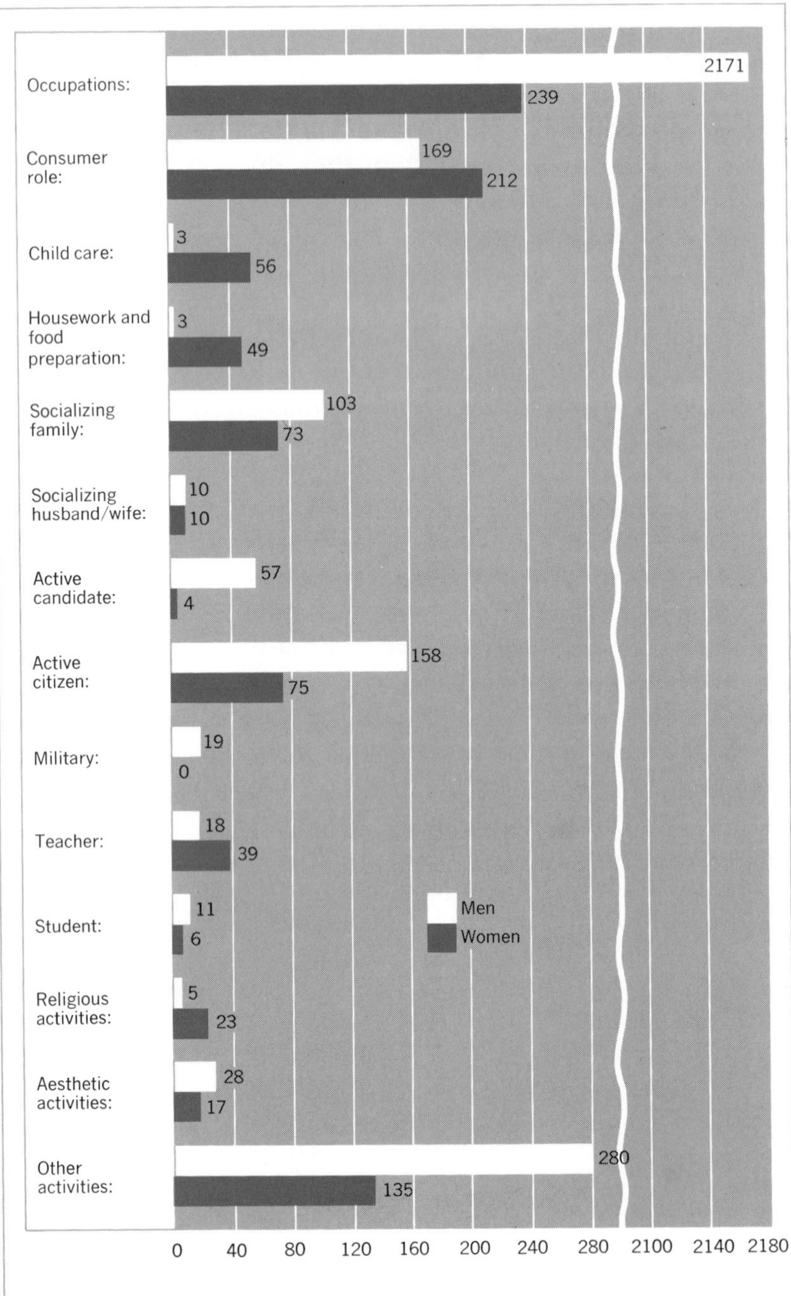

cause they frequently do not even realize that other roles, other life-styles, and other futures are open to them. Female socialization is one of the major social instruments for the oppression of women, and is a clear case of *victim socialization.*

ADULTS AND ALTERNATIVE SOCIALIZATION AGENTS

Thus far we have been discussing the socialization process that primarily affects children and that takes place in the family. It is important to realize, however, that socialization is not finished when the child grows up, for the process continues all through life. To be sure, most social psychologists and sociologists believe that a major portion of the socialization impact occurs at a young age and that patterns crystallized early affect a person the rest of his life. However, social learning continues in a variety of settings outside the family.

Peer groups, for example, teach new skills and new attitudes that are sometimes different from the family's influence. Peer influence is especially high during adolescence, and particularly in reference to dating and sexual behavior.

Schools, of course, are also a major agent for socializing both children and adults. Schools teach general attitudes and values (honesty, patriotism) and specific skills (reading, math). In addition, schools furnish the setting for the heavy peer interaction that has such great impact on the informal learning process. (See Chapter Ten for a discussion of education's role.)

Work organizations are socialization agents that have grown more and more important in modern societies. Even before adolescents enter the labor force they normally experience some "anticipatory socialization" for their future jobs. That is, they begin to develop the skills, attitudes, and personal life-styles they believe are appropriate for their occupational goals. Moreover, many work organizations carefully train their employees in the skills and attitudes necessary for occupational performance. Many people gradually develop an "occupational personality" that fits the work setting—the doctor's bedside manner, the librarian's meticulous habits, the lawyer's keen eye for contradiction, the scientist's passion for evidence. These occupational styles literally become part of the individual's personality.

The *mass media* are certainly important agents. We live in a culture where the modern mass media—particularly television—provide instant coverage of events all around the world and programs that teach social values. Children spend hours watching television. In fact, the average child today spends about 1080 hours a year in the formal school classroom, but probably over 1500 hours in front of that electronic teacher, the TV. More than 95 percent of the nation's families own televisions; about 100 million sets are currently operating in the United States.

Certainly the child—and adult for that matter—learns much from the media. Social values are constantly pressed on the viewers. They are taught that material possessions, sex appeal, and being "with it" are very important. The right car, the right refrigerator, the right drink are indicators of economic success; the latest deodorant, the latest toothpaste, the latest hair-grooming discovery bring instant popularity; and a certain hair style, a certain musical preference, certain clothing are "in" and must therefore be adopted. Viewers are also taught political attitudes (one should be informed about public affairs, not voice too many objections to the government, and support the "democratic processes"); they are taught a particular view of women's role in the society ("good" wives stay home and cook, care for the children, and devote themselves to their husbands). All these values are open to question and subject to debate, but the flickering tube continually molds and shapes the pliable minds of its viewers. Sandwiched in among the soap operas, the used car ads, the monster movies, and the variety shows are lessons about how one should think, act, buy, love, and live in a modern society. This mass socialization permeates the society without regard to social class, race, or region.

Finally, every society has agencies established to *resocialize* people, to change them and remold them into new roles, attitudes, and beliefs. Prisons, concentration camps, mental hospitals, and military organizations are examples of "total institutions" that resocialize people.

SOCIAL CHANGE AND ITS IMPACT ON THE FAMILY

Although socialization occurs in many different ways, the family is still the society's chief socialization agent. At the beginning of the chapter Figure 4.1 showed that the family links the individual to cultural values on one hand, and to institutional values on the other. As the cultural and institutional structures of society change—as they are doing so rapidly these days—the family must adapt to the new scene if it is to meet the human needs of its members. In the next few sections we will discuss some institutional and cultural changes that are affecting the family and its role as a socialization agent. Let us begin with family responses to political upheaval, using Russia as an example.

POLITICAL CHANGE AND FAMILY RESPONSE: RUSSIA

Russia is an excellent case of rapid family change promoted by a political revolution. Before the twentieth-century revolution Russia was ruled by czars in one of the most autocratic, totalitarian dictatorships in the Western world and was considered one of the most backward countries, for social repression and isolation from the world combined to hinder both material and social progress. It was not until 1861 that the serfs, the rural farmers who were virtually slaves, were given their legal freedom. Even after their emancipation there was not much change in their life conditions because land was so expensive and the peasants so poor that many continued working the land of the aristocracy as they had before emancipation. (Burgess, et al., 1963, p. 102.)

The Russian economic base at that time was largely agricultural. The family was of the "extended" type, with several generations living under one roof as a family unit. The extended family provides much cheap labor, both in the fields and in the household, where tasks not yet performed by machines are time consuming and arduous. Furthermore, except in times of crop failure, such a family structure is economically cheaper, since the large number of individuals in the extended family can be fed, clothed, and housed right off the land with little added expense.

The internal control of the prerevolutionary family paralleled the control that the czarist government had over the peasant. The head of the household, almost always the oldest male, ruled his subordinates (his wife, children, their wives, and any other relative).Wife beating was not only common, but had been institutionalized by an ordinance drawn up by Pope Sylvester, head of the Russian Orthodox Church. This ordinance gave careful instructions regarding the use of the whip, informing the user in the techniques that

The family in prerevolutionary Russia.

would not maim or kill—thus rendering the wife unfit for further service—but that would be painful and effective in obtaining future obedience.

If a wife refuses to obey, and does not attend to what her husband tells her, it is advisable to beat her with a whip according to the measure of her guilt; but not in the presence of others, rather alone. And do not strike her straight in the face or on the ear; be careful how you strike her with your fist in the region of the heart, and do not use a rod of wood or iron. For he who allows himself to be carried away to such actions in anger may have much unpleasantness if, for instance, she loses her hearing or goes blind or breaks a bone in her hand or foot or elsewhere. Keep to a whip, and choose carefully where to strike; a whip is a painful and effective deterrent, and salutary. (Quoted in Mace and Mace, 1964, p. 94)

It was customary for the father of any bride to give the prospective groom a whip to be used exclusively on the wife. This whip was ceremoniously hung over the bridal bed. In spite of the new freedoms that had been gained by the serfs in the period between 1861 and 1917, wife beating was still practiced just prior to the revolution. Oppression within the family existed even as oppression from the czars was reduced.

CHANGES AFTER THE RUSSIAN REVOLUTION

After the 1917 revolution the larger society changed drastically, and the family was clearly affected.

During the twenty years immediately following the Revolution, the Soviet government sought to bring into being the ideas of the family developed by Marx, Engels, and Lenin. Central to these conceptions was the emancipation of the woman from subordinate status and household chores and her active involvement in economic and political life. To achieve this goal, the government relied principally on two measures: first, it promulgated legislation guaranteeing women equal status in all walks of life, freeing them from traditional marriage bonds by permitting marriage and divorce on an almost casual basis, and granting freedom of abortion. Second, it sought to provide communal facilities for the upbringing of children, as well as for dining, cooking, and performing other household chores. (Bronfenbrenner, 1972, p. 120)

After the revolution the situation changed rapidly and today the Russian family shows far more democratic practices. Although these new family forms were not solely the result of the Bolshevik revolution (they were also brought about by rapid industrialization), the more democratic form of government was incompatible with the prerevolutionary authoritarian family system. In czarist Russia the head of the household or sometimes the local aristocracy had complete authority over the marriage of children—determining whom they would marry, regardless of their personal wishes. Women and children were held in low esteem. Women, in fact, had no legal rights and were totally economically dependent on their husbands or fathers.

Today, however, conditions have changed. Marriages are made with the permission and by the desire of the individuals concerned. Divorce has been liberalized, allowing women the legal as well as the practical right to separate from husbands for whom they have no personal feelings or who treat them cruelly. In addition, women have been granted legal equality with men, thus insuring them the right to a livelihood of their own and freeing them from the whims of autocratic husbands.

Moreover, many of the cares of the family have been eased by changes in the Soviet society. Medical care is available to all who need it, thus eliminating the constant worry over who is to pay the bills and the fear that because of poverty there will be no doctor when needed. Education is also available to children without regard for the parents' ability to pay for it, thus erasing the inherited elitism of prerevolutionary Russia where only the children of the aristocracy were allowed an education.

In short, the Russian family in the decades after the revolution changed dramatically from its traditional form. To be

The Russian society changed and so did the family.

sure, it would be wrong to attribute all that change to deliberate policy by the communist state, for as Bonfrenbrenner points out, many other social forces were impinging on the family.

What brought about the change was not so much government policy vis a vis *the family . . . as the broader social and economic crises taking place. . . . The chaos and strain of the Revolution . . . the subsequent collectivization, famine, and purges, together with the concomitant mass migration to the new industrial centers, led almost inevitably to the weakening and disruption of the family. . . . Husbands, wives, and children were separated. . . . In addition, both the rapidly increasing demands for manpower . . . and the decreasing standard of living and value of wages drove increasing numbers of women out of the home into the fields and factories. . . . Finally, family life was further disrupted by heavy and irregular work schedules. It is impressive evidence of the strength of traditional institutions that Russian patterns of marriage and family life maintained some stability despite these sweeping changes. (Bronfenbrenner, 1972, pp. 121-122)*

It is obvious that the changing political, economic, and social institutions of the Soviet society had caused monumental changes in the family, just as the rush toward industrialization had done in the United States a few decades earlier—an historical change we will examine next.

SOCIAL CHANGE AND THE AMERICAN NUCLEAR FAMILY

Sociologists identify a number of family types, but two are critical for our discussion. The *nuclear family* is composed of a husband, wife, and their children, usually living separately in a house of their own. By contrast, an *extended family* is essentially a combination of several nuclear families, with an older couple maintaining a residence in which several other generations live. Most commonly a couple would have sons and their wives and children living with them, while daughters would have gone to join other extended families.

It is important to understand that the type of family is very closely related to the economic system of the larger society. Most societies with extended family systems are traditional, depending very heavily on agriculture as the basic economic system. The extended family allows the economic advantages of one generation to be passed down to the next, especially when the land itself is the critical factor. As nations have industrialized they typically shift from an extended family type to a nuclear family.

INDUSTRIALISM'S IMPACT ON THE FAMILY

In early agricultural America the extended family was the dominant style.

But as America industrialized, rural agricultural life styles gave way to the demands of industry, reshaping the lives of those living under the new technology, and producing a nuclear family life-style. For example, industry needs many workers and, since one industrial plant often needs the services and products of other industrial plants, they must be located within a short distance from one another. For this reason hundreds of thousands of workers must live nearby, eliminating the possibility of individuals living on large land holdings. Indeed, as a city develops, land prices skyrocket, so that living on even one acre of land is economically and spatially out of the question for most workers. In effect, this means packaging families together in apartment buildings that use little land, but settle family after family in upward-expanding buildings. With the invention of the car, many workers have been able to escape to homes in surburbia, but modern surburbia is very different from the rural living of a century ago. Today one strives for a down payment on a three-bedroom tract home built on a 50 by 100-foot lot. The rooms are small, the garden area miniscule, but geographically and economically such housing serves as an alternative to the urban apartment for many workers.

A further need in an industrial society is *geographic mobility* for workers. Factories open up and close down. Workers are needed for short periods of time, then the need in that area slackens, and the worker looks elsewhere for employment. These conditions make mobility a key factor in the size of a family; it is easier to move if the family is small. Moreover, unlike the agricultural society where children were a benefit, children today are an economic liability. It costs huge sums of money to rear a family; in fact, the Presidential Commission on Population estimates that it costs about $59,000 to bring up one child to adolescence. All these factors combine to press for a smaller nuclear family in industrial societies.

CONTEMPORARY TRENDS

Today the pace of social change is accelerating even faster than it did during the Industrial Revolution, and many more profound changes are occurring in the family.

The Family as a Consumer Unit. Within our industrial capitalistic system, the family is no longer a *production* unit producing agricultural products and crafts; instead the production occurs outside the home, and the family has become a *consumer* unit. The man supports the family, the mother bears the children and then remains home to care for them. In many ways the function of children in our society is to consume, and the role of the mother is to spend what the husband earns. The nuclear family is perhaps the model of ultimate consumption. Most American nuclear families have a tremendous investment in kitchen appliances, furniture, plumbing, and electricity, and automobiles that are used only a fraction

Does the structure of the house affect the lives of the people?

of the time. The average middle-class kitchen could be used to prepare meals for twenty as well as for four or five, and the plumbing facilities could service many, but our values indicate that each isolated family unit must have all this expensive equipment—to keep the economy moving if for no other reason. In addition, because it is part of our culture to rear our children in the isolated home, each family invests large sums of money in the implements and toys of childhood, most of which are discarded after brief use. In short, the whole complex of family activities is in some sense tied to its economic function as the primary consumption unit in the modern society.

The Impact of Changing Technology. Technology has and will change our family lives. The automobile radicalized interpersonal relationships—a "bedroom on wheels," somebody noted—and perhaps its pollution will radicalize social relations just as much. Many of these changes in technology result in changes in the family. For example, as technology progresses, services that were once performed in the home become professionalized. Childbearing no longer takes place in the family home with a midwife in service; instead, the prospective mother is rushed to the hospital—with a consequent increase in the cost of having a child. Education, too, becomes more formalized, takes longer, and is removed from the home.

Multiplying these problems is the fact that as the technology increases, the expectations rise about the desired standard of living. A hundred years ago a middle-class family might have been satisfied with separate chamber pots for each bedroom. Today the expectations are for at least two elaborate bathrooms in the modern urban household. Furthermore, as more and more people are crowded together in small spaces, luxuries of a century ago become necessities. No health department of any large city would allow housing to be built without the elaborate plumbing and electricity that we now take for granted, but the increased cost is expensive.

All the changes in technology affect the family in a number of ways. Because technology is expensive the family income must increase to cover expenditures for items now considered desirable, if not necessary, for family living. The smaller family size and the paraphernalia for mechanized housework free women from many of their previous responsibilities in rearing a family. Together these factors enable the woman to find employment outside the home. And as mother and father spend more time outside the confines of the family, so too do the children. As they reach the teen years, children find more of their time devoted to institutions outside the family. In short, the family becomes less of a production unit with members working together to produce their basic needs, and becomes more of an economic consumption unit where money earned outside supports the family.

VALUE STABILITY AND VALUE CHANGE

Industrialization, political upheaval, and technological advances all have profound impact on the *value systems* of the society, especially as they apply to the family. Some family values have remained stable for years, while others have changed rapidly in recent times.

STABLE FAMILY VALUES

There has been remarkable stability about some family values. Of course, not everyone always agrees about values in a complex society such as the United States, and there are many exceptional styles of family life, especially among the extreme upper and lower social classes. However, to a remarkable extent some of the following values are widespread and stable.

Everyone Should Marry. One widespread assumption is that everyone should get married and, in fact, most of us expect this for ourselves. Children, particularly girls, fantasize about their future marriages. Popular songs, movies, and comic strips assume that everyone will marry and, furthermore, that everyone wants to. There are many discriminatory practices against those who remain single, including taxes and insurance rates that are frequently higher for the single individual. In addition, many businesses are reluctant to hire or promote the single individual. Moreover, the social stigma felt by a single person often acts as persistent encouragement to marry.

Statistical evidence showing pressure toward marriage is indicated in Figure 4.4, which shows that a relatively small percent of the people age 18 and over are unmarried. The normative pressure seems to be getting stronger, for even fewer people remain unmarried today than at the turn of the century; in fact, twice as many remained unmarried in 1900 (32.3 percent for males) than in 1970 (16.5 percent for males).

Moreover, getting married is not enough. One must also do it by a certain age if he is to escape the pressures of raised eyebrows and solicitous friends. Statistics indicate that the vast majority of people are married by age 25, many having done so prior to their twentieth birthday. College men and women surveyed in 1973 showed a preferred age of marriage at about 24 for men and 22 for women, slightly younger than students surveyed in 1939. Thus, our value system dictates that we should get married, and that we should do it at a relatively early age.

Personal Choice. Complicating the matter somewhat is a very strongly held value that each person marries a partner on the basis of personal choice. In contrast to the values of many traditional societies (e.g., India) where mates were picked by parents, American values dictate that only the individuals involved have the

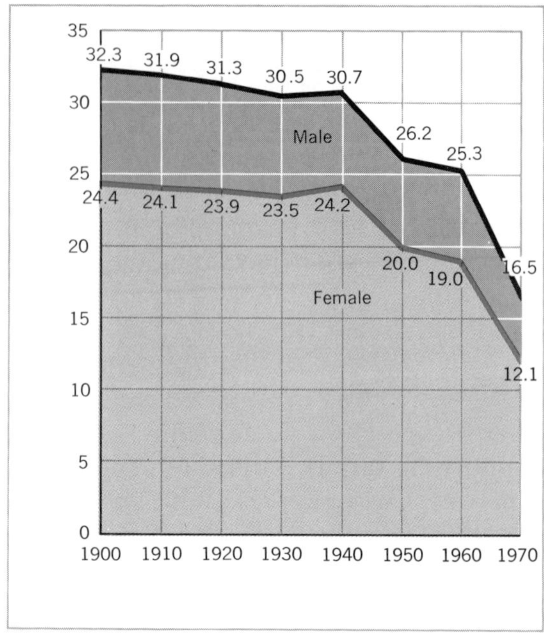

Figure 4.4
Percent of population, single, never married, age 18 and over.

right to determine their partners. Granted, many American parents do take a hand in the mate selection of their offspring, but they do it in a subtle manner. A family may move from one neighborhood to another, offer a European trip, or allow the young person the chance to go to college as techniques to manipulate the range of choice a son or daughter has in mate selection. Nevertheless, in spite of all of the social pressures put on young people, in the final analysis the legal and moral rights of mate selection belong to each individual.

Living Alone. Accompanying the idea of emancipation from parental authority, our normative order instructs us to live apart from either set of parents. We are advised by clergy, marriage counselors, and advice columns in newspapers to form a single household composed of the marital partners and their children. The building industry mirrors this ethic by producing housing that allows little room even for this limited family—much less the addition of Grandma or Aunt Suzie, who would place intolerable strain on the physical dimensions of most households.

Have Children. The American value system advises us to get married early, live alone, and complete the cycle by producing children. The social pressures felt in the decision to marry are felt even more strongly on this point. Mass media and anxious mothers-in-law continually reinforce this principle. In addition, the woman herself is frequently anxious to become a mother. Our society has taught women not to prepare themselves for careers outside the home, and thus women often find themselves in unrewarding occupations. For many, the alternative of motherhood is an all too seductive status. Figure 4.5 indicates the preferences among college men and women in the number of children desired. Although the trend is to smaller families, there is still a strong social value toward having children.

CHANGING FAMILY VALUES

Although the values listed above have remained fairly stable, there are other family values that are changing rapidly. Two seem particularly important.

Changing Roles. First, the *traditional male-female roles* are changing rapidly. Earlier in this chapter we discussed sex role socialization, with particular attention to the socialization of women. By the time people are young adults they have very clear notions of male-female role differences. Males should work, usually outside the home, for wages, while women serve generally as household help without fixed wages. Children are socialized early into these patterns. By the age of four many boys already have fantasies about the occupations they will pursue, fireman and policeman being two popular choices. On the other hand when asked about adulthood, girls frequently reply that they want to be mommies. With this kind of training few men balk at the prospect of working outside the home and, up to now, most women have accepted their housebound role.

While these rigidly defined roles may be functional for an industrialized society, it is questionable how beneficial they are to the individuals forced to occupy them. If the women's liberation movement is voicing objection to womens' assigned roles, so, too, are many men who, battered and ulcerated from the competitive work world, are now asking for a choice in their life's assignments. Popular magazines are beginning to print stories of role reversals where the wife earns the salary while the husband tends the home chores. While little would be gained by a complete reversal of roles, there is much to be said for a relaxing of the boundaries between the sexes. Many experiments are being tried, with husbands and wives sharing both wage earning and child care. Most families are still traditional, but changing roles are quite common among some social groups, especially upper-middle class families where both husband and wife pursue careers and share family responsibilities.

Changing Norms About Sex Behavior. The second area of normative change concerns sex relations. Like all other societies, ours prescribes the conditions under which people can be sexually involved. Until recently the norm, no matter how often violated, was that sex should occur only after marriage, and with the marital partner. Furthermore, some kind of sex acts were permitted, others were not. Many states still have laws that punish those who indulge in "unnatural" acts. It perhaps goes without saying that sexual norms usually assume

Figure 4.5 **Preferences regarding age at marriage and number of children**

	At What Age Should People Marry?		How Many Children Should Couples Have?	
	Men Prefer	Women Prefer	Men Prefer	Women Prefer
1939	25.1	24.0	3.3	3.5
1956	24.9	22.9	3.6	3.9
1967	24.5	22.5	2.9	3.3
1973	24.4	22.4	2.7	3.1

Source: Gallup Poll Index, June 1973.

that those acts that are permitted will take place between two people of the opposite sex, and will be done in private.

Today, however, there is enormous conflict over these sexual norms. Headlines of local newspapers tell stories of wife swapping and group sex sessions. In addition, controversies rage over the use of contraceptive pills, nude bars, abortion, and child care centers. Obviously there is no consensus over the question of morality. Instead we have a pluralistic value system, with many different moralities adhered to by members of different groups. There are different sexual norms for college students, married suburbanites, hippies in their communes, and Wall Street stockbrokers. The society is in flux, new ideas are being created, and some of the old ideas are being revived. Norms concerning the proper morality within the family change accordingly.

In spite of all the public support of sexual fidelity, there are cracks in that normative wall. The actual amount of sexual infidelity is unknown; obviously there are no random samples of the population giving accurate counts of the married people who engage in such activities. However, conservative estimates indicate that about 25 percent of all married women engage in extramarital activity as do about 50 to 60 percent of all married men. Although we may not have good data on sex *behavior,* we do have public opinion polls that show that *attitudes* are becoming more liberal, as shown in Figure 4.6.

PROBLEMS IN THE AMERICAN FAMILY

Social change, then, is affecting the traditional values of the family. Whenever social change is occurring, there are likely to be major upheavals in the institution affected. The next sections examine some of the major problems facing the family today.

DIVORCE

Divorce can be viewed both as a problem and as a solution to other problems. While acting as a solution to an unworkable marriage, it can create problems of an emotional and financial nature. The

Figure 4.6

Attitudes on sex are rapidly becoming more liberal: Gallup Poll results 1969–1973

United States Opinions

Percent Saying Premarital Sex Is "Wrong"

	1969	1973	Pt Chng
Nationwide	68	48	−20
Under 30 years	49	29	−20
30–49 years	67	44	−23
50 and over	80	64	−16
Men	62	42	−20
Women	74	53	−21
Married	X	51	—
Single	X	27	—
College background	56	41	−15
High school	69	45	−24
Grade school	77	60	−17
Protestants	70	53	−17
Catholics	72	45	−27
East	65	38	−27
Midwest	69	51	−18
South	78	58	−20
West	55	41	−14

Percent Saying Nudes In Magazines Objectionable

	1969	1973	Pt Chng
National	73	55	−18
Under 30 years	56	35	−21
30–49 years	73	51	−22
50 and over	83	74	− 9
Men	66	44	−22
Women	80	65	−15
Married	X	56	—
Single	X	37	—

Percent Saying Nudes In Plays Objectionable

	1969	1973	Pt Chng
National	81	65	−16
Under 30 years	67	45	−22
30–49 years	82	62	−20
50 and over	88	82	− 6
Men	73	55	−18
Women	88	73	−15
Married	X	67	—
Single	X	42	—

Percent Saying Topless Waitresses Objectionable

	1969	1973	Pt Chng
National	76	59	−17
Under 30 years	64	45	−19
30–49 years	73	53	−20
50 and over	84	76	− 8
Men	63	45	−18
Women	87	72	−15
Married	X	61	—
Single	X	41	—

X No data available

A: Premarital sex should be avoided under any circumstances

B: Premarital sex is all right if couple is in love

C: Premarital sex is all right even if couple is not in love

International Comparisons

Views Of Youth in Ten Nations On Premarital Sex

	A	B	C	No Ans
Sweden	4	56	38	2
West Germany	6	65	23	6
Switzerland	8	68	23	1
France	10	65	22	3
United Kingdom	14	68	15	3
Yugoslavia	18	75	7	—
United States	23	57	19	1
Japan	27	68	4	1
Brazil	40	48	12	—
India	73	23	4	—

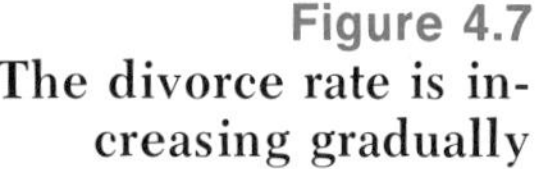

Figure 4.7
The divorce rate is increasing gradually

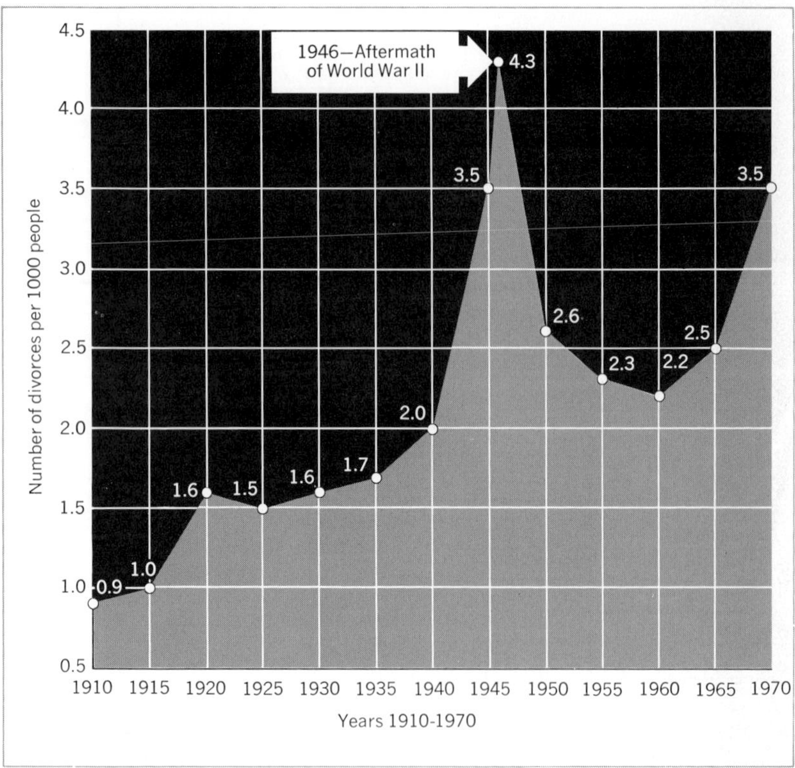

adults involved often feel shame or failure; after all, they picked their partners. They have no one else to blame—except each other.

Financially, divorce can be devastating. Often families barely surviving financially find their expenses increased. Two households must be established where one existed before, and lawyers' fees must usually be paid. These expenses put heavy strain on an already overworked budget. The nuclear family is particularly hard hit because of its institutionalized isolation from other familial groups, such as parents, brothers, or sisters.

The divorce rate is gradually increasing, as Figure 4.7 shows. What is not obvious from the rates themselves, however, is the accumulated amount of divorce. In 1955 about 10.5 percent of all marriages ended in divorce; in 1971 about 16.7; if current trends continue, by 1980 about 25 percent of all marriages will end in divorce. In certain parts of the nation, such as California, nearly half of first marriages already end in divorce.

DEATH AND THE NUCLEAR FAMILY

Death, of course, occurs in all societies, but when the nuclear family predomi-

In a youth-oriented society, it is difficult to adjust to old age.

nates, the impact is particularly hard. If a parent dies while children are young, then half of that child's world is gone. In societies with extended families, the aunts, uncles or grandparents can fill in for the deceased, but with the isolation of the nuclear family, these relatives are not readily available. Adults, too, suffer more severely under these conditions. Functions formerly undertaken by the deceased must now be taken over by the remaining partner or remain undone; death may also place severe financial burdens on the remaining members of the family; emotional worlds built around the deceased mate collapse. In short, the heavy trials and griefs of death are exaggerated in the nuclear family.

OLD AGE

The ideal of living alone in the nuclear family creates special hardships for the aged. What does Grandma do when Grandpa dies? She is at the point where strength and vigor are lacking, and she needs someone to mow her lawn, to help her carry groceries, and to engage in a loving conversation now and then. She, too, dreads losing her independence by moving in with her children and feels that she has nothing to offer them. Thus, when she can no longer manage a household by herself, she is packed off to a retirement community to decay in the midst of other "senior citizens," that is, if the family can afford the very expensive price tag. If she does not have the price of admission for a comfortable retirement, she is forced to make it alone on a small Social Security check, or she is carried away to a charity home. If there are worse living conditions than these charity homes for the aged, short of a maximum security prison, they have yet to be described in the literature. These places generally lack the necessary refinements to allow the aged to live and die in peace and dignity. But our culture goes on; the young are socialized to the value of living alone, and it is not until many years later that this paradise begins to turn sour.

SUMMARY

Although people are born with some biological instincts, they still must be carefully trained into the cultural values and institutional forms of their society, primarily through the activities of the family. All major theories of personality—whether they be the social interactionists, Freudians, behaviorists, or modeling theorists—argue that social interaction is a key to developing the "self." A person is not really human until he learns about himself and the society around him through social interaction. The family, of course, is the key institution in this learning process.

The socialization process teaches many things to the child, but among the most important are the *statuses* (social positions) the person will hold and the *roles* (social behaviors) that he will play. Among the most important social behaviors are *sex roles,* the culturally trained activities that men and women learn to associate with their sex. In addition, many social groups experience "victim socialization," a process by which minorities, women, and other disadvantaged social groups are taught to accept inferior social statuses. Although resocialization efforts sometimes overcome the negative impact of victim socialization, it is nevertheless true that child-rearing practices, school curriculums, and the mass media often reinforce the negatively stereotyped roles that disadvantaged groups are taught. Witness, for example, the victim socialization process that inflicts second-class statuses on women. The family shares its socialization function with many other groups in the society. Peer groups, schools, work organizations, and "total institutions" (prisons, mental hospitals) all have a part in the teaching or resocialization process. To be sure, the family has prime responsibility for socialization, but as social change occurs, the family's role changes in response. For example, both the Russian and American family patterns have changed drastically in the last century, the former in response to a massive political revolution and consequent modernization, and the latter in response to rapid industrialization. As social change of this type occurs it obviously has great impact on the *cultural values* that govern the family. Although many values remain the same (getting married, having children, living in a nuclear family), many values shift rather substantially (husband and wife roles, sexual morality). In such a changing society the family is faced with a number of critical problems, including a mushrooming divorce rate, nuclear families that are totally disrupted by the death of a mate, and difficulties in dealing with old age in a youth-oriented society. Nevertheless, in spite of all these problems, the family is still the critical socializing linkpin between the individual and the cultural values and institutions of the larger society.

REFERENCES

Asch, S. E. "Effects of Group Pressure Upon the Modification and Distortion of Judgments" in Eleanor E. Maccoby, Theodore W. Newcomb, and Eugene L. Hartley (eds.), *Readings in Social Psychology* (New York: Holt 1958), pp. 174-183.

Ashcraft, Norman "The Isolated, Fragile Modern Family," *Los Angeles Times,* May 21, 1972. Section I.

Bandura, A., and R. H. Walters. *Social Learning and Personality Development* (New York: Holt, 1963).

Barry, H., III, M. K. Bacon, and I. L. Child. "A Cross-Cultural Survey of Some Sex Differences in Socialization," *Journal of Abnormal and Social Psychology,* 55, 1957, pp. 377-382.

Bell, Robert. *Marriage and Family Interaction* (Homewood, Ill.: Dorsey Press, 1967).

Bem, S. L., and D. J. Bem, "Case Study of Nonconscious Ideology: Training the Woman to Know Her Place," in D. J. Bem, *Beliefs, Attitudes and Human Affairs* (Belmont, Calif.: Brooks-Cole, 1971).

Bettelheim, Bruno. "Feral Children and Autistic Children," *American Journal of Sociology,* 54, March 1959.

Bronfenbrenner, Urie, "The Changing Soviet Family," in Michael Gorden (ed.), *The Nuclear Family in Crisis,* (New York: Harper and Row, 1972), pp. 119-142.

Brown, Roger. *Social Psychology.* (New York: Free Press, 1966), pp. 69-80.

Burgess, Ernest W., Harvey J. Locke, and Margaret Thomas. *The Family,* 3d ed. (New York: American Book Company, 1963).

Cadwallader, Mervyn. "Marriage as a Wretched Institution," in Joann S. and Jack R. Delora (eds.), *Intimate Life Styles* (Pacific Palisades, Calif.: Goodyear Publishing, 1972), p. 169.

Child, I.L., E.H. Potter, and E.M. Levine "Children's Textbooks and Personality Development," *Psychological Monographs,* 60 (3), 1946, pp. 1-7 and 43-53.

Clark, G., and H.G. Birch. "Hormonial Modification of Social Behavior," *Psychosomatic Medicine,* 7, 1945, pp. 321-329.

Denfeld, Duane, and Michael Gordon, "Mate Swapping: The Family That Swings Together Clings Together," in Arlene and Jerome Skolnick (eds.), *Family in Transition,* (Boston: Little, Brown, 1971).

Embree, Alice. "Media Images I: Madison Avenue Brainwashing - The Facts" in Robin Morgan (ed.), *Sisterhood is Powerful* (New York: Vintage, 1970), pp. 175-191.

Etzioni, Amitai. "Sex Control, Science, and Society," *Science, 161,* September 13, 1968, pp. 1107-1112.

Freud, Sigmund. *Civilization and Its Discontents,* Translated by Joan Riviere (London: Hogarth Press, 1946).

Friedan, Betty. *The Feminine Mystique* (New York: W. W. Norton, 1963).

Frisof, Jamie Kelen. "Textbooks and Channeling," from *Women - A Journal of Liberation, 1,* (1), Fall 1969, pp. 26-28.

Goldberg, Phillip. "Are Women Prejudiced Against Women?" *Transaction, 5,* April 1968, pp. 28-30.

Goldberg, S., and M. Lewis. "Play Behavior in the Year-Old Infant: Early Sex Differences," *Child Development,* 40, 1969, pp. 21-31.

Goldfard, W. "Effects of Psychological Deprivation in Infancy and Subsequent Stimulation," *American Journal of Psychiatry,* 15, 1945, pp. 247-255.

Heiskanen, Veronica Stolte. "The Myth of the Middle-Class Family in American Family

Sociology" in *The American Sociologist,* 6, (1), February 1971, pp. 14-18.

Henry, Jules. *Culture Against Man* (New York: Random House, 1963).

Hess, Robert, and Judith Tornsy. *The Development of Political Attitudes in Children.* (Garden City, N.Y.: Doubleday Anchor, 1968).

Heym, Leah. "Children's Books," in *Women - A Journal of Liberation,* Fall 1969.

Hilgard, E.R., and D.G. Marquis, *Conditioning and Learning* (New York: Appleton-Century-Crofts, 1940).

Hinton, William. *Fanshen* (New York: Vintage Books, 1966), pp. 42-43.

Levy, Marion J., Jr. *The Family Revolution in Modern China* (New York: Atheneum, 1968), pp. 41-60.

Mace, David and Vera Mace. *The Soviet Family* (New York: Dolphin Books edition, 1964; Doubleday, 1963).

Mann, Thomas, *Buddenbrooks* (New York: Random House, Vintage Books, 1952).

Markarenko. A. S. *The Collective Family: A Handbook for Russian Parents* (Garden City, Anchor Books, 1967).

Mead, George H. *Mind, Self and Society* (Chicago: University of Chicago Press, 1934).

Mead, Margaret. *Male and Female* (London: Victor Gollancz, 1950).

Mead, Margaret. *Sex and Temperament* (New York: Morrow, 1935).

Miles, Betty. "Harmful Lessons Little Girls Learn in School," *Redbook,* March 1971.

Milton, Nancy. "Women in China," *Berkeley Journal of Sociology, XVI,* 1971-1972, pp. 106-120.

Moore, Barrington. "Thoughts on the Future of the Family," in Maurice Stein, Arthur J. Vidich, and David Manning White (eds.), *Identity and Anxiety* (New York: The Free Press, 1960).

Neubeck, Gerhard. "Two Clinicians and a Sociologist" in Gerhard Neubeck (ed.), *Extra-Marital Relations,* (Englewood Cliffs, N.J.: Prentice-Hall, 1969).

Newsweek, "Runaways: A Million Bad Trips," 76, (17), October 26, 1970, pp. 67-68.

Pavlov, I.P. *Conditioned Reflexes and Psychiatry,* translated and edited by W. H. Gantt (New York: International Publishers, 1941).

Porter, Paige. "The Definition of Women," mimeographed, Stanford University, 1971.

Roebuck, Julian, and S. Lee Spray. "The Cocktail Lounge: A Study of Heterosexual Relations in a Public Organization," in Berhardt Lieberman (ed.), *Human Sexual Behavior* (New York: Wiley, 1971), pp. 261-269.

Scott, J.P. *Aggression* (Chicago: University of Chicago Press, 1958).

Sears, R.R., E.E. Maccoby, and H. Levin. *Patterns of Child Rearing* (Evanston, Ill.: Row, Peterson, 1957).

Skinner, B.F. *The Behavior of Organisms: An Experimental Analysis* (New York: Appleton-Century-Crofts, 1938).

Spira, Melford. *Children of the Kibbutz* (Cambridge: Harvard University Press, 1958).

Spitz, René A. "Hospitalism" in Rose L. Caser (ed.), *The Family* (New York: St. Martin's Press, 1964), pp. 399-425.

Spitz, R.A. "The Role of Ecological Factors in Emotional Development in Infancy," *Child Development,* 20, 1949, pp. 145-156.

Steele, Brandt F., Carl B. Pollock, "The Battered Child's Parents," in Arlene S. and Jerome H. Skolnick, (eds).), *Family in Transition* (Boston: Little, Brown 1971).

Terman, L.M., and M.H. Oden, "Psychological Sex Differences" in L. Charmichael (ed.), *Manual of Child Psychology,* 2nd ed. (New York: Wiley, 1954).

Time, "The Battering Parent," 94 (19), November 7, 1969, pp. 77.

Trecker, Janice Law. "Women in U.S. History High School Textbooks," *Social Education,* March 1971, pp. 249-260 and 338.

Udry, J. Richard. *The Social Context of Marriage* (New York: J.B. Lippincott, 1966).

Weitzman, Lenore J., et al. "Sex Role Socialization in Picture Books for Pre-school Children," A paper read at the American Sociological Association Meeting in Denver, September 2, 1971.

Yang, C.K. quoted in *The American Sociologist,* 7 (5), May 1972, pp. 1-19.

Zalba, Separio R., "Battered Children," in *Transaction,* 8, (9-10), July-August 1971.

FIVE STRATIFICATION DYNAMICS AND THE SOCIAL CLASS SYSTEM

TILLMON AND GENEEN

Case Number One—Johnnie Tillmon, Resident of Watts, Los Angeles.

I'm a woman. I'm a black woman. I'm a poor woman. I'm a fat woman. I'm a middle-aged woman. And I'm on welfare. In this country, if you're any one of those things—poor, black, fat, female, middle-aged, on welfare—you count less as a human being. If you're *all* those things, you don't count at all. Except as a statistic. I am a statistic. I am 45 years old. I have raised six children.

I grew up in Arkansas, and I worked there for fifteen years in a laundry, making about $20 or $30 a week, picking cotton on the side for carfare. I moved to California in 1959 and worked in a laundry there for nearly four years. In 1963, I got too sick to work anymore. My husband and I had split up. Friends helped me to go on welfare. . . .

Each month I get $363 for my kids and me. I pay $128 a month rent; $30 for utilities, . . . $120 for food, . . . $50 for school lunches. . . . This leaves exactly $5 per person per month for everything else—clothing, shoes, recreation, incidental personal expenses and transportation. This check allows $1 a month for transportation for me but none for my children. That's how we live. (Tillmon, 1972, p. 111)

Case Number Two—Harold S. Geneen, President of International Telephone and Telegraph Company.

International Telephone and Telegraph, the conglomerate which has been much in the news this year, is the nation's eighth largest industrial corporation but it ranks first in one category: It pays its top man better than anyone else.

Harold S. Geneen, the chairman and president of ITT, collected a base salary of $382,492 in 1971 and then—for selling all the Wonder bread and renting all those Avis cars and Sheraton rooms—he picked up a bonus of $439,000 for a tidy package of $812,492, or $15,625 per week. Thus, for the second year in a row, Geneen retained his position as the highest-paid executive in the business world. . . .

While 1971 was the year of the wage-price freeze, there were some spectacular pay boosts in the executive suites. (Moskowitz, June 3, 1972, p. 33)

The opening sketches of Johnnie Tillmon, the black woman from Watts, and Harold S. Geneen, President of ITT, reveal much about modern U.S. society. Here are two twentieth-century Americans who might as well live on different planets as far as their experiences of this society are concerned. In this and the next two chapters we will be examining the stratification process in modern society that divides people into different social classes and gives them radically different life-styles. Think about the differences that separate Mrs. Tillmon and Mr. Geneen:

1. They are clearly in different *social classes*, Tillmon in the lowest and Geneen in the highest, and there is very little chance that Tillmon could ever have enough *social mobility* to catch up.

2. The *economic system* of the society is the fundamental social process that defines their relative social positions.

3. They represent opposite ends of the *income and wealth continuum*, with almost unimaginable differences between their life chances.

4. Tillmon is a black woman, while Geneen is a white man; on both counts (*black* and *woman*) Tillmon faces enormous discrimination that makes it almost impossible for her to have an equal chance.

5. The *legal system* of the society helps Mr. Geneen avoid taxes and obtain subsidies for his company, while it denies equal opportunities for Mrs. Tillmon at almost every turn.

6. Mrs. Tillmon is one of the millions of Americans who fall into the *poverty* category, and she receives *welfare* to help her survive; some, but not much, of Mr. Geneen's taxes goes to help her.

The three upcoming chapters will examine the social web in which Tillmon and Geneen are bound, and the processes that have put them in such different positions. In this chapter we will look at the social class system that is linked to the distribution of wealth in the society, and at some theories that try to explain why social classes are found in all societies. Chapter Six will examine the processes of social mobility in modern society, with special focus on the racial, sexual, and legal barriers that hinder mobility for so many people. Finally, in Chapter Seven we will discuss one of the major consequences of the stratification system, the enormous poverty that is apparent even in such a rich nation as the United States. In that same chapter we will study some of the social and cultural belief patterns—"ideologies"—that are used to justify poverty, and at the hopelessly inept welfare system that is supposed to help to alleviate it. Thus, these three chapters are closely related, each in turn examining a different aspect of the stratification network that has so strongly affected the lives of Johnnie Tillmon and Harold Geneen.

SOCIAL CLASSES AND THE FUNCTIONALIST THEORY OF INEQUALITY

In every society people are divided into relatively distinct social classes. In some societies, for example, in the Indian caste system, there is a sharp demarcation between classes, and mobility between them is highly restricted. In other nations, including most of the modern industrial nations, instead of sharp breaks between the classes, there is an almost unbroken continuum from the upper-class elite groups on one end to the lower-class, poverty-stricken groups at the other. Most people in the society do, however, identify psychologically with some social class.

Many explanations have been offered to explain why social classes form in all societies, and one of the most influential approaches was the *functionalistic* theory, proposed by Kingsley Davis and Wilbert Moore. Davis and Moore argued that every society divides its goods, wealth, and services on the basis of the importance of the jobs, that is, on the "function" that each job performs for the society. Some jobs are more critical—more functional—to the society than others; consequently, it is highly important for the society to fill those jobs. Davis and Moore assumed that the more important jobs are more difficult and require longer periods of training; therefore people are unwilling to take them. As a result it is necessary for the society to reward those jobs more highly in order to lure people into taking them. (Davis and Moore, 1945)

The Davis-Moore theory might be summarized as "the great race" theory. Society needs a number of jobs, which vary by importance and difficulty. In order to insure that the most talented people will get the most critical jobs, society holds a great "talent race." Those who win—those who have the most talent—are rewarded highly with wealth, prestige, and power. The losers obviously have less talent and consequently are given lower statuses, less critical jobs, and fewer rewards. It is, then, the great talent race that determines who gets what. Thus, the functionalist theory bases inequality on the *nature of the occupational system.* As Davis and Moore stated in an often-quoted passage, "Social inequality is thus an unconsciously evolved device by which societies insure that the most important positions are conscientiously filled by the more qualified persons."

How valid is the functionalist theory of stratification? Many sociologists today argue that the functionalist analysis misses the mark widely, for a number of reasons. First, it is extremely difficult to rank jobs in terms of their importance. Is it really true that the society needs businessmen, scientists, professors, and doctors—the highly rewarded jobs—more than it needs farmers, trash collectors, and factory workers? The society needs th[illegible] of *all* these people, so it [illegible]e to argue that some are more [illegible]an others.

[illegible]e importance of the job does [illegible]be the critical factor in deter[illegible]ards. For example, if im[illegible]termines rewards, why is it [illegible] some criminals, bookmakers, cigarette-company executives, and resort real-estate developers often make so much money? Surely their jobs are not "critical" for the society. Job importance seems to have very little relation to the reward structure in society.

Postage and Fees P
Department of the
DoD-317

Third, it seems strange that the functionalists argue that it is necessary to reward physicians, professors, and businessmen more highly to get them to do their work. On the contrary, these jobs are more interesting, more self-satisfying, and more intrinsically gratifying than the less prestigious jobs. It seems that the functionalists really should reverse their argument; the dirty tasks of society should be rewarded more highly if the functionalist theory is really true. It would seem more logical that trash collectors, heavy industry workers, teachers in the ghetto, and farm laborers should be the ones who are paid most highly in order to lure them into the less pleasant jobs of society.

In short, the importance of jobs is simply not related to the rewards people get. As C. H. Anderson put it: "Who has the evidence to demonstrate that the doctor who writes a drug prescription is more important than the pharmacist who fills it, the truck driver who transports it, the worker who produced it . . . or the chemist who discovered it? Without any one of these persons, the sick person would not safely get his drug" (Anderson, 1971, p. 87). If the basic link between "importance" and "reward" breaks down, then the whole functionalist theory collapses. (For a critique of the whole Davis-Moore approach, see the collected papers in Bendix and Lipset, 1966.)

THE CONFLICT/POWER THEORY OF STRATIFICATION

The functionalist theory of stratification has so many glaring weaknesses that a number of sociologists have recently proposed an alternative explanation called the "conflict and power theory," described here by Leonard Reissman.

[The] opponents of functionalism draw the line at the proposition that inequality is unavoidable . . . they argue that, in reality, . . . a system of stratification tends to continue because the members of a society who are in the highest strata want the system to continue

unchanged. Power, not functional necessity, is the key to understanding stratification. Chiefs, kings, aristocrats, or the upper class all have the same intent: to secure their position, to discourage outsiders, and thereby to control power relations so completely that they alone determine who can enter their circle. What looks like functional necessity, therefore, is really elite control. What may once have been functionally necessary must become dysfunctional [harmful to the society] because those in power seek to stay in power. (Reissman, 1967, p. 207)

BASIC IDEAS OF THE CONFLICT/POWER THEORY

The conflict/power theory takes an entirely different approach to the explanation of social inequality, suggesting that the "great race" of the functionalists is very unfair. In a sense there is a "hobbled race" in which some people have great disadvantages, and the prize jobs and the wealth of society are *not* fairly distributed on a talent basis. Instead, people inherit most of their wealth and opportunities, obtaining good jobs because their parents were able to give them special advantages—good home lives, health care, and higher education. There is a race for the best jobs, to be sure, but some people start way ahead, and it is no surprise that they stay ahead. Thus power and special advantages determine who will win the race, get the best jobs, and corner the most wealth. The British sociologist T. D. Bottomore says it clearly: "Indeed, it would be a more accurate description of the class system to say that it operates largely through the inheritance of property, to ensure that each individual maintains a certain social position, determined by his birth, and irrespective of his particular abilities" (Bottomore, 1968, p. 11). With all the weaknesses in the functionalist explanation, it seems that the power and conflict theory is a much more accurate description of the stratification processes in modern society.

There are important *political value judgments* implied in each of the theories. The functionalist explanation leans heavily toward a *conservative* interpretation of society, since it provides a theoretical justification for the *status quo.* If it were true that there is a great race for the highly valued, difficult jobs, then the people who hold them would, in fact, be the most talented and would have just claim to them. Thus, the functionalist argument essentially affirms the social class system as a legitimate and just arrangement for distributing scarce resources. The conflict theory, on the other hand, tends to be a *liberal* and *radical* theory, because it argues that the current situation is an artificial result of power manipulations in the society. The conflict theory denies that the present inequalities are necessary and thereby undermines the legitimacy of those who hold the prime positions in society. The functionalist theory at least implicitly suggests that there is no need for change, since the stratification system is "necessary" for the society to work. The conflict theory, on the other hand, argues that change is needed, since the stratification system is largely based on the naked exercise of power.

The remainder of this chapter will be based on the power/conflict interpretation of stratification. There are two out-

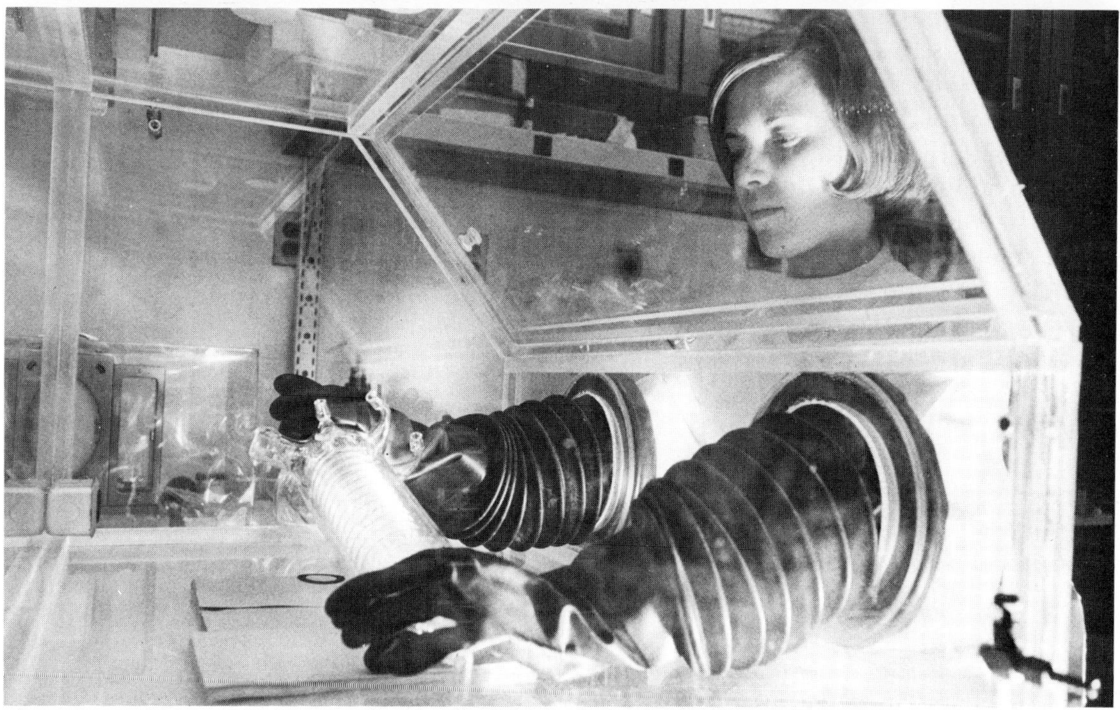

The jobs of society: Why are some highly rewarded and others not? The "Functionalist" theory says it is necessary to reward difficult jobs, so the scientists, businessmen, and doctors get more. But the "Conflict" theory says it is power and inherited position, not social need or skill, which determine who is rewarded more.

standing theories that are largely based on this analysis. One is the famous explanation of the class system advanced by Karl Marx; the other is a recent reinterpretation of the stratification process by Gerhard Lenski.

THE MARXIST MODEL OF CLASS FORMATION

Karl Marx was one of the most influential social theorists of the modern age, and his analysis of the class structure has probably influenced sociologists more than any other. Marx never wrote a single, unified analysis of social class, but his concern for the issue is scattered throughout his major works *(Capital, Economic and Philosophic Manuscripts, The German Ideology).* His insights into the nature of modern society were visionary at the time he wrote, and his ideas must be carefully considered by any responsible social scientist. Essentially, Marx argued that the class structure was based on power, not on the needs of society; power, in turn, was based on the technological and economic system of the society.

Marx's Basic Argument. *Marx was an economic determinist.* He believed that the methods of economic production in a society largely determined its social structure. Technology provides the material base for the society, and all ideas, beliefs, and social institutions are a reflection of the methods of production; they are merely "superstructures" built on top of the material base. Thus, government, the family structure, and even religion are reflections of the economic system in modern society.

The methods of production produce social classes. Marx argued that in capitalist societies there is a rigid class system based on ownership of the production system. He notes:

> *Insofar as millions of families live under economic conditions of existence that divide their mode of life, their interests and their culture from those of other classes, and put them in hostile contrast to the latter, they form a class. (Marx,* Eighteenth Brumaire, *no date, p. 109)*

Although Marx realized that there were many social classes, he emphasized only two: the *bourgeoisie* (owners of property and the systems of production) and the *proletariat* (workers).

The owner classes (bourgeoisie) dominate the worker classes (proletariat). According to Marx, in all societies the few people in the owner classes have dominated the many people in the worker classes, particularly in capitalistic nations. The government enforces this domination, for the political system is the servant of the ruling economic classes.

"Class consciousness" is necessary for social change. Marx felt that the owners were able to dominate the working classes because the workers were so disorganized and so brainwashed by the owners that they did not even recognize their common plight and thus could not band together for effective political action. A class that shares a common plight but does not work to correct it Marx called a "class-*in*-itself." He believed, however,

Marx believed social class resulted from inequalities in social power as determined by the economic system. The oppressed workers of early industrial England.

that eventually the working class would become aware of its underprivileged position and would become a class self-consciously fighting for itself and its rights, that is, the working class would become what Marx termed a "class-*for*-itself." When this happened, capitalism, because it had so badly exploited the now-revolting workers, would have planted the seeds for its own destruction and the new classless society would result.

The awakened proletariat would overthrow the bourgeois society. Once they have awakened to their plight the workers would organize and strike back at the capitalist society that suppressed them, producing massive social revolution. After the revolution was successful the proletariat workers would rule but, since workers represent the majority of the people, a true democratic socialism would result—a government run for the benefit of all classes, not merely for the welfare of the rich owners. The means of production, the technology, would then be in the hands of the people through a socialistic system. Class domination and exploitation would end. Figure 5.1 summarizes Marx's argument.

Without doubt Marx's ideas have been among the most important contributions to an economic interpretation of social stratification and social change. Although their establishment of a communist society has certainly not lived up to Marx's dream of a classless, democratic socialist society, the leaders of the Russian Revolution believed they were acting out the historical changes Marx predicted. Marxism has been a critical element in the spread of communism and socialism throughout the world. In addition, modern social theorists in every society have used Marx's ideas as a cornerstone in theories of stratification.

Comments on Marx's theory. Marx's ideas have, however, been criticized on a number of points. First, his view of the class structure of society was very limited, for modern capitalistic nations have many social classes, defined not only by their role in production but also by education, prestige, and life-style. Marx's two classes simply do not conform to reality in a complex society.

Second, the "class consciousness" among the workers in capitalistic societies has not developed nearly as far as Marx expected. The rise of trade unions, for example, won many advances for the workers that made it unnecessary for political revolution. Likewise, the extension of political suffrage to all social classes and the general rise in the standard of living has taken some of the sting out of the workers' oppression. Marx's social revolution did not occur in capitalistic England, nor in any other fully industrialized nation; both Russia and China were at a precapitalistic stage when their communist revolutions occurred. As Anderson commented:

There have been no class revolutions in places where they were supposed to occur, i.e., advanced capitalist societies. Owing to ameliorative change and reform in economic organization within capitalist society, the proletariat has been placated, class consciousness stunted, and class conflict averted or routinized. Similarly, Marx underestimated the capacity of capitalist society to create

Figure 5.1
The Marxist Model of Social Stratification: the Capitalist System and Proletarian Revolution

System of production

"Material base"
Major example:
English capitalism of 19th century

Creates →

System of ideas and beliefs to support current situation

"Ideal superstructure"
Example: Bourgeois democracy

Creates →

Social classes

Two most important:
Bourgeois-owners
Proletariat-workers

↓

Class domination

In all societies a few in upper classes have ruled the many in the lower classes. In capitalist society the bourgeois rules the proletariat. The government is a reflection of the economic system. It serves the bourgeoisie and oppresses the proletariat.

←

Class struggle

If the proletariat wakes up and becomes a self-conscious class (a class for itself), then a revolution will occur. Thus, capitalism carries the seeds of its own destruction, it creates a revolutionary worker class:
WORKERS OF THE WORLD UNITE!

←

The classless society and the socialist system of production

When the proletarian revolution succeeds all classes will be abolished, and production will be handled by the "people" in a socialist system with all sharing equally.

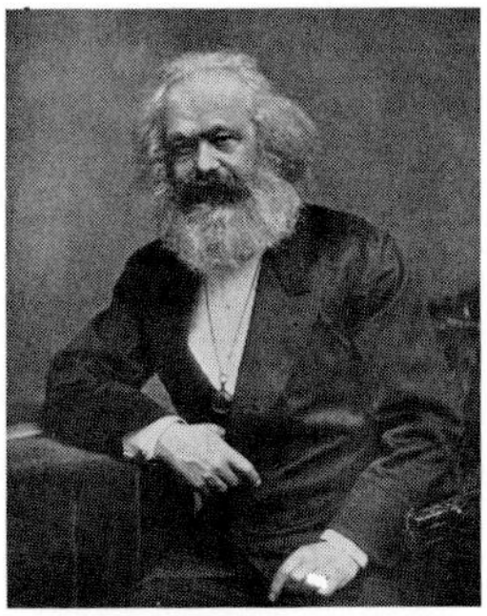

Karl Marx (1818-1883)
One of the most important social thinkers of modern times, Marx believed that technology ("forces of production") shaped the social structure. Capitalism, one type of technology, would produce class conflict and eventually destroy itself. Out of this destruction, however, a classless society would emerge, based on socialistic modes of production. His most important work was Capital, published in 1909.

and sustain relatively high levels of employment, thus far avoiding the accumulation of large reservoirs of restive and discontented unemployed and idle persons. By way of sustaining Marx, however, the closest thing to self-conscious social revolution that this country has ever witnessed, the New Deal, was instituted as a result of massive unemployment and the collapse of capitalist economic machinery. . . . (Anderson, 1971, p. 78)

Finally, Marx's thesis that the government is always in service of the bourgeoisie in capitalistic nations is not always borne out by history. The New Deal in the United States, the extension of civil liberties to oppressed groups, and the gradual democratization of most Western nations are historical currents that Marx never anticipated.

Marxist Theory: Power and Social Change. In spite of these limitations Marxist theory has played a great role in social change in the twentieth century. One third of the world's people live under social systems that adhere to Marxist world views in some form or another. Moreover, the major contributions of his thoughts are once again receiving serious attention by Western social scientists. In terms of our discussions, two points about Marxian thought should be mentioned.

First, Marx's theory of social stratification is directly based on concepts of power and conflict. Power, in turn, is based on the technological and economic system, specifically, on the methods of production in an industrial society. Consequently, the Marxist analysis, which explicitly rejects any notion that it is "necessary" to have inequality in the society, is the major foundation for power/conflict theories of social stratification.

Second, it should be noted that Marxism is not merely a theory of stratification, but also includes an analysis of how the stratification system will *change* over time. The unequal distribution of resources between the bourgeoisie and the proletariat is the foundation of inequality but, as class consciousness increases among the workers, a social revolution will occur to upset the unequal class structure. This theory of change has indeed come true in many of the social revolutions of the twentieth century, although never exactly in the form Marx predicted. Consequently, Marx is important as a social-change theorist and as a stratification theorist.

GERHARD LENSKI: THE DISTRIBUTION OF SOCIETY'S SURPLUS

In *Power and Privilege* (1966) Gerhard Lenski offers a theory of stratification that is primarily based on a power interpretation. Lenski argues that a very small proportion of a society's resources are distributed according to *need,* whereas the majority of those resources are distributed according to *power.* Lenski makes the following statement:

Men will share the product of their labors to the extent required to ensure the survival and continued productivity of those others whose actions are necessary and beneficial to themselves. *This might well be called the first law of distribution, since the survival of mankind as a species depends on compliance with it. This first law, however, does not cover the entire problem. It says nothing about how any* surplus, . . . *will be distributed. This leads to what may be called the second law of distribution. If we assume that in important decisions human action is motivated almost entirely by self-interest or by partisan group interests, and if we assume that many of the things most desired are in short supply, . . . this surplus will inevitably give rise to conflicts and struggles aimed at its control. If, following Weber, we define power as the probability of persons or groups carrying out their will even when opposed by others, then it follows that* power will determine the distribution of nearly all of the surplus possessed by a society. *(Lenski, 1966, p. 44)*

Lenski's argument, then, is quite simple; the society will divide a bare minimum of resources equally so that it can keep functioning, but surplus resources of the society will be divided on the basis of power. This is Lenski's answer to a question he asked earlier in his book: "Who gets what, and why?"

Lenski argues that this hypothesis helps explain the inequality of any given society, and he has amassed much comparative data from a number of societies, both past and present, to show that this thesis holds true. In very simple economies, where there is little if any surplus, there is very little inequality based on power and wealth; but in agricultural economies, which develop more surplus, inequalities begin to appear in rather sharp form. Finally, in early industrial societies the inequality grows at an even more rapid rate. Thus, the more technologically advanced an economy becomes, the more surplus is available for powerful people to corner and the greater the inequality of distribution. However, Lenski did find one outstanding exception to this rule; in the modern industrial nations with extremely high surpluses the distribution of wealth and power begins to equalize.

Figure 5.2 shows a chart of Lenski's data linking technological surplus with inequality. The general trend is clear; more surplus leads to more inequality, except that extremely high surpluses begin to diminish the inequality. Why is this the case? Lenski suggests that in these advanced industrial nations there is such abundance that goods can be redistributed more equitably without hurting the wealthy. In addition, the working classes in these highly developed nations begin to assert their political power so that the trend toward greater inequality is reversed through the actions of the government. Whether this pattern is only a temporary phenomenon for advanced industrial nations, or whether equality may actually grow as the technology grows, is an open question. Perhaps Lenski's hope for more equalization in advanced technological societies will come true in the long run, and there is some evidence that conditions are getting better. Nevertheless, the unhappy fact is that gross inequalities in income, wealth, and power still exist, even in advanced nations such as the United States, as we will see in the next section.

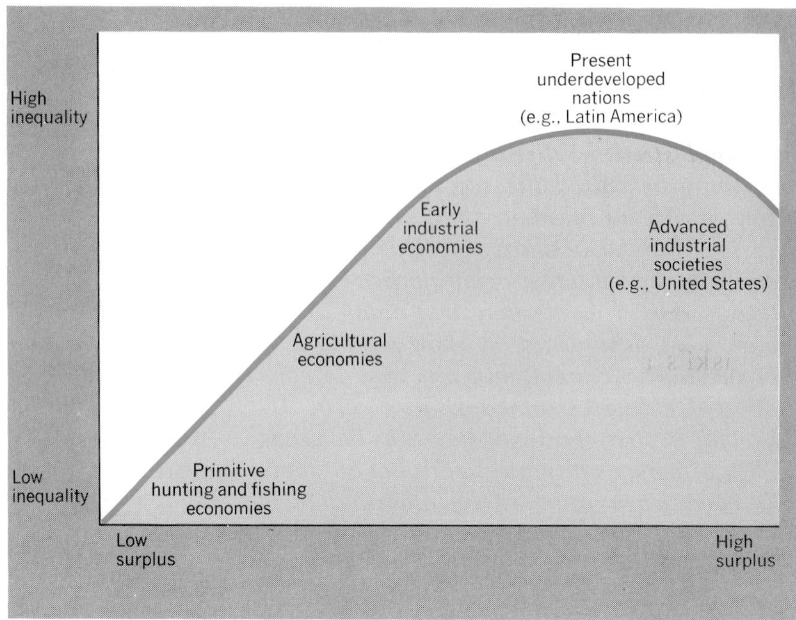

Figure 5.2
Lenski's hypothesis: Increasing surplus produces greater inequality, except in extreme cases.

UNEQUAL DISTRIBUTION OF INCOME AND WEALTH

Power is a tool that enables its holders to gain more of the material benefits of life, because power buys wealth. Most power and wealth are *inherited,* passed along from one generation to the next. Although popular myth says that people can struggle upward by working hard—the old rags-to-riches story—the fact is that most people end up in life with little more than they started. There are exceptions, of course, but they are just that—exceptions. Although, because of rising economic conditions, most people are slightly better off than their parents, few people make much progress in climbing the social class ladder. Let us examine some of the facts.

INCOME DISTRIBUTION

Some of the most reliable figures about the distribution of material resources in the society are income statistics. Figure 5.3 takes all American families and divides them into five groups, each group representing 20 percent of the total number of families. The chart then shows how much of the national income each group of families earns. Note that the top fifth of the families corners an enormous share of the nation's income, whereas the bottom fifth has only a very small share. In fact, families in the upper fifth earn nearly 10 times as much as families in the lower fifth! It is clear, then, that income is drastically unequal. In fact, the noted economist Paul Samuelson once observed that, "If we make an income pyramid out of a child's blocks, with each layer portraying $1,000 of income, the peak would be far higher than the Eiffel Tower, but almost all of us would be within a yard of the ground."

This chart also indicates that the distribution of income has changed only slightly in the period from 1929 to 1969. The three lowest groups have virtually a constant proportion of the national income, with the lowest (Group E) hovering between 4 and 5 percent. At the upper end, on the other hand, the highest (Group A) has gone down from 54 percent to 43 percent with most of that reapportioned income going to the middle groups instead of to the lower. Thus, over the 40-year period from 1929 to 1969, income was drastically malproportioned, with the highest fifth of the families receiving almost half of the income.

These figures refer to *family* incomes, but many economists argue that such figures hide the fact that for many lower-class families it takes both husband and wife to make the income. Thus, family-based figures hide many inequities that might show up if only individuals were examined. Henle (1973) carried out such an individual analysis for the Department of Labor and concluded that incomes are actually more unequal than in previous years. From 1958 to 1970, for example, the people in the upper 20 percent income brackets increased their share from 42.8 percent of all income to 45 percent; at the other end of the scale, the lowest 20 percent of the people decreased their share from 2.8 percent to 2.2 percent. Two facts are startling: the huge inequality between the upper and lower groups (45 versus 2.2 percent of the income captured) and the fact that incomes are growing more unequal over time—conditions are getting worse.

Henle argues that four economic conditions account for the growing inequality. First, more people are working part-time and, when their wages are averaged with full-time workers, it depresses the overall average. Second, many very young people have joined the labor force and are willing to work for lower wages. Third, the occupational structure has changed so that there are more highly paid professionals and managers at the top, thus pushing up the income averages at the top. Finally, industry has given higher wage increases to people at the top of the scale than at the lower, a pattern of giving more to the rich—who also happen to be the powerful who are making the decisions about pay increases. In short, the changing occupational patterns and distribution of wages all press for greater inequalities in American society.

But do other nations have as much inequality as the United States? The major industrialized nations, such as the United States, Japan, Great Britain, and Canada, have similar income distributions. And, although none of these nations have an equal distribution of in-

Figure 5.3
Income distribution in the United States, 1929–1969.

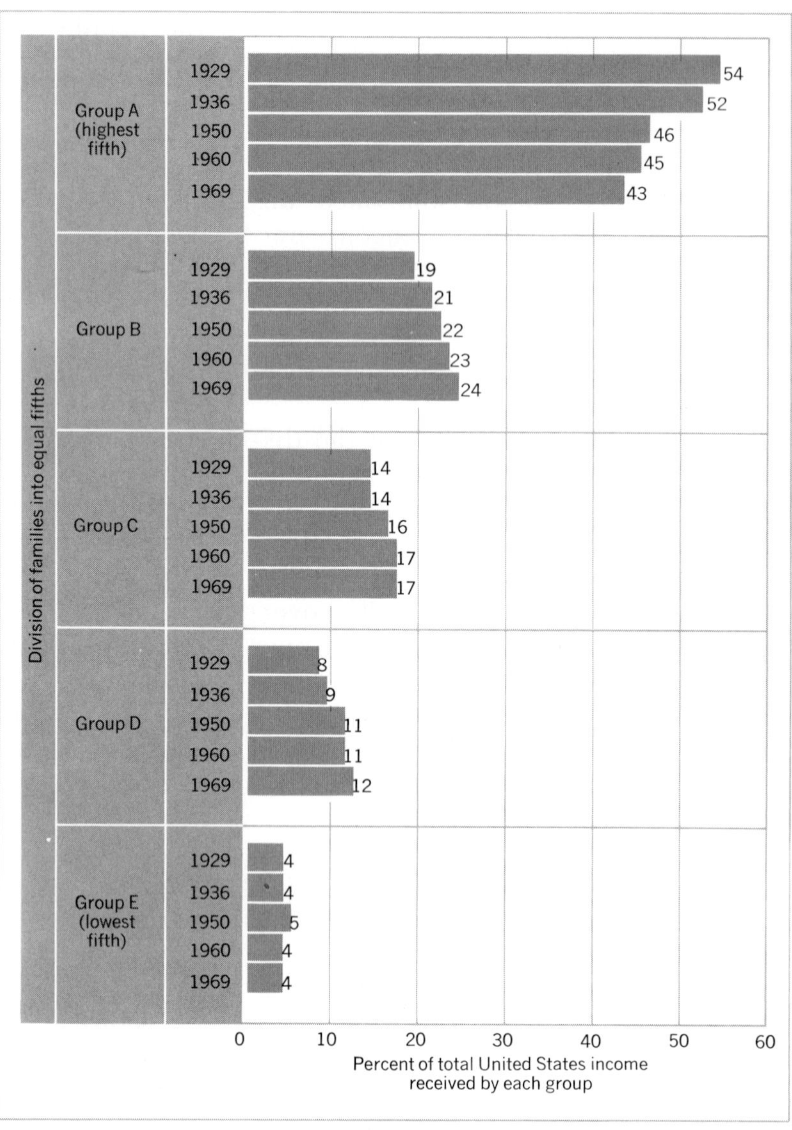

Source: Historical Statistics of the United States and *Statistical Abstract of the United States*, 1971: both by U. S. Department of Commerce, Bureau of the Census, published in 1960 and 1972, respectively.

come, their wealth is more equally divided than in less developed nations such as India, Indonesia, Brazil, Egypt, and Mexico. A number of nations do have more equal distributions than the United States. These nations—all with relatively homogeneous populations—include Denmark and the other Scandinavian countries as well as Israel and the Netherlands. The overall trend, then, seems to be that highly industrialized nations have more equal income distributions than nondeveloped nations do and that nations with relatively homogeneous populations have even more equal distributions.

Many sociologists argue that the comparative equality of income distribution in the industrialized nations, at least relative to that of underdeveloped nations, has led to increased political stability in these nations. Because people in the industrialized nations are more satisfied with their lot, they are unwilling to undertake massive social upheavals. General economic prosperity has blunted their zeal for change.

Certainly there are some exceptions to this rule, as is the case in the minority group revolutions in America. Dissatisfaction can develop even if a country has a more equally distributed income pyramid than most others. Obviously the dissatisfaction of minorities and poverty groups within the United States demonstrates that groups comparing themselves against the more affluent in their own society become dissatisfied because of their *relative* status, even if the overall average within the society is better than for underdeveloped nations. Three things must be said simultaneously: (1) the developed nations have more equal income distributions than the underdeveloped nations; (2) but the industrialized nations should not be too satisfied, for they still have badly distributed incomes; and (3) social discontent in industrial nations is bred by *relative deprivation* that the poor sense when they compare themselves to the wealthy within their own society.

THE DISTRIBUTION OF WEALTH

F. Scott Fitzgerald once commented to Ernest Hemingway that "The rich, Mr. Hemingway, are different from you and me." Hemingway was reported to have answered, "Yes, Mr. Fitzgerald, they have more money." Hemingway's sarcastic reply was supposed to mean that the *only* difference was money. But actually, money buys a great many other advantages in life—education, travel, good health. Yes, the rich *do* have more money, and the difference is astonishing. Income measures the amount of money coming into a family in a given year; *wealth,* on the other hand, is a measure of the amount of money a family has managed to accumulate over a long period of time. While income is a fairly good measure of the year-by-year flow of money, wealth is a much better indicator of how money is passed down from generation to generation. It is very difficult to get accurate figures on the distribution of wealth in the society because most statistics kept by the government do not deal directly with such figures. Most statistics on wealth are fairly old, but, although the exact dollar figures may vary over time, most sociologists think these figures still represent the *relative* situation today.

The data suggest that approximately 10 percent of the families in the United States account for about 60 percent of all the private holdings of wealth, omitting those held by the government and by corporations. In 1962, for example, the 4132 people who had incomes of more than $60,000 had cornered a total of $670 billion worth of private wealth. In fact, the richest 1 percent of American adults control a solid one third of all the nation's private wealth, including nearly all of the state and local government bonds (which are tax exempt), almost 40 percent of the federal bonds, 36 percent of all mortgages, and about 30 percent of the nation's currency. (See Lundberg, 1969.)

The maldistribution of wealth is also clearly shown by examining ownership of corporation wealth. Corporations have become the prime wealth holders in modern society, controlling much more of the national income and capital than any given individuals. A handful of people control most of this corporation wealth. In fact, about 1 percent of the American adult population owns nearly 80 percent of all corporate stock—a staggering $500 billion. Moreover, even this estimate may not indicate the true concentration of corporate wealth, for much corporation stock is held by private foundations that are often only front organizations for wealthy individuals. In short, about 250,000 families control the vast majority of the corporate assets in this society, and this enormous wealth represents the largest single block of nongovernment money in the United States. Naturally, the nation's millionaires are found in this group. In 1970 there were about 110,000 millionaires representing less than 0.05 percent of the population. These fortunes were largely acquired by *inherited* wealth, not by earned income.

Two other startling facts should be added to this dismal picture about the concentration of wealth. First, over the past few decades this maldistribution of wealth has actually gotten worse; the amount of wealth in a few hands has actually grown. Second, there is a remarkable continuity in the families that hold wealth; rich families hand their wealth down from one generation to another, thus preserving intact the radical concentration of power and money.

But whereas only 1 percent of the population controls most of the nation's financial reserves, 11 percent of U. S. families are deeply in debt, and another 34 percent have assets of less than $5000. If you take into account the 15 percent who have assets between $5000 and $10,000 it is clear that the majority of the population owned less than $10,000.

Thus, wealth in the United States is very poorly distributed, with only a handful of people controlling the lion's share. While 35 percent or more of the nation lives in poverty, at the other end of the scale less than 1 percent controls the overwhelming majority of the national money. Moreover, as mentioned above, among those who hold enormous wealth the vast majority report to the Internal Revenue Service that they inherited most of it; the rich did not get wealth by earning it, they usually got it by the accident of being born into a wealthy family.

THE LINK BETWEEN ECONOMIC DISTRIBUTION AND SOCIAL PROBLEMS

It is important to understand that most of the critical domestic social problems in the United States—particularly poverty problems—are caused by this radical maldistribution of power and wealth in the society. The conflict between the races, poverty in the midst of affluence, and most of the other critical issues that we associate with urban decay and social conflict have their roots directly in the problem of poorly distributed income, wealth, and political power. It is the central thesis of this book that social problems and social conflict are primarily the result of social *system* problems, not the fault of evil individuals.

The blame for social crisis should not be laid on the popular, stereotyped villains: "lazy welfare bums," "radical hippies," "outside agitators," or "malcontent blacks." These are nothing more than the elusive witches in a massive social witch-hunt; they are not the causes of the trouble, but they serve to distract the public from the real problems. No, the real source of social crisis is the fundamental maldistribution of the economic system, the extremes of wealth and poverty, coupled with generous portions of racial prejudice, and a feeling of political impotency among the majority of the people. These issues, not the convenient bogey-men of popular stereotype, are at the root of social crisis in the United States.

SOCIAL CLASSES

Up to this point this chapter has been discussing the *causes* of social stratification in society—the economic distribution system and the political power that supports an unequal distribution of income and wealth. Now let us turn our attention to the *patterns* that social stratification takes, to the class structure in modern society. American sociologists have always been fascinated by the class structure, and many studies have shown that people in the United States recognize several broad classes: the upper class, which includes the wealthy and the powerful, the middle class, which includes white-collar and professional workers, the working class, which includes the blue-collar and industrial workers, and the lower class, which includes the poor, poverty-stricken groups.

FACTORS THAT DEFINE SOCIAL CLASS

Why is a person in one class rather than in another? In general, studies have shown that the public defines social classes by three major factors: (1) income and wealth, (2) educational levels, and (3) occupation.

Income and wealth are among the most important factors for defining social classes, since money determines, to a certain extent, one's life-style, and life-style determines status. The upper classes can, for instance, afford to buy services and goods that set them apart from the middle and lower classes. At the other end of the social scale, the poverty stricken are basically in that plight because of the distribution of income in the nation. Thus, wealth and income distributions are at the very heart of the class system in any society.

Education is the second major factor that places a person in a particular social class because it is a key to occupational advance that, in turn, helps to gain more money. Money is also a critical determinant of personal life-styles that so often separate people in different social classes. Consequently, those who have higher educations are generally considered to be higher in social class than those who have not had similar advantages.

Occupation is the third important factor in the definition of social class. Throughout the world different occupations hold different levels of prestige, with professionals, managers, and intellectuals at the high end of the scale and manual workers at the low end. Figure 5.4 shows a survey taken in the United States in 1963 in which a sample of the general public was asked to rank a number of occupations in terms of how desirable they were. In general, major public officials, physicians, college professors, lawyers, and top business executives head this list; such white-collar workers as public school teachers, accountants, artists, and building contractors hold the middle; and janitors, taxi drivers, cooks, and truck drivers fall at the lower end. The researchers who did this study point out that this rating is more or less consistent throughout the world and that it has remained essentially constant in time as far back as sociological evidence goes.

Why are some occupations rated higher than others? This is a difficult question to answer, but it is possible to take a guess. First, occupations that require long periods of training or education at high levels of intellectual skill are rated high. Second, high ratings go to those jobs that are associated with cleanliness and autonomy of one's working conditions—the professionals, the technicians, and the white-collar workers. Finally, jobs that have power, such as public officials, judges, and congressmen, are all rated high on the occupational scale.

It is important to understand that the three factors that define social class—income, education, and occupation—are highly correlated with each other. That is, if a person is high on one of these factors he is very likely to be high on the others. Education is associated with good jobs, and good jobs are associated with high incomes. There are some exceptions, to be sure, such as school teachers who earn low salaries but nevertheless have high prestige, or plumbers who earn high salaries but have very little social prestige. But, because in general, each of these three factors is closely related to the others, sociologists often use only one of these factors as the defining criterion, assuming that the others will also be present.

THE FIVE MAJOR SOCIAL CLASSES

Sociologists do not completely agree about how many classes there are in America because classes overlap considerably, and there are no sharp breaks between them. It is generally possible, however, to identify five or six basic social classes. W. Lloyd Warner (1942) found that people in a small New England town he called "Yankee City" identified six classes; A. B. Hollingshead found that people in Midwestern Elmtown (1949) and in New Haven, Connecticut (1958) more or less divided themselves into five classes. Hollingshead used a fairly complex measure of social class, combining education, occupation, and place of residence. Harold M. Hodges (1969) studied the San Francisco Peninsula area, a major urban region, and found essentially the same kind of class breakdown as did Hollingshead. Using Hollingshead, Warner, and Hodges as our information sources, let us examine the characteristics of the five basic social classes. (See also Figure 5.5.)

Class I: The Upper Class. The upper class is composed of the community's business and professional leaders—business executives in the major companies, lawyers, doctors, accountants, professors, and other major professionals. In addition, the cream of this crop are independently wealthy—the upper-upper classes who have *inherited* their wealth. Some sociologists (e.g., Warner) separate this extreme elite into an upper-upper class, but they constitute such a small proportion of the population that it seems unnecessary to do so.

The members of the upper class generally live in expensive homes, in the best neighborhoods, and earn extremely high incomes relative to the rest of the population. Among the upper-upper group wealth is inherited, and family background, tradition, and prestige are important to them. Almost all of the people in the upper class are college graduates, often with advanced degrees from good private institutions; their wives usually have slightly less education but almost always some college.

The upper class is not showy in displaying its wealth, because this is considered "crude" and a characteristic of people who are struggling instead of those who have made it. The upper class tends to be quiet in their wealth; they often do not drive the newest cars, wear the flashiest clothes, or give the largest parties. Instead, they go in for more conservative activities such as attending the opera, traveling, reading, and intimate entertaining.

The family patterns of the upper class are relatively stable, for in spite of the widespread publicity given to upper-class divorces, the divorce rate is actually much lower than in the rest of the population. Politically the upper class is rather conservative, since the business elites and independent professionals (doctors, lawyers, accountants) tend to vote Republican, and to oppose any change in the class structure. On the other hand, the smaller group of intellectuals among the upper class (professors, journalists, clergymen) tend to be more liberal in their political attitudes, to vote Democratic, and to act as leaders for social change movements. All members of this upper class are "heavy joiners," participating in many clubs and political organizations.

Figure 5.4 **The public's ranking of occupations. Public opinion polls conducted by the National Opinion Research Center showed that the general public ranked occupations in this order of prestige. International studies show similar ratings, and available historical evidence shows remarkable stability in the ratings over time.**

Occupation	NORC Score	Rank
U.S. Supreme Ct. Justice	94	1
Physician	93	2
Nuclear physicist	92	3.5
Scientist	92	3.5
Government scientist	91	5.5
State governor	91	5.5
Cabinet member in the Federal Government	90	8
College professor	90	8
U.S. Representative in Congress	90	8
Chemist	89	11
Lawyer	89	11
Diplomat in the U.S. Foreign Service	89	11
Dentist	88	14
Architect	88	14
County judge	88	14

Occupation	NORC Score	Rank
Building contractor	80	31.5
Artist who paints pictures that are exhibited in galleries	78	34.5
Musician in a symphony orchestra	78	34.5
Author of novels	78	34.5
Economist	78	34.5
Official of an international labor union	77	37
Railroad engineer	76	39
Electrician	76	39
County agricultural agent	76	39
Owner-operator of a printing shop	75	41.5
Trained machinist	75	41.5
Farm owner and operator	74	44
Undertaker	74	44

Occupation	NORC Score	Rank
Plumber	65	59
Automobile repairman	64	60
Playground director	63	62.5
Barber	63	62.5
Machine operator in a factory	63	62.5
Owner-operator of a lunch stand	63	62.5
Corporal in the regular army	62	65.5
Garage mechanic	62	65.5
Truck driver	59	67
Fisherman who owns his own boat	58	68
Clerk in a store	56	70
Milk route man	56	70
Streetcar motorman	56	70
Lumberjack	55	72.5
Restaurant cook	55	72.5

Occupation	Score	Rank
Psychologist	87	17.5
Minister	87	17.5
Member of the board of directors of a large corporation	87	
Mayor of a large city	87	17.5
Priest	86	21.5
Head of a dept. in a state government	86	21.5
Civil engineer	86	21.5
Airline pilot	86	21.5
Banker	85	24.5
Biologist	85	24.5
Sociologist	83	26
Instructor in public schools	82	27.5
Captain in the regular army	82	27.5
Accountant for a large business	81	29.5
Public school teacher	81	29.5
Owner of a factory that employs about 100 people	80	31.5
Welfare worker for a city government	74	44
Newspaper columnist	73	46
Policeman	72	47
Reporter on a daily newspaper	71	48
Radio announcer	70	49.5
Bookkeeper	70	49.5
Tenant farmer—one who owns livestock and machinery and manages the farm	69	51.5
Insurance agent	69	51.5
Carpenter	68	53
Manager of a small store in a city	67	54.5
A local official of a labor union	67	54.5
Mail carrier	66	57
Railroad conductor	66	57
Traveling salesman for a wholesale concern	66	57
Singer in a nightclub	54	74
Filling station attendant	51	75
Dockworker	50	77.5
Railroad section hand	50	77.5
Night watchman	50	77.5
Coal miner	50	77.5
Restaurant waiter	49	80.5
Taxi driver	49	80.5
Farm hand	48	83
Janitor	48	83
Bartender	48	83
Clothes presser in a laundry	45	85
Soda fountain clerk	44	86
Share-cropper—one who owns no live-stock or equipment and does not manage farm	42	87
Garbage collector	39	88
Street sweeper	36	89
Shoe shiner	34	90

Source: Robert W. Hodge, Paul M. Siegel, and Peter H. Rossi, "Occupational Prestige in the United States: 1925–1963" in Richard Bendix and Seymour Martin Lipset, *Class Status and Power* (New York: Free Press, 1966), pp. 324–325.

Class II: The Upper-Middle Class. The upper-middle class is composed of people in minor managerial positions and in the lesser ranking professions, such as public school teaching and social work. The income level of this group is quite high, but little money is inherited, almost all of it coming from salaries. Members of the upper-middle class live in one-family houses in better residential areas. Most of the people in this class are upwardly mobile, working their way up from lower classes primarily through the benefit of higher education that enables them to get better jobs. Their educational level is quite high, most of them having finished college. The general picture, then, is a highly educated group in relatively high occupational categories, with moderately large incomes.

The upper-middle-class people tend to be more obvious in their consumption patterns, preferring to drive luxury cars, to dress in the latest styles, and to entertain with great flair. Other leisure time is spent in the fine arts—ballet, opera, and the theater. They rarely watch television or go to sporting events except when these are related to their colleges.

The family pattern of the upper-middle class is very stable. Less than 10 percent are divorced or separated, the average family size is relatively small, and the family is the focus for psychological satisfaction. The upper-middle class, too, is a joiner group, although they tend toward the service clubs such as Rotary, Lions, and Chambers of Commerce, while the children usually are members of Boy Scouts, Girl Scouts, and church groups. Politically the upper-middle class tends to be conservative, usually voting Republican.

Class III: The Middle Class. The middle class is composed of the "average Americans" who make about the national median income (around $12,000), who graduated from high school, and who are the sales people, the white-collar workers, the factory foremen, and the highly skilled laborers. The middle-class family typically lives in a subdivision home in the suburbs, surrounded by other families of very similar social status.

The consumption habits of the middle class are typical American fare: movies and magazines such as *Reader's Digest* and the *Ladies' Home Journal* are popular, but television is the big source of entertainment. When the family goes out it is usually for a camping trip, a ride in the country, or an occasional sports event. Members of the middle class are not great readers, nor do they participate much in the so-called "fine arts."

Rigidity in moral standards and strictness about sexual behavior characterize the home life of the middle-class family. Divorce rates are higher than the upper classes, but the family patterns are nevertheless basically stable. This class is the most religious of any social class, with most of its members typically being Roman Catholics, Lutherans, Methodists, or Baptists, depending on the region of the country. The Protestant ethic governs much of the behavior of this class: hard work, frugality, and success in occupations are important moral values for the members of the middle class. Politically the middle class is split: about half its members vote Republican and about half Democratic. This group has the highest rate of switchovers during election periods, depending on current issues and the personality of the candidates.

Class IV: The Working Class. What are the characteristics of the working class? In the United States there is a great deal of blurring between the middle and working classes, since they often overlap in income and life-style. However, there are some minor differences. The father is likely to be a skilled laborer, a worker in a factory, or an operator of heavy machinery; father and mother may have finished high school but more likely did not quite make it; the average income is somewhere between $6000 and $9000; the family is likely to live in an apartment, a duplex, or a small tract home.

Family life is the center of many activities for working-class people. Visiting relatives is the main recreation outside the home, except for an occasional sporting event. The family spends much time watching television, and there is an occasional trip to the movies. The father is the dominant figure in the family, for this social class is very patriarchal and father's word is the law. Many families are broken up because of divorce (divorce rates for the working class are very high), separations, and desertions.

Politically, people in the working class are Democrats; they hope for more government intervention to help the workingman and consider themselves politically liberal on economic issues. This political liberality does not, however, extend to civil-liberty issues; members of this class are often prejudiced against and intolerant of minority groups and unusual behavior. The blue-collar worker in this class is usually just above the economic status of minority groups and is determined not to lose out in the status race. Consequently, he is the most likely to be opposed to the civil rights movements and other liberal social concerns.

Class V: The Lower Class. "Life is tough, that's all there is to it." This sentence, stated by a lower-class person in San Francisco, well summarizes the plight of the lower classes. Assailed by basic problems of economic insecurity, poor health, and a vicious circle of deprivation, the lower classes carve out a living in the face of an environment that must seem extremely hostile. Lower-class members often belong to a racial minority and work as unskilled laborers, if they work at all, for unemployment is likely to be a constant plague. This is the man last to be hired and first to be fired, a man who barely scrapes enough together each week to feed and clothe the family. Most people in this social class drop out of school in their middle teens just short of the eighth grade, marry early, and have large families.

Home is usually a very small, crowded apartment, often at the level of a slum dwelling. Privacy is always a problem, for the whole family may live in an extremely small space with very few facilities. Home life is the whole world to the lower-class person, but it is a rough life to say the least. The divorce rate in this group is the highest of any class when desertions are taken into account, for the

Figure 5.5
Profiles of five social classes

Class levels	Approximate Percent of Population*	Likely Occupation	Likely Education	Religious Affiliation	Approximate Annual Income (Some Overlap Between Classes)	Residential Neighborhood	Leisure Time Activities
I. Upper class	3.4	Independently wealthy Lawyers Professors Doctors Accountants Executives	17 or more years of school College and beyond	Jewish Episcopalian Congrega–tional A few Roman Catholics	Over 17,000 Some extremely high Much inherited wealth	Very elite neighborhood Expensive houses	Music, cultural Travel "Serious" reading Elite clubs Active sports (tennis, sailing)
II. Upper-middle class	9.0	Small businessmen Teachers Social workers Managers of small firms	Around 15 years College	Congrega–tional Jewish Some Catholics	Between 13,000 and 17,000 Most earned income by salary	Good neighborhoods Moderately expensive homes	Cultural events Formal parties Travel Family outings
III. Middle class	21.4	Administrative Clerical Chain store managers Technicians Salesworkers	High school	Methodist Many Catholics	8000 to 14,000 Salary Some wages	Private homes Medium sized Some tract homes	Visiting friends Television Movies Some "light" reading
IV. Working class	48.5	Skilled labor Industrial workers	10 to 12 years	Methodist Baptist Many Catholics	6000 to 9000 Hourly wages	Apartments Small tract homes	Visiting relatives Television Detective novels, "Girlie magazines" Observer sports (baseball, football)
V. Lower class	17.7	Unskilled labor Unemployed	Elementary school	Baptist Pentecostal Extreme fundamen–talist groups	Under 5000 Poverty and welfare	Slum areas Poor apartments	Television Visiting Relatives

legalities of divorce are often sidestepped by a husband who simply disappears. People in this class report a great deal of strife between husband and wife, and there is constant "in-law trouble." The lower classes try to stick together as family groups, however, rushing to the aid of relatives in need. Many of the families are headed by females, and welfare is often the source of family income. But when father is around he is king, for male dominance is widely practiced in this class. Children are disciplined severely and are expected to do as they are told under all circumstances.

Sociologists often report that the lower classes are trapped in a vicious circle, for the objective conditions of low income and poverty greatly influence psychological attitudes. Members of the lower class are often unwilling to take risks in order to advance their occupational status, since they often lost such gambles in the past. They usually do not have as much "achievement motivation" as people in the other classes, but this is a very realistic attitude for people whose achievement has always been stopped by hostile social conditions. In general, lower-class people are apathetic to political issues, they do not join the labor unions, and they are not involved in social clubs.

The general picture of the lower class is of an isolated, apathetic, and downtrodden group. It is important to realize, however, that this situation is more because of the social circumstances and the economic system than the people themselves. Attitudes of apathy and resignation are realistic and hardly faults for which the lower classes should be blamed. The responsibility for this vicious circle should be laid squarely where it belongs: on the economic system, the political sphere, and the system of racial prejudice and discrimination.

OTHER FACTORS ASSOCIATED WITH SOCIAL CLASS

The description of the five social classes, summarized in Figure 5.5, gives a general overview of the divisions in American society. It is important to understand, however, that these general profiles are not necessarily accurate for all people or for all regions of the country. Classes overlap considerably, and the attitudes described as characteristic of one class may be found in other classes. Thus, although the general patterns are correct, the reader should not fall into the trap of seeing these as hard and fast, air-tight compartments that completely separate people into social categories. In fact, there is much fluidity among the classes and many common values and common life-style patterns. But it is because certain attitudes and activities do correlate fairly consistently with different social classes that sociologists are concerned with class divisions. Knowing a person's social class allows you to predict a great deal about his life-style, his attitudes, and his life chances. In addition to the relationships summarized above a few additional factors are linked to social classes.

1. *Life Chances.* The death rate varies by social class, with members of the upper classes living considerably longer than those of the lower classes. It is estimated, for example,

that males in the upper classes will typically live to be 70 years or older, whereas males in the lower classes average about 60 years.

2. *Fertility Rates.* In general, the higher the social class the fewer children in the family. This finding holds true for almost all societies and is one of the most constant characteristics of the class structure. The one exception to the rule, however, is that the upper classes at the very peak of the pyramid often have large families very much like the lower classes. At all steps in between, the lower classes have more children than the classes above them.

3. *Illness.* Lower-class members suffer more illness, both physical and mental, than upper-class people. The finding that there is a higher incidence of mental illness among lower-class people (see pp. 61–64) contradicts the public stereotype of the upper-class executive suffering more mental breakdowns and having more ulcers.

4. *Membership in Organizations.* In general, the upper classes are much more prone to be "joiners" of voluntary associations and political organizations. The one exception is that blue-collar workers frequently belong to unions.

5. *Sex Behavior.* The famous Kinsey reports of the late 1950s startled the world by their finding that the upper classes were more liberal and experimental in their sexual behavior than any other social class. The variation in sex behavior tended to be consistent with the class position; the higher the social class the more sexual experimentation and liberal attitudes.

6. *Political Attitudes.* The higher the social class the more likely it is that a person will be conservative. Thus, in the United States upper classes will tend to be Republican, whereas the lower classes will tend to be Democratic. There are, of course, exceptions to this rule, one of which is that upper-class intellectuals sometimes break ranks with their more conservative fellows, voting Democratic and holding liberal political philosophies.

One's potential for an adequate life, health, education, and income, then, are all dependent on the chance factor of one's birth into a social class. The pattern is quite clear; the lower classes are trapped in a vicious cycle of economic deprivation, psychological defeatism, and hopeless despair. This cycle is more a result of the general economic situation and a spin-off of the enormous inequality in society than it is a characteristic of the people themselves. The upper classes, on the other hand, have advanced education, high incomes, careful health service, and sophisticated life-styles. Social-class position and social-class dynamics are indeed important characteristics of society.

SUMMARY

Every known society, past and present, has been divided into distinct social classes. What causes the huge social inequalities that we note all around us in the society? Why is it that some people are rich and powerful, while the majority is not? Why is there a substratum of poverty and discrimination in a nation that prides itself on equality? Certainly it is *not* because of the importance of some jobs and the need for the society to reward them more—the heart of the functionalist theory of stratification. No, the more likely explanation is that inequality is caused by the manipulation of power in the society, as Marx so well argued years ago. In fact, the conflict theory of stratification seems to get at the heart of the matter, and at the heart are the *power* and *economic systems.*

Usually classes are defined by wealth, occupational prestige, education, or some combination of these three factors. Many societies have had extremely sharp distinctions between classes, but in the modern industrial nations, people are distributed along a continuum, from upper classes to lower; divisions between the classes are not very sharp, and there is much overlap between them. But this does not mean that modern states are classless societies; on the contrary, people still identify with specific social classes, and there are still significant behavioral differences between people in different groups.

In general, sociologists identify about five classes in America. Life chances for these various classes are dramatically different: the upper classes corner most of the advantages of life—wealth, health, education, social prestige. Life habits are different, too, with divergent styles of family living, religion, political activity, and recreation.

REFERENCES

Anderson, C. H. *Toward a New Sociology* (Homewood, Ill.: Dorsey Press, 1971).

Bendix, Richard, and Seymour Martin Lipset, eds. *Class, Status, and Power,* 2nd ed. (New York: Free Press, 1966).

Bottomore, T. B. *Classes in Modern Societies* (New York: Vintage Books, 1968).

Dahl, Robert. *Who Governs?* (New Haven: Yale Press, 1961).

Dahrendorf, Rolf. *Class and Class Conflict in Industrial Society* (Stanford: Stanford Press, 1959).

Davis, Kingsley, and Wilbert Moore. "Some Principles of Stratification," *American Sociological Review, 10,* 1945, pp. 242–249.

Gans, Herbert. *The Levittowners* (New York: Pantheon, 1967).

Henle, Peter. "Exploring the Distribution of Earned Income," U.S. Department of Labor, *Monthly Labor Review,* December 1972, pp. 16–26.

Hodge, Robert W., and Donald J. Treiman. "Class Identification in the United States,"

American Journal of Sociology, 73, March 1968, pp. 535–547.

Hodges, Harold M. "Peninsula People: Social Stratification in a Metropolitan Complex," in Clayton Lane (ed.), *Permanence and Change* (Cambridge, Mass: Schenkman, 1969), pp. 5–36.

Hollingshead, August B. *Elmtown's Youth* (New York: Wiley, 1949).

Hollingshead, A. B., and Frederick C. Redlich. *Social Class and Mental Illness* (New York: Wiley, 1958).

Jackson, J. A., ed. *Social Stratification* (Cambridge: Cambridge University Press, 1968).

Kahl, Joseph A. *The American Class Structure* (New York: Holt, 1957).

Lampman, Robert. *The Share of Top Wealth-Holders in National Wealth* (Princeton, N. J.: Princeton University Press, 1962).

Lenski, Gerhard. *Power and Privilege* (New York: McGraw-Hill, 1966).

Lundberg, Ferdinand. *The Rich and the Super Rich* (New York: Bantam, 1969).

Marx, Karl. *The Eighteenth Brumaire of Louis Bonaparte* (New York: International Publishers, n.d.).

Marx, Karl. *Economic and Philosophical Manuscripts* (New York: International Publishers, 1844).

Marx, Karl, and Friedrich Engels. *The German Ideology* (New York: International Publishers, 1846).

Marx, Karl. *Capital* (New York: International Publishers, 1909).

Moskowitz, Milton. "Salaries in the Year of the Wage Freeze," *San Francisco Chronicle,* June 3, 1972, p. 33.

Olsen, Marvin E. "Social and Political Participation of Blacks," *American Sociological Review, 35,* August 1970, pp. 687–694.

Reissman, Leonard. "Social Stratification," in Neil J. Smelser (ed.), *Sociology: An Introduction* (New York: Wiley, 1967).

Shostak, Arthur. *Blue Collar Life* (New York: Random House, 1969).

Tillmon, Johnnie. "Welfare is a Woman's Issue," *Ms,* Spring 1972, pp. 111–116.

Veblen, Thorstein. *The Theory of the Leisure Class* (New York: Macmillan, 1912).

Warner, W. Lloyd, and Paul S. Lunt. *The Status System of a Modern Community* (New Haven: Yale Press, 1942).

SIX
SOCIAL MOBILITY: RACIAL, SEXUAL, AND LEGAL BARRIERS

BLACK BOY

In the autobiography of his childhood, Richard Wright tells of the kindly white man in Mississippi who gave him a job and promised that he could learn a trade, practice on the job, and move ahead occupationally. The other two men in the small optical factory did not, however, like this idea, and they proceeded to make life miserable for him.

The climax came at noon one summer day. Pease called me to his workbench; . . . "Richard, I want to ask you something," Pease began pleasantly, not looking up from his work.

"Yes, sir."

Reynolds came over and stood blocking the narrow passage between the benches; . . . I looked from one to the other, sensing trouble. . . .

"Richard, Reynolds here tells me that you called me Pease," . . .

I stiffened. A void opened up in me. I knew that this was the showdown. He meant that I had failed to call him Mr. *Pease. I looked at Reynolds; he was gripping a steel bar in his hand. . . . (He) grabbed me by the collar, ramming my head against a wall.*

"Now be careful, nigger." snarled Reynolds, baring his

In the paragraphs above Richard Wright described the agonizing plight of a black man trapped in the vicious cycle of prejudice and discrimination. Here was a black man who wanted desperately to work his way up, to capture the American Dream of rising to a better life for himself and his family. But he was caught, locked into his social position by prejudice and racial barriers.

In this chapter we will examine social mobility, the processes by which people change their social classes. First, we will look at some of the general patterns of mobility and some of the factors that promote it. Second, we will discuss the racial, sexual, and legal barriers that so effectively hinder the social mobility of millions of talented Americans.

SOCIAL MOBILITY

Having noted some of the characteristics of the different social classes in America in the last chapter, our next question has to do with how people move between classes. Do people often move out of the class in which they are born? If so, what *teeth. "I heard you call 'im Pease. And if you say you didn't you're calling me a liar, see?" He waved the steel bar threateningly.*

If I had said: "No sir, Mr. Pease, I never called you Pease," I would by inference have been calling Mr. Reynolds a liar; and if I said: "Yes, sir, Mr. Pease. I called you Pease," I would have been pleading guilty to the worst insult that a Negro can offer to a southern white man. . . .

"Richard, I asked you a question!" Pease said. Anger was creeping into his voice.

"I don't remember calling you Pease, Mr. Pease," I said cautiously. "And if I did, I sure didn't mean." . . .

"You black sonofabitch! You called me Pease, then!" he spat, rising, slapping me till I bent sideways over a bench.

Reynolds was up on top of me demanding:

"Didn't you call him Pease? If you say you didn't, I'll rip your gut string loose with this fucking bar, you black granny dodger! You can't call a white man a liar and get away with it!"

I wilted. I begged them not to hit me. I knew what they wanted. They wanted me to leave the job.

"I'll leave," I promised. "I'll leave right now." (From Richard Wright, Black Boy, *1937)*

are the conditions that promote or hinder that movement, termed social mobility?

The United States has often been called a "land of opportunity," a nation where a person can rise in social class by hard work, education, and talent. Is it true that social mobility is available for most people, or is this belief largely a myth? To answer this question we must define some terms. Mobility is usually measured by the amount of change in occupational position, since occupations are usually considered to be the major indicators of social class. Given the male dominance in occupations, sociologists usually studied only men when they examined social mobility. There are two types of occupational mobility. The first is called *intergenerational* (between generations) mobility, the change in occupational position from father to son. That is, intergenerational mobility is said to occur when a son has a different job from his father's. Downward mobility involves a move into a less prestigious job, whereas upward mobility entails a move into a better job. Another type of mobility deals not with the relationship between fathers' and sons' occupations, but with the life career of a single person. This is generally called *intragenerational* (within a generation) mobility. Usually sociologists are more concerned with *intergenerational* mobility, the difference between the occupational positions of fathers and sons, and most research concentrates on this type.

PATTERNS OF SOCIAL MOBILITY

Over the last few decades sociologists have amassed quite a bit of data about social mobility in the United States. Peter M. Blau and Otis Dudley Duncan wrote one of the most important books in the study of social mobility, *The American Occupational Structure* (1967), in which they rated occupational groups into 17 categories, with professionals and managers at the top of the scale and farm workers at the bottom. Blau and Duncan then proceeded to measure the amount of movement between these occupational groups. Their conclusions are very interesting.

1. The vast majority of sons do not end up in the same occupational group as their fathers.
2. Most of the moves, however, are only one or two steps upward or downward from the father's occupation. This is social mobility, but it is *short range* in nature.
3. There is much more upward than downward movement, that is, the son is likely to have a higher status job than his father.
4. The 17 occupational groups listed by Blau and Duncan seem to break into three basic clusters: white-collar workers, blue-collar workers, and farm workers. There is little mobility between these three clusters.

Most of the social mobility from one job to another occurs *within* these three groups, although there is some movement upward from the lower groups into the higher. There is very little movement downward; white-collar workers almost never move into blue-collar jobs, and blue-collar workers rarely go into farm jobs. It is not unusual, however, for craftsmen in the upper part of the blue-collar segment to move upward into clerical or sales jobs, or for farmers to move up into the blue-collar section as laborers.

The American Dream is in some sense true. There is opportunity for people to advance socially in the United States and to obtain jobs ranked higher than their fathers'. But that dream is limited; although upward social movement does occur, most of it is of limited range. Thus, a son may change from being a farmer to being a construction worker—an improvement in many respects—but he is unlikely to change from being a farmer to being a corporation manager or a school teacher. Blau and Duncan have assembled historical data, and they believe that the conclusions listed above have held for at least the last 40 years in the United States.

SOCIAL FACTORS THAT PROMOTE SOCIAL MOBILITY

Two groups of factors promote social mobility: (1) the structural features of the society and (2) the characteristics of the individual himself. Let us begin by concentrating on the social circumstances that have helped to promote social mobility in the United States, the most important of which has been the shift in the occupational structure itself. This shift has resulted in an ever increasing number of high-prestige jobs and a diminishing number of low-prestige jobs. It is obvious that in such a circumstance most workers would have more opportunities for upward mobility simply because more high prestige jobs are available.

As indicated in Figure 6.1, approximately 40 to 50 years ago the largest bloc of workers held farm and blue-collar jobs. With increased automation and farm mechanization, however, the occupational pyramid began to change. Farm jobs decreased rapidly while professional and white-collar jobs increased dramatically.

In addition, upper-class groups have much lower birth rates than do other classes and consequently do not reproduce themselves. Thus, top occupational jobs have been expanding, upper-class people have not been reproducing themselves, and lower-class groups have been moving up in the occupational structure to fill the vacuum. Migration has also influenced upward mobility. First the European immigrants to this country moved in and filled the lower-prestige jobs; later the great rural-to-urban migration filled the same function. When all these factors are taken into account—expansion of better jobs, lower birth rates of upper classes, and migration patterns—it should be obvious why most people in the United States experience some upward mobility, at least in comparison to their father's position.

INDIVIDUAL FACTORS THAT PROMOTE SOCIAL MOBILITY

The changes in the occupational structure outlined above explain why a majority of people will experience some upward social mobility. These general trends do not, however, explain why any *particular individual* will move up in the occupational structure. There must, then, be some individual characteristics that make people more or less likely to succeed occupationally. Extensive research on this subject has demonstrated that certain characteristics do, indeed, stand out among those who move upward in the social structure. Certainly we would assume that aggressiveness, intelligence, and hard work are individual characteristics that would help in achieving upward mobility—not to mention a generous portion of good luck! In their study of occupational mobility Blau and Duncan identified four additional factors that are extremely important in determining whether an individual rises socially.

The first two factors concern the educational and the occupational level of the father. The higher the father's education or occupation, the more likely it is that his son would be able to get ahead in the occupational structure, largely because advantages from one generation are passed on to the next. Income derived from the father's good job is plowed back into the son's education, leading to better job possibilities for the son.

The other factors were characteristics of the son—his education and the nature of his first job. It is more and more true that education is a linkpin for social mobility, for those who have higher education are consistently ahead in their ability to obtain higher prestige jobs (in Chapter Twelve we will explore this relationship extensively). Finally, Blau and Duncan suggest that a person's first job is very important in setting the trend for the rest of his life. If the first job is a good one and has real chances for advancement,

Figure 6.1
Factors in the economic system that promote upward mobility (Chart shows rough percentage distribution of various jobs: solid line equals present; dotted line equals approximately 1920).

Blau and Duncan Categories

		Blau and Duncan Categories
Upper classes do not reproduce themselves, must be replaced from below		Professional and managerial jobs 1. Self-employed professionals 2. Salaried professional 3. Managers
High-prestige jobs expanding	1974 / 1920	White collar jobs 4. Salesman 5. Proprietors 6. Clerical 7. Retail salesman
		Blue collar and skilled labor 8. Manufacturing craftsmen 9. Other craftsmen 10. Construction 11. Manufacturing operations 12. Other operatives 13. Service
Low-prestige jobs contracting	Farmers pushed off farm	Farm jobs and unskilled labor 14. Manual laborers 15. Other laborers 16. Farmers 17. Farm laborers

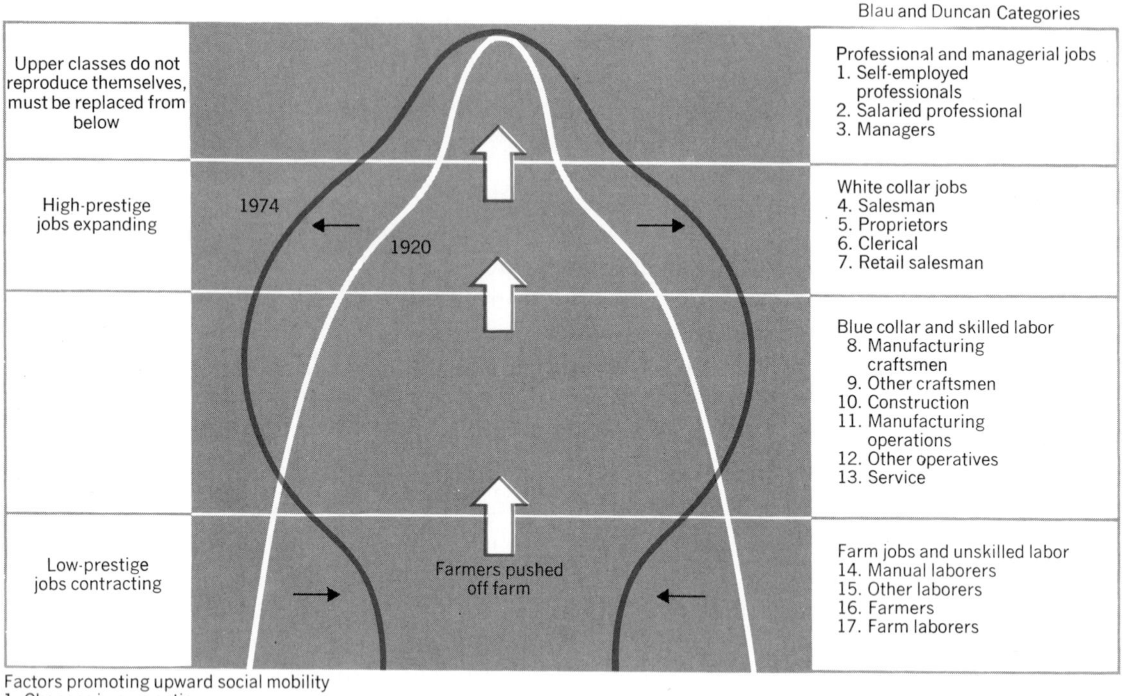

Factors promoting upward social mobility
1. Changes in occupation:
   Low-prestige jobs are contracting; high-prestige jobs are expanding, especially white collar service jobs.
2. Differential fertility:
   Upper classes do not reproduce themselves, so they cannot even fill the former jobs, much less fill the expansion. Therefore lower groups move up to fill the vacuum.
3. Migration:
   Lower groups migrate to urban areas where higher prestige jobs are available. First it was the European migration, now it is the rural-to-urban migration.

then the subsequent patterns of social mobility are more open. Thus, if a man wants to achieve a better job position than his father, he should do several things: choose parents who have high-prestige jobs and good incomes (we should all be so lucky!), work out the best educational training he can possibly achieve, and make sure his first job has advancement possibilities built into it.

All of this sidesteps the question of talent and ability, the stuff out of which the great American Dream is built. The ideology of American capitalism has always said that talented, hardworking, bright, energetic people get ahead in life, whereas the lazy and unintelligent become the social failures. All of the information above suggests that this belief misses the point widely, since it does not take into account the built-in advantages that children of the rich inherit. In reality, there is only limited mobility, and most of what there is can be accounted for by such sociological factors as changes in the economic system and the social class origin of the person. In some ways this is a dismal conclusion, because it downgrades the role of talent and hard work.

Nevertheless, it is true that talent and hard work do have their rewards. Certainly not all social mobility can be explained by the structure of the economy or by the class origin of a person's family. This leaves some room for those with high talent and high ability to maximize their potential for social mobility. Of course, people who have everything going for them at once—educated parents, high social-class background, education, *and* talent—will find the road much easier than people who have only some of these characteristics. On the other hand, people who have other social characteristics—especially if they are minorities or women—may find their mobility severely limited; they may even find themselves locked into a "caste" status.

CASTES IN AMERICA?

A caste is a class that is rigidly defined. As Gerhard Lenski notes:

Caste, like class, has been defined in a variety of ways. Underlying all or nearly all the definitions, however, is the idea of a group whose membership is rigidly hereditary. When caste and class are used as contrasting terms, castes are thought of as groups out of which and into which mobility is virtually impossible. . . . Actually, however, there is no need to treat caste and class as separate phenomena. In the interest of conceptual parsimony one can quite legitimately define caste as a special kind of class. . . . Thus we may say that a class is a caste to the degree that upward mobility into or out of it is forbidden by the [*social norms*]. *(Lenski, 1966, p. 77)*

Societies differ greatly in their class structure, especially regarding the social mobility that is possible between classes. In some nations the class system is relatively fluid; by hard work and by education people can raise their class position, change jobs, and achieve a higher lifestyle. On the other hand, there are many societies where it is almost impossible to move from one class to another; birth determines which class people will be in, and no amount of work or education can move them out of it. The more fluid situation is called an *open-class society,* while the more rigid case is called a *caste system.*

India is the classic example of a nation with a rigid caste system. Traditionally, everyone in the society was born into a caste and lived his life within the confines of that social situation. The individual was virtually helpless either to change his own caste or to help his children advance. The barriers between the castes were very high; places of worship, type of occupation, intermarriage, political activities, and religious responsibilities were carefully circumscribed for each caste. The society even specified different roads that the various castes might use. A lower-caste person, or "untouchable," had a position so low that he was literally outside the whole caste system and could never raise his social position regardless of his personal achievements. On the other hand, the upper-caste Brahmin was at the top of the social ladder regardless of how much he failed in occupational or economic terms. Mobility between the castes was virtually unknown. Since India's independence in 1949 the government has attempted to eliminate the caste structure, but has met with widespread social resistance to changing such a deeply ingrained social value.

Thus, India represents one end of the continuum as a closed-mobility society; it is very difficult, however, to name societies that really have open-mobility systems. In fact, in all the world's societies social position is greatly affected by the social position of the individual's parents and the economic benefits or liabilities that come through family connections. However, there are some societies with more flexible class systems; most of the industrial nations of Western Europe and America have more social mobility than other nations.

Our concern at this point is with caste structures and their effect on social mobility. Is it possible that even in advanced nations such as the United States there are elements of a caste system that restrict social mobility? This point has been under continued debate. A number of social scientists argue that minority groups in America are essentially in caste situations, since their social mobility is greatly restricted and their life chances are almost entirely determined by the accident of birth. In a caste society the lower castes face extreme hardship, obtain fewer of the society's economic benefits, and are constantly harassed by prejudice and discrimination. Moreover, mobility from the lower caste into upper levels of society is virtually prohibited. Certainly minorities in the United States face these problems. However, with the rapid change occurring in the United States it is doubtful that minorities here can be considered real castes; although mobility is restricted, it is hardly as rigid as a true caste system.

THE RESTRICTED MOBILITY OF RACIAL MINORITIES

Generally, it is very difficult for minority people to move out of their own situation into social positions in the white society. Their class membership is determined almost entirely by race, and this accident of birth is more important than ability or personal competency. In fact, throughout most of American history it has been illegal for blacks and whites to intermarry; prohibiting intermarriage is a common feature of a caste system. It has also been true that whites, regardless of their social position, have felt superior to minority members, even if those people were in more prestigious occupations or earned more money. In the United States today at least three major minority groups seem to face the problems that we normally associate with a lower castelike status: 9 million Spanish-speaking Americans (including Chicanos in the Southwest, Puerto Ricans in the Northeast, and Cubans in Florida), half a million native American Indians, and 23 million blacks. In the sections that follow we will briefly examine some of the social conditions that hinder mobility for each of these groups, as well as some of the rising activism that accompanies their attempts to break out of the castelike statuses that have been forced on them so long.

BLACK AMERICANS

Approximately 11 percent of the people in the United States are black. Emerging from a tradition of rural southern slavery, after World War I blacks began to migrate from the rural areas to the cities, and from the South to the rest of the nation. Today about half the blacks live outside the South and, whether living in the North or the South, they are concentrated in large urban centers. Unfortunately, regardless of where they have lived, blacks have faced systematic discrimination—in schooling, jobs, housing, and almost every other area of life. Generally they have filled the lowest, unskilled jobs, and have been isolated in miserable ghettos in central cities. As a result of this systematic discrimination blacks have faced hardships in almost every sphere of social life, as Figure 6.2 clearly shows. But blacks are on the move, and over the past two decades a strong black social movement has been fighting to promote social reform in the United States. With charismatic leaders like Malcolm X and Martin Luther King minority groups in the United States began to fight more aggressively against the oppression they were facing. The first efforts were spent in resocialization (black is beautiful), in developing an ideology that defined the white man's power structure and white racism as the cause of oppression, and in building a movement that could survive the harrowing experiences of sit-ins, marches, and jails. The authorities did not stand by passively, however; the white man's police, tear gas, and police dogs always barred the way. In the face of such harassment it was not easy building a movement, developing leaders, and marshalling a committed body of followers. However, slowly, painfully, and doggedly the movement grew and flourished even in the barren soil of a hostile society.

At first, the goals of the black movement were simple, specific, and limited; the demand was for integrated schools, integrated transportation, and social welfare laws. The tactics, too, were limited and calm: appeals to justice, legal court claims, demands on the "Christian conscience" of the nation. But the limited goals were resisted, and the milder tactics were usually ignored.

As the bone-weary years dragged on, progress toward racial equality alternated with serious setbacks. In 1954 the Supreme Court ruled that segregated schools are unlawful, but determined whites dragged their feet. A half-hearted federal government made many sympathetic noises, but was slow in taking real action against segregation and discrimination. The Civil Rights Act of 1964, a

Figure 6.2
Statistical profile of black Americans

I. Median income of nonwhite families as a percent of white income

Year	Nonwhites[a]	Blacks	Whites
1950	54		100
1955	55		100
1960	55		100
1965	55	54	100
1970	64	61	100
1971	63	60	100

II. Persons below the poverty income level (percent)

Year	Blacks	Whites
1960	55	18
1965	42	11
1970	34	10
1971	32	10

III. Unemployment rates

Year	Nonwhite	Whites
1950	9.0	4.9
1955	8.7	3.9
1960	10.2	4.9
1965	8.1	4.1
1970	8.2	4.5
1971	9.9	5.4

IV. Percent of persons 25-29 who have completed high school

Year	Blacks	Whites
1960	38	64
1966	48	74
1970	54	79
1971	54	81

V. Percent of persons 25–34 who have completed four years of college

Year	Blacks	Whites
1960	4.3	11.7
1966	5.7	14.6
1970	6.1	16.6
1971	6.3	17.2

VI. Infants dying within 28 days of birth (per 1000 live births)

Year	Nonwhite	White
1940	39.7	27.2
1950	27.5	19.4
1960	26.9	17.2
1965	25.4	16.1
1968	23.0	14.7
1969	21.6	14.1
1970	21.6	13.5

VII. Percent of families with female head

Year	Nonwhite	White
1950	17.6	8.5
1955	20.7	9.0
1960	22.4	8.7
1966	23.7	8.9
1971	28.9	9.4
1972	30.1	9.4

VIII. Number of recipients of aid to dependent children

Year	Nonwhite	Blacks	Percent of Blacks in United States Receiving Aid
1960	1.8 million	1.3 million	7
1971	5.8 million	4.8 million	21

Source: Current Population Reports, Series P-23, No. 38 "The Social and Economic Status of Negroes in the United States, 1970," U.S. Department of Commerce, Bureau of the Census; Ben Wattenberg and Richard M. Seammon, "Black Progress and Liberal Rhetoric," *Commentary,* April 1973, pp. 35–44; *Current Population Reports,* Series P-23, No. 42; *The Social and Economic Status of the Black Population in the U.S., 1971,* U.S. Census Bureau.

major step forward, was marred by the death of Martin Luther King. The end of *de jure* segregation in the South was coupled with the awareness that Northern *de facto* segregation was even more effective in separating the races. The progress toward desegregation that began to pick up steam in the late 1960s and early 1970s ran head-on into the busing debate that became a major domestic issue in the 1972 presidential election. Progress was constantly coupled with reversals.

Thus, as the struggle wore on, the early tactics and goals of the movement were often seriously questioned by black people who felt the demands were too limited or the tactics too mild. Gradually the goals were escalated to include ending the oppression of *all* minorities, opening up employment opportunities, developing strong minority political parties, ending residential segregation, and ridding the nation of its pervasive, deep-seated racism. The escalation of goals was paralleled by an escalation in tactics: the riots of Watts, Newark, and Detroit; open warfare between the police and the Black Panthers; prison riots at Attica, New York and in other parts of the nation.

Meanwhile the relentless court actions went on, with many favorable court judgments but constant delaying tactics by whites in power. Schools throughout the nation were ordered to integrate, but ceaseless rounds of appeals coupled with housing segregation kept most segregated. Richmond, Virginia was ordered in 1972 to unite with its suburban neighbors so that integration would be promoted between the majority black inner city and the majority white outer fringe, but the Supreme Court overturned the decision. In an historic case attacking Northern *de jure* segregation, Denver, Colorado was ordered to integrate its schools even though the basis was residential patterns instead of forced segregation. Many court cases opened up new possibilities for blacks, but white resistance often stifled those opportunities.

In spite of the reversals and difficulties blacks have experienced, the black movement of the past decades has indeed paid off in improved conditions for its people. Although it is important to say that America still has a long way to go before blacks have equal rights—it is also important to stress that the black revolution has actually secured many gains. Figure 6.2 shows that in most areas of life blacks have come a long way in the last two decades: (1) moving from a median income that was only 54 percent of the white median in 1950 to 65 percent in 1971, (2) reducing the number of blacks below the poverty level from 55 percent in 1960 to 34 percent in 1970, (3) increasing the number who have completed high school (38 percent in 1960 to 56 percent in 1970) and college (4.3 percent in 1960 to 6.1 percent in 1970), and (4) reducing sharply the infant death rate from 39.7 percent in 1940 to 23.0 percent in 1968. To be sure, whites advanced during the same period, but on most of these issues black gains outpaced the white gains. After reviewing many statistics on the

Blacks on the move in America. March on Washington led by Martin Luther King.

progress of blacks over the past decade Wattenberg and Scammon conclude:

Judging progress is of necessity a cold and comparative discipline. We believe, however, that on the basis of the statistics we have examined, it is fair to say that for American blacks generally in the 1960's a huge amount of progress was made—although there is still a substantial and necessary distance to traverse before some rough level of parity is reached. *Moreover, those three in ten blacks who remain trapped in poverty also made statistical economic progress in these years, although on balance this progress may with justice be considered nullified by the stunning rise of violence in the worst areas of our nation.*

Now, is all this better than what it replaced? The answer is an uncompromising "yes." In a society that prides itself on being middle class, blacks are now moving into the middle class in unprecedented numbers. In a society that scorns the high-school drop-out and offers work to the high-school graduate, blacks are now finishing high school and significant numbers are going on to college. In a culture that has a clear idea of what is a good job and what is not, blacks are now moving into good jobs. There can be little doubt that all these socioeconomic developments are better than what they replaced. (Wattenberg and Scammon, 1973, p. 41)

In spite of the progress, however, some glaring problems persist. First, although progress has been made over previous years, blacks are still far behind on most of the statistics; they have come far, but there is still much to do. Second, the statistics on family problems among blacks are very discouraging. Families with female heads where husbands have divorced or deserted have continued to increase sharply, up from 17.6 percent in 1950 to 30.1 percent in 1972. Part of this can be blamed on the welfare systems that force unemployed or underemployed fathers to flee their homes in order to allow wife and children to obtain government support. In addition, the number of blacks on Aid to Dependent Children Welfare rose from 1.3 million (7 percent of all blacks) in 1960 to 4.8 million (21 percent of all blacks) in 1971. This is largely because better welfare procedures now include people who need help, instead of denying them because of trumped-up regulations as was often the case in the past. However, not all the increases are due to changes in the welfare laws, and these are signs of serious problems.

In short, in spite of all the progress there are still major issues to be won in the battle for black equality. As a consequence, the black revolution that began in the 1950s still continues, and with many different minority groups joining in the struggle, some of which will be examined in the next sections.

CHICANOS OF THE SOUTHWEST

Since Texas became independent in 1835 and the United States annexed the Southwest in 1848, Mexican-Americans (Chicanos) have been considered foreigners, inferior persons who filled a need for inexpensive farm labor. The popular negative stereotype portrayed them as people who were prone to act out a biological inclination for alcohol, violence, and crime. When they were needed for cheap labor, Mexican nationals were welcome; millions of them were "imported," and at one point they constituted 85 percent of the common labor in agriculture, railroading, mining, and industry in the Southwest. But, when jobs became scarce during the Depression, 312,000 Mexicans were deported to lighten the welfare load. Some of the deportees were actually American citizens.

Chicanos employed as farm workers have historically endured the most wretched conditions. Moving from farm to farm to follow the seasonal work, they generally live in housing supplied by farm owners. Typically the quarters were extremely cramped and lacking in even the most obvious features, such as decent plumbing. Nor is this phenomenon limited to the Southwest and Texas; Chicanos also provide agricultural labor in much of the Northeast, Midwest, and Northwest.

Even in recent times, the wages of farm workers have been pitifully low. In California in 1967 the 700,000 Chicanos employed in agriculture earned an average of $1.78 an hour, and could work only enough to average $1709 a year. Such low annual income is typical of seasonal labor and keeps many Chicanos in utter poverty and completely dependent on farm owners for housing. Still worse, the low wages virtually force wives and children to work. This necessity of working from a very early age, combined with the constant migration, almost destroys any chance for Chicano children to acquire a decent education. In turn, poor education insures the continued isolation of the Chicano people culturally, linguistically, economically, and socially. Figure 6.3 profiles some of the social conditions of Chicanos as compared to the total U. S. population.

Language has been used as a subtle but effective means of keeping Chicanos in the lowest social positions. Until a few years ago a good command of English was necessary to vote, to obtain an education, to acquire a driver's license, and to fill out an application for even menial jobs. Although there have been some reforms, especially in areas with heavy concentrations of Chicanos, the problem remains. Ironically, the federal government finally acted to aid speakers of Spanish (as in the Bilingual Education Act of 1967) only after large numbers of Cuban middle-class refugees immigrated to America. The far larger population of Mexican-Americans had received and *still* receives a much cooler reception.

Although receiving little notice until recently, violence against Chicanos has been formidable. In the 1930s and 1940s there were actually more Chicanos lynched in the Southwest than blacks in the entire United States. Furthermore, there have been, especially during the 1940s, wholesale riots in which urban Chicano populations have been attacked (e.g., the Los Angeles "zoot-suit" riots). The Mexican government filed formal protests against these outrages. In recent years such overt violence has subsided, but more subtle forms of persecution and discrimination have continued. But Chicanos, too, have become more activist, and are now demanding their rights, led

Figure 6.3
Statistical profile of Chicanos (Mexican-Americans) compared to total U. S. population

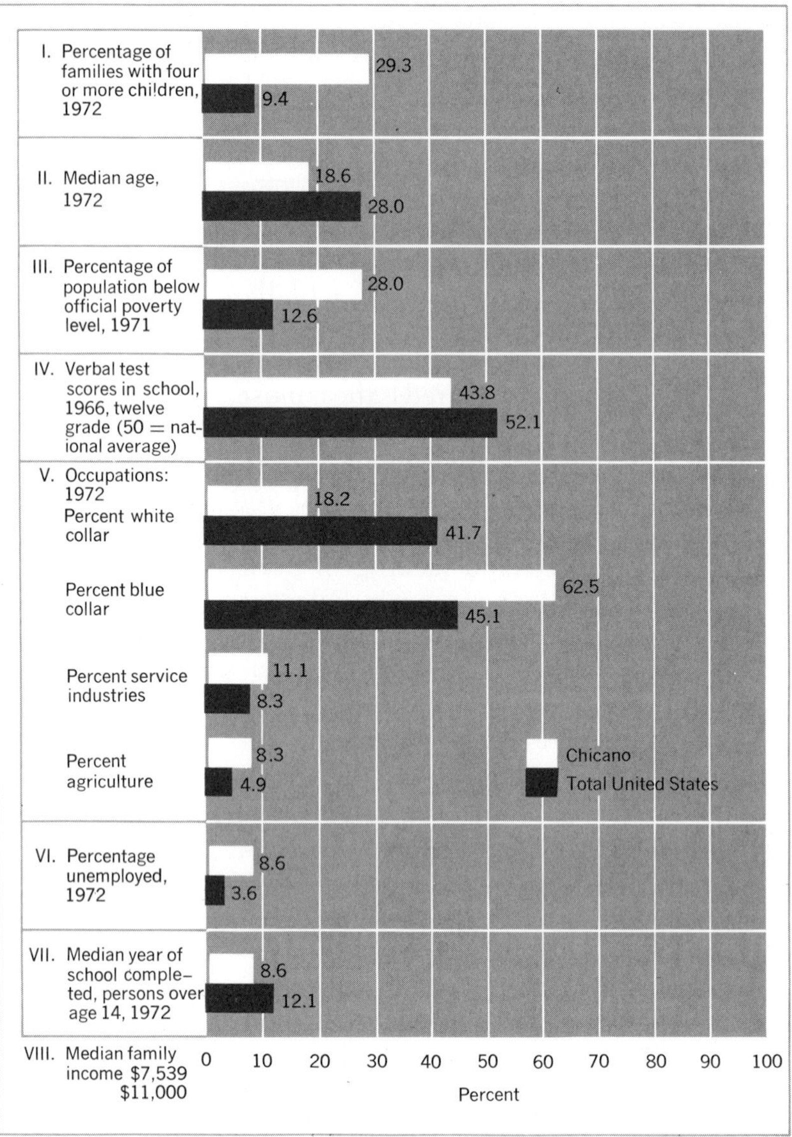

Sources: U.S. Bureau of the Census, *Current Population Reports,* Series P-20, No. 224, "Selected Characteristics of Persons and Families of Mexican, Puerto Rican, and Other Spanish Origin: March 1971," U.S. Government Printing Office, Washington, D.C., 1971; U.S. Bureau of the Census, *Current Population Reports,* Series P-20, No. 213, "Persons of Spanish Origin in the U.S., Nov., 1969," U.S. Government Printing Office, Washington, D.C., 1971. *Statistical Abstract of the United States, 1971,* U.S. Government Printing Office, Washington, D.C., 1971, p. 119; *Persons of Spanish Origin in the U.S., March 1972 and 1971,* Current Population Reports, U.S. Census Bureau, Series P-20, No. 250.

by dynamic leaders such as Cesar Chavez.

Cesar Chavez and the Chicano Farm Workers. Cesar Chavez was himself a migrant worker until his ability to work with people earned him a position with the Community Service Organization (CSO), a group dedicated to helping Mexican-Americans. Although the CSO was helpful, Chavez felt that only a labor union ultimately could make it possible for the migrants to earn a decent living and to provide their children with greater opportunities. Consequently, in March 1962 Chavez temporarily forsook his chance to escape poverty and personally started to organize the grape workers of Delano, California.

Chavez had chosen to begin with the grape workers of Delano because grapes require much attention, and the growers would therefore feel the pressure of a strike almost immediately. Furthermore, these workers were already the highest paid of farm workers, earning an average of $2400 a year at 90 cents an hour. Because they already were making progress, Chavez believed they would be more likely to fight for the future. Thus the movement was begun where the chance, not the need, for success was greatest.

In the fall of 1965 a three-year agricultural strike—the longest in California history—began. Because the union was still young and weak and the workers were too poor to endure a long strike, help had to come from outside. Fortunately, Chavez was a master at working with existing organizations to build a broad coalition. Previously he had taken his workers into the AFL-CIO, which automatically meant an alliance with one of the most powerful labor organizations in the country. The AFL-CIO directly contributed $10,000 a month to the farm workers' cause and also arranged for collections to be taken among such member unions as the Garment Workers', Seafarers', Packinghouse Workers', and others.

While he was receiving help from established labor organizations, Chavez and his aides also sought the support of militant civil-rights groups, particularly the Student Nonviolent Coordinating Committee and Congress on Racial Equality. They supplied picket captains experienced in confrontations. Chavez also pulled in members of the clergy and volunteers from such organizations as the Students for a Democratic Society and the W.E.B. Dubois clubs. Added to this were young volunteers attracted to the farmworkers' cause as an ideological extension of the civil rights movement.

Meanwhile, Chavez's own rank and file needed to be motivated and united in their cause, because a weakening of grass-roots support among the Chicano workers themselves would have been a death blow to the movement. Again, the union leadership proved very capable. Just as the courage of the workers was used as a theme to solicit outside support, so outside support was used to strengthen the courage of the workers.

Chavez also managed to gain support from the Catholic Church, the traditional church of his followers. And on March 17, 1966, the day after he had received unqualified backing from the eight Cath-

Cesar Chavez and the Chicano farmworkers strike.

olic bishops of California, Chavez began a procession from Delano to Sacramento to arrive on Easter Day. Although in many ways this was a traditional political protest, in one sense it had a special twist, a religious bent. Its symbol was La Virgen de Guadalupe. Furthermore, Chavez suggested that, like the Lenten processions of Mexico, the theme be penitential—atonement for past sins of violence on the part of workers and picketers regardless of what provocation may have been involved. The non-Chicano members of the movement found this attitude difficult to comprehend; this is hardly a normal tactic for even the least militant of labor unions. In any case the growers had not offered any atonement for *their* sins of violence and oppression. Nevertheless, the march was extremely successful in bringing the strikers together under traditional religious symbols and in gaining publicity.

Predictably, the workers alone could not wield enough power, so they changed tactics, hoping to force a settlement by seeking a nationwide boycott. In this effort the machinery and outside connections of the movement as well as its broad-based support proved decisive in creating a massive response. One by one the wine-grape growers agreed to sign contracts, and when the last, Paul Masson Vineyards, signed in September 1968, this phase of the struggle was over.

In terms of the number of workers actually protected by contracts, the campaign against the wine-grape producers was only a preliminary step. Most field workers, especially the poorest paid, labored on other crops. But a powerful organization with experienced personnel and strong alliances and with a broad spectrum of outside organizations had been built. This may have been the first time that many Chicanos had worked together to gain meaningful improvements in their lives, but, from that time on, the Chicano movement has established itself as a political and social force to be recognized.

Today that movement is still active, but gradual change has occurred in the agricultural production industries, most likely as a result of the gains forced by Chavez. The growers, in an effort to stop the UFW, have encouraged protective legislation for field workers covering bargaining, improving work conditions, and raising wages. These efforts have not produced national legislation, but many western states are considering agricultural labor relations legislation.

Another change has been that the Teamsters Union has undercut Chavez's United Farm Workers Union by signing contracts with the growers, taking them away from the UFW. Unlike the UFW, the major organizational thrust of the Teamsters is not farm workers. Many growers view contractural arrangements with the Teamsters as the lesser of two unavoidable evils. The UFW claims that the Teamsters have negotiated "sweetheart" contracts, going easy on the growers and deliberately trying to hurt the UFW. The future of Chavez's movement, as it faces the double-edged threat of the giant Teamsters Union and the growers, probably depends on either strengthened boycotts or protective legislation insuring supervised elections for field workers. (For descriptions of the Chicano farmworker's fight for equality see Dunne, 1971, and Gomez, 1971.)

Chicanos in Urban Areas. But the story of Cesar Chavez and the farm workers is only part of the Chicano struggle; in fact, in some ways it is almost a sideline story. As heroic as it is, the fight of the farm workers will eventually be overshadowed by urban struggles. Many of the growers struck by Chavez were themselves in desperate financial straits. They were not going hungry, as many of their workers were, but many of these farms were heavily mortgaged, and their owners were contending with 9 to 10 percent interest rates plus the uncertainties of the agricultural markets. With or without the unions many of the present farms will go out of business; the number of farms in California was cut in half between 1945 and 1970. In 1971 4 percent of the owners held 70 percent of the land, and 8 percent of the owners employed 80 percent of the labor. Since these larger farms are much more mechanized, the demand for Chicano labor is likely to dwindle. Not only does this put them in a very weak bargaining position, but it threatens to destroy even the marginal jobs they now hold. Plagued by illiteracy, poor education in general, and historical prejudice, it does not seem that persons so displaced by mechanization could easily be absorbed into another part of the economy. The new battle will be to break into the urban life of America.

Already 80 percent of Chicanos live in urban areas, mostly in ghettos called "barrios." Here they have encountered conditions fairly similar to those of black Americans, with the added element of a language barrier. As a more and more urban and organized group, Chicanos have already won many improvements. With the change from rural farms to urban barrios has come a growing revolution in the attitudes and expectations of Chicanos and at least the beginnings of change in the attitudes of others toward them. (For additional material on Mexican-Americans see Burma, 1970, and Moore, 1970.)

THE FIRST AMERICANS AND THE LAST AMERICANS—INDIANS

It is bitterly ironic that American Indians now occupy, as a group, one of the least favorable socioeconomic positions in American society. They have literally become the "last" group in what was once exclusively their continent.

After Indians first encountered Europeans it was only a short time until the invaders began to displace these former inhabitants. Intermittent warfare against superior technology and a better organized enemy took a terrible toll of Indian lives. Worse yet, the Europeans brought to America diseases against which the Indians had no natural immunity. There are documented cases of Europeans using these diseases as a form of biological warfare; for instance, "gifts" of blankets may have been collected from small-pox hospitals. Ultimately the Indians did succeed in saving themselves from extermination by agreeing to live on "reservations" designated by the whites. Typically this was the worst land in the nation and, most important, it was not able to support the Indian with either his own technology or with the new agricultural-grazing technology compatible with his culture. The Indians were thus turned into beggars—dependent on whites for even a meager existence.

Unlike most other minorities, Indians remain isolated in largely rural areas. Thus, the problems of minority status are compounded with rural poverty. Within

Indians protest centuries of oppression by capturing Alcatraz Island in San Francisco Harbor.

the 23 states that contain almost all of the Indian population, about 9 out of every 10 Indians live on reservations. Conditions on these reservations have often been abominable. As early as 1926 a government study directed by Lewis Meriam found the Indians to be "extremely poor, in bad health, without education and lacking adjustment to the dominant culture around them." More recently, in 1964, a Bureau of Indian Affairs survey of 14 reservations found that median family income varied from $900 to $3600 a year; only one reservation had a median income above $2500. It is not hard to see where this problem develops; in 1967, a prosperous year, 37.3 percent of reservation Indians were unemployed versus 2.3 percent of the non-Indian population. The previous year a special survey of 14 reservations showed that the unemployment rate varied from a "low" of 20 percent to an incredibly high 79 percent.

Perhaps it is the health problems that have hit hardest and most directly at the Indian spirit. American Indians have a tuberculosis rate almost seven times the national average and contract dysentery 49 times as often. The huge gap in death rates between Indians and whites has been gradually closing; infant mortality was still up to 30.8 per 1000, versus 19.7 for the white population. Figure 6.4 gives more statistical data on Indian social life and living conditions.

But these are only dry statistics that do not fully reveal the human side of the tragedy. The hopelessness, despair, and alienation that are all too common on the reservation and among Indians everywhere destroy pride, separate families, and lead to a terrible problem of alcoholism. The following case studies, drawn from many produced by the Economic Research Service, give some impression of how these problems hit at the personal level.

Case B. *Mr. and Mrs. B are 29 and 27 years old, respectively. They are the parents of seven children ranging in age from one through nine, living in a small, one-story house they rent for $30 a month. Living space of about 500 square feet is something less than adequate for a family of nine. . . . The house construction is poor, with outside wall covering of tar-paper-composition material, and there are no inside plumbing facilities, no public sewage disposal . . . nor septic tank. Their water must be carried from a well. . . . Mr. B has been unemployed for three years because he sustained an injury while working in a lumber mill. The accident required surgery, during which time the mill replaced him. . . . Mr. and Mrs. B both completed nine grades of school. Three of their children are in school; the other four are preschoolers. The sole source of income . . . was $1924 from Mr. B's unemployment compensation. He did . . . better in 1965 when he earned $2374, but far below the poverty threshold. . . .*

Case C. *The parents in this family are 47 and 36 years old. . . . They have eight children whose ages range from three to nineteen. The family is housed in a one-story wood dwelling which allows only about 100 square feet of living space per family member. These rented quarters contain no indoor plumbing facilities . . . and no sewage disposal system. . . . Mr. C, partially disabled by inactive TB,*

Figure 6.4
Statistical Profile of American Indians Compared to Total U.S. Population

Social Characteristics	Total U.S. Population	Indians
I. Population, 1970	201,722,000	798,000
II. Percent of school age population in school, 1971	98.7%	92.0%
III. Infant mortality, 1968 (deaths under 1 year per 1000 births)	21.8	30.8
IV. Maternal deaths per 10,000 births, 1964	3.4	6.3
V. Deaths due to tuberculosis per 100,000 people, 1967	3.5	15.8
VI. Median age, 1970	28.1	20.5
VII. Life expectancy	70.2	63.5
VIII. Cases of tuberculosis per 100,000 people, 1964	26.6	184.1
IX. Accident rate per 100,000 people, 1968	41.6	100.5
X. Percent males unemployed, 1967	2.3%	37.3%
XI. Median income of males, 1964	$5710	$1800
XII. Average achievement test scores, Grade 12, 1966 (50 = average)	52.1	43.7

Sources: Joint Economic Committee, Congress of the U.S., *American Indians: Facts and Future* (New York: Arno Press, 1970); *Statistical Abstract of the U.S. 1972* (Washington, D.C., U.S. Govt. Printing Office, 1971), p. 119; U.S. Dept. HEW, Office of Public Health, *Vital Statistics of the U.S.*, 1967; *Illness Among Indians,* Indian Health Service (Washington, D.C.: U.S. Govt. Printing Office, 1971); *General Social and Economic Characteristics: U.S. Summary* (U.S. Census Bureau, 1972).

works only part-time, as a laborer. . . . Mrs. C . . . would like to learn to be a typist. . . . Mr. C has had no formal schooling, cannot read and can write only his name. . . . This family's income is derived from welfare payments, amounting to $1950 . . . plus Mr. C's earnings [of] . . . $466.

Case G. *Mr. and Mrs. G, aged 74 and 70 are now living alone. . . . The aging parents own their single-story house of wood siding. Space is ample for the two of them . . . but there is no indoor plumbing, no public sewage system, and no septic tank. . . . In 1960 Mr. G retired from . . . farming. . . . Mr. G had only one year of schooling and his wife had none. Neither can read, and Mr. G can write only his name. Their oldest son graduated from high school, but he is the only one of their ten children who completed more than six years of school. . . . This couple lives on a monthly check of $105 from the Veterans' Administration. . . .*

Conditions have, however, actually been improving. Reservation Indians have lately become more militant, organizing and seeking aid for initiating economic development projects. Other projects include improving education, not only to give Indian children more opportunity, but also to give them an understanding of the worth of their native culture. Indian self-consciousness is rising, and major confrontations between Indians and whites occurred during the early 1970s, particularly when they seized control of the abandoned federal prison on Alcatraz Island in San Francisco Bay (1971) and the small town of Wounded Knee, South Dakota (1973). In other cases tribes have, through the courts, won substantial settlements for land previously seized and have used this money to generate jobs and to improve social services. It is conceivable that the reservation system, originally an instrument of oppression, might provide a basis for social action and organization to restore American Indians to something more closely approximating their proper conditions in the country that was first theirs. (For more information on Indians see Subcommittee on Economy in Government, 1970, Cahn, 1969, Fisher, 1969, and Steiner, 1967)

THE RESTRICTED MOBILITY OF WOMEN

Although racial minorities form the largest pocket of people with restricted mobility, women of all racial and ethnic groups also face unique problems. Although it is true that women have generally acquired their social class based on their father's or husband's status, it is more and more the case that they contribute significantly to that joint status through their occupations outside the home. In addition, a sizable number of women are striking out on their own, remaining single, and through their occupations determining their own social position.

Parallels between the social conditions of women and of blacks are sometimes drawn by those who feel that the status of women is similar to that of the severely discriminated-against blacks. Sociologist Helen Hacker suggested the basic analogy as early as 1951, and her comparative chart is reproduced in Figure 6.5. It must be stressed, however, that this is only one viewpoint. Many militant blacks and feminists emphatically reject the analogy, insisting that it is absurd to compare the relatively minor (by the militant's assessment) disadvantages of middle-class women to the basic fight for survival faced by many racial minority groups. Hacker's proposal that women are a caste is probably inaccurate, but even if their status is not that bad it *is* clear that they face serious discrimination that hinders their social mobility and life chances.

Discrimination against women is examined in several chapters, but it might be helpful to summarize some of these factors in conjunction with the discussion of women's social mobility chances.

1. *Women face severe discrimination in occupations.* (See Chapter Twelve.)

- They hold low-skill, low-pay jobs.
- They receive much lower pay even for comparable work.
- There are many barriers at job entry that effectively prohibit women from the best jobs.
- There are few women in the high-paying professions (although they are heavily represented in teaching, social work, and nursing—the lower-paid professions).

2. *Women are socialized into lower statuses and more restricted self-images.* (See Chapter Four.)

- Early childhood training and play ac-

Black militant Angela Davis on trial in San Jose, California. Minorities are arrested and prosecuted far out of proportion to their numbers. Miss Davis, who was found innocent of all charges, maintains that the government silences black dissent by constantly harassing the leaders with legal action. This keeps them quiet and out of action, even if later they are found innocent—as most have been in the rash of "political" trials since the mid-1960s.

Figure 6.5

Comparison of the caste-like status of blacks and women. Hacher's comparison is probably incorrect; white women hardly face the same discrimination as blacks, but in 1951 when it was written the point had to be made strongly in order to emphasize the dormant issue of women's rights.

	Blacks	Women
1. High Social Visibility	a. Skin color, other "racial" characteristics b. Distinctive dress	a. Secondary sex characteristics b. Distinctive dress
2. Ascribed Attributes	a. Inferior intelligence, smaller brain, less convoluted, scarcity of genius b. More free in instinctual gratification. More emotional, "primitive" and childlike. Imagined sexual prowess envied c. Common stereotype "inferior"	a. Inferior intelligence, smaller brain, less convoluted, scarcity of genius b. Irresponsible, inconsistent emotionally unstable, lack strong superego, women as temptresses c. "Weaker"
3. Rationalization of Status	a. Thought all right in his place b. Myth of contented Negro	a. Woman's place is in the home b. Myth of contented woman—"feminine" woman is happy in subordinate role
4. Discriminations	a. Limitations on education, should fit "place" in society b. Confined to traditional jobs —barred from supervisory positions c. Deprived of political importance d. Social and professional segregation e. More vulnerable to criticism	a. Limitations on education, should fit "place" in society b. Confined to traditional jobs —barred from supervisory positions c. Deprived of political importance d. Social and professional segregation e. More vulnerable to criticism
5. Accommodation Attitudes	a. Supplicatory whining intonation of voice b. Deferential manner c. Concealment of real feelings d. Outwit "white folks" e. Careful study of points at which dominant group is susceptible to influence f. Fake appeals for directives; show of ignorance	a. Rising inflection, smiles, laughs, downward glances b. Flattering manner c. "Feminine wiles" d. Outwit "menfolk" e. Careful study of points at which dominant group is susceptible to influence f. Appearance of helplessness

tivities tend to emphasize more passive, dependent roles for women.

■ Early picture books give extremely stereotyped views of the options open to women in life.

■ School textbooks almost uniformly neglect women, and when they are included it is only in minor roles.

■ The mass media (television, radio, newspapers, novels) tend to portray women in secondary roles and to play up the stereotyped homebound mentality.

3. *Women face serious legal discrimination.* (See later sections in this chapter.)

■ The right to vote was extended to women only a few decades ago.

■ So-called "protective" laws limit the occupational advancement of women in many states.

■ Property laws often favor men.

■ Abortion and contraceptive laws limit the rights of women to control their own bodies.

■ Welfare laws often treat women as second-class citizens.

4. *Educational opportunities are unequally distributed between men and women.* (See Chapter Eleven.)

Almost the same number of men and women graduate from high school but fewer women go to college.

■ Admissions and scholarship policies discriminate against women in many colleges.

■ Women receive fewer higher degrees—masters, professional degrees, and doctors—except in lower-paying professions such as teaching.

■ Many factors combine to limit educational opportunities for women, such as the lack of women professors and widespread prejudices against scholastic achievement for women.

We could easily extend the list to include a number of other issues, but it does seem clear that women in this society face considerable discrimination and that their mobility into the most privileged statuses in the society is sharply limited. Thus, although minority groups and women do not actually constitute true castes in this society, it does seem reasonable to suggest that these groups form an extremely rigid class—and the consequences for the life chances of the group members are very important. They face much prejudice and are constantly harassed by discrimination of all kinds.

THE LAW AND SOCIAL MOBILITY

Whenever people face discrimination it invariably hinders their social mobility. Job discrimination stifles the mobility possibilities of those affected; residential segregation causes ghettos and segregated schools, cutting into people's desire for better housing and schools; educational discrimination severely hampers a person's ability to move ahead economically and socially. One area that is sometimes overlooked is legal discrimination, the laws that have enormous impact on people's ability to have social mobility. If laws discriminate by promoting school segregation, or job inequalities, or unequal application of criminal prosecution, then the victims are sharply restricted in their mobility opportunities. Let us examine some of these legal hindrances.

VICTIMLESS CRIMES

There is a class of laws that covers such activities as drug abuse, prostitution, gambling, and other activities that have no victims; no one is injured with the possible exception of the person who is doing the act. Police departments around the nation spend much time prosecuting these "victimless crimes." In fact, in a recent study the San Francisco police department was reported to spend nearly one half of all its man-hours pursuing drunks, prostitutes, gamblers, and drug users. Police effort is thus diverted away from real criminals and instead directed at petty vices. The prosecution of victimless crimes is an important hindrance to social mobility for many people, especially those in minority or poverty areas where victimless crimes are used as an excuse for police to harass people. A police record obtained in this manner can follow people all their lives, hindering their social mobility chances whenever they apply for a job.

All victimless crimes are an invasion by the state into the private lives of individuals who are doing something the state has labeled a "vice." In almost every other area of life we demand that the state keep hands off unless a citizen's activity is hurting someone else. However, in the area of "vice" the state feels that it has the wisdom to define criminal acts even if the people are mature adults doing something from which they personally derive satisfaction.

In every historical age this category of crime has shifted with the customs of the day. While almost every age has prohibited murder, violence against people, theft of property, and other major crimes, the definition of victimless crimes has varied dramatically, depending on which social groups had power. In many societies, for example, prostitution, the use of drugs, and gambling have not been illegal. The definition of the crimes to be outlawed is always the prerogative of the middle and upper classes, since the whole process is an outgrowth of class custom and class norms instead of universally held human values. Almost always the "vices" are the habits of the lower classes, minorities, and young people, essentially powerless groups in the society, instead of the vices of the middle classes or the older generation. When a vice is practiced enough by the white middle and upper classes it no longer is a criminal offense; cigarette smoking, the use of liquor, and gambling in state lotteries are classic examples of practices that were once defined as vices, but are now legal simply because they are practiced by most of the people.

On the other hand, the habits of minorities, the poor, or the young are often defined as crimes. For example, research studies on marijuana have shown varied results about its harmfulness—unlike the deadly, but legal, use of cigarettes or liquor. But smoking grass is mostly the habit of the young, the lower classes, and the powerless, and the possession and sale of marijuana are illegal. The wide range of laws, their interpretations, and the penalties against marijuana use have served to undermine the trust that young people have in the legal system. (See Braden's comments in Insert 6.I.) People in urban ghettos frequently are harassed by police using arrests for prostitution, gambling, and drugs as methods for "controlling undesirables." Naturally, this constant harassment and the police records that follow it are serious obstacles for anyone who wants to break out of the ghetto's vicious cycle of poverty.

It is bad enough that victimless crimes are prosecuted at all, but in addition, there is another accompanying problem. In their overly zealous attempts to stamp out victimless crimes the police of the nation have gradually eroded a number of fundamental constitutional rights. In order to stamp out the use of marijuana the District of Columbia passed in 1970 a crime bill that provided for a number of severe police tactics, including "preventative detention" practices that allow police to hold arrested persons without bail, "no knock" searches by which the police can crash into private residences, a series of mandatory minimum sentences that remove a judges' discretion on the punishment given to criminals, and a rash of new wire tapping regulations. The American Civil Liberties Union expressed fear that these police tactics, in their hurried attempt to tackle minor vices, would greatly erode civil liberties. This is a clear case in which the cure is much worse than the disease, since these minor vices become the excuse for police departments to obtain strong "law and order" laws that were most often used against militant groups.

In the last few years many civic leaders and intellectuals have argued that all criminal penalities for victimless crimes should be lifted. In fact, the report of a presidential commission (1970) recommended that laws against pornography and against sexual acts between consenting adults be abolished—the entire report was categorically rejected by President Nixon. In spite of some public concern among civic leaders, it appears that the

INSERT **6.1**

TRYING TO ENFORCE THE UNENFORCEABLE

In this article Tom Braden, a syndicated columnist published in many newspapers, comments on the "war between the generations" that results from laws against marijuana.

Like a great many other fathers in this country I have a child who was arrested not long ago for possession of marijuana. I risk a personal account because it seems to me to point to a general conclusion.

The episode was memorable for a number of reasons. First, it was a physical shock. Anybody who tells you that you can take a telephone call from a son who is in jail and not reflect upon it for weeks to come is a person who doesn't care about his children.

Second, it posed a moral problem. A father likes to think of himself as protector of children and defender of the upright. A son who is in jail for violating the law is a problem in allegiance.

Allegiance once decided, the episode was costly. To be reasonably certain that a child does not serve the mandatory three-year jail sentence, it is necessary to hire a lawyer who can convince the prosecuting attorney that his duty may be fulfilled by permitting the child to plead guilty to the offense for which a policeman had stopped him (a defective taillight). Even so, this particular child served three days in jail.

Fourth, and most important, the episode taught me a lesson that I didn't want to learn, namely that there is justice in the prevalent view of the young that they are the victims of bad law and of policemen who enforce bad law selectively.

"Why did you lower the penalty?" a police officer from a small town in upper Michigan asked an official for the Bureau of Narcotics at a meeting earlier this summer. "The only way that

bulk of the white middle and upper classes—the power holders among the electorate—is content to leave the situation as it is. Reform may be a long time coming.

To summarize, victimless crimes simply cannot be understood unless it is clear that *the definition of vice is essentially a type of social conflict in which the older generation, the wealthy, the racial majorities, and the powerful define as criminal, the activities of the young, the poor, the minorities and the powerless,* we can get rid of long-haired kids on the Michigan peninsula is to stop them on a traffic violation and toss them in jail after we find the stuff."

The official from the Narcotics Bureau was nonplussed. He had been attempting to explain President Nixon's new federal legislation which makes first offense possessors guilty of a misdemeanor and subject to sentences of not more than a year. It had not occurred to him that the law against marijuana was a law against a generation.

And yet it can't be anything else. According to a recent poll, 39 percent of all college students call themselves "frequent" users of marijuana. The figure is up 15 percent from last year. And 62 percent of all college students have tried marijuana from one to three times. Shall we enforce the law? Shall we toss millions of our children into jail?

President Nixon has taken a small step in the direction of permitting us to escape this impossible choice. The new federal legislation is intended to serve as a model of the states. It lowers the penalty for possession and makes it possible for judges to suspend sentences and expunge records.

But it does not prevent policemen from harassing the young for doing what nearly all the young are doing. Nor does it satisfy one generation that it is not being chivied about by another. As the Surgeon General of the United States, Dr. Jesse L. Steinfeld has remarked, "I know of no clearer instance in which the punishment for an infraction of the law is more harmful than the crime."

Meantime, we continue to spend time and money trying to enforce the unenforceable, confusing ourselves by linking marijuana with dangerous drugs and giving our children an excuse for saying that we are unfair to their generation.

Source: San Francisco Chronicle, Thursday, September 16, 1971, p. 45.

enforcing laws against the behavior that is quite legitimately accepted within those subgroups. As a consequence, thousands of people in minority and poverty groups get police records that haunt them all their lives, hindering their social mobility opportunities at every turn.

INEQUITY IN THE APPLICATION OF LAWS

In addition to laws that effectively discriminate against powerless groups, there is much favoritism and inequality in the application of laws that are supposed to affect all citizens equally, a fact that has major impact on the social mobility of people who are discriminated against. For example, social position is a very important factor in determining whether a person will be arrested, and if he is arrested whether he will be tried. All crime statistics consistently show that lower-class and minority people are arrested in numbers way out of proportion to their percentage in the population. Part of this overrepresentation is because the dismal social conditions of the poor and minorities do lead them to commit more crimes than do middle- and upper-class people. But much of this overrepresentation is clearly because police harass these people and because lower-class and minority group people are subject to arrest and trial when middle- and upper-class people would have been warned and turned loose.

Philip H. Ennis (1967) conducted a study to determine some of the patterns of law enforcement in the United States (see Figure 6.6). The outstanding finding is that out of 2077 crimes only 50 went to trial. In most cases the victims did not even notify the police; the police came in 787 cases, an actual arrest was made in only 118 cases, and 50 were prosecuted.

Most of those who were arrested and tried were blacks, poverty-stricken whites, or young people, in short, the powerless and outcasts of the society. The influence of social class on arrest and trial rates is one of the most clearly established facts in criminal justice, since frequently with the aid of high-priced lawyers the wealthy can get off from almost any crime. Police arrests for victimless crimes are almost always directed against members of the lower class, although the upper classes also commit many victimless crimes. A person from the slums who is caught with marijuana is put in jail; a person from the suburbs is let off with a warning. The person from the ghetto who steals hubcaps is taken to police headquarters; the white-collar worker who steals equipment from his office is often ignored.

White-collar criminals, like juvenile offenders, receive special treatment that in effect removes the stigma of crime and does not brand them as criminals. A study of 547 cases of white-collar crime in which unlawful behavior was *proved* showed that in only 9 percent were these rulings made by a criminal court (Wolfgang, et al., 1970). Many cases were handled in civil courts or settled before coming to court at all. This study showed that violations of copyrights, patents, and trademarks, as well as antitrust and false advertising suits very rarely go to criminal court even when there is solid evidence of a criminal violation. State prosecutors are reluctant to pursue cases of white-collar criminals who manipulate shady stock deals, of industries that falsely advertise products and pollute the air and water, of businessmen who cheat on local taxes and pay off politicians for favors, even though, as E. H. Sutherland asserts, "The financial cost of white collar crime is probably several times as great as the financial cost of all the crimes which are customarily regarded as the "crime problem."" (Sutherland, 1949, p. 8)

In effect, the criminal law is largely exercised against lower-class criminals and their particular kinds of crime: steal-

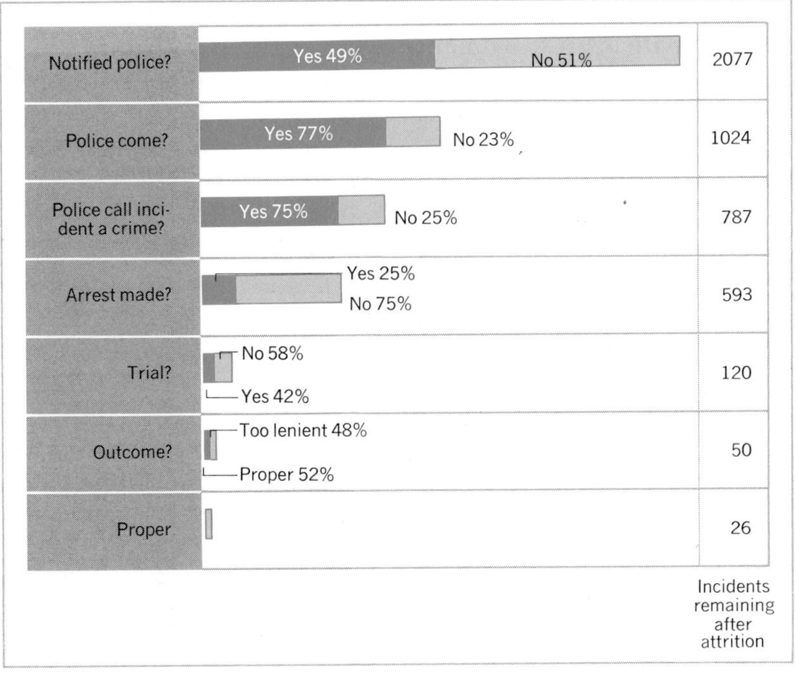

Figure 6.6
Patterns of criminal prosecution in reported crimes. In a national survey a random sample of Americans was asked whether they had ever been the victim of a crime. Of those who had been (2077) here is what happened:

Source: Philip H. Ennis, *Criminal Victimization in the United States* (Chicago: National Opinion Research Center, 1967).

ing, crimes of violence, and petty vices such as drinking and gambling—all crimes that are quite unnecessary for the affluent. As it has been said, "The rich and poor alike are forbidden to sleep under the bridges of Paris—but why would the rich need to?"

Another type of law that traditionally has been unfairly administered deals with the regulation of voting. Voting plays a critical role in the political processes of a democratic society, but until recently the right to vote was denied to large groups of people. Throughout the nation so-called "literacy laws" effectively prohibited blacks and many poor people from voting, since they were unable to pass very strict reading tests; these same reading tests were rarely administered to whites and members of the elites. With the concerted drive by civil-rights activists to register more minority members and poor people throughout the nation, coupled with recent court rulings that outlawed most of the more blatant forms of voting restrictions, there has been an upsurge in the number of registered voters from depressed socioeconomic groups.

HOW LAWS DISCRIMINATE AGAINST WOMEN

In the last few pages we have been discussing the ways in which the laws of the society discriminate against the powerless, the poor, and members of minority groups, and consequently reduce their social mobility opportunities. Laws often discriminate against women as well, even though women are just as likely to represent middle- and upper-class segments of the society as are men. In many ways women occupy a status not unlike that of the poor and other powerless groups. All people clearly are not equal under the law, in spite of our naive beliefs to the contrary. It is almost always true that social groups to whom the society assigns lower status are discriminated against by the legal system, whether those groups are blacks ("separate-but-equal" laws, Jim Crow laws), welfare recipients (household search without benefit of normal protection), or homosexuals (arrest and harassment). Women, for example, are faced with a number of discriminatory laws that apply to them but not to males.

The battle for women's equality in the legal system did not end in 1920 when women voted for the first time in a national election. Even today there are many laws that severely limit women's rights. For instance, women have never had the same rights as men over property; they usually were forced to have a man (husband or father) hold title to their possessions. When a woman sold property it was with the permission of men, and usually with the signature of a man who would be "responsible" for her actions. Such property laws have discriminated against women, virtually making them wards of men. Although "common property" laws in many states have now given women equal rights over material goods, there are still many laws unfavorable to the property rights of women. In 1966, for example, the U. S. Supreme Court upheld a Texas law that prohibits a married woman from entering into binding legal contracts without her husband's approval—yet the husband could do so without the wife's approval.

Many other discriminatory laws limit the rights of women.

- The Social Security laws treat women as second-class citizens, giving them more benefits as wards of their husbands in most cases than they receive from their own payments.
- Although courts have consistently ruled against the exclusion of minority groups from juries, the Supreme Court has never overruled local laws that discriminate against women on juries. In Boston nearly three times as many men are called for jury duty as women, by deliberate policy of the county jury clerk.
- The so-called "domicile" laws almost universally specify that a husband may choose where the family is to live, and the woman must accept his choice or be guilty of desertion from her family.
- It is still quite legal for colleges and universities to discriminate on the basis of sex, but not on the basis of race, creed, or religion. Recent rulings are gradually eliminating this sex bias, but the practices are nevertheless widespread.
- So-called "nepotism" rules in many companies, universities, and government agencies prohibit relatives from working in the same company. Such a policy effectively excludes wives from working in the same professional area as their husbands, and these rules have been upheld by courts.

Several other laws have a negative impact on women. Many laws were passed during the early years of this century to protect women from the terrible conditions that then existed in factories and mills. Although these protective laws served a useful purpose at the time, they have become barriers against women in the modern job market. Some of these laws, for example, prohibit women from lifting heavy loads, working overtime, or working at strenuous jobs. The effect of these laws is that women are kept out of high-paying jobs on the pretense that they are strenuous. For example, in 1966 the Colgate-Palmolive Company attempted to fire female workers because the Indiana state law said women could not lift more than 35 pounds. In a court suit (*Sellers, et al.* vs. *Colgate-Palmolive Company*) the U. S. Court of Appeals in Chicago ruled in 1969 that the law had been used to discriminate against women workers, excluding women from jobs they were perfectly competent to do.

A whole group of laws about sexual behavior and abortion hit women especially hard. Laws against prostitution are hardly fair in their unequal treatment of the female prostitute (who goes to jail) and her male client (who goes home). Many school boards prohibit pregnant women who are unmarried from attending school, while the fathers go right on studying. The laws against birth control, very common until only a few years ago, were particularly cruel to women who wanted to limit the size of their families and to gain some measure of control over their own bodies. Abortion laws even today typically make it a criminal offense to end an unwanted pregnancy. California, New York, Hawaii, and other states have begun to administer legal abortion, but there still is an underground of quacks who make money from women who must resort to illegal abortions because of the law's rigidity.

The laws are gradually changing, especially under the pressure of militant women's liberation groups. In 1963 Congress passed the "Equal Pay for Equal Work" act that, at least legally, ended the frequent practice of paying women lower wages than men in the exact job. However, many firms get around this law by retitling the men's jobs and upgrading them on the payscale, although the job is essentially the same that a woman holds with a lower title. In 1964 the Civil Rights Act added "sex" to race, creed, and religion as prohibited bases of discrimination. Since that time the Equal Employment Opportunity Commission, an agency set up to implement the employment provisions of the civil-rights law, has spent nearly one-third of its time investigating complaints of discrimination based on sex. In 1972 Congress passed a constitutional amendment to guarantee women full protection under the Constitution. Progress, though in evidence, has been painfully slow.

SUMMARY

Social mobility is the movement between classes, usually defined by changes in occupational status between fathers and sons. Today there are many structural changes occurring in American society that promote social mobility: changes in the occupational structure, the lower fertility of the upper classes, and the rural to urban migration. Because of these changes there is a considerable amount of social mobility in the United States, with most sons rising slightly above the social status of their fathers. The bulk of upward intergenerational social movement results from changes in the structure of the society, not from the individual characteristics of the people themselves. Individual ability, education, and hard work do, however, help to predict which particular people will rise in the new occupational structure.

In spite of the high level of social mobility, a number of groups in the society are rigidly confined to lower statuses. Although the United States does not have as rigid a "caste" system as, for example, India, it does nevertheless have some sharp divisions within the population that hinder social mobility. Minority groups—especially Spanish-speaking Americans, native American Indians, and blacks—find it extremely difficult to move out of their disadvantaged status into the more privileged positions that whites normally reserve for themselves. In addition, women seem to face very similar kinds of social-mobility barriers. Racial discrimination, discrimination against women, and the lack of equal educational opportunities for all citizens are only a few of the barriers to social mobility.

In addition, the legal system has a number of built-in inequities that hinder the social mobility of many social groups. For example, victimless crimes constitute one of the most important classes of discriminatory law. In effect, laws against victimless crimes are a method by which the middle and upper classes and the powerful in society attempt to control the behavior of the powerless and the lower classes. Although most laws are theoretically written so that they treat everyone impartially, in reality there are vast differences between the treatment that different social groups receive at the hands of the law. Minority groups, youth, and the poor are arrested in proportions that are way out of line for their percentage in the population. Although some of this discrepancy may be accounted for by actual higher rates of crime in these groups, much of it is because the police harass these groups more than they do the middle and upper classes. Finally, we find that the law systematically discriminates against women in almost all areas of life. Taken together, all of these facts about the law and its application suggest that the political system is not functioning so that all social groups have equal opportunities for basic life chances and social mobility.

Society is not static, however, and the social mobility situation has been changing over the last two decades. Certainly the advantages and opportunities for minorities and women to advance within the society are greater now than they have been in many years. To be sure, progress is extremely slow, and the advancements are often balanced by major steps backward. It may be that the class lines that are presently defined by minority status and by sex roles will eventually break down, but these lines are clear at the present time. Until these barriers can be lowered significantly it is premature to talk about the fulfillment of the American Dream where everyone's social class is based on his talent, hard work, and ability. That day is still a long way off.

REFERENCES

Blau, Peter M., and Otis Dudley Duncan. *The American Occupational System* (New York: Wiley, 1967).

Burma, John H., ed. *Mexican Americans in the United States* (San Francisco: Canfield Press, 1970).

Cahn, Edgar S., ed. *Our Brother's Keeper: The Indian in White America* (New York: World, 1969).

Dunne, John G. "To Die Standing," *Atlantic Monthly, 227* (6), June 1971, pp. 39–45.

Ennis, Phillip H. *Criminal Victimization in the United States* (Chicago: National Opinion Research Center, 1967).

Fisher, A. D. "White Rites Versus Indian Rights," *Trans-Action, 7,* November 1969, pp. 29–33.

Glazer, Nathan, and Daniel P. Moynihan. *Beyond the Melting Pot,* rev. ed. (Boston: M.I.T. Press, 1970).

Gomez, David F. "Chicanos: Strangers in Their Own Land," *America, 124,* (23), June 26, 1971, pp. 649–652.

Hacker, Helen. "Women as a Minority Group," *Social Forces, 30,* 1951, p. 65ff.

Liebow, Elliot. *Tally's Corner* (New York: Little Brown, 1967).

Lipset, S. M., and R. Bendix. *Social Mobility in Industrial Society* (Berkeley: University of California Press, 1958).

Moore, Joan. *Mexican Americans* (Englewood Cliffs, N. J.: Prentice-Hall, 1970).

Pinkney, Alphonso. *Black Americans* (Englewood Cliffs, N. J.: Prentice-Hall, 1969).

Report of the National Advisory Committee on Civil Disorders. (Washington, D.C.: U. S. Government Printing Office, 1968).

Rose, Arnold. *The Negro in America* (New York: Harper and Row, 1964).

Simpson, G. E., and J. Milton Yinger. *Racial*

and Cultural Minorities, 3rd ed. (New York: Harper and Row, 1965).

Spilerman, Seymour. "The Causes of Racial Disturbances: A Comparison of Alternative Explanations," *American Sociological Review, 35,* August 1970, pp. 627–649.

Steiner, Stan. *The New Indians* (New York: Delta, 1967).

Subcommittee on Economy in Government, Joint Economic Committee, Congress of the United States, *American Indians: Facts and Future, Toward Economic Development for Native American Communities* (New York: Arno Press, 1970).

Sutherland, Edwin H. *White Collar Crime* (New York: Dryden Press, 1949).

Wattenberg, Ben J., and Richard M. Scammon. "Black Progress and Liberal Rhetoric," *Commentary,* April 1973, pp. 35–44.

Wolfgang, Marvin E., Leonard Savitz, and Norman Johnston. *The Sociology of Crime* (New York: Wiley, 1970).

Wright, Richard. *Black Boy* (New York: Harper and Row, 1937).

SEVEN
POVERTY IN AMERICA

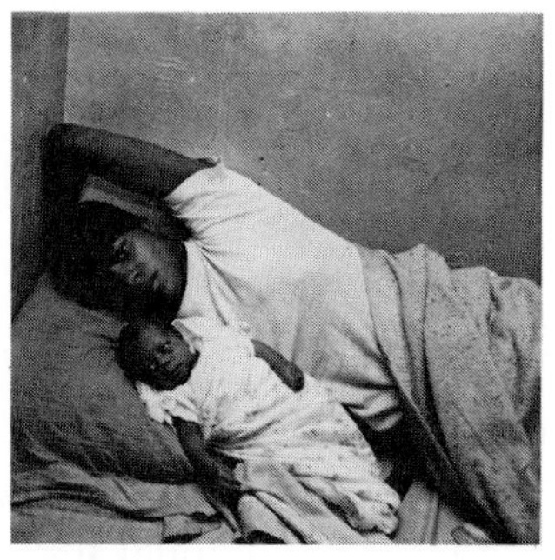

HARRY MARTIN

"I'm going to be a lawyer," said Harry, aged six. "Lawyers make good money. I'm going to keep my money."

It was midafternoon but the tenement was dark. Grey plastic sheeting was tacked to the insides of the living room windows except for one window where a stick was propped against the collapsed Venetian blind to keep it against the cracked glass. Plaster was off an expanse of ceiling and walls, and strands of hair on the laths trembled with the passing wind from outside. A double doorway gave onto the kitchen which was almost invisible. Its windows, too, were sealed with grey plastic, presumably to preserve heat. But the darkness was thickened by a crisscross of clotheslines that filled the room with the hangings of what looked like shapeless cloth. In one corner of the kitchen was a small refrigerator, in another a table with three legs and one chair. There was a stained stove bearing a basin full of children's clothes soaked in cold soapy water. Next to the clothes basin was a pan of cold red beans and beside that an iron frying pan containing a single short rib congealed with fat. Through one kitchen door was a bathroom dominated by a toilet covered by boards; it had frozen and burst during the winter. Through another door was "the kids' room" a murky chamber with one window insulated by a roller shade tacked at the top and held down at the bottom sill with a stone. In this room slept seven children, in two beds. Neither bed had a mattress. The children slept on the springs. . . .

Outside, Sister Mary William . . . said:

"You figure out what's going to happen to Harry Martin when he finds out he's never going to be a lawyer. And his brother's never going to be a doctor. And his sister's never going to be a nurse. The worst most of us have to resign ourselves to is that there's no Santa Claus. Wait until this hits those kids." (Bagdikian, 1964)

In the previous chapter we examined the *causes* and the *patterns* of social stratification. Now we will examine one of the major *consequences* of stratification—the poverty that so severely affects the lives of millions of Americans such as little Harry Martin in the opening quote. In the midst of previously unknown affluence, in a society where wealth and material goods are abundant, it is discouraging to discover that a large portion of the people live in economic need. Poor housing, insufficient health care, and malnutrition are not uncommon in America.

Concern over poverty in the United States is not a new issue; since the earliest days of the republic there have been political movements primarily concerned with the equalization of economic benefits. And from the mid-1960s, when the Johnson Administration declared with fanfare that it was about to begin a War on Poverty, to the present, there has been great concern over poverty in America. Thousands of pages of journalistic articles, conference reports, government documents, and academic monographs have been written on the topic. The mass media have reported extensively on the problem of poverty. The Johnson Administration's programs never made much of a dent in poverty, however, and the advent of the Nixon Administration in 1968 signaled the end of the government's primary drive against poverty. Nevertheless, poverty and the associated social crises are still of crucial concern.

THE NATURE OF POVERTY IN AMERICA

It is obvious that Harry Martin and his family are trapped in the vicious cycle of poverty, but we need to know more about the people that share Harry's fate, the people that constitute the great lower caste of poverty in this affluent society.

THE DEFINITION OF POVERTY

There are many different definitions of poverty; some describe the living conditions of the poor, others depend on such objective standards as income levels. The Social Security Administration defines a household as being "poor" if its annual income is less than three times the cost of a minimal diet for the people in that family. Since this definition depends on food prices, it shifts each year. In 1973 the poverty-level income for an urban family of four was over $4000—less than half of the 1973 national median income of about $11,000 per family.

But not all people agree with setting the poverty level at three times the food budget. Some would set a constant amount, such as $4000, and others would use an arbitrary figure, such as one half of the median income. In short, there is no single definition of poverty with which all social scientists would agree. It is, however, widely agreed that between 20 and 30 percent of American families are now living in poverty. Throughout the rest of this discussion we will use the

Social Security Administration's definition because most government statistics are based on those figures.

Of course, it could be argued that the poor in the United States are actually much better off than many people in the rest of the world whose earnings are considerably under $4000. But poverty is a *relative* matter. It makes little sense to compare people in the United States with people in underdeveloped nations because the reference group for the American poor are those wealthier people around them. To be sure, many people in the world are literally starving and have no place to live, whereas even the "poor" American is not on the verge of starvation and does not have to sleep on the street. These relative comparisons, however, are not meaningful because the American poor—and the rest of the society—judge poverty on a relative scale, comparing social groups within the United States rather than across national boundaries. Victor R. Fuchs stated the point well.

Recent surveys of low income families have reported a high percentage owning television sets, washing machines, telephones, and other consumer goods that would be considered luxuries by most of the world's population—and would have been considered luxuries by most Americans thirty years ago. By the standards that have prevailed over most of history, and still prevail over large areas of the world, there are very few poor in the United States today. Nevertheless, there are millions of American families who, both in their own eyes and in those of others, are poor. As our nation prospers, our judgment as to what constitutes poverty will inevitably change. When we talk about poverty in America, we are talking about families and individuals who have much less income than most of us. When we talk about reducing or eliminating poverty, we are really talking about changing the distribution of income. . . . (Fuchs, in Will and Vatter, 1970, p. 17)

FACTS AND FIGURES ABOUT POVERTY

Figure 7.1 indicates that in 1972 a little over 24 million people—11.9 percent of the total population—lived below the poverty level—a figure larger than the entire population of Canada, or half the population of England or France! Figure 7.1 also shows that the number of poor people decreased rather significantly from 1959, when almost 40 million people (22.5 percent of the total population) lived below the poverty level. But, even though these figures indicate that there has been some improvement in the problem of poverty over the last few years, the fact that 24 million people still live in poverty is a social crisis of monumental proportions. Moreover, many economists argue that much of what appears to be a reduction in the number of poor people actually only reflects a generally higher per capita income and that there has been no significant increase in the *proportion* of the total income that the poor receive. Thus, while in absolute money terms the poor are better off than they have been in many decades, the unfortunate truth is that by *relative standards* the poor's position has not actually improved. In fact, Victor R. Fuchs suggests that this situation may have grown worse. He noted that in 1947 19 percent of the population earned less than one half the median income, but in 1969 20 percent did so.

Figure 7.1
Americans below official poverty level: 1959 and 1972 compared

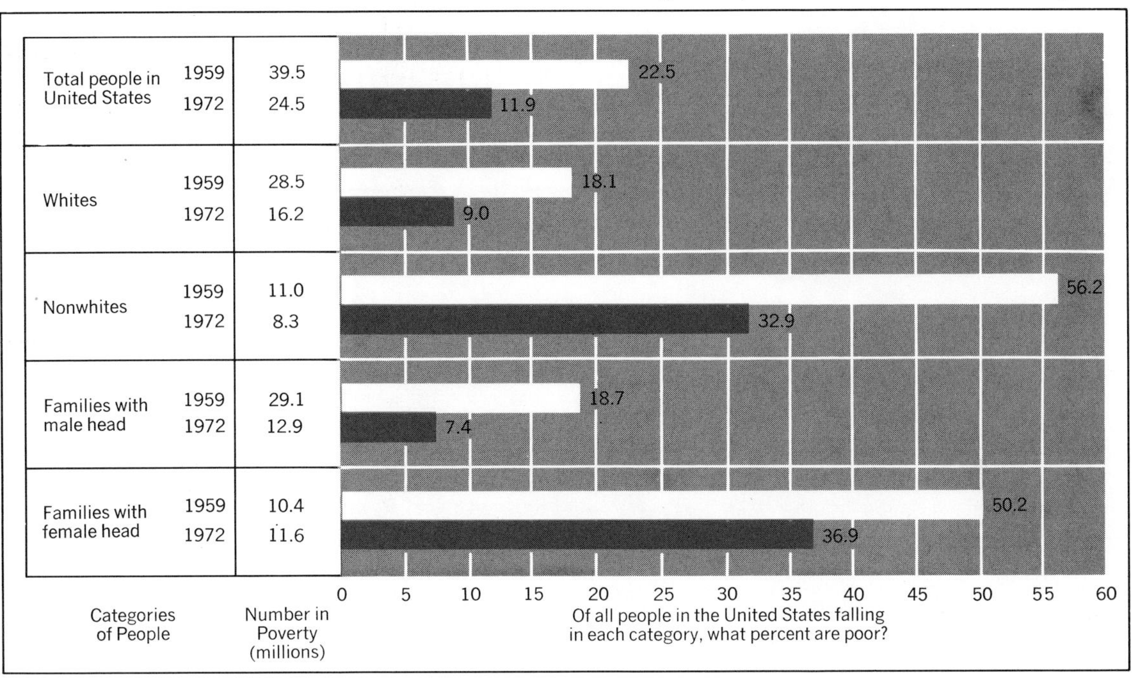

Source: U.S. Bureau of Census, *Statistical Abstract of the U.S.*, 1973; *Current Population Reports,* Series P-60, No. 88, June 1973.

These are some major characteristics about poverty in the United States.

1. Although about half of all poor people live in metropolitan areas, rural areas have proportionately much more poverty than metropolitan areas do. Approximately 24 percent of all families on farms are poor as opposed to about 10 percent in metropolitan areas.

2. Central cities have much higher rates of poverty than do suburbs (13.4 percent and 7.3 percent, respectively).

3. The probability of a nonwhite being poor is three times as great as for a white person, but, even though proportionately whites are underrepresented, they constitute about 69 percent of all people living in poverty because they are a much more numerous group. Thus, in *absolute numbers* most of the poor are white; nevertheless, in *proportionate* terms nonwhites have much greater rates of poverty.

4. Families with female heads of household are nearly five times as likely to be living in poverty as those with male heads (38.3 percent of families with female heads are in poverty as opposed to only 8 percent of families with male heads).

Figure 7.2 gives more statistics on the poor in America, this time asking the question "Of those who are poor, what are their characteristics?" By looking at Figures 7.1 and 7.2 you can get an overview of the facts and figures on poverty. It is tricky to summarize those facts,

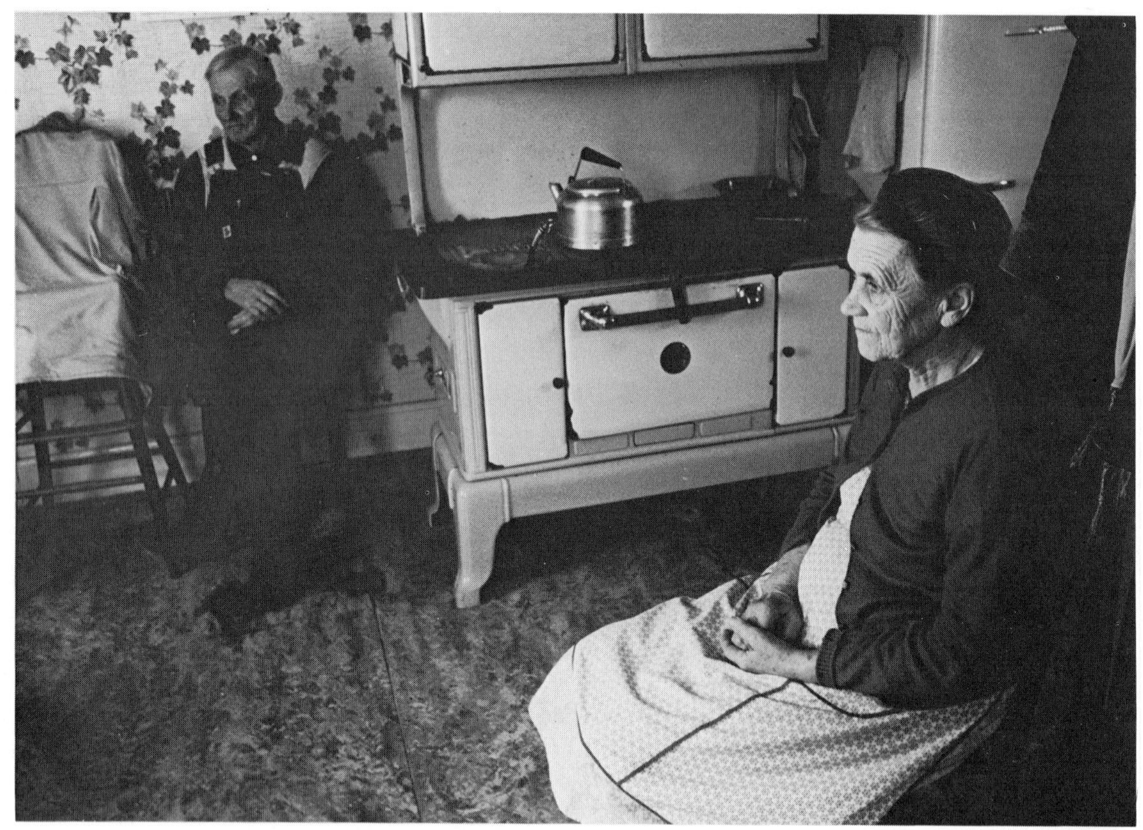

One of the largest groups of poverty-stricken people is the aged. The problem of the aged is one of the most serious social crises in this youth-oriented society. And abject poverty is often their lot.

however, because you must clearly separate the *absolute numbers* from the *rates* of poverty in any social groups. For example, because they constitute such overwhelmingly large numbers in the total population, people in white, male-headed, under 65, or urban families constitute the largest *absolute numbers* of the poor. However, there are much higher *rates* of poverty in nonwhite, female-headed, elderly, or rural families. Because the people with the higher rates are such small groups to begin with, they are not a majority of the people in poverty. It is also interesting to note the type of family that does *not* fall into the poverty category very often: a white family headed by a male skilled worker or professional, living in an urban area.

PATTERNS OF LIFE IN POVERTY

Dry statistics about poverty are helpful in understanding the broad picture, but they hardly show the real life-style of people living at the bottom of the social system in America. Most of the poor are either

Figure 7.2
Who Are the Poor? (24,460,000 total poor, 1970)

Category	Subcategory	Percent
I. Race	White	69
	Nonwhite	31
II. Residence	Urban	51
	Rural nonfarm	33
	Farm	16
III. Age	18 and under	42
	19-64	40
	Over 64	18
IV. Head of household	Male	52.9
	Female	47.1
V. Other characteristics*	Elderly	18.3
	Children under 18	42.2
	Adults in female-headed household	17.6
	Adults in family headed by disabled male	3.0
	Adults in family headed by unemployed male	7.0
	Adults in family headed by employed male	11.9

0 10 20 30 40 50 60 70 80

Of those who are poor, what percent fall into each category?

*Based on the poor in metropolitan areas only — 12,871,000, about half the total poor. These were the best figures on this type of breakdown, and total figures vary very little.

Source: Anthony Downs, *Who Are the Urban Poor?* (New York: Committee for Economic Development, 1970) p. 20; U.S. Bureau of the Census, *Statistical Abstract of the U.S.*, 1971, p. 322.

elderly, or children, or adults living in female-headed families with no husband/father to support them. Often they are on public welfare, like Antonia Matos, a Puerto Rican woman living in New York City.

Antonia Matos is a tall, overweight, 26-year-old with a pretty face, large warm brown eyes, three small children and no husband. She is also a special sort of poverty statistic—an entry on the relief rolls. . . .

The only money that comes into the family's three-room apartment, which is badly in need of paint and floor covering, is a $94 check from the city every 15 days. Life depends on this check, on the monthly free Federal surplus foods and free medical care.

The very existence of Miss Matos and her family, a 7-year-old son and two daughters, rests with her welfare investigator and his little black book—the omnipresent Manual of Policies and Procedures. The book tells the agent in minute detail what an individual's "entitlement" is, depending on age, sex, employment and physical condition.

Exclusive of rent, utilities and a few other recurring items, the official daily budget, which is required by state law, comes to $1 for the mother, 90 cents for the son, 74 cents for the 4-year-old daughter and 66 cents for the baby. These allowances must provide food, clothing, personal care and household supplies. . . .

Each month she gets about 19 packages of food with a retail value of $17.50—eight pounds of meat, two pounds of peanut butter, 10 pounds of flour, five pounds of cheese, four pounds of butter and two pounds of lard. There is also rice, cereal, cornmeal and powdered milk. Next month a pound of powdered eggs will be added.

The investigator arranges for the check-like voucher for these staples. He also arranges for grants for such items as suits, overcoats and overshoes.

When the investigator visits he always checks on the receipts for rent and utilities. Many persons on relief fall behind on gas and electricity payments because the bills come bimonthly and they have failed to save for them.

"I don't owe nobody," Miss Matos said with pride. (Dougherty, 1964)

In poverty families life is ringed in by a hostile environment, especially the harsh economic realities of unemployment and underemployment. Because of fewer childhood opportunities, lack of education, job discrimination, poor health, and dozens of other factors the poor find themselves in the lowest status, unskilled jobs that are plagued with low wages and uncertain employment. This economic situation is largely beyond the control of the poor, because the national economic policies that so affect them are made in the councils of government and industry. Nevertheless, the impact on their lives is clear: poor and crowded housing, inadequate health care, a general life-style that lacks the basic material resources that most Americans would consider essentials.

The stress of these economic and physical conditions on the social life in poverty families is enormous. The very fabric of human relationships is torn and battered. Children are forced to leave school to get jobs that help support the family. In-laws and relatives are frequently crowded into small apartments, and family conflict is common. There is a high rate of divorce, abandonment, and desertion in poverty families, with a consequence that many are headed by females who have to live on public welfare. When husbands and fathers, confronted by the hostile economic system in the outside world, become failures at providing for their wives and children, they often flee from the helpless situation where they are daily confronted with their economic impotence. That desertion sometimes takes the form of suicide.

Recently a man who had been unable to find work and in despair committed suicide, left a note to his wife, saying: "I have gone forever; there is one less in the world to feed. Good-bye. God help you to care for Tony; don't put her away." This is the fear and dread of pauperism; "don't put Tony away" is the last thought of the man whose misery caused him to take his own life. (Hunter, p. 61)

The patterns of life in poverty are grim, but people in poverty nevertheless share the common American hopes for advancement, a good job, and a stable family life. Why can they not gain those hopes, why are they trapped in this vicious cycle—what are the *causes* of poverty?

COMMON AMERICAN IDEOLOGIES ABOUT THE CAUSES OF POVERTY

Before we explore the real causes of poverty we will first have to dismiss the popular explanations because they are almost entirely wrong. In fact, there is a deeply ingrained belief system that distorts reality and lays the blame on the poor themselves instead of on the economic system that is the real source of poverty. Let us examine that inaccurate popular myth. People in the middle and upper classes try to justify the inequal distribution of wealth in the society with value statements and rationalizations. It is not enough simply to have wealth and power; that privileged position must be "legitimate," it must be "right." For this self-justifying purpose, the wealthy and powerful develop "ideologies."

KARL MANNHEIM: THE CONCEPT OF "IDEOLOGY"

Karl Mannheim wrote a famous book entitled *Ideology and Utopia* (1936) in which he discussed "ideologies" that were rooted in the self-interest of a social class and used to maintain its privileged position against demands for reform. Mannheim held that an ideology had four components. First, there is a *belief system,* a set of ideas that justifies the existing world structure and supports the privileges that the social class has obtained. Second, the ideology always has an element of *distortion* in it; the belief system warps reality to justify social privileges. Third, the ideology is almost always *unconscious,* and those who are distorting reality are not even aware of it themselves. Finally, the ideology serves a specific purpose, that of holding down nonprivileged classes and *maintaining the status quo,* thus preserving the advantages of the wealth and power elites.

In short, Mannheim suggested that powerful social classes support their power with cultural beliefs. For example, the royalty in Europe often justified their claim to the throne on the weak ideological theory of the "divine right of kings." By proposing such a theory they were able to justify intellectually their seizure of control. In America the expanding nation articulated a new ideology called "manifest destiny," which sanctioned American westward expansion. Manifest destiny was an ideological justification for a form of political exploitation in which many native American Indians and Mexicans were killed or dispossessed from land that the Europeans wanted for their own purposes.

EARLY AMERICAN IDEOLOGIES ABOUT WEALTH AND POVERTY: SOCIAL DARWINISM

"Social Darwinism," a widespread ideology during the nineteenth century, argued that every social class is like a biological species and that there is a great struggle for the "survival of the fittest" in the social arena. The most fit are obviously the rich and the powerful, for they survived and flourished in the great social battle. Obviously the poor and the weak are not biologically fit, and it is "right" that they should be poor. Herbert Spencer, an early sociologist who strongly believed in Social Darwinism, stated it rather directly.

The well-being of . . . humanity, and the unfolding of it into this ultimate perfection, are both secured by that same [natural law] . . . to which the [animal kingdom] at large is subject: a discipline which is pitiless in the working out of good: a . . . law which never swerved for the avoidance of partial and temporary suffering. The poverty of the incapable, the distresses that come upon the imprudent, the starvation of the idle, and the shoulderings aside of the weak by the strong . . . are the decrees of a large, farseeing [natural law] . . . It seems hard that widows and orphans should be left to struggle for life or death. Nevertheless, when regarded not separately, but in connection with the interest of universal humanity, these harsh fatalities are seen to be full of the highest [social benefit] —a [social benefit] . . . which brings to the early graves the children of diseased parents, and singles out the low-spirited, the intemperate, and the debilitated as the victims of an epidemic. (Spencer, 1880, pp. 353–354)

Thus, Spencer believed not only that the poor had been the source of their own trouble, but that it was also a good thing they met misfortune and died early, because this was a law of nature that purified the human race. Conversely, the Social Darwinists had only the highest praise for the rich, who, according to Albert Keller, were

a product of natural selection, acting on the whole body of men to pick out those who can meet the requirement of certain work to be done. . . . They may fairly be regarded as the naturally selected agents of society for certain work. They get high wages and live in luxury, but the bargain is a good one for society. There is the most intense competition for their place and occupation. This assures us that all who are competent for this function will be employed in it, so that the cost of this will be reduced to the lowest terms. . . . (Keller, 1914, p. 90)

Thus, the Social Darwinists divided the world into two neat camps: the hard-working, frugal people who would rise to the top and be "naturally selected" to become rich and the lazy; and the "low-spirited" ones who would sink to the bottom and be wiped out by natural forces. Moreover, this is the way it *should* be, it was nature's law, and any interference was tampering with nature. In fact, Spencer had nothing but scorn for people who wanted to reform society and help the poor.

Blind to the fact, that under the natural order of things society is constantly excreting its unhealthy, imbecile, slow, vacillating, faithless members, these unthinking [social reformers] . . . advocate an interference which not only stops the purifying process, but even increases the [problem] . . . absolutely encourages the multiplication of the reckless and incompetent . . . and discourages the multiplication of the competent and provident. . . . And thus, in their eagerness to prevent the . . . sufferings that surround us, these sigh-wise and groan-foolish people bequeath to posterity a continually increasing curse. (Spencer, 1880, p. 354)

In the early 1900s there was a rash of novels in the Social Darwinist mode that attempted to justify the great wealth inequalities that were growing rapidly. As the Rockefellers and Stanfords accumulated their millions from the rapid expansion of industrialism and the massive growth of railroads, the Social Darwinist ideology justified the robber barons and their economic exploitation. Among these were the famous Horatio Alger stories, which came out in a series of small novels around the turn of the century. In the typical Horatio Alger story a young man from the lower classes moves to the city and by hard work and industrious effort, he climbs up the social ladder until he is one of the wealthiest and respected members of society. The moral was simple: work hard and you, too, can succeed. The contrary lesson was also clear: the poor have only themselves to blame for their plight, since they obviously do not work hard and are incapable of surviving in the great social race. All reputable social scientists today have rejected Social Darwinism, but this ideology did provide a rationale for the economic rape of American lower classes throughout much of the nineteenth century—and unfortunately similar ideas are widespread today.

CONTEMPORARY IDEOLOGIES ABOUT WEALTH AND POVERTY: "THE CULTURE OF POVERTY"

Charles Wilson, a former official of General Motors and the Secretary of Defense under President Eisenhower, made the infamous statement that "I always thought what's good for General Motors is good for the nation." Wilson obviously believed that the interests of the holders of corporate wealth were parallel to those of the nation, and he was not even aware of the obvious ideological characteristics of his statement.

Unfortunately, like the Social Darwinist ideologies of the last century, similar social justifications for inequality in modern life are just as false. In truth, wealth and power have not usually come to those who work hard and who struggle for success; West Virginian coal miners with blackened lungs and Chicano farm laborers certainly work hard but have little to show for it. In reality most of the massive wealth of the society is held by those who inherited it. Today the common complaint against welfare programs is that they are overloaded with lazy, unproductive members of society who simply do not wish to work and who could get ahead if they only tried harder. Ronald Reagan, the former Governor of California, said "taxes should hurt," but he managed to pay no income taxes in many years. As he attacked the lower classes for being on welfare, he proclaimed an upper-class ideology that was carefully designed to mask a simple fact: the power elites of society have created the social conditions that produce the massive poverty they are crying against. Elites in every society have manufactured belief systems that justify their social privileges and that attack anyone who tries to reform the social system.

Today it is quite common for conservative politicians to attack welfare as a popular public issue, concentrating their attention on supposed abuses by the poor and ignoring the massive abuses that are constantly committed by corporations and the wealthy. Recently a San Francisco newspaper ran a huge headline about welfare abuses in the State of California, proclaiming that nearly 11 percent of the welfare recipients in the state were in violation of welfare rules. If you took the time to read the fine print, however, the charge had been made by a conservative politician up for reelection and was based on no evidence whatsoever. On the same front page, but under a headline of smaller type, was a report of a suit against the Bank of America and its BankAmericard system for allegedly fixing credit rates with other credit agencies—a practice that is clearly illegal and that costs customers millions of dollars. Moreover, buried in the back pages of that same newspaper was a statement to Congress by Representative Charles A. Vanik, who reported that many large corporations avoided paying their fair share of taxes over the last decade. Vanik said that five large corporations—Continental Oil, MacDonnell Douglas, Gulf and Western Industries, the Aluminum Company of America, and Signal Companies—made profits in 1971 but paid no tax at all. Vanik added that approximately one third of the top 100 corporations listed by *Fortune* magazine had managed to avoid their share of taxes; they paid less than 10 percent of their profits in taxes, a rate considerably below that of the average assembly-line worker in their plants. Vanik went on to say that the unusually low tax rates were not illegal, for loopholes had been carefully exploited in order to keep taxes down.

Thus the alleged welfare abuses of the poor were in a headline banner across a major newspaper, while the abuses of huge corporations and the credit-fixing

The American ideology about poverty: False, but widely believed. (Reprinted by permission, Sawyer Press, Los Angeles, Calif. 90046)

activities of the world's largest bank were relegated to small items buried in minor articles. It appears that the newspapers—like most of the rest of the society—still believe in Social Darwinism, since they stress the shortcomings of the poor but ignore the deliberate activities of the wealthy corporations. Of course, it is easy to harp on defenseless welfare mothers, but it would take real nerve to criticize the giant corporations that control the newspaper purse strings with their advertising.

But it is not only the conservative politicians and major newspapers who blame the poor while ignoring the socially harmful activities of the major corporations and the wealthy upper classes. In addition, the average citizen is often convinced by a mild form of Social Darwinism. The political scientist Robert E. Lane conducted an intensive study of attitudes toward political, economic, and social issues in a sample of people in a large Atlantic city, which he called "Eastport" (Lane, 1962). Lane reported that the average citizen of Eastport believed that the lower classes and the poor got what they deserved, that their laziness and lack of ability stood in the way of their success. Lane quotes one factory worker in Eastport as saying:

You get a lot of people who don't want to work; you got welfare. People will go on living on that welfare—they are happier then hell. Why should they work if the city will support them?

Lane concludes that the average lower-middle class person in Eastport was very much opposed to welfare and to social services for the poor. Lane made the following conclusions:

In general, there is little sympathy given to those lower in the scale, little reference to the overpowering forces of circumstance, only rare mention of sickness, death of a breadwinner, senility, factories moving out of town, and so forth. The only major cause of poverty to which no moral blame attaches is depression or "unemployment"—but this is not considered a strikingly important cause in the minds of the Eastport men. . . .

In a lower-middle stratum of the population one can reach upward and engage the behavior of the ruling classes in a moral grip, or downward and pick out the violations of the moral code of the unrespectable, the outré, *the failures. There is gratification to be had either way, but Eastport's common man chooses to moralize downward, not upward. He spends more time condemning the failures of the poor than in condemning the extravagance, the sinful living, the exploitative behavior of the rich. The poor are under his nose, while the rich are not. . . . (Lane, 1963, p. 43)*

Lane's conclusions are supported by public opinion polls that usually show that the general public believes that "poverty is the fault of the poor." For example, one nationwide opinion poll found that 34 percent of the general population believe that poverty is caused by a lack of personal effort among the poor, 25 percent said it was due to circumstances beyond the control of the poor, and 38 percent said both personal failure and circumstances combined (Free and Cantril, 1968, p. 28). Most people blamed the poor themselves, not the economic system that put them there.

It is interesting to note that those who receive the most benefits from public subsidies are also the ones who cry the loudest against welfare. In a fascinating study of attitudes among people in Madera County, California, Robin Yeamans reported that farm owners who were receiving huge government subsidies were nevertheless unhappy that the poverty stricken around them were receiving government help (Yeamens, 1969).

There are 185 Madera County growers who were paid \$5000 to \$133,555 each in U. S. subsidies. Miss Yeamans sought their views on aid to the poor and drew such responses as these:

From a grower who received \$18,000 in government subsidies but opposed federal assistance to the poor: "The Bible says a man should work."

From a wife of a grower who got \$29,000 in crop price supports: "Giving causes loss of pride."

The wife of another grower who got \$16,000 from the government came up with this classic: "I can't understand having things handed to you."

Among other growers drawing handsome subsidies from Washington there were such responses as: "We don't want to create a generation of idle people." "Everyone should have it as hard as I did." And the baffling proclamation that "they [poor people] make more than anyone today."

A summary of the Madera survey noted that the closer a federal poverty program paralleled the kind of federal assistance the growers received, the greater their hostility. Ninety-four percent of the growers opposed providing $4000 a year to a family of five to avoid depressing wages during high periods of unemployment; 81 percent opposed a $4500 guaranteed annual income for a family of seven; 57 percent opposed federal assistance for the poor. But the U. S. food-stamp program, which helps take some surplus food off the open market and thus helps sustain crop prices, won the approval of 85 percent. Only 8 percent saw any parallel between the government subsidies that they received and the aid to the poor that they opposed. As further substantiation for this finding, Senator James Eastland of Mississippi, one of the most vociferous senators in opposition to welfare, was paid $211,364 in 1969 for *not* planting corn on his vast acreage.

Thus, there is still strong sentiment at all levels in the society that argues that poverty is the fault of the poor. Again we have a classic case of "blaming the victim" instead of blaming the economic system that produced poverty in the first place. All of the belief patterns we have been discussing reflect the characteristics that Karl Mannheim called "ideology." First, the belief system justifies the world as it is presently structured and supports the privileges of the upper classes. Second, the belief system distorts reality, ignoring the real causes of poverty, blaming the victims, and not considering the social realities that produce the problem. Third, the ideologies are largely unconscious, for those who act according to them are often unaware of their belief. Taken together, all of these factors reinforce the privileged positions of the upper and middle classes, giving them a rationalization to explain their own advantages and a method of shifting the blame from the society onto the victims of poverty.

THE REAL CAUSES OF POVERTY

Although it is popularly believed that the poor are lazy, shiftless people who are unwilling to work and who live off public welfare, the truth is that the vast majority of the poor are either helpless and unable to earn their own way or are victims of economic circumstances beyond their own control. By examining some of the underlying causes of poverty, we may be able to smash the popular stereotype once and for all.

THE ECONOMIC AND SOCIAL SITUATION OF POVERTY FAMILIES

Looking back at Figure 7.2 you can see that most of the poor are helpless victims of social circumstances far beyond their own control. Eighteen percent of the poverty stricken are over 65; 42 percent are children under the age of 18; 28 percent are in families headed by people who are unable to earn a living—females who must take care of children, males who are physically disabled, and males who are unemployed. Moreover, about 12 percent of the poor are in families headed by males who do work. These male family heads, although working, are trapped in a circle of unskilled labor that does not bring in enough income to get their families above the poverty level. In addition, there is a complex set of institutional barriers that reinforce the poverty cycle, as discussed by Anthony Downs in Insert 7.1.

These facts stand in extreme contrast to the popular image of lazy, nonworking poor people. How we can possibly expect children, who compose the largest single block of poor people, to be earning their own way in a society that has high unemployment rates even among able-bodied adults? The elderly can hardly be expected to earn their own living, and even in the middle and upper classes it is assumed that the elderly should not have to work. It is also clear that men who cannot find work and women who must take care of children are hardly the lazy types of the popular image.

It is even more interesting to note that among the poor, 12 percent are headed by men who are working. These people cannot be blamed for failing to bring their families out of poverty, since they are doing the best they can. In fact, they often are working more than fulltime and earning less than the poverty level. The Committee on Economic Development, after studying a number of government statistics, reported that poverty is primarily a matter of inability, dependency, illness, and old age. The economists on this committee found that among those who were *able* to work the majority were in fact working.

The outstanding fact emerging from these studies is that most of the poor in the working-age brackets, who might reasonably be expected to be in the labor force, in fact were in the labor force and a large proportion were employed. In other words, by 1969 the great majority of the presumptively able-to-work were actually working, at least part-time. (Committee for Economic Development, 1971, p. 43)

Thus the problem of poverty is not that the poor do not work, it is that the poor *cannot* work. They are ill, they are children, they are mothers with small children, they are the elderly, they are the unemployed, and they are the underpaid. Certainly there are likely to be poor people who cheat on welfare and who choose to be lazy if they possibly can, just as the popular image suggests. All known facts show, however, that laziness and welfare cheating are not more widespread among the poor than among all other classes. It appears that the poor are doing their best under inordinately difficult circumstances.

Although inability, youth, and old age all contribute to the likelihood that one will be poor, we cannot neglect the fact of widespread racial discrimination. The chances of being poor if a person is nonwhite are one out of three, but only one of ten if one is white. Does this difference mean that nonwhites are lazier, have less ambition, or are less willing to work? This is the popular stereotype, of course, but the facts indicate that the plight of nonwhites results more from discrimination than from the personal characteristics of the minorities them-

INSERT **7.1**

INSTITUTIONAL FACTORS THAT CAUSE POVERTY

For many people, poverty is not just a lack of income. It also involves a deprived and defeatist state of mind, a persistent lack of capability for improving one's own situation, and an inferior or dependent position in society. Moreover, major social institutions repeatedly reinforce these maladies—even when those institutions are specifically intended to alleviate poverty. In fact, almost every analysis of urban poverty has concluded that the system of institutions in which the poor are enmeshed tends to perpetutate their poverty. Consequently, attempts to eliminate poverty which provide direct aid to poor persons are bound to fail in the long run unless they also significantly alter the institutional systems surrounding the poor. . . .

In this brief paper it is impossible to provide a detailed or comprehensive analysis of how social institutions reinforce poverty. . . . Instead, a few important examples have been summarized.

1. Retail prices for food and other staples paid by residents of big city, low-income neighborhoods are often higher than those paid by residents of higher-income areas. This occurs mainly because poor people tend to shop in small local stores, rather than because of price differentials in larger chain stores.

2. Poor residents of big cities pay much higher prices and interest rates for merchandise purchased on credit than wealthier residents pay for exactly the same goods. A Federal Trade Commission study showed that prices of such goods averaged 50 percent higher in low-income areas.

3. Housing in low-income areas is far more expensive in relation to the quality of service received—especially in Negro areas—than in middle-income neighborhoods. For comparable or only slightly lower rents, poor households receive smaller

units in worse physical condition with poorer services and neighborhood amenities.

4. Poor citizens have fewer opportunities to improve their own housing than wealthier citizens because most lenders will not provide mortgages for either purchase or improvement in very low-income areas. . . .

5. In most parts of the world, poor migrants to urban areas are allowed to build their own housing on vacant land at the edges of the urbanized areas. . . .

In the United States, middle-class construction standards enforced by building codes and zoning laws make new construction of low-cost housing on vacant land impossible. Consequently, in U. S. metropolitan areas, most poor in-migrants are concentrated in older central-city neighborhoods in units which are extremely difficult to upgrade through self-help.

6. Poor people are a minority group in the United States, so few policies or programs benefiting them are politically viable unless they provide simultaneously equal or even larger benefits for middle-income and upper-income groups. As a result, most subsidies benefit the wealthy far more than the poor. Three examples are:

Housing Subsidies. The largest of such subsidies consists of income tax deductions allowed for property tax and interest payments made by home owners. . . . As a result, the per capita housing subsidy received by the wealthiest 20 percent of the population is twice that received by the poorest 20 percent.

Urban Renewal Benefits. Land write-downs inherent in urban renewal programs benefit mainly real estate developers, high-income renters of renewal-project housing, downtown property owners, and local governments. In contrast, such projects displace low-income families without paying adequate compensation and cause an increased shortage of housing available to these families, [compelling them] to pay higher rents.

Federal Sewer and Water Grants. Most of these subsidies are used in communities which have a low proportion of poor households.

7. Schools of the lowest quality, with the least qualified teachers and often the oldest buildings and equipment, are usually concentrated in poor neighborhoods, especially in the big cities. . . .

8. Urban highways are often deliberately routed directly through low-income areas, especially Negro neighborhoods, but bypass wealthier residential districts. The resulting displacement imposes heavy costs upon those forced to move and those living in nearby poor neighborhoods. . . .

9. Poor neighborhoods in large cities normally receive the lowest quality of city services (such as garbage collection and police protection) as measured in quality of output.

10. New jobs are being created mainly in suburban areas distant from central-city low-income areas, especially in Negro areas. The many unemployed persons living in the central cities are therefore handicapped in getting jobs. . . .

11. Police practices in low-income areas maximize the probability that young men, particularly Negroes, will develop official police records for acts that would not create such records in higher-income suburbs. Yet these records may seriously impede the employment or educational opportunities of the young people concerned, thereby impairing their ultimate income-earning capabilities. [Moreover,] once a poor person is arrested on suspicion of any crime, existing bail practices may compel him to remain in jail for months even if he is completely innocent, simply because he cannot raise bail. . . .

12. Employers frequently add unnecessary requirements to job specifications which make it harder for poor persons with little educational attainment or a past police record to qualify. Racial prejudice is another factor in the rejection of potential employees who are poor. . . .

These institutional perversities, and many more, tend to make escape from poverty extremely difficult for many of the persons who become trapped in it by birth or changing circumstances.

Source: Anthony Downs, *Who Are the Urban Poor?* (New York: Committee for Economic Development, 1970).

selves. For instance, blacks face enormous discrimination in job opportunities, so even if they want to work employers are more likely to throw barriers in their way. In addition, blacks are discriminated against in housing; they pay much higher rents than poor whites, and they pay a much larger proportion of their incomes for housing. Schools in nonwhite neighborhoods are usually much poorer than those in white neighborhoods, thus insuring that the disadvantages of the parents will be passed on to the children. Credit and loans for nonwhites are difficult to arrange, and the nonwhite poor person often finds himself trapped by high interest rates, foreclosures on loans, and other types of financial discrimination. To be nonwhite in America increases the chances of being poor many times over.

INEQUALITY BEFORE THE LAW

Incapacity, old age, childhood dependency, underemployment, and racial discrimination; these are the pieces of the puzzle that cause poverty in America. That is not the whole story, for not only is the *economic* system stacked against the poor, but the *legal* and *political* systems also reward the rich and penalize the poor—as the next section describes.

THE EFFECT OF TAX LAWS ON WEALTH AND POVERTY

Tax laws offer the rich a wide variety of loopholes, while the lower and middle classes pay more than their fair share. This is in spite of the fiction of a graduated income tax under which the rich supposedly pay more. The so-called "impartial" tax laws are rigged to favor the rich and to soak the poor. For example, Joseph Pechman (1968) reports that people who earn less than $2000 per year pay for all federal, state, and local taxes–a total of nearly 44 percent of their income. Those who earn from $2000 to $15,000 pay about 27 percent. And those who earn over $15,000 pay 38 percent. That is, the middle-income group pays the lowest tax rates, the highest-income group the next lowest, and the poorest the highest. This is in direct contradiction to the theory of a graduated income tax, and it shows that those who have power and wealth have been able to influence the law for their personal benefit.

Millionaires, in fact, tend to pay a percentage of taxes that is really no greater than the average wage earner and considerably less than the average victim of poverty. Most extremely wealthy people obtain much of their income from "capital gains," that is, from property and other material that has gained in value between the time it was bought and sold. It is interesting to note that capital gains—the income source of only the richest people—is taxed at the lowest rate. For example, if a family of four earned $10,000 all from wages its federal income tax would be about $905.00, but if the $10,000 came from capital gains the tax would only be $98.00! In fact, although

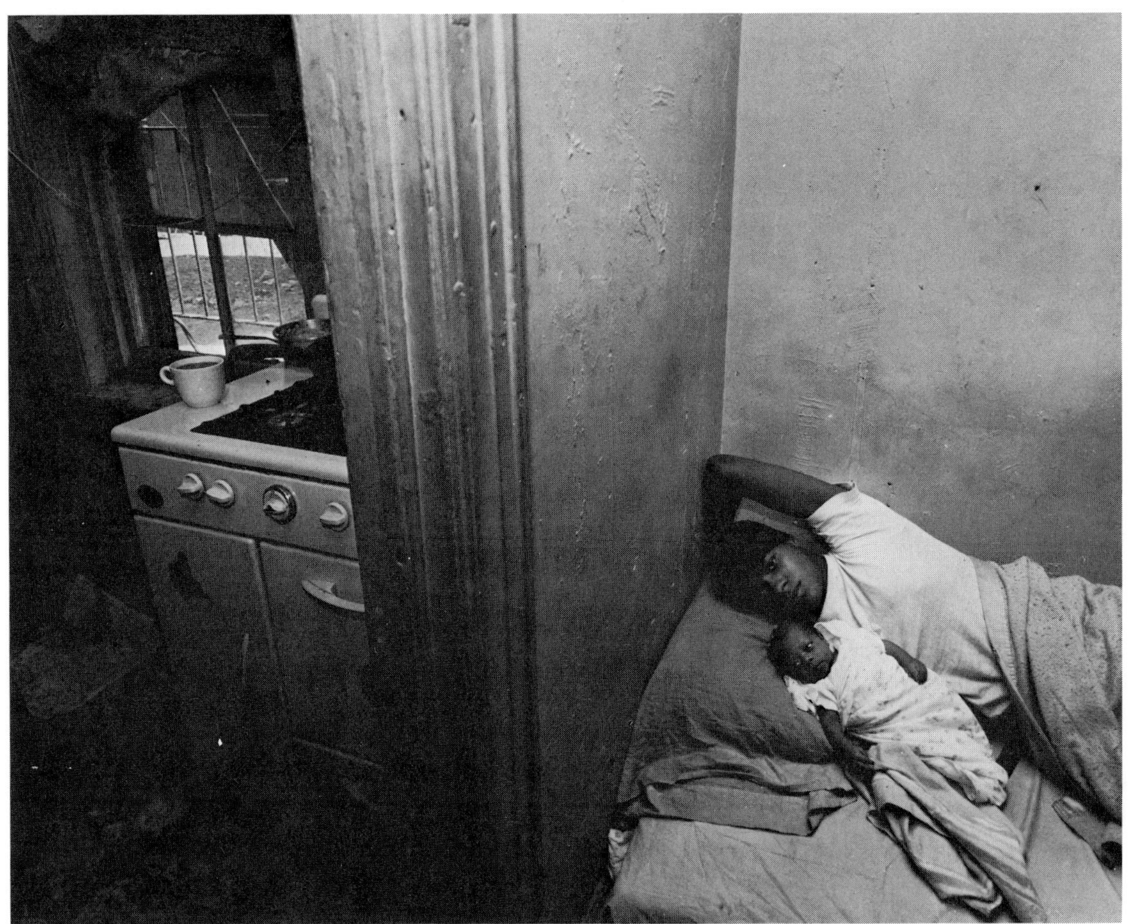

Public opinion says the poor are lazy: But the reality is they cannot help themselves.

the millionaire in theory is supposed to pay about 70 percent of his income in taxes, the reality is that when his income is derived from capital gains he usually pays only about 4 percent when all the tax loopholes are carefully exploited.

There are many other inequities in the tax laws. For example, single people usually pay higher taxes than married people, reflecting the family-oriented, small-town perspective that has dominated legislatures in the past. In an age when overpopulation is a critical problem the continued tax breaks for married people make little sense; nevertheless the marriage-oriented view still dominates the legislatures. As another example, corporation taxes have been gradually going down—a trend that increased under the former Nixon Administration. Local tax laws, too, are often unfair. In fact, some economists suggest that local tax laws are even more "regressive" (i.e., tax the poor more) than federal laws. For example, Felmeth talks about sales taxes and property taxes.

The regressivity of local taxes is well known. The sales tax is a consumption tax. The poor must pay a greater share in relation to their income since a larger portion of their income is spent on consumptive needs, as opposed to land or securities investment. But the property tax is even more regressive. It is inherently regressive because it taxes the value of housing. Since the poor tend to devote a larger percentage of their income to the necessary provision of housing than do the wealthy, they pay a higher percentage of their income in taxes, usually in the form of high rents. (Felmeth, 1971, pp. VI–23)

Taken together, these facts indicate that the tax laws are geared to favor the power elites themselves.

SPECIAL PRIVILEGE LAWS

Recently I was discussing the problems of the poor and the issues of welfare with an anthropologist. During the course of the discussion he made an interesting statement: "Oh, Americans definitely believe in welfare. The only problem is they don't believe in the welfare going to the poor; they want it to go to the rich." This seemingly contradictory statement turns out to be an accurate assessment of the welfare practices and policies in the United States today. In Insert 7.II, Charles McCabe of the *San Francisco Chronicle* points out that the vast sums of federal monies that go into "welfare" go largely to rich corporations and to defense-related industries in the form of subsidies, to the rich in the form of tax loopholes, and to the middle classes in the form of housing and highway benefits. The poor actually receive a very small percentage of the nation's subsidies. Whereas money given by the government to poor people is called "welfare," a term that has negative connotations, when the government gives money to the rich and powerful it is called a "subsidy." In either case the government is handing out money, but the words used to describe it reflect the dominant value systems of the society. To be on welfare is bad; to be receiving a subsidy is in many respects good.

What kinds of subsidy are handed out by the federal government? Four billion dollars annually goes to support farm prices. It is interesting to note that the farmers who receive these subsidies are by and large huge landholders and massive corporations rather than small-farm owners.

In addition to farm subsidies there are literally hundreds of other programs that underwrite business and industry in this nation. Senator William Proxmire, Chairman of the Senate Joint Economic Committee, stated that subsidies to transportation, housing, farming, shipping, and many other industries amount to at least $63 billion a year. Lockheed Aircraft Corporation, for example, received about one quarter billion dollars to prevent its bankruptcy in the early 1970s. Shipping industries, for instance, are underwritten to a large degree by the federal government; the government provided nearly $3 billion to cover shipbuilding costs between 1970 and 1972, and nearly $2 billion will be paid over the next few years to shipowners to enable them to hire domestic laborers. Airline companies

INSERT **7.II**

WHO'S ON WELFARE? YOU'D BE SURPRISED!

Charles McCabe, writer for the *San Francisco Chronicle,* wrote a series of columns on "welfare" to the giant corporations and the wealthy of society. Presented here in abbreviated form, McCabe shows how arguments against welfare are merely ideologies used by social elites to distract attention from their own expensive government subsidies.

Ponder, some words written by the former Chief Justice of the U. S., Mr. Earl Warren: "Perhaps welfare to needy individuals can someday be discussed with the same equanimity as subsidy to industry. The efforts of the government to relieve great suffering among large segments of our population invariably met with resistance from those who believe that our concern should be limited to the poor-house as Dickens depicted it in Oliver Twist. . . . When hundreds of millions of dollars are given to bankrupt railroads, failing defense manufacturers, shipping interests and the like, the words 'welfare' or 'relief' are not used."

How true, how true! The word welfare, in our time, has made an almost complete about-face. From a word suggesting generosity, it has been transmuted into our favorite pejorative. People who are awarded welfare by the state are objects of our scorn, often our hatred. In the popular mind, welfare almost immediately conjures black people who refuse to work, and spend their time, on our money, engaging in gin and riot, and illicit mating for the purpose of getting a lot of little bastards on the public payroll. Government, we tell ourselves righteously, has no right to use our money for these purposes.

Yet the portly Texas oilman, picking up huge tabs at 21 and The Four Seasons; the longshoreman hoisting containers onto freighters, the guy who builds a pretty house with federal assistance; the railroad engineer; the wheat and rice and every other kind of farmer—all these are just as clearly on relief as the blacks. They are, in the national mind, upright and decent citizens, there is nothing in the least wrong with their accepting large federal subsidies to support their ways of life.

It is hardly a secret, though Congress doesn't want the point labored, or if possible even mentioned, that transportation, housing, farming and shipping are all on welfare. A short time back the airlines, and the conglomerates and the film makers came to Congress, hat in hand. What happened to Lockheed is, in a sense, the new American dream. Lose money, whimper publicly, get bailed out by Congress, meaning us.

The class most vocal in its exertions against welfare recipients, the blue collar brigade, is very heavily into federal funds for housing. In 1970, Congress concocted a housing scheme for home buyers in the $7000 to $12,000 a year income bracket. Since the days of FDR at least $20 billion have been disbursed by the Federal government to provide housing for one sector or other of the voting public. Yes, billions.

And what of good old middle America, the farmer? For years Congress has voted annually $3.8 billion to support farm prices. That is, to assure that virtually no sizeable farm property will lose money. These farm payments, as clearly welfare as a bowl of soup given on a breadline are almost permanently built into our system.

In a sense everybody in this country is on relief, not merely those people with the funny skin and the bad habits. Subsidies to the transport, housing, farming, shipping, and many other economic entities not excluding Lockheed, cost the taxpayer at least $63 billion last year.

Senator William A. Roth in 1970 claimed to have unearthed 1350 individual charity programs spread among 57 departments and agencies of government. He estimated that total federal aid outlay in 1971 was nearly $80 billion. And, as *The New Republic* wryly observed recently, ". . . Nobody in Congress or the executive branch has the foggiest notion what good these subsidies do. All we know for sure is that they benefit the rich more than the poor."

Like the guys who build ships. The Merchant Marine Act of 1970 provides citizen subvention to shipyards of some $2.7 billion to cover the extra cost of building 300 ships in domestic yards rather than abroad. As Senator Roth discovered when he started poking into the matter of subsidies, it is hard to get the true poop about them. In the first place, they are seldom called subsidies. Most likely: aid, supply assistance, tax incentive, loan or tax credit.

This secrecy and evasiveness has thrown up an entire new profession—grantsmanship. Smart cats sit in offices in Washington, find out where the loot is buried, and sell the info to their clients for a nice profit. "'Meaningful information' is the 'Open Sesame' to federal assistance programs, because most of them require that action to be initiated by those needing the aid. As a result, lack of adequate information has resulted in advantaging the advantaged and disadvantaging the disadvantaged."

The truth would seem that our federal charity programs discriminate against those who need charity the most, the truly poor and unemployed and mostly black. When next you sadly wag your head, in unison with Governor Reagan and the rest of the troglodyte pack, at the exigencies of those who get rent and food money from the state, give a thought to those highly efficient grantsmen back in the Capitol. Not to speak of the oilmen with their depletion allowances, the airport developers, businessmen who invest in new machinery, people who set up foundations, investors with capital gains—all of whom get subsidies.

LET'S GET THE RICH OFF WELFARE.

Source: Charles McCabe, "Who's on Welfare," *The San Francisco Chronicle,* Wednesday and Thursday, May 17 and 18, 1972, pp. 41 and 39, respectively.

have been subsidized for years, ostensibly to pay for air mail service, but in reality as a direct subsidy for expenses. Trucking industries are subsidized because their share of highway developments are far more expensive than the taxes they pay; landlords receive special tax benefits that allow them to depreciate their properties far faster than they actually deteriorate; public utilities are constantly pampered by the so-called "regulatory agencies" that are in fact captives of the very industries they are supposed to regulate.

Subsidizing the rich, then, is an important aspect of welfare in this nation and is a direct result of the power and political domination that the wealthy and affluent hold over the political process. The political system that supports these subsidies is not nearly so generous when it comes to welfare for the poor, a topic that we will examine in the next section.

WELFARE: PROBLEMS AND PROPOSALS

So far we have been examining some of the patterns of poverty in America, and some of the real *causes* that promote it—the economic system, the built-in inequalities of social institutions, and the domination of the legal and political system by the rich and powerful. Now we turn our attention to the welfare system that is supposed to help alleviate the harsh realities of poverty—but that generally fails.

WHO IS ON WELFARE?

A rather startling fact about American welfare is that of the 24 million people in poverty, only slightly more than 12 million receive any government assistance. Surely this is in direct contradiction to the popular notion that the poor are living out of the public pocket. Of those who do receive help from the government large amounts come from the Social Security Administration and the Veteran's Administration—both of which are *earned* benefits and are available in greater amounts to members of the middle class than to the poor. In fact, this type of earned "welfare" represents about half of the welfare payments to the poor. The public assistance programs, which the public is generally thinking about when it talks about "welfare," really accounts for less than 13 percent of the total welfare bill. For example, of the $33 billion in federal money given in aid to the poor in 1971, approximately one third came from the Social Security Administration and approximately 10 percent from the Veteran's Administration. In fact, only about 20 percent of the poor actually receive help from public assistance funds, such as old-age benefits or aid to dependent children.

Direct federal aid to the poor constitutes only a tiny percentage of the federal budget—almost nothing compared to the enormous sums spent on defense. The state and local governments are hardly overexerting themselves to aid the poor either; they spend twice as much on highways as they do on the problem of poverty. It is difficult, then, to understand the public outcry against the poor and against those who receive welfare. Perhaps it is part of the nation's value system to emphasize economic competition and to look down in vengeance and scorn on those who have not survived in that competition.

To summarize, several facts must be remembered about the welfare system.

1. About half of the poor do not receive welfare payments of any kind. The society has provided no mechanism at all for these poverty-stricken people to stay alive.
2. Of those 50 percent who receive payments, about one half receive *earned* payments, mainly from the Social Security and Veteran's administrations.
3. Of the remaining 25 percent of the poor who are receiving general public assistance payments, the vast majority are helpless—the young, mothers with small children, the blind, and the disabled.
4. Finally, the few who are receiving public assistance receive so little that the majority still are in the poverty bracket.

The overall picture, then, is that the poor in America are a neglected, abused substratum of the population. Unfortunately this dismal picture is reinforced by the very welfare system that is supposed to help these people.

REGULATING THE POOR: THE WELFARE SYSTEM

In theory the welfare system is designed to help those who cannot help themselves—the blind, incapacitated, weak, young, and unemployed. The well-off in the nation, so the theory goes, establish humane systems for helping the less fortunate. The truth, however, is considerably less idealistic, because in reality the welfare system is used as a device for regulating the poor instead of a system for alleviating their misery. In *Regulating the Poor: The Functions of Public Welfare* (1971), Piven and Cloward argue that welfare is basically designed to control the work habits of the poor, expand services when the poor are unruly and violent, but expell them from relief when domestic peace returns. Thus, the welfare rolls expand and contract depending on the unhappiness and behavior of the poor.

The key to an understanding of relief-giving is in the functions it serves for the larger economic and political order, for relief is a secondary and supportive institution. Historical evidence suggests that relief arrangements are initiated or expanded during the occasional outbreaks of civil disorder produced by mass unemployment, and are then abolished or contracted when political stability is restored. We shall argue that expansive relief policies are designed to mute civil disorder, and restrictive ones to reinforce work norms. In other words, relief policies are cyclical—liberal or restrictive depending on the problems of regulation in the larger society with which government must contend. (Piven and Cloward, 1971, p. xiii)

"Welfare rights" demonstration at Chicago's federal building protesting unfair welfare cuts and demanding more jobs and courtroom justice.

Piven and Cloward describe several welfare cycles over the past 50 years. The Depression of the 1920s threw millions of people out of work and brought untold misery to the poor of the United States. The federal administration under Herbert Hoover took few effective measures to alleviate the problems, and massive unrest, riots, and social upheaval resulted.

The election of Franklin Roosevelt and an overwhelmingly Democratic Congress resulted in major expansions of the welfare rolls, work programs such as the Work Projects Administration, and unemployment payments. These measures placated the poor, and social unrest decreased rapidly. As domestic peace returned, however, there were public outcries against the "loafers" on the welfare rolls, and "reforms" were made to enforce work and to get people back into the economy's private sector. World War II started and the economy mushroomed, reducing the welfare rolls as people moved back into private employment.

The 1940s and 1950s had fairly small welfare rolls, caused at first by high levels of employment, and later by the restrictive government policies that kept people off the rolls even when economic conditions worsened. In the late 1950s economic conditions took a severe downturn, the black revolution began, and the poor of the nation began to show definite signs of violence and unrest. The move of blacks out of the southern agricultural economy into the large urban centers, the urban riots in Detroit, Newark, Watts, and other cities, and the advent of the Johnson Administration with its liberal welfare policies were conditions that led to a literal explosion of the welfare rolls. During the 1950s the number of people on relief increased about 17 percent, but during the 1960s the increase was an amazing 107 percent, most of which occurred after 1964.

The cycle, then, is very clear; severe economic crisis creates unrest, misery, and potential violence among the poor. In order to quell the violence the government expands the welfare rolls, placating the poor and restoring domestic peace. When the violence is safely past, however, the public belief in individualism and the work ethic leads to outcries for welfare reform and a restoration of work. In short, welfare is not so much a process of public charity and concern as it is a response to fear and a method of regulating the work habits of the poor.

In the early 1970s the welfare rolls swelled, domestic peace was largely restored—at least on the surface—and the conservative administration of Richard Nixon moved once more to reduce the welfare rolls. The classic cycle was at the peak of expansion and there was much concern to reduce the rolls as much as possible. Once more the public, hoping to rebuild the work ethic, called for welfare "reform."

WELFARE REFORM STRATEGIES

The welfare program has been subjected to an enormous amount of criticism from all quarters—from liberals, from conservatives, from those who are on welfare, from those who administer the programs, and from those who want to improve the system. The Committee on Economic Development made an extensive study of the welfare system in the United States and published a monograph entitled *Improving the Public Welfare System* (1971). In its opening statement the Committee made the following comment.

The present welfare system of the United States was brought into being in the 1930's when one third of the nation was described as "ill housed, ill clothed, and ill fed." The transient problems then facing the country were massive unemployment and the need to devise emergency measures that would provide for sustenance for millions of Americans. The welfare structure inherited from this emergency is entirely inadequate to cope with the problems of poverty in a high-employment economy. (Committee for Economic Development, 1971, p. 9)

The committee's study of the welfare system is one of the most thoughtful in many years and has been a basis of government planning for revamping the program. In their analysis the committee found that the welfare system had a number of major flaws and proposed a series of reforms that might result in a more effective, fair, and efficient plan of welfare. Let us examine a few of the criticisms and some of the proposals for reform.

Reaching the Poor with Assistance. First, the welfare system fails to reach more than half of the poor in America. Millions of people who live in abject poverty are excluded from the public assistance programs for reasons that are not justified. The major group excluded are those who are working, even though these workers may earn well below the poverty level because of racial discrimination or lack of education or of skills. The Committee on Economic Development believes that excluding the working poor from welfare punishes the very people in the poverty bracket who are trying the hardest to get out of it.

Consequently, the committee argues that a federal system of national minimum income should be established to provide government help to anyone who needs it, whether the need results from inadequate earnings or the inability to work. This would close an enormous gap in the welfare system, offering help to the working poor and to other people in the poverty bracket who are presently excluded from the welfare system because of various technicalities, such as residence requirements. Essentially the recommendation calls for a guaranteed minimum income for all families in the United States, based on need instead of on any other formula. As a starter the committee suggests that a family of four should receive $2400 a year in income support. The Nixon Administration accepted these guidelines as a basis for a series of recommendations to Congress, although the Administration's proposal allows for only $1800 instead of $2400 for a family of four. Unfortunately in the years since that proposal was made no action has been taken on it by Congress.

Rewarding Work. The second problem identified by the committee was that under the present system people receiving government help are punished if they go to work because every dollar they earn is subtracted from their welfare payments. In effect, this practice amounts to a 100 percent tax on the money poor people earn and removes any incentive for them to break out of the poverty cycle by working. It is actually much more advantageous for a poor person *not* to work than to work under the present welfare system. Thus the committee urged that the government establish a bonus plan whereby people on poverty could keep a certain percentage of money they earn without having their welfare payments reduced. Of course, after a family was earning a sizable amount the welfare payments would be reduced accordingly and gradually tapered off. This would allow for a family to increase its earnings gradually without being cut off welfare until it had broken out of poverty.

Support Services. The third set of recommendations deals with support facilities for the poor. Much of the problem of poverty can be traced to two factors: (1) lack of skills, which lead either to unemployment or to such poor employment that the income is still below the poverty level; and (2) inability of women with small children to work. The Committee on Economic Development believes that these two problems are major barriers to bringing people off the welfare rolls and into the work force. Consequently, they recommended that all able-bodied people on welfare be required to receive work training in order to continue on public assistance. This would make an expanded program of work training an integral part of the family-income-maintenance program. In addition, it was recommended that a federally supported program of day-care centers be established so that mothers receiving public assistance would be able to supplement their incomes by working and by receiving job training. These two support programs—job training and day-care centers—would be major backup facilities to encourage the poor to upgrade living conditions.

Equalizing State Assistance. The committee found large variations among states in the amount paid welfare recipients and in the quality of services offered. Thus it was much more advantageous to be on the welfare rolls in New York or California than in Mississippi or Alabama. In 1968 Mississippi had a maximum of $55 a month for aid to dependent children, whereas New Jersey had a maximum of $332—nearly seven times as much as Mississippi. The Committee for Economic Development argued that this disparity among states is one of the most serious inequalities in the entire welfare system and should be remedied immediately. The most logical procedure, they argued, would be to remove the welfare programs from the administration of the states and place it entirely under the control of the federal government. Currently only two states in the country offer a family of four enough welfare to pull them out of poverty! The other 48 states offer welfare services and payments that are under the amount that the federal government has established as a poverty-level income. For this reason the committee urged the federal government to continue upgrading the quality of services and payments to the point that every family in America could be assured of an income equal to or above the poverty level at any given time. This would require assistance far above the $2400 the committee presently wants to achieve, and over twice as high as former President Nixon's figure of $1800 for a family of four.

Eligibility Standards. Finally, the present procedures for establishing eligibility for welfare services was found to be inefficient, inflexible, and demeaning to the poor people who were forced to go through the bureaucratic red tape, and frustrating to professionally trained welfare workers who do not wish to be used primarily as clerks. At present most of the welfare administration's effort goes into investigating welfare clients' eligibility, and most of the social workers' time is spent in bureaucratic procedures instead of in helping the people. Included in the eligibility procedure are such humiliating activities as middle-of-the-night raids on mothers with dependent children to make sure they are not sexually involved with men who might support them. The present eligibility system is costly in personnel time, inefficient in its application, and humiliating to the welfare recipients.

The Committee for Economic Development suggested a very simple reform procedure. Each family would simply sign an affidavit attesting to its needs under penalty of perjury, and all other certification procedures would be eliminated with the exception of spot checks based on small scientific samples. This would remove the demeaning practices of eligibility investigation and would free the welfare workers to do what they're paid to do—to help the poor.

From "Services" to an "Income" Strategy. The final set of proposals represents a revolutionary new way to handle the welfare program. The committee suggested that there should be a shift from the *services* approach to the *income* approach. The former approach assumes that the government will provide services such as health care, family planning, dental care, and low-income housing. Under this procedure most of the money is spent on middle-class social workers and administrators who supposedly provide services for the poor at no cost.

The income approach, on the other hand, assumes that the poor are able to buy their own services on the open market. Consequently, the strategy should be simply to give them money and let them buy their services wherever they wish. Under the income strategy the giant bureaucracy of the welfare establishment would be largely eliminated, and instead the poor would receive assistance checks by mail directly through some agency such as the Social Security Administration. Under this plan the poor could then go out to the open market and buy whatever housing and health and social services they need without the interference of social workers and governmental bureaucracies.

The income strategy represents a fundamental shift in handling welfare and poverty assistance. The services approach assumes that the poor cannot judge for themselves what they need; the income approach assumes that they can and that they will buy what they need if they have the money. It seems that the income strategy is now gaining widespread support as it becomes clear that the services strategy is inadequate to deal with the problem of poverty.

BASIC SOCIAL REFORM

It is not clear whether the proposals for welfare reform as suggested by the Committee for Economic Development and as presented to Congress by the Nixon Administration will gain sufficient support to be implemented. It *is* clear, however, that there is a rising discontent with the present welfare program and a continuing recognition that poverty is a central crisis in modern society. Hopefully, dissatisfactions will result in new procedures for dealing with poverty, although ultimately a more basic reform of American economic and political systems is needed to eliminate the fundamental inequities based on an unequal distribution of power, income, and wealth in the society.

The patchwork rebuilding of the welfare system, as necessary as many of the reforms are, cannot solve the basic underlying problem of an economy that has built-in inequality, discrimination, and long-standing pockets of poverty. The only real solution is serious economic reform and the reduction of inequalities. Piven and Cloward state the issue clearly.

In principle, there are two ways of dealing with relief explosions and the underlying economic and social dislocations which they reflect. One is by reforms in economic policy that would lead to full employment at decent wages, and the other is by relief reforms. If jobs were created on a large scale, whether by public or private investments, and the wages paid were adequate, many AFDC mothers would immediately take jobs. Over the long run, however, basic economic reforms would reduce the rolls by a more fundamental process: that of restoring lower-class occupational, familial, and communal patterns. Since men, for example, would no longer find themselves unemployed or employed at wages insufficient to support women and children, they would be able to resume breadwinning roles. A dramatic impact on the relief system would result, for fewer women would be forced to ask for assistance for lack of adequate male support. (Piven and Cloward, 1971, p. 345)

However, as Piven and Cloward point out, there is little hope that a viable political coalition can be put together to produce serious economic reform. Until that happens, they take the unusual position that the welfare system should *not* be reformed. On closer examination, their argument appears to be the humane choice of allowing swelled welfare rolls until such time as serious reform is accomplished in the entire economy.

We are opposed to work-enforcing reforms. The basis for our opposition is that when similar reforms were introduced in the past, they presaged the eventual expulsion of large numbers of people from the rolls, leaving them to fend for themselves in a labor market where there was too little work and thus subjecting them once again to severe economic exploitation.

In the absence of fundamental economic reforms, therefore, we take the position that the explosion of the rolls is the true relief reform, *that it should be defended, and expanded. Even now, hundreds of thousands of impoverished families remain who are eligible for assistance but who receive no aid at all. (Piven and Cloward, 1971, pp. 347–348)*

SUMMARY

Poverty is a relative thing. Although poor people in the United States are better off than the poor in other parts of the world, their comparison point is the wealthy and affluent all about them. The United States has, in fact, many pockets of poverty, constituting about one eighth of the population. In the popular mind the poor are lazy and individually at fault for their plight. In fact, many "ideologies" have grown up to explain—and to justify—the social inequality in the society, to show why the rich are deserving of their good fortune and the poor have only themselves to blame. The facts, however, indicate that the major causes of poverty are legitimate: illness, chronic unemployment, old age, physical disability, broken homes, and the responsibilities of caring for small children. Much of the problem is, therefore, caused by the economic system. On one hand, the laws of the nation are designed to give special privileges to the powerful, through subsidies to industry and tax breaks to the wealthy. Similar subsidies to the poor are called by the negative term "welfare." And the sums that come through that method to the poor are dismally small when compared to the huge sums given to industries and to wealthy individuals.

The myth of endless streams of lazy poor feeding out of the public pocketbook is invalidated by examining the welfare system. First of all, the welfare system is primarily a mechanism for returning *earned* payments to people through the Social Security and the Veteran's administrations. Only a very small portion of the welfare program is in the controversial "public assistance" categories—unemployment and Aid to Families with Dependent Children. Of 100 poor people only about 50 get any help from welfare and of that 50, less than 20 get help from public assistance programs. Moreover, even with welfare help the vast majority of the poor are still living in miserable conditions. A number of proposals have been made for revamping the entire program: extending coverage to more people, rewarding work instead of cutting benefits when people earn outside money, building up support services for job training and child care, and revising the eligibility standards. The basic proposal for meeting these objectives is to turn the system over to the federal government, to create a guaranteed minimum income, and to eliminate the inequities that are built into the state programs. In addition, many proposals suggest that the "services" strategy that has so long dominated the welfare program be replaced by an "income" strategy. An "income" approach allows the poor to buy their own services on the open market instead of being dependent wards of the welfare bureaucracies.

REFERENCES

Bagdikian, Ben H. *In the Midst of Plenty: The Poor in America* (New York: Holt, 1964).

Downs, Anthony. *Who are the Urban Poor?* (New York: Committee for Economic Development, 1970).

Dougherty, Philip. "Family on Relief: Study in Poverty," *The New York Times,* April 5, 1964.

Free, Lloyd A., and Hadley Contril. *The Political Beliefs of Americans* (New York: Clarion Books, 1968).

Fuchs, Victor R. "An Alternative Income-oriented Definition," in Robert F. Will and Harold G. Vatter, eds. *Poverty in Affluence* (New York: Harcourt, Brace, and World, 1970).

Hunter, Robert. *Poverty* (New York: Holt, 1912).

Improving the Public Welfare System (New York: Committee for Economic Development, 1971).

Irelan, Lola M., Oliver C. Moles, and Robert M. O'Shea. "Ethnicity, Poverty, and Selected Attitudes: A Test of the 'Culture of Poverty' Hypothesis," *Social Forces, 4,* June 1969, pp. 405–413.

Keller, Albert, ed. *The Challenge of Facts and Other Essays* (New Haven, Conn.: Yale Press, 1914).

Lane, Robert E. *Political Ideology: Why the American Common Man Believes What He Does* (Glencoe, Ill.: Free Press, 1962).

Lewis, Oscar. *La Vida* (New York: Random House, 1966).

Mannheim, Karl. *Ideology and Utopia* (New York: Harcourt, Brace and World, 1936).

Pechman, Joseph. "The Rich, the Poor, and the Taxes They Pay," *The Public Interest, 17,* Fall 1968, pp. 21–43.

Piven, Frances Fox, and Richard A. Cloward. *Regulating the Poor* (New York: Pantheon Books, 1971).

Ryan, William. *Blaming the Victim* (New York: Pantheon Books, 1971).

Rytina, Joan Huber, William H. Form, and John Pease. "Income and Stratification Ideology: Beliefs About the American Opportunity Structure," *American Journal of Sociology, 75,* January 1970, p. 712.

Spencer, Herbert. *Social Status* (New York: Appleton, 1880).

Vallentine, Charles A. *Culture and Poverty* (Chicago: University of Chicago Press, 1968).

Will, Robert E., and Harold G. Vatter, eds. *Poverty in Affluence* (New York: Harcourt, Brace and World, 1970).

Yeamens, Robin. "Double Standard," *Progressive Magazine,* February 1969, p. 5.

EIGHT THE POLITICAL PROCESS: THE STATE AND INTEREST GROUPS

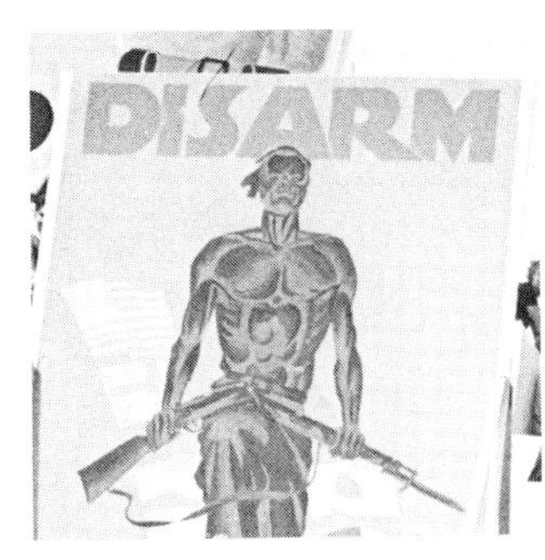

THE POWER ELITE

As the means of information and of power are centralized, some men come to occupy positions in American society from which they can look down upon, so to speak, and by their decisions mightily affect, the everyday worlds of ordinary men and women. . . . The power elite is composed of men whose positions enable them to transcend the ordinary environments of ordinary men and women; they are in positions to make decisions having major consequences. . . . For they are in command of the major hierarchies and organizations of modern society. They rule the big corporations. They run the machinery of the state and claim its prerogatives. They direct the military establishment. They occupy the strategic command posts of the social structure, in which are now centered the effective means of the power and the wealth and the celebrity which they enjoy. (From C. Wright Mills, *The Power Elite*)

In the three previous chapters we have been discussing the stratification system, a network that is primarily built on inequalities in the economic distribution of money—*income* and *wealth.* In this chapter we turn to a different, but closely related issue—the unequal distribution of *power.*

Every known society, both historical and contemporary, has had sharp inequalities in the distribution of power. This is just as true today in the United States as it has been in any other nation; in fact, C. Wright Mills argues in the opening quotation that it is even *more* true today because a "power elite" controls many of the institutions of society. The inequalities of power and those of wealth are closely related because power inequalities lead to dramatic differences in the amount of political influence that people in the society hold, which leads, in turn, to an unequal distribution of the society's wealth. The elites who gain control over power and wealth then translate their advantages into formal systems of authority—into law, into corporate structures, and into legal and political systems. Groups who are not members of the elite sometimes find themselves powerless, poor, and without effective influence over their social lives. Most important, these powers and inequalities are reinforced and undergirded by the *state,* the social institution that now dominates all others.

EXPANSION OF THE MODERN STATE

The state is now one of the most crucial social institutions in modern society. The degree to which the state is involved in our private lives is astonishing. The state registers our births, controls the conditions in the hospital where we are born, and regulates the licensing of the attending physicians. The state protects us in our childhoods by regulating the treatment our parents may give us. The state provides schools for us and requires that we attend. And the list goes on. The state regulates the operation of motor vehicles and regulates working conditions and labor unions. Furthermore, the state records our marriages, collects our taxes, provides services, piles up social security funds to support us in our old age, and even registers our deaths and regulates the burials. To say the least, people in modern society are political beings.

From an historical perspective the expansion of services provided by a contemporary state is a very recent phenomenon. In fact, the traditional view has been the old saying, "That government is best which governs least." By contrast, modern governments have extended their activities to the point that virtually no area of life is left untouched.

The expansion of the government's domain seems to be a trend throughout the world, regardless of the political system. In communist nations, such as the

Soviet Union and China, the expansion of governmental services from prerevolution to postrevolution was staggering. Following the socialist logic of Marx, who said the state must control the economy to prevent the capitalists from exploiting the workers, the communist states moved into areas never before seriously influenced by the government—especially in economic and production areas. In the third-world nations—the developing countries—the expansion of government has been dramatic, for nationalism and socialism have accompanied modernization. Mao's China, Nehru's India, and Castro's Cuba are only three of the many developing nations that saw a sizable growth of governmental services. In the modern Western nations the expansion of government has also been continuous—in peace and war, under liberal and conservative administrations.

The relentless expansion of American government can be seen most easily by examining the share of the gross national product (the total value of all goods and services produced by a society in a year) spent by all branches of the government—federal, state, and local. In almost every year since colonial times the government's share has increased. The most reliable statistics start with 1929 and are shown in Figure 8.1. Note that from 1929 to 1971 the share of the gross national product spent by all levels of government rose from 8.2 percent to 22.2 percent, an increase of nearly 300 percent. During that same period the number of people employed by governments increased by 319 percent, while the number employed by private sectors of the economy increased only about 104 percent. The size of the government's role in American society is increasing in both absolute and relative terms.

CONTROLS OF THE POLITICAL PROCESS

But the critical question for observers of modern society is not only the *size* of the contemporary state, but the *control* of the political process. How is power distributed, who influences the central political decision processes? For whom does the government function? Who receives the benefits of the government's services? What social groups are served by the political process? Are some groups more disadvantaged than others, and do vested interest groups get more than their share of the political benefits? Radical critics of society argue that, although the state is supposedly democratic and supposedly serves everyone impartially, in reality the state is frequently the tool of vested interest groups and power elites. In short, power is just as unequally distributed as we have seen wealth to be. Let us examine one of the most important controversies over this question, the debate about the "power elite."

WHO GOVERNS? IS THERE A POWER ELITE?

Does the government serve the people or is it the servant of small elite groups? C.

Figure 8.1
Government expenditures compared to gross national product,* absolute dollars and percent, 1929–1971

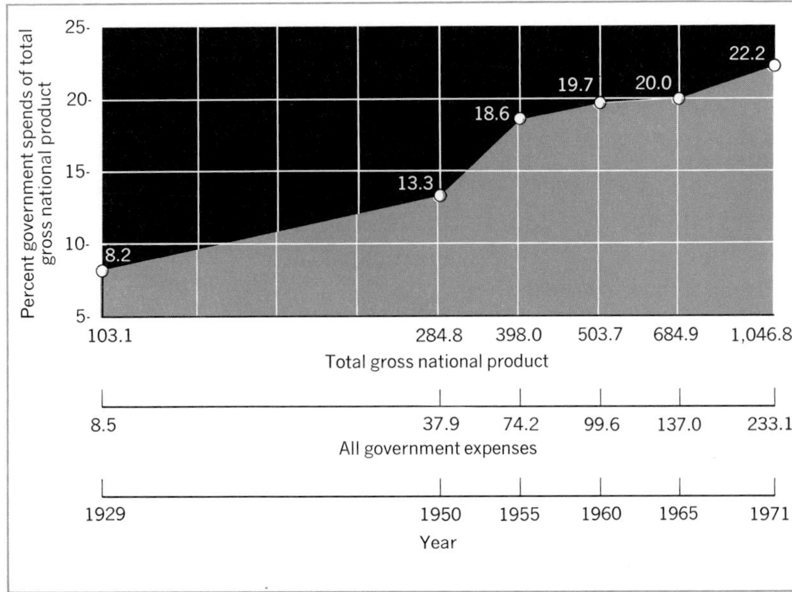

*"Gross national product" is the total money value of all goods and services produced in a nation for a year.

Wright Mills, a famous Columbia University sociologist who died in the late 1950s, proposed in *The Power Elite* (1956) that the government was actually the servant of three very small groups of elites in the *government*, the *military*, and the large *corporations*. The quotation from Mills at the beginning of the chapter summarized his basic argument.

Main Tenets of the Power-Elite Theory. The power-elite theory suggests the following:

1. Small groups of elites control most of the governmental decisions that influence national policies.

2. The major elites are the heads of giant corporations, top officials in the government, and key military personnel.

3. The three different types of elites are closely associated because very often corporation executives become military heads, military heads move into government posts, and government officials become corporation officials.

4. Although there are occasionally deliberate conspiracies among these powerful people—as there was in the infamous Watergate scandal in the early 1970s—conspiracies are usually unnecessary because common interests and common backgrounds are enough to insure that decisions are made for the benefit of the in-group elites.

5. The members of the power elite hold their influence by virtue of their offices in critical bureaucracies—the state, the corporations, and the military—instead of by their personal influence as individuals.

6. Directly under the power elite there is a group of people, such as Congressmen, state government officials, and lower members of the military, with "middle-range power." These middle-range elites carry out the orders of the power elites.

7. When all these factors are taken together the government is seen to be essentially undemocratic; it serves small vested interest groups and systematically discriminates against the masses of people.

It is no surprise to any critical observer that the poor, minorities, women, and the young are excluded from power. But, if Mills is correct, then it is also true that the great masses of middle-class, white, educated citizens are also shut out of power. Effective decision making on most major issues affecting millions of people—decisions on war and peace, on welfare and taxes, on education and health—are centralized in the hands of a few powerful people. The Vietnam war, for example, was begun without even a Congressional declaration of war; prestigious Congressmen did not even have influence over that fateful decision, much less the average citizen!

These decision makers are the same people who reap the lion's share of the wealth, prestige, and social privilege. The power elites are also the wealth elites and the prestige elites. Although there are rarely conspiracies among the powerful, there is, nevertheless, a deep common concern among the elites for preserving their advantages, a shared interest that acts just as effectively as a conspiracy. The outcome is that the elites act in a unified manner to maintain their privileges.

Empirical Support for the Power-Elite Theory. There is empirical support for the power-elite theory. Many studies have pointed to a single power structure that is dominating the decision process, particularly on the national level, but also on the local level. One example is the government's close connections with business through the Department of Defense. The Pentagon controls most of the federal budget—about $80 billion per year—and spends much of this money buying military hardware from huge corporations whose managers and directors are often ex-members of the military establishment itself. In fact, of the largest 100 corporations in the United States over half are directly concerned with military hardware.

Military chiefs and industrial chiefs move back and forth between the government and the private sector, carrying their common concerns with them. Robert McNamara, for example, was Secretary of Defense under President Johnson, having moved there from the presidency of Ford Motor Company, which does enormous amounts of defense contracting. David Packard, Deputy Secretary of Defense in the Nixon Administration, was one of the coowners of the Hewlett-Packard Company, a prime defense contractor. It is not difficult to find many other examples of people in power moving from one segment of society to another: Dean Rusk, Secretary of State under Kennedy, was head of the Rockefeller Foundation, which holds a major share of the Standard Oil Company of New Jersey. Henry Kissinger, a member of the academic elite at Harvard, moved directly into foreign policy under President Nixon; Walt Rostow and McGeorge Bundy were also academics who made the transition to government posts.

In short, there is an interplay between the chiefs of the government, the corporations, the military, and the academic world. There may not be a conspiracy among the power elites, but there is certainly an interchange of personnel and ideas that forms a common frame of reference and a mutual interest. Major national decisions are shaped by the intricate web of connections among these powerful people.

Relations Between Elites Within Each Sector. Not only are there connections among different segments of public life, but *within* each sector there are also many interlocking power elites. The most obvious are the close interconnections among the powerful corporations. The managers and directors of these corporations have multiple holdings, controlling several industries at the same time. For example, H. L. Nieberg (1966) reports that his study of 74 nationwide corporations revealed that 1480 directors and managers held a total of 4428 corporate positions; each man held nearly four different positions in four different companies. This overlapping control effectively reduces the competition among the companies and increases the likelihood that corporate interests will be coordinated in opposition to the public interest.

In addition to the overlap in top personnel there are even more direct connections through corporate mergers. In the last few decades the number of corporate mergers has skyrocketed, both vertically (buying up your own suppliers) and horizontally (buying up your competitors). In fact, the top five manufacturing companies have been able to accumulate power to the point that they account for 20 percent of the profit in the manufacturing industries. Through mergers and expansion the top 500 companies account for 80 percent of the holdings of physical plants, property, and corporate profits. That means that only 20 percent of corporate wealth is held by the remaining 400,000 firms. The accumulation of corporate power and wealth in so few hands suggests that a corporate power elite must in fact exist. With such power and wealth at their fingertips, it would be inconceivable that the captains of industry do not influence national policy in a major way.

Systems of Authority Support the Inequality of Power. As the discussion above shows, the power elite do not necessarily control decisions by their own personal wealth and power. Instead, their prime control is exercised through the organizations they run, the giant political and economic bureaucracies. Thus, power and wealth are concentrated in a few hands and are translated into stable institutional forms. Powerful families and individuals hold huge amounts of power and wealth, but they cannot fully exercise their power without the institutional forms that support them. Power held by individuals is translated into governmental policy, the law, and bureaucratic authority systems. The Ford, Mellon, Rockefeller, Firestone, Hughes, and Kennedy families hold vast reserves of private wealth, but their most critical leverages of power are through the corporations they control, through the laws they promote, and through the government positions they influence.

Other Power-Elite Studies. C. Wright Mills' description of the national power elite has evidence to support it, and other studies back it up. Robert Presthus confirms many of Mills' arguments in his study of major corporation executives, published in *Men at the Top* (1964). John Kenneth Galbraith agrees with the power-elite theory in his book, *The New Industrial State* (1968), in which he analyzes the nature of an economic system that is concentrated in the hands of government and big business.

Studies of national decision making are also supplemented by studies on the local level. Floyd Hunter (1953) analyzed local decision making in Atlanta, Georgia, and essentially confirmed the power-elite thesis. In Atlanta, for example, most of the critical decisions about city policies and local law were decided by a small clique of government officials and major businessmen. Hunter argued that the democratic process did not function, for on most of the major decisions the majority of the people were shut out of effective influence as a tiny group of prestigious, wealthy people shaped and molded the critical policies.

WHO GOVERNS? THE PLURALISM THEORY

Mills' power-elite theory has been the source of a constant debate in modern sociology because, although many people agree with his general thesis, there are also many social scientists who believe his vision was too restricted. The "pluralist" theory, offered by some sociologists and political scientists as a balance to Mills' theory, argues that instead of a small power elite there are many competing interest groups struggling for power. Because these groups are fighting against each other they tend to form countervailing pressure groups, thus eliminating the dominance that any one group might gain. Whereas the power-elite theory suggests that the government is controlled by vested interest groups and as a consequence is very undemocratic, the pluralist theory proposes that the struggle between interest groups allows democracy to work, since no single group can gain power.

Robert Dahl, a Yale political scientist, is a prime proponent of the pluralist theory. Dahl studied the decision-making processes in the city of New Haven, Connecticut under the administration of Mayor Richard Lee and found that his results contrasted sharply with Hunter's analysis of Atlanta. Dahl argued that in New Haven there definitely was not a single power elite controlling all of the major decisions. Instead, he found many different interest groups, pushing and pulling the mayor in many directions. In fact, Mayor Lee—who would have been the major power elite if Mills and Hunter were correct—was nothing more than a broker who stood between different interest groups. Instead of dominating the decisions, Mayor Lee simply became the focal point for cross pressures from various veto groups. Dahl describes the mayor's plight in the following.

The mayor was not at the peak of a pyramid but rather at the center of intersecting circles. He rarely commanded. He negotiated, cajoled, exhorted, beguiled, charmed, pressed, appealed, reasoned, promised, insisted, demanded, even threatened, but he most needed support and acquiescence from other leaders who simply could not be commanded. Because the mayor could not command, he had to bargain. (Dahl, 1961, p. 204)

In light of his studies of New Haven, and in light of a number of other studies of similar decision processes, Robert Dahl and Nelson Polsby (1963) have proposed a different set of assumptions about political decision processes.

1. Instead of one single power elite there are *multiple interest groups* pushing and pulling the decision makers in every direction.
2. No one interest group is usually powerful enough to dominate the decisions. Instead, the different groups exercise *veto power* over the decisions, frequently mustering enough power to stop a decision but rarely having the power to force its own opinion on the decision makers.
3. It takes a major *coalition* of different interest groups to get a decision made. Therefore, many groups must be involved in the decision and no single group can ever have complete control.
4. Not only are there different interest groups, but there are also *many different elites* who make the decisions. The power-elite theory had argued for a single dominant elite, but the pluralistic theory says that even the elites themselves are splintered into different camps.
5. The pluralist theory rejects the notion of secret, hidden power that is exercised by the dominant elite. Instead, the pluralists say that decisions are actually made more or less democratically. This does not mean that modern society is a perfectly working democracy, but it does mean that decision making is more democratic than the power-elite theorists proposed.

David Riesman, another of the major supporters of the pluralist theory, extends the argument beyond local issues. National politics, he argues, are not controlled by a power elite but by the constant interaction of "veto groups" who never control much power individually but who collectively work to move the political system. In his book *The Lonely Crowd* he lists some of the many groups that have veto power.

One might ask whether one would not find, over a long period of time, that decisions in America favored one group or class . . . over others. Does not wealth exert its pull in the long run? In the past this has been so; for the future I doubt it. The future seems to be in the hands of the small business and professional men who control Congress, such as realtors, lawyers, car salesmen, undertakers, and so on; of the military men who control defense and, in part, foreign policy; of the big business managers and their lawyers, finance-committee men, and other counselors who decide on plant investment and influence the rate of technological change; of the labor leaders who control worker productivity and worker votes; of the black belt whites who have the greatest stake in southern politics; of the Poles, Italians, Jews, and Irishmen who have stakes in foreign policy, city jobs, and ethnic, religious and cultural organizations; of the editorializers and storytellers who help socialize the young, tease and train the adult, and amuse and annoy the aged; of the farm-

ers—themselves a warring congeries of cattlemen, corn men, dairymen, cotton men, and so on—who control key departments and committees and who, as the living representatives of our inner-directed past, control many of our memories; of the Russians and, to a lesser degree, other foreign powers who control much of our agenda of attention; and so on. (Riesman, 1953, p. 257)

Riesman believes that because there are so many divergent interest groups they prevent the formation of a single power elite. Certainly there is some evidence that countervailing interest groups are pushing and pulling on all sides of decisions at the national level, just as Riesman suggests. For example, under strong pressure from conservationists and environmental groups, the government established the Environmental Protection Agency, which has moved against the pollution practices of big business. Although many ecology groups do not feel that the EPA has moved fast enough or far enough, that EPA exists and has had some measure of success indicates that government can be an active agent against the interests of the power elites in big business and for the interests of the general public. As another example, the welfare system has expanded in the last few years even in the face of determined opposition from most conservative politicians and business interests. The power-elite theory alone cannot explain how minorities and the poor have been able to expand welfare programs—even though the welfare programs have been largely ineffective in promoting real social change.

In short, there is some evidence that at both local and national levels there is some diversification of power, just as the pluralist theory suggests. It is doubtful, however, that the rosy picture of carefully balanced veto groups functioning within a well-oiled democracy is true for many situations.

POWER ELITE AND PLURALISM: COMMENT

Figure 8.2 compares some of the major aspects of the power-elite and the pluralist theories. Although the two theories disagree on most issues, they share the common concern that the democratic process may not be functioning properly. The power-elite theorists base that concern on the fear that a small bloc has cornered most of the effective influence; the pluralists base it on the paralysis that results when conflicting veto groups halt effective political decision making.

Which of these theories is more nearly correct? Although there is abundant evidence to show that both theories have a certain amount of truth, the available evidence does seem to substantiate the power-elite theories, at least on the national level. Local politics may indeed have many of the characteristics described by the pluralists; the national scene, however, appears to be best understood by the power-elite analysis. On most critical national decisions, decisions that affect the life, health, and well-being of most citizens, the general public has

Figure 8.2

Comparison of power elite and pluralism theories

Two Portraits of the American Power Structure

Power structure	Mills—Power Elite	Riesman—Pluralism
Levels	a. unified power elite b. diversified and balanced plurality of interest groups c. mass of unorganized people who have no power over elite	a. no dominant power elite b. diversified and balanced plurality of interest groups c. mass of unorganized people who have some power over interest groups
Changes	a. increasing concentration of power	a. increasing dispersion of power
Operation	a. one group determines all major policies b. manipulation of people at the bottom by group at the top	a. who determines policy shifts with the issue b. monopolistic competition among organized groups
Bases	a. coincidence of interests among major institutions (economic, military, governmental) b. social similarities and psychological affinities among those who direct major institutions	a. diversity of interests among major organized groups b. sense of weakness and dependence among those in higher as well as lower status
Consequences	a. enhancement of interests of corporations, armed forces, and executive branch of government b. decline of politics as public debate c. decline of responsible and accountable power—loss of democracy	a. no one group or class is favored significantly over others b. decline of politics as duty and self-interest c. decline of effective leadership

Source: William Kornhauser, "Power Elite or Veto Groups," in R. Bendix and S. M. Lipset (eds.), *Class, Status and Power*, 2nd ed. (New York: Free Press, 1967), p. 215.

very little control over those who make the fundamental policies.

Issues of war and peace, international policy, and taxation are concentrated largely in the hands of a few powerful politicians and industrial chiefs. Small power blocs are still quite capable of shaping public policy to their own benefit, as illustrated in the giant subsidies that were given to the Lockheed Aircraft corporation when it almost went bankrupt or in the subsidies that are regularly extended to railroads. Vested interest groups have also been able to stop much progressive legislation as, for example, the ability of real estate interest to block legislation that would protect the California seacoast (see pp. 272–275).

Although both the power-elite and the pluralist theories help explain the dynamics of political decision making, the bulk of the evidence suggests that the power-elite thesis better explains the inequalities of modern society, the unresponsiveness of the government to the needs of its people, and the continued existence of a sharply unequal class system. In the next section we will discuss *how* this domination occurs, how certain powerful interest groups manage to control the state through pressure tactics and lobbying efforts.

CORPORATE ELITES AND THEIR LOBBYING ACTIVITIES

How do the power elites control political decisions? C. Wright Mills argued that the power elites use a number of tactics, chiefly placing people in positions where they can simultaneously control industrial, military, and governmental decisions. In addition, the corporate powers of society spend untold amounts of money on lobbying efforts to influence governmental decisions. Major interest groups have paid experts who work at state and federal legislatures trying to get laws passed favorable to their clients—labor unions, businesses, professional groups, and so on. The lobbying activities at the California legislature in earlier years are described in the following quotation.

The activities of lobbyists in the first session of the California Legislature at San Jose in 1850 *led it to be called the* "legislature of a thousand drinks." *In the next century, lobbying in California became virtually synonymous in the public mind with bribery. For example, between 1900 and 1914 during the legislative sessions* the chief counsel of the Southern Pacific saw to it each week that a weekend round-trip ticket to San Francisco was left on the desk of each member. *The correspondence of Collis P. Huntington, one of the "big four" who ran the railroad, contains long lists of corruptible officeholders and discusses frankly the costs of obtaining favorable legislation. The nefarious lobbying activities of the Southern Pacific largely provoked the reform regime of Hiram Johnson, but in the 1940's, the Sacramento scene was much the same.* Governor Warren admitted that the liquor lobbyist, Artie Samish, had more power than he. *As Samish boasted,* "I'm the Governor of the Legislature. To hell with the Governor of the State." *While Mr. Samish ultimately went to jail, an investigation of his activities revealed that "some of his clients undoubtedly paid more in fees to Mr. Samish than they paid in taxes for the support of all legitimate functions of state government." Many of the laws these fees bought remain on the books. (Fellmeth, 1971, pp. VIII–4)*

But lobbying efforts did not stop with the early days of California, for today there are over 500 registered lobbyists in Sacramento. Lou Cannon described one meeting between legislators and lobbyists for the Southern Pacific Railroad.

The cobblestones in the courtyard of the Firehouse shone damp and polished in the rain of early spring that March evening of 1967 when California's political leaders met for dinner with the lobbyists. . . . The lobbyists knew all the legislators and the legislators knew them. It had been that way ever since the days of the old Southern Pacific. . . . They were experienced men, these lobbyists, and they represented clients who mattered. . . . They know how to put on a dinner. . . . The waiters brought seven kinds of vintage wine and turtle soup with sherry. . . . Californians have always cared for important men and men of economic influence. (Cannon, 1969, p. 44)

Lobbying activities are a subtle combination of many different influence strategies; they constantly act to influence political decisions by force of logical argument, friendship between lobbyists and legislators, and many types of legal and illegal sidepayments and bribes. In addition, threats and coercion are common—removing campaign funds, fighting against a legislator's pet bills, exposing damaging personal information.

Let us take some concrete examples of lobbying activity on the ecology issue. Public concern over the environment and pollution has risen tremendously since the late 1960s and early 1970s. Public outcries against the pollution of the air, water, and land have been great, but progress still seems to be very slow. The public wonders why, with all this concern, the movement toward better environmental policies has not gotten far. If we examine the lobbying activities of real estate groups, lumber industries, oil companies, utility agencies, and transportation groups, we can better understand the barriers to environmental progress.

Fellmeth and his associates (1971) found that in the 1970 California legislature alone there were 235 lobbyists who represented oil, real estate, lumber, construction, and other groups with a vested interest in environmental exploitation. These lobbyists spent $3,600,000 (an average of $30,681 per legislator!) trying to persuade the legislature to resist ecology-minded conservation moves and to preserve the privileged positions these power blocs had built up over the years. And, since a few powerful committee chairmen can effectively block new legislation, the lobbyists had to concentrate that $3.6 million on a handful of the key legislators. One lobbyist turned in an expense report after a weekend with a few legislators that read, "$2,000, deer hunting, goodwill." Meanwhile, the ecology and conservation groups could only mus-

INSERT **8.I**

PARTISAN INFLUENCE TACTICS: THE CASE OF THE *SEA RANCH*

Although most people want to protect the seacoasts and to preserve public access to them, miles of the coast have been isolated by private development. The *Sea Ranch,* a second-home development in northern California, is an excellent illustration of how commercial interests can override the majority of people.

The law of California states that all tidelands from the mean high-tide line on out are the property of the state. The difficulty is access to these lands when most or all of the property fronting on them is privately owned. The state Constitution provides that:

> *No individual, partnership, or corporation claiming or possessing the frontage or tidal lands of a harbor, bay, inlet, estuary, or other navigable water in this State, shall be permitted to exclude the right of way to such water whenever it is required for any public purpose, nor to destroy or obstruct free navigation of such water; and the Legislature shall enact such laws as will give the most liberal construction to this provision so that access to the navigable waters of this State shall be always attainable for the people thereof.*

Unfortunately, the Legislature never really spelled out the necessary details and by tradition private land owners have been able to deny access across their property.

The *Sea Ranch* covers over 10 miles of the Sonoma county coast and was a project of Oceanic Properties, a subsidiary of Castle and Cooke, Inc., of Hawaii. Their original use permit

ter two lobbyists, with a pitiful budget of about $50,000.

It is no wonder that bills for the protection of the seacoast, control of oil drilling, and other conservation issues consistently fail in the legislature. The condition in local governments is not much better—perhaps worse. Read Insert 8.I about the lobbying activities that helped a land-development company block off part of the California seacoast for its housing development, even though the activity was supposedly against the law.

Lobbying attempts are generally aimed

stipulated that they must present a development plan which dealt with the problem of public access to the ocean. In January 1968 *Sea Ranch* officials met over lunch with four or five members of the Sonoma County Board of Supervisors and presented their plans, which called for deeding 100 acres of land at one end of the *Sea Ranch* to Sonoma County for a park. This was to be the public access while the remaining beach—over 10 miles—was to be the exclusive domain of the owners of *Sea Ranch,* "guarded by a full-time security patrol." The County Planning Department recommended accepting this offer, but when the plan was announced an outraged public wrote 1400 letters of opposition to the *Sea Ranch* (versus 300 in favor), and in early April opponents of the project filed an appeal with the County Board of Supervisors. The appeal was rejected by a vote of four to one.

The appeal process had really exhausted the normal means of blocking a use permit, but in May 1968 a group called Citizens Organized to Acquire Access to State Tidelands (COAAST) began a signature drive to place a referendum on the ballot. The measure they designed called for public access to all state tidelands through "corridors" crossing private property—such corridors being through naturally occurring terrain features such as ravines. All development plans would have to include such provisions. Since the *Sea Ranch* had agreed to abide by any new regulations passed within one year following the original approval of their plan, the new requirement would apply to them.

The Sonoma County Supervisors did not react kindly to this attempt to take the matter out of their hands. One even called the effort "subversion." Nevertheless COAAST had gathered 9158 valid signatures by August (only 6342 are needed to place an issue on the ballot).

But the supervisors and land developers were not to be bypassed so easily. The supervisors, meeting on September 3, refused to put the initiative on the fall ballot, stating that the

at the legislature, but sometimes the vested interest groups have to take a different tack. In California there is a provision that groups who cannot get effective action from the legislature can put propositions on the ballot at election time. In effect, the voters can bypass the legislature completely in order to put laws into effect. For many years the environmentalists have been so badly beaten in the well-controlled legislature that they have tried the proposition tactic. Unfortunately the public, too, can be swayed by vested interest groups.

county legal counsel had found it to be "not a proper subject for an initiative petition." While the refusal to list the referendum was obviously illegal, the supervisors knew that delay of any sort would put off any action until after the one-year deadline. The real estate developers would win by delay. An outraged COAAST appealed and within two weeks the California Supreme Court ordered the initiative measure placed on the ballot as Proposition B.

Immediately after the court order, Joseph McClelland, director of the *Sea Ranch* project, announced the formation of the Citizens Committee for Preservation of Property and Conservation Together (PPACT). As you might guess, PPACT opposed Proposition B. During the next month and a half Oceanic Properties spent an estimated $50,000 attacking Proposition B with newspaper ads, television messages, and letters to the original signers of the initiative petition. One local paper opposed to Proposition B said support for the proposition had come from "a vociferous group of students and their professors." Against this onslaught the pro-ecology advocates of the measure relied on volunteer aid and a budget of $2300.

PPACT used three arguments against the proposition, none of which was reasonable. It is also true, however, that the hastily organized advocates of Proposition B never put together coherent counterarguments. PPACT claimed, first, that the taxpayers would have to pay to purchase the proposed "corridors" to the coast. Although the legal question could only be answered by the courts, there was an excellent chance that purchase would not be necessary if the corridors were a zoning requirement. Second, the *Sea Ranch* asserted that there were virtually no good beaches in the area and even ran cartoons on their ads showing a family, outfitted with beach gear, peering over a steep cliff at the end of a corridor. In fact, however, a County planning report found six usable beaches in one-third of *Sea Ranch* alone

For example, in the 1970 California elections a group of conservationists gathered enough petitions to place Proposition 18 on the ballot. This measure would have allowed 25 percent of the gasoline taxes to go toward the construction of mass transit systems or air pollution projects, instead of 100 percent to road construction as current law provided. The conservationists argued that the bill would help the state to clean up its smoggy air, provide matching money for federal projects, and encourage public transit systems to lessen the pollution mess from private cars.

In the early days of the campaign Prop-

and the advertising for the development in San Francisco papers boasted of "great white beaches and coves. . . ."Somebody was fooling somebody: the ads for *Sea Ranch* proclaimed beaches, but *Sea Ranch* itself paid for cartoons saying Proposition B was useless because there were no beaches!

Finally, PPACT pointed out there there were two studies regarding access to the beaches being made by the State Legislature and the "definitive legislation" was expected by mid-1968. They suggested that "hasty" action under Proposition B might frustrate these studies. They did not, of course, point out that the irretrievable loss of over 10 miles of beach was an even more hasty action that would certainly frustrate the state's attempt to save the coast.

After the great publicity campaign by the real estate bloc it is no great surprise that Proposition B lost 55 percent to 45 percent and that the *Sea Ranch* project went on. Ironically, a year later the state passed a new bill essentially similar to Proposition B. The bill provided that no city or county had the right to approve a subdivision fronting on the ocean unless reasonable public access was provided. Furthermore, such access must be in the form of corridors from public highways to land below the mean high-tide level. No compensation was to be paid for such easements. Although even this act still has some loopholes it does give a strong weapon to local citizens' groups. Unfortunately, the bill exempted all developments currently existing or for which plans had been approved. *Sea Ranch,* of course, managed to slip under the wire, and today, in spite of the law 10 miles of the Sonoma Coast is effectively closed to the public.

Source: Robert C. Fellmeth, *Power and Land in California,* Volume I, (Washington, D.C.: Center for Study of Responsive Law, 1971), pp. IV–130–136.

osition 18 had an impressive group of backers: almost every public interest organization in the state, most major public officials, local Chambers of Commerce, and conservation groups. Preliminary polls showed that Proposition 18 would win by two or even three to one. But the trucking, highway construction, automobile, and oil groups had prevented such legislation for years with their effective lobbying, and were not about to stand by idly while the conservation groups won a ballot victory. Fellmeth and his associates described the situation as follows.

A massive public relations campaign was launched chiefly by the above-named interests [oil and construction]. Billboards appeared all over the State exhorting in stark yellow letters:

"MORE TAXES? NO! NO. 18."

Of course Proposition 18 had nothing whatsoever to do with the tax rate. This claim was augmented by a series of distorted and contrived ads alleging that road construction funds were depleted (untrue), that gas tax money could already *be used for air pollution control if the State Legislature so decided (the same interests argued before the Legislature that it lacked such authority), that motor vehicle registration money was already being used for these purposes (not the vast receipts affected by this legislation), that it would mean coerced mass transit (untrue—only by local vote). The ads proclaimed that roads would deteriorate (also untrue considering that road* maintenance *money is unaffected by Proposition 18). . . . Films of cars going through toll booths warned Californians that "the bells will ring" if they vote for Proposition 18. (Fellmeth, 1970, p. VII–15)*

What was the outcome of Proposition 18? Polls taken at intervals before the election showed that the sentiment favoring the proposition gradually eroded as the scare campaign escalated, until the final election return was 54 percent No, and 46 percent Yes. A major environmental bill that the public had originally favored was drowned in the flood of propaganda and distortion put out by the automobile and oil interests. It is no wonder; the conservationists had a tiny budget of $22,721 to fight for the measure, but the auto and oil interests spent a staggering $348,785 on their campaign to defeat it. Once again the lesson is clear; the massive vested interest groups can afford to use their vast resources—originally obtained by exploiting the environment—to run lobbying and publicity campaigns to obtain laws that allow further exploitation of the environment. The vicious circle is complete.

INTEREST GROUPS AND PRESSURE TACTICS

Lobbying by corporations is, however, not the only kind of influence process that goes on in the political arena. Social scientists have lately given much attention to a spectrum of interest groups that are working throughout the political process. William A. Gamson made the following comment about the rising interest in pressure groups and interest groups as subjects for sociological investigation.

Under the influence of Harold Lasswell and Arthur Bentley among others, political scientists broke out of the sterility of treating politics as the study of formal governmental institutions. The alternative they proposed focused on the political process and assumed that "of the vast variety of activity involved in political situations, that of the persons within the governmental and party structure is only a manifest and small part when compared with the importance of non-governmental social groups." Thereafter, political scientists became increasingly interested in the operation of social class and ethnic ties as a basis of political activities. Interest groups and pres-

sure groups were urged as the primary units of political analysis rather than formal governmental structures. . . . The chief vehicles for the expression of group interest are political parties and pressure groups. . . . The study of politics in this view, becomes the study of influence and conflict among such groups with some attention to the functions of government as a broker and referee. In other words, it is important to study how any government manages and regulates conflict, but the "principal driving forces in politics are class interests and group interests; they make themselves felt regardless of the kind of government or social organization that exists. . . ." (Gamson, 1970, pp. 3–4)

Our focus in this section, then, will be on the *influence* process, by which people try to get decisions made for their benefit.

AUTHORITIES AND PARTISANS

In order to understand the dynamics by which groups influence decisions it is very helpful to examine the work of William A. Gamson, the author of *Power and Discontent* (1970), and on whose work much of this section is based. Gamson divides the world into two types of political actors: *authorities* and *partisans.* Authorities are people who hold power and have been vested with the right to make decisions for the society. Usually these are government officials, but the theory also applies to officials within an organization. Partisans, on the other hand, are people who do not have the right to decide, but who nevertheless want to influence decisions so that their concerns are protected. The distinction between partisans and authorities gets blurred sometimes because the two groups frequently overlap, but nevertheless the distinction is useful for clarifying political processes.

One way of understanding partisan groups is to look at their *organization.* Starting with an individual as the most simple case, partisan groups become increasingly complex as they organize to attack greater goals. Four types of partisan organization levels are frequently noted.

1. *Individual partisans.* Individuals who try to obtain the preferred decisions.
2. *Interest groups.* Collections of individuals who share a common desire for a particular kind of decision.
3. *Social movements.* Large bodies of people who press for change, usually composed of several interest groups.
4. *Political parties.* An even larger assembly of interest groups and social movements that try to take over the decision-making power by controlling the government.

These are not four clean categories, but the distinction is not that critical, for the basic *influence processes* are about the same, regardless of which partisan group influences decisions.

Influence processes are the activities that partisans undertake to obtain favorable decisions from authorities on issues that are critical to the partisans. Figure 8.3 outlines four steps in the influence process. Step One shows the two groups involved—authorities and partisans. Step Two shows the *goals* that partisans have when they make influence attempts. Step Three outlines the *tactics* of both authorities and partisans. The authorities use tactics for social control, to resist the

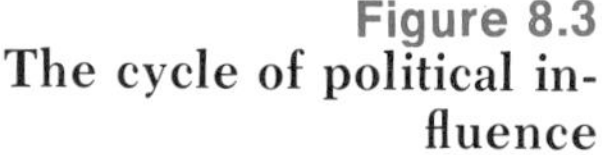

Figure 8.3
The cycle of political influence

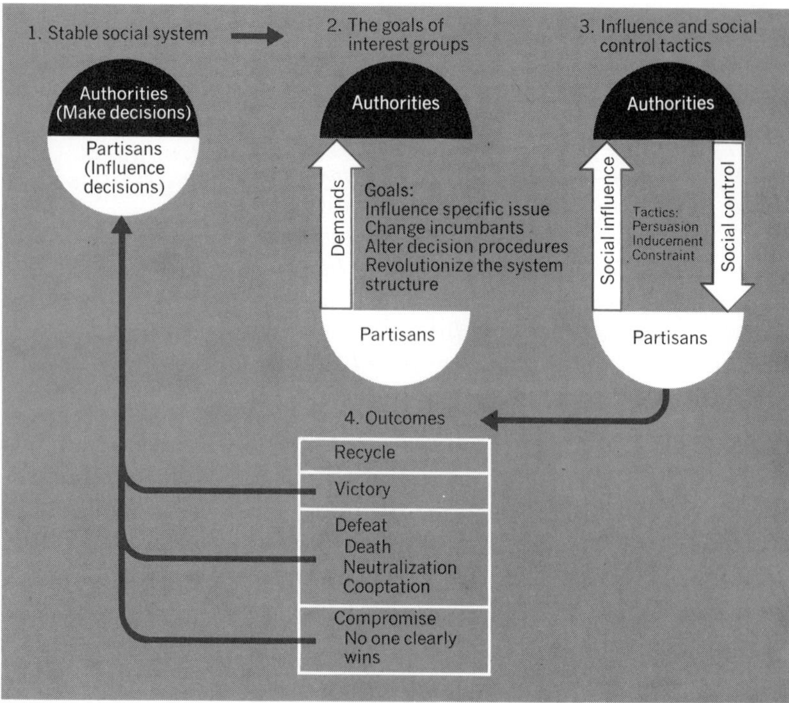

partisans' advances and to keep them in line. The partisans use tactics for social influence to force the authorities to make the favorable decisions. Step Four specifies the *outcomes* that are likely: victory, defeat, or compromise. The next few sections will expand on these four steps.

GOALS OF PARTISANS

The goals of partisans range from fighting for or against busing in schools, to demanding rights for women, to working for civil rights, to ending wars. Every interest group has its own unique goals, and it would be impossible to catalog them all. Gamson suggests that there are at least four broad categories of goals, each one more comprehensive than the last.

Specific Issues. An interest group's first demand is that the authorities change the policy on some concrete issue, such as fluoridation of the water supply or integration of schools. If the partisans win their demands at this level they may either end their influence activities (if they are relatively well satisfied with their general station in life) or move on to some new issue (if they have more generalized discontent). Wealthy or middle-class groups are most likely to quit once they have won the single battle, whereas the poor and minority groups, facing general life problems not solved by a single victory, are likely to pick a new issue and escalate their demands.

Changes in Incumbents. On the other hand, if the interest group *fails* to achieve its goals on the specific issue, it will try to oust the decision makers and replace them with more sympathetic officials. Frequently, for example, interest groups pressuring a local school board simply will not accept an unfavorable decision by the board. Instead they will mount a recall election or work to throw out the board members at the next election. "By golly," the sentiment goes, "if you won't decide things the way we want we'll just throw you out on the street."

Changes in Decision Process. If the partisans lose on both counts—if decisions go against them, and they cannot get the officials out—then they are likely to insist that the system is stacked against them. In this situation they will want a completely different *procedure.* For example, if the local zoning board has approved a new high-rise apartment building in a neighborhood, the opponents will first try to get the decision reversed or the zoning commissioners ousted. Having failed at both those options, however, they may take the case to the city council or to court, that is, they will bypass the previous method of decision making and attempt to influence a new procedure at a higher level. Appealing up the line is a method of demanding a new *decision procedure.*

Changes in Social Structure. When all else fails, partisans are likely to view the entire social system as the enemy. When blacks, Spanish-speaking Americans, welfare mothers, and American Indians find that they are ignored and discriminated against, when every "legitimate" channel is unresponsive, then they begin to suspect that the whole society is rigged against them, that the entire class structure is arranged so they remain on the bottom. Under such circumstances talk of revolution is almost inevitable, for how else can their goals be achieved if the normal influence channels are deaf to their pleas?

This process of increasing demands—called "goal escalation"—occurs in city politics, state politics, and at the national level, and is a practice common to all interest groups who have serious goals at stake, goals that are vital to their interests and worth fighting to win. Let us shift now from the topic of interest-group goals to the topic of *tactics.* What does a group do in order to reach its goals?

INFLUENCE TACTICS

Although partisans use a wide variety of tactics to influence authorities, Gamson suggests that there are three basic types of influence tactics open to a partisan group: persuasion, inducements, and constraint.

Persuasion is a nonviolent approach that uses logic, intellectual appeals, and moral concerns to sway the decision makers. This is usually a partisan group's first move, for it is the least costly tactic and is not likely to make the authorities fight back. The civil rights movement based its earlier requests for social change on arguments about social justice, Christian morality, and human rights; the early feminists waged a verbal war against injustice to women, primarily on the basis of moral claims and intellectual persuasion; and the ecology movement today is based primarily on ethical and

Partisan goals vary: French workers in 1936 call for disarmament—just before war once more engulfs them!

logical appeals to the general public and to specific officials. The idea behind persuasion is that the authorities should do as the partisans want because it is right, moral and just.

If the persuasion tactic does not work, however, the partisans have another influence weapon: *inducement.* Essentially inducements are some type of payoff from the partisans to the authorities. Usually these are perfectly legal, such as help in a political campaign, money contributed to a campaign fund, or public support for some official. Of course, inducements can also be under-the-table payoffs or bribes. Inducements, then, are a way of paying for help.

The third major type of influence tactic is *constraint.* Constraint is a violent tactic used by groups who are alienated and frustrated and who have usually exhausted all other alternatives. Constraints may be direct violence: attack, burning and bombing, outright war. Or constraints may be indirect coercion: sit-ins, passive resistance, nonviolent protests, strikes. There certainly have been many violent influence attempts throughout history. Revolutions, riots, murders, and assassinations are the more vivid examples, from the great historical revolutions to the assassinations that have plagued modern America. Nonviolent coercion is also a common practice. Gandhi, Martin Luther King, Susan B. Anthony, and Cesar Chavez all led nonviolent protests at some point in their struggles. In effect, constraint threatens disruption of some sort.

Suppose a partisan group has been using mild tactics to influence decisions, but continues to get no results. If they constantly lose, the people affected by the decision are likely to up the ante in tactical terms, moving from the nonviolent stages of persuasion and inducement to the violent phase of constraint. As goals and tactics increase, however, so do the costs. The major points about these "tactical escalations" are:

1. Moving from persuasion, to inducement, to constraints represents *an upward scale of force and violence.* It is more forceful at each stage, but this does not necessarily mean it is more effective.

2. Escalating tactics is not necessarily more effective because with every move up the scale toward constraint the *cost* of applying the influence tactic goes up. Authorities may not give in easily; they are especially likely to fight back when coercion is used against them. Remember, the authorities have methods of resisting, too, such as police power.

3. Groups that are more *alienated and frustrated are likely to use constraints and violence,* whereas groups that are satisfied and relatively confident in the authorities are more likely to use persuasion or inducements.

SOCIAL CONTROL AND INFLUENCE OUTCOMES

Up to this point we have been discussing the goals and tactics of partisans as they influence decisions. We must not forget, however, that the authorities are making countermoves, for they have a number of *social control* possibilities.

The authorities could, of course, simply accept the demands of the partisans and reshape social policy accordingly. However, there are a number of resistance factors that make giving in difficult. First, there is the natural inertia that comes with tradition, and it does take trouble and high cost in money and manpower to make changes. In addition, the authorities themselves may be part of the elite who would be hurt by partisan demands, or they may be personally conservative and opposed to change.

Even if they favor the changes, however, the authorities are likely to be caught in *cross pressures.* Meeting the demands of one partisan group may bring the wrath of another power bloc down on their heads. Authorities are never entirely free to decide issues as they please, especially if they are elected officials and their constituencies oppose change. The controversy over busing to achieve racial balance in the schools is an excellent example of the dynamics of cross pressures, for while the courts and the Office of Education pushed for more busing there were enormous cross pressures from local communities demanding that these policies be reversed.

Should the authorities decide that they cannot meet the partisan demands they have an arsenal of weapons similar to those of the partisans, but different in certain critical details. Authorities, too, can use *persuasion, inducements,* and *constraint.* In fact, they are likely to match the influence tactics used against them. For example, if partisans primarily use persuasion then the authorities will generally respond with persuasion, appeals to reason, propaganda, and calls for cooperation in "gradual change." If the partisans escalate tactics, attacking with coercive violence or nonviolent passive resistance, the authorities are likely to respond in kind; police will be called,

A question of tactics. (© 1970 Jules Feiffer. Courtesy Publishers-Hall Syndicate)

arrests made, students expelled, and underground leaders flushed out and even killed. Of course, the authorities may sometimes *start* the violence cycle; it is not only the partisans who escalate.

In fact, as the encounter goes on both the partisans and the authorities get into a vicious circle, each one raising the tactical level until sharp crisis becomes almost inevitable. The history of social conflict often displays this vicious circle of escalating tactics. The civil rights movement, the student peace movement, and the French and Russian revolutions all share the common characteristic that they started with tactics based on persuasion and inducement. When change did not come, however, the conflict gradually escalated into violent struggle.

Although dramatic, violent conflicts attract the most attention, generally the interaction between partisans and authorities never reaches that stage. The *outcome* of an influence attempt is most likely to be compromise and some commitment to gradual change. Usually the partisans cannot get as much as they want, and usually the authorities have to change more than they would have liked.

There are rare situations, however, where compromise is impossible because the authorities refuse to respond or because the partisans increase their demands after each favorable response. In such cases *power* determines who will win. If the partisans can muster enough public support, money, and manpower, they can force the authorities to meet their demands. The authorities, however, almost always have the overwhelming advantage because they control the armed forces of the society. Consequently, most

Social control in action: Demonstrators confront riot police.

extreme cases of violent conflict between partisans and authorities are won by the authorities. It is for that reason that successful social movements and revolutions—special types of partisan groups—are so rare.

PARTISAN INFLUENCE ACTIVITIES: SUMMARY

Let us draw together some of the threads about partisan groups and influence tactics. Influence on political decision making by partisan interest groups is a critical part of the political process. It would be folly to concentrate entirely on the formal structure of government, on the legislatures, the courts, and the executive bureaucracies, for these formal processes are only part of the story of political decision making. The section above outlined the "cycle of influence" by which partisan groups try to influence decisions. Some of the more critical points are:

1. Every political system may be divided into two parts: the *authorities* who make binding decisions and the *partisans* who influence those decisions.

2. Partisans have a number of political *goals* that they want to press on the authorities. Usually their goal is to obtain a favorable decision on some specific issue. If they are not able to win on the issue, however, they may escalate their goals to include changing the incumbents, changing the decision procedures, or changing the political structure.

3. Partisan groups may use a number of *tactics* that fall generally into three categories: persuasion, inducements, and constraints.

4. Groups that are highly alienated from the political process are more likely to use constraint tactics, whereas groups that are basically satisfied with their social circumstances are more likely to use persuasion or inducement tactics.

5. Authorities respond to social influence attempts by using *social-control* tactics, which are similar to partisan influence tactics: persuasion, inducements, and constraints.

6. The *outcome* of an influence cycle may be a clear win for the partisans, but it is more likely that compromises will be made, and the partisans will rarely achieve all of their goals. Thus the stage is set for the partisan groups to attempt once more to influence the authorities.

In the next section we will examine one more important influence procedure by which partisans influence authorities in democratic societies—voting.

VOTING BEHAVIOR IN A DEMOCRACY

Because voting is such a critical method of influencing political processes, political sociologists and political scientists have studied voting behavior extensively, primarily through public-opinion polls and analysis of election results. In an effective democracy the election is the court of last resort. Although pressure tactics and other covert practices undoubtedly affect political decisions constantly—as we have shown earlier in this chapter—it is nevertheless true that the voters hold power at the ballot box. The election is always a crucial political cut-

(© 1970 Jules Feiffer. Courtesy Publishers-Hall Syndicate)

Many nonvoters feel frustrated—with good reason!

ting point, since the battles lost and won with the ballot affect all the other political processes. Sociologists and political scientists have learned much about voter behavior and its relation to religion, social class, occupation, education, and a host of other social factors. The following sections list a few summary points.

VOTER APATHY AS A SOCIAL PROBLEM

One of the basic assumptions of a democracy is that everyone should vote, thus insuring the "will of the people." However, it is a fact that for most elections most people stay home. Only in national presidential elections do more than half the people turn out. The national elections usually average about two thirds of the eligible voters; local and state contests not tied to a national election usually attract only about a one third vote. Does this kind of apathy indicate a sick democracy?

In most ways the answer has to be Yes, for low turnout certainly indicates that many people are not having any influence on the political process. Studies of nonvoters indicate that they are likely to be uninformed, uninterested, and alienated from the political process because they feel ineffective: "Whether I vote or not won't matter, the same power groups will run the society anyway." Indifference, ineffectiveness, and lack of information seem to be most characteristic of lower classes and poorly educated groups, and public opinion polls show that the nonvoter is likely to be younger, in a low income bracket, and have little education. Feelings of political ineffectiveness and apathy are probably reason-

Figure 8.4
Characteristics of Voters and Nonvoters

High Probability of Voting	Median Probability of Voting	Low Probability of Voting
Income $10,000+	Income $3-10,000	Income $3000-
Professionals Businessmen	Skilled workers White collar workers Farmers	Manual workers
College educated	High-school educated	Grade-school educated
Live in metropolitan areas or live in very small towns	Live in towns or small cities	
Jews	Protestants or Catholics	
Easterners and westerners	Midwesterners	Southerners
Those over 50 years of age	Middle-aged persons	Young persons (under 30)
Republicans	Democrats	
Whites	Whites	Nonwhites
Old residents of a community		New residents of a community

Source: Gallup Opinion Index, November 1970, No. 65.

able attitudes for minorities and the poor, because they have seen their hopes dashed all too often, their influence attempts frequently ignored, and their interests systematically undermined by other power groups that dominate the political process. To be indifferent and apathetic are realistic attitudes for people in the lower strata of the society, and it is no wonder that they choose to opt out of a political system that fails to meet their needs. Figure 8.4 summarizes the findings of one study of voters and nonvoters. The data indicate that one segment of the

Lower social classes and minorities often fail to vote because they do not have proper information, because they feel so defeated that they opt out, or often because they have been denied the right by discriminatory laws. For the older Chicanos who could not read, the Raza Unida party in Crystal City, Texas composed sample ballots showing which boxes to mark.

population, an underprivileged segment that badly needs to exert its influence in its own interests, is virtually unrepresented in the political process.

Some observers suggest, however, that apathy may not be as bad as it seems, for two reasons. First, apathy may imply that there is a *basic consensus* among the various groups of the society, that they generally feel the government is responding to their needs and it is, therefore, unnecessary to vote. Second, the characteristics of some nonvoters tend to be rather authoritarian: (1) they tend to prefer authoritarian, strong-man solutions for social problems; (2) they tend to be intolerant of political views other than their own; (3) they often show strong racial prejudices; and (4) they often oppose progressive public measures such as fluoridation and school bonds. (See Greer and Orleans, 1962, for a review of the literature on characteristics of nonvoters.) In fact, when larger voter turnouts draw in people who are usually apathetic, it is generally a sign of intense community conflict over some issue such as school integration or fluoridation. The typical reaction of the previously inactive voters is to oppose social change.

From the above discussion it is obvious that the effect of voter apathy on the democratic process is quite complex. On one hand, it might be argued that nonvoters would be more likely to hamper the democratic process than strengthen it

INSERT **8.II**

VOTER CHARACTERISTICS: A SELF-TEST

TRUE-FALSE

1. Poor people are very likely to vote.
2. Persons in metropolitan areas are less likely to vote than farmers.
3. Republicans vote more regularly than Democrats.
4. Protestants vote more often than either Catholics or Jews.
5. Young people are more likely to vote than people over the age of 55.
6. Westerners vote more often than Midwesterners.
7. Southerners are about as likely to vote as Easterners.
8. Nonwhites are more likely to vote than whites.
9. Businessmen vote more frequently than farmers.
10. Those persons with college educations are very likely to vote.

MULTIPLE CHOICE

1. The group most likely to vote among these is:
   a. Catholics
   b. Jews
   c. Protestants
   d. Blacks

if they participated in elections. On the other hand nonvoters are also likely to be in the lower classes, or among the oppressed minorities of society who desperately need to be politically effective. Excluding them from the political process is likely to allow politicians to ignore them, thus reinforcing their social position and making them politically impotent, thus increasing their apathy. Consequently, the nonvoter and his plight constitute one of the major dilemmas of a democratic society.

SOCIAL CHARACTERISTICS AND PARTY AFFILIATION: A PROFILE OF VOTERS

We have been discussing the characteristics of nonvoters, but what about the voters? Before you read this section stop for a moment and take the quiz in Insert 8.II to indicate how much you know at this point about voters. The answers are given on p. 289, but read the text and study Figure 8.4 before you look; see if you would change any of your answers after reading the text, then look at the answers.

2. A region of the country with higher voter turnout is:
   a. The South
   b. The Midwest
   c. The West
   d. None of these
3. The persons least likely to vote are:
   a. High school graduates who did not finish college
   b. Democrats
   c. New community residents
   d. Small town residents
4. The occupational group least likely to vote is:
   a. Manual workers
   b. Farmers
   c. Businessmen
   d. Professionals
5. The person most likely to vote would be:
   a. White, Protestant, and a farmer
   b. Black, democratic, and under 30
   c. Jewish, 50 years old, living in New York
   d. Midwestern, middle-aged, living in a small city

Answers to true-false

1-F, 2-F, 3-T, 4-F, 5-F, 6-T, 7-F, 8-F, 9-T, 10-T

Answers to multiple choice

1-b, 2-c, 3-c, 4-a, 5-c

Studying voter characteristics has been a favorite game of political scientists and sociologists for a long time. Research indicates that social factors such as social class and religion are closely related to how a person votes. In all democratic nations, for example, there are political parties that represent the "working man" and others that represent the "upper classes," with political affiliations fairly sharply divided along social class lines. Religion, too, is an important feature in determining political behavior, with Catholics usually voting differently from Protestants, depending on the unique situations in each nation. Figure 8.5 summarizes many of these studies, with various social groups placed along a continuum from political "left" to "right." The political labels "left" and "right" derive from seating patterns in the French Assembly, where liberals and socialists sit on the left and conservatives sit on the right. Figure 8.5 is important and should be studied closely because it contains much information.

Figure 8.5
Characteristics of voters: left to right political continuum

Political Label	"Left"	"Moderate"		"Right"
Political stance	Revolutionaries	Social reformers	Conservatives	Reactionaries
Political parties	Weathermen Progressive Party Communist Party Socialist Party Peace and Freedom Party	Democratic Party	Republican Party American Independent Party (George Wallace's Party)	Minutemen John Birch Society
Goals of parties	Drastic social changes, revolution	Moderately progressive social reform	*Status quo* Protect privileges of upper classes	Turn back the clock Deny civil rights Increase privileges of upper social groups
Examples of party goals	Sharp redistribution of wealth, oppose military. Extreme form: overthrow government and set up radical democracy	Welfare expansion, Greater Civil Rights, Reform political process, Prounion	"Law and order" Subsidies to industry, Anti-union, Pro-big business	Subsidies to industry, oppose welfare and civil rights laws, expand the military. Extreme form: overthrow government and set up dictatorship
Social groups affiliated with these parties	Intellectuals Radical students	Manual workers Poor Union members	Farmers	Businessmen Doctors
Social class affiliated with parties	Lower-classes Some upper middle class intellectuals		Middle classes	Upper classes
Religious groups affiliated with parties	Jewish	Catholic Baptist	Most Protestants Methodist	Episcopal Congregational

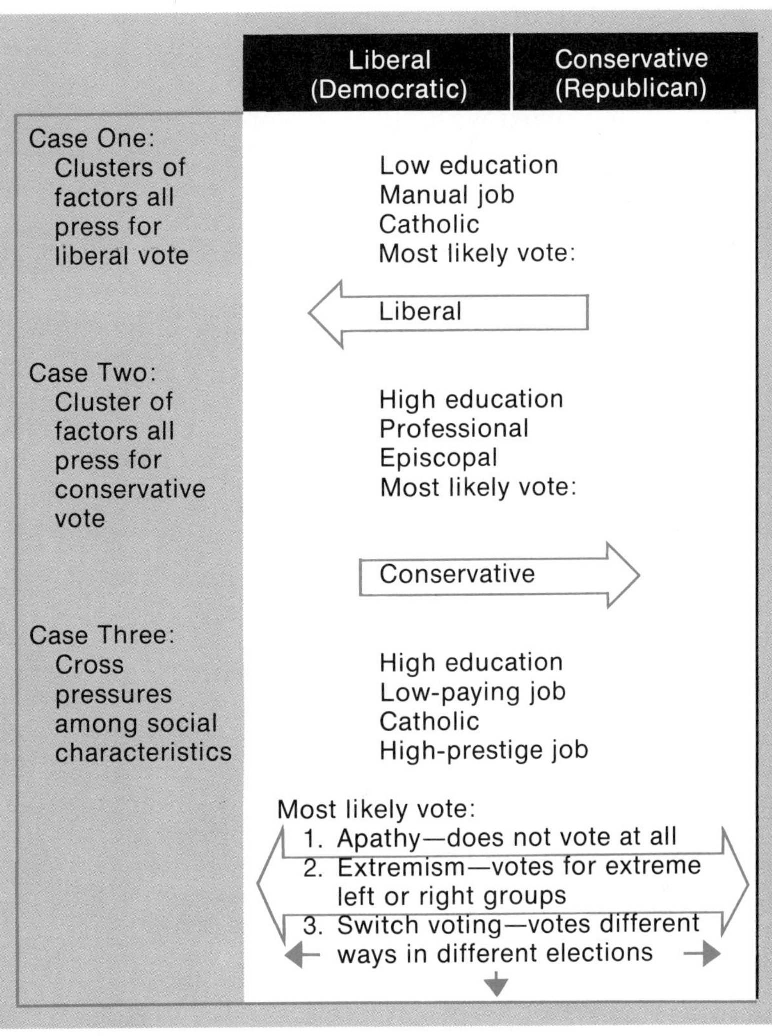

Figure 8.6 Cross pressures and voting. The typical voter's characteristics tend to *cluster*, so that most of his social relations push him in one direction—toward either a "liberal" or a "conservative" political position. Sometimes, however, a person's social characteristics pull in opposite directions, resulting in "cross pressures." Such a voter is likely to display unusual voter behavior

Several words of warning should be offered about Figure 8.5 First, the "left-right" continuum is very hard to draw in many nations because conservatives and liberals sometimes work together; moderate groups, in particular, may shift left or right depending on the issue. Second, by no means *all* the people in a given social group vote the same way; most workers vote Democratic in the United States, but a sizable group always goes Republican; most businessmen vote Republican, but many vote Democratic. There are many factors that make for individual differences. It should never be assumed that because *most* people in a group vote in a particular way that the group is a monolithic bloc with no variations.

CROSS PRESSURES AND VOTING

Most of the time social characteristics tend to cluster. For example, a person who has little education and a manual job will also tend to have low income and a fundamentalistic religion—all of which tend to be associated with "liberal" voting. Or he might have the opposite cluster—high education, professional job, and high income—pressuring him toward a "conservative" position. Sometimes, however, a person has contradictory social characteristics. He may have a high-prestige job, and high education but relatively low pay (the college professor) or he may have high pay but low education (successful used-car salesman).

What happens when such unusual combinations occur? Typically such people experience strong inner conflicts, for they cannot decide which way to vote. The three possible results are (1) *apathy*—simply do not vote, (2) *extremism*—vote for extremist left- or right-wing groups who promise to upset the current social order, and hopefully establish a new society in which the current cross pressures are eliminated, or (3) *switch voting*—change parties often, and remain relatively detached from party allegiences.

The concept of cross pressures has been used to explain a number of "strange" voting patterns, including college professors who tend to vote liberal when their social position would dictate conservative, rich Jewish merchants who vote liberal when their business connections would press toward conservative, and "new rich" families whose wealth dictates conservative but who vote liberal because they have not achieved enough social prestige. The problem with the cross-pressure concept is that it is seldom adequate to predict precisely which option a person will take; will he not vote, or vote extremist, or switch votes? It is difficult to predict in advance, but at least the cross-pressure idea helps explain odd voting patterns once they are discovered. Figure 8.6 shows the concept of cross pressure in graphic form.

SUMMARY

The state is now the dominant social institution in modern society. This has not always been the case, for in less complex and less industrialized societies the state's role was relatively limited. In contemporary industrialized societies, however, the state has loomed ever larger, dominating the society more and more—much more so than the family, the church, the educational institutions, or even the economic system.

Who is served by the political process? Many sociologists suggest that there is a power elite composed of corporation heads, government officials, and military chiefs who dominate most of the national decision making. There is much persuasive evidence that the power-elite theory is true in many respects. The interlocking relationships among the government, the military, and the corporations suggest that a community of common interests prevails among the elites. In addition, only a handful of gigantic corporations control most of the wealth and most of the political influence in the corporate world, and they have major impact on political decisions through lobbying, advertising, and placement of industry officials in government positions.

On the other hand, however, there are a number of political scientists who argue that decision making is best described by a "pluralistic" theory. According to the pluralistic model, competing interest groups balance each other's power to the point that they become "veto groups," capable of stopping action but rarely able to force their own purposes on the political decision makers. Although the pluralistic theory has some merit, it does not seem as accurate as the power-elite theory.

Informal interest group activities are an extremely important aspect of the political process. Authorities in the formal government system are constantly pressured by informal partisan influence. Partisans have a wide variety of goals, and use many different tactics. Authorities, too, can use a variety of tactical defenses in their social control attempts. The outcome of influence attempts is usually a compromise, for partisans rarely get all they desired.

One specific type of partisan activity is voting, an area of great concern for social scientists who study democratic nations. Studies of voter apathy, the failure to vote, show a number of conclusions. First, nonvoters are likely to be less informed about political issues and candidates, less educated, and hold more extreme viewpoints than voters. Voter apathy may be partly related to social status, since people with the above characteristics frequently belong to the lower classes. But voter apathy may also result from a general consensus that the political system is functioning fairly well. When things are going well people may not vote because they feel it unnecessary. Voter apathy may, then, indicate either that citizens are satisfied with their social conditions or that socially deprived groups are denied an opportunity to change their social conditions.

Voting behavior is related to other social characteristics

such as religion, social class, and occupation. In general, upper-class people with high incomes, high education, and high-prestige jobs tend to vote conservative, that is, Republican in the United States. On the other hand, people with lower incomes, lower-prestige jobs, and lower education tend to vote liberal, that is, Democratic in the United States. There is, however, no rigid pattern in these voting trends. Often unusual voting patterns are related to some specific issue or some specific candidate. Unusual patterns are also related to cross pressures that voters experience when their social characteristics pull them in different directions.

REFERENCES

Cannon, Lou. *Ronnie and Jesse* (New York: Doubleday, 1969).

DeTocqueville, Alexis. *Democracy in America* (New York: Alfred A. Knopf, 1945).

Fellmeth, Robert C. *Power and Land in California,* Vols. I and VIII (Washington, D. C.: Center for Study of Responsive Law, 1971).

Galbraith, John Kenneth. *The New Industrial State* (New York: Signet Books, 1968).

Gamson, William A. *Power and Discontent* (Homewood, Ill.: Irving Press, 1970).

Greer, Scott and Peter Orleans. "The Mass Society and the Parapolitical Structure," *American Sociological Review,* October 1962, pp. 634–646.

Hunter, Floyd. *Community Power Structure* (Chapel Hill: University of North Carolina Press, 1953).

Kornhauser, William. "Power Elite or Veto Groups," in Reinhard Bendix and Seymour Martin Lipset (eds.), *Class Status and Power* (New York: Free Press, 1966, pp. 120ff).

Lipset, S. M. *Political Man* (New York: Doubleday Anchor, 1963), pp. 48–67.

Mills, C. Wright. *The Power Elite* (New York: Oxford University Press, 1956).

Murdoch, George. "Feasibility and Implementation of Comparative Community Research," *American Sociological Review,* December 1950, p. 716.

Nieburg, H. L. *In the Name of Science* (Chicago: Quadrangle Books, 1966).

Polsby, Nelson W. *Community Power and Political Theory* (New Haven: Yale Press, 1963).

Presthus, Robert. *Men at the Top* (New York: Oxford University Press, 1964).

Riesman, David. *The Lonely Crowd* (New York: Doubleday, 1953).

Weber, Max. *The Theory of Social and Economic Organization,* translated by A. M. Henderson and Talcott Parsons (New York: Oxford University Press, 1947).

NINE SOCIAL MOVEMENTS AND REVOLUTION

DECLARATION OF INDEPENDENCE

Picture the scene. Here they are, the revolutionaries gathered in a room plotting the overthrow of the government. There is a police unit out looking for most of them; the governor has personally ordered his agents to put a stop to the affair; undercover agents have been watching this alienated pack of men for a long time. But until now there has not been enough concrete evidence to arrest them.

Look around the room. These are serious people; they worry a lot about the state of society. These are idealistic men; they think they can create a utopia by destroying the state. These are revolutionaries; they have turned against the establishment. These are dedicated fanatics; they have pledged to fight until their very honor, fortunes, and lives are expended for the cause.

Think about their recent actions. In the last few months this band of revolutionaries has gone on a rampage, tearing up property, holding demonstrations, shooting at the authorities, and bombing buildings. They have stored a huge arms supply, and they are secretly training men who will form the central core of an armed rebellion. They have formed a close-knit "movement" that constantly engages in harassment techniques against the police. It is no wonder that secret agents have infiltrated the movement to sabotage it.

The scene described above took place on July 4, 1776, in Philadelphia. The cast of radicals included Thomas Jefferson, John Adams, John Hancock, and Benjamin Franklin—revolutionaries to the man. The inflammatory document called for overthrowing the government, for war, if necessary, to upset the establishment, for ultimate commitment by the revolutionaries to their cause. The document was the Declaration of Independence; the movement culminated in the American Revolution.

This chapter is about social movements, about dedicated social groups that try to upset the normal course of society and thrust it in a new direction. In this chapter we will focus our attention on the four issues central to this book—*power, conflict, social problems,* and *change.* Social movements are one of the major forces for change in any society; they usually enter or create a situation of intense social conflict, and they are almost always closely linked to a pressing social problem. All of these elements were very

Look at them. They have gathered to make plans for the future. There are left-wing intellectuals, land owners, and businessmen in the group who think they should write a document to show their reasons for striking at the establishment. They had a committee prepare the paper, and now they are using "participatory democracy" to debate the issue. One man is going to read the revolutionary manifesto out loud, so let's listen to him.

When in the Course of human Events, it becomes necessary for one People to dissolve the Political Bands which have connected them with another, and to assume among the Powers of the Earth, the separate and equal Station to which the laws of Nature and of Nature's God entitle them, a decent Respect to the Opinions of Mankind requires that they should declare the causes which impel them to the Separation.

We hold these Truths to be self-evident, that all Men are created equal, that they are endowed by their Creator with certain unalienable Rights, that among these are Life, Liberty, and the Pursuit of Happiness—That to secure these Rights, Governments are instituted among Men, deriving their just Powers from the Consent of the Governed, that whenever any Form of Government becomes destructive of these Ends, it is the Right of the People to alter or to abolish it, and to institute new Government. . . .

much present in the American Revolution.

There are, however, many kinds of social movements. In the United States alone there are the New Left, the John Birch Society, the Klu Klux Klan, and the Youth for Christ, as well as movements centered on such issues as population control and environmental protection. Many of the great social and political changes in history resulted from a successful social movement, such as the rise and spread of Christianity, the overthrow of the Russian Czar in the 1917 revolution, and the Nazification of Germany under Hitler.

Throughout the 1960s and early 1970s there was almost unprecedented activity arising from the efforts of various social movements. And much of this activity was highly visible; television has brought to millions of viewers scenes of rioting blacks, demonstrating students, marching peace advocates, parading welfare mothers, chanting Chicano farm workers. While these forces for reform racked the nation, counterreform movements such as the John Birch Society, the Ku Klux Klan, the Minutemen, and the pro-Wallace organizations became active in order to forestall change. Counterdemonstrations, staged by construction workers, the "hard hats," highlighted the growing conflict in the American nation.

Of course, as the 1970s matured the overt violence and public upheaval cooled considerably—the student movement and the antiwar movement became dormant as the United States withdrew from Vietnam. Nevertheless major social movements have continued in more subtle form, often taking to the courts instead of the streets. The minority rights movements, the women's movement, and the ecology movement are still very much alive and active.

We have all had experience—either direct or indirect—with these movements. But in this chapter we will analyze the characteristics of social movements from a sociological perspective. We will look at their origins, organizations, tactics, and outcomes.

WHAT IS A SOCIAL MOVEMENT?

The upsurge in social protest and social movements has prompted sociologists to be more interested in this subject over the last few years than ever before. In general, previous research has been on the topic known as collective behavior, which includes studies of riots, panics, fashions, fads, and crowd behavior. Generally the sociological approach has been to do a case study of a single incidence of riot or panic, and simply to describe it, emphasizing the irrational, mob-psychology elements in it.

The current emphasis, however, has shifted to the analysis of deliberate social movements that endure for longer time periods and are overt, conscious attempts to change society. Some of the older studies of crowds and panics may have stressed the mob-psychology aspects of collective behavior, but the study of social movements stresses the role of deliberate organization, conscious leadership, and skillful use of tactics to promote social change.

A DEFINITION OF SOCIAL MOVEMENTS

A SOCIAL MOVEMENT IS A FORM OF COLLECTIVE BEHAVIOR IN WHICH A DEDICATED GROUP OF PEOPLE ORGANIZE TO PROMOTE OR TO RESIST CHANGE. THE MOVEMENT HAS DEFINITE GOALS, AN ORGANIZATION STRUCTURE, AND A CLEAR, CHANGE-ORIENTED IDEOLOGY. THE MOVEMENT CONSCIOUSLY AND PURPOSEFULLY PROMOTES THE POLICIES IT DESIRES, USUALLY THROUGH POLITICAL OR EDUCATIONAL ACTIVITIES.[1]

[1]This definition substantially agrees with the emphases of major current theories of social movements. Compare Turner and Killian (1957), Smelser (1963), Toch (1965), Blumer (1951), and McLaughlin (1969).

It will be helpful to break up this definition to understand better the four major points.

1. *A dedicated group of people.* A movement is not simply a collection of individuals, or individuals acting alone; it is an activity that demands heavy group commitment and action over a long period of time.

2. *Organized to promote or to resist change.* Sociological attention has usually focused on movements that promote change; lately there has also been concern about conservative movements that are organized specifically to resist change.

3. *Has definite goals.* In its early stages a movement may not have clear goals but, as it matures, it will focus on a few concrete goals. As a movement begins to define its goals more clearly, its organization will get tighter and its leaders stronger. Often the ideology and social program will then be written into a movement literature.

4. *Consciously and purposefully promotes change through political and educational activities.* A movement presses for or even demands social changes. It uses a variety of tactics: riots, propaganda, persuasion, voting, lawsuits, changes in laws. Most movements try to affect public opinion and public values through education and to change public policy through the political system.

CHARACTERISTICS OF SOCIAL MOVEMENTS

There have been and are today so many different social movements that meet the above criteria that it is almost impossible to make sense out of the variety. Joseph R. Gusfield described the hodge-podge of studies about social movements in these terms.

> *Historians, political scientists, and sociologists have published studies of the following phenomena: Liberalism, the American Revolution, the Chinese Revolution, the Methodist movement, Temperance, the Civil Rights movement, Populism, the Sepoy rebellion, the Taiping rebellion, the Labor movement, "cargo cults," McCarthyism, Pan-Africanism, the Peace movement, Technocracy, Messianism, Zionism, the Free Love movement, the New Right, the New Left, the Natural Childbirth movement, Surrealism, Feminism, Freudianism, Progressivism, Neorealism, and Antisdisestablishmentarianism. (Gusfield, 1970, pp. 1–2)*

And even this list is incomplete and could be expanded to include literally hundreds of others. There have been many attempts to classify social movements into different types, but there has never been agreement on a single classification. Ralph Turner and Lewis M. Killian (1957) proposed a widely used classification of social movements: *power oriented, value oriented, personal-expressive,* and *resistance.* This classification is not entirely satisfactory, since movements never fall neatly into one of the types and they change rapidly, emphasizing first one thing then another.

In the next few pages we will use the Turner-Killian ideas, but instead of forcing different social movements into one type we will say that every movement has all of these characteristics: every movement tries to gain political power, convince people of its values, provide personal enhancement for its members, and resist attacks from the outside world. However, they vary in *emphasis,* stressing some aspects more than others during different periods in their lives.

Power Orientation. Most movements try to gain some control over the key power networks in a society in order to force a change in the social system. Social movements often emerge from a long period of oppression; the goal is to capture enough control over the political processes to right the wrongs they have suffered. Sometimes movements are *reformist* or *evolutionary* in their power orientation; their followers try to promote change by legal means (lawsuits, pressure on lawmakers, voting). The National Association for the Advancement of Colored People is a good example of a movement stressing evolutionary approaches. Others are more *revolutionary;* having given up hope that the society will ever change by peaceful means, some groups resort to riots, bombings, violent demonstrations, stockpiling of illegal arms, and even outright warfare. The Irish Republican Army is an outstanding contemporary instance.

The American Revolution of 1776, the French Revolution of 1789, the Russian Revolution of 1917, and the Chinese Revolution of 1949 were all based on social movements with strong revolutionary power orientations. In contemporary America there have been scores of influential social movements with heavy stress on gaining power, including the New Left, the Chicano movement, and the student revolt. Among the strongest social movements of this type in America today is the black movement.

Value Orientation. Although movements usually have some power orientations they also work by persuasion, trying to mold public opinion about new values, norms, and belief systems. A prime task is to reeducate the society about value questions, to highlight wrongs that the society is committing, and to press for a reshaping of normative standards. The tactics for bringing about value changes are more likely to be persuasion, propaganda, education, and appeals to justice.

Of the many movements with important impact on the current American scene two stand out vividly as stressing value changes: the women's liberation movement and the ecology movement. Both groups are trying to break down traditional social attitudes and to build a new value orientation by using persuasion, education, and propaganda. Of course, the strategy is not entirely oriented to value changes; they are also interested in moving their activities to the political arena. Although they are most heavily involved in value and normative issues, if they find that change is not coming, they often switch to political action and influence tactics. That is exactly the kind of transformation that we now see, in the women's liberation movement. See Insert 9.I for discussion of an earlier movement that started with heavy emphasis on value changes but that ended up primarily stressing political power—Prohibition.

Personal-Expressive Orientation. Sometimes movements reverse their focus; instead of pressing for change in the larger society, they turn inward to change the personal lives of the members in the movement. Often the movement's individual focus is a realization that the

INSERT **9.1**

THE PROHIBITION MOVEMENT

Those who advocated the prohibition of alcohol eventually lost their battle against the "demon rum." But for several decades they held the balance of power in the United States and succeeded in having their program written into the Constitution. This was a degree of success enjoyed by very few protest movements.

Initially prohibitionists, centered in the rural North, combined temperance with religious revivalism, abolitionism, and humanitarianism. These people were suspicious of the rapid growth of industrial cities and disgusted by social and physical conditions in the new urban centers. They were also perturbed by the influx of Catholic immigrants, especially the Irish, whose boisterous, hard-drinking life-style seemed appalling. When Samuel Burchard chided the Democrats as being identified with "rum, Romanism, and rebellion," he was reflecting the feelings of many people against liquor, against Catholics, and against the South.

But the organized campaign against alcohol really began in the city of Boston around 1826. Very quickly groups such as the Sons of Temperance and the American Society for the Promotion of Temperance sprang up. At first they were not politically powerful, but they projected a very prestigious, almost aristocratic image that encouraged imitators throughout the North.

By 1840 these self-appointed reformers were beginning to have some impact. Agitation for their cause was now centered in numerous "Washington societies"—George Washington, who enjoyed his Madeira, would probably have been opposed to this use of his name. Encouraged by the success of Father Theobald Matthew in Great Britain and Ireland during the 1830s and 1840s, Neal Dow, a leading figure among the Maine prohibitionists, finally rallied enough support to make his state the first to outlaw alcohol in 1846. By 1856 13 states in the North and West had passed similar laws, but this early success was to be largely undone by the approaching Civil War.

Liquor taxes provided an important part of government revenues at the time, and the North needed money desperately to carry on the war. Concurrently the alcohol industry began intensive lobbying efforts and probably succeeded in delaying for decades the eventual prohibition of their product. Only two of the original 13 "dry" states retained their laws against alcohol up to 1920.

After the Civil War the movement began anew. In 1869 a Methodist minister, John Russel of Michigan, led a group of prohibitionists in taking control of a chapter of the Masonic Lodge, which was, not coincidentally, a Protestant, nativist organization at that time. The lodge became the forerunner of the Prohibition party by sponsoring a convention to nominate candidates. At their first convention in Chicago during September 1869, it was clear that they would have little effective political power. Nevertheless, a movement was growing. This was also the first American political convention to allow women to participate on equal terms, thus reflecting the prominence of women in the prohibition campaign.

After the Chicago convention the movement became increasingly emotional and populist, quickly losing its upper-class, aristocratic connotation. Although the health and socioeconomic costs of alcohol have always been very serious, the movement chose to emphasize more dramatic and heartrending themes. An excellent example of this rhetoric can be found in a portion of George Young's poem (written about 1900) "The Lips that Touch Liquor":

Though in silence, with slighted affection I pine,
*Yet the lips that touch liquor shall never touch mine.**

In the last analysis it was the highly political, mass-based Anti-Saloon League that carried through the successful fight to pass the prohibition amendment. James Cannon, a Methodist bishop, ran the Anti-Saloon League during its crucial years, displaying a keen sense of power politics as well as righteous indignation. Instead of backing the Prohibition party exclusively, Cannon's followers swayed their votes to any candidate who would oppose liquor. Gradually the League built strong bipartisan support for the movement and developed antiliquor factions within each party. As early as 1887 President Grover Cleveland felt compelled to issue an executive order banning liquor in the territory of Alaska. During the next administration President Benjamin Harrison banned alcohol from White House functions, thereby producing great moral support for the prohibitionists. One by one the states succumbed to pressure and outlawed alcohol. By 1920, the year the prohibition amendment passed, 33 states, covering 63 percent of the population and 95

*Incidentally, the term "teetotaler" came into usage because abstainers would write the letter "t" after their names (to signify temperance) on the membership rolls of early antialcohol societies.

percent of the nation's land area, were "dry."

Ironically, by the time victory was achieved, the rural-Protestant-nativist sentiment that had supported prohibition was beginning to lose its grip on American society. It was quickly apparent that making liquor illegal was not going to stop people from indulging. When Herbert Hoover called prohibition "a great . . . experiment, noble in motive and far-reaching in purpose," he meant just that—it was an experiment, and it failed miserably.

At first illegal liquor could easily be landed along America's long seacoasts, and during the early 1920s the schooner *Rosie* became legendary for firing whiskey-filled torpedoes to shore. Slightly later forged doctor's prescriptions became a widespread source of "medicinal" alcohol. But many people turned to denatured alcohol. Small-time "distillers" cooked out poisonous substances and added color and flavoring to produce "gin, bourbon, Scotch" or whatever was desired. When carefully executed the process worked, but countless people suffered paralysis, blindness, and even death from improperly made liquor. With these unexpected by-products of the "noble experiment" some people began to have second thoughts about prohibition.

Finally organized crime moved in on the small entrepreneurs of bootlegging. Bloody gang wars erupted over the lucrative illegal liquor market, making headlines in the newspapers and enemies for prohibition. Although the government struggled to enforce the law, there was enough profit in bootlegging to bribe almost any official. Occasionally this corruption was spotlighted, and the decay of public trust added another nail in the coffin of the prohibition movement. In 1929 a clandestine "summit conference" was held in Atlantic City, New Jersey, for the purpose of dividing markets among various elements of organized crime. This infamous meeting was attended by such notables as Al Capone, the Detroit "Purple" Gang, and most other important underworld figures who had survived the bloody 1920s. Although 1550 federal agents were arrayed against them they were simply no match for organized crime, implicitly supported by the millions of citizens who daily violated the law.

In the end the public outrage became so great that in 1933 the Twenty-First Amendment was passed to repeal the Eighteenth. After 13 years the "great . . . experiment" died, and with it died one of the most active U. S. social movements of the century.

larger society will not change and that the movement does not have the strength to force revolution; even if the society cannot be transformed, the individual's *reaction* to his circumstances can be.

Throughout history religion has been the basis for most social movements stressing personal-expressive interests. Advocates of social change have often strongly condemned the retreatist attitude of movements that ignore larger social problems and concentrate on the individual's small world. Karl Marx, for example, vigorously attacked religion as a conservative force that acted as the "opiate of the people," keeping them personally satisfied although the larger society refused to change its oppressive social system. Often movements that stress personal expression encourage the individual to endure personal adversity because he will get his reward in heaven or within himself. The movement's promise is that other people who have benefited from the social situation—the upper-class exploiters, the powerful, the rich—will be overthrown whereas the righteous, those who have borne the burdens of current social life, will be richly rewarded.

Religious revivals periodically sweep most societies, and contemporary United States is no exception. The "Youth for Christ" movement, the campus revivals, and the Billy Graham Crusades are features of American life today. Moreover, the whole "encounter" and "sensitivity" group phenomena have been widely interpreted as secular personal-expressive movements that are having a strong impact among some people.

Resistance Orientation. Although social movements generally struggle to promote change, they sometimes assume a resistance posture, working to prevent social change and to reaffirm traditional values. Movements sometimes assume resistance postures in reaction to another movement promoting change. Among the most common resistance movements in America today are the organizations fighting civil rights changes. In recent years successes of the civil rights movement have generated a cadre of opposition groups: the White Citizens Councils, the George Wallace movement, the revived KKK, and a host of antibusing organizations. Another important resistance movement is the John Birch Society, a political action group that fears the nation is becoming too liberal, even communistic.

WARNINGS ABOUT SOCIAL MOVEMENT CHARACTERISTICS

Although this classification system (see Figure 9.1 for a summary) provides a framework for distinguishing various emphases of social movements, several warnings must be made about its use. First, *social movements do not stress only one characteristic.* Instead, they vary in *emphasis,* stressing one aspect, but never completely eliminating the other aspects. For example, the women's liberation movement is primarily value oriented at this point, but some groups in the movement are certainly power oriented and seeking change through political means. Moreover, the members derive personal-expressive benefits from the movement. The same is true of almost every movement; it stresses one aspect, but

The Ku Klux Klan: A movement resisting change.

Figure 9.1
Characteristics of Social Movements. (1) Movements usually stress one aspect but may contain elements of the others. In fact, most movements have *some* of all four elements, but they concentrate on one. (2) Over time a movement may shift its emphasis

Characteristic	Major Focus	Examples of Movements Stressing This Characteristic
Power orientation	Oriented to change through political power and influence. May be *reform* oriented or *revolutionary*	New Left Chicano Movement Black Rebellion Student Revolt Nazi Party Facist Movement
Value orientation	Oriented to changes in cultural values, norms, and belief systems—usually by persuasion, propaganda, and education	Women's Liberation Ecology Movement Counterculture Peace Movement
Personal-expressive orientation	Oriented to the personal improvement of people *within* the movement instead of promoting change in the larger society	Religious Revivals Encounter and Sensitivity Groups Youth for Christ
Resistance orientation	Oriented to stopping social change instead of promoting it. A conservative reaction to rapid social change; often tried to reestablish a previous condition	John Birch Society Minutemen Ku Klux Klan Nativistic Movements McCarthyism White Citizens Councils

usually contains a mixture of the other concerns.

Second, *a movement is very likely to change over time.* For example, the Prohibition movement started out primarily focusing on personal-expressive concerns; the Women's Christian Temperance Union (WCTU), one of the major forces in the Prohibition movement, was originally dedicated to individual pledges of nondrinking among its members. Later it shifted to value changes, working on a campaign to change the public attitude toward alcohol. And finally the WCTU, along with the Methodists, the Anti-Saloon League, and other antidrinking groups, converted from public opinion and value orientations to direct political action. The antidrinking lobby in Congress spent untold sums of money and devoted thousands of man-hours to get the Eighteenth Amendment passed. Thus, over time the Prohibition movement passed through a whole series of transformations, from personal expressive concerns, to value orientations, and finally to power politics. Other movements often exhibit this step-by-step transformation.

THE LIFE CAREER OF SOCIAL MOVEMENTS

Now that we have defined social movements and have shown some of their major emphases, we can turn to another very interesting topic: how they develop, carry out their activities, and change society. Figure 9.2 shows that a social movement passes from a set of premovement conditions into an awakening stage, then gradually organizes itself in a "movement-building" phase. Finally, when it is powerful enough, it attacks the power structure, attempting to achieve its goals. Meanwhile, the power holders in the society are likely to be fighting back; they will be using social control processes to stop the movement. After an extended period of influence and counterinfluence the outcomes are decided. The movement may win its objectives, or it may be beaten. Most likely there will be some kind of compromise. (See Smelser, 1963, for a similar life-cycle of collective behavior incidents.)

Throughout the rest of the chapter we are going to look at the stages in the life of a social movement, constantly referring to the women's liberation movement as the key example. You may want to refer back to Figure 9.2 occasionally, since it outlines the items in the discussion. Although each step will be presented as if it were neatly separate from the others, in reality the phases often overlap. The point to remember is that the steps are only roughly sequential and may, in fact, be occurring simultaneously.

PREMOVEMENT SOCIAL CONDITIONS

Social movements emerge slowly and painfully, from a set of unique conditions, typically including a long period of social *discrimination and oppression* coupled with a short period of progress that generates *rising expectations.* When expectations outrun progress, a revolutionary social movement is likely to develop. Both of these factors—oppression and rising expectations—usually combine to produce a movement.

SOCIAL OPPRESSION PROMOTES SOCIAL MOVEMENTS

Workers of the world unite! All you have to lose are your chains! With these words Karl Marx and Frederic Engels called the workers of the world to join the social revolution against capitalist society. They were essentially proclaiming a theory about the origins of social movements; the conditions are so bad, the chains are so heavy, that there is nothing to lose by

Figure 9.2
The life-career of social movements

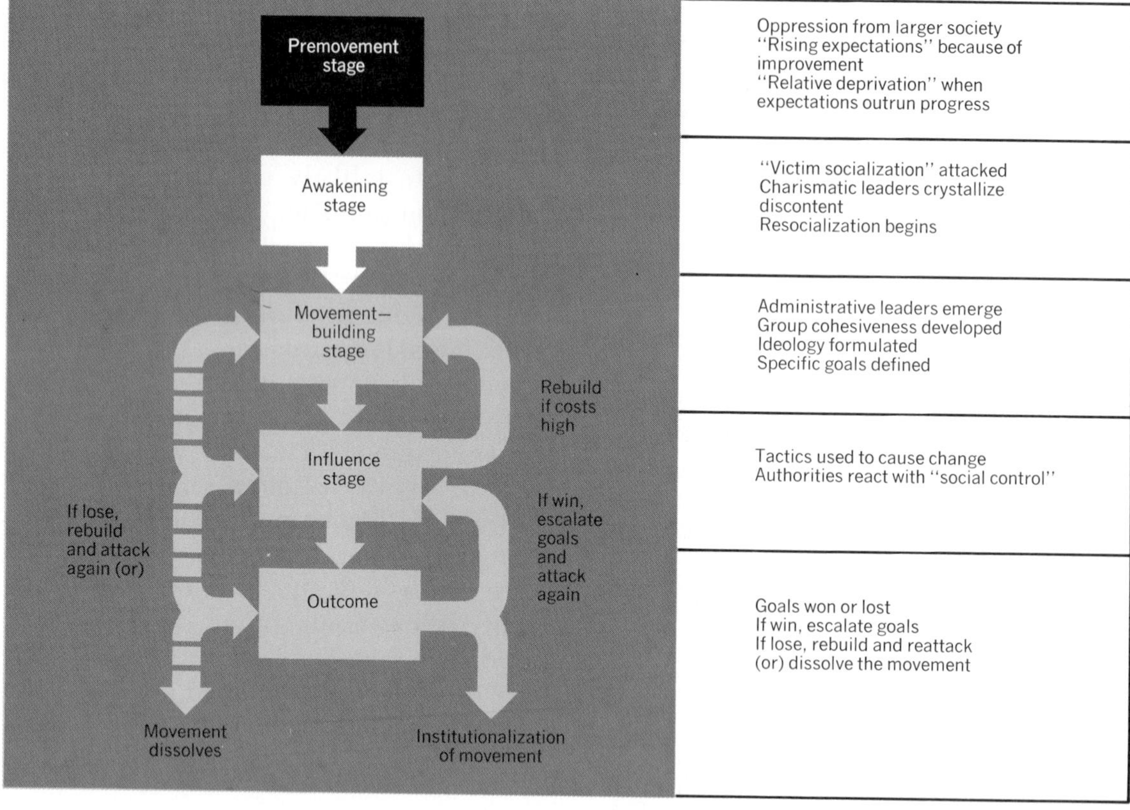

joining a revolutionary social movement. Through the centuries social theorists, activists, and historians have pointed to the social conditions that precede social movements: poverty, class divisions, racial hatred, clashes over power.

Social groups can be oppressed in many different ways. Job discrimination is clearly one of the most important, for the economic success of any group influences its opportunities in almost every other area of life. Education, housing, material goods, health, and even life expectancy itself are usually limited for oppressed groups. Political impotency is another crucial element of oppression, for without real political power, without effective influence over decision-making, a group is helpless before the demands of those with power. In short, the whole intermeshed fabric of life is woven differently for oppressed groups. In some settings, the very existence of some oppressed groups is threatened by genocide, the process of killing off an entire race. Genocide is rare but not unknown, as vividly shown by the Nazi attacks on the Jews and the white man's attacks on the

Genocide: Social oppression in its worst form. Our popular folklore pictures the brave U.S. Cavalry rushing to aid the defenseless settlers from savage redmen. In actuality our social policy toward the Indians was one of systematic genocide, the killing off of a whole race. We were much more effective than the Germans were with the Jews. It is estimated that about 80% of the native Americans were killed, either in fighting, by white man's imported diseases, or by the hardships of relocation into "reservations"—the wastelands where they were for all practical purposes condemned to death.

American Indian. This kind of oppression and degradation breeds social upheaval, social movements, and revolutions.

The anticolonialist movement since World War II is a specific instance of a movement bred by oppression. After centuries of European domination the colonial nations of Africa and Asia threw off the yokes of European control—just as the American colonies had done two centuries earlier. In each case there was a strong power-oriented movement that fought against the Europeans, the most famous of which was probably Mahatma Ghandi's anti-British movement that led to Indian independence in 1949. Certainly the drastic upheaval that has occurred over civil rights in the United States grew out of centuries of oppression. The story of black oppression in America is now common knowledge, and the impressive civil rights and black power movements that swept the nation over the last few years clearly have their roots deep in the soil of human misery and social discrimination. Women, too, have faced serious discrimination, and a revitalized women's liberation movement is pressuring for social change.

RISING EXPECTATIONS PROMOTE SOCIAL MOVEMENTS

Although the classic explanation of the origin of social movements follows Marx in stressing oppression, there is an alternative explanation that suggests pressure for change occurs only *after* a group has started making progress and conditions are improving. According to this argument social groups at the very bottom rarely revolt because they are too busy staying alive; they are eking out their lives with barely enough energy for daily existence, much less social revolution. It is only when conditions are getting better, when the daily round of mere survival is broken, when people's hopes and aspirations start rising, that powerful social movements grow.

According to this analysis, it is the *gap between expectations and reality* that is critical in promoting revolutionary activity, not the absolute level of oppression itself. When things are at their worst people expect little, but when things begin to improve the expectations and hopes may run ahead of reality, producing intense frustration. Alex de Tocqueville, the French social theorist of the nineteenth century, offers this comment about improving conditions as they affected the French Revolution.

So, it would appear that the French found their condition the more unsupportable in proportion to its improvement. . . . Revolutions are not always brought about by a gradual decline from bad to worse. Nations that have endured patiently and almost unconsciously the most overwhelming oppression often burst into rebellion against the yoke the moment it begins to grow lighter. The regime which is destroyed by a revolution is almost always an improvement on its immediate predecessor. . . . Evils which are patiently endured when they seem inevitable become intolerable when once the idea of escape from them is suggested. (de Tocqueville, as quoted in Davies, 1962)

James C. Davies adds to these ideas in the following proposition: *"Revolutions are most likely to occur when a prolonged period of objective economic and social development is followed by a short period of sharp reversal"* (Davies, 1962, p. 6). What de Tocqueville and Davies say about large-scale political revolutions also holds true about social movements, even when they do not reach the revolution stage. In Figure 9.3 Davies graphically shows how aspirations which grow faster than objective progress can lead to social unrest. The French Revolution, the Russian Revolution of 1917, the black rebellions in contemporary America, and the women's liberation efforts are clear cases of revolutions and social movements promoted because aspirations and expectations outran real improvements.

In the following sections we will examine the women's liberation movement as an example of the general dynamics of social movements.

DISCRIMINATION AGAINST WOMEN IN MODERN SOCIETY

In the beginning God created the heaven and the earth. . . . And God said, "Let us make man in our image, after our likeness; and let them have dominion over the fish of the sea, and over the fowl of the air, and over the cattle, and over all the earth." . . . And the rib, which the Lord God had taken from man, made he a woman and brought her unto the man. . . . And the Lord God said unto the woman, "What is this that thou has done?" And the woman said, "The serpent beguiled me, and I did eat." . . . Unto the woman He said, "I will greatly multiply thy sorrow and thy conception; in sorrow thou shalt bring forth children; and thy desire shall be to thy husband, and he shall rule over thee." (Abridged from Genesis 1, 2, 3)

Today few serious theologians argue for a literal interpretation of the biblical story of creation, but the attitude expressed in the passage above—that woman is subservient to, weaker than, man—has been accepted for most of recorded time. With minor exceptions the history of mankind has been the history of male supremacy, male dominance of the social system. No caste or racial discrimination has ever had the pervasive, enduring character of sex discrimination. Kate Millett, the literary critic and women's liberation advocate, calls the historical dominance of males *sexual politics*.

In introducing the term "sexual politics," one must first answer the inevitable question "Can the relationship between the sexes be viewed in a political light at all?" The answer depends on how one defines politics. This essay does not define the political as that relatively narrow and exclusive world of meetings, chairmen, and parties. The term "politics" shall refer to power-structured relationships, arrangements whereby one group of persons is controlled by another. . . . The word "politics" is enlisted here when speaking of the sexes primarily because such a word is eminently useful in outlining the real nature of their relative status, historically and at the present. . . . In America, recent events have forced us to acknowledge at last that the relationship between the races is indeed a political one which involves the general control of one collectivity, defined by birth, over another collectivity, also defined by birth. Groups who rule by birthright are fast disappearing, yet there remains one ancient and universal scheme for the domination of one birth group by another—the scheme that prevails in the area of sex. . . . What goes largely unexamined, often even unacknowledged (yet is institutionalized nonetheless) in our social order, is the birthright priority whereby males rule females. Through this system a most ingenious form of "interior colonization" has been achieved. . . . This is so because our society, like all other historical civilizations, is a patriarchy. (Millett, 1970, from p. 23, 24, and 25)

Sexual politics, then, refers to the dominance of men over women in almost every area of life: occupational, financial, legal, educational, political. Discrimination against women in a male-dominated society is certainly not new, but it is being attacked today more than at any

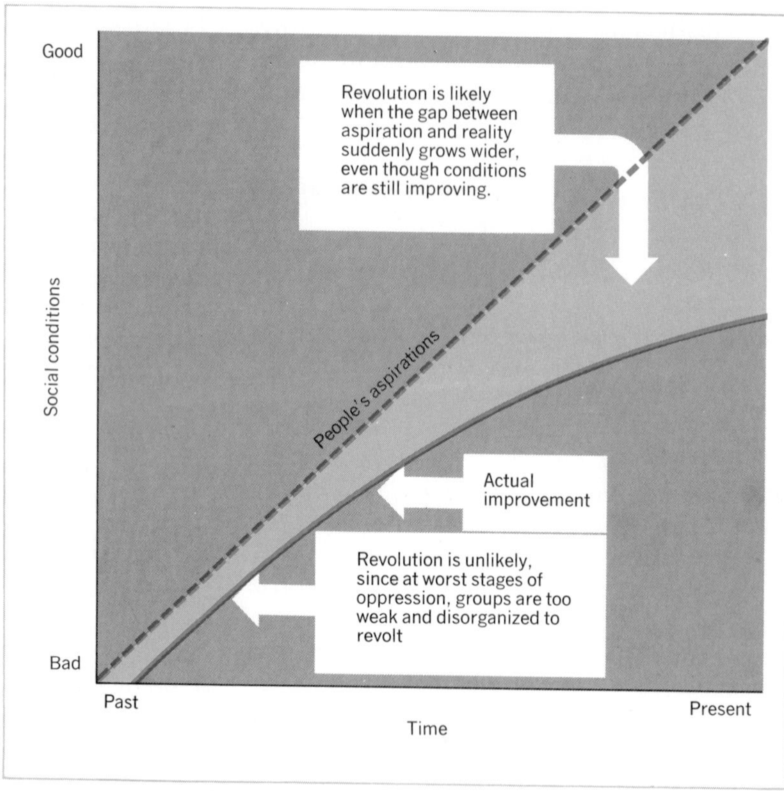

Figure 9.3
When aspirations outrun real progress, social unrest is likely

Source: Revised from James C. Davies, "Toward a Theory of Revolution," *American Sociological Review, XXVII,* 1962, p. 7.

other point in history. We seem to be standing on the edge of a number of social movements demanding equality in the world—the poor, minority groups, homosexuals, native Americans, and certainly women.

Women face serious discrimination and have their life opportunities sharply restricted by the social prejudices and unconscious sexism that pervades the social system. It is important to keep this pattern of discrimination in mind because it is the key to the rising consciousness and the political activism that now characterizes the growing women's movement. If social discrimination causes social movements—and that is the thesis of this chapter—then it is almost inevitable that women will organize to force changes in the society.

However, as we have said earlier, social discrimination alone usually does not produce a social movement, since *a steady improvement in conditions* is usually needed to promote a movement. Women are probably better off now than they have ever been in modern history, but the conditions have not improved fast enough to keep up with their legitimate expectations. The taste of equality is there, but the meat is still missing; the feeling of *relative* deprivation is clearly linked to *real* deprivation. As conditions slowly improve oppressed peoples chaff at the bit even more than when they were totally oppressed. In addition, they now realize that political pressure *can* produce improvement.

AGITATION AND AWAKENING

There are at least two factors that help to mobilize a complacent group into action: charismatic leaders and a process of "re-socialization."

LEADERS

Leaders are particularly important for galvanizing social unrest into an effective social movement. The soapbox orator, the quick-witted writer, the flaming preacher—these are the leaders who transform many oppressed individuals into an organized social movement. Every great movement points with pride to its firebrand leaders: Hitler, Jesus, Susan B. Anthony, Martin Luther King, and Malcolm X, were different in many respects, but they shared the ability to rouse their followers, to enlist committed allies, and to charge against the movement's enemies. The leader crystallizes the vague unrest of the people and translates it into concrete organization. The leaders become the focal point, the apex of the movement—in fact, to many people the leaders in some sense *are* the movement.

The leaders of the women's liberation movement, for example, broke with tradition and began to chart new courses in the face of widespread opposition from both men and women. The early voices raised against injustice to women also opposed slavery, for abolitionism and women's rights were closely related before the Civil War. Frances Wright was one of the first women to achieve public fame in the women's cause. Other women came to the forefront as the nineteenth century women's movement got under way in earnest. Lucretia Mott and Elizabeth Cady Stanton were instrumental in organizing the famous convention for women's rights in 1848 at Seneca Falls, New York. After the Seneca Falls conference the women's movement steadily gained ground under the leadership of a mixed group of powerful leaders. Susan B. Anthony organized the militant National Women's Suffrage Association; in England the Pankhurst sisters, Emmeline and Christabel, founded the strong political union called the English Women's Organization; Sarah Bagley upset the mill-towns of the Northeast with her militant women's labor union; by 1913 there was a powerful, politically active band of suffragettes demonstrating and picketing in Washington under the dynamic guidance of Alice Paul (who later founded the National Women's Party). These figures denied the shackles of

Frances Wright. Among the first women to speak publicly in this country and to advocate women's rights.

EARLY LEADERS OF THE WOMEN'S LIBERATION MOVEMENT IN AMERICA.

Lucretia Mott. (Below left) Called the Seneca Falls convention for women's rights in 1848.

Elizabeth Cady Stanton and Susan B. Anthony. (Below right) Worked with Mott in calling Seneca Falls convention, organized the militant National Woman Suffrage Association.

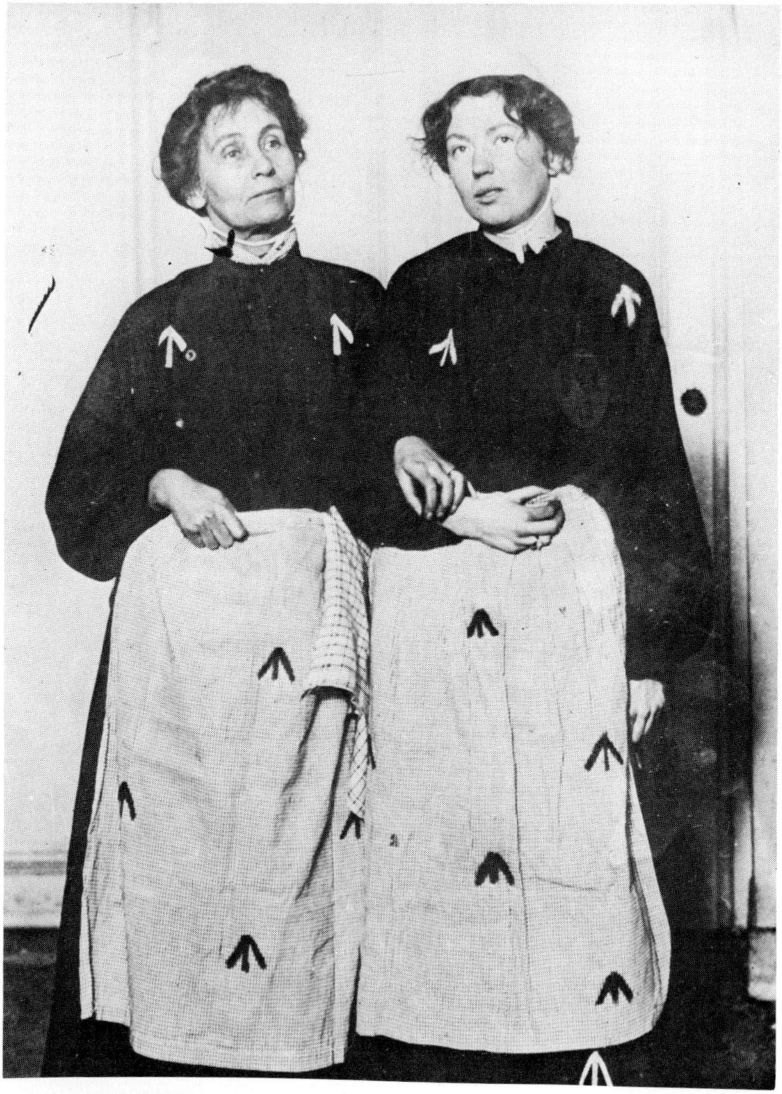

Emmeline and Christabel Pankhurst. Leaders of the English Women's organization, the women's social and political union, which included many working class women, founded in 1903.

Alice Paul. In 1913 organized a suffrage parade of 8000 women in Washington, D.C. Founded the National Women's Party in 1916.

tradition current in their day and stirred the consciousness of women around the nation.

RESOCIALIZATION

"Resocialization" is always part of a movement's first stages; the movement's followers must throw off years of training in "knowing their place" and build their self-confidence enough to strike back at their oppressors. Resocialization is necessary because oppressed groups frequently accept their oppressors' definition of them. They actually believe that they are inferior, worthless, and somehow deserve the miserable treatment they are receiving; *they become socialized to their victim status.* Psychologists often report that victims identify with their oppressors, wish they could change roles, and hate their own group. Studies of women, blacks, concentration-camp inmates, and other socially oppressed groups have shown that victim socialization is so strong that the victims not only adjust to their low status and accept it as "natural," but may even fight against members of their own group who dare to upset the status system. It is certainly not unusual to find black "Uncle Toms" who accept their status and refuse to push for change; the women's liberation movement is often opposed by women who do not see that they are oppressed; even some inmates of Nazi concentration camps adopted their captors' view that they were "Jewish poison" that had to be exterminated.

Thus, one of the first steps of an emerging social movement must be a campaign of resocialization, a deliberate attack on the group's victim status, and an awakening to its true plight. Sojourner Truth, a black abolitionist of the nineteenth century, traveled around the country trying to wake up women—especially black women—to their disadvantaged plight. At the 1851 women's rights convention in Akron, Ohio, she made a speech that blasted the current image of women as meek, helpless creatures who could not care for themselves.

> *. . . Well, chilern, whar dar is so much racket dar must be something out o'kilter. I tink dat 'twixt de niggers of de Souf and de women at de Norf all a talkin' 'bout rights, de white men will be in a fix pretty soon. But what's all dis here talkin' 'bout? Dat man ober dar say dat women needs to be helped into carriages, and lifted ober ditches, and to have de best place every whar. Nobody ever help me into carriages, or ober mud puddles, or gives me any best places, . . . and ar'nt I a woman? Look at me! Look at my arm! . . . I have plowed, and planted, and gathered into barns, and no man could head me—and ar'nt I a woman? I could work as much as a man (when I could get it), and bear de lash as well—and ar'nt I a woman? I have borne five children and I seen 'em mos' all sold off into slavery, and when I cried out with a mother's grief, none but Jesus heard—and ar'nt I a woman? (Quoted in Liberation Now, p. 187)*

In the contemporary scene women are engaged in all kinds of consciousness-raising meetings that try to cut through decades of socialization. Merilyn Salzman Webb wrote an insightful article (1969) attacking some images of women that are common in the popular mentality. Webb's anguished cry is that women have been locked into six roles: secretary, sexpot, spender, sow, civic actor, sickie. Secretary symbolizes the low-paid jobs women get, sexpot is the *Playboy* sex symbol, spender is the useless consumer role of buying luxuries merely to keep the economy rolling, sow is the bearer of children who loses her own personality to service the population explosion, civic actor is the dabbler in civic good deeds who lets the men have the real power, and sickie is the neurotic suburbanite who depends on her psychiatrist for identity and meaning. Webb's goal—and the goal of the consciousness-raising activities of women's liberation—is to smash these sick, oppressive images and allow women to see the vital, exciting options that should be open to them.

In short, the resocialization process is an attempt to bring the oppressed group to understand and appreciate its own strengths, to cast off the *negative stereotypes* the masters have hung round their necks. For over a century blacks in America have been fighting to rid themselves of the slave identification, the slave mentality, and the slave self-concept. In the last decade the campaign has made remarkable progress; "Black is beautiful!" is a startling slogan that follows decades of negative stereotypes proclaiming black to be dirt. The new pride, the new strength that blacks now have is vivid testimony to a successful movement's ability to resocialize its people.

THE MOVEMENT-BUILDING STAGE

Out of the oppressive premovement social conditions a group of charismatic leaders prod the movement from its complacency and a program of resocialization shatters the group's negative images and substitutes powerful new self-concepts. This is a crucial point for the movement, a point at which a number of issues come to the forefront, particularly the need for organization.

ADMINISTRATIVE LEADERSHIP

Charismatic leadership got the movement started; it provided the lively, emotional charge that awakened the movement's members to their common plight. If the movement is to flourish, however, it now needs a different kind of leader, an *administrator,* who can organize the work, raise funds, and marshal social support. The administrative leader is a pragmatist. Although he accepts the rhetoric and idealism of the charismatic leader, he is more concerned about very practical items such as money, organization, and communication with the larger society. He is more willing than the charismatic leader to deal with the power structure of the outside world in order to get things done. Often the charismatic leader and the administrator exist side by side—the former giving speeches, leading marches,

Sojourner Truth

and going on hunger strikes, while the latter is busy organizing practical support behind the scenes.

GROUP COHESION AND ORGANIZATION BUILDING

As a movement grows, it encounters serious problems of *coordination and group cohesion.* Initially the prime goal is to awaken people, to stir them up to the changes that are needed. Once this is accomplished, the prime task, a task requiring the skills of the administrative leader, is to organize the movement's followers, to weld them into a strong political force, and to direct their actions toward concrete goals. The movement is very likely to form an "association" or a "complex organization" such as the NAACP, CORE, the Ku Klux Klan, the Minutemen, the Fascist Party, or the White Citizens Councils. Any large-scale movement such as women's liberation, the civil rights movement, or the peace movement is likely to be an association of any number of separate organizations. In that sense it is not one movement, but many separate minimovements working on the same problem.

For example, the women's suffrage movement of the nineteenth century spawned dozens of organizations including the National Woman's Suffrage Association (under the leadership of Elizabeth Cady Stanton and Susan B. Anthony), the American Woman Suffrage Association, the English organization called the Woman's Social and Political Union, and the militant International Ladies Garment Workers Union (ILGWU). During the opening years of this century these organizations fought doggedly for women's rights, but except for the ILGWU most of these organizations faded away after women gained the right to vote.

Currently the scene is flooded with new women's rights organizations. As the movement once again gathers strength, its organizations are growing and flexing their muscles. In 1966 the National Organization for Women (NOW) was formed by Betty Friedan, author of *The Feminine Mystique,* as one of the original founders. Currently it is one of the most active, widespread groups. Literally hundreds of other women's organizations have been formed all over the United States.

IDEOLOGY AND BELIEFS

As the social movement grows it begins to develop an *ideology and a belief system* to account for the oppression of its people and to proclaim the new Utopia that will arrive when the movement takes over the world. The development of such a movement ideology requires a third type of leader. We have already noted that it takes a "charismatic" leader to get the movement started and an "administrative" leader to get it organized. Producing an appropriate ideology, however, requires an *intellectual* leader, one who can translate the feelings, hopes, frustrations, and dreams of the movement into persuasive, action-oriented words. Typically these intellectual leaders will produce two different kinds of materials. One leader, such as Karl Marx, may write intellectual ideological materials that are addressed to the intelligentsia of a society. Another intellectual leader, however, may produce popular ideology addressed to the general public. Malcolm X and Germaine Greer, for example, have been popularizers of the causes of blacks and of women, respectively.

Definition of the "People." The intellectual leaders develop an ideology to define the true "people." The members of the movement and their allies are the genuine people whereas outsiders are the enemies who are holding back the "true believers" (as Eric Hoffer calls the most dedicated members of the movement). The slogan, "If you are not part of the solution, you are part of the problem," is indicative of the sharp distinction between friend and enemy. The movement's ideology defines the in-group and out-groups, attributing pure motives to insiders and oppressive motives to outsiders. Of course, the definition of the "people" is a shifting thing with political implications. All social movements—religious, politically right, politically left—spend much energy trying to rally allies to their cause and asserting that its followers are the "real people." "Power to the people" is a common slogan, but the definition of the "people" means different things to different folks.

Definition of the "enemy." Defining the people simultaneously defines the *enemy*. Members of movements often see conspiracies behind every bush, for this viewpoint allows them to personify otherwise vague, hidden social forces that are causing their problems. Without a clear enemy, the movement has nobody to fight. Hitler found it easy to explain Germany's plight: a Jewish conspiracy. The John Birch Society and Joseph McCarthy shared a common fear of a communist state. The student revolutionaries suspected an "establishment" and its "military-industrial complex" of endless oppression. The women's liberation groups strike back at the male chauvinist power structure that oppresses them. This crystallized stereotype of the enemy gives the movement a clear objective to attack.

Visions of Heaven and Hell. The enemy and the present conditions under the oppressor are the epitome of the hell the movement is fighting, whereas the movement itself is the vanguard of the Utopian heaven. All social movements tend to divide the world into these two kingdoms —oppressor's hell and movement's Utopian heaven—and it is one of the prime tasks of the movement's leaders to define those issues. Adolph Hitler put it very sharply: if the Nazis won, Germany would rise gloriously from its ashes and *"Deutschland Uber alles"* would come true; if the Nazis lost, hell would arrive on the wings of a communist, Jewish-controlled Europe in which a defeated Germany cowered as a defeated puppy. Jesus Christ contrasted "this world" of sin to the eternal Kingdom of Peace that he would bring. Right-wing extremists fear a hell in which the United States will be overrun by "pinkos," "radi-libs," communists, and other evildoers; if the right's efforts prevail, however, the nation will be a Utopia where true-blue, red-blooded Americans can live safely without the fear of a red conspiracy.

Developing Specific Goals. In its latest phases the movement moves beyond the vague defintions of heaven and hell. In particular, the movement sharpens its definition of what is wrong; it begins to specify *limited, concrete goals.* In the early stages it is enough to protest the injustices faced or to cite the dangers feared. As the movement grows, however, the vague ideology must be replaced by specific goals that can be achieved by direct action. The general call for "liberation" gives way to demands for voting reforms, more equitable division of wealth, or a progressive income tax. The ambiguous goals of civil rights, for example, slowly crystallize into a battle over school integration (although that trend is now reversing and the civil rights goals are becoming diffuse once more). The vague claims for women's equality finally focused on the right to vote; the temperance movements that had their origins in unfocused opposition to "vice" of all kinds gradually narrowed to a constitutional amendment prohibiting alcoholic beverages. Every successful movement gradually refines its concerns and proceeds to wage a concentrated fight to achieve those few specific goals. Insert 9.II, for example, is a shortened version of the political platform of a West Coast-based group called the Coalition, a platform that states a set of concrete political demands. When a movement has reached this point it moves out of the preparation stages into the attack stage, the stage in which it is no longer building up its internal resources but is instead trying to influence other groups.

INFLUENCE ACTIVITIES AND OUTCOMES

The movement is now ready for action. From its humble beginnings it has been aroused by charismatic leaders, resocialized its members so they are ready to act, developed administrative and intellectual leaders, proclaimed its ideology, and built an effective organization. Now the group turns its attention to influence activities, attempting to persuade the larger society to accept and implement its goals. Actually, the influence attempts have probably gone on for quite a while, for even as it is getting organized it is testing its influence capacities.

In the previous chapter we looked at interest-group activities and explored William Gamson's discussion of the conflict between "authorities" (the decision makers and power holders) and "partisans" (people who do not have the power themselves but who want to influence the decisions). The social move-

INSERT **9.II**

THE "COALITION" PLATFORM ON SEXISM*

The Coalition proposes that:

1. Legal discrimination against women must be eliminated.
   a. The U. S. Congress should pass, and the states should ratify, the Equal Rights Amendment to the Constitution giving women a specific Constitutional guarantee of equal rights under the law.
   b. Certain states maintain discriminatory laws against women, regarding jury service, property rights, rights to make binding contracts, severity of punishment for crimes, identification as heads of households, and in sexual relations. We oppose these laws.
   c. Protective legislation, initially written to lessen hardships on female workers, now serves to justify sex discrimination. These laws must be eliminated or extended to cover all workers.
   d. Vice laws must be rewritten to end the prosecution of prostitutes and the regulation of sexual behavior between consenting individuals.
   e. Federal and state legislation must ensure the right of women to be educated to their full potential, equally with men. All discrimination and segregation by sex, written or unwritten, must be eliminated at all levels of education, including colleges, graduate and professional schools, loans and fellowships, and Federal and State training programs such as the Job Corps.
   f. We must eliminate "man-in-the-household" welfare laws that preclude child-support payment if a man lives in the house.

*The "Coalition" is the West Coast radical-reformist group.

ments we are now studying are like large combines of interest groups, all struggling for similar goals. Consequently, it will be helpful for you to keep in mind the earlier discussion of interest-group behavior.

MOVEMENTS EXERT INFLUENCE

Partisans—in this case social movements—try to influence decisions and bring about social change through a wide variety of tactics. They appeal to the public conscience; they insist on reason-

g. Women in prisons should obtain work furloughs from prisons to the same extent that men prisoners do. The understaffing of female prisons must be corrected.

h. Women in the armed forces should be promoted on an equal basis with men.

2. We must rearrange our social organization to give women an equal position in the society.

   a. The society should not control women's reproductive functions. We must eliminate laws that limit access to birth control information and devices, or that govern abortions. The government should support birth control and abortion clinics staffed by qualified personnel.

   b. Legislation must protect the right of women to return to their jobs within a reasonable time after childbirth without loss of seniority or other accrued benefits. Women should be paid maternity leave as a form of social security and/or employee benefits or accumulated sick leave.

   c. The responsibility of caring for children should not rest entirely on women, but should be assumed by both parents and/or by the wider society.

      The standard work day should vary in length, with workers choosing the amount of time spent at work and the amount spent with the family—this would let both parents contribute to the care of their children.

      Fully equipped child care centers for children preschool through adolescence should be provided as a public service. On-the-job child care facitilities should be provided for nursing mothers.

      Income tax laws should include deductions for home and child care for working parents.

3. Widespread beliefs about female competence and decision-making ability have inhibited women from participating

able treatment; they plead for social change. The mass media and the printed word are exploited to their fullest advantage for the cause. If their concerns are not met the movement turns to peaceful public demonstrations and perhaps even to violence and revolutionary activities. Many of the major social movements of this century have gone the entire route from public appeals and persuasion to demonstrations to violence and revolutionary activity. The antislavery, women's fully in political and occupational roles. We must root out these beliefs.

a. The media—radio, television and newspapers—cater to these beliefs, facilitating further discrimination against women. We must get rid of the stereotyped, negative portrayals of women by public media, including the incompetent woman so often depicted in advertisements. Stereotypes that portray men as aggressive and dominant and women as passive and supportive should not be aired on public media.

b. Education does not expose women children to the full range of available occupations, but mostly teaches them about "female" occupations; male children also fail to receive information about traditionally "female" occupations—male children fail to receive information about traditionally female concerns such as child care and homemaking. Legislation must eliminate references in school textbooks to male supremacy, unique male competence and female ineptness. Textbooks must present the full range of occupations as occupied by both men and women workers, including portraying men occupied at domestic tasks.

4. Homosexuals, both male and female, suffer from discrimination in employment, education, government, the military, and the society at large. The fundamental right of consenting individuals to engage in sexual behaviors of their own choosing must not be abridged by legislation. We must eliminate all laws that legislate sexual behavior in the private lives of any consenting individuals, as well as all education, occupational, governmental, military and social legislation that discriminates against homosexuals.

suffrage, and unionization movements were some outstanding examples in the 1800s and early 1900s; the civil rights movement, women's liberation, and the student rebellions were more recent illustrations. In each case there were constant appeals to the public conscience, demonstrations with massive bands of followers, and finally, when demands were not met, instances of violence. The details differ in each case, but the overall pattern remained essentially the same.

RESPONSE OF THE AUTHORITIES

Meanwhile, the authorities, the power wielders who could hinder or promote social change, respond to the movements' demands in different ways. In each of the four instances mentioned above—unionization, women's rights, student rebellion, and civil rights—the authorities were slow to act. From a sociological perspective the slowness of the authorities' response is certainly understandable, for each movement was demanding fundamental shifts in the social value systems, in the power distribution of the society, and in the allocation of wealth, income, and prestige—shifts not easily accomplished.

Often the authorities not only fail to respond, they actively try to destroy the movement. Police action is sometimes used against the movement, for *force* is an option open to both the partisan movements and the authority powerholders. The police marched with vicious dogs and electric cattle prods against civil rights demonstrators in Mississippi in the 1950s, the National Guard shot and killed four students at Kent State in 1971, federal troops beat and arrested suffragists in Washington (1916), Pinkerton guards kicked and mutilated union organizers in the 1930s.

However, there are also many cases where the force of the authorities is marshalled behind a progressive social movement: federal troops and marshals backed up the civil rights movement many times even as local police were harassing it; police power has frequently been used against right-wing Minutemen and the Ku Klux Klan; the FBI occasionally hunts down a right-wing bomber. In general, however, the power structure of the society is dedicated to the status quo, to preserving vested interest groups, and to upholding the stratification system as it presently exists.

OUTCOMES

Change comes slowly; change-oriented movements usually run into stone walls. Whites have vested interests in keeping blacks down: it means power over them; it means money to be made from them; it means social influence is denied to them. Employers are obviously concerned about their advantages over workers; it costs money to pay a decent wage and to provide reasonable working conditions, and unions upset the power equation that once favored the owner. And now, unions too have a vested interest in the status quo and are excluding blacks, other minorities, and women in order to maintain their own position. Men have distinct reasons for keeping women "in their place," for certainly more women in the professions, in high-paying jobs, and in powerful political positions will deny men the privileged positions they have always assumed. In each case, then, a change-oriented social movement is confronted with ingrained habits, vested interests, and conservative political power structures fighting for the status quo. This is not to say that change never happens, but that it comes only with blood, sweat, and tears—and slowly, very slowly.

The women's liberation movement, for example, has had a spotted career. It gradually emerged in the pre-Civil War years as an offspring of the abolitionist movement, a development that has strong parallels in the contemporary women's movement that has spun off from the civil rights and student protest movements of the 1960s. The drive for women's rights received a strong lift by the social conditions of the Civil War, then moved on to the suffrage movement, eventually achieving the Nineteenth Amendment, allowing women to vote. After women's triumphant participation in the presidential election of 1920 the movement fell apart, an event that leaders today blame on the movement's exclusive, almost fanatical emphasis on the vote as the key to women's rights. After World War II the nation was too busy licking its wounds and regaining normalcy to worry about rights—for women or anyone else.

The civil rights drive of the late 1950s and early 1960s again opened up broad social reform issues, laying the groundwork for the rising expectations of women. Irritated by their second-class role in the civil rights and student movements, the women split off into their own active bands. From that spin-off the contemporary movement sprang. To catalog the accomplishments and failures of the women's liberation movement would take another whole book, but a few of the more important events have been drawn together in the chronology of the movement in Insert 9.III. You will want to examine it closely to get a feel for the historical and sociological events that have gone into this massive social change.

WINNING, LOSING, AND THE DEATH OF MOVEMENTS

In some sense a social movement is like an organism; it is born; it grows; it does its work, and then it dies. Most movements do not last very long, for the truth of the matter is that most fail miserably in their quest for social change. Although we have discussed moderately successful movements throughout this chapter, most movements die an early death, failing to organize, failing to make an impact, failing to bring about change. The history books never discuss the failures, in fact, they are lost on the sands of time, usually with little record of their birth. To take the organism analogy one step farther, most movements are stillborn.

Many others get *coopted* by the power structure, that is, they are simply picked up and merged with the existing power system. Most third political parties in the United States, for example, never get off the ground because the two dominant parties eventually insert their ideas into their own political platforms. However, cooptation is a two-sided sword; the establishment buys some peace and quiet by giving in a little and incorporating the movement, while the movement buys a little progress at the price of losing its most serious demands. For example, the women's movement in the 1920s bought the vote—a moderate reform—by giving up most of its other radical demands for reshaping the role of women in the rest of society.

A few movements—a mere handful—are able to grow, prosper, and make serious changes in the society. Unionism, civil rights, and women's suffrage have actually been successful social change agents; they have made the society inch forward to progressive reform. To be sure, they never get the whole cake, and the progress is slow and frustrating, but there is serious social reform under their prodding. They are potent political and

INSERT **9.III**

CHRONOLOGY OF THE AMERICAN WOMEN'S LIBERATION MOVEMENT

The women's liberation movement in America has had a long, checkered career. Over the past century the conditions of women have steadily improved, under the persistent pressure of many individual women and organized groups. At times there has been much overt public activity, such as women's participation in abolition movements before the Civil War, the suffrage movements of the early twentieth century, and the current reawakening. At other times the movement has been virtually dormant, as right after the Civil War, and in the 30-year period from the early 1930s to the early 1960s. The following chronology is certainly not exhaustive, but at least it marks some of the high points.

Colonial Period	Many colonies and early states allowed women to vote, but between 1699 and 1807 most states enacted laws that took away the few rights women had.
1837	Mount Holyoke, the first college for women, opened; it was followed shortly by Oberlin and Vassar.
Pre-Civil War	Women's rights groups gradually grew in partnership with the abolitionist movement. Almost every prominent women's rights fighter was first an abolitionist. Susan B. Anthony and Lucy Stone were key leaders at this point.
1848	The Seneca Falls, New York conference on equal rights for women was the world's first and marked the official opening of the women's suffrage movement. Two abolitionists, Lucretia Mott and Elizabeth Cady Stanton, called the meeting.
Civil War Period	The Civil War was a time of major upheaval for women, for they entered government jobs in great numbers, replaced the soldiering men in the teaching profession (which had been a male stronghold until then), and opened many colleges for women.
1869	The territory of Wyoming was first to give women the vote; Utah did so the next year; Colorado and Idaho followed shortly.

1913	Alice Paul organized a suffrage parade in Washington, D.C., with several thousand women. She and others were expelled by conservative elements in the women's suffrage movement in 1913.
1916	The National Women's Party, headed by Alice Paul, exerted intense pressure on top officials to change legislation affecting women's working and voting. While picketing the White House they were mauled and had their banners destroyed by observers. On June 22 many were arrested and sent to prison; in prison they received brutal treatment. They were released on March 3, 1917 and started picketing again in June. This group seems to have been successful in forcing the Senate to vote on the suffrage issue.
1919	The Senate approved the Nineteenth Amendment allowing women to vote, but it took one more year for state ratification.
1920	Women received the right to vote and participated in the 1920 presidential election.
1930s–1950s	Having expended its energy in a successful campaign to obtain the vote, the women's movement faded. The Great Depression, World War II, and the conservative 1950s produced social forces that undermined women's progress. For 30 years the movement remained nearly dormant.
1964	The Civil Rights Act was passed, declaring it illegal to discriminate on race or sex. Originally the addition of sex to the act was a plot by conservative legislators to stop the law, but since its passage it has opened many opportunities for women.
1966	The National Organization of Women was formed with Betty Friedan as founder and first president. This group is concerned with "making women *visible* as people in America, as a conscious political and social power, to change our society now, so all women can move freely, as people, in it."
1972	Under intense pressure from over 90 organized groups, Congress passed the Equal Rights Amendment to the Constitution, designed to eliminate discrimination on the basis of sex.
1974	An International Feminist Congress met in Europe to plan policy and strategy for the planned 1975 United Nations Conference on the status of women.

sociological forces that must be reckoned with.

Generally a "win" for a movement will not lead to its disbanding; instead, it is likely to ask for more, to translate its gains into more radical demands. This has happened in most successful major movements. After much effort a movement may be institutionalized, that is, its major goals and values may be accepted by the larger society and translated into stable political reforms such as laws, political parties, and legislative realignments. Only the most successful movements reach institutionalization, but some, like the union movement, become formidable establishment institutions after long periods as partisan revolutionaries.

SOCIAL MOVEMENTS AND REVOLUTIONS

In their most dramatic form social movements may lead to revolutions. Some of the most important political changes in history have occurred during the violent upheavals of revolutions, most of which emerged out of the activities of social movements that grew so powerful they took over the political reins. The American Revolution of 1776, the French Revolution of 1789, the Russian Revolution of 1917, and the Chinese Revolution of 1948 all changed the face of the modern world in ways that it is almost impossible to imagine. In each case the revolution began as a large social movement or as a coalition of several social movements. The communist party, for example, was basically a massive social movement before it took control in Russia and China.

Although revolutions have some unique qualities, some social scientists argue that they tend to have similar patterns and that regularities of revolutionary behavior can be discovered. Crane Brinton's classic book, *The Anatomy of a Revolution* (1938), outlined some patterns exhibited by revolutionary social movements. Let us examine the steps which Brinton outlined.

SOCIAL CONDITIONS PROMOTING THE REVOLUTION

Earlier in this chapter we noted that social movements tended to grow out of two related social conditions: intense social oppression or conflict, coupled with a period of improvement when aspirations outrun real progress. The same dynamics that promote social movements are also the prime forces behind revolutions. The Russian Revolution of 1917, for example, came after years of food shortages, battlefield losses in the war with Japan, and the general decline in the Russian economic system. In addition, by 1917 the disastrous war with Germany was draining Russia of its last ounce of blood. When Nicolas, the last of the Romanov Czars, abdicated the throne in 1917, he left a nation under siege, ripped to pieces by social crisis and miserable conditions. Almost every major revolution shows this kind of deep-seated social misery as its starting point.

Revolutions also emerge from social situations where there is steady improvement, since expectations are likely to be running ahead of real progress. Although conditions in Russia were miserable when Nicolas abdicated, it was also a fact that Russia had seen steadily improving social conditions in the period from 1850 to the revolution in 1917. The serfs had been freed, the power of the czar had been decreased, the Duma (legislature) had been established, and general standards of living had been improved for most of the people. However, Davies (1962) argues that it was exactly this improvement, combined with the sharp reversals and problems that came at the turn of the century, which sparked the revolution. In short, revolutions essentially depend on the same social forces that social movements rest on: social oppression, steady improvement, and sharp reversals in progress.

THE DEFECTION OF THE INTELLECTUALS

Brinton argues that almost every revolution is aided because the intellectuals of the society—the scholars, writers, editors, and often the clergy—turn against the government and join the masses in attempting to overthrow the regime. The intellectuals become the focal points around which the masses gather because they do most of the public speaking, turn out most of the revolution's writing, and usually help seize control of the mass media. Nikolai Lenin, for example, was at the same time the intellectual leader of the Russian Bolsheviks and their political captain. This is exactly in line with Karl Marx's argument that the workers would need the guidance and the support of the intellectuals if they were ever to break their apathy and organize an effective revolution. The Russian Revolution demonstrates the truth of Marx's thesis.

THE REVOLUTIONARY OUTBREAK

Most revolutions are preceded by a series of minor outbursts that are effectively put down by the government's military. In the American Revolution, for example, the Boston Tea Party was an early outbreak; the Boston Massacre showed that the government had the ability to put down dissension, at least in its early stages. In the Russian Revolution a number of events occurred long before 1917, with the demonstrations and the massacre at the Winter Palace in 1905 being the most dramatic. As events begin to build one major event usually provides the spark that sets the revolution afire. The storming of the Bastille in France in 1789 became the symbolic action welding together many revolutionary groups who then turned their hostility against the king. In each case there is some outstanding event that demonstrates the demands of the revolutionaries while highlighting the government's oppressive measures. If the conflict continues to rage, however, the government itself will become badly splintered; although it may respond in a bloody fashion, the regime's response is often symbolic of its weakness. At this point the regime begins to waver and its military apparatus begins to crumble as common soldiers refuse to fire on average citizens. This was the case in the Russian Revolution, for most of the armies under the Czar's control refused to fight, either against the Germans on the western front or against the revolutionaries back home.

THE RULE OF THE MODERATES

As the intellectuals draw their allegiance away from the established government they usually form a "parallel" government—a "shadow" government that is ready to take over if the regime falters. Usually the intellectuals form a moderate government, dedicated to changing the more dramatic abuses, but not dedicated to totally upsetting the system. When the Russian Czar Nicolas abdicated in 1917, the legislature elected the moderate Alexander Kerenski as President. The moderates, however, inherit a difficult situation, since the government they have seized is already on the brink of collapse and typically the people who have assumed power are politically inexperienced. Moreover, at this time of social crisis the moderates are unwilling to take dramatic steps to suppress mass violence, since they themselves have arrived at power on the back of populist concerns. The moderates are inclined toward compromise and are hesitant to curb those who are more radical. This paves the way for their downfall, for the radicals are not at all hindered by such moderate attitudes.

TAKEOVER BY RADICALS AND THE REIGN OF TERROR

The moderate government in Russia, under Kerenski, lasted only about seven months before the radical Bolsheviks under Lenin managed to seize control. In France the picture was very similar, for the radical Jacobins threw out the moderate government that had taken the reins from the king. In both instances a wild period of terror followed on the heels of the radical takeover. In France and Russia the monarchs were killed by radical revolutionary leaders, and there was a systematic purge of government officials who were either killed, exiled, or imprisoned. Although the radicals usually proclaim that they are going to set up a strong democracy, in reality the reign of the radicals often turns into a totalitarian dictatorship. Nevertheless, at the same time the radical regime takes steps to overcome the worst abuses of the previous government. In the Russian Revolution, for example, the Bolsheviks immediately sued for peace with the Germans; once peace was secured they set about major programs of land reform and industrial reorganization designed to help the peasants and the workers. However, their terrorist tactics usually go to such extremes that fears arise that the society will be torn apart unless the radicals are stopped. This leads to a resurgence of the moderates.

THERMIDOR

The radical Jacobins during the French Revolution were led by Robespierre, a man whose reign of terror left the French society completely splintered, and on July 27, 1794 he was deposed and executed.

Under the new French calendar July was called Thermidor, and the so-called Thermidor revolution was led by moderates determined that the radical excesses

Alexander Kerenski led the moderates as they took over from the Czar. . . .

But Nicholai Lenin's radical communists quickly ousted the moderates and formed the Soviet regime.

of the Jacobins should not be allowed to destroy the French Society completely.

Every major revolution has its Thermidor, a period when moderates decide that they have had enough and regain control of the government. This does not mean they return to the old system, but it does mean that some of the more radical excesses are stopped. Typically this reaction leads to a strong leader: Bonaparte in France, Stalin in Russia, and Mao in China. Under this new strong man the revolution slowly cools down and most of the radical terror tactics are crushed. The regime tries to reestablish some sense of normalcy, and the government bureaucracies once again start functioning. Meanwhile the regime works to build up legitimacy in the international community, attempting to become recognized as an effective, legitimate government. The revolution is now over, but its gains are institutionalized in the new government. Although revolutions rarely achieve all that the radicals had hoped, they usually go far beyond the old system they replaced.

SUMMARY

Social movements are well-organized groups that act either to promote or to resist change in the social system. All social movements have at least four major concerns, although each one may tend to emphasize one more than another: (1) power orientation, an attempt to gain political influence and power, (2) value orientation, an attempt to change values and norms through education, publicity, and propaganda, (3) personal-expressive orientation, an attempt to serve the personal needs of movement members, and (4) resistance orientation, an attempt to guard against other movements with contradictory values and goals.

Social movements have life careers, just as biological organisms do. In the *premovement stage* oppression, rising expectations and relative deprivation are elements in the complex pattern of social forces that lead to the birth of a social movement. During the *awakening phase* charismatic leaders prod the oppressed group members into recognizing their "victim" status, into a resocialization process, and into a redefinition of their self-image so they will believe in themselves and assert their rights. Then the *movement-building* process begins; pragmatic, administrative leaders develop tight-knit organizations, while intellectual leaders coin a movement ideology that gives a vision of the hellish life under the oppressors and the Utopian life under the successful movement. Finally, the movement begins to define goals more sharply, as ambiguous hopes for the future become crystallized political platforms. The movement is ready for attack.

The final phases—*influence* and *outcome*—are the heart of the matter, since in those stages the movement begins to lash out at the larger society, demanding change, pleading for reasonable reforms, and pushing on to confrontation. The authorities may now respond in a number of ways, including granting the demands, coopting the movement, or suppressing it with counterviolence. It is the rare movement that actually translates its demands into effective social policy and social change. Most fail; most vanish. However, if a movement has its fundamental concerns implemented, it is likely to embark on a new round of activity, escalating its goals and pushing its reforms even farther. Or the basic concerns of the movement may be institutionalized, written into law, and enshrined in social policy. In the extreme case social movements become revolutions, upsetting the entire political system. Successful social movements are in the vanguard of social change and are among the most potent forces for transforming the social system.

REFERENCES

Bem, S. L., and D. J. Bem. "Case Study of a Nonconscious Ideology: Training Woman to Know her Place," in D. J. Bem, *Beliefs, Attitudes, and Human Affairs* (Belmont, Calif.: Brooks/Cole, 1970).

Blumer, H. "Collective Behavior," in A. M. Lee (ed.) *New Outline of the Principles of Sociology* (New York: Barnes & Noble, 1951).

Brinton, C. C. *The Anatomy of Revolution* (New York: Vintage Books, 1957).

Davies, James C. "Toward a Theory of Revolution," *Amer. Soc. Review, 27,* February 1962, pp. 5–19.

Edwards, Lyford P. *The Natural History of Revolutions* (Chicago: University of Chicago Press, 1927).

Epstein, Cynthia Fuchs. *Woman's Place* (Berkeley: University of California Press, 1970).

Friedan, Betty. *The Feminine Mystique* (New York: W. W. Norton, 1963).

Gusfield, Joseph R. *Protest, Reform, and Revolt* (New York: Wiley, 1970).

Hacher, Helen. "Women as a Minority Group," *Social Forces, 30,* p. 65.

Lang, D., and Lang, G. E. *Collective Dynamics* (New York: Crowell, 1961).

Liberation Now! (editors unidentified) (New York: Dell Paperback, 1971).

McLaughlin, Barry. *Studies in Social Movements* (New York: Free Press, 1969).

Millett, Kate. *Sexual Politics* (New York: Doubleday, 1970).

Morgan, Robin. *Sisterhood is Powerful* (New York: Vintage, 1970).

Smelser, N. J. *Theory of Collective Behavior* (New York: Free Press of Glencoe, 1963).

Toch, H. *The Social Psychology of Social Movements* (Indianapolis, Ind.: Bobbs-Merrill, 1965).

Turner, R. H., and Killian, L. M., *Collective Behavior* (Englewood Cliffs, N.J.: Prentice-Hall, 1957).

Webb, Marilyn Salzman. "Woman as Secretary, Sexpot, Spender, Sow, Civic Actor, Sickie," *Motive,* March–April 1969, pp. 49–59.

TEN
EDUCATION AND SOCIAL MOBILITY

THE SOCIETY'S CHANGING EDUCATIONAL NEEDS

Americans have a recurrent fantasy that schools can solve their problems. Thus it was perhaps inevitable that, after we rediscovered poverty and inequality in the early 1960s, we turned to the schools for solutions. Yet the schools did not provide solutions, the high hopes of the early-and-middle 1960s faded, and the war on poverty ended in ignominious surrender to the *status quo.* In part, of course, this was because the war in Southeast Asia turned out to be incompatible with the war on poverty. In part, however, it was because we all had rather muddleheaded ideas about the various causes and cures of poverty and inequality.

. . . the reforms of the 1960s were misdirected because they focused only on equalizing opportunity to "succeed" (or "fail") rather than on reducing the economic and social distance between those who succeeded and those who failed. The evidence we have reviewed suggests that equalizing opportunity will not do very much to equalize results, and hence that it will not do much to reduce poverty.

. . . even if we are interested solely in equalizing opportunities for economic success, making schools more equal will not help very much. (Bane and Jencks, 1972, p. 37)

The opening statement by Christopher Jencks raises the central question of this chapter. Is education a tool for social reform, can it help equalize social opportunities in the society? Or is education impotent to cause real change, to equalize job opportunities, to reform social problems? In this chapter we will examine some of the links between education and social mobility, and some of the crucial barriers that diminish education's potential as a source of social change.

EDUCATION AND SOCIAL MOBILITY

One of the major impacts of education on the individual is its effect on occupational careers. The modern industrial society has an enormous appetite for trained manpower—manpower to run factories, build computers, design airplanes, teach

The changing shape of a day's work: Modern society demands highly trained labor.

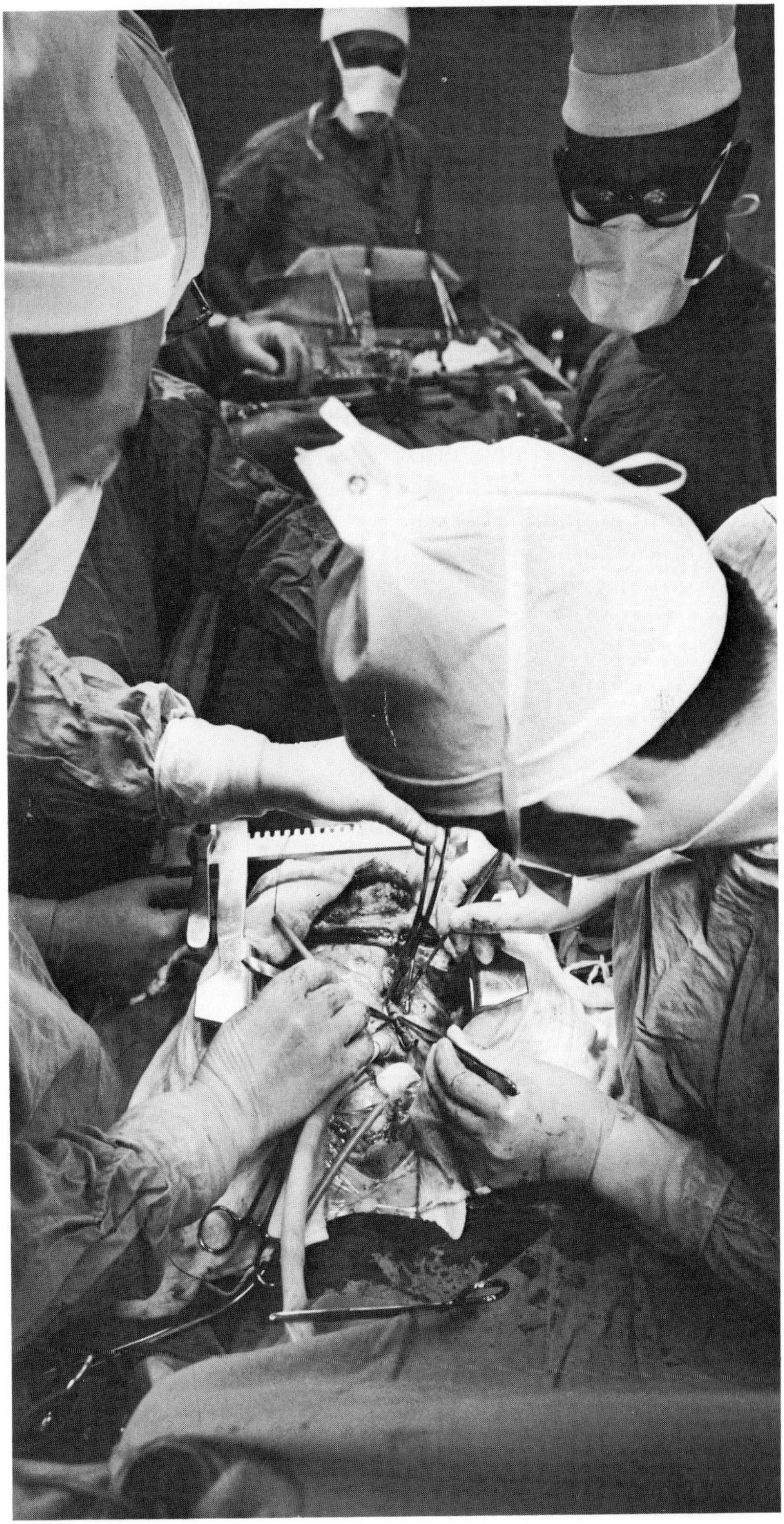

young people, generate nuclear power, and perform heart transplants. People in a frontier society needed strong muscles and a keen eye; people in the modern industrial state need education and training. The work structure has changed radically, and hunters, farmers, laborers are no longer needed in as huge numbers as formerly. Work in modern society has shifted from *primary* industry (agriculture, mining, lumbering) to *secondary* industry (manufacturing, building, transportation) and more lately to *tertiary* industry (service work, professional labor, retail trade, finance). And every shift in the occupational structure has increased the need for education.

EDUCATING THE EXPERT SOCIETY

Because of the sweeping changes in the occupational structure, Burton R. Clark calls this the "expert society," a society in which the expert reigns king and the nonexpert is usually unemployed (Clark, 1962). Everywhere more skilled, more highly trained manpower is needed. Michael Young has named this expert-hungry society *meritocracy,* meaning a society in which the people with the highest technical qualifications will form new elites and replace those based on money, power, or inherited aristocracy (Young, 1958). The new meritocracy will be staffed by experts trained by the formal education system. Even now training for most occupations can no longer be left to chance or to on-the-job training, but instead requires concentrated, systematic education over long periods of time. Education has become the society's "gatekeeper," determining who will advance and who will be left behind.

THE RISING "EDUCATIONAL THRESHOLD"

Not only has there been a growth of new high-skill jobs, but there has also been an increase in the educational requirements for the same jobs. Once insurance salesmen could get by with a high-school education; they are now expected to be college graduates. Once policemen did not need a high-school degree; they are now urged to have at least some college. Once farmers needed only to know about a few simple tools; they now must know about mechanics, agricultural science, and chemistry. In field after field the *"educational threshold,"* the lowest level of education required to enter a field, is going up, and many people who previously had more than enough education to hold a particular job are becoming technologically and educationally obsolete.

Modern America is more and more becoming a "credentialed" society, for to enter a particular occupation a person must bear the proper credentials, display the appropriate labels, and be able to sign the right degrees after his name. Many critics argue, however, that the credentials are not always necessary; how much education do salesmen, policemen, and farmers really need? The problem is that without the proper credentials many capable, talented people are often not even considered for the job. This has the effect of closing doors in the faces of many people, particularly minority members

The "educational threshold" is rising

who, having faced terrible disadvantages in getting any kind of education, are now told that their credentials are not adequate. To compound the problem there has been a drastic "credential inflation" over the last few years. Just as it takes more money to live in an inflationary period, it takes more credentials just to get the same jobs now. Where it once took only a high school degree to get more jobs, a college education is now required.

The society is in many respects overtrained already—look at all the unemployed schoolteachers, engineers, scientists, and Ph.D.'s all over the nation. Nevertheless, the requirements keep going up. Thus in a society where education is supposed to open up opportunities, the credential system is effectively closing out many people. Before we go on let us examine more carefully the link between the educational and occupational worlds.

EDUCATION AND OCCUPATIONAL SUCCESS

The changing occupational structure and its increasing demands for high skilled labor plus requirements for educational credentials is putting heavy responsibilities on the educational system to provide trained manpower. In the modern, "expert" society education is one of the critical factors determining whether a young person can get a job, earn a reasonable living, and "get ahead" in life. In fact, *the more education people have, the more likely they are to have a prestige job, to earn higher average yearly and lifetime incomes, and to achieve better job positions than their parents.* On the other hand, low education leads to a low-level job requiring few skills; unemployment is always a risk; the possibility for breaking out and advancing to a better job is cut off. Much evidence can be offered for these statements.

EVIDENCE SUPPORTING THE EDUCATION-OCCUPATION LINK

There is a wealth of data to show that advanced education helps in acquiring and holding good jobs.

The More Education, The More Likely a Person Is To Have a High-Prestige Job. In a major study of occupations and education Blau and Duncan (1967) found that people with more education had a better chance to work in a professional or technical capacity, whereas people with less education more probably had low-paying, unskilled jobs (see Figure 10.1).

The More Education, The Greater The Income. Census Bureau figures show year after year that higher education increases earning capacity, with the differences between the upper and lower levels of the educational scale amounting to huge sums. Figure 10.2 shows how much difference education makes in earning power, both on an annual basis and over a person's lifetime.

The More Education, The More Upward Social Mobility. Not only do people with lower education make less money, hold lower prestige jobs, and have higher chances of unemployment, but they also face the unpleasant fact that they are very likely to *stay* in this unfortunate position. People with higher levels of education, however, have good opportunities for *social mobility*—for getting a better job, earning more money, and maintaining a better life-style. In their study of occupations in the United States Blau and Duncan (1967) found that the most important factor affecting whether a son moved to a higher social position than his father *(intergenerational mobility)* was the amount of education. The more education, the more likely a son was to advance, but with lower levels of education the more likely a son was to remain at the same position. Figure 10.3 shows, for example, that among those who had no formal education only 12 percent moved to a higher occupational position than their fathers, but of the sons who had five or more years of college 76 percent rose in social standing.

QUESTIONS ABOUT THE EDUCATION AND OCCUPATION LINK

Although most of the evidence shows that education is strongly linked to occupa-

Figure 10.1
With different levels of education, what kinds of jobs do people hold? (Males, white, 25–64 years old, March 1972)

	Less than four years of high school	Four years of high school	One to three years of college	Four or more years of college
Professional	1.5	6.7	20.1	55.7
Managers	7.5	14.6	23.6	24.5
Sales workers	2.2	6.3	11.6	9.3
Clerical	4.0	8.8	9.6	4.0
Craftsmen	28.6	29.2	15.6	2.5
Operatives	29.4	18.9	9.1	1.0
Nonfarm laborers	10.5	4.1	2.2	0.5
Service workers	9.3	7.7	5.9	1.7
Farmers	4.5	3.2	2.1	6.7
Farm laborers	2.4	0.4	0.2	0.2
Total %	100.00	100.0	100.0	100.0

Source: Current Population Reports, P20–243, March 1972, Bureau of the Census.

tional progress, recent research questions that basic assumption. The questions come in several forms: (1) Does advanced education really bring higher economic and occupational rewards? (2) Do people really need the advanced education to perform on the job? (3) Will advanced education guarantee occupational success? Let us comment briefly on each of these questions.

Is Education Linked to Job Success?

First, Christopher Jencks and his associates at the Harvard School of Education have challenged one of the most cherished beliefs of educators, sociologists, and liberal social reformers by claiming that their data—based primarily on government studies—do *not* show a strong relation between education and income or occupational status (see Jencks, et al., 1972). In fact, the Jencks analysis suggests that less than 15 percent of the variation in occupational success can be accounted for by educational and family background *together.* As a result schools can have little effect on occupations, and any hopes that improved education can help to solve inequalities in the job field are doomed to failure. Jencks' argument raised a national storm of controversy, because, if it is correct, society is spending huge amounts of money on education when it should be attacking other social problems.

How can we evaluate Jencks' attack on the idea that education is a prime factor in occupational success? The central thesis is that education is not really related to increased income, and on that score there is much evidence to refute Jencks. Almost every other statistical analysis, including major studies by Bowles and Gintis (see Levin, 1972, p. 51), shows much stronger ties between education, occupation, and income. Moreover, Levin (1972) argues that Jencks handled his data very poorly, and proper reanalysis would show a much stronger impact of education on income and occupation. In addition, census data—such as in Figures 10.1 and 10.2—suggest Jencks is incorrect. In spite of the national attention given to Jencks'

Figure 10.2
Median annual and lifetime income of groups with different education levels

Years of School	Family Heads Annual Income, 1971	All Males Expected Lifetime Income (1968 Data)
Less than eight	5714	196,000
Eight	7687	258,000
Nine to eleven	9088	294,000
Twelve	10,829	350,000
One to three college	12,339	411,000
Four or more college	15,883	586,000

Source: Statistical Abstract of the United States, 1972, p. 111.

research, he is probably wrong in his assertion that education makes no difference in occupational advancement and income. (We will hear more about the controversy over Jencks' research in Chapter Thirteen.)

Irrelevant Curriculum and Inflated Credential Requirements. A second chorus of criticism concerns the relevance of the curriculum in schools and colleges to the world of work. Many critical books, such

Figure 10.3
Advanced education aids upward mobility. Percentage of sons who achieved higher occupational levels than their fathers, by sons' educational levels

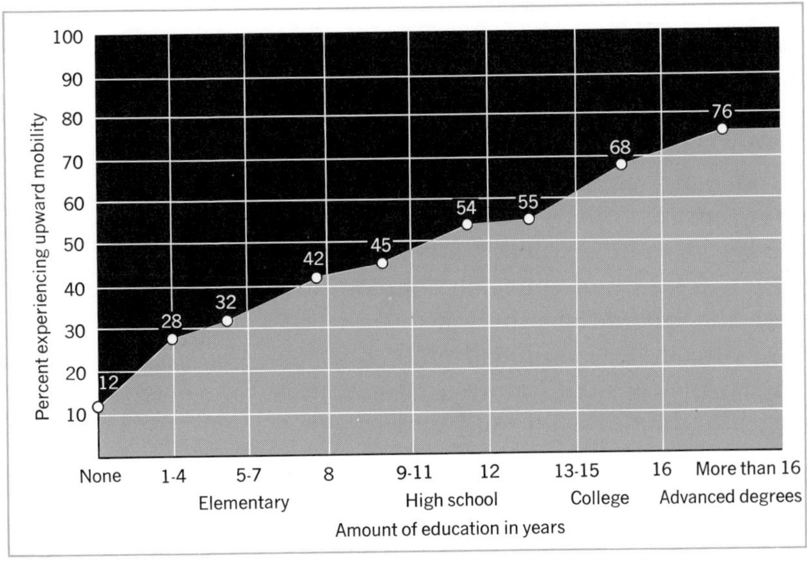

Source: Adapted from Peter M. Blau and Otis Dudley Duncan, *The American Occupational Structure* (New York: Wiley, 1967), p. 157.

as Berg's *The Great Training Robbery* (1971), have argued that schools are really not preparing people for the jobs they take. The public, Berg asserts, is being robbed because of education's failure to train people in the skills that are really needed. In addition, the critics suggest that there is little need for the high educational requirements placed on many jobs. In effect, the high credential requirements serve as barriers, keeping out those who cannot afford the luxury and expense of advanced education. To these critics, education is actually *hindering* the occupational progress of many social groups who are trained in irrelevant curriculums and then denied the better jobs because of inflated credential requirements that are quite irrelevant to the needs of the jobs. In short, education may often be a barrier to occupational success for underpriviledged social groups, while it is simultaneously advancing the careers of the fortunate who can afford high degrees.

Education Cannot Guarantee Good Jobs. Finally, it is more and more obvious that having an education does not *guarantee* a person a good job. One of the major difficulties in the economic condition of the nation over the past few years has been the unemployment of highly educated people. Of course, employment fluctuations occur frequently, and the unemployment of highly qualified people may only be a momentary, passing condition. Nevertheless, for many people who struggled through years of school it is crushing to discover that they are overqualified and cannot get jobs that reflect their qualifications. Engineers who drive cabs, Ph.D.s who teach elementary school, and space scientists who sell insurance are victims of the economic situation, just as other groups are. However, the lesson to be learned is *not* that education is a waste of time; on the contrary, with the credential inflation and the rising threshold of educational requirements, the fact that many qualified people are unemployed only means they will press others farther down the scale completely out of work. The link between education and having a job is even more clear in times of unemployment; the educated still get the jobs, even if not the top jobs they want; the uneducated still are most likely to have the poorest jobs or to be unemployed. Unfortunately, the job equation is rather one-sided; having a good education does not necessarily lead to a good job, but having a poor education almost surely means a poor job.

THE AMERICAN EDUCATIONAL SYSTEM: OPEN OR CLOSED?

In spite of all the criticisms it is still true that education is one of the crucial keys to social opportunity, occupational advancement, and social mobility. It is, therefore, extremely important to provide educational opportunities for all people if the society is to be open, democratic, and just.

COMPARISON OF THE "OPEN" AND "CLOSED" MODELS

Two educational models are of concern in this chapter—the "open" system and the "closed" system.

1. *The "Open" Education Model.* If a society's social system were completely open and fair, *ability* would determine people's educational possibilities. They would go on to higher education if they were intelligent, worked hard, and achieved in educational activities. Accidental factors—birth position, social class, sex, race—would not determine educational opportunity. Turner (1960) called this "contest" mobility; social progress is like a great race in which all participants have an equal chance if they run hard. This type of social mobility is "achieved," since it depends on achievement instead of on social background.

2. *The "Closed" Educational Model.* If the social system were unfair, if everyone did not have equal educational opportunity, we would expect much "channeling." That is, accidental factors such as family wealth, race, and social class would channel a person into higher or lower educational levels. Ability would not be the major determinant of success. Turner called this "sponsored" mobility, for some people would then have special advantages over people who were not spon-

sored by the luck of birth; they would be sponsored by accidental social factors. This is "ascribed" social mobility.

Which model—open or closed—best describes the American educational system? The answer is complex, for, although the American system is more open than those of most other societies, it does have many built-in inequities and unfair practices. One of the most glaring problems is that of discrimination against minority groups, a topic to be discussed at length in Chapter Thirteen. But there are many other inequities that should be spotlighted. In order to judge how well the American educational system lives up to the dream of equal opportunity, we will examine both the factors that tend to open up educational opportunities and the pressures that tend to limit these opportunities.

EDUCATION FOR THE MASSES: OPENING UP EDUCATIONAL OPPORTUNITIES

One of the most important developments in contemporary society that is pressing for an "open" educational system is the explosion of educational opportunities and achievements for all social classes. Once education was for the elite of the society. Today, however, education is extended to the masses and the "democratization of education" is spreading in the advanced industrial nations. (See Figure 10.4 for illiteracy rates in different nations.)

Several pieces of evidence show how dramatically the educational level of the United States has risen. Not only has the absolute number of students aged 5 to 17 increased (from about 17 million in 1910 to over 50 million in 1970) but, even more interesting, the *percentage* of children attending school has also risen steadily. As shown in Figure 10.5, in 1910 about 70 of every 100 children in the school-age bracket went to school, whereas in 1970, 96 of every 100 did so.

In addition, more people are staying in school for longer periods of time. Forty years ago only one out of every eight Americans had finished high school; in 1973 the figures showed about 65 percent of the total population had at least a high school education, and the percentage is rising rapidly. The median level of education in the United States is now over 12 years of schooling, a figure that only a few decades ago would have been unbelievable. College enrollments are also rising, as Figure 10.6 indicates. Although this trend does seem to be leveling off, it is nevertheless true that more people than ever before are going to college. Moreover, the level of educational attainment of the nation will continue to rise, if only because older people who did not have high educations are constantly being replaced with younger people who have more years of schooling. Of course, this trend has massive, largely unmeasurable, effects on the nation—on voting behavior, the job market, cultural values, child-rearing practices, and dozens of other factors that are closely related to educational levels. In short, there are clearly many educational opportunities in this society, opportunities that indicate we have a fairly "open" educational system.

Figure 10.4
Illiteracy rates in different nations. Although modern industrial states have low illiteracy rates, many nations still have much illiteracy

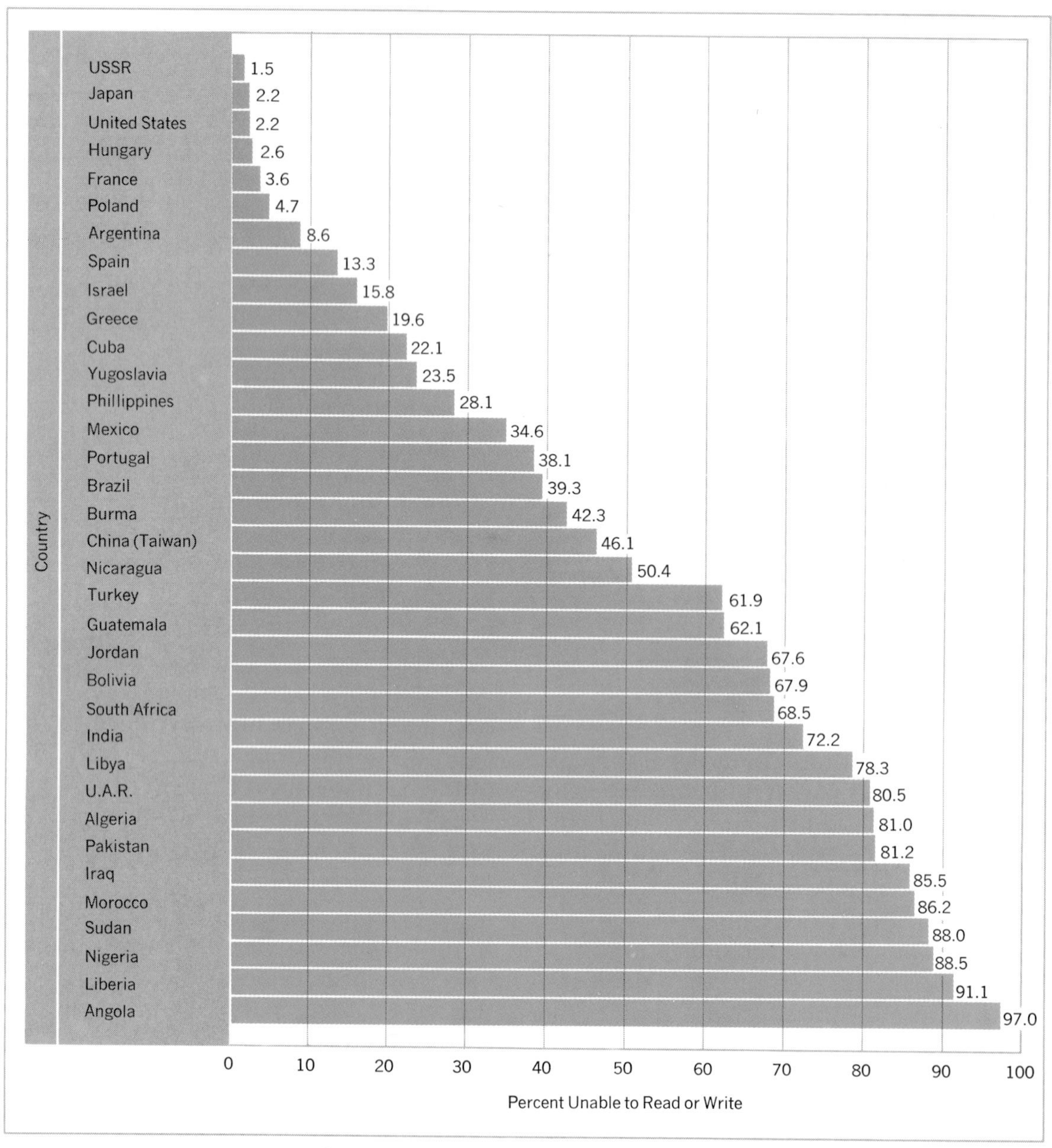

Source: Statistical Office of the United Nations, New York, N.Y., *Statistical Yearbook* 1969; United Nations Educational, Scientific, and Cultural Organization, Paris, France, *Statistical Yearbook,* 1969 and 1972.

Figure 10.5
Educational attainment: Percent of school-age youth enrolled in school—United States

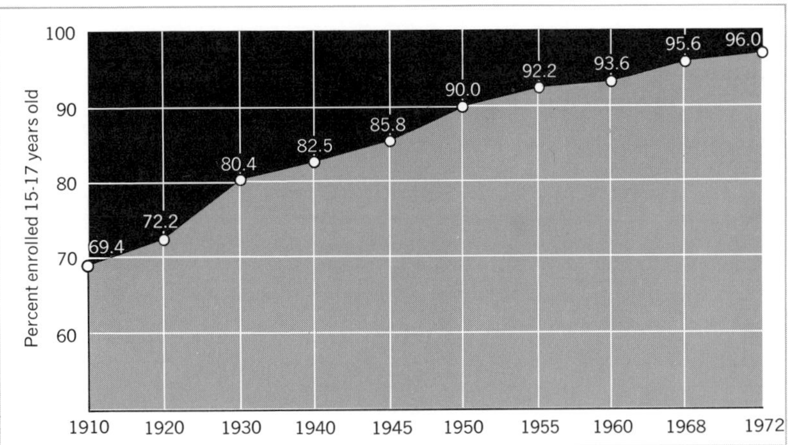

Sources: Statistical History of the United States from Colonial Times to the Present. Series H 383-394, p. 214; "Population Characteristics," *Current Population Reports,* Series P-20, No. 162, March 24, 1967. U.S. Department of Commerce, Bureau of the Census, p. 7; "Population Characteristics," *Current Population Reports,* Series P-20, No. 167, August 30, 1967. U.S. Department of Commerce, Bureau of the Census, p. 10; "Population Characteristics," *Current Population Reports,* Series P-20, No. 179, March 4, 1969, U.S. Department of Commerce, Bureau of the Census, p. 2.

BARRIERS TO EDUCATIONAL OPPORTUNITY

In spite of the many forces pressuring for greater educational opportunity in modern society there are also many barriers to educational advancement that make it more "closed."

TEACHER ATTITUDES, TRACKING SYSTEMS, AND COUNSELING

Let's do an experiment. Let's divide a group of students in half arbitrarily by using their locker numbers—even numbers go into one group, odd numbers into the other group. Now we will tell the teachers that group one is a very "high-potential" group and will learn very fast, whereas group two consists of slow learners. Since each student was assigned to a group at random, there is no reason to expect the two groups to have different test scores at the end of the year. The only distinction between the groups is that the teachers expect *the students to perform differently. Do you think the students will make better test scores if they are favored by their teachers?*

The experiment posed above was actually conducted by Robert Rosenthal and Lenore F. Jacobson (1968) in a predominantly Mexican-American elementary school in California. Over a two-year period the test scores for the fake "high-

Figure 10.6
Enrollment in institutions of higher education

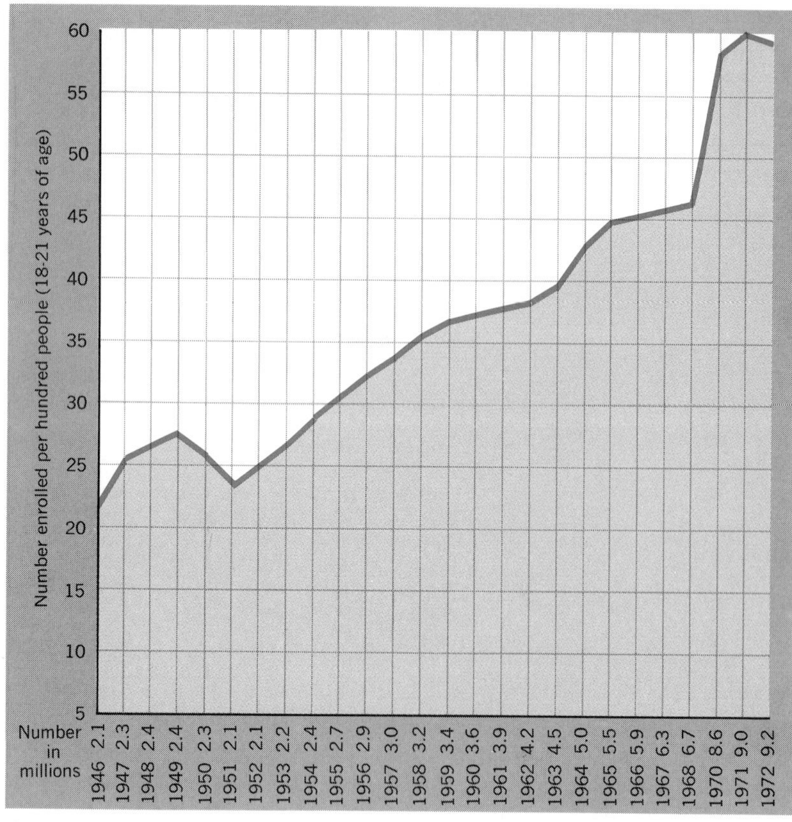

Source: Digest of Educational Statistics, U.S. Office of Education, U.S. Government Printing Office, Washington D.C., 1970; *Current Population Reports, Population Estimates and Projections,* Department of Commerce, Bureau of the Census, Series p-25, No. 473, January 1972; *Chronicle of Higher Education,* December 18, 1972, p. 2.

ability" group were much higher than the scores for the fake "low-ability" group. The *teachers' attitudes* had in fact influenced the children's learning; the children's real ability (approximately the same in both groups) was submerged under the teachers' expectations. This experiment has far-reaching ramifications because there are many factors that influence teachers' perceptions. Do teachers treat lower-class children differently from upper-class children? Are blacks and other minorities encouraged and helped as much as whites? Are female students discriminated against? There are many factors that help form teachers' perceptions of their students, and all these characteristics become bases on which the teachers "channel" students into lower-ability performance. The social prejudices and middle-class biases of the teachers impinge heavily on the students. In some cases it is the teacher's expectations instead of the student's ability that determine the student's success in school.

The psychological expectations of the teachers informally channel students into different achievement levels. In addition, there is the more formal channeling process, the *tracking system,* by which students are divided into curriculum tracks based on tests and other criteria. Since tracking often begins early in the child's school career, it tends to reinforce whatever disadvantages the child starts with. Belonging to the Bluebirds (slow readers) may destroy the student's self-confidence and does take him away from other children who might help him read better. Moreover, since middle-class children generally have a better home background for success in school than lower-class children, the tracking system tends to resegregate classrooms around social class and racial lines. Quite rightly, the tracking system is under heavy attack by civil rights advocates and educational reformers.

Moreover, the counseling system in high schools appears to be biased in the direction of middle-class children. Two sociologists, Aaron Cicourel and John Kitsuse, studied the counseling system in a large high school and discovered that the social class of the parents was a major factor in the quality of counseling the students received, regardless of individual talent. In addition, they found that students were assigned to curriculum tracks on the basis of tests of doubtful value, of subjective factors that biased the counselors, and of personal judgments about the student's future life that often were not at all realistic. Cicourel and Kitsuse summarized their findings this way.

In one sense, the influences of social class on the treatment accorded students has become a built-in feature of the organizational activities of the modern comprehensive high school, particularly those with highly developed counseling programs. Insofar as the high school is committed to the task of identifying talent and increasing the proportion of college-going students, counselors will tend to devote more of their time and activities to those students who plan and are most likely to go to college and whose parents actively support their plans and make frequent inquiries at the school about their progress—namely, the students from the middle and upper social classes. Thus, as between two students of equal ability who are reported as failing in their course, if one is a college-going middle-class student and the other a non-college working-class student, how is the counselor likely to handle them? If our assumption is valid, the upper-middle-class student will be called to a conference, inquiries will be made among his teachers, and his parents will be informed of his problems, while the lower-class student, unless he is considered exceptionally bright, may be ignored. (Cicourel and Kitsuse, 1963, p. 145)

Teacher attitudes, the tracking system, and the counseling system all combine *to reinforce the social characteristics that students bring with them to school.* Instead of breaking down social barriers, the school helps to crystallize the class, race, and social distinctions that rule the larger society. In many respects, instead of being the avenue of escape and social mobility, the school becomes an agent of the outside status structure, channeling the student into his "proper place." The school becomes a sorting system, separating children along class and racial lines, funneling the wealthy and affluent into prime jobs, while condemning the poor and the minorities into the leftovers.

THE JOYLESS CLASSROOM

The charge that the schools reinforce the social class system has been coupled with another powerful critique—that the educational curriculum is irrelevant and joyless for most students. Many social critics have argued that American schools are repressive, juiceless, drab places where individual creativity and curiosity are slowly squeezed out of the students; where conformity and neatness are rewarded instead of energy and excitement; where obedience and discipline are the concerns of the teacher instead of learning and knowledge; where respect for the teacher is valued above self-expression and self-determination. Rote learning, memorization, meaningless objective tests, and dull textbooks are all part of the drab mixture that stifles children. Albert Einstein, the great atomic scientist, has complained that the rigidity of the school system almost forced him away from intellectual activities.

One had to cram all this stuff into one's mind, whether one liked it or not. This coercion had such a deterring effect that after I had passed the final examination, I found the consideration of any scientific problems distasteful to me for an entire year. . . . It is in fact nothing short of a miracle that the modern methods of instruction have not yet entirely strangled the holy curiosity of inquiry; for this delicate little plant, aside from stimulation, stands mainly in need of freedom; without this it goes to wrack and ruin without fail. It is a very grave mistake to think that the enjoyment of seeing and searching can be promoted by means of coercion and a sense of duty. To the contrary, I believe that it would be possible to rob even a healthy beast of prey of its voraciousness, if it were possible, with the aid of a whip, to force the beast to devour continuously, even when not hungry—especially if the food, handed out under such coercion, were to be selected accordingly. (As quoted in Goodman, 1962)

Not only is the curriculum often irrelevant and dull, but many schools are run like prisons. John Holt, an outstanding educator and social critic, wrote that "what is most shocking and horrifying about public education today is that in almost all schools the children are treated, most of the time, like convicts in a jail." In all too many respects schools are like "total institutions" (see pp. 57–59); they strip children of their identities, subject them to endless rules and regulations, bunch them together in similar groups, and run their lives like a time clock. The pupil must ask permission to go to the toilet and carry a hall pass in the process. One teacher told this story about his school.

There is no physical freedom whatever at Milgrim (High School). That is, there is no time at which, or place in which a student may simply go about his business. Privacy is strictly forbidden. Except during class breaks, the toilets are kept locked, so that a student must not only obtain a pass but find the custodian and induce him to unlock the facility. My mother, who had a certain humor about these matters unusual in her generation, had a favorite story about a golfer who, in a moment of extreme need, asked his caddy to direct him to the nearest convenience. The poor boy, unfortunately, stuttered; and the desperate golfer finally interrupted him, sadly, saying "never mind, now son; I've made other arrangements." How often this occurs at Milgrim I do not know, but when it does, the victim is undoubtedly sent for detention.

Milgrim High's most memorable arrangements are its corridor passes and its johns; they dominate social interaction. "Good morning, Mr. Smith," an attractive girl will say pleasantly to one of her teachers in the corridor. "Linda, do you have a pass to be in your locker after the bell rings?" is her greeting in reply. There are more different kinds of washrooms than there must have been in the Confederate Navy. The common sort, just marked "Boys" and "Girls" are generally locked. Then, there are some marked "Teachers, Men" and "Teachers, Women," unlocked. Near the auditorium are two others marked simply "Men" and "Women," intended primarily for the public when the auditorium is being used for some function. During the school day a cardboard sign saying "Adults Only" is added to the legend of these washrooms; this is removed at the close of the school day. (Friedenberg, 1963, pp. 29–30)

Teachers, counselors, and administrators hold different expectations—often based on the student's social class, race, and sex instead of on ability—that affect the student's performance. Moreover, these attitudes become institutionalized in the tracking system: lower-class and minority students are funneled into vocational education and manual training; middle- and upper-class students are pushed into college-prepatory classes that will move them into better jobs. If you add to these factors the biased, dull curriculum and the repressive atmosphere of many schools, the whole environment of the schools does not meet our expectations of an open system. This is not, however, the whole story, for as students go on to college the situation does not usually improve.

FINANCIAL SUPPORT OF THE SCHOOLS REINFORCES INEQUALITY

One of the critical debates in education has been the financing of schools. Combined, the federal, state, and local governments of the United States spend more than $60 billion on education in the United States each year, but although this sum seems huge it is reasonable when compared to other American expenditures. The Department of Defense alone spends more money than all the educational systems in the United States combined. The outlay for cosmetics and liquor are more than the expenditures for education; the income of insurance companies is almost as great as educational funds; the amount of money spent on automobiles—purchase, repair, and upkeep—is enormous compared to educational expenditures. This low level of educational commitment is reflected in the poor physical facilities and supplies, low teachers' salaries (median income in 1972 was under $8,000), and overcrowded conditions.

This low level of funding also affects the research and development (R and D) resources available to education. It is now widely recognized that R and D funds are critical to expand knowledge in a field; consequently, the Department of

Defense, private industry, and other government agencies spend huge sums of money on R and D activities. Defense spends about $6 billion on R and D each year and private industry spends about $8 billion. Federal money spent on research and development in education, by contrast, was only $104 million in 1971. The ratio between defense and education is 60:1, and between industry and education is 80:1. Is education so unimportant that making better bombs or automobiles should get such fantastically larger research budgets? The financial investment in education is one of the best examples of the sometimes warped social priorities of the nation.

And there are other financial issues at state and local levels. The following are all data that have emerged from social science research in the last decade.

1. Because of their unequal wealth, different states spend vastly different amounts of money on their pupils (see Figure 10.7). Once again the accident of birth largely determines a student's chances—this time the accident of which state he was born in.

2. The distribution of educational funds *within* states are very unequal; rich districts give their children much better educations than poor districts. This inequality is largely the result of funding schools through property taxes within each district. Rich districts can afford better educational facilities. For example, in 1972 in California, Beverly Hills had a tax base of $40,885 per student, whereas nearby Baldwin Park had only $3706 per student. Obviously children from Beverly Hills had far better educational facilities than those from Baldwin Park. This type of inequity prevails in every state in the nation. In 1972 two court decisions—one in California (*Serrano* vs. *Priest*) and one in Texas (*Rodriguez* vs. *San Antonio*)—ruled that an unequal distribution of funds within states was unconstitutional. If these decisions had been upheld by the U. S. Supreme Court they would have forced every state to equalize its school expenditures among districts and in the process would have reshaped the whole property-tax system throughout the nation. Unfortunately, these court decisions that held so much promise for educational reform were overturned by conservative judges of the U. S. Supreme Court that had only months before been appointed by President Nixon.

3. Even within the *same* district school funds are unequally divided, with upper-class, white schools consistently getting more money, better facilities, and more experienced teachers than poor or minority schools. This pattern has been demonstrated in a number of sociological studies throughout the country, including a large midwestern city (Sexton, 1961), Atlanta (Burkhead, 1967), and Chicago (Coons, 1962).

The overall pattern is that social-class background and the luck of birth into the right state or district greatly influences a child's chances to obtain a good education. Once more the ideal of an open educational system is confronted with the hard fact that in many respects the system is closed, this time in regard to financial expenditures.

WHO GOES TO COLLEGE?

We have been exploring inequality in education, primarily at the elementary and secondary level. With college more often being a requirement for entry to high-prestige jobs, it is particularly distressing that the general patterns of dis-

Figure 10.7
State variations in income and school expenditures.

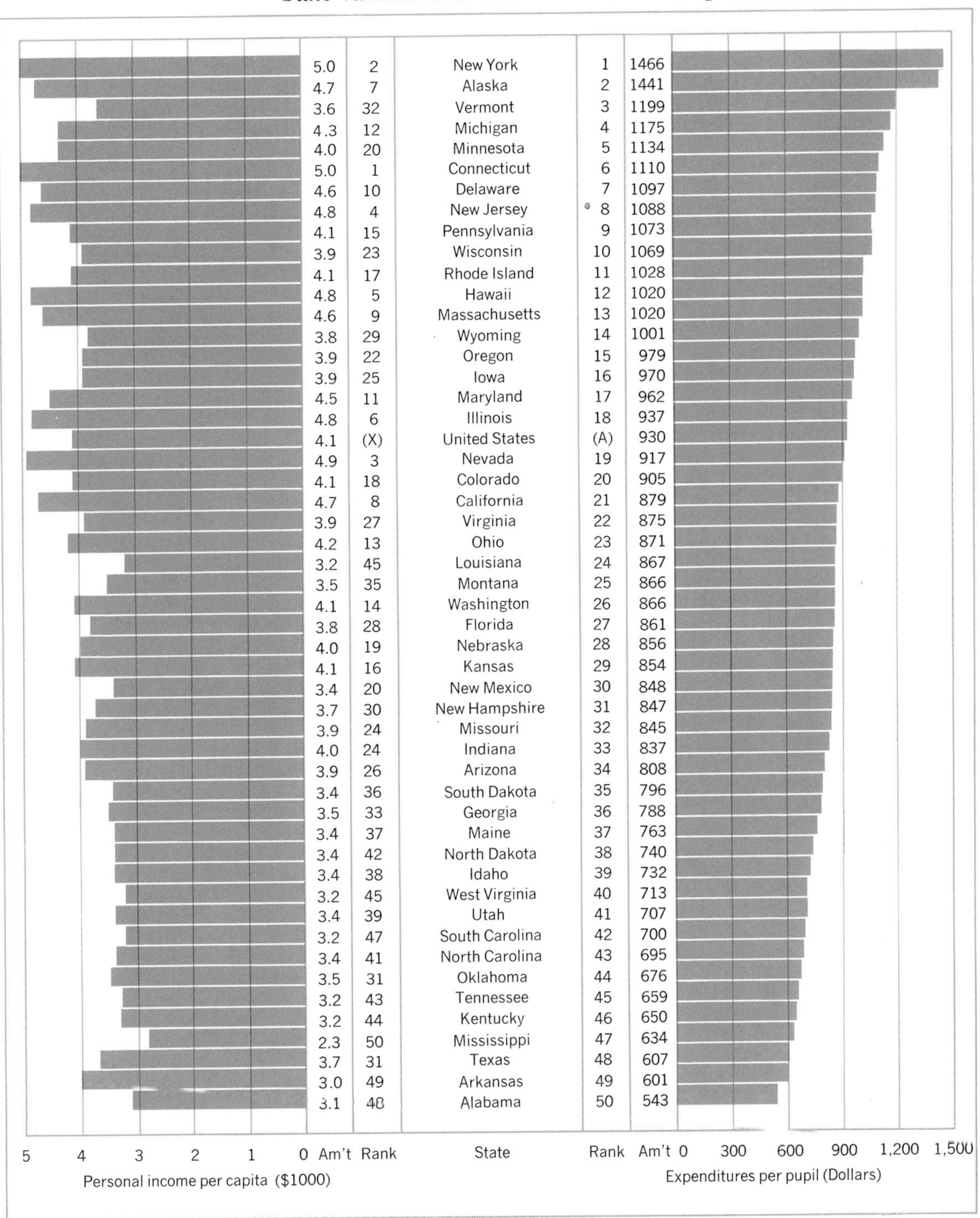

Am't	Rank	State	Rank	Am't
5.0	2	New York	1	1466
4.7	7	Alaska	2	1441
3.6	32	Vermont	3	1199
4.3	12	Michigan	4	1175
4.0	20	Minnesota	5	1134
5.0	1	Connecticut	6	1110
4.6	10	Delaware	7	1097
4.8	4	New Jersey	8	1088
4.1	15	Pennsylvania	9	1073
3.9	23	Wisconsin	10	1069
4.1	17	Rhode Island	11	1028
4.8	5	Hawaii	12	1020
4.6	9	Massachusetts	13	1020
3.8	29	Wyoming	14	1001
3.9	22	Oregon	15	979
3.9	25	Iowa	16	970
4.5	11	Maryland	17	962
4.8	6	Illinois	18	937
4.1	(X)	United States	(A)	930
4.9	3	Nevada	19	917
4.1	18	Colorado	20	905
4.7	8	California	21	879
3.9	27	Virginia	22	875
4.2	13	Ohio	23	871
3.2	45	Louisiana	24	867
3.5	35	Montana	25	866
4.1	14	Washington	26	866
3.8	28	Florida	27	861
4.0	19	Nebraska	28	856
4.1	16	Kansas	29	854
3.4	20	New Mexico	30	848
3.7	30	New Hampshire	31	847
3.9	24	Missouri	32	845
4.0	24	Indiana	33	837
3.9	26	Arizona	34	808
3.4	36	South Dakota	35	796
3.5	33	Georgia	36	788
3.4	37	Maine	37	763
3.4	42	North Dakota	38	740
3.4	38	Idaho	39	732
3.2	45	West Virginia	40	713
3.4	39	Utah	41	707
3.2	47	South Carolina	42	700
3.4	41	North Carolina	43	695
3.5	31	Oklahoma	44	676
3.2	43	Tennessee	45	659
3.2	44	Kentucky	46	650
2.3	50	Mississippi	47	634
3.7	31	Texas	48	607
3.0	49	Arkansas	49	601
3.1	48	Alabama	50	543

Source: U.S. Bureau of the Census, *Statistical Abstract of the U.S.*, (Washington D.C.: U.S. Government Printing Office, 1972).

crimination and inequality persist in higher education. Of the students who complete high school about half of the men and a third of the women *start* college, but only about 22 percent of the men and 15 percent of the women actually graduate. So, in spite of the marked increases in college attendance, only a small minority of citizens actually complete higher education. There are a number of factors involved in determining who goes to college. In our idealized model of a completely open social system the people who go to college would be the brightest and hardest working. But, although intelligence is important, other factors—social class, family background, the ability to pay, parents' educational backgrounds—are at least as critical. Let us look at some of the evidence.

1. *The Higher the Socioeconomic Status of the Family, the More Likely the Children Are to go to College.* The more money the family has, the higher the prestige of the father's occupation, and the higher the social class of the family, the more likely a child is to have the encouragement and the financial resources to attend college.

2. *The Higher the Child's IQ, the More Likely He or She is to go to College.* This, of course, is what we would expect in an "open" system, and is true to some extent. At least as IQ has been measured traditionally, IQ scores are highly correlated with other predictors of college entrance. However, there is a great debate about measure of intelligence, and any explanation of factors that stimulate college attendance should be sensitive to cultural bias. But as Figure 10.8 indicates, ability interacts with the class background of the family. This figure, from Stouffer's study of boys in the Boston school system (1950), shows how many boys plan to go to college in given IQ levels and in given categories of family background. As you move up the left side of the chart the socioeconomic status of the family increases (from unskilled labor up to major professional groups). At the same time, as you move across to the right of the chart the IQ scores of the boys go up. Now notice that at almost every step of the ladder in IQ more boys plan to go to college, but this is also the case at every step of the *occupational level* of the family. As you can see, from the high-IQ/high-family-background corner (upper right) to the low-IQ/low-family background corner (lower center), there is 10 times more college orientation in the upper group. From this chart three things are clear: (a) the higher the IQ, the more college plans; (b) the higher the family background, the more college plans; and (c) IQ and family background are *both* important to college plans; they interact very much.

3. *Students From Large Cities are More Likely to Attend College Than Students From Smaller Communities.* Large cities have several advantages; more educational opportunities are available, and students can live at home and commute to school. In addition, city high schools probably have better counseling services to direct students toward college.

4. *The More the Students' Peers Plan to go to College, The More Likely They Will go to College.* This is especially true for the lower classes. Among working-class students in California Irving Krauss (1964) found that strong pressure toward college among a student's friends led to over 80 percent of the youth making college plans, whereas only 29 percent wanted to go if peer pressure for college attendance was weak.

5. *The Higher Parent's Educations, The*

Figure 10.8
Higher IQ and higher social class work jointly to increase college attendance. Proportion of boys enrolled in college preparatory courses and definitely planning to go to college in Boston schools, by IQ scores and occupational background of family.

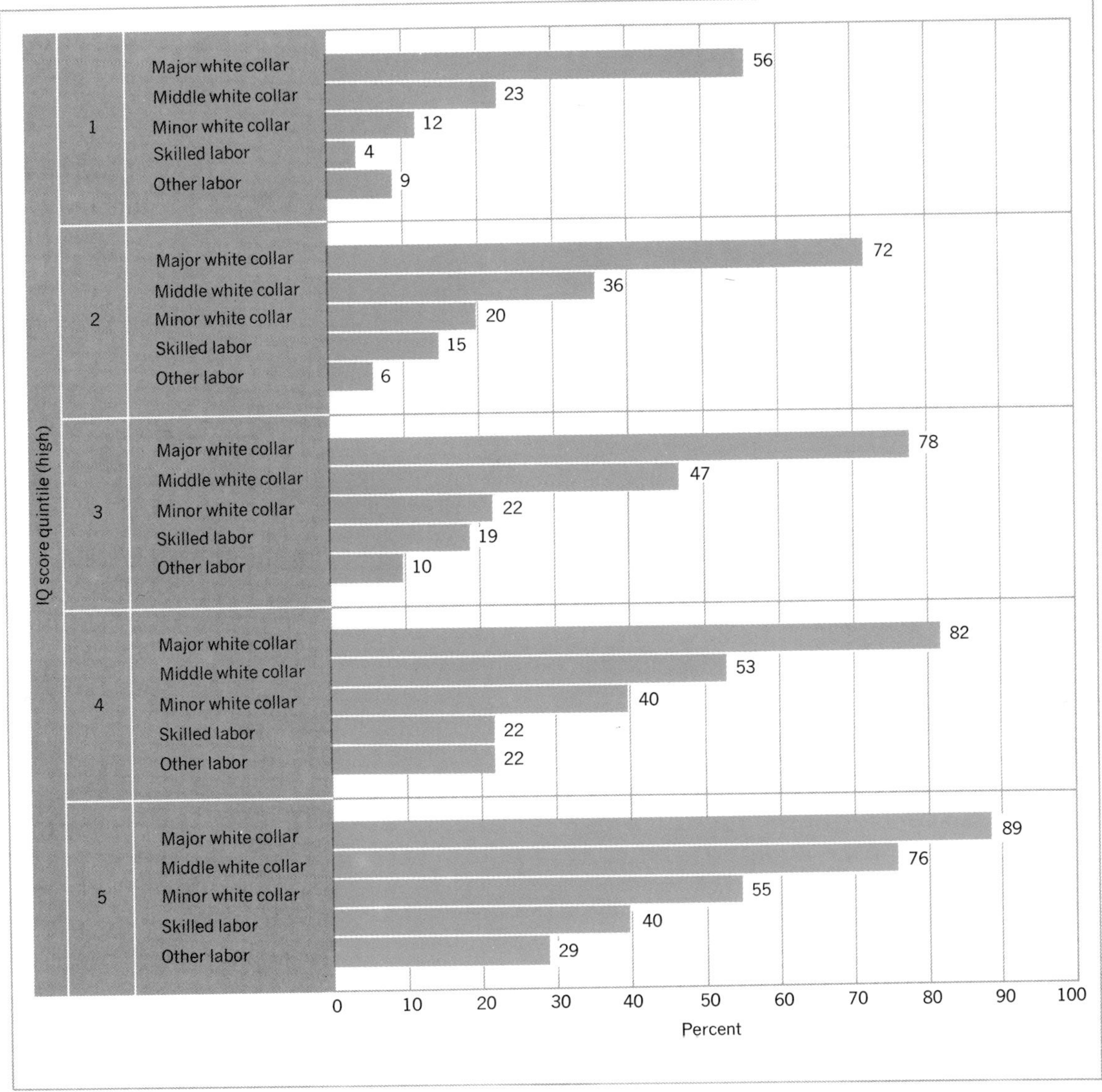

Source: Samuel Stouffer, "College Aspirations, IQ, and Family Background," *American Journal of Sociology,* Spring 1950, pp. 116–121.

More Likely a Student is to Attend College. Highly educated parents realize that education influences occupational and social success, and they are much more likely to encourage their children to attend college. In a study of over 9000 high school seniors in Wisconsin, Sewell and Shah (1968) found a direct correlation between parents' educational attainment and children's plans for college. Whereas only about 37 percent of the children whose parents had low educations wanted to go to college, 92 percent of the children whose parents had high educational backgrounds wanted to go on to higher education.

Taking all these factors into account, there are four major theories that help to account for who goes to college. The first is the *modeling* theory; if parents are highly educated then they are probably going to encourage their children to remain in school, and they are likely to have friends and relatives who model the life patterns that higher education affords. The second is the *opportunity* theory; children from higher income families and who live in large cities have more opportunity to attend college because they have colleges available and they have the money to pay for it. Theory three is the *reference group* idea; if students are surrounded by friends and peers who want to go to college, they, too, are likely to plan in that direction. Finally, there is the *ability* theory; those who work the hardest and have the highest IQ's tend to go to college. (See Chapter Thirteen for a discussion of culturally biased measures of intelligence).

These are certainly not mutually exclusive theories because in fact all of them work together. In addition all the factors seem to *compound.* That is, if people have one of these factors going for them, they are also likely to have the others. If people are born into upper-class families, for example, they are likely to have educated parents, live in a cosmopolitan city, go to a college-oriented high school, have peer friends interested in college, and have the money to pay for higher education. People born in lower-class families sometimes have none of these other advantages. Clearly social status and social background factors impinge on the educational system to a great degree, opening it more to the middle and upper classes and closing it off for the lower classes. Once again we see the "channeling" effect by which the social status system of the larger society is reflected in the educational system.

THE EDUCATION OF WOMEN: SOCIAL "CHANNELING" IN REFERENCE TO SEX

We have been examining a very important question: Is the educational system "open," do all citizens have an equal chance, or is it "closed" to many groups and social classes? The evidence we have gathered thus far—about high school tracking and counseling, the curriculum, biased intelligence tests, and entry to higher education—presents us with some very serious problems. In many ways educational opportunity is sharply limited. Let us look at another more specific example of the "closed" character of the educational system: sex discrimination. Women constitute one of the groups who are disadvantaged in education.

In Chapter Four we discussed how, in general, women are socialized to accept an inferior status. M. Horner conducted an experiment (Horner, 1969, as quoted in Bem and Bem, 1970) that illustrates how strong an impact this socialization has on women's attitudes toward scholastic achievements. College women were asked to complete the following story. "After first-term finals, Anne finds herself at the top of her medical-school class." Here are some examples of the responses.

Anne starts proclaiming her surprise and joy. Her fellow classmates are so disgusted with her behavior that they jump on her in a body and beat her. She is maimed for life.

Anne is an acne-faced bookworm . . . . She studies twelve hours a day, and lives at home to save money. "Well, it certainly paid off. All the Friday and Saturday nights without dates . . . . I'll be the best woman doctor alive." And yet a twinge of sadness comes through—she wonders what she really has . . . .

Anne doesn't want to be number one in her class . . . . She feels she shouldn't rank so high because of social reasons. She drops to ninth and then marries the boy who graduates number one.

In contrast, when the college women were asked to finish the same story about a man, John, the endings were very different.

John has worked very hard, and his long hours of study have paid off . . . . He is thinking about his girl, Cheri, whom he will marry at the end of med school. He realizes he can give her all the things she desires after he becomes established. He will go on in med school and be successful in the long run.

The revealing thing about this sad little experiment is that *women*, not men, were telling the stories that portrayed Anne in such a difficult position. The women who told the stories were affected, like other people in the society, by an unconscious prejudice against high educational success for a woman. Horner comments that "unusual excellence in women was clearly associated for them with the loss of femininity, social rejection, personal or social destruction or some combination of the above." For men there is no contradiction between success and acceptance; for women there is.

STATISTICS ABOUT THE EDUCATION OF WOMEN

The effects of social pressure against the education of women is all too clear in the statistics. Although about the same number of men and women complete high school (1,541,000 men and 1,561,000 women in 1971), there are more men completing college (473,000 men and 344,000 women). Women receive an even smaller number of master's and doctor's degrees. Figure 10.9 shows the percentage of each degree awarded to men and women from 1900 to 1969. Notice that men consistently receive the vast majority of the doctor's degrees, nearly two thirds of the master's degrees, and considerably more than half of the bachelor's degrees. There seems to be some progress in equalizing educational levels for men and women, but it is very slow. At some times, in fact, the trend has reversed; the percentage of women awarded higher degrees went down sharply in 1950 and by 1969 had only barely managed to reach 1930 levels. Doctor's degrees for women have actually gone down from 1930 to 1969.

Moreover, there are differences in the *subjects* that men and women study in college (see Figure 10.10). Men tend to major in the sciences and social sciences and in professional areas such as engineering. Women, on the other hand major in education, humanities, and the social sciences—subjects that prepare them for lower-paying, less prestigious jobs. All of these facts add up to a generalized pattern of underachievement and lack of opportunity for women in education.

Figure 10.9
Percent of degrees earned by women and men, 1900–1969

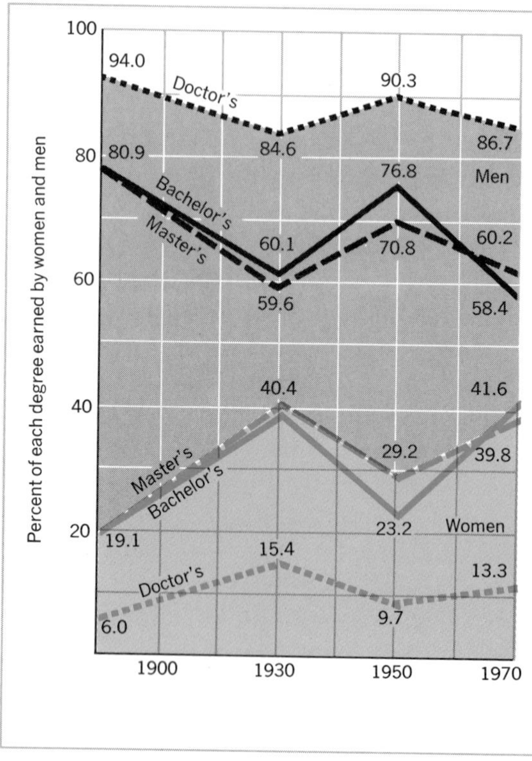

Source: Department of Labor, *1969 Handbook of Women Workers,* Bulletin 294 of the Women's Bureau, p. 191; Bureau of the Census; *Statistical Abstract of the U.S.,* 1972 NOTE: This chart should be read as follows. "Of all the Doctor's degrees given in 1900, 94.0 percent went to men, and 6.0 percent to women." The top and bottom lines are doctor's degrees, and add up to 100 percent for any given year. The same is true for each degree.

BARRIERS TO THE EDUCATION OF WOMEN

Of course, many people would argue that the educational disparities between men and women are not the result of discrimination but rather of the personal choice of women: "After all, nobody is *stopping* them, women can get an education if they want to." However, a moment's reflection suggests that really it is not that simple. There are, in fact, many social barriers to the education of women.

First, as mentioned above, women are *socialized* from early childhood not to desire too much education. Oh, to be sure some education is necessary but only a minimum. The prime task for a girl, she is constantly told in subtle ways, is to catch a man and settle down in a family. Higher levels of education may be a problem, since many "eligible" men may already be married and since men may feel

Figure 10.10
Percent of degrees at each level earned by women in various fields, 1970

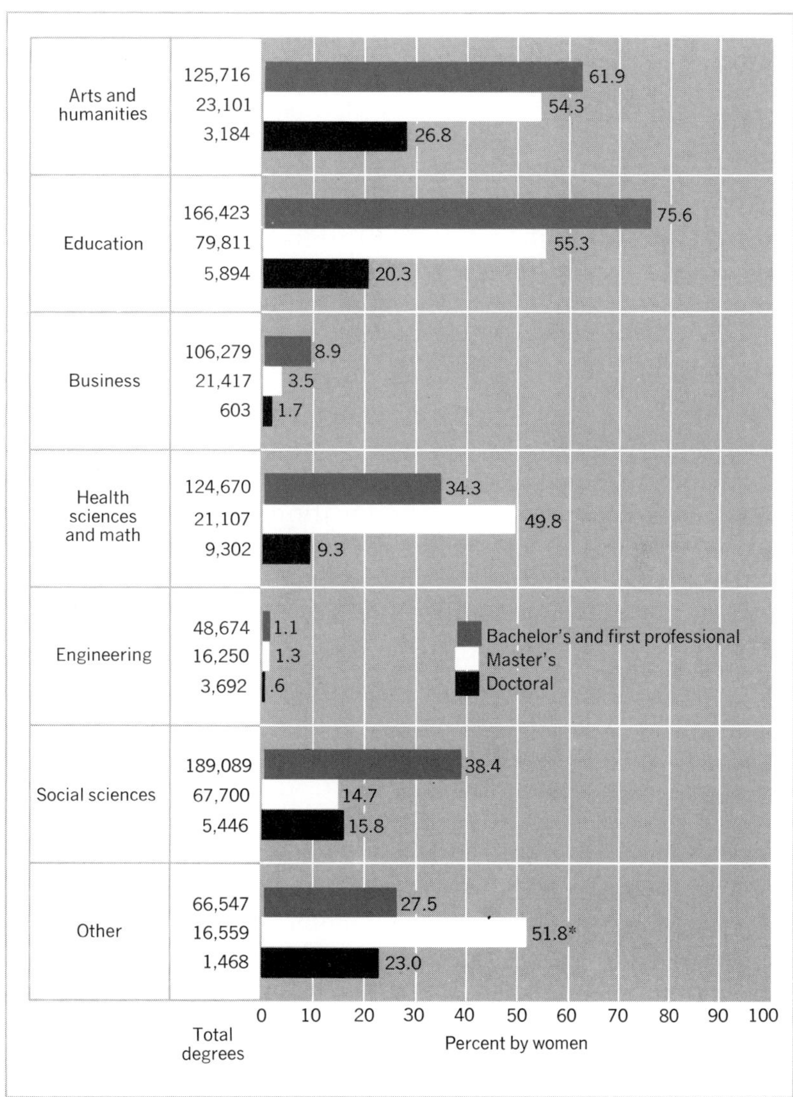

*This high figure is largely due to Master's Degrees in Library Science, which accounted for 5436 of 6544 Master's Degrees carried by women in this field.

Source: Statistical Abstract of the United States, 1972, p. 133.

threatened by highly educated women who compete with them. The parents are much more likely to encourage a son to go on to college, but the daughter is apt to go only if there is a surplus of funds. In a study of parental aspirations for their children, Sewell and Shah (1968) found that in every social class, regardless of parents' education, both mothers and fathers encouraged their male children to go to college more than they encouraged their female children. Figure 10.11 shows one of their findings.

Second, there are serious discriminatory practices in higher education that systematically limit a woman's chance for educational achievement. There is discrimination in admission policies; many of the highest prestige universities in the nation maintain exclusive or quota policies against women, including Harvard, Brown, Dartmouth, Connecticut Wesleyan, the military academies, Princeton, and Cornell. Only recently Congress outlawed sex discrimination in graduate schools that receive federal money, and other federal agencies have begun to move against sex discrimination in undergraduate schools. The discrimination is further illustrated in the scholarship and loan aid given to men and women—the 1971 average for men was $760, but for women $518.[1]

The barriers continue throughout a woman's college career, chiefly in the absence of female role models. Whereas men are surrounded by successful male professors, deans, and presidents, there are few successful female models for a woman to imitate or with whom she can emotionally identify. The informal social pressure to conform is subtle; nobody *tells* her that she had better play down intellectual achievement but, in many ways the message is drummed into her head.

Women, in fact, actually begin to believe that men are better scholars. Philip Goldberg (1968) did a very simple experiment to show how well established this belief was. Goldberg asked female college students, separated randomly into two groups, to rate some professional articles from six different academic areas. The exact same articles were given to each group, but one group's articles listed men as the authors whereas the other groups' listed women. The women consistently rated the male-authored articles higher than the female-authored articles—even though they were actually identical. Even in traditionally female areas, such as elementary education and dietetics, the women rated the male author higher! When the experiment was repeated with male subjects a similar pattern of favoritism toward male authors was found. Both men and women shared the common prejudice that women could not perform as well as men in academic subjects—in spite of all the scientific evidence suggesting men and women are about equal in mental capacities.

The forces of discrimination against women are powerful: socialization that deemphasizes education, less financial help from family, less scholarship aid,

[1] Testimony entered into the *Congressional Record* by Senator Birch Bayh, February 28, 1972.

Figure 10.11
Parents encourage sons to attend college more than daughters in sample of Wisconsin youth. (percent receiving parental encouragement to go to college)

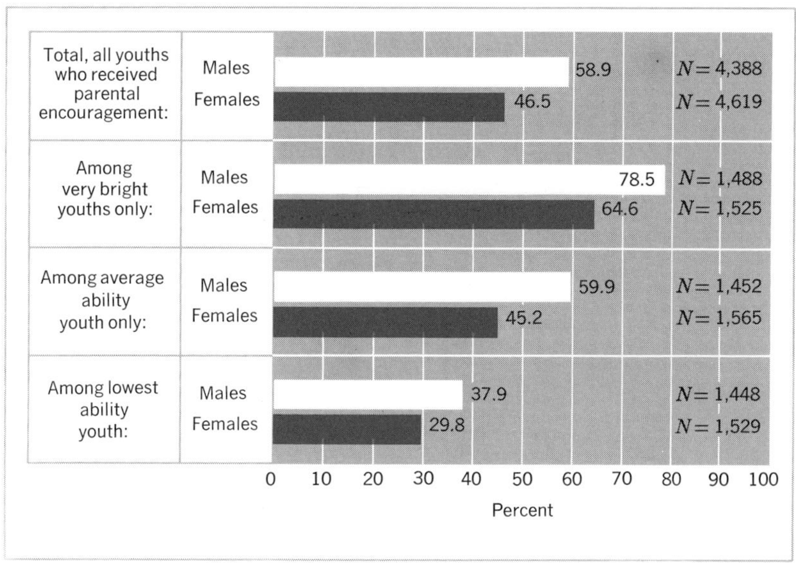

Source: William H. Sewell and Vimal P. Shah, "Parental Education and Children's Aspirations and Achievements," *American Sociological Review, 33* (2), April 1968, pp. 196–197.

fewer role models to pattern their academic lives after, and a widespread prejudice against women's achievement in academic fields. By way of contrast, men do not face these barriers. Families are much more likely to urge them on to college and to sacrifice financially for them. On entering college men have fewer restrictions on admissions, receive bigger scholarships, and find many more role models among the faculty for emotional and professional identification. In addition, men face less pressure to get married—or if they marry they are likely to have a working wife to support them. The disadvantages women face in the educational sphere have immense ramifications in other areas of life, especially in the occupational world.

SUMMARY

Americans have always pointed with pride to their educational network, and with some real justification because it is better than that of most other societies, past and present. In some respects it is an open system. Ability is still important and often rewarded even for minority and lower-class students. Public education is expanding, especially in the community college sector. Public expenditures for education have been consistently rising for many decades. There has been serious—although extremely slow—progress in the area of racial discrimination; access to higher education is greater than at any other point in history.

But we have also noted a series of problems that suggest that educational opportunities are closed for major segments of the society. Minority, lower-class, and female students face serious disadvantages: the teachers' attitudes, the counseling system, the tracking system, and the testing system. And all students must put up with irrelevant curricula that stifle the creative possibilities children bring to the school and reinforce the inequities of social stratification that exist in the larger society. Access to higher education—important for occupational and social advancement—is sharply limited by social background. Students whose parents are well-educated and financially successful and who go to good high schools with good students are likely to be more successful academically than less advantaged students of comparable ability. Finally, the whole educational experience is systematically stacked against women students because a multitude of barriers stand in their way.

When we take all these factors together, the picture is complex. In many ways the system is "open," but in many respects it is closed to huge segments of the population. As we have stressed many times, power, wealth, social prestige, and social class factors are impinging on the social system so that certain groups are disadvantaged and other groups have unearned advantages that help them get far ahead. Unfortunately the education system reflects—and reinforces—these tendencies toward inequality.

REFERENCES

Berg, Ivar. *Education and Jobs: The Great Training Robbery* (Boston: Beacon Paperbacks, 1971).

Bane, Mary Jo and Christopher Jencks. "Schools and Equal Opportunity," *Saturday Review of Education,* October 1972, pp. 37-42.

Blau, Peter M., and Otis Dudley Duncan. *The American Occupational Structure* (New York: Wiley, 1967).

Brim, O.G. *Sociology and the Field of Education* (New York: Russell Sage Foundation, 1958).

Burkhead, Jesse, et al. *Input and Output in Large-City High Schools* (Syracuse, N.Y: Syracuse University Press, 1967).

Cicourel, A.V., and J.I. Kitsuse. *The Educational Decision-Makers* (Indianapolis: Bobbs-Merrill, 1963).

Clark, Burton R. *Educating the Expert Society* (New York: Chandler, 1962).

Coons, John E. "Chicago" in U.S. Civil Rights Commission, *Civil Rights U.S.A.: Public Schools North and West* (Washington: U.S. Government Printing Office, 1962).

Friedenberg, Edgar. *Coming of Age in America* (New York: Vintage, 1963).

Goodman, Paul. *Compulsory Mis-education* (New York: Vintage Books, 1962).

Halsey, A.H., Jean Floud, and C.A. Anderson, eds. *Education, Economy and Society* (New York: Free Press, 1961).

Hodgson, Godfrey. "Do Schools Make a Difference?" *Atlantic*, January 1973, pp. 36-46.

Holt, John. "Education for the Future," in Robert Theobald (ed.) *Social Policies for America in the Seventies* (New York: Doubleday, 1969).

Jencks, Christopher, et al. *Inequality: A Reassessment of the Effect of Family and* Organization," *Harvard Education Review, 34*, 1964, pp. 428-455.

Katz, Fred E. "The School as a Complex Organization," *Harvard Education Review, 34*, 1964, pp. 428-455.

Krauss, Irving. "Sources of Educational Aspiration among Working-class Youth," *Amer. Soc. Review, 29*, December 1964, pp. 867-879.

Levin, Henry M. "Schooling and Inequality: The Social Science Objectivity Gap," *Saturday Review*, November 11, 1972, pp. 49-51.

Lieberman, Myron. "Professors Unite!" *Harper's Magazine*, October 1971, pp. 61-70.

Neill, A.S. *Summerhill, A Radical Approach to Child Rearing* (New York: Hart, 1960).

Rosenthal, Robert, and Lenore F. Jacobson. *Pygmalion in the Classroom* (New York: Holt, 1968).

Sewell, William H., and Vimal P. Shah. "Parent's Education and Children's Educational Aspirations and Achievements," *American Soc. Review, 33* (2), April 1968, pp. 191-208.

Sexton, Pat. *Education and Income* (New York: Viking Press, 1961).

Turner, R.H. "Sponsored and Contest Mobility and the School System," *Amer. Soc. Review, 25*, 1960, pp. 855-867.

Young, Michael. *The Rise of the Meritocracy 1870-2033* (London: Thames & Hudson, 1958).

ELEVEN
TECHNOLOGY AND THE ECONOMIC SYSTEM

TOFFLER

There is, as yet, no widely accepted or wholly satisfactory term to describe the new stage of social development toward which we seem to be racing. Daniel Bell, the sociologist, coined the term "post-industrial" to signify a society in which the economy is largely based on service, the professional and technical classes dominate, theoretical knowledge is central, intellectual technology—systems analysis, model building, and the like—is highly developed, and technology is, at least potentially, capable of self-sustaining growth. The term has been criticized for suggesting that the society to come will no longer be technologically based—an implication that Bell specifically and carefully avoids. Kenneth Boulding's favorite term, "post-civilization," is employed to contrast the future society with "civilization"—the era of settled communities, agriculture and war . . . . Brzezinski's choice is the "technotronic society," in which he means one based heavily on advanced communications and electronics . . . . Then, of course, there is McLuhan's "global village" and "electric age"—once again an attempt to describe the future in terms of one or two rather narrow dimensions: communications and togetherness . . . . My own choice . . . is "super-industrial society." . . . It is intended to mean a complex, fast-paced society dependent upon extremely advanced technology and a post-materialist value system. (From Alvin Toffler, *Future Shock*, p. 491)

Toffler, in his book *Future Shock*, spends much time examining the impact of technology on social life and projecting that impact to the future. Toffler's concern is well chosen, for almost nothing affects your daily life more than the technological and economic system under which you live. Your job, your home, the thousands of inventions you use, and the nature of your family life and your government are in large part reflections of the technological system of contemporary society. It is obvious, then, that any adequate sociological treatment of modern society must consider economic and technological factors.

The sociologist's concern is not with the operation of the economy in itself—with banking, interest rates, business cycles, and other such issues. Instead, the sociologist is interested in the *relationship between the economic and technology systems and other social institutions of society*—family, religion, government, education. How does the economic system affect the employment of minorities and women? How has religious belief influenced the development of industrial society? How is automation affecting leisure time? How is the distribution of wealth in America affected by the growth of the business corporation? We will examine the economic and technical aspects of society by looking at some of the contemporary trends in the economic sector.

THE CONTEMPORARY TECHNOLOGICAL SOCIETY

The economic and technical changes of the past several centuries have essentially created a whole new world. Let us examine a few of the critical features of modern technological society.

THE DIVISION OF LABOR IN SOCIETY

One of the main characteristics of industrial society is its intense *specialization of labor.* As industrialism developed, workers became specialists and exchanged their services with one another through the medium of money. The French sociologist Émile Durkheim wrote a classic book entitled *The Division of Labor in Society* (1893) in which he took the labor specialization in modern society as a key feature for understanding contemporary life. Durkheim contrasted two different kinds of social integration.

1. *Mechanical solidarity* is the social integration characteristic of traditional, premodern societies. In these societies, Durkheim argued, there is little specialization of labor, everyone fulfills essentially the same roles, and there are "common values" that reinforce the social system. These common values are rigidly enforced, and any deviation

from the norm is punished severely by "repressive laws" based on force.

2. *Organic solidarity* is the social integration characteristic of modern societies with a high degree of labor specialization. Since there are many social roles a more complex value system emerges, a "pluralistic" value structure in which there is much more freedom and many more options. In such a highly differentiated society there would be high *interdependence*; people would depend on each other more because they have to exchange specialized services.

Contemporary sociologists agree with Durkheim's far-sighted analysis, for extreme job specialization is the order of the day in modern society. Doctors, lawyers, and plumbers now come in so many stripes that the average man is bewildered by the number of specialities and subdivisions that make up most jobs. To be a specialist today is to be the man in the know; to be a generalist is to be a shallow thinker who is not to be trusted with important tasks. In fact, according to the U. S. Department of Labor, there are now over 35,550 job specialties in the American economy. Moreover, intense job specialization does lead to a pluralistic value structure. People with different jobs tend to think differently, to hold different goals, and to espouse different values. People in different job settings do not see the world the same way. They seek diverse political goals, they have different aspirations for their children, they hold divergent religious beliefs, and they think differently about the family structure. In a very real sense specialized jobs create a Weltanschauung, a specific world view. Varied life-styles, different occupational "jargons" (see Insert 11.I), and different outlooks on the world—these are some of the consequences that stem from intense job specialization.

THE GROWTH OF A SERVICE ECONOMY

Sociologists usually divide work activities into three main subtypes.

1. *Primary industries* deal directly with obtaining raw materials from nature and include agriculture, mining, fishing, hunting, and forestry.

2. *Second industries* convert raw materials into usable products or distribute these products. Manufacturing, heavy industry, chemical refining, construction, and transportation are examples.

3. *Tertiary industries* are personal services such as medicine, education, barbering, and entertainment as well as services to the whole society such as trade and communication.

Through history there has been a steady progression from primary activities (especially agriculture) to secondary activities (especially manufacturing) to a service economy. It took several hundred thousand years for man to move from primary industries into manufacturing, but it has taken only a few hundred for the advanced industrial nations to move to a service economy. In the early 1960s the United States became the first nation in the world to have over half of its nonfarm labor force in service industries. Figure 11.1 shows how the labor force of

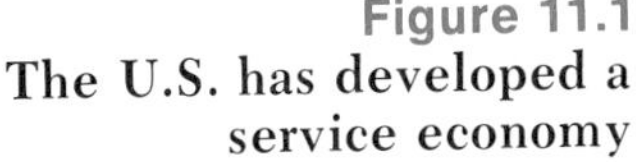
Figure 11.1
The U.S. has developed a service economy

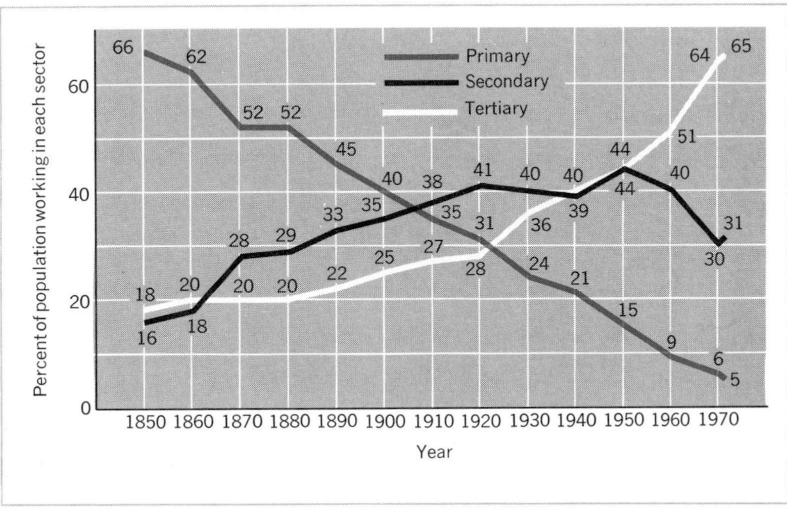

Source: U.S. Bureau of Census, *Historical Statistics of the U.S., Colonial Times to 1957; Statistical Abstract of the U.S.*, 1972.

the United States has changed over the last decades. Note how steadily the primary and secondary groups have decreased, and how dramatically the service group has grown, starting in the 1920s. It is important to realize, however, that most societies are still largely agricultural or manufacturing. It is the advanced industrial nations that have service economies.

The shift from agriculture and manufacturing to a service economy has many consequences for your daily life, including:

1. The statistical odds are that, because of this shift in the economy, *you will be employed in a service occupation*, whereas your father was most likely in a secondary industry—industry, refining, construction, transportation. Of course, there are plenty of exceptions, but "on the average" chances are that your job career will be different from your father's.

2. Service industries require *more skills*, so your job will probably require more education and training than your father's.

3. There will be a better chance for you to have *social mobility* because the service jobs are generally considered higher in social prestige, are better paid, and are usually white-collar activities. Of course, since so many other people will also be employed in service jobs, their prestige value may go down, relatively speaking. It is still true, however, that the statistical odds are that you will gain in social status over your parents.

Of course, none of the above things may actually happen to you personally, but at least across the whole population the odds are stacked in that direction. It is interesting that all these changes are likely to happen to you because of changes in the economic system, not necessarily because you worked any harder than your parents' generation. Once more the nagging suspicion arises that social status, wealth, and prestige are due at least as much to accidents of birth as they are to hard work.

TRIUMPH OF THE CORPORATE BUREAUCRACY

The economic world is different from the past in many ways, as the preceding pages testify, but one of the changes that dominates all others is the growth of the bureaucratic corporation. For most of human history work was carried on in the family; then it moved outside the family to a small craft shop, and later to the small, owner-run business with father and son cooperating in the enterprise that was handed down from generation to generation. Today, however, the small family business has been replaced by the giant corporation, owned by absentee stockholders, operated by professional managers, and organized in a bureaucratic fashion. The corporate bureaucracy now dominates the American economy and has definite organizational characteristics.

The corporation is jointly owned—no one man holds it, but a large group of stockholders share the ownership. The corporation has many advantages over private ownership, since many stockholders together can raise large amounts of capital and, in the event of a business failure, no one stockholder can be held liable. The capital-raising abilities and the shared liability make the corporation an excellent system for economic expansion and massive capital investment. An important consequence of this system is that *ownership is separated from control.* That is, the stockholders as the legal owners turn the operation of the enterprise over to professional managers who are salaried employees. A board of directors supposedly oversees the management but, in many respects, management acts as if it owned the company. Critics have argued that this system leads to many abuses, for the managers can take advantage of their professional knowledge, their closeness to the everyday operation, and the lack of unity among the stockholders to take effective control of the company.

The corporation is organized bureaucratically. Max Weber argued that the true sign of a modern economy was the rise of bureaucracies over the private family-dominated work units of the past. Instead of the private personal whims of an owner, a bureaucracy has the advantage of rules and regulations, careful assignment of work, and a system of rewards based on standard salaries. The modern worker is a creature of the office, the bureau, and the corporation instead of the man of the field, the craftshop, or the family-run business. And this trend toward bureaucratization will increase as the service industries take over even greater sections of the economy.

What does all this say about the modern worker? We can draw a few conclusions about his work in modern society.

1. The modern worker will probably be a wage earner or a salaried employee instead of being self-employed.

2. He will be an "organization man," working in a bureaucracy—whether that bureaucracy is General Motors, Methodist Hospital, The Federal Reserve Bank, or Yale University.

3. He will work under a professional manager and will rarely see the "owners," the faceless stockholders of the company.

In short, the modern worker will be quite different from past periods in history; he will be working at a specialized job, in a bureaucratic corporation or government agency, in a service occupation. Of course, not everyone will be in this type of job setting, but this will be the predominant mode. We need to look also at some other issues about the modern economy, especially the role of women and minorities in the occupational world.

WOMEN AND MINORITIES IN THE OCCUPATIONAL WORLD

Together, minorities (male and female) and women make up nearly one half of the labor force in the United States, with white men comprising slightly more than half. Minorities, the vast majority of whom are black, account for about 11 percent of the civilian labor force, and about one third of all the workers in the United States (as in most other industrialized nations) are women. Over 30 million U. S. women are in the labor force, almost 10 million above the World War II employment peak in 1944. There has been a steady increase in the percentage of the total labor force represented by women: 18 percent in 1900, 25 percent in 1940, 36 percent in the peak war year of 1944, and 37 percent in 1972. The increased employment of women has resulted from a number of factors. First, there are presently more women than men in the society, and as the expanding economic system demanded more workers, there have not been enough men to do the work. Second, service occupations—teaching, social work, personal services, saleswork, all of which have traditionally been women's occupations—have expanded rapidly since World War II. Third, laborsaving devices, prepared foods, and increased school time for children have combined to free women from many of their traditional home-related activities. Finally, there has been a widespread shift in values, since both men and women now consider it more appropriate for women to work.

A few general statements about the characteristics of women workers can be made.

1. Most women workers (about 60 percent) are married.

2. Although in absolute numbers there are more white women workers, *proportionately* more nonwhite women work.

3. Most women work out of economic necessity, not merely as a way of earning luxury extras. Many women workers are without husbands, and often they are supporting children. Many more are from low-income families and provide basic support. It is estimated that two thirds of all working women work because of serious economic need.

4. In recent years the employment of women has increased at a much faster rate than that of men (See Figure 11.2).

Figure 11.2
More women are going into the labor force

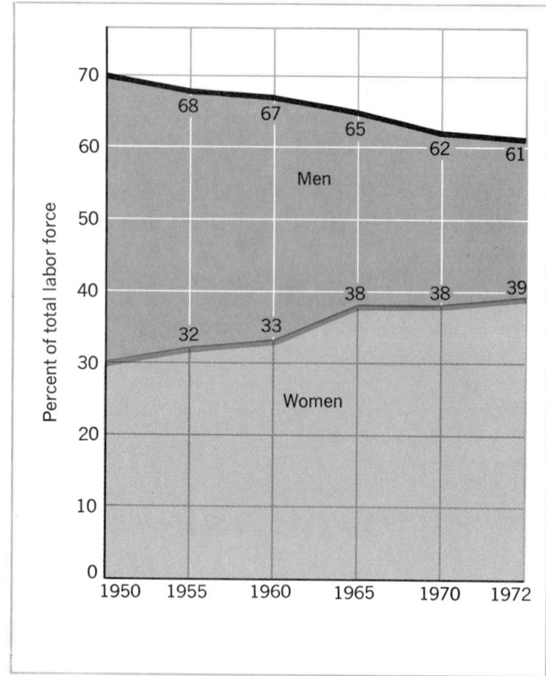

Source: U.S. Census Bureau, *Statistical Abstract of the U.S.*, 1972, p. 217.

There are, then, a huge number of employed women who make a major contribution to the economy. Moreover, their public labor is in addition to the significant contribution that women make in housework and child care.

The problem, however, is that minorities and women in the work force are systematically discriminated against, kept in lower-paying jobs, denied equal opportunities for advancement, and laid off quicker than white men. Almost every minority or female worker faces obstacles that do not burden white men, and the psychological cost is enormous. Not surprisingly, minority groups experience the least social mobility and face enormous discrimination in the economic sector. As Blau and Duncan have commented:

Negroes chances of occupational success in the United States are far inferior to those of a Caucasian. Whereas this hardly comes as a surprise to anyone familiar with the American scene, it is noteworthy that Negroes are handicapped at every step in their attempts to achieve occupational success. . . . Disproportionate numbers of Negroes live in the South, where occupational opportunities are not so good as in the North. Within each region, moreover, Negroes are seriously disadvantaged. They have lower social origins than whites, and they receive less education. Even when Negroes and whites with the same amount of education are compared, Negroes enter the job market on lower levels. Furthermore, if all these differences are statistically controlled and we ask how Negroes would fare if they had the same origins, education, and career beginnings as whites, the chances of occupational achievement of Negroes are still considerably inferior to those of whites. Within the same occupation, finally, the income of Negroes is lower than that of whites. The multiple handicaps associated with being an American Negro are cumulative in their deleterious consequences for a man's career. (Blau and Duncan, 1967, p. 404-405)

Women, too, face discrimination in the occupational field and find it extremely difficult to advance in social status, except through the status they gain from their husbands. What are some of the disadvantages faced by minorities and women in the occupational world?

MINORITIES AND WOMEN: OCCUPATIONAL PATTERNS

Minorities and women are primarily located in jobs that require lower skills, less education, and offer lower pay than the jobs held by white men. Of course, not every woman or minority member holds a poorer job than every white man, but the overall pattern is in that direction. Figure 11.3 is very important and should be studied carefully because it shows the types of job held by three groups: (1) all workers, including whites, and minorities, men and women, (2) minorities alone, and (3) women alone. Several important conclusions can be made from the data presented in Figure 11.3.

1. Women are concentrated in *clerical* jobs and *service* jobs (hairdressers, secretaries, laundry workers, maids). Clerical and service jobs are notoriously underpaid and generally offer little possibility for advancement.
2. Women are badly underrepresented in skilled craftsmen and managerial occupations, jobs that are highly paid and have good advancement opportunities.
3. Minorities are overrepresented in *service*, *operative* (truck drivers, deliverymen), and *manual-labor* jobs. In short, most of the unpleasant, dirty jobs go to minorities.
4. As you might expect, minorities are underrepresented in the high-paying jobs (professionals, managers, and craftsmen) and in the low-paying, white-collar occupations generally held by women (clerical). About 38 percent of all minorities are in white-collar jobs, compared to about 51 percent for whites.

The professional category is actually very misleading. Among the representatives of minorities in this category the vast majority are low-paid teachers and clergymen; proportionately very few are engineers, professors, doctors, accountants, or lawyers. The women may look better off, in their share of professionals (14.4 percent for women, 14.2 percent for total population). But this, too, is very deceptive, since most professional women are teachers and nurses who, compared to other professionals, are poorly paid. In 1972, for example, it was reported that of 1625 faculty posts in 36 prominent law schools, only 35 were held by women. Commenting on this situation, Cynthia Fuchs Epstein makes the following statement.

Figure 11.3
Compared to the whole work force, what occupations do nonwhites and women hold?

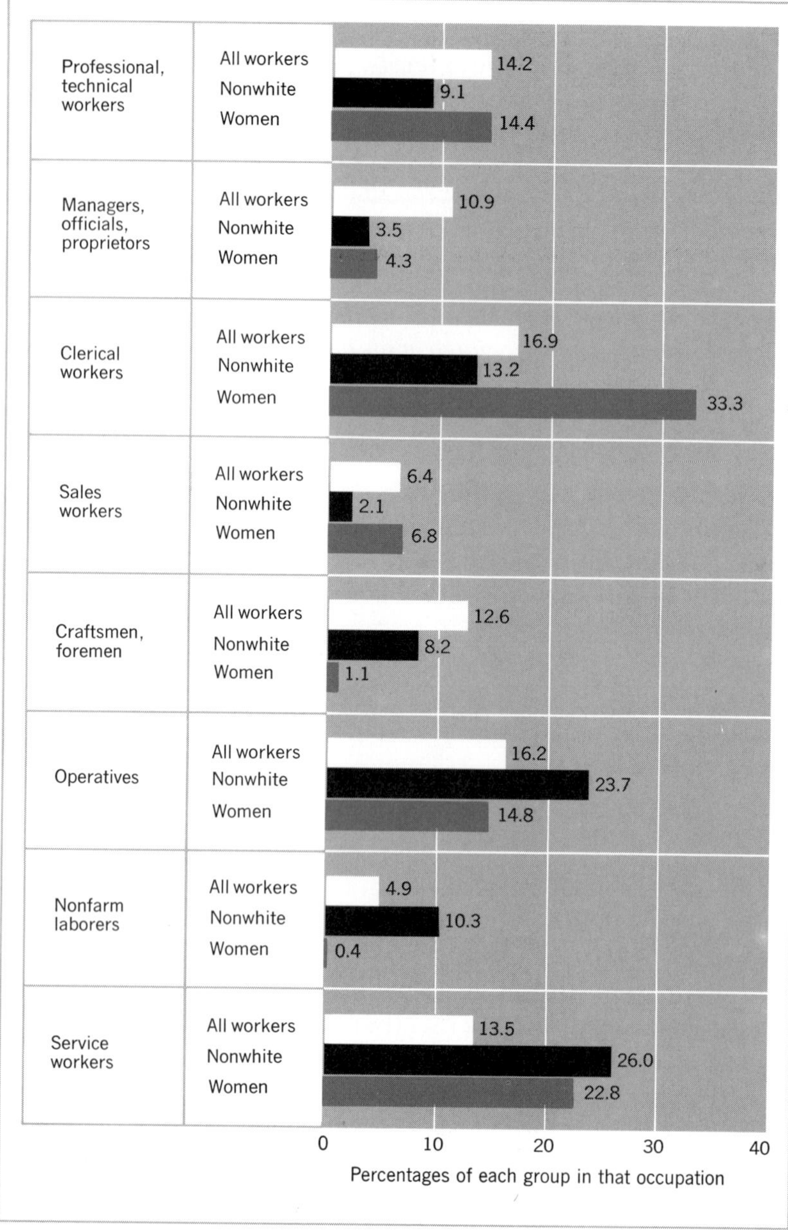

Source: U.S. Department of Labor, *1969 Handbook of Women Workers,* Bulletin 294 of the Women's Bureau, p. 92; U. S. Bureau of the Census, *Statistical Abstract of the U.S.,* 1971, pp. 222–223.
All workers = 78,204,000. Nonwhites = 8,445,000. Women = 29,469,000.
This table should be read as follows, taking "professionals" as an example of all workers, 14.2% were professional; of all nonwhite workers, 9.1% were professional; of all women workers, 14.4% were professional.

American women's participation in the prestige professions has remained constant during the past seventy years, increasing slightly since 1960 though not enough to constitute a change of level. This static situation has persisted in spite of astounding advances in the legal and social position of women in the United States and throughout the world. Women who have chosen careers in the elite professions are as deviant (in comparison with most American women) in 1968 as they were in 1898 . . . . Although the number of women in the labor force is enormous . . . women who work have settled for a fraction of the job possibilities offered by the economy. And their failure to advance into the jobs which are valued most highly in our society—the upper strata of business and the professions—is striking. Only a handful have joined the professions of law, medicine, teaching in higher education, engineering, or those linked to the nature sciences . . . . The ministry and the military are the most enduring male preserves, and the proportion of women in them is negligible. A recent survey by the Harvard Business Review *states that there are so few women in management positions that "there is scarcely anything to study." (Epstein, 1971, p. 6)*

UNEMPLOYMENT RATES OF MINORITIES AND WOMEN

Minorities and women are the last hired and the first fired. When unemployment goes up, women and minorities suffer the most because they are usually in vulnerable positions. For example, in 1971 the Vietnam war was winding down, the aerospace industries were suffering, and general unemployment under the Nixon Administration was extremely high. With nearly 6 percent of the total work force unemployed, the pattern of discrimination against women and minorities was very vivid. For white males the unemployment rate was 4.8 percent, but for white women the rate was 5.9 percent. Minorities were hurt even worse, with unemployment rates of 8.1 percent for men and 10.8 percent for women. This is a pattern that often repeats itself in the occupational field; white men are always the most advantaged, and black women are always the most disadvantaged. White women and black men usually are in the middle position, always well behind the white men but ahead of minority women. Figure 11.4 shows the huge disadvantage of minorities when unemployment is high, for although they represent only 11 percent of the work force, blacks always represent a much greater proportion of those who are unemployed or underemployed (working some, but not as much as is necessary to earn a living wage).

INCOME DIFFERENCES

One of the most depressing aspects of employment discrimination against women and minorities is that they earn much less than white men, even when doing the same work. Women are underrepresented in labor unions; only about one out of seven female workers belongs to a union, whereas about one out of three male workers do. Minorities, too, are badly underrepresented because unions have been especially slow about lowering racial barriers. Consequently minorities and women belong to a powerless, nonorganized sector of the work force that can easily be manipulated into accepting less money. The part-time nature of many women's careers, a career pattern that has in-and-out paths during child-rearing ages, and the insecurity of many women's positions make them particularly vulnerable to lay-offs, salary discrimination, and low ceilings on advancement opportunity. Minorities, of course, face similar problems.

Figure 11.5 shows the *relative incomes* of several social groups. Four groups are compared: (1) white and Chicano men, (2) Asian, Indian, and black men, (3) Chicano and white women, and (4) Asian, Indian, and black women. Taking white and Chicano men as the 100 percent level for any given year, the chart shows the relative percentage that each other group earned. Not until the 1970 census were Spanish surname data separated from white census data. Therefore, the percentages do not accurately reflect the low relative incomes for both male and female Chicano incomes. For example, in 1939 for every dollar the white men made (top line) the Chicano and white woman made 60.8 cents (the second figure down), Asian, Indians, and black men made 45 cents (third figure down), and Asian, Indian, and black women made 23 cents (the fourth figure down). You should be able to follow the chart across the years now, always comparing any group back to the white and Chicano men at the top.

Figure 11.4
Profile of Black employment

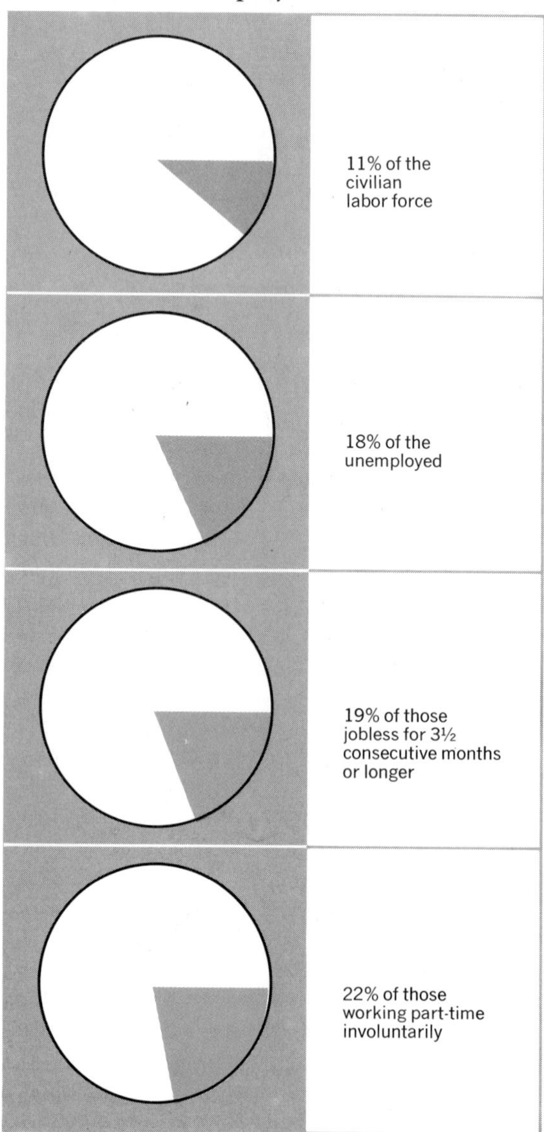

Source: U.S. Department of Labor, *Black Americans: A Chartbook,* 1971, p. 23.

Last hired and first fired. Minorities and women experience much higher levels of unemployment than white men.

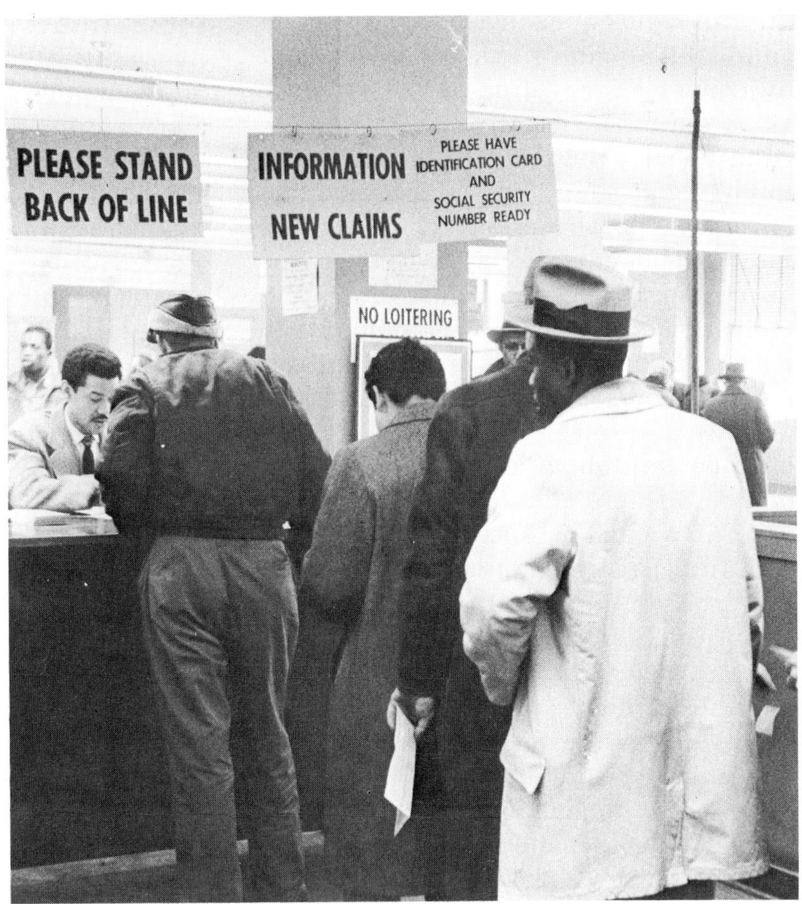

From Figure 11.5 it is obvious that white and Chicano men are clearly at the top of the occupational ladder in earnings. White and Chicano women, and Asian, Indian, and black men are in the middle, with the men pulling slightly ahead of the women in recent years. Finally, Asian, Indians, and black women are consistently at the very bottom; they are definitely the most disadvantaged, and dramatically so, in every year. The overall pattern is depressingly clear; whites are always ahead of blacks, and men are always ahead of women.

BARRIERS TO EQUAL EMPLOYMENT

There are many factors that contribute to this dismal picture of discrimination. First, minorities and women do not reach the same educational levels as white men; although they finish high school at about the same rate, they drop out (or are *pressured* out) of higher education. With the educational requirements of jobs continually going up, these educational disadvantages have serious consequences for employment. Second, most women have major roles as housewives and mothers and consequently are unable to work full-time with the same regularity as men. Of course, for many women this is not the case, since they are unmarried or have no children at home, but there is a definite in-and-out pattern to the careers of many women because of home responsibilities. This irregularity keeps them in low positions, ruins their chances for seniority, and blocks their professional advancement.

A third critical factor limiting the occupational advancement of women and minorities is outright discrimination. By and large white men control the occupational field, and many barriers are erected against others who want to advance in it. As minorities and women enter jobs, they find that white men have the system sewed up. Until recently newspapers, help-wanted ads were separated into male and female categories with higher paying and trainee jobs listed under the "male" heading. There is also much outright discrimination at the point of employment; women and minority members are often not hired in the better job categories.

PRESSURES IN THE JOB SITUATION

Assuming by some lucky chance a minority member or a woman gets a job, there are many subtle—and not so subtle—factors that hold them back. For example, many "protective laws" were written at an earlier period to protect women from the unbearable work of nineteenth century sweat shops, but these same laws are now used to stop the advancement of women. Many states, for instance, have limits on how much weight a woman can lift. Job descriptions of high-paying tasks often state that heavy lifting is required even though the lifting is done by machine—thus effectively shutting out women. Other laws specify that women cannot work overtime—to protect their health, mind you—but the men who do work overtime accumulate extra money and chances for advancement. Many of these protective laws are being challenged, and some are being eliminated, but many are still in effect.

In addition, there is endless, petty discrimination on the job where women are competing with men. A woman is constantly forced to prove herself, to insist that she is a "person" as well as a woman, and to pressure men into accepting her as a professional equal. Often men cannot adjust to having women in a professional role. There is an amusing case of a woman who was appointed a judge in England several years ago. Only four women had ever earned a position as

Figure 11.5
Relative incomes of four occupational groups. White and Chicano males are the baseline. For any year they represent 100, and all other groups are ranked *relative* to White and Chicano males. For example, in 1968 White and Chicano men made an average of \$8047; Asian, Indian, and Black men made \$5518 (68.6 percent of earnings of White and Chicano men). Although the exact figures vary from year to year, the chart reports the *relative* position without discussing exact dollar amounts. Consequently, the reader does not have to mentally adjust to changing dollar values.

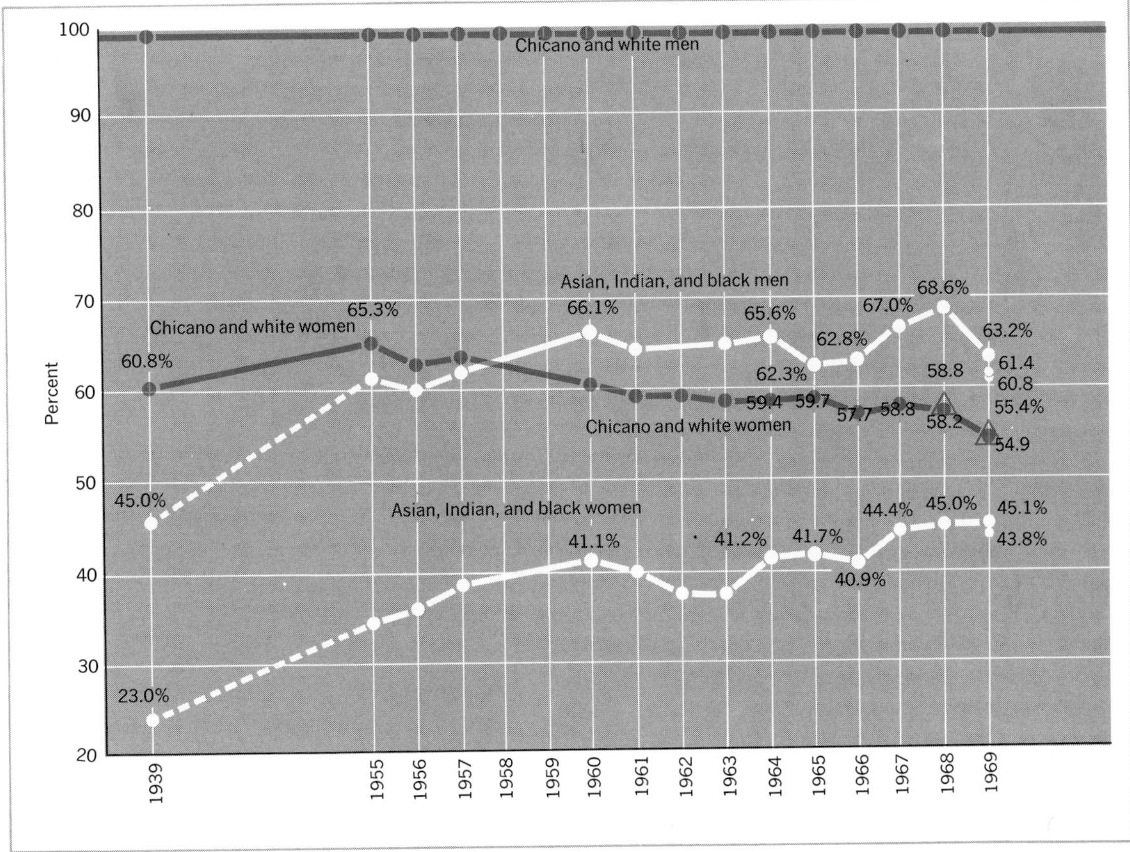

Source: Nancy Jewell Cross, "Relative Total Money Incomes by Sex-Race of People Paid for All-year Work, 1939–1969" (Menlo Park, Calif.: Mimeographed), p. 1., updated from U.S. Census Bureau, Current Population Reports, Series P-60, 1972.

senior barrister in England up to 1965. One of those, Mrs. Elizabeth Lane, was finally appointed to the High Court of Justice, touching off a characteristically British protocol crisis: what should she be called in the courtroom?

Visually, Mrs. Elizabeth Lane, 60, will look little different from her male colleagues when she dons her gown and wig and joins four other new appointees as the first woman among the High Court's 62 justices. But the problem is: what should lawyers call her. "My lord" seemed confusing at best, while traditionalists cringed at the sound of "Mrs. Justice." After grave deliberation, the Lord Chancellor's office has duly issued its decision: henceforth Mrs. Lane will be Mr. Justice Lane and may indeed be called "My Lord." "There simply isn't any precedent for calling a woman anything different," argued a harassed official. "We've taken what seems the least absurd decision." His Lordship, Mr. Justice Lane, is also entitled . . . to a bachelor knighthood . . . . (From Time, *August 27, 1965, p. 40; quoted by Epstein, 1971, pp. 88-89)*

The daily psychological adjustments that women face on the job are very discouraging. Cynthia Fuchs Epstein interviewed many women professionals and recounts some of the daily frustrations.

The woman is like a "stigmatized" person . . . who feels he is "on," having to be self-conscious and calculating about the impressions he is making, to a degree and in areas of conduct where he assumes others are not. . . . Women in professions often asserted, during interviews, that they spent more time on work than a man would because they "must be better than a man." One woman expressed the feeling vividly: " . . . if you're a woman, you have to make less mistakes . . . a woman must put greater effort into her work . . . because if you make a fool of yourself, you're a damn fool woman instead of just a damn fool." . . . Women may also try to be as unobtrusive as possible, and not attract attention ["create trouble"] by holding back in conversation or accepting work which keeps them in invisible positions, such as library work or government work in which they do not have individual clients. . . . Men in the professions manifest similar discomfort in their interactions with female colleagues. They, too, overrespond. They feel uneasy and may try to compensate by being overly solicitous, congenial, courtly—or by demanding too little of a woman, or too much. (Epstein, 1971, from pp. 190–193)

Women, of course, are not the only ones who face on-the-job discrimination, for this has always been a curse against minorities. The opening paragraph of Chapter Six, for instance, related Richard Wright's experience as a black man on the job with whites who were determined to make him quit and succeeded. In short, the list of occupational barriers against minorities and women is impressive: equal educational opportunities, discrimination at entry, laws that hold them down, discrimination in promotion and salary, and a whole complex of psychological tensions in the job setting. And this discrimination persists even though many changes have occurred in the last few years.

INSERT **11.1**

THE OCCUPATIONAL STRUCTURE HAS BECOME VERY SPECIALIZED: JOB TITLES AND JARGON LANGUAGE

The first edition of the *Dictionary of Occupational Titles* listed 17,452 jobs in 1939; the second edition found 22,028 jobs in 1949. For some reason not stated the current 1965 third edition counted only 21,741 jobs—a slight decrease. In addition, the current dictionary lists 13,809 job titles that are synonymous with or subsumed under one of the 21,741 titles regarded as distinct occupations. Some unusual titles were these.

Alligator farmer

Blintze roller

Cork inspector

Corset stringer (listed under "lacer")

Cuff turner

Diamond-dust technician

Dividend-deposit-voucher quoter

Dust brusher (shoe manufacturer)

Ear-muff assembler

Egg-breaking machine operator

Cherry bomb finisher

Flower-pot-press operator

Germ-separator man (corn processing)

Heel pricker

Inner-tube deflator

Kiln-door builder

TECHNOLOGY AND SOCIAL CHANGE

Up to this point the chapter has been discussing the characteristics of the economic and occupational structure of modern society. Let us turn now to another critical issue, the link between technology and social change. This book has argued that a critical sociology must examine *social problems* (such as those of minorities and women in the occupational world) and *social change.* Much of the time we have been *describing* change, showing what is happening to political systems, the family, religion, and education as the society is transformed. At

Last putter-away (A "last" is a shoe mold)	Quill-buncher-and-sorter
Lozenge-dough mixer	Rag inspector
Mercury-washer	Rug measurer
Mobile-lounge driver	Safety-pin-assembling machine operator
Opera-hat-brim coverer (an "opera hat" is a top hat)	Scallop trimmer
Mud-analysis district supervisor (listed under petroleum engineer)	Screw remover Umbrella tipper (machine)
Pillowcase turner	Weather forecasting service salesman

JARGONS: SPECIAL LANGUAGES FOR SPECIAL JOBS

JARGON-WORD	WHO USES?	COMMON TRANSLATION
Abbey-lubber	Sailors (19th century)	Loafer
All alive	Tailors	Poorly made garment
Bad-work girl	Garment makers	Woman in charge of reworking cloth incorrectly sewn
Boom	Journalists	A sensational story designed primarily to increase circulation
Comped	Printers	Set up, or "composed," matter
Corn	Skiers	Granular snow
Duck	Soldiers	An amphibious vehicle (during World War II: an inductee)

other times, we have been trying to explain the *origin* of change, to show what forces cause rapid shifts in the social world. Technology is a major cause of social change, and in this section we will examine its role.

TECHNOLOGY AS A CAUSE OF SOCIAL CHANGE

Today technology is confronting us with new possibilities and new threats: heart transplants raise all sorts of moral issues; contraceptive pills throw the church into

Entalpy	Physicists	The sum of a fluid system's internal and external energy
Howgozit curve	Pilots and navigators	Graphic representation of the flight of an aircraft
Knee shot	Television cameramen	A picture of a performer from the knees up
Loss leader	Storekeepers	An article sold below cost to attract customers
In the mud	Radio technicians	Having too little volume
Percentage shop	Labor organizers	A business that maintains a certain ratio of union to nonunion employees
Pubit	Sailors (navy)	A sailor in transit (*p*oor *u*niformed *b*astard *i*n *t*ransit)
Red-baiting	Politicians	Persistent and extreme criticism of communists
Sludge	Doctors	An agglomeration of red blood cells
Transculturation	Sociologists	Cultural change in a transitional period from an old to a new culture
Viscerotonia	Clinical psychologists	A temperament characterized by slowness to act and uninhibited emotional expression

Source: U.S. Department of Labor, *Dictionary of Occupational Titles,* 3rd ed.; Albert Berrere and Charles Leland, *A Dictionary of Slang, Jargon, and Cant* (London: Ballantyne, 1889); and Eric Partridge, *A Dictionary of New Words* (New York: Philosophical Library, 1955).

fits; test-tube babies may be just around the corner with untold consequences for the family; automation will probably change the job structure of the society and provide increased leisure time; computer-directed automation is moving the modern world toward the postindustrial era; the atomic bomb may yet completely evaporate humanity. To say the very least, technology is one of the greatest forces for social transformation.

Throughout history technological innovation has often been a moving force: (1) changes in agricultural technology resulted in the food surpluses necessary for the growth of cities; (2) changes in weapon technology have often upset empires and nations (the iron chariot in Asia Minor, the long-bow in Europe, and the atomic bomb in Japan are examples); (3) the introduction of steam power pushed the world into the Industrial Revolution; (4) the invention of the cotton gin revitalized a dying slave trade and helped plant the seeds for the horrible American Civil War (see Insert 11.II). What are the processes by which technology has such profound impact on the social system?

KARL MARX AND THE "TECHNOLOGICAL DETERMINISTS"

We have discussed Marx's social theories at various places earlier in the text. You will remember that Marx predicted that the greatest social upheaval of modern history would be the revolution of the working classes, a prediction that has come true in several countries of the world. The *cause* of that revolution, Marx argued, would be the technological arrangement of the capitalist society, a system that divided the population into workers and owners and gave the owners enormous power. In effect, the private property system, coupled with a capitalist production network, would eventually sow the seeds of its own destruction. As the workers realized that they were mere pawns in the production system, they would band together to overthrow the system and establish a Utopian communist state.

Fundamental to the Marxist theory of social change, then, is the idea that the "forces of production," the economic framework, are the prime cause of social change. It is not the force of ideas or religion or patriotism (the forces Marx called the German word *Idealfactoren*) that would transform the world, but rather the industrial relations, the technological system (*Realfactoren*). People who believe with Marx that technology is the determining factor in social change are often called "technological determinists."

THE "CULTURAL-LAG" THEORY OF SOCIAL CHANGE

Among the more important sociologists who, although not a technological determinist himself followed the technological determinst reasoning, was the American William F. Ogburn, who coined the term "cultural lag." Essentially, a cultural lag exists when one part of the culture changes, but the other parts associated with it do not adapt rapidly enough. Ogburn offered several examples of cultural lag. First is the relation between the automobile and the highways; as automobiles increased their speeds, the highways were not improved rapidly enough, resulting in many more highway accidents. Second is the connection between home production and the role of women; as industry assumed most of the homemaking tasks (sewing, weaving, soapmaking), the role of women did not change; consequently they felt their status lowered and their work meaningless.

INSERT **11.II**

TECHNOLOGY AND SOCIAL CHANGE: THE COTTON GIN

Occasionally a relatively minor technological innovation can have an enormous impact on the social structure. In the late eighteenth century the institution of slavery was declining in the United States. Politicians in both the North and the South generally agreed to end slavery, even in the Southern states where 94 percent of the slaves were located by 1790. The American Constitution provided for the end of the slave trade, and this bill was not vehemently opposed in the South. By 1804 every state north of the Mason-Dixon line had abolished or arranged to "phase out" slavery, and even in the South the general feeling was that slavery would soon be phased out. The reason was a matter of simple economics: industrialization was making slavery obsolete. Men were no longer required for their brute strength but for their skilled labor or for their ability to tend machines. The rising industrial society required a more mobile and adaptable labor force than slavery could provide.

Yet at the same time that industrial development seemed to be making slavery an anachronism, it was also creating a demand for cotton. Inventions like the spinning jenny, flying shuttle, and power loom were revolutionizing the textile industry, but it was floundering because of a shortage of raw cotton. The shortage was caused by a technological bottleneck—the seeds had to be laboriously picked out of the fibers by hand. This problem limited production so much that the widespread growing of cotton was not practical.

In 1793 Eli Whitney invented the cotton gin, a very simple machine to remove the seeds. With it the amount of cotton that a

Third is the link between industrial technology and workmen's compensations; as more men were injured by complicated machinery, it took nearly 75 years for adequate insurance programs to be instituted.

As Ogburn put it, there were four steps in understanding a cultural lag.

1. *Two factors* have to be identified that are closely related (autos and highways).
2. A previous state of *adjustment* between the factors must be demonstrated (slow autos and curvy highways are compatible).
3. A *change* in one factor must be noted, without sufficient change in the other (autos increased speed).

man could process was at least tripled. The cotton gin was crucial in promoting the expansion of the textile industry in England and Northern America and of plantation agriculture in the South.

In a matter of decades the Anglican slaveholders moved from their former limited enclaves around Chesapeake Bay and the coasts of the Carolinas and Georgia, gradually displacing the nonslaveholding Scots-Irish farmers who had previously controlled the interior South. This latter group either left the Southern rural areas, acquired plantations and slaves of their own, or became the "poor white trash" of a later era. Meanwhile the number of slaves soared. In 1776 their number was estimated at 502,000, of whom 47,000 were in the North. By the beginning of the Civil War, however, there were over 4 million slaves in the South.

In the North antislavery movements were organized. As moral outrage grew in the North, however, Southerners who now could profitably grow cotton, began to justify it. Inevitably these and other conflicting interests led to war. But even the Civil War could not utterly obliterate slavery; slaves simply became tenant farmers, a fate that they shared with an increasing number of poor whites who lost their own farms in the destruction and economic dislocations of Reconstruction.

In the end it seems that technology undid its own work. In the twentieth century cotton is more and more being replaced by synthetics, and what cotton agriculture remains is almost completely automated. The blacks of the rural South became excess labor, and one of the greatest migrations in history began as blacks moved from the farms into the cities of both the South and the North. The old "cotton belt" was the chief source of black Northern migration in the post-World-War II period. The slaves, who might have been freed well over a century earlier had it not been for the cotton gin, finally entered the industrial society.

4. A *maladjustment* results (auto accidents increase).

Ogburn's prime focus was on technological changes that in turn affected social institutions, and he was convinced that technology was the prime mover in social change.

I attempted . . . to cite many hypotheses of cultural lag, and in nearly all cases the independent variable—the causer of change proved to be a scientific discovery or mechanical invention. For instance, the invention of the steam engine led to the factory, and only afterwards to the change in the legal rights of women. These illustrations lead to a charact-

erization, by some, of the theory of cultural lag as a technological interpretation of history. I stated, however . . . that the independent variable could very well be an ideology or a non-technological variable. . . . For instance, it is quite probably that religion and not technology was the cause of most social changes in India 2,500 years ago at about the time of Buddha. . . . But in our times in the Western world. technology and science are the great prime movers of social change. . . . *(Ogburn, 1957, pp. 171–2, emphasis added)*

Ogburn's basic thesis—social institutions do not keep up with advances in the technology—is evident all around us. Among the most obvious are the growth of mass transportation, communications, and regional industry that make small suburban governments ineffective and wasteful. There is very little sign, however, that regional governments will be developed soon to deal with massive traffic congestion, water and air pollution, and school equality. A horrifying example of cultural lag is the gap between the technology of atomic warfare and worldwide social controls over atomic weapons. Insert 11.III discusses the impact of changing technology on social relations, using the example of the steel ax in an Australian tribe.

MAX WEBER AND THE "PROTESTANT ETHIC" THEORY

Up to this point we have been discussing social change from the perspective of the technological determinist who believes technology reshapes social behavior. However, there are many sociologists who believe that the impact can run the other direction as well; social organization and social ideas can affect technology.

Max Weber, the impressive German economist and sociologist, took as one of his major life works the study of one important social change—the rise of the modern capitalist society. Unlike Marx, who attributed change to technological developments, Weber tried to show how cultural ideas and beliefs—the *Idealfactoren*—had as much impact as technology and economics—the *Realfactoren.* In his major work on this subject, *The Protestant Ethic and the Spirit of Capitalism* (1930) he argued that the religious beliefs of Puritan England were one of the major causes of modern capitalism (see Figure 11.6). Calvinism was the dominant religion in England and New England in the seventeenth century at the beginning of the industrial revolution. Weber proposed a series of steps that linked Calvinism and capitalism.

1. *The doctrine of predestination.* Calvinism held that a man was condemned to hell or rewarded in heaven by the arbitrary will of God, and no amount of "good works" on earth made any difference.
2. *The problem of assurance.* The critical question for a Calvinist was whether he was saved or would go to hell. How could he get assurance he was among the "elect"?
3. *The concept of "vocation."* Although Calvinist thelogians denied that there was any way to determine election, in the popular mind and in popular preaching it was widely held that a man who served well in a "Christian vocation" was obviously among the elect if he worked hard and especially if he were economically successful.

INSERT **11.III**

THE STEEL AXE AND THE YIR YORONT CULTURE

The Yir Yoront aborigines of southeastern Australia depended on the stone axe as their most basic and essential tool for many centuries. The axe was more than a tool for them; it was a symbol of status, of male dominance, of the fundamental rights of ownership, of strong relations with distant trading partners in an extended commercial network. This whole value system began to change when the Yir Yoront encountered Europeans in the Nineteenth Century.

The native Australians discovered that white men possessed fine axes made of steel, a material completely unknown to them. Gradually the cattle "stations" (ranches) of the Europeans began encroaching on the homeland of the Yir Yoront. Some of the ranchers horribly abused the natives, killing them or abducting them as slaves or "housegirls." Finally the government took action and established a string of church missions to provide protection and surveillance as well as to "improve the savages." Although Christianity itself did not prove to be very popular, the Yir Yoront did accept one gift of the whites very eagerly—the steel axes.

The Europeans hoped that with this more efficient tool, the natives would make "progress." The impact of the steel axe was greater but it did not lead to "progress" but rather to a drastic upheaval of the social structure of the tribe. According to anthropologists, the steel axe had the following effect.

Decreased self-reliance	Previously a man who needed an axe would trade for an axe head and then construct the rest of it himself from materials he found. Now, in order to get a steel axe, it was necessary to go to the mission and act "deserving, industrious, and dependent."
Upset the status relations between young and old	The possession of an axe had been considered a mark of status and manhood but the Europeans sometimes gave axes directly to young men and even children.
Upset the status relations between the sexes	Previously no woman could "own" an axe. When she needed to use one for her work, she had to borrow it from her male kin and return it promptly and in good condition. The Europeans often gave axes to women to use as their own.

Destroyed orderly trading relations	In the past the Yir Yoront had to obtain axe heads from trading partners far to the south. These relations were quite systematic and provided for regular contact among widely scattered groups. The introduction of steel axes upset the usual terms of trade and often completely destroyed the need for trading relationships.
Made tribal gatherings less important and less pleasurable	Ceremonies had previously provided for the simultaneous meeting of many trading partners. These were festive occasions that also provided the opportunity to obtain axe heads—perhaps a whole year's supply. With the trading relationships weakened, however, the gaity as well as the practical function of these ceremonies gradually faded.
Forced the leader-group form of organization on the tribe	The collective activities of the Yir Yoront had been directed by a complex system of kinship relations. Almost anyone was subordinate to a few others and superordinate to a few. There was no overall leader or chief. When dealing with the whites, however, they found it necessary to appoint one or two spokesman who gradually acquired more power than they were entitled to traditionally.
Increased the incidence of stealing and trespassing	The indiscriminate gift of steel axes to those who traditionally could not own them diluted the whole notion of ownership itself. As people became less sure of the norms of ownership, they became more ready to violate them and, in the general confusion, more likely to get away unpunished.
Weakened faith in religion	The Yir Yoront attempted to explain the origins of every important artifact they possessed with some myth showing how the article was given them by a distant mythical ancestor. Since they had very few artifacts and since their technology was virtually stagnant, it was quite possible to believe these stories. There was, however, no mythical explanation for the origins of the steel axe—its source was obvious. Their result was to cast suspicion on the other myths as well as on the whole structure of the religion.

Source: Condensed from Peter R. Hammond, *Cultural and Social Anthropology* (New York: Macmillan, 1966), pp. 84–94.

Technology affects the social system: How does the automobile affect your daily life?

4. *Hard work, discipline, and material success.* The logical outcome of the Calvinist doctrine was that hard work and competitive striving were highly valued among the Calvinists. These were outward signs of a man's inner Christianity, and obvious symbols of his election.

5. *The growth of capital.* Moreover, since wasting money on worldy goods and pleasures was contrary to Calvinist belief, the successful businessman plowed his profits back into the business. This practice insured more hard work, more discipline, more material success—and more assurance of being saved.

Thus the Calvinists of England and New England worked hard and put their money back into their businesses, in this way providing the economic basis for the development of capitalism. Weber's thesis has been constantly debated, but there is no conclusive proof whether he was right or wrong. Many scholars believe that Weber provided an accurate description of the *origins* of modern capitalism, but they argue that, once started, the growth potential and *continuance* of capitalism did not depend on Calvinism or any other religion. So while Calvinism may have been the starter, the engine of capitalism had its own momentum.

Some sociologists argue that other belief systems can provide the necessary impetus for the growth of industrialism, and that Calvinism was only one example of a widespread historical phenomenon. Robert Bellah (1957), for example, suggests that the Tokugawan religion, which stressed hard work and economic success as religious values, provided the same thrust for Japan's industrialization. Other writers propose that the quasireligious fervor of communism and nationalism provided the ideological push for the industrialization of socialist nations and of underdeveloped nations. In light of these arguments, Weber's general thesis can be broadened: (1) some deeply held belief system must foster the values of hard work and capital saving in order for industrialism to get its start—whether that ideology be Calvinism, Tokugawan religion, communism, or some other belief system; (2) once begun, the industrial movement develops a force of its own and becomes largely independent of the belief system that started it.

Max Weber (1864–1920)

TECHNOLOGY AS A SOURCE OF SOCIAL CHANGE: A SUMMARY

Let us summarize the observations about technology and social change.

1. Technology is one of the key sources of social change. It has been in the past and is even more so today.
2. Technological change is occurring at an ever increasing pace. One invention feeds another until the speed of technological change is almost overwhelming.
3. Technology greatly affects other social institutions. In fact, the technological determinists believe that most changes in social institutions are caused by technology.
4. Cultural lags arise when the technology changes at a different rate than the social institutions associated with it, causing a serious maladjustment.
5. Social institutions also affect technology. Institutionalized science, for example, is a major social institution that seriously impinges on technology. Belief systems—such as Calvinism—probably affect industrial development.

Social ideas affect the economic system. John Calvin was the leader of the Protestant group whose beliefs may have affected the growth of modern capitalism.

Thus the relation between technology and social change is a complex, important issue. In fact, the growing development of advanced technological systems is a major factor pushing us to an entirely different kind of future society; the current industrial system is rapidly giving way to the "postindustrial" society, a topic we will examine next.

POSTINDUSTRIAL SOCIETY

Where is the industrial state going? A number of social scientists argue that industrial society is reaching its conclusion and that shortly the most advanced nations will move into another stage of development. The opening quotation in this chapter is a description of one probable new society toward which we are moving.

The variety of terms used to describe this new stage is bewildering—postindustrial, superindustrial, technotronic, postcivilization, global village—but the same basic idea runs through all the terms. They refer to the end of industrial society as we know it and the emergence of a new, radically different way of life. In Insert 11.IV some general patterns about the probable shape of the emerging new technological system are outlined.

Moreover, the changes in *technology* raise a host of *social* issues. Technology does not exist in a vacuum; as the technology changes, other social institutions adjust, and these institions in turn influence technology. As we look to the future a number of issues seem critical.

THE IMPACT OF AUTOMATION

Amid all of the other changes occurring in society there is a quiet, ceaseless revolution that may alter practically all aspects of social existence. This is the "silent revolution" of automation—or "cybernation," as it is sometimes called —a shift in the way the society does its basic work. C. H. Anderson summarizes the essential features of automation.

Figure 11.6
The link between Calvinism and modern capitalism: Max Weber's "Protestant Ethic" theory

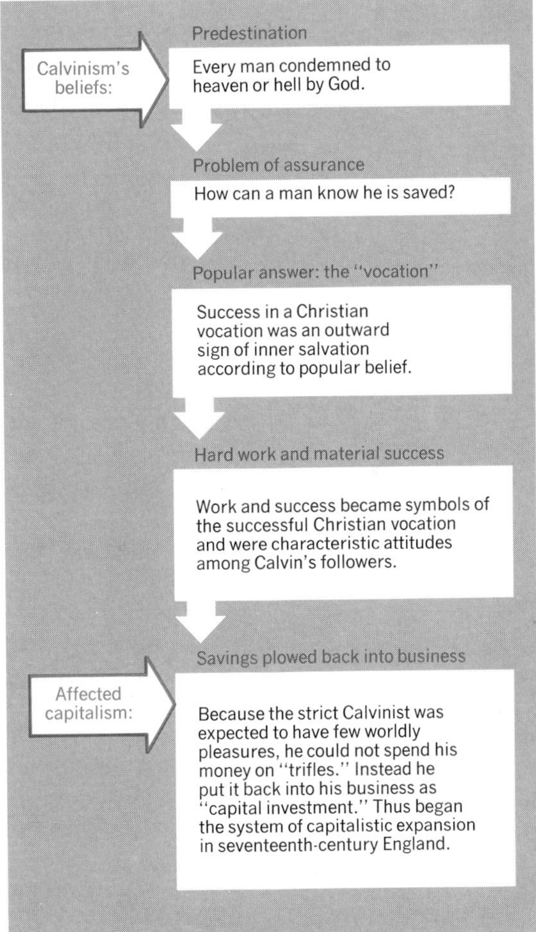

What is automation? Automation refers to the use of a whole range of electronically regulated machinery to control production processes, monitor the quality of the product, and adjust production to correct for deviations. In effect, whereas men are required to control and operate industrial machines, automated machines control and operate themselves. What's more, automated machines are infinitely more efficient, accurate, and safe than industrial machines. The ordinary person usually thinks of automation mainly in terms of "Detroit automation," the integrating and linking of machines by means of electronical-

INSERT 11.IV SUPERINDUSTRIAL SOCIETY

Many terms have been coined to describe the next stage of economic development after industrialism: superindustrial, postindustrial, technotronic, postcivilization. Whatever the terms, most scholars agree that the new society will be:

Science and knowledge based	Industry based on "practical know-how" and mechanical power will be replaced by sophisticated scientific systems. Knowledge is the new "raw material" for industry.
Communications oriented	Complex electronic communications system will be needed as never before. If knowledge is the new raw material, then communication is the new "transportation" system.
Electronics dominated	Simple mechanical systems will be replaced by complex electronic networks.
Highly automated	Technology will be so highly automated that it will take care of itself and even repair and reproduce itself, freeing people for more meaningful tasks.
Dependent on professional and service occupations	Human tasks will more and more change from production jobs (taken over by automation) to professional, educational, and service tasks.
Dominated by higher skill levels	Almost without exception, jobs in the future will require more education and higher levels of skill.
Rich in leisure time	As automation takes over more of the production tasks, people will be freed for more leisure activities, a challenge for them to use their time meaningfully.
Oriented to a new value system	The most highly debated question about the postindustrial society is this: now that material things can be produced in almost unlimited quantities, can man deal with his *social* problems? Hopefully a "postmaterialism" value system will develop.

ly controlled transfer mechanisms. The reduction of an assembly operation to the push of a button, originally utilized in the automobile industry but soon applied in meat-packing, baking, and many other industries involving transfer processes, is an important but not the only type of automation. Also important are process control systems—computerized operation of process plants in oil, mineral, and chemical industries. . . . Basic to all automation, but specialized for the automatic handling of information and data in administration and decision making, is an assortment of computers. (Anderson, 1971, p.221)

There are many vital social issues linked to the growth of automation. First, there is the impact on the occupational system, for it is likely that automation will cause job displacement as machines take over the tasks that people once held. In fact, the economy may grow substantially even while unemployment increases. For example, unemployment has held steady at high rates even while the national output has increased in recent years. The meat-packing industry has automated extensively and has managed to increase productivity by 50 percent while cutting its work force by 40,000 jobs. The automobile, steel, railroad, and mining industries have all had significant drops in employment while maintaining or increasing their productivity. Much of the displacement occurs because jobs are upgraded, with lower skilled groups being eliminated. Thus it seems safe to say that automation will upgrade the standards for many jobs and replace many workers. How can the society deal with this mass displacement? Who will bear the social costs—the luckless worker, business, government, unions, the consumer? Will there be a more unequal distribution of wealth and income as the power of automation is concentrated in the hands of powerful corporations and as thousands are displaced from their jobs?

A second issue raised by automation is the *quality of life in the job setting.* What will it be like to tend machines, to work on a task in which the worker can have little satisfaction, to be a cog in an industrial machine that has little need for human creativity in the work setting? Several studies of automobile assembly plants (Faunce, 1958; Blauner, 1964) have suggested that there is little social interaction among workers, widespread alienation and worker discontent, a lack of opportunity for workers to advance into managerial jobs, and a pervasive "atomization"—feelings that the worker is no more than an interchangeable part in a huge impersonal system. Often these feelings well up into massive strikes and labor unrest, a problem that continually plagues the automobile industry (see accompanying picture of the Lordstown Chevrolet plant, a scene of major labor unrest).

Although it is possible that automation may increase the number of jobs that resemble automobile assembly lines, it is also quite possible that it may eliminate many more.In fact, only about 5 percent of all American workers actually work on assembly lines, and the development of a service economy—discussed earlier—means that most new jobs will not be in the industrial sector that is so highly mechanized. In addition, automation is displacing many people who work in those settings, so that the quality of life in the job setting may actually increase because of automation.

Finally, automation will probably reduce the amount of physical labor in work and will increase the leisure time available to most people. It may be that in the future workers will not need to work as many hours each week as they do today; this is certainly the case in production industries and may even be true in the service activities of the future. The American mentality has for centuries been tied to the Protestant Ethic of hard work, striving, and competition. Can it adjust to a society where work is not the central feature of life and meaning must be found in other areas—in the family, in leisure, in public service?

DISTRIBUTION OF INCOME IN THE POSTINDUSTRIAL SOCIETY

Perhaps the silent revolution of automation will transform the society, making material goods available in quantities never before dreamed of, and making professional service available in a scope that defies present imagination. But what of the *distribution* problem? How will the social system adapt to the increased wealth? Will it continue to hold untold thousands of people in wretched poverty while the luxury piles deeper and deeper all around them? Income in the United States is certainly not evenly distributed, as we have shown many times. Of course, the poor in America are richer than most of the world's poor, but *relative* to the wealth all about them they must feel even more stress. Unless we devise a social system capable of adequate distribution and reasonable equality, then all the advances in technology will seem hollow and meaningless in the face of increasing social unrest and upheaval.

Devising a more equitable system is not merely a technical problem, it is more fundamentally a *political* one. We already have the resources and the techniques; the missing ingredient is a public will to make the necessary changes. A number of social critics are now arguing that the old link between jobs and income must be broken and that some type of guaranteed annual income is both possible and desirable (see Insert 11.V for a discussion of the impact of cybernation and automation on the distribution of income). Even more radical proposals suggest that most of the basic goods of society can be distributed free, as Frank Lindenfeld suggests.

The key idea is that a small number of standardized subsistence items can be produced in such quantity as to be given away freely, thus forming the backbone of a subsistence economy. Almost any commodity can be produced cheaply and well by machines. A technologically advanced society can support the automated production of several varieties of standard items which can be given away: shoes, shelter, bread, milk, radios, bicycles, telephone service, etc.

Automation in the auto industry: The Nova plant at Lordstown, Ohio. General Motors takes pride that this is one of the most highly automated plants in the United States, yet this very plant was the scene of unending labor strife in the early 1970s. Will automation cause more discontent and alienation on the job, or will it eliminate most jobs such as these on the assembly line?

Some items, like teaching and medical service, shouldn't and probably couldn't be provided completely by machines, and so it would be necessary to find some people who would desire to serve their fellow human beings by providing such services. My guess is that even if there were not huge profits in medical practice, a large number of people could be found who would be willing to volunteer for some of the same reasons people have volunteered for the Peace Corps.

A luxury economy could exist side by side with the subsistence economy, allowing those who did not want the standardized goods or services to join with others in producing their own variants. If you wanted to lie on the beach and do nothing, you could obtain the necessities of life produced in abundance by machines; if you wanted non-standardized or luxury items, you could make them yourself or enter the luxury market system as entrepreneur or worker. But nobody would be

INSERT **11.V**

CYBERNATION'S EFFECT ON THE DISTRIBUTION OF INCOME

This statement is written in the recognition that mankind is at a historic conjuncture which demands a fundamental reexamination of existing values and institutions. . . .

THE NATURE OF THE CYBERNATION REVOLUTION

Cybernation is manifesting the characteristics of a revolution in production. These include the development of radically different techniques and the subsequent appearance of novel principles of the organization of production; a basic reordering of man's relationship to his environment; and a dramatic increase in total available and potential energy.

The fundamental problem posed by the cybernation revolution in the United States is that it invalidates the general mechanism so far employed to undergird people's rights as consumers. Up to this time economic resources have been distributed on the basis of contributions to production, with machines and men competing for employment on somewhat equal terms. In the developing cybernated system, potentially unlimited output can be achieved by systems of machines which will require little cooperation from human beings. As machines take over production from men, they absorb an increasing proportion of resources, while the men who are displaced become dependent on minimal and unrelated government measures, and, are less able to disguise a historic paradox: that a growing proportion of the population is subsisting on minimal incomes, often below the poverty line, at a time when sufficient productive potential is available to supply the needs of everyone in the United States.

There is no question that cybernation does increase the potential for the provision of funds to neglected public sectors. Nor is there any question that cybernation would make possible the abolition of poverty at home and abroad. But the industrial system does not possess any adequate mechanisms to permit these potentials to become realities. The industrial system was designed to produce an ever-increasing quantity of goods as efficiently as possible, and it was assumed that the distribution of the power to purchase these goods would occur almost automatically. The continuance of the income-through-jobs link as the major mechanism for distributing effective demand—for granting the right to consume—now acts as the main brake on the almost unlimited capacity of a cybernated productive system.

An adequate distribution of the potential abundance of goods and services will be achieved only when it is understood that the major economic problem is not how to increase production but how to distribute the abundance that is the great potential of cybernation. There is an urgent need for a fundamental change in the mechanisms employed to insure consumer rights.

FACTS AND FIGURES

No responsible observer would attempt to describe the exact pace or the full sweep of a phenomenon that is developing with the speed of cybernation. Some aspects of this revolution, however, are already clear:

The rate of productivity increase has risen with the onset of cybernation.

An industrial economic system postulated on scarcity has been unable to distribute the abundant goods and services produced by a cybernated system or potential in it.

Surplus capacity and unemployment have thus co-existed at excessive levels over the last six years.

The underlying cause of excessive unemployment is the fact that the capability of machines is rising more rapidly than the capacity of many human beings to keep pace.

A permanent impoverished and jobless class is established in the midst of potential abundance.

NEED FOR A NEW CONSENSUS

We believe . . . that the industrial productive system is no longer viable. We assert that the only way to turn technological change to the benefit of the individual and the service of the general welfare is to accept the process and to utilize it rationally and humanely. The new science of political economy will be built on the encouragement and planned expansion of cybernation. . . .

But major changes must be made in our attitudes and institutions in the forseeable future. . . . What is man's role when he is not dependent upon his own activities for the material basis of his life? What should be the basis for distributing individual access to national resources? Are there other proper claims on goods and services besides a job?

Because of cybernation, society no longer needs to impose repetitive and meaningless (because unnecessary) toil upon the individual. Society can now set the citizen free to make his own choice of occupation and vocation from a wide range of activities not now fostered by our value system and our accepted modes of "work. . . ."

PROPOSAL FOR ACTION

As a first step to a new consensus it is essential to recognize that the traditional link between jobs and incomes is being broken. The economy of abundance can sustain all citizens in comfort and economic security whether or not they engage in what is commonly reckoned as work. Wealth produced by machines rather than by men is still wealth. We urge, therefore, that society, through its appropriate legal and governmental institutions, undertake an unqualified commitment to provide every individual and every family with an adequate income as a matter of right. This undertaking we consider to be essential to the emerging economic, social and political order in this country. We regard it as the only policy by which the quarter of the nation now dispossessed and soon-to-be dispossessed by lack of employment can be brought within the abundant society. The unqualified right to an income would take the place of the patchwork of welfare measures—from unemployment insurance to relief—designed to ensure that no citizen or resident of the United States actually starves.

We do not pretend to visualize all of the consequences of this change in our values. It is clear, however, that the distribution of abundance in a cybernated society must be based on criteria strikingly different from those of an economic system based on scarcity. . . .

The present system encourages activities which can lead to private profit and neglects those activities which can enhance the wealth and the quality of life of our society. Consequently national policy has hitherto been aimed far more at the welfare of the productive process than at the welfare of people. The era of cybernation can reverse this emphasis. With public policy and research concentrated on people rather than processes we believe that many creative activities and interests commonly thought of as non-economic will absorb the time and the commitment of many of those no longer needed to produce goods and services. Society as a whole must encourage new modes of constructive, rewarding and ennobling activity. Principal among these are activities, such as teaching and learning, that relate people to people rather than people to things. Education has never been primarily conducted for profit in our society; it represents the first and most obvious activity inviting the expansion of the public sector to meet the needs of this period of transition.

THE TRANSITION

We recognize that the drastic alterations in circumstances and in our way of life ushered in by cybernation and the economy of abundance will not be completed overnight. . . . We must develop programs for this transition designed to give hope to the dispossessed and those cast out by the economic system, and to provide a basis for the rallying of people to bring about those changes in political and social institutions which are essential to the age of technology.

. . . In our opinion, this is a time of crisis, . . . Public philosophy for the transition must rest on the conviction that our economic, social and political institutions exist for the use of man and that man does not exist to maintain a particular economic system. This philosophy centers on an understanding that governments are instituted among men for the purpose of making possible life, liberty, and the pursuit of happiness and that government should be a creative and positive instrument toward these ends.

Source: The Ad Hoc Committee, "The Triple Revolution," *Liberation,* April 1964 in *Radical Perspectives on Social Problems,* Frank Lindenfeld, ed. New York: Macmillan 1973, pp. 207-218 *forced by economic necessity to work for somebody else or take a job he did not like. Those who didn't want the free standard commodities could support a craftsman or make their own.*

The existence of computer and automation technology would allow the production and distribution of commodities without the need for very much human labor; the more advanced technologies could even supply more variation in the end products than older assembly line techniques, at no extra cost. Of course, all of this would not obviate the need to make certain political decisions. Indeed, it would clarify the political nature of economic decisions. When you can make practically anything in large quantities and provide it on a free basis, then it becomes a political *question as to whether a particular item—automobiles, for instance—should or should not be made for general distribution. (Lindenfeld, 1968, p. 216)*

Proposals such as the guaranteed annual income and the free distribution of goods and services suggest that it is at least conceivable that the postindustrial society may devise new and unique solutions to the age-old problem of resource allocation.

However, these changes will involve more than changes in the United States, for one of the most serious crises emerging in the new superindustrial state is its relation to the rest of the hungry, underdeveloped world. The maldistribution of wealth internationally is even more staggering than inside the United States. Figure 11.7 shows how great is the maldistribution of wealth among the nations of the world. Will the industrialized nations of the world continue to exploit the nonindustrialized countries? And if so, will the peoples of the "third world" continue to allow themselves to be exploited? These are questions that affect us all, because the balance of world peace and the hopes of civilized man depend on the answers.

SOCIAL PLANNING AND SOCIAL VALUES

Critics of the technological society argue that the wild expansion of technology has raped the environment, created social upheaval, and stamped out many of our cherished values. Once again Alvin Toffler makes an insightful statement.

The speed-up of diffusion, the self-reinforcing character of technological advance, . . . the intimate link-up between technology and social arrangements—all these create a form of psychological pollution, a seemingly unstoppable acceleration of the pace of life.

The psychic pollution is matched by the industrial vomit that fills our skies and seas. Pesticides and herbicides filter into our foods. Twisted automobile carcasses, aluminum cans, nonreturnable glass bottles and synthetic plastics form immense kitchen middens in our midst. . . . We do not even begin to know what to do with our radioactive wastes—whether to pump them into the earth, shoot them into outer space, or pour them into the oceans.

Our technological powers increase, but the side effects and potential hazards also escalate. We risk thermopollution of the oceans . . . we concentrate such large masses of population in such small urban-technological islands, that we threaten to use up the air's oxygen faster than it can be replaced. . . . Through such disruptions of the natural ecology, we may literally . . . be destroying this planet as a suitable place for human habitation. (Toffler, 1971, pp. 419–430)

With such enormous side-effects facing us it is critical to begin planning. Unfortunately the American "free-enterprise" mentality has so ingrained the profit motive and the antigovernment-interference idea that it is difficult to get systematic planning on the massive scale that is required. Government has largely taken a "hands-off" attitude toward industry, and industry has responded by putting profits above the environmental and human social cost. Without serious planning by government, business, industry, and science we may find that the technological servant has become a dragon in our midst.

To put it another way, what kind of social *values* will dominate in the post-industrial society? Many people fear that the consumption mentality may corrupt us entirely, that things, things, and more things may become a way of life, with the consequent death of cherished values. Visitors from other countries experience culture shock as they encounter the materialism of Americans. Peace Corps volunteers returning after several years in underdeveloped nations are stunned by the pervasive materialism that now is so shockingly apparent to them. The selfishness of a nation that has huge pockets of poverty in the midst of untold wealth cannot fail to impress sensitive people, foreign or native. Somehow the nation must deal with its own value issues if it is to move into the future with a soul as well as with a silver-lined pocketbook.

SUMMARY

The modern industrial society is extremely dependent on its advanced technology. A number of oustanding characteristics dominate: (1) an extremely complex division of labor, with many specialists trading their knowledge and services, and with highly complex systems of interdependence among all its parts; (2) an economy that is shifting more and more to service occupations, with fewer people in agriculture and mining, and a somewhat smaller percentage in manufacturing than was the case 50 years ago; (3) a system of social bureaucratic management in which the corporation is now dominant; (4) widespread occupational discrimination against women and minorities.

Technological and economic changes are major determinants of social change. Many sociologists have studied the

Figure 11.7
International comparisons of gross national product (GNP) and growth rates (1960–1970)

Country	GNP per Capita (US Dollars)	Growth Rate (Percent)
United States	4,240	3.2
Sweden	2,920	3.4
Switzerland	2,700	2.6
Canada	2,650	2.8
France	2,460	4.8
Denmark	2,310	3.7
Australia	2,300	2.9
New Zealand	2,230	2.0
Germany, Fed. Rep. of	2,190	3.7
Norway	2,160	4.0
Belgium	2,010	3.5
Finland	1,980	3.9
United Kingdom	1,890	1.8
Netherlands	1,760	3.1
Germany (*Eastern*)†	1,570	4.1
Israel	1,570	5.3
Libya, Arab Rep. of	1,510	21.7
Austria	1,470	3.9
Japan	1,430	10.0
Puerto Rico	1,410	6.0

Country	GNP per Capita (US Dollars)	Growth Rate (Percent)
Uruguay	560	−0.8
Jamaica[2]	550	3.0
Chile	510	1.7
Costa Rica	510	2.9
Portugal	510	4.9
Mongolia†	460	1.0
Albania†	430	4.9
Nicaragua	380	2.8
Saudi Arabia	380	7.1
Guatemala	350	1.9
Iran	350	4.9
Turkey	350	3.4
Malaysia	340	3.8
Peru	330	1.4
Iraq	310	3.0
China, Rep. of	300	6.3
Colombia	290	1.5
El Salvador	290	1.9
Zambia	290	5.4
Cuba†	280	−3.2
Dominican Republic	280	0.4

Country	GNP per Capita (US Dollars)	Growth Rate (Percent)
Sierre Leone	170	1.2
Bolivia	160	2.4
Egypt, Arab Rep. of	160	1.2
Thailand	160	4.7
Cameroon	150	2.0
Mauritania*	140	4.6
Viet-nam, Rep. of	140	1.8
Central Africa Rep.	130	0.0
Kenya	130	1.5
Khmer Rep.	130	0.5
Yemen, People's Dem. Rep. of	120	−4.6
India	110	1.1
Laos*	110	0.2
Malagasy Rep.	110	0.0
Pakistan	110	2.9
Sudan	110	0.6
Uganda	110	1.7
Indonesia	100	0.8
Togo	100	0.0
Afghanistan	—	0.3

Italy	1,400	4.7
Czechoslovakia†	1,370	3.9
USSR†	1,200	5.6
Ireland	1,110	3.5
Hungary†	1,100	5.5
Argentina	1,060	2.6
Venezuela	1,000	2.5
Poland†	940	5.1
Trinidad and Tobago	890	3.8
Bulgaria†	860	6.7
Romania†	860	7.5
Hong Kong	850	8.7
Greece	840	6.2
Spain	820	6.5
Singapore	800	4.5
South Africa[1]	710	3.3
Panama	660	4.8
Lebanon	580	2.1
Mexico	580	3.4
Yugoslavia	580	4.6

Jordan*	280	4.7
Korea (*North*)†	280	5.9
Brazil	270	1.4
Algeria	260	
Honduras	260	1.1
Syria, Arab Rep. of	260	4.7
Ecuador	240	1.2
Ivory Coast	240	4.7
Paraguay	240	1.0
Rhodesia	240	0.4
Tunisia	230	2.1
Angola	210	1.4
Korea, Rep. of	210	6.4
Mozambique	210	3.3
Papua New Guinea	210	2.0
Philippines	210	1.9
Liberia	200	1.3
Senegal	200	−0.1
Ceylon	190	2.1
Ghana	190	0.0
Morocco	190	3.4

Burma	—	1.8
Burundi*	—	0.0
Chad	—	−1.3
China (*Mainland*)†	—	0.8
Congo, Dem. Rep. of	—	0.2
Dahomey	—	0.9
Ethiopia	—	2.3
Guinea	—	2.6
Haiti	—	−1.0
Malawi	—	1.0
Mali	—	1.2
Nepal	—	0.4
Niger	—	−0.9
Nigeria	—	−0.3
Rwanda	—	−0.8
Somalia*	—	1.5
Tanzania[3]	—	1.6
Upper Volta	—	0.1
Viet-Nam (*North*)†	—	3.2
Yemen, Arab Rep. of*	—	2.3

Source: International Bank for Reconstruction and Development, *World Bank Atlas*, (Washington, D.C.: 1971).

[1]Including Namibia.

[2]The estimate of growth of GNP per capita of 0.8% in the 1970 Atlas was in error; the correct figure should have been 2.6%.

[3]Mainland Tanzania.

* Estimates of GNP per capita and its growth rate are tentative.

†Estimates of GNP per capita and its growth rate have a wide margin of error mainly because of the problems in deriving the GNP at factor cost from net material product and in converting the GNP estimate into US dollars.

—Estimated at less than 100 dollars.

impact of technology on the social structures of society, and they have developed complex theories to show how the interaction occurs. The most famous theory was Marx's analysis of industrial changes in England, but other "technological determinists" have clarified the link between change and technology. One important theroist was William F. Ogburn, who developed the "cultural-lag" thesis, a theory that argues that social transformation in modern societies almost always comes after technology has made it necessary. But not all sociologists have agreed that technology is the prime force. Max Weber, for instance, demonstrated that cultural values and ideals can change the economic system—a reversal of the technological-determinism theory.

What will the economic and technological systems of the future be like? Nobody knows for sure, of course, but a number of basic characteristics seem to be emerging. The postindustrial society will be highly dependent on automation and on a production system that will be able to produce most of the goods needed by the society with a small work force. The impact on our social institutions should be enormous. In the midst of this social upheaval it will take imagination and creative social planning to insure that the fruits of the postindustrial society are distributed equitably, justly, and without harm to the physical environment.

REFERENCES

Anderson, C. H. *Toward a New Sociology* (Homewood, Ill.: Irwin-Dorsey, 1971).

Bellah, Robert. *Tokaguwa Religion* (Glencoe, Ill.: Free Press, 1957).

Bendix, Reinhard. *Work and Authority in Industry* (New York: Wiley, 1966).

Birnbaum, Norman. *The Crisis of Industrial Society* (New York: Oxford University Press, 1969).

Blau, Peter M., and Otis Dudley Duncan. *The American Occupational Structure* (New York: Wiley, 1967).

Blauner, Robert, *Alienation and Freedom: The Factory Worker and His Industry* (Chicago: University of Chicago Press, 1964).

Burke, John G., ed. *The New Technology and Human Values* (Belmont, Calif.: Wadsworth Publishing, 1969).

Darwin, Charles. *Origin of the Species* (New York: Appleton, 1859).

Durkheim, Emile. *The Division of Labor in Society,* trans. by G. Simpson (Glencoe: Free Press, 1933).

Epstein, Cynthia Fuchs. *Woman's Place*

(Berkeley: University of California Press, 1970).

Faunce, Robert. "Automation in the Automobile Industry" *American Sociological Review, 23,* August 1958, pp. 403–406.

Lindenfeld, Frank, ed. *Radical Perspectives on Social Problems* (New York: Macmillan, 1968, 1973).

Marcson, Simon, ed. *Automation, Alienation, and Anomie* (New York: Harper and Row, 1970).

Marx, Karl, and Friedrich Engels. *The German Ideology,* (New York: International Publishers, 1947).

Moore, Wilbert. *The Conduct of the Corporation.* (New York: Random House, 1962).

Morgan, Lewis. *Ancient Society* (Cambridge, Mass: The Bellnap Press, 1964, first published 1877).

Ogburn, William F. "Cultural Lag as Theory", *Sociology and Social Research, 41,* January-February 1957, pp. 167–174.

Smelser, Neil. *Social Change in Industrial Society* (Chicago: University of Chicago Press, 1959).

Toffler, Alvin. *Future Shock* (New York: Bantam, 1971).

Weber, Max, *The Protestant Ethic and the Spirit of Capitalism,* trans. by Talcott Parsons (New York: Scribner's, 1930).

Whyte, William. *The Organization Man* (New York: Simon and Schuster, 1956).

TWELVE POPULATION AND URBANIZATION

EHRLICH ON POPULATION

I have understood the population explosion intellectually for a long time. I came to understand it emotionally one stinking hot night in Delhi a couple of years ago. My wife and daughter and I were returning to our hotel in an ancient taxi. The seats were hopping with fleas. The only functional gear was third. As we crawled through the city, we entered a crowded slum area. The temperature was well over 100, and the air was a haze of dust and smoke. The streets seemed alive with people. People eating, people washing, people sleeping. People visiting, arguing, and screaming. People thrusting their hands through the taxi window, begging. People defecating and urinating. People clinging to buses. People herding animals. People, people, people, people. As we moved slowly through the mob, hand horn squawking, the dust, noise, heat, and cooking fires gave the scene a hellish aspect. Would we ever get to our hotel? All three of us were, frankly, frightened. It seemed that anything could happen but, of course, nothing did. Old India hands will laugh at our reaction. We were just some overprivileged tourists, unac-

Ehrlich's description of overcrowding in India and his data on the population explosion present a sobering picture for all mankind because the very existence of human life is at stake. In addition to a more general concern about population, sociologists have become more interested in the effect that population factors have on human social life. In this chapter we will examine two important features of population—the growth of population itself and the progressive concentration of that population into urban areas.

THE POPULATION EXPLOSION

The world population is growing at a fantastic pace (Figure 12.1). An important concept to remember in connection with the population explosion is the *doubling time,* that is, how long it takes the world population to double. It probably took 1 million years for the world's population to double from 2.5 to 5.0 million, the level reached about 8000 B.C. From this point humans began redoubling about every 1000 years, and by A.D. 1650 there were about 500 million people on the customed to the sights and sounds of India. Perhaps, but since that night I've known the *feel* of overpopulation.

It has been estimated that the human population of 6000 B.C. was about five million people, taking perhaps one million years to get there from two and a half million. The population did not reach 500 million until almost 8,000 years later—about 1650 A.D. This means it doubled roughly once every thousand years or so. It reached a billion people around 1850, doubling some 200 years. It took only 80 years or so for the next doubling, as the population reached two billion around 1930. We have not completed the next doubling to four billion yet, but we now have well over three billion people. The doubling time at present seems to be about 37 years. Quite a reduction in doubling times: 1,000,000 years, 1,000 years, 200 years, 80 years, 37 years. Perhaps the meaning of a doubling time of around 37 years is best brought home by a theoretical exercise. Let's examine what might happen on the absurd assumption that the population continued to double every 37 years into the indefinite future.

If growth contined at that rate for about 900 years, there would be some 60,000,000,000,000,000 people on the face of the earth. Sixty million billion people. This is about 100 persons for each square yard of the Earth's surface, land and sea. (From Paul Ehrlich, *The Population Bomb,* 1968)

earth. It then took only 200 years to double again, to 1 billion people in 1850. The next doubling required only 80 years, so that by 1930 there were about 2 billion living persons. We have not yet attained the next doubling; the world's population is estimated by the United Nations to be slightly over 3.7 billion in 1974. At the current growth rate the population of the world would double every 36 years. Look at these doubling times: 1 million years, 1000 years, 200 years, 80 years, 36 years. The facts are staggering; will the population soon be doubling every decade?

Although the population growth today is a subject of much concern, we are certainly not the first generation to notice the problem. In fact, during the industrial revolution Europe was growing so fast that some people began to predict a disaster as the population outgrew the food resources. One of the most vocal of these prophets of doom was an English clergyman named Thomas Robert Malthus (1766–1834).

In his major work, *Essay on the Principle of Population,* first published in 1798, Malthus noted that populations were normally held down by three *positive* checks: disease, famine, and war. Although war had not been reduced, disease and famine had been. Consequently the population was growing rapidly. The

Figure 12.1
The long-term growth of world population

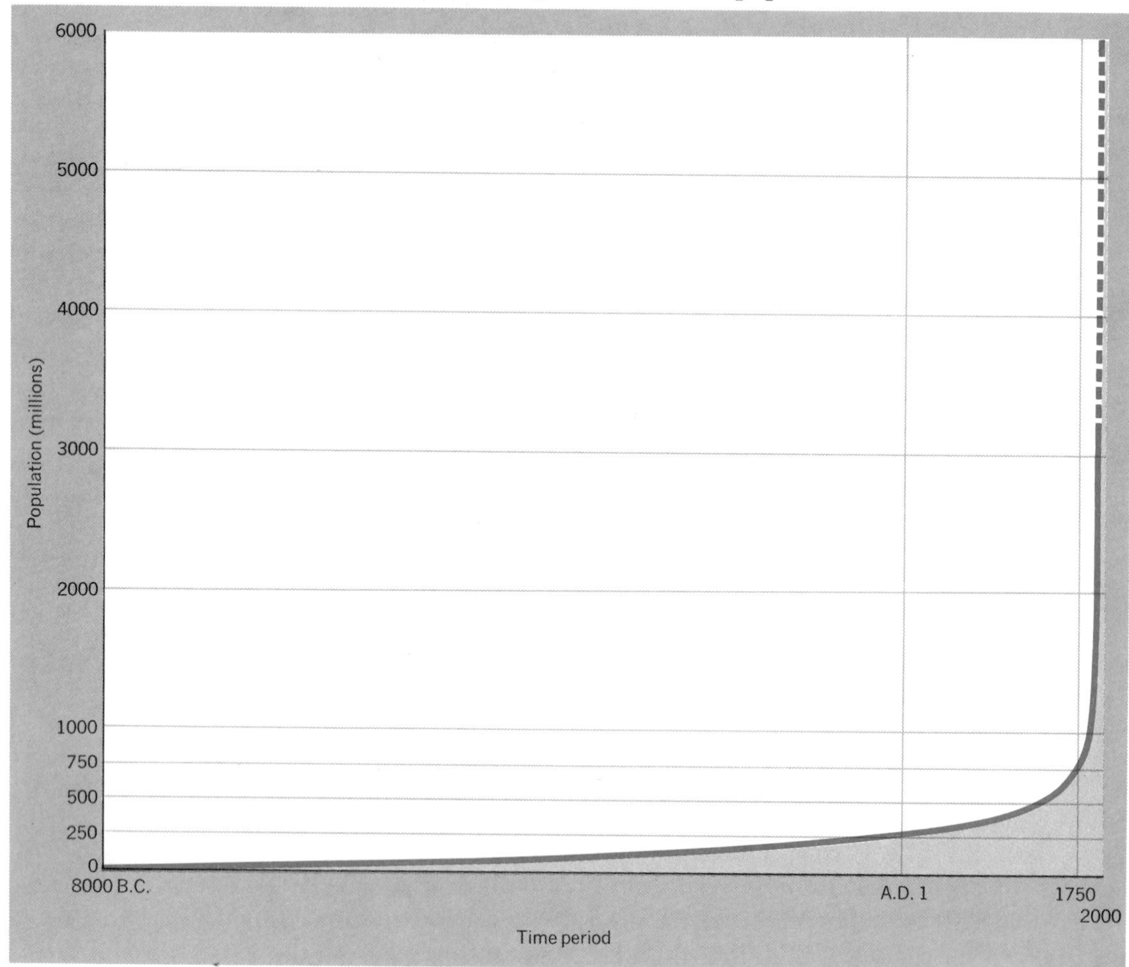

Source: Population and Society, Charles B. Nam. Houghton Mifflin Co. 1968

question then was whether technology and food production could keep pace with a growing population for very long. Malthus concluded that they could not, basing his thinking on sound demographic and economic principles. Population grows proportionally to the present population. Thus if the rate of growth is constant, the total population increases at a geometric rate in the same way that money accrues with compound interest. Food supplies, on the other hand, cannot grow indefinitely at a geometric rate, according to Malthus. The economic "law of diminishing returns" indicates that increasing inputs of labor or capital on the same area of land will eventually be of little help in raising yields. Since the supply of agricultural land is limited, Malthus concluded that the production of food would inevitably fall behind population growth until famine, disease, or war again brought down the numbers and reestablished an equilibrium between population and the environment.

Malthus was in a good position to observe the rapid growth of population during the industrial revolution and to be alarmed by it. And, although he was wrong in some respects, Malthus was probably correct to say that Europe, and England in particular, could not have improved its standard of living permanently had population continued to grow at the nineteenth-century pace.

For a time migration to the New World helped drain off part of the population growth. Between 1820 and 1930 official records indicate that over 32 million Europeans left for the New World (including Australia), and the actual number may have been greater than the records show. But, as was apparent to Malthus and most students of demography, this exodus could not continue indefinitely; eventually the birthrate must decline or the death rate rise. Malthus was not particularly optimistic about a decline in births, since the marriage and birthrates seemed to rise in times of economic improvement. Moreover, being a minister, Malthus did not believe in the practice of contraception, which he considered a "vice." He believed instead that a powerful morality was needed to support the delayed marriage and sexual abstinence necessary to control population growth.

Thomas Robert Malthus (1766–1834). English clergyman who predicted that overpopulation would gradually lead to disaster for the human race unless the birthrate was drastically lowered. Malthus was, however, very pessimistic about the possibility of reducing the birthrate. Improved technology and agriculture have reduced the threat of starvation, proving Malthus wrong—at least for the present. Many people, however, fear that in the long run his gloomy predictions may yet prove accurate.

Malthus has often been criticized, sometimes unfairly and somtimes not. Some economists have suggested that Malthus was far too pessimistic in assessing the limits of technology; sociologist and communist writers have objected strongly to Malthus' observations on poverty, which he tended to attribute to the prolific birthrate of the poor rather than to the economic system. In defense of Malthus it must be said that he did consider these criticisms and softened his conclusions considerably in later versions of the *Essay.*

CONTEMPORARY POPULATION TRENDS

The crisis that Malthus predicted has not occurred in the industrialized nations for two reasons. First, there were major technological breakthroughs in food production, such as the introduction of new grains, the potato, and fertilizers, that made the same amount of agricultural land capable of supporting much larger populations. Second, there has been a trend in the industrial nations toward a sharply reduced birthrate. Since population trends in industrialized and nonindustrialized nations differ considerably, they must be treated separately. Let us first examine the population dynamics of the industrialized nations.

THE DEMOGRAPHIC TRANSITION

The "demographic transition" in Western nations was a population shift that occurred in three stages. Stage One, the most common situation of mankind before the Industrial Revolution, was a high death rate-high birthrate condition under which the population was low and fairly stable.

Stage Two began at about the time of the Industrial Revolution with a series of technological and health advances. The *death rate* began to drop sharply as a consequence of better food, the control of disease, and better health facilities. However, the *birthrate* remained at its previously high levels, and the population began to grow enormously. This was the approximate period of Malthus' writing and it appeared at the time that runaway population growth would overwhelm the world. Between 1650 and 1850, for example, the population of Europe jumped from 103 million to 274 million—and this did not include millions of Europeans who moved to America.

Stage Three, however, saw a sharp drop in *birthrates.* The Industrial Revolution produced a growing middle class that voluntarily lowered its birthrate and valued highly a small family. Particularly as people moved from farm life to industrial life children became less of an asset and more of a liability. As the birthrate decreased then, the population growth slowed down rapidly. In the new stage of low birthrate-low death rates most industrial nations stabilized with very slowly increasing populations.

The lowered birthrates began first in northern and western Europe, then gradually gained momentum from about 1875 to 1935. The birthrate was decreasing at about 0.3 of a point per year until it reached extremely low levels in the depression. Since then birthrates have fluctuated slightly, but not enough to reverse the basic trend downward. In fact, in 1973 the United States had for the first time lowered its birthrate to the point that in the long run its population would stop growing and stabilize.

In central and southern Europe the decline of birthrates appears to have begun slightly later than in northwestern Europe. In southern Europe, except for some of the more industrial parts of Italy, the decline of the birthrate came slowly. At this rate it took from the end of the nineteenth century to midtwentieth century to complete the transition, and even then the birthrate was still higher than it had been in northwest Europe during the 1930s; since then, however, the birthrate has declined further in southern Europe. Central Europe, on the other hand, made rapid progress. The birthrate decline began in the late nineteenth century and was fairly complete before World War II.

Finally, in the early 1900s, the demographic transition began in east Europe, which was at the time a "frontier" area. Possibly for this reason the birthrate was extremely high at the onset of the transition—around 40–50 instead of the 35–40 more common in eastern and northern Europe. When natality decline did begin, however, lost time was quickly made up. The demographic transition was generally completed between about 1900 and 1960, despite the interruptions of terribly destructive wars that hindered social progress. Today the countries of east Europe have some of the lowest birthrates in the world.

Small families, a pattern that was once a peculiarity of the upper classes of industrial countries, had become the dominant life-style of all of Europe by the midtwentieth century. Generally speaking the rest of the world was not so fortunate—the only exception being Japan, which for uncertain reasons, entered the demographic transition about the same time as eastern Europe and proceeded as quickly.

Japan was the first distinctly non-European nation to industrialize and experience the demographic transition. In fact, it was so far ahead of other non-European societies (probably about 50 years) that it really must be considered a special case. The first data for Japan are for 1920, but by then both the death rates and birthrates appear to have fallen already. They continued to drop regularly as Japan became one of the most powerful industrial nations on earth. By the early 1960s the Japanese birthrate fell to an all-time low. Some demographers believe that the postwar decline in birthrates was greatly speeded by the Eugenics Protection Law, which offered legal, inexpensive abortions on demand.

POPULATION TRENDS IN MODERN INDUSTRIAL NATIONS

Having discussed major population trends of the industrial nations, we will now examine three more specific aspects of the general trend: (1) death rates, (2) birthrates, and (3) fertility differentials (differences in birthrates associated with different social groups).

The Death Rate in Industrial Societies

The death rate (the number of deaths per 1000 population) is uniformly low in all societies that have experienced the demographic transition because premature death from infectious disease has been all but eradicated. Expectation of life at birth is around 70 years, slightly higher for females.

The principal causes of death in modern societies are cancer and degenerative diseases of the heart, cirulatory system, lungs, and kidneys. The maladies largely affect older people and are difficult to cure, since they reflect chronic bodily weaknesses instead of specific outside infections. Probably for this reason improvements in life expectancy have greatly slowed down, and it is unlikely that there will be any further large decreases in death rates without some dramatic scientific breakthrough.

Those few people who die prematurely are often the victims of accidents, suicides, or homicides. Only in infant mortality is there still room for improvement; the infant death rate in some developed countries, notably the United States, has not fallen as much as it could. The United States probably has a higher infant mortality rate than many advanced nations because of the uneven availability of medical care, with minorities and the poor having less access to medical care than other groups—one more piece of evidence that shows how inequality affects life chances in America. Recently, however, there has been a decline in the death rates of American infants, perhaps as a result of government programs designed to extend medical attention to minorities and the poor.

It is interesting that, as infectious diseases were reduced, the life span of women became longer than that of men. Various theories have been advanced to explain this fact, but many demographers now believe that it is mainly a result of two factors. First, there may be some slight biological advantage of women—a greater resistance to the kinds of diseases that are currently the major causes of death. Second, men are generally subject to greater occupational stress, higher risk of accident, and harder physical tasks. Men also appear to cultivate more health-damaging habits, such as smoking. Presently the death rate of men is higher than that of women in all age groups, including those during which women are exposed to the risk of childbearing. (Of course, at these younger ages men are plagued by a high accident rate, which any auto insurance company will be glad to tell you about.)

Birth Rates. Whereas in the past the death rate fluctuated greatly, it is now the birthrate that periodically rises and falls and is thus the major dynamic factor in determining population growth. The basic long-term trend, as stated earlier, has been gradually downward (see Figure 12.2). There have been fluctuations, however. For example, the 1900 birthrate (figures are number of births per 1000 of total population) was 30.1; it decreased to a low of 18.7 in 1935; then shot back up after World War II until it peaked at 25.0 in 1955. This postwar "baby boom" may have reflected the greatly improved postwar economic situation; partly it may have been the result of births being "made up" that had been postponed during the war and depression.

In any case, this upward trend has subsided. From a postwar high of 25.0 in 1955, the birthrate fell steadily to about 15.6 in 1974. Perhaps the recent declines

Figure 12.2
U.S. Birthrate per 1000 people. The long-term trend is down

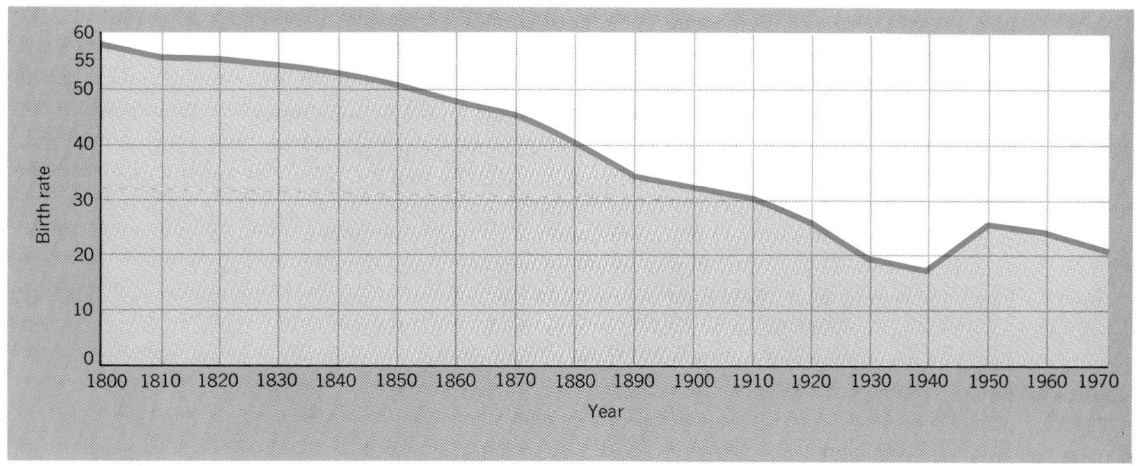

Source: U.S. Census Bureau, *Historical Abstracts of the U.S., Colonial Times to 1957,* and *Statistical Abstract of the U. S.,* 1972.

are the result of a worsening economic climate or of the longer period of formal schooling. On the other hand, they may be due to the availability of effective oral contraceptives, coupled with a general feeling that population growth is undesirable. Other western societies have generally shown a birthrate pattern similar to that of the United States, although they usually had shorter and milder "baby booms."

Fertility Differentials. Finally, something should be said about fertility differentials—differences in birthrates associated with religion, ethnic backgrounds, race, socioeconomic class, and residence. Let us summarize some of the more important differences.

1. *Rural life and poverty.* Since the demographic transition began, and even before, the poor and the rural dwellers have had more children. Although this trend is still true, currently the differences are modest and we might anticipate that they will become even less significant in the future.

2. *Religion.* Religion has continued to be a major determinant of fertility differences. Western societies with large Catholic groups almost invariably have moderately higher birthrates than those that are predominantly Protestant. Research suggests that this is not because of the Papal ban on contraception, which is regularly violated by large numbers, but because of a sincere desire among Catholics for a strong family life. The Catholic-Protestant differences are especially apparent among the higher socioeconomic classes; Catholics who are economically successful actually seem to have more children than those who are less well off, in direct contrast to the traditional low fertility of the Protestant upper classes. However, in recent years the differences between Protestant and Catholic family sizes seem to be narrowing, with both tending toward smaller families.

3. *Race.* Nonwhite populations in the United States have always had a higher birthrate than whites, but also a much higher death rate, so the actual percentage of nonwhites in the population has actually declined (this tendency was aided by the influx of many white immigrants). The differences in birthrates are fairly substantial, with nonwhites averaging about a 50 percent higher rate. For example, the white birthrate in 1950 was 23.0, the nonwhite 33.3. By 1970 both rates were considerably lower, but nonwhites still maintained their advantage: white 16.6, nonwhites 24.2. The long-term historical tendency, however, suggests that nonwhites' rates are decreasing as education levels, income, and other socioeconomic factors improve.

THE URBANIZATION OF THE HUMAN POPULATION

The size and growth of population is only part of our study, for people are not evenly distributed over the earth. One of the more important aspects of the *distribution* of population is the trend toward urbanization. Although there were many cities in earlier periods of history, the growth of highly urbanized populations is a very recent phenomenon. Before 1850 no society had a majority of its population living in urban areas, and by 1900 only Great Britian did. Today, however, nearly all of the industrial nations are highly urbanized and the nonindustrial nations are moving in that direction.

And the pace of urbanization has been quite rapid. In the United States, for example, the first census, taken in 1790, reported only 5.1 percent of the nation's population as urban. In each census thereafter the percentages increased sharply: 19.8 in 1860, 28.2 in 1870, 39.7 in 1900, and 51.2 in 1920. Thus it was just after World War I that more than half of the American people began living in cities. By 1950 the percentage had risen to 63.7 and by 1971 was up to 71 (data from Bogue, 1955, and U.S. Census, 1970).

Rapid urbanization has actually become a worldwide phenomenon. All over the world the rate of increase of cities is much higher than the rate of growth of the general world population. It is estimated that more than 20 percent of the world population now lives in the cities of 100,000 people or more. This is a new phenomenon, since it is only in the last century and a half that people have begun to live in cities to any great extent. In the next few sections we will examine a number of urban trends and problems that are seriously affecting social life.

THE DOMINANCE OF URBAN VALUES

Life in urban society is considerably different from life in the rural society that humans have known for thousands of years. Obviously there are physical differences that set off the city from the country: huge concentrations of people in small spaces, high-rise buildings that maximize land use, intricate networks of highways that carry millions of cars, huge traffic jams that strangle transportation, and decaying housing and pollution that scar the landscape. Our interest, however, is not in the physical shape of the city, but in the *social consequences* of urban life.

Ferdinand Tönnies (1855–1936), an early German sociologist, suggested that social life could be divided into basic patterns depending on the social behaviors expressed (Tönnies, 1887). At one end of a continuum is the *Gemeinschaft,* or community that is normally associated with rural life. The rural community has the following characteristics.

1. A small population with low density levels.
2. Very close social relations, since everyone in the community knows everyone else.
3. Informal methods of social control, with gossip and personal persuasion used to keep behaviors in line with the community norms.
4. Strong kinship ties, heavy involvement with family, and strong focus on family life styles.
5. A simple division of labor, with only a few jobs available.
6. Extremely close attachment to the local community and intense provincialism.

Urban areas, by contrast, are larger, have more superficial relationships, depend more on formal social control (police and courts), understress family relations, and have more cosmopolitan outlooks. Throughout the early twentieth century sociologists and popular writers often wrote about the "loss of community" and the unfortunate decline in rural values as urban attitudes spread. Many writers felt that the decline of rural values meant that human life was growing more impersonal, harsher, and more unfeeling as city attitudes began to dominate. There was a touch of romanticism in many of these theorists, however, because they often idealized rural life, which in reality had its own problems: provincialism, constant meddling in neighbors' affairs, limited job and educational opportunities.

In recent years the debate over whether urban or rural ways of life are "better" has subsided somewhat, for now it is widely recognized that both ways of life have their own unique advantages and disadvantages. (See Figure 12.3 for an outline of some of the social opportunities and problems of urban life.) In any event, urban patterns of life are more and more dominating the American social scene as more people move to the city and as the mass media impose urban values all over the nation, regardless of where people live.

THE GROWTH OF MEGALOPOLIS AND SUBURBANIZATION

Not only are cities growing rapidly, but they are also beginning to overlap. Where there were once miles of countryside between cities, there are now many areas of the nation where cities run into one another without breaks. Such an area is called a *megalopolis.* The Northeast coast, from New Haven to Newark, is one huge city; the same is true of the San Francisco Bay area, the Los Angeles area,

Figure 12.3
Positive and negative social aspects of urban life

Positive	Negative
Cities allow occupational specialization and a wide range of services unavailable elsewhere.	The occupational specialization of cities insures that most lower-class persons will either be unqualified for employment or work at boring, demeaning jobs.
By bringing together significant numbers of people with similar interests, the city encourages and supports the cultural life of society—theater, music, museums of art and of natural history.	By bringing together people with similar interests, the city also insures that many deviant groups, some harmful to society, will be able to exist; for instance, the distribution of heroin would be prohibitively expensive unless there were many users in a small area.
The city offers anonymity and freedom that allows a person to "try on" new roles and identities; to be known by everyone in a small town can be fine unless you want to change in some way.	The city is sometimes a group of strangers in which a person is cut off from *meaningful* groups that could otherwise define his role and identity; this may leave the city dweller in a state of anomie, or normlessness.
In a psychological sense the city is where the action and the excitement are; it would be absurd to complain about crowding on New Year's Eve in Times Square or during Mardi Gras in New Orleans, since the crowding is part of the attraction of these events.	The city and its crowds can overstimulate the mind until a person becomes numbed by the crush of humanity and oblivious to others as individuals; this allows a person to watch passively while another is raped or murdered.
By bringing together people of various ethnic-cultural backgrounds the city destroys the normative tyranny of any one single group to dictate the standards of acceptable behavior.	Ethnic-cultural diversity also tends to break down the normative control previously provided by subgroups, thus allowing crime and violence to proliferate.
The predominance of casual relationships, called secondary, or *gesellschaft*, prevents people from getting involved with everyone they meet, allows them to choose their friends, and insures privacy. In a secondary relationship people encounter each other only in narrowly defined aspects such as "clerk" and "customer."	The predominance of secondary roles tends to minimize the warm, all-encompassing primary relationships that involve whole personalities and tend to persist over time.
The city provides a more comfortable life than is usually possible in rural areas.	The city cuts people off from nature and destroys the natural environment.

the southern end of Lake Michigan around Chicago, and the Greater London complex in Great Britain. Population experts suggest that the growth of such massive urban complexes will increase to the point that 70 percent of the U. S. population may live in megalopolises by the year 2000. Figure 12.4 shows where those urban concentrations will probably be.

Within these huge urban concentrations there is a new pattern of growth called *suburbanization,* the growth of fringe communities. Most urban growth is now occurring in these suburban rings instead of in the central core of the city. In fact, many major cities in the United States have actually experienced population decreases in their central areas—New York, Boston, Detroit, San Francisco, Chicago, and Pittsburgh among them. Presently about one third of the nation's population lives in central cities, one third in suburban areas, and one third outside urban regions. Suburban areas have grown sharply over the last few years, central cities have decreased slightly, and nonurban areas have decreased rapidly.

This rapid growth of the suburbs is aggravating several social problems of urban areas. First, the fragmentation of local governments with all the accompanying problems is increased. Second, segregation lines are hardened because the exodus from the city consists largely of middle-class citizens who leave behind minorities and the poor. School integration, for example, is now almost impossible in most large cities because the white middle-class children live in different school districts. Integration cannot be accomplished without crossing governmental lines, and this has never been successfully done. The one major attempt—Richmond, Virginia's plan to unite the several suburbs—was ruled down by the Supreme Court.

Finally, the flight of middle-class taxpayers to the suburbs leaves the cities burdened with enormous problems but a much lower tax base. Of course, most of the suburbanites will work in the city and use city services, but do not pay city taxes. Some cities have tried to tax suburbanites who work in the city. New York City, for example, has a tax on income earned by suburbanites working in the city. Most of these plans have failed before they started. In short, the growth of suburban fringes is creating a complex set of problems for the central cities: governmental fragmentation, residential and school segregation, loss of city tax bases.

GOVERNMENTAL FRAGMENTATION AND DEMOCRATIC REPRESENTATION

The growth of huge metropolitan areas with their suburban fringes causes a number of problems, but one of the worst is the extreme fragmentation of governments. In any large urban area the local governments are splintered into many small units, none of which is able to serve the needs of the entire region. Today urban problems are regional, not merely confined to the political borders of a single city. Pollution of air and water, school integration, police protection, transportation, and utilities all require

Figure 12.4
The urbanization of America: Megalopolis map of the year 2000. Like most other industrialized nations, the United States has become an urban society. Urban specialists predict that by 2000, 70 percent of the people will live in great urban clusters called megalopolises, shown on the map.

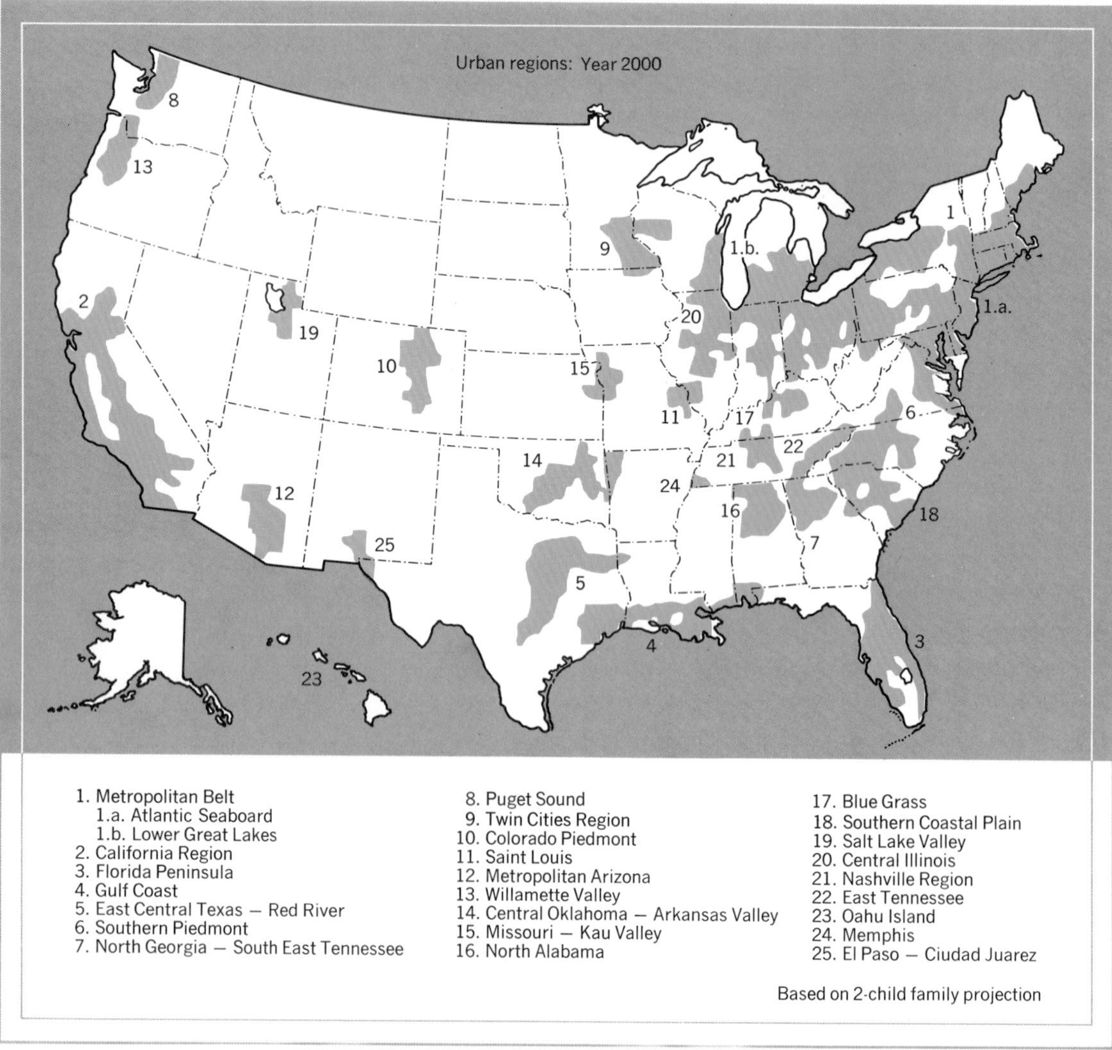

Source: Presidential Commission on Population and the American Future (Washington, D.C.: U. S. Government Printing Office, 1972)

close cooperation among various governmental units. Under the present outdated structures, however, urban areas are so hopelessly splintered that the necessary cooperation is rarely achieved. In fact, the residents of a small community on Long Island could not get the necessary cooperation among various government units to put in a needed traffic light (see Insert 12.I).

In addition, because there are so many overlapping governmental units the taxpayer often has to pay for needless, wasteful duplication of services. Why, for example, should a city dweller pay city taxes to support a police force and at the same time pay county taxes for the sheriff's department? In may other areas of governmental services—transportation, pollution, and housing codes among them—there are massive inefficiencies because of duplication or because regional problems are attacked piecemeal by local agencies.

Thus far, few urban areas have been innovative about handling their regional problems. A few cities such as Nashville and Miami are now experimenting with "Metro" governments that combine the central city and its suburbs into single governmental units. Other areas have created special regional districts for specific problems, such as the Port of New York and New Jersey Authority, which handle all ports in the region, and the Bay Area Rapid Transit District, which built a unified transportation system in the San Francisco Bay region. Unfortunately, most urban areas have not yet faced up to their regional problems, and governmental fragmentation still strangles most creative efforts.

In addition, democratic values are seriously threatened by this governmental fragmentation. How can a voter vote intelligently when the governmental system is hopelessly confused? The average urban area is divided and subdivided into special tax districts, county governments, city governments, school districts, and towns. For example, Santa Clara County, California (where the city of San Jose lies) has 96 separate local governments: 15 cities, 37 school districts, 44 special districts (flood control, parks, etc.). The types of governmental agencies in Santa Clara County are overwhelming:

1. County Board of Supervisors
2. Municipal governments.
3. Elementary school districts.
4. High school districts.
5. Junior college districts.
6. Special water conservation districts.
7. Special fire districts.
8. Special soil conservation districts.
9. Special water districts.
10. Special sanitation districts.
11. Special park districts.
12. Special hospital districts.
13. Special cemetery districts.
14. Special memorial districts.

It is no wonder that the voters of Santa Clara County are bewildered by their governmental structure. In a survey made by a group working for Ralph Nader (Fellmeth, 1971, pp. 31–36) it was found that only 60 percent of the eligible voters

INSERT **12.1**

THE WAR FOR A STOPLIGHT: THE BALKANIZATION OF SUBURBIA

Port Washington is a comfortable community of 35,000 residents located on the north shore of Long Island. Its size and the combined education and political awareness of its citizens should make it a good example of government in the tradition of "home rule." In fact, however, Port Washington is divided into a maze of jurisdictions and special districts, mostly run by part-time, impotent local politicians. This is a situation all too typical of the suburbs—Long Island outside of New York City has 13 townships, 92 villages, 807 special districts, and approximately 100 unincorporated areas. Confusion results, making home rule a cruel farce.

The people of Port Washington felt that a traffic light to protect children walking between a school and a library was needed and soon discovered just how bad their situation was. The library was in the village of Baxter Estates. The school was in an unincorporated area although it was run by the Port Washington school district. The street itself was maintained by the county but patrolled by the Port Washington police district, which is smaller than the Port Washington school district. Traffic lights on this road were the responsibility of the county but parking was regulated by the town. It is not surprising that no governmental body wanted to take responsibility for the traffic-light project.

After much effort by residents, the request for the traffic light

registered and that only 20 percent of these people actually voted. Thus only 12 percent of the voters elected local officials. In addition, the same survey found that the average voter was almost totally ignorant of the local government structure: only 12 percent knew the county had a Board of Supervisors; only 26 percent of the city dwellers knew the form of government the city had and one of the elected officials; only 5 percent could name their school district and at least one school official. In short, the voters of Santa Clara County have such a confused governmental system that they really are ignorant about the local authorities. They pay taxes for services that are duplicated by many different governments, they send their children to school districts where they rarely bother to elect was turned down by the county, which recommended that the town restrict parking on the street to increase visibility. This was only the last of a long series of buck-passing maneuvers that had lasted three months, a time during which countless children had crossed this street. When the police district received the recommendation from the county it proposed parking restrictions to the town board. The townspeople were frustrated and angry. Predictably the town board scheduled the meeting for a week-day morning, hoping that husbands would not be willing or able to miss work to attend. The board declared it had no jurisdiction over traffic control.

By this time the local citizenry would not be put off by such excuses. Under pressure, the board did approve a new parking ordinance and pledged to help work for the traffic light. This effectively pacified the opposition. A year after the question was first brought before the local government, however, there was still no traffic light.

As Americans flee to the suburbs, they seek to protect their new communities under the doctrine of home rule. What they have so far is a patchwork of local governments that cannot serve even their simplest needs. Protected by apathy, local politicians act as custodians for an archaic system of governance. If it is to work, the ideal of home rule must be backed by hard, sweeping reforms. If it is impossible merely to get a stoplight, is it any wonder that the really serious social problems are neglected?

Source: Samuel Kaplan, "The Balkanization of Suburbia," *Harper's Magazine, 243* (1457), October 1971, pp. 72–74.

the school officials, and they usually fail to vote because of the confusion. Yet Santa Clara County is not an atypical example; Los Angeles County has nearly four times *more* governmental districts than Santa Clara. To say the least, local government is hardly a model of effective democracy. Political fragmentation, voter apathy, and duplication of services at high tax prices are some of the costs the nation pays for the growth of huge urban areas.

HOUSING PROBLEMS AND PHYSICAL DECAY OF THE CITIES

The physical decay of cities is the most visible problem of urban life. The United States faces a chronic housing shortage, especially among poorer people, and slums are mushrooming all over the nation. The poor are the major victims of inadequate housing, just as they are the victims in most other areas of modern life. Yet, the people with the lowest incomes pay the highest percentage of their income for housing—and invariably receive poorer quality housing for the money they spend (see Hartman, 1972).

Income Bracket	Average Percentage Paid for Housing
Less than $2000	35
$2000–$3000	30
$3000–$4000	25
Over $4000	15

Racial segregation, scalping by slum lords, poorly administered housing projects, and the reluctance of banks to lend money to poor people; these are only a few of the social forces that press the poor into relatively expensive but inadequate housing.

Unfortunately, the public policies and programs designed to overcome these problems have done little or nothing to alleviate them. As Chester Hartman notes:

An even larger number of families are being forced either to live in substandard and overcrowded quarters and neighborhoods or pay an excessive portion of their incomes—25 percent, 35 percent and higher—in order to obtain a decent place to live.

The public housing program is bankrupt. The cancer of abandonment permeates whole sections of our major cities. Scandal, profiteering and dysfunction characterize the newer subsidy programs for moderate-income families. Suburban areas continue to erect legal and de facto barriers to prevent the construction of housing for low- and moderate-income families. (Hartman, 1972, p. 30)

Public housing programs designed to alleviate housing shortages for the poor have often been badly planned, replacing small slums with "high-rise slums," the great, grey monsters of public housing that have become crime ridden and that decayed shortly after being built. In St. Louis, for example, the massive Pruitt-Igoe housing project, built in 1954, was designed to house 10,000 people in a 57-acre area of high-rise buildings. Now almost the whole area lies vacant, the great, empty buildings stand with smashed windows, weedy lawns, and ripped-out plumbing—void of human habitation. Poor planning, inadequate police protection, chronic unemployment, poor schools, and miserable city services created a wasteland of failure in this so-called "model" development. It is unfortunate that the nation cannot house its citizens—although we seem to be able to do most other things we want, such as sending men to the moon.

Other physical aspects of the urban environment present problems. After years of civil rights efforts the nation is still largely segregated in its housing, and as whites move to the suburbs, leaving the decaying central cities to minority groups, the lines of division are actually growing sharper. This tendency is often aided by realtors as well as deliberate governmental policy through zoning regulations, housing restrictions, rent-control policies, and low-income housing activities. The nation is cursed with a hard-core racial segregation that is growing worse all the time.

Urban housing problems are difficult to solve. Urban slums like these were replaced by huge "urban renewal" housing projects in St. Louis. But the housing units were soon abandoned because of poor police protection, inadequate services, and tenant neglect. Eventually the "model" development was torn down for yet another urban renewal effort.

Meanwhile the physical pollution of rivers, air, and land is wrecking the environment. The issue is really not one of technology, since most of the technological developments necessary to clean up the environment have been made. Like so many other social problems pollution is basically a political and economic issue: who will pay the increased cost for cleaner environments? Powerful interest groups—oil companies, chemical industries, etc.—are fighting to influence government policy so they do not have to pay their share. In the last analysis the consumers will have to pay the bill and, if past history is any indicator, the poor and the socially disadvantaged will probably pay more than their share. Like so many other issues, the physical decay of the cities—slums, inadequate housing and transportation, pollution—is all tangled up with the political processes by which social decisions are made and by which the powerful maintain their privileges at the expense of the poor and powerless. All these issues are aggravated by the continuous population growth that so quickly wipes out many social improvements as fast as they are made. Let us turn back now to that critical population issue because it influences urban life at least as much as any other social force.

POPULATION AND THE FUTURE

What about the future of the planet Earth? Is overpopulation a real threat, as we hear so often in the popular press? Are there any hopeful signs that the population explosion will subside? Is there hope for improving the quality of life, or will overpopulation wipe out the opportunities? Will urban problems be continually aggravated by excessive population?

THE POPULATION EXPLOSION

As noted previously, Malthus argued in the nineteenth century that the world was headed for doom because of overpopulation. His predictions have not come true in the industralized nations, but many people believe he may yet be proven correct, for they argue that we are headed for an ecological disaster as the population once again threatens to outrun the food supply. One of the most outspoken advocates of population control is Stanford biologist Paul Ehrlich, who proclaims the problem vividly in the following words.

The facts of today's population crisis are appallingly simple. Mankind at first gradually, but recently with extreme rapidity, has intervened artificially to lower the death rate in the human population. Simultaneously we have not, repeat have not, intervened to lower the birthrate. Since people are unable to flee from our rather small planet, the inevitable result of the wide discrepancy between birth and death rates has been a rapid increase in the numbers of people crowded onto the Earth. The growth of the population is now so rapid that the multitude of humans is doubling every 36 years. Indeed in many underdeveloped countries the doubling time is between 20 and 25 years. Think of what it means for the population of a country like Colombia to double in the next 22 years.

But, it seems highly unlikely that 22 years from now, in 1990, Colombia will have doubled its present population of 20 million to 40 million. The reason is quite simple. The Earth is a spaceship of limited carrying capacity. The three and one half billion people who now live on our globe can do so only at the expense of the consumption of non-renewable resources, especially coal and petroleum. Today's technology could not maintain three and one half billion people without "living on capital" as we are now doing. . . . Somewhere between one and two billion people are today undernourished (have too few calories) or malnourished (suffer from various deficiencies, especially protein deficiencies). Somewhere between 4 and 10 million of our fellow human beings will starve to death this year. Consider that the average person among some 2 billion Asians has an annual income of $128, a life expectancy at birth of only 50 years, and is illiterate. A third of a billion Africans have an average life expectancy of only 43 years, and an average annual income of $123. Of Africans over 15 years of age, 82% are illiterate. Look at the situation in India, where Professor Georg Borstromg estimates that only about one person in fifty has an adequate diet. . . .

No, we're not doing a very good job of taking care of the people we have in 1968—and we are adding to the population of the Earth 70 million people per year. . . . We have an inadequate loaf of bread to divide among today's multitudes, and we are quickly adding more billions to the bread line.

The death rate could rise in several ways. Perhaps the most likely is through famine. The world has very nearly reached its maximum food production capacity. . . . Plague presents another possibility for a "death rate solution" to the population problem. . . . Indeed, if a man-made germ should escape from one of our biological warfare labs we might see the extinction of Homo Sapiens. It is now theoretically possible to develop organisms against which man would have no resistance . . . . Finally, of course, thermonuclear war could provide us with an instant death rate solution. . . . (Erhlich, 1970, pp. 1–3)

In order to understand Ehrlich's fear look again at Figure 12.1. Notice that the world population increased very slowly through most of mankind's history, but in the last few centuries the population has taken off at an astronomical rate, doubling itself in ever shorter periods of time and rushing headlong toward 8 and perhaps even 12 billion people. Certainly these figures reinforce the concern that the world may be facing mass starvation, overcrowding, and a general lowering of the quality of human life.

The population explosion is fundamentally the result of a sharp decrease in world *death rates*, not because of increased birthrates. The difference between low death rates and high birthrates is the villian producing such high increases in population. The problem is clear if you examine Figure 12.5. In the advanced industrial nations both the death rates and birthrates have dropped, with a resultant low rate of population increase. In the less developed nations, however, the death rate is down sharply but the birthrate remains high; the result is runaway population growth.

WORLD DIFFERENCES IN POPULATION GROWTH

Figure 12.5 suggests that the population explosion does not effect all nations in the same way. The world's nations may be

Figure 12.5
Difference between birth rates and death rates determine population growth

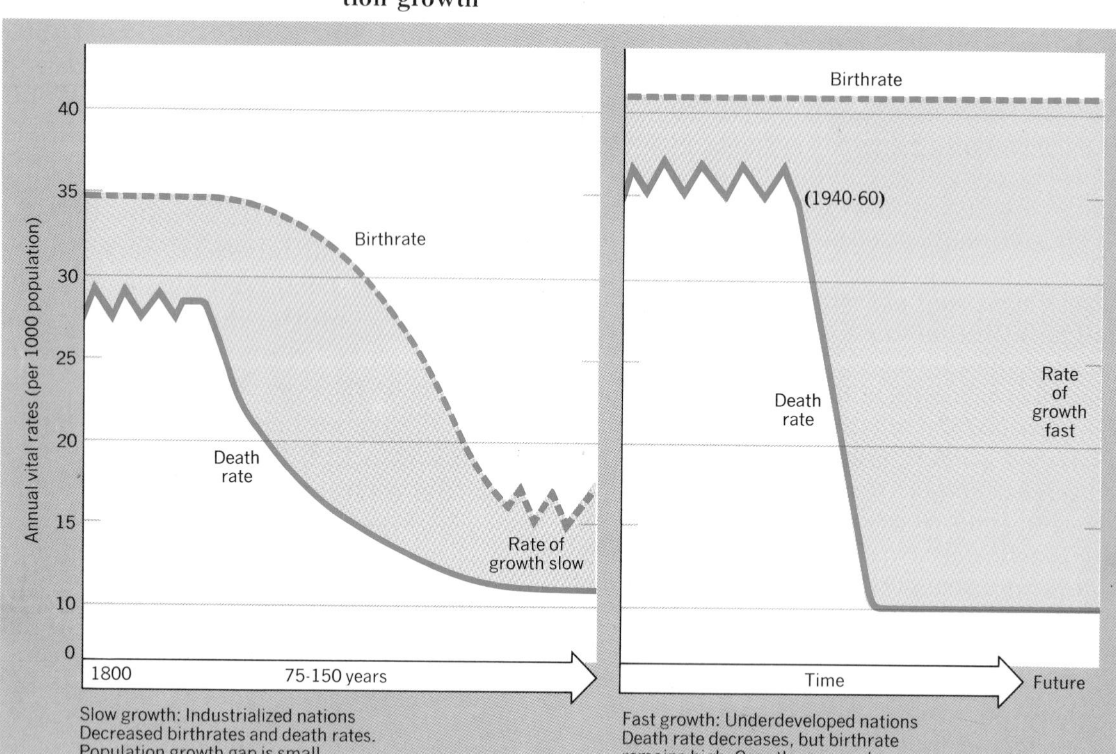

Source: Committee on Science and Public Policy, National Academy of Sciences, *The Growth of World Population,* Washington, D.C., 1963), p. 10, p. 15.

divided into approximately three groups, according to their population growth.

Group I includes the western industrial nations that have managed to achieve very low death rates and at the same time relatively low birthrates. Populations of this group grow slowly relative to those of other nations. Examples of nations that fall into this block include the United States (with a growth rate of 1.4 percent), the United Kingdom (0.7 percent), the USSR (1.4 percent), Denmark (0.8 percent), and Western Germany (1.1 percent).

Group II includes nations that have a sharply declining *death rate* but only slightly declining *birthrate.* In these nations both the population growth and the level of industralization are moderate. Although the population increase in this group is higher than for Group I, it certainly is not a runaway population explosion. Included in this block are China with a population growth of 1.5 percent and India with a population growth of 2.5 percent. It is extremely interesting that these two giants are actually in the moderate growth group instead of in the extremely high growth group. But, given the massive population base from which they started, even moderate growth levels will result in astronomical population increases in India and China over the next century. Others in this moderate group include the nations of southern and eastern Europe, Japan, Argentina, and most of the Caribbean nations.

Group III includes the nations that have virtually exploding populations. As a region Latin America probably shows the highest rates of increase. In the late 1960s Costa Rica was growing by 3.8 percent annually, enough to double the population in only 18 years. Comparable figures for other nations in the region were Mexico (3.4 percent), Colombia (3.4 percent), and Venezuela (3.4 percent). Most of Southeast Asia also has extremely high rates, averaging about 2.8 percent per year. Africa has a somewhat more modest growth rate. These nations whose populations are increasing so rapidly face famine and starvation unless effective measures can be found to reverse the process.

Figure 12.6 gives some startling information about the effect of the population explosion on different nations. By projecting the current trends to the year 2000 this chart shows that the developed, industrialized nations will grow very slowly, while the developing nations of Africa, Asia, and Latin America will grow increasingly faster. In fact, the whole pattern of population distribution will change, with the percentage in the developed nations going down sharply at the same time the percentage in the underdeveloped nations rises rapidly. Figure 12.6 should be studied carefully because it shows the dismal fact that the nations already facing starvation and poverty are the ones whose populations are exploding.

If the population explosion continues, what will happen to the quality of human life? In some sense it depends on which block of nations we are talking about. Assuming that there is no nuclear war and that the underdeveloped nations do not carry off a successful revolution against the developed nations, it will almost certainly be the underdeveloped nations that will face mass starvation, famine, and constant social upheaval. It does not take a population specialist to imagine what would happen if a nation such as India doubled its population in the next few years. Although there may be technological breakthroughs in food production, it is almost inconceivable that advances could support such huge population growths. Consequently, these nations must either limit their population, obtain food from the more developed nations, or face mass starvation. Many people believe that mass starvation is the most likely result. Although there have been extensive birth control campaigns in China, India, and Latin America, these attempts can only be labeled failures at this point. The population is still climbing at unbelievable rates.

POPULATION AND THE AMERICAN FUTURE

What difference will the population explosion make to America, one of the more industralized nations with a low growth rate? In 1972 the Presidential Commis-

Figure 12.6
Estimated and projected populations for developed and developing areas in the twentieth century

Year		Developed[a]	Developing			
			Total	Africa	Asia[b]	Latin America
1900 1925 1950 1975 2000	Population in Millions	554 700 838 1,115 1,448	996 1,207 1,659 2,741 5,459	120 147 199 331 663	813 961 1,297 2,107 4,145	63 99 163 303 651
1900–1925 1925–1950 1950–1975 1975–2000	Percent Increase	26.4 19.7 33.0 29.9	21.2 37.4 65.2 99.2	22.5 35.4 66.3 100.3	18.2 35.0 62.5 96.7	57.1 64.6 85.9 114.8
1900 1925 1950 1975 2000	Percent of World Total	35.7 36.7 33.6 28.9 21.0	64.3 63.3 66.4 71.1 79.0	7.7 7.7 8.0 8.6 9.6	52.4 50.4 51.9 54.6 60.0	4.1 5.2 6.5 7.9 9.4

Source: Irene Taeuber "Population and Society" in Robert E. L. Faris (ed.) *Handbook of Modern Sociology* © 1964 Rand McNally & Co., Chicago, p. 94.
a Europe, U.S.S.R., Australia, New Zealand, Japan, Northern America
b Excluding Asian portion of U.S.S.R. and Japan

sion on Population Growth and the American Future reported to the President and to the general public. Some of the Commission's major findings are helpful in assessing the importance of population increases on the daily life of American citizens. The basic finding of the Commission is the following.

We have found no convincing argument for continued national population growth. On the contrary, the pluses seem to be on the side of slowing growth and eventually stopping it altogether. Neither the health of our economy nor the welfare of individual businesses depends on continued population growth. In fact, the average person will be markedly better off in terms of traditional economic values if the population growth slows down . . . . (Presidential Commission, 1972)

The Commission assumes that families in the United States over the next century will average between two and three children. Even if the family size were immediately reduced to only two children, however, the population would continue to grow for nearly 100 years because the number of women of childbearing age is still increasing. Thus, even if the 20 to 35 age group limits their families to two children, there are so many people in this age bracket that the population will increase in absolute numbers and, for a time at least, the number of births will exceed the number of deaths.

What would be the difference in the quality of life in the United States if the average family had two instead of three children? Figure 12.7 indicates that an average of two children would lead to 307 million people in the United States by the year 2020, whereas, an average of three would lead to 477 million. This difference in population would have enormous consequences for the quality of life in the United States. For example, the Commission argues that with the larger population the general standard of living would be decreased for most American families, that extreme overcrowding would occur in metropolitan areas, that mineral resources and water supplies would be drastically overtaxed, that food supplies would rarely meet the demand and food prices would go up significantly, and that environmental pollution of all kinds would be substantially increased. Insert 12.II summarizes several of the Commission's important conclusions on the effects of increased population. The overall conclusion is that the American people must reject the long-held notion that booming growth alone is always a good thing.

What can be done about the problem of overpopulation? The Presidential Commission made several suggestions.

1. Universal sex education should be available to all children.

2. Abortion should be readily available on demand by any woman wishing it.

3. Contraceptive information and devices should be freely distributed to all people, including minors.

4. All formal and informal restrictions against voluntary sterilization should be removed immediately.

The Commission hoped that a combination of these remedies would help hold down the birthrate and consequently improve the quality of life. What are the chances that these recommendations will actually be carried out?

Conservative forces against the limitation of population seem to be extremely large. In fact, President Nixon immediately repudiated the recommendations of his own Presidential Commission, insisting that many of the recommendations were immoral. The Catholic Church attacked the Commission's recommendations, arguing that they were contrary to the moral teachings of the Catholic faith. And yet the environmentalists who favored population control were unhappy with the Commission—because they did not think the Commission went far enough. In short, there was strong opposition to the Commission's report, even though most social scientists would agree that they were reasonable recommendations designed to help alleviate a monumental problem.

The widespread opposition to the population report is not the only cause for believing that changes in population growth will be extremely difficult to accomplish. Birthrates are affected by basic value orientations toward family life, and

Figure 12.7
U.S. population: Two- versus three-child family

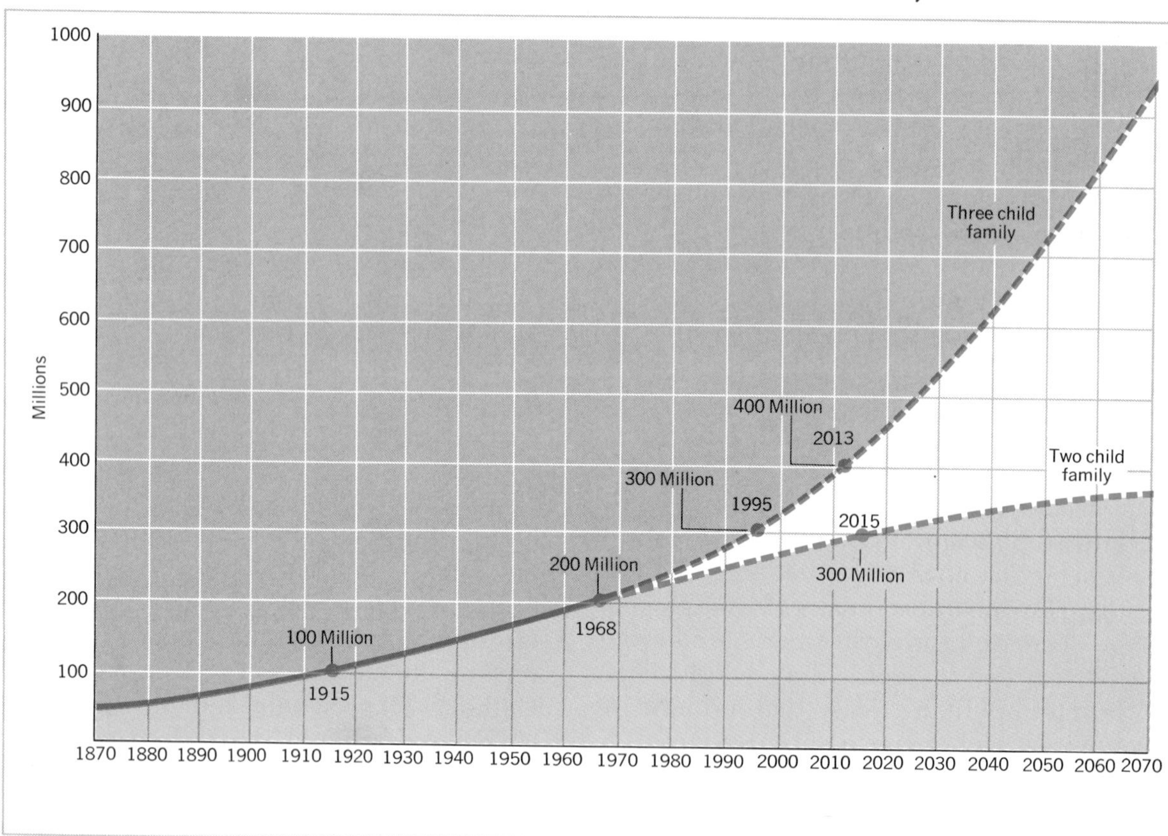

Source: Presidential Commission on Population Growth and the American Future, *Interim Report* (Washington: U.S. Government Printing Office, 1971), p. 10.

these values are among the most cherished human concerns. Religious beliefs, for example, have great impact on family size and structure. The relations between spouses and with the extended family are basic to the value system dealing with family size.

The values concerning family size are very difficult to change by public policy. For example, almost all European nations before World War II tried to encourage population growth to build manpower for military establishments. Policies designed to increase the birthrate were vigorously pursued all over Europe, but at the same time the birthrate continued its downward drop. In Germany Hitler succeeded in raising the birthrate during the 1930s, but this was mostly because of increased employment opportunities. A number of European nations have deliberately tried to increase their birthrates with almost no success; as early as 1666 England exempted married people from

INSERT **12.II**

WHAT DIFFERENCE WILL A LARGER U.S. POPULATION MAKE?

The U.S. Commission on Population Growth and the American Future, a blue-ribbon panel of lawmakers, businessmen, and educators established by Congress to study population problems in America, made its report in March 1972. The Commission urged that the U.S. population growth be slowed somewhat, suggesting that an average number of two children per family would greatly increase the quality of life compared to larger families. The following areas would be affected by the population.

Production and income	Total increase in goods and services—the gross national product—would increase with larger populations, but the effect on *each individual* would be better if the population did not increase as much. This is because a larger proportion of the people would be working in the slower growth situation, whereas there would be more unemployment in the faster growth situation.
Pollution	A higher birth rate would greatly accelerate the pace of environmental pollution. By the year 2000 the faster growing population (three children per family) would have nearly 12 percent more air pollution than a slower growing population (two children).

certain taxes and fathers of 10 children were awarded a pension; during the colonial period the French government sent boatloads of women to overseas colonies and made it illegal for men not to marry them; in Italy during the Fascist period a "bachelor tax" was levied on all unmarried men; in Germany under Hitler SS officers were provided weekend leaves in order to impregnate women selected for them by the Nazi party; in the Soviet Union Stalin encouraged higher birthrates by levying special taxes on the unmarried and on parents with small families. Every one of these was a major attempt to increase the birthrate; every one of them failed. And it will probably be just as difficult to *lower* birthrates as it has been to *raise* them.

In light of all these discouraging facts Paul Ehrlich believes that the population bomb will continue to explode over the next few decades. His assessment of the situation is grim, for he believes that overpopulation will occur in spite of optimistic predictions made by some people. Ehrlich argues that the general public has a set of hopeful

National Resources	Faster population growth would deplete the natural resources at a more rapid rate. Many states, for example, are already critically short of water, and this shortage would dramatically increase if the population grew rapidly.
Urban Growth	The faster the population grows, the more people are crowded together in urban areas. If the population grows rapidly, nearly 85 percent of the people would be crammed into urban areas by the year 2000. Unfortunately, even if it grows more slowly, about 80 percent of the people would be living in urban areas.
Educational costs	Presently the United States spends about 7.5 percent of the gross national product on education. With rapid population increase, however, the percentage would shoot up to about 13 percent by the year 2000. This would mean that other vitally needed social services would be shortchanged.
Recreation	Increased populations would make even further strains on our already overtaxed natural recreation areas. With high population growth people would probably find it impossible to get away into natural environments for recreation; there just would not be many natural environments left!
Food	Although the United States is probably in no danger of mass starvation—as some other nations are if their populations increase—the food prices would rise drastically if the population increased rapidly because unprofitable, poor land would have to be used to supply enough food.

myths about population that are absolutely false.

1. *Myth 1.* The population explosion is over, at least in the United States, because the birthrate is at an all-time low. Ehrlich's answer: although the U. S. population is low the overall rate for world population growth is still astronomically high.

2. *Myth 2.* The United States has no population problem, it is only a problem for the underdeveloped nations. Ehrlich's answer: The United States is actually using up its natural resources faster than any other nation. Even if we were not overpopulated we would face revolution by the underdeveloped nations. Therefore it is in our benefit to consider the problem ours as well as theirs.

3. *Myth 3.* Much of the earth is empty land and could be used for growing food. Ehrlich's answer: most of the vacant land is impossible to use under any known method of agriculture. Virtually all of the land suitable for agriculture is already being used for that purpose.

4. *Myth 4.* We will be able to farm the sea for more food when the land supply runs out. Ehrlich's answer: most of the sea is a biologi-

Can the population explosion be stopped?

cal desert, and we are already beginning to overharvest the world's waters. In fact, all the signs point to a reduction of the food yield from the sea, not an increase.

5. *Myth 5.* We could solve the crowding problem on our planet by migrating to other planets. Ehrlich's answer: nonsense, no planet that we know of could support human life nor do we have any conceivable method of transportation that would move billions of people to these planets.

6. *Myth 6.* Family planning is the answer to the population explosion. Ehrlich's answer: family planning has not worked even in highly industrialized nations such as Japan. It certainly cannot be expected to work in more underdeveloped nations such as India and Latin America.

THE POPULATION EXPLOSION: IS THERE ANY HOPE?

With all this unhappy news about the difficulty of lowering the birthrate it appears to be a hopeless task. Are we inevitably going to face overpopulation, or is there any chance of reversing the trend? There are a few hopeful signs that this may not be a completely impossible task. The only question is, however, whether the birthrate can be lowered fast enough to avert the population explosion and widespread starvation that so many people are predicting. What are some of the more hopeful signs?

Hopeful Signs. Donald J. Bogue (1967) believes that by the twenty-first century the world population will grow at a much slower rate. He bases this conclusion on several pieces of evidence. Improved technology for contraception that can be used for mass adoption by uneducated people is being developed, and increased funds are being allocated in most countries for professional and medical services to accompany those technologies. Moreover, most of the political leaders of the underdeveloped nations have publicly advocated birth control and have thrown their prestige behind the fight to lower the birthrate. In addition, the population growth may slow down because we seem to have reached a point of diminishing return in death control. Most societies are already capable of controlling the major infectious diseases, the worst threats to health. Now we can expect little more population increase because of improvements in death control procedures. When all these factors are taken together, Bogue argues, the population will be growing at a drastically lower rate over the next hundred years. Bogue admits, however, that this decrease in the birthrate will still not be enough to stop population growth completely.

Finally, there is some hope that attitudes about family size may be changing. Public opinion surveys throughout the world show that the preference for smaller families is increasing regardless of where the surveys are taken—although there are still wide variations between countries. For example, Gallup Poll results indicate that over the years more Americans have begun to favor small families. Figure 12.8 shows that by 1971 77 percent of the people wanted families of three of fewer children. Notice also that Figure 12.8 breaks the population down by various groups; men are more apt to favor small families than women, young people more than older people, Protestants more than Catholics, and people with advanced education more than people with little education. It is particularly interesting that younger people—the ones who will be bearing children—favor smaller families. All this is hopeful news, suggesting that the need for a lower birthrate may be reflected in changed attitudes throughout the public.

Underdeveloped Nations: A New Demographic Transition? In addition to the hopeful signs in the industrialized nations there is now some hope that the underdeveloped nations may be experiencing their own demographic transitions. It has long been obvious that the runaway population growth of the poorest nations, where the rate of increase often reached 3 percent per year (enough to double in about 23 years), could not go on indefinitely. Sooner or later the less developed countries would encounter famine, disease, war, and the death rate would rise again. Some people have been openly predicting mass starvation in the very near future.

A temporary solution to the problem was to expand the production of food in the poorer nations. New types of seed, more efficient farming techniques, and better irrigation have produced a "green revolution" in some underdeveloped areas. Even these advances, however, could only provide a "breathing space" of a few years or, at most, decades. Eventually the birthrate would have to come down if mass disaster were to be avoided. Happily there is *some* evidence that this is beginning to occur. Unfortunately the evidence is slim, since for most of the world's population we do not have enough accurate information to tell what is really happening.

The birthrate was fairly high in the giant nations of India, China, and In-

Figure 12.8
The trend is to lower desired sizes

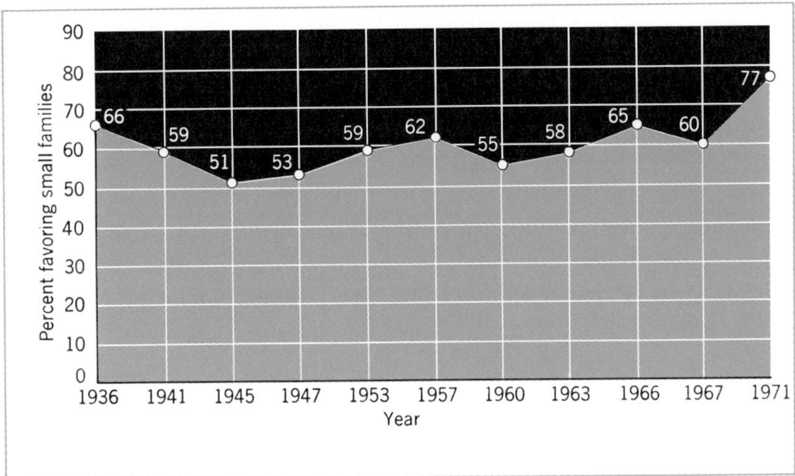

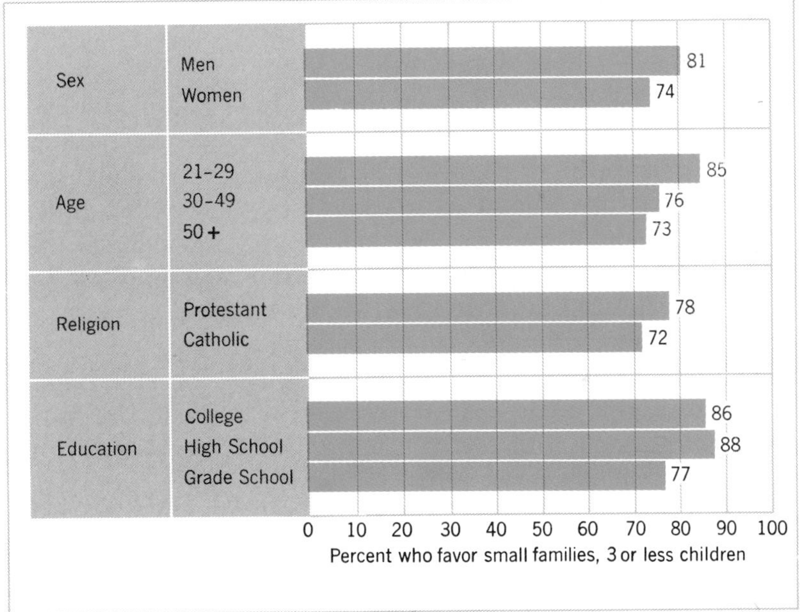

Source: Gallup Opinion Index, March 1971, No. 69, pp. 18–19

donesia, but it is very difficult to tell if it is declining. India and Indonesia have had massive birth control campaigns and official government figures proclaim some decrease in the birthrate, and we do know that the birthrate in parts of India has fallen. Moreover, some Chinese populations outside the People's Republic, notably in Taiwan and Singapore, have decreased their birthrates considerably. Since about 40 percent of the earth's people now live in these three areas of Asia, the future world demographic situation will obviously depend on what happens there to a great extent. Unfortunately, the picture is unclear at this point.

The picture is less cloudy, however, for some other nations. All over the world there are smaller countries in which the birthrate is falling. Figure 12.9 shows those nations in which the trend is fairly well established. You can see that they are drawn from many different regions, cultures, religions, and political systems. In addition, although many underdeveloped nations start late, once their birthrate begins to drop, it drops rapidly. Most of these nations are moving fast enough to reach American birthrate levels in about 30 years—*if* present trends continue. And, in a few cases, the recent reductions in the birthrate have been spectacular, often averaging a point a year or more, as in Taiwan, South Korea, Tunisia, Singapore, and (West) Malaysia.

In explaining why some societies have experienced rapidly falling birthrates, we should note that many, but not all, have had massive family-planning programs aimed at disseminating and encouraging the use of contraceptives. In addition, it is important to note that the nations with declining birthrates are by and large the most advanced of the underdeveloped countries, the richest among the poor. This is not surprising, of course, since economic change has often gone hand in hand with social change, making possible new attitudes toward children, sex, and family. In general, and especially recently, the developing countries have been making great strides not only in agriculture but also in industry, health, education, commerce, and organization of all kinds. Many demographers believe that these are the factors that may allow the demographic transition to succeed all over the world. These are the same forces that produced the demographic transition in the industrialized nations.

We have covered a lot of ground in this section, and only part is based on solid evidence. The rest consists of educated guesswork. Unfortunately the availability of demographic data is such that very little can be said with certainty about the underdeveloped world. We do not know that the countries currently reducing their birthrates will continue to do so. If they do, we do not know that they will be able to keep up the pace they have set thus far. We *certainly* do not know whether other, larger nations such as India and China are following their lead. But there is some reason for hope.

The Prospect for the Future of Mankind. The debate continues over the population explosion and its important consequences for the future of the human race. The debate has no complete answer

Figure 12.9
Nations with previously extremely high birth rates are now experiencing declines

Source: Dudley Kirk and Steve Beaver, Food Research Institute, Stanford University

based on current sociological information. Some competent sociologists and biologists are arguing that the population explosion will engulf the world regardless of what we do—that human values are too entrenched and that the population drive is too forceful to stop it in time to avert the disastrous consequences of overpopulation. Other reasonable and competent sociologists, however, believe that there is some hope—that human values do change, that birthrates are falling, and that people around the world are becoming more concerned about the problem. Of course, any optimism about falling birthrates must be balanced with the fact that even lower birthrates will not solve the problem of population increase. It will grow astronomically for years to come even if the birthrate were drastically decreased.

The debate continues, and there is no answer to it. Yet the fate of mankind probably hinges on this issue as much as on thermonuclear war and other major social issues. Population growth is one of the forces that is shaping human life and leading, perhaps, to catastrophe.

SUMMARY

One of the most important influences on social behavior is the growth of population and its concentration in urban areas. Throughout most of human history the population was severely limited by the food supply. The advent of agriculture, the control of infectious diseases, and the development of technology during the Industrial Revolution, however, enabled the population to grow at fantastic rates. In fact, the growth was so rapid that it outstripped food supplies in many parts of the world, leading many people—most notably Thomas Malthus—to predict that the world would soon be faced with mass starvation.

Malthus' dismal predictions did not come true, however, for a variety of reasons. Food production increased, new technologies developed, and birth control techniques were improved. Most important, however, the industrialized nations experienced a major demographic transition, a shift to lower death rates and subsequently to lower birthrates. Although the reasons for this transition are not entirely clear, it seems that attitudes associated with industrialization and urban living somehow affect people's attitudes toward family size. Presently in the industrialized nations birthrates are rather low, death rates have dropped to all time lows, and the population growth is continuing to slow down.

At the same time, the world is experiencing a sustained trend toward urbanization. Although there were major cities in ancient times, it has only been recently that most of the population, especially in industrialized nations, has lived in cities. It now appears that urban growth patterns and urban values will dominate most of the world, even in the underdeveloped nations that are just beginning to urbanize.

Massive population growth and prolonged urbanization have created a host of critical social problems. Huge metropolitan areas, called megalopolises, now dominate the urban landscape, with cities running together without a break, surrounded on all sides by suburban fringes. These urban complexes are fragmented into many small governmental units, creating enormous inefficiencies in dealing with regional problems and extreme voter apathy regarding complex local issues. In addition, the growth of suburbs has reinforced racial segregation, undermined the tax base of the cities, and created regional problems that no single unit of government can handle. Coupled with all these problems is the physical decay of the city: the growth of slums, the general inadequacy of housing, snarled traffic congestion, and widespread pollution of air, land, and water.

Compounding these difficulties is the continued threat of a population explosion. Malthus' predictions about overpopulation may yet come true, especially in the underdeveloped areas of the world where population growth is running wild. Even in the United States overpopulation may become a problem. The Presidential Commission on Population argues that a slower growth rate would increase the quality of life, but its suggestions for slowing the growth have unfortunately been attacked by many people.

Is there any hope for averting the overpopulation disaster? There are a few hopeful signs; public opinion polls indicate that attitudes now favor smaller families, contraceptive techniques are now highly developed, and the underdeveloped nations seem to be entering their own transition to lower birthrates. Many population experts, however, fear we may already have passed the point of no return, that the population will explode out of control in spite of these hopeful signs. The history of mankind hangs in the balance on this question, and social life as we now know it may live or die depending on the outcome.

REFERENCES

Bogue, Donald J. "The End of the Population Explosion" *The Public Interest,* No. 7, Spring 1967, pp. 11–20.

Bogue, Donald J. "Urbanism in the United States, 1950," *American Journal of Sociology, 60,* March 1955, pp. 471–486.

Ehrlich, Paul. *The Population Bomb* (New York: Ballantine Books, 1968).

Ehrlich, Paul. "The Population Explosion: Facts and Fiction" (Palo Alto, Calif: Zero Population Growth, 1970).

Fellmeth, Robert. *Power and Land in California,* Vol II (Washington, D. C. Center for Study of Responsive Law, 1971).

Hartman, Chester. "The Politics of Housing: Introduction" *Society, 9* (9), July/August 1972, p. 30.

Kaplan, Samuel, "The Balkanization of Suburbia," *Harpers Magazine,* 243 (1457), October 1971, pp. 72–74.

Mumford, Lewis. *The City in History* (New York: Harcourt, 1961).

Nam, Charles B. *Population and Society* (Boston: Houghton Mifflin Co., 1968).

Presidential Commission on Population Growth and the American Future. *Report to the President and Congress.* (Washington, D.C.: U.S. Government Printing Office, 1972).

Russel, J. C. "Late Ancient and Medieval Population," *Transactions of the American Philosophical Society.* Vol. 48, Part 3, 1958.

Sjoberg, Gideon. "The Origin and Evolution of Cities" in Scientific American, *Cities* (New York: Knopf, 1967), pp. 25–39.

Taeuber, Irene B. "Population and Society," in R.E.L. Faris. *Handbook of Modern Sociology* (Chicago: Rand McNally, 1964).

Thompson, Warren S. *Population Problems* (New York: McGraw-Hill, 1953).

Tönnies, Ferdinand. *Gemeinschaft und Gesellschaft* (Leipzig: 1887; Berlin: K. Curtius, 1926).

Wrong, Dennis. *Population* (New York: Random House, 1962).

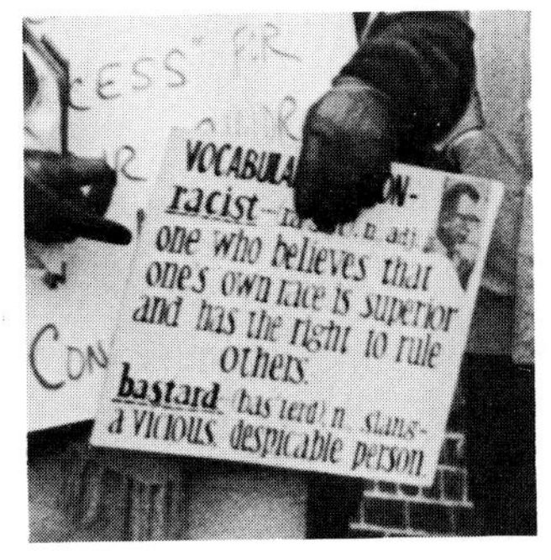

THIRTEEN
SOCIAL REFORMISM: RACE AND EDUCATION

MALCOLM X

I kept close to the top of the class, though. The topmost scholastic standing, I remember, kept shifting between me, a girl named Audrey Slaugh, and a boy named Jimmy Cotton.

It went on that way, as I became increasingly restless and disturbed through the first semester. And then one day, just about when those of us who had passed were about to move up to 8-A, from which we would enter high school the next year, something happened which was to become the first major turning point of my life.

Somehow, I happened to be alone in the classroom with Mr. Ostrowski, my English teacher. He was a tall, rather reddish white man and he had a thick mustache. I had gotten some of my best marks under him, and he had always made me feel that he liked me. He was, as I have mentioned, a natural-born "advisor," about what you ought to read, to do, or think—about any and everything. We used to make unkind jokes about him: why was he teaching in Mason instead of somewhere else, getting for himself some of the "success in life" that he kept telling us how to get?

I know that he probably meant well in what he happened to advise me that day. I doubt that he meant any harm. It was just in his nature as an American white man. I was one of his top

The story of Malcolm X, a brilliant young black who, although at the top of his class, was told to be a carpenter, is the heartbreaking tale of educational discrimination against American minority groups—a story of talent wasted, dreams shattered, hopes dashed, pride broken. Sociology provides an approach that is useful in analyzing inequalities of educational opportunities and by understanding them, helping to *solve* the problems.

SHOULD SOCIOLOGISTS TRY TO SOLVE SOCIAL PROBLEMS?

What can scientific sociology—the sociology of college courses, scholarly journals, and statistical reports—say about the educational problems that crushed Malcolm X's dream? By posing this question we have opened one of the hottest students, one of the school's top students—but all he could see for me was the kind of future "in your place" that almost all white people see for black people.

He told me, "Malcolm, you ought to be thinking about a career. Have you been giving it thought?"

The truth is, I hadn't. I never have figured out why I told him. "Well, yes, sir. I've been thinking I'd like to be a lawyer." Lansing certainly had no Negro lawyers—or doctors either–in those days, to hold up an image I might have aspired to. All I really knew for certain was that a lawyer didn't wash dishes, as I was doing.

Mr. Ostrowski looked surprised, I remember, and leaned back in his chair and clasped his hands behind his head. He kind of half-smiled and said, "Malcolm, one of life's first needs is for us to be realistic. Don't misunderstand me, now. We all here like you, you know that. But you've got to be realistic about being a nigger. A lawyer—that's no realistic goal for a nigger. You need to think about something you *can* be. You're good with your hands—making things. Everybody admires your carpentry shop work. Why don't you plan on carpentry? People like you as a person—you'd get all kinds of work."

The more I thought afterwards about what he said, the more uneasy it made me. It just kept treading around in my mind. (*The Autobiography of Malcolm X,* 1966)

debates in modern sociology. Is it the proper role of sociologists to get involved in solving problems or should they just gather information and hope that somebody else solves them? Should sociologists try to be social engineers or should they remain theorists? (See Figure 13.1.)

In Chapter One, two views of the proper role of sociologists were contrasted: the "scientific, theory-oriented" view and the "critical, policy-oriented" view. Both definitions have been accepted and advocated by competent sociologists, and the field has always had scholars who did both activities. Throughout most of the book we have examined the methods and research activities of the scientific, theory-oriented school of sociology; in this chapter we will explore the research activities of the critical, policy-oriented school. It is important to understand that these approaches are not contradictory or mutually exclusive, because actually the same research tools and methods are employed in both. The main difference between the two views is that the theory-oriented approach stresses knowledge for its own sake whereas the policy-oriented approach emphasizes using knowledge to improve social conditions. Cronbach and Suppes (1969) call these two different approaches "conclusion-oriented" and "decision-oriented" research; one type is taking conclusions and building theories, while the other is using the results for policy decisions to improve society.

Some people argue that sociologists should stay out of the battle to change the world, at least in their role as sociologists. As private citizens, they will very likely take positions, but as professional sociologists their role should be to search for truth, whether it has practical consequences or not. One argument against involvement is that it is difficult for sociologists to be objective if they already have value positions. If sociologists put on the knight's armor to battle society's evils, they may lose the scientific objectivity necessary for good research. In addition, sociologists are not trained to deal with politicians who make most of the decisions. Moreover, some politicans demand quick, easy answers, and frequently serious mistakes are made when scholars yield to these demands for simple solutions. In light of all these problems, many people argue that the sociologist should stay out of "policy-oriented" research.

On the other hand, some people argue that since sociologists have the scientific information about social problems, they should use it to prevent its being misused by uninformed people. This activist view is held by many sociologists, and several journals and magazines are devoted to social problems. *Society* (formerly called *TransAction)* is a policy-oriented magazine, and *Social Problems,* the journal of the Society for the Study of Social Problems, is more practically oriented than most scholarly journals. Moreover, a group of young sociologists, members of the "Sociology Liberation Front," are demanding that academic sociologists take a stand on social issues.

The debate over a theory versus a policy orientation continues, and there are legitimate arguments for both views. But throughout this book we have advocated that sociologists should take an activist position. In fact, one of the prime goals of a "critical" sociology is to press for more policy-oriented research, for more high-quality scientific activity that can be translated into sound policy decisions to improve the society.

HOW CAN SOCIOLOGY HELP TO SOLVE SOCIAL PROBLEMS?

If sociologists are to tackle social problems they must have a way of approaching the task. At least five steps are involved. Although for the sake of clarity we will separate the various steps, in real research the distinctions between the various activities are not so clear and the steps overlap considerably.

Figure 13.1
The great debate: should sociologists help solve social problems?

Pro	Con
Reasons Sociologists Should:	Reasons Sociologists Should Not:
1. Sociologists have appropriate training for researching social problems.	1. Sociologists are not skilled in handling political consequences of involvement.
2. Sociological knowledge will be misused if sociologists do not get involved.	2. Policy makers demand "instant decisions," and sociologists rarely have quick answers to complex problems.
3. By getting involved in the "real world" sociologists can escape the "ivory tower" and make their research better.	3. By getting involved sociologists take sides in the controversy thus losing their scientific objectivity.
4. When the sociologists get involved it helps the policymaker understand the need for research before hasty policies are made.	4. Policymakers often prostitute the sociologists' position, not really listening to the research, but using the sociologists as window-dressing to "prove" scientifically that the politician's preconceived ideas are right.
5. Most importantly, the society desperately needs help and sociologists should offer their services even though they are aware they have few answers that will actually solve the problems.	5. Too much practical involvement may reduce the attention to basic research that may help to solve problems "in the long run."

STEP ONE: IDENTIFYING THE SOCIAL PROBLEM

It may seem like a simple thing to identify a problem; who needs a sociologist to tell us that something is wrong? But identifying the problem is not usually that simple, and can be a critical roadblock. For example, is there a problem with minority admissions to colleges? Who knows until the evidence is assembled? Are blacks underrepresented in high-paying jobs that require advanced education? It takes statistics to prove the answer. Does segregated education hinder the learning of minority groups? Without the sociological information, the facts, all we have is a hunch. In other words, the first step is to determine as carefully as possible *what* is wrong; only then can research begin to suggest *why*, and what to do about it.

For example, during the 1950s and

1960s it was popularly believed that physically run-down schools were a major cause of poor achievement among minority groups. In fact, many school districts have spent huge sums on building programs to improve their schools—and to avoid desegregation. But sociological research now suggests that the physical condition of a school is *not* a major influence on achievement, and the money could have been better spent on other things, such as hiring better teachers or reforming the curriculum. In short, the problem has been diagnosed wrongly, as is often the case with social problems. Sociological insights, theories, and research can help to define the problems and marshal the evidence.

STEP TWO: GATHERING NEW SOCIAL SCIENCE DATA

Once a problem is identified and carefully analyzed the next step is to design special studies to find out more about the problem. Additional information is especially important when the available data are fragmentary, confusing, and contradictory—as they usually are. For example, if we diagnosed low achievement in schools as being a problem of poor teachers, then we would mount a study to determine more precisely the characteristics that separated good and bad teaching, and the strategies that might improve it.

STEP THREE: INTERPRETING THE NEW INFORMATION

The sociologist goes to the field or the laboratory, investigates a problem and brings back his mountain of IBM cards, observations, and survey information. Now all he has to do is take the "hard facts" and make a decision about solving the problem, right? Wrong. The "hard facts" usually are not as hard as we would like, in fact, they tend to be a little on the mushy side. "The facts speak for themselves" is an old proverb, but the proverb is wrong. Somebody has to act as the interpreter who takes the "facts" and makes some sense out of them.

To take a nonsociological example, it is a known "fact," shown by hundreds of insurance reports, that the more fire engines sent to a fire, the more damage done to the building. More fire engines must cause more damage, and the "facts" prove it, at least until someone interprets the facts differently. For instance, more fire engines go when there is a bigger fire, and it is the bigger fire that causes the extra damage, not the number of fire engines.

The same kind of interpretation goes on constantly in the social sciences. For example, the "facts" show that black children do poorly on IQ tests. Does this prove they are not as intelligent? Not necessarily so; another interpretation is that the IQ tests are biased at the start in favor of the white, middle-class children. For the black children, competing on the biased test is like running a race with both legs tied together. So the point is simple; all "hard facts" have to be carefully interpreted, and finding out "why" is one of the sociologist's major roles as he helps to solve social problems.

STEP FOUR: PROPOSING IMPROVEMENT STRATEGIES

After we have identified a problem, gathered new data, and interpreted this information, the next step is to propose "improvement strategies," courses of action that will solve—or at least lessen—the problem. To continue the example we have been using, suppose we have found that some minority groups do not achieve as well as middle-class whites in school and that, according to our research, the reasons are more problematic home lives, less competent teachers, and an outdated curriculum. What do we propose as a solution to this problem? Improvement strategies might include integration and community control of local schools. Usually sociologists propose a number of different improvement strategies, and public debate among citizens and policy-makers helps to determine which strategy will be used. Rarely, however, are decisions made solely on the basis of the information gathered; public passion, values, and power plays are major forces in shaping decisions.

STEP FIVE: ANALYZING SOCIAL AND ECONOMIC BARRIERS

The problem has been identified, the information has been painstakingly assembled, the data have been carefully interpreted, and improvement strategies have been proposed. Now we can relax. After turning all this valuable information over to the proper authorities we can go on to the next problem, secure in the knowledge that a solution will be forthcoming soon. Right? Wrong, the process cannot stop there.

What happens to all our careful research? Most likely, nothing. After all this work the results will probably be ignored, the plans put in a folder and filed away, and the pleas for change greeted with polite smiles but no action. Why is this usually the case, why is social change so difficult even when we have assembled all the sociological information? There are many factors that impede change, and part of a policy-oriented sociologist's task is to go beyond the immediate problem and look at the broader social, political, and economic context that surrounds the problem.

For example, after all our research on educational discrimination we may not be able to change the situation because of ingrained prejudices, the inept administration of the educational bureaucracy, the slow pace of government action, or hostile reactions to busing children outside their neighborhoods. Moreover, limited tax bases do not provide enough money to bring ghetto schools up to equality, and the middle-class whites are unwilling to give up the educational advantage that gives them a definite economic advantage. This is a long list, but it includes only a few of the factors that might block our plans for improving the schools. Examining all these factors is a difficult assignment, but if social science is to have a real impact we must take the assignment seriously.

Having completed the five steps—steps that often overlap and are sometimes so joined that they are indistinguishable—one of the critical remaining tasks is to spread the information as widely as possible so that potential policymakers can use it. This dissemination also allows other sociologists to criticize and improve the suggestions. Policy suggestions must not be buried in scholarly journals if they are to be translated into policy. (See Figure 13.2 for a summary of this research process.) Now let us turn to the problem of educational discrimination.

IDENTIFYING THE SOCIAL PROBLEM: DO WE HAVE EQUAL EDUCATIONAL OPPORTUNITY?

American schools are supposed to do many things—teach reading and writing, develop "citizenship," help children to prepare for their future occupations, and open up avenues of social mobility. The public school system works remarkably well for some people, but has failed a great many others: blacks, Mexican-Americans, Puerto Ricans, "slow learners," and others who are consistently left behind.

Recently at a school board meeting in Louisiana a black father leaped to his feet in the middle of a public hearing over school integration and shouted:

Man, let's get the picture straight! This "system" you call a school is killing my kid! My kid can't read worth a damn, and he's in the ninth grade. My kid can hardly spell his name. My kid is so far behind that he'll never catch up, he'll never make it, man. And you smart guys sitting up there—you principals, and teachers, and school board guys—what the hell are you doing about it? I used to think you were right—my kid's "culturally deprived," and its the kid's fault, my fault, my wife's fault. But, man, that day is over. I come to this rotten school with its broken windows, its super-middle-class textbooks, its up-tight teachers, and its wild, crazy, hostile system—and man, I'm tired of taking the blame! Your damn school is no damn good, and it's raping my kids! And what are you going to do about it?!

The important thing about this father's anguished cry is that he is dead right; the school system is, in fact, condemning many minority children to social and occupational failure in a society that demands good education for success.

Concern over educational opportunity for minorities began developing after World War II. Since the early 1900s most school in the United States had been racially segregated. In the South segregation was specified by law *(de jure)* and, in the rest of the nation, it was the practice by custom and very often based on residential patterns *(de facto).* For years the various states had argued that segregation was not harmful if the facilities for all races were approximately equal—a doc-

Figure 13.2
Sociologists help to solve social problems

trine the Supreme Court had earlier upheld. But in the 1954 *Brown v. Topeka (Kansas) Board of Education* ruling the Court decreed that the "separate-but-equal" doctrine was inherently discriminatory because of the negative educational and psychological results it produced. Although there was sustained effort throughout the late 1950s and 1960s by civil rights groups and the federal government to see that schools were integrated, integration did not proceed fast enough for many people. A major social crisis developed: race riots broke out in dozens of cities during the mid-1960s; antibusing sentiment led to serious disruptions in the public schools.

More and more sociological evidence was accumulated to show how educational discrimination was hurting minority children, but there was virtually no social science information about solving the problem, and what was available was almost useless. Government and school officials needed more information. What was wrong? How could it be solved? These questions led to new research on the problem.

GATHERING NEW INFORMATION: CONGRESS COMMISSIONS THE COLEMAN REPORT

In 1964, a time of massive conflict over school integration and educational opportunity, the Congress of the United States called for a major study of educational opportunity in the nation. In setting up the study Congress directed that:

The Commissioner [of Education of the United States] shall conduct a survey and make a report to the President and the Congress, within two years of the enactment of this title, concerning the lack of availability of equal educational opportunities for individuals by reason of race, color, religion, or national origin in public educational institutions at all levels in the United States, its territories and possessions, and the District of Columbia.

In late 1965 a staff of sociologists, educators, and psychologists headed by James S. Coleman of Johns Hopkins University began this study, one of the largest sociological surveys ever conducted. The study was officially entitled "Equality of Educational Opportunity" (Coleman, 1966), but is commonly known as the Coleman Report. Over 4000 school districts and 645,000 pupils participated in this project. The quality of the schools and school facilities, and characteristics of teachers, the opportunities for special classes, the extent of segregation and integration, and the academic achievement of pupils were among the topics ex-

The Supreme Court's integration ruling was resisted in many places. Federal troops open the way for black students at Little Rock High School.

amined. Using this report and other sources we can piece together some general ideas about educational opportunity in the nation. Although the Coleman Report is not current, it is still the largest single study on this topic and is generally supported by subsequent research.

THE EXTENT OF MINORITY SEGREGATION IN AMERICAN EDUCATION

The Coleman Report showed that in 1964 the overwhelming majority of American children still went to schools that were largely segregated by race. Considering

As late as 1974, most schools were still segregated.

all the efforts that had been directed toward integration, the figures were astonishing. In the South, for example, almost all students of both races attended totally segregated schools, and the national averages were hardly better; in the twelfth grade over 99 percent of white children attended schools that were at least 50 percent white; about 66 percent of black children attended schools that were at least 50 percent black. This pattern of segregation held true in large and small school systems, in urban, suburban, and rural areas of both North and South. And it was not until after 1970 that this situation changed significantly.

DIFFERENCES IN SCHOLASTIC ACHIEVEMENT

The Coleman Report also showed enormous differences in *academic achievement* between racial groups and between sections of the country (see Figure 13.3). White students consistently scored well ahead of black students; city students ahead of rural students; students in the Northeast ahead of students in the South. Moreover, from the first grade to the twelfth the gap between black children and white children *grew wider.* Black children, starting behind whites on a verbal test in the first grade, actually fell farther behind with each passing year.

For whatever reasons—such as poor schools, poor social environment, and unstable family conditions—minority children did not learn at the same rate as whites; in addition, minority children did not stay in school as long. However, that disparity is closing rapidly, for among the younger people that are examined, the new generation of minorities coming out of schools today has approximately the same level of education as among whites (see Figure 13.4).

School enrollment is considerably more confused. On the secondary-school level the races are equal, with almost 99 percent of blacks and whites in school. But only 14 percent of blacks between the ages of 20 and 24 are enrolled in college, compared with 21 percent of whites. Thus, although blacks are catching up with whites in median number of school years completed (if not in the amount learned during those years), college en-

Figure 13.3
Verbal achievement test scores: Negro versus white, northeast versus south, 1965

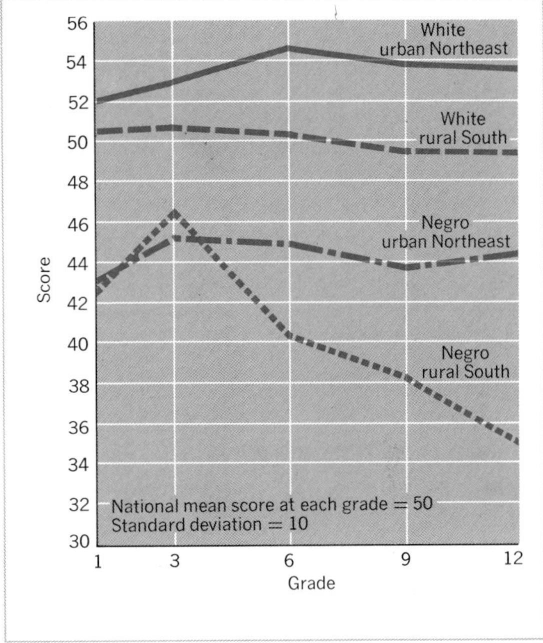

Source: James S. Coleman, "The Concept of Equality of Educational Opportunity," *The Harvard Educational Review, 38* (1), Winter 1968, p. 20.

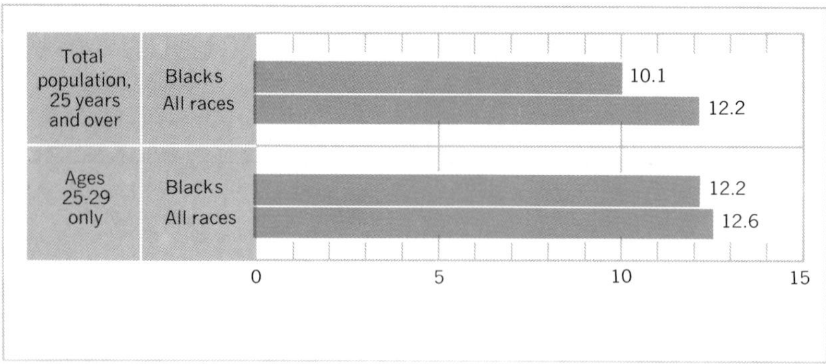

Figure 13.4
Median school years completed: Blacks versus all races, 1971. Comparing overall figures blacks are behind but, among younger groups coming through school recently, the gap is rapidly closing

Source: U.S. Census Bureau, *Statistical Abstract of the U.S.*, 1972, p. 111.

rollment of blacks is still far behind that of whites.

What do all these facts and figures put together show? First, minority groups are catching up in *enrollments,* and in *number of years of school completed,* especially at the secondary school level. However, minority groups are still far behind in *achievement* as measured by test scores, and considerably behind in *college attendance.* In some respects the picture is getting better, but there is much left to be done. Before we can change the situation, however, we must know *what causes the differences*—we must interpret the data.

ANALYZING THE DATA: WHAT CAUSES THE DIFFERENCES IN ACHIEVEMENT?

The reasons for these differences in educational opportunity for different groups are complicated. The Coleman Group, in its attempt to understand the causes of low achievement among minority groups, stated four critical findings.

1. Surprisingly, the *quality of the school* itself—the number of books in the library, the kinds of special programs, the condition of the building, and other physical features—has little impact on children's achievement. Only the quality of teachers has much effect, and even that is relatively small.

2. One of the most important influences on school achievement is the *family background* of the child, since learning patterns are established long before school age. Children who come from poor families, whose parents are divorced, whose parents have little education, and whose parents place little stress on education tend to have low achievement. Unfor-

tunately, many minority children have such a background.

3. A second major influence on achievement is the *nature of the student body,* that is, the social class, race, and motivation of fellow students. In essence, the more achievement-oriented one's classmates, the better one's own achievement. Probably competition and the "role model" the other children offer causes the higher success.

4. Some *individual attitudes* are important, especially the ideal of "fate control," that is, students who feel that success is a matter of fate achieve less than those who feel that hard work overcomes barriers.

Although neither the Coleman Report nor any subsequent study can provide all the answers, these four points are a basis for considering what policy changes might improve the situation.

SCHOOL FACILITIES

As mentioned earlier it had been thought that poor achievement among minority group children might be a result of poor school facilities, such as teachers, buildings, curriculum, libraries, and special problems. The Coleman Commission did find patterns of minority children going to inferior schools; in many cases minority schools had bigger classes, poorer teachers, smaller libraries, lower teacher salaries, fewer special programs for advanced students, and fewer science laboratories (see Figure 13.5). Puerto Rican, Indian, Mexican-American, and Oriental-American schools tended to fall somewhere between the largely black and largely white schools in terms of facilities. These differences, however, were *not* extremely large, a fact that surprised the team of sociologists who studied the data. While there were minor differences, they could not possibly account for the massive differences in achievement between whites and minorities.

Although the surprising finding was that on the national average, minority schools were not very different physically from white schools, it is nevertheless true that there are pockets of serious problems in many inner-city situations. The statistics of the Coleman Report have often been contradicted by flesh and blood accounts that come out of the ghetto schools. Stories of poor buildings, prejudiced teachers, irrelevant middle-class curriculums, and shoddy textbooks are often told. Jonathan Kozol, a teacher who served in a depressed school in Boston, gives a vivid picture of conditions in his school in Insert 13.1. In spite of these problems, however, the overall statistics simply could not justify an interpretation that physical facilities were the real cause of the problem—a fact that surprised everyone and led to a search for other causes.

THE CHILD'S HOME ENVIRONMENT

One of the most important influences on educational achievement is the home environment of the child. Although the school is the major institutionalized agent of education, it actually does only part of the educational task; the home, friends, work, and daily life also contribute. Consequently, it is no great surprise that children who have improverished social backgrounds usually do not do as well in school as children who come from ad-

Figure 13.5
Differences in elementary school facilities, by race, 1965

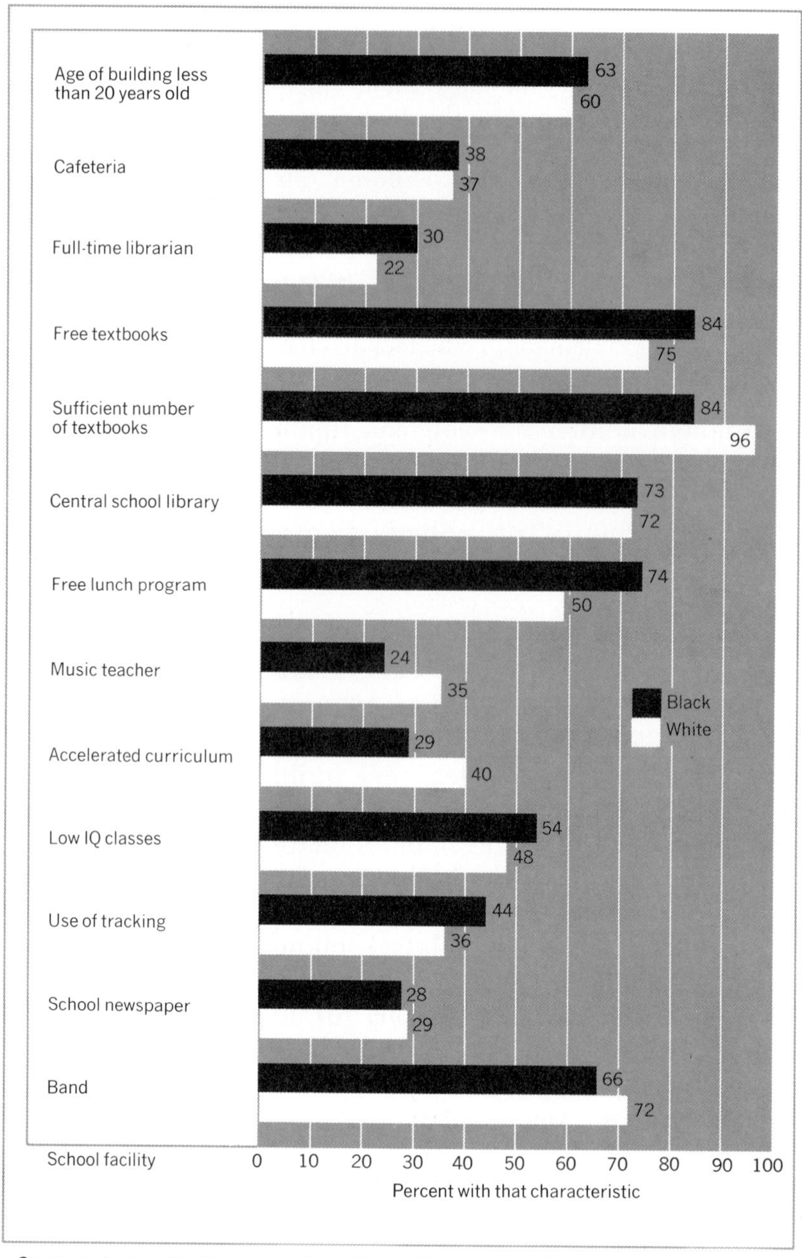

Source: James S. Coleman, *Equality of Educational Opportunity,* U.S. Dept. of HEW, 1966, pp. 10, 13.

INSERT **13.1**

"DEATH AT AN EARLY AGE" (OR) HOW TO GET ALONG IN THE BOSTON PUBLIC SCHOOLS

Jonathan Kozol was a teacher in the Boston public school system who wrote the best-selling, explosive book *Death at an Early Age.* In his book Kozol discusses some of the trials and tribulations of children trapped in the vicious environment of a ghetto school, one of the forgotten outposts of the Boston school system. In this excerpt Kozol discusses some of the physical conditions in his school, where he taught his classes in the auditorium.

"Soon after I came into that auditorium, I discovered that it was not only our two Fourth Grades that were going to have their classes here. We were to share the space also with the glee club, with play rehearsals, special reading, special arithmetic, and also at certain times a Third or Fourth Grade phonics class. . . . One day the sewing class came in with their sewing machines and then that seemed to become a regular practice in the hall. Once I counted one hundred and twenty people. All in the one room. All talking, singing, yelling, laughing, reciting—and all at the same time. Before the Christmas break it became apocalyptic. Not more than one half of the classroom lessons I had planned took place throughout that time.

"Mr. Kozol—I can't hear you."
"Mr. Kozol—What's going on out there?"
"Mr. Kozol—Couldn't we sing with them?"

vantaged homes. The child can be just as intelligent, but he is likely to fall behind other children when there is a broken home, when there is insufficient money for health services, when the parents have little education, when the community is ridden with crime and economic deprivation, when the family is so large that children are neglected, or when the father is unemployed or gone.

In general, the research picture shows the following: (1) children of higher socioeconomic classes do better than children of lower economic classes; (2) children from urban areas generally do better than children from rural areas; (3) children in the North do better than children from the South; (4) children from homes with both parents do better than children from broken homes; and (5) children from white families tend to do better than minority children.

Figure 13.6 shows some of the variation in achievement test scores of ninth

One day something happened to dramatize to me, even more powerfully than anything yet, just what a desperate situation we were really in. What happened was that a window whose frame had rotted was blown right out of its sashes by a strong gust of wind and began to fall into the auditorium, just above my children's heads. I had noticed that window several times before and I had seen that its frame was rotting, but there were so many other things equally rotted or broken in the school building that it didn't occur to me to say anything about it. . . .

First there was a cracking sound, then a burst of icy air. The next thing I knew a child was saying: "Mr. Kozol—look at the window!" I turned and looked and saw that it was starting to fall in. It was maybe four or five feet tall and it came straight inward out of its sashes toward the heads of the children. I was standing, by coincidence, only about four or five feet off and was able to catch it with my hand. But the wind was so strong that it nearly blew right out of my hands. A couple of seconds of good luck . . . kept glass from the desks of six or seven children and very possibly preserved the original shape of half a dozen of their heads. . . . I soon realized I was not going to be able to hold the thing up by myself and I was obliged to ask one of the stronger boys in the class to come over and give me a hand. Meanwhile as the children beneath us shivered with the icy wind . . . I asked one of the children in the front row to run down and fetch the janitor.

When he asked me what he should tell him I said: "Tell him the house is falling in. . . . "

Source: Jonathan Kozol, *Death at an Early Age,* p. 114.

graders, varying by their family situation. From this figure it is obvious that children who have fathers at home do much better at school. Figure 13.7 shows the discouraging information that on top of all their other disadvantages black children are much more likely to be fatherless—and the 1970 census shows a sharp increase in fatherless black families above these figures from the 1964 Coleman study. The overall picture indicates that the home background of the child has an impact on the child's performance in school and that minority groups have more of these problems. Of course, these are overall statistics, and any *specific child* may be an exception to the rule. By no means *all* children from lower classes do poorly in school; by no means *all* children from broken homes have trouble. This only means that *on the average* children with socially impoverished home characteristics tend to fall behind children with more advantages.

Even the best schools would have difficulty making up for home environments such as these.

SOCIAL CLIMATE OF THE SCHOOL AFFECTS PERFORMANCE OF CHILDREN

A third finding of the Coleman Commission was that the *social composition* of the school greatly affects achievement. Even if children are from disadvantaged homes and are attending run-down schools, they will still learn better if the school has a good mixture of social classes and races. The value of socially mixed classes is that they give children from minority groups and socially impoverished backgrounds more associations abling them to learn the values of academic success and adopt attitudes that will help them succeed in school. In short, lower-class children, in mixed classes, have models to follow in learning to achieve academically. This finding was one of the conclusions of the Coleman Report, but even more important, contrary to popular belief, the lower-class children did not hold back the middle-class children. A heterogeneous mix in the school improves the performance of disadvantaged children without hurting the performance of the more advantaged child.

Figure 13.6
Verbal achievement test of ninth graders: Different regions and different family situations, 1965

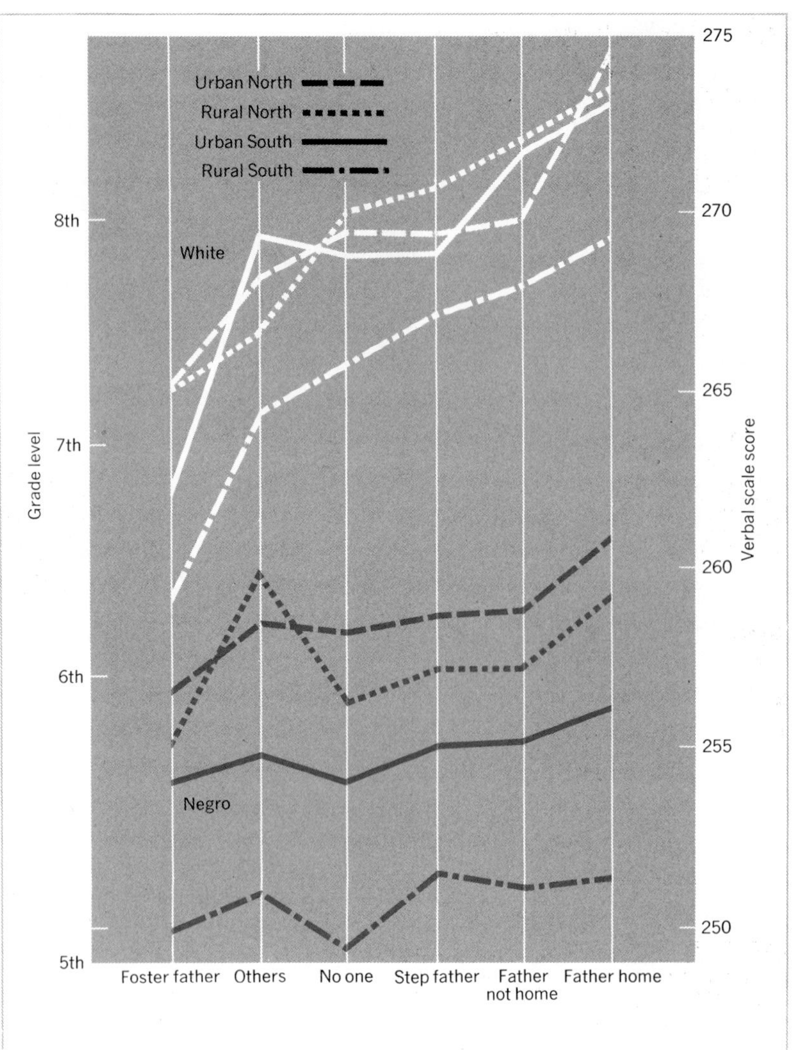

Source: Daniel P. Moynihan, "Sources of Resistance to the Coleman Report," *Harvard Educational Review,* 38 (1), Winter 1968, p. 32.

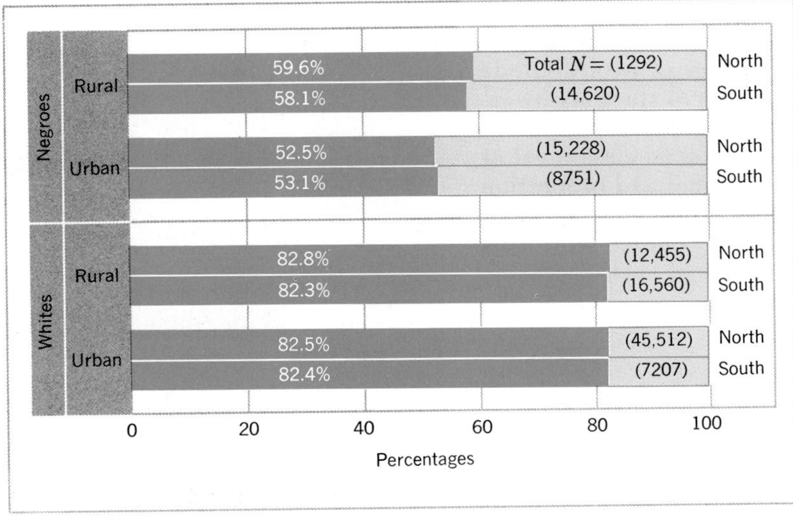

Figure 13.7
Percentages of ninth graders with fathers at home, 1965. In general Negro children are more likely to be in fatherless homes

Source: Daniel P. Moynihan, "Sources of Resistance to the Coleman Report," *Harvard Educational Review*, 38 (1), Winter 1968, p. 34.

Figure 13.8 shows some of the data from the Coleman Report about the academic performance of twelfth-grade black students in the Northeastern United States. This table indicates that the social composition of the school is a major factor in determining the academic success of a child. Looking at the table, notice that children from higher social classes do better than lower-class children (compare group "A" with group "B"), but that children in schools of higher overall social class do better than their peers in schools of lower overall class (compare "C" with "D" and "E" with "F"). Next, if you compare the bars in each group of four, you will note that blacks who attend schools where there are more whites generally do better than black children in highly segregated schools.

FATE CONTROL

One additional factor found to have impact on academic achievement was "fate control," a belief in one's ability to achieve success through one's own effort. Children with low fate control were likely to say that luck, not skill, determined whether they made good grades. Children living in broken homes and struggling to stay ahead in a hostile ghetto environment often feel powerless against outside forces. This feeling of "everytime everthing seems to be going well something or somebody interferes and I can't make it" is a major barrier to achievement of any kind. What good is working hard when all the cards are stacked against you? Not surprisingly, children who expressed these feelings did more poorly than other children who had experienced

Figure 13.8
Average grade level performance of twelfth-grade Negro students by individual social class origin, social class level of school and proportion white classmates last year; metropolitan Northeast

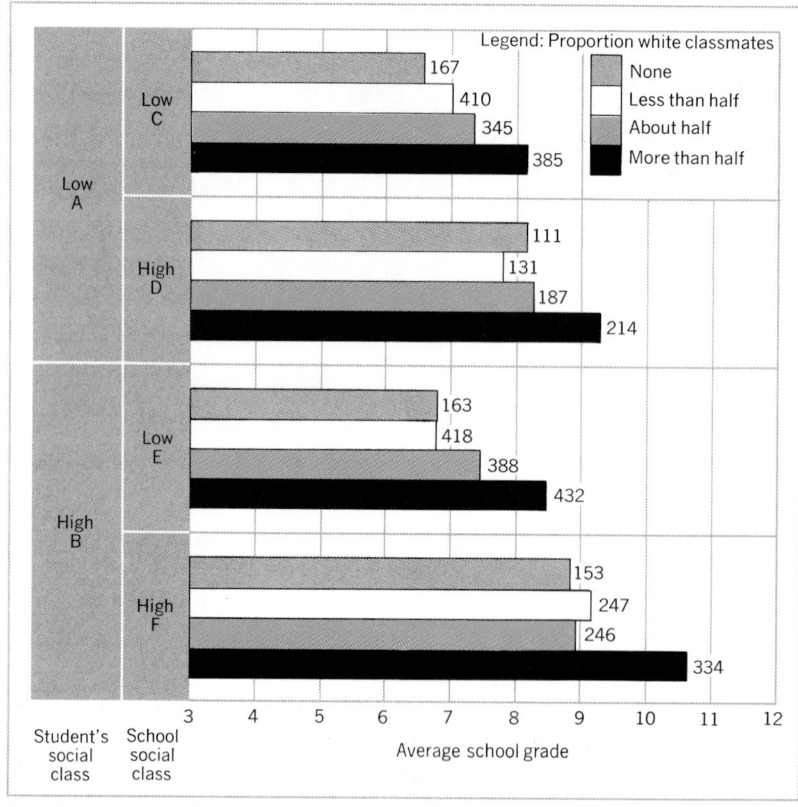

Note: The numbers outside the bars represent the number of cases.

Source: Racial Isolation in the Public Schools, op. cit., p. 90.

success and who felt that they had some power to affect their environments.

ANALYZING THE DATA: SUMMARY OF WHAT WAS FOUND

Coleman and his associates believed that they could arrive at a fairly good description of the causes of poor academic performance of minority children.

1. Minority children attended schools that had relatively poor facilities and relatively ill-prepared teachers. However, the differences were *not* as great as had been originally thought.

2. The minority children's home social environments were not as helpful in promoting positive attitudes toward school achievement.

3. When children attended segregated schools, whether the segregation was based on social class or race, they did not have as many role models for academic success. Consequently they did more poorly than children who went to integrated schools.

4. Children who felt helpless and victimized by their environments did more poorly than those who felt that hard work would lead to success.

REACTIONS TO THE COLEMAN REPORT

This discussion of race and education has been based on the Coleman Report because it is an important work on the subject of minority education. It must be noted, however, that this report—like any other major research—has been seriously criticized by scholars and community leaders. The criticisms fall into two major classes: (1) criticisms of the sociological methodology and (2) criticisms of the implied policy recommendations.

The *methodology criticisms* are varied and serious. The Coleman study was one of the largest social research projects ever undertaken, but Congress allowed only two years to complete the task. Because of the time pressure a number of errors were made. The sample of schools and pupils had flaws, including the refusal of many schools and teachers to cooperate with the study. Many items on the complex questionnaires were not answered by the teachers, administrators, and students. Moreover, children were asked difficult questions that they may have answered incorrectly (do third graders know their fathers' exact occupations?). Finally, a number of errors were made in data analysis that opened questions about the interpretations that Coleman and his associates made. Taken together, these methodological problems posed questions about the report's findings.

But in spite of these problems most of the reinterpretations that tried to correct the errors came out with substantially the same results. The federal government commissioned further analyses of the data (*Racial Isolation in the Schools*, 1966), and members of the Harvard faculty undertook a series of reanalyses published in *On Equality of Educational Opportunity* (Mosteller and Moynihan, 1972). Both of these major works supported the Coleman Report's basic findings. Although the various methodological problems should not be ignored, the evidence seems to support the basic validity and importance of this research. Research should never be accepted uncritically and without careful study of its flaws; neither should it be rejected too lightly without evaluating its strengths.

The *policy implications* of the Coleman Report raised an even greater storm than the methodological problems. Liberal scholars, black community leaders, educational specialists, and segregationists all found fault with the report because they did not want to accept the implied policy recommendations. Liberal scholars and black community leaders were incensed that the family instead of the school was being blamed for the academic failure of minority children. The Coleman Commission's findings did indeed argue that minority children were already at a disadvantage by the time they entered school, but in subsequent years the debate was cooled somewhat, with people on all sides agreeing that early-childhood education programs are necessary to enrich the preschool learning environment of children.

The educational community was shocked that the quality of the school made little difference in equalizing the opportunities of minority children. Educational leaders, of course, wanted to argue that increased funds for schools and more rational policies about allocation of resources would improve conditions, but the Coleman Report gave little support to that cherished belief. In spite of the finding that school facilities make little difference in achievement, the educational establishment has continued to argue that improving facilities and distributing resources more equally is a good social policy.

Finally, the findings that blacks in integrated schools learn better than blacks in segregated schools raised hopes among some groups and produced controversy among others. People who favored integration welcomed these findings; community-control advocates who had given up on integration and begun to fight for black control of black schools were dismayed that the report seemed to argue that community control would not work as long as schools were segregated. Finally, segregationists were furious that the government had sponsored a study that urged integration.

In short, the Coleman Report was greeted with mixed reactions. It made almost everybody mad—liberals and blacks because it implicitly criticized the black family; conservatives because it stressed the need for more integration; sociologists because it had methodological flaws; black leaders because it gave more emphasis to integration than to community control.

There are several critical points that this review of the reactions to the Coleman Report make clear.

1. *Never accept research uncritically, but do not disregard a study simply because it has problems.* Be alert to errors and methodological problems. Never put all your faith in a single study because it may have serious problems or the researchers may also have a special interest in proving one thing or another. On the other hand, pointing out a study's problems does not discredit the research. Of course, you *should* discredit it if the balance of evidence seems to be against it, but be reasonable and sophisticated about what to accept and reject. In general, for example, the Coleman Report's findings must be taken seriously in spite of its flaws.

2. *Look for the policy implications a study may have.* Even theory-oriented research may have a practical application. In this case the policy implications were fairly clear: more integration, more stress on the early childhood years and the strength of the family, and more attention to teacher qualifications.

3. *Be aware of the political and social biases of the critics.* All the critics we listed above had their own vested interests, liberals, conservatives, black community control leaders, and black integrationists all read something different into the report based on their interests. Power and self-interest often determine reactions as much as—or more than—scientific criticisms.

IMPROVEMENT STRATEGIES: WHAT CAN BE DONE?

We have been playing the sociological detective. A crime has been committed, the crime that educational opportunities are not equally available in America, that lower-class and minority groups are systematically discriminated against in education, that these groups cannot perform as well as other children in academic areas. What are the social, economic, education, and home factors that cause this crime to be perpetuated in American society? We have found so far that poor schools, inferior teachers, irrelevant curriculum, disadvantaged home environments, and almost universal segregation by race and social class are the chief problem areas.

Now let us switch roles. We have done our detective work and it is time to pick up our social engineer roles. Although we certainly do not know all the causes of unequal educational opportunity, we at least have a basis for investigating and evaluating possible solutions. The three different strategies that have been proposed to eliminate educational discrimination are integration, compensatory education, and community control of schools.

IMPROVEMENT STRATEGY ONE: INTEGRATION

As we mentioned earlier, the Supreme Court ruled in 1954 that segregated schools are by definition discriminatory and the evidence assembled by the Coleman Commission clearly supported that ruling. Segregation of races and social classes was indeed one of the factors that hindered the educational progress of many children. Yet today the schools are still largely segregated. The federal government has at times been quite vigorous in pushing for integration, but at other times it has been extremely lax.

In spite of much opposition and changes in federal administration and public mood, the country seemed finally to be making some progress toward integration by the early 1970s. The Department of Health, Education and Welfare began a major push against slow-moving Southern school districts in 1970, and the effect was a rapid dismantling of the Southern dual school system. For example, in 1967 only 4.3 percent of Southern black children were in integrated school districts; by 1969 the figure was 27.2 percent; and in 1971 the total leaped to over 90 percent. However, these are figures for integrated *districts*, not necessarily for specific schools. That is, the district could be in compliance with the law, but still have many individual schools segregated because of housing patterns. As a result, while over 90 percent of southern districts met the legal requirements, only 43.9 percent of black students actually attended schools that were at least half white. Even so, these figures represent substantial progress over a four-year period.

Interestingly enough, in the North and West only 27.8 percent of blacks attended schools where at least half the students were white; the South is integrating much faster than the rest of the nation. The main barrier to effective integration in the North and West is that neighborhoods, and consequently the schools, are largely segregated. And the massive move of white, middle-class families to the suburbs has made it increasingly difficult to integrate inner-city schools. Moreover, in an important 1971 decision the Supreme Court ruled that busing is legal if used to stop *de jure* segregation, but refused to impose the same standard on *de facto* segregation. In other words, Southern segregation based on law was outlawed, but Northern segregation based on residence was untouched.

The 1971 ruling on busing caused a surge of antibusing sentiment in both the North and South. Although busing has been used for years to transport children to their assigned schools, busing for racial balance was opposed by many blacks as well as whites. *Newsweek* magazine reported in March 1972 that a national Gallup Poll found that children of only 3 percent of the parents interviewed were involved in busing for racial balance. Yet 69 percent of the people surveyed opposed busing to achieve racial balance. Around 50 percent of the black parents opposed busing and expressed the opinion that it was always *their* children who were taken out of their familiar neighborhood school and bused across town.

In another development, a potentially far-reaching 1972 court decision in Richmond, Virginia ruled that the Richmond school district (65 percent black) must be merged with the suburban Chesterfield and Henrico county school districts (90 percent white) in order to achieve racial balance within an entire metropolitan area. This decision argued, in effect, that suburbanites who very often have fled the city to avoid urban problems would be required to participate in overcoming those problems. In 1973 the U. S. Supreme Court overturned this ruling, so inner-city schools again are unable to integrate even if they wish to because most of the whites have moved out.

Many forces have promoted integration, but the grim fact remains that the majority of children still attend segregated schools. Many whites have been very resistant to integration, blocking it with court suits, delaying tactics, and outright hostile opposition. And, as indicated by the reactions of blacks to busing, many minority group members now oppose integration. Their argument is that integration will put their children in hostile environments and wipe out many of the unique features of their culture. Community control of schools, which will be discussed later in the chapter, is now the preferred strategy of some black parents. All in all, the picture is confused, and progress is very slow.

Not only are the schools still generally segregated, but in many cases desegregation has not actually produced high social interaction across racial lines. In many cases there is segregation *within* a school even if it is legally desegregated. One cause of this internal segregation has been the academic tracking system, which places low-achievers with other students with low test scores, and high achievers with other high achievers. This practice effectively resegregates the schools internally because the differing test scores of blacks and whites usually funnels them into different academic tracks. In addition, many schools seem to be socially segregated outside the classroom, with little interaction in social situations and extracurricular activities. The U. S. Commission on Civil Rights, therefore, makes a distinction between *integrated* schools, where children go to the same classes and interact socially, and *desegregated* schools, which theoretically have mixed classes but, in fact, are internally segregated by tracking systems and by segregation in the social life of the school. The Commission believes that the favorable impact of integration noted in the Coleman Report holds true only in the truly integrated school, not in the desegregated school.

Overall, the integration picture can be summarized as follows:

1. The schools are still largely segregated, and opposition to integration from white parents and, more and more, from more militant minority parents continues.

2. Although the government's position on integration has been inconsistent, the courts, from 1954 to the early 1970s moved steadily toward greater support for integration. However, the more conservative Nixon-appointed court of the 1970s shows serious signs of backing down on that long-standing commitment by, for example, overturning the Richmond strategy of busing from suburbs to the city.

3. "Busing" of children has become an emotional issue, supported or opposed for a variety of reasons. To a large extent, busing has become a symbol of the antiintegration forces that are reluctant to oppose integration on purely racial grounds. (Busing is opposed as being contrary to the American tradition of the neighborhood school.)

4. Recent statistical reports show that Southern *de jure* segregation is actually breaking down much faster than Northern and Western *de facto* segregation.

5. Integration generally leads to improvement of the disadvantaged children with no loss of progress among the middle-class children. This optimistic picture, however, is clouded by racial tension and internal segregation, which wipe out the advantages. On the whole, truly *integrated* schools show much progress; schools that are merely *desegregated* do not.

IMPROVEMENT STRATEGY TWO: COMPENSATORY EDUCATION

Integration is strategy directed toward improving the social climate of the school by altering its racial and social-class mixture. In comparison, *compensatory education* is an improvement strategy directed at the *school facilities*—improvements in buildings, teacher qualifications, and curriculum—regardless of the social composition of the school. The 1965 Elementary and Secondary Education Act provides federal money for literally hundreds of projects that are supposed to improve minority education without necessarily integrating the schools. The projects have a variety of goals: to provide special tutoring for children, to improve teacher quality, to establish special classes or tracking systems, to enlist parental support, to provide teacher aides, and to reduce class sizes.

In New York, for example, the More Effective Schools program, run largely by the American Federation of Teachers, tried to improve the academic performance of ghetto children by reducing class size, hiring community people as teacher aides, and developing special curriculums and special classes. And Head Start, a federal program geared to very young poor children, was supposed to help overcome some of the disadvantages that resulted from an impoverished social environment and family situation. This policy emerged from the Coleman Commission findings about the effect of family backgrounds on academic performance.

Unfortunately, dozens of research projects have assessed the compensatory education efforts and arrived at this conclusion: up to this point they do not seem to work. Head Start has had mixed results; in some situations it seems to help, in others it does not. But in general, the academic performance of children is not helped by compensatory education programs. As one researcher put it:

> *After a few years of experience with such efforts, what have the results been? By now the existing evidence is fairly well known: compensatory programs in schools isolated by race and social class have resulted in no substantial or lasting improvement in students' academic competence. Evaluations have been undertaken in a number of different school systems, on programs with different emphases, under varying conditions of expenditure for school improvement. The data are scarce and imperfect, but the uniformity of* [NEGATIVE] *results cannot be ignored. (Cohen, 1970, p. 117)*

Why have the compensatory education programs failed? Although there are many explanations, the most important factor seems to be that these programs have occurred in *segregated* schools, and all the evidence from the Coleman Report suggests that improving school facilities *without integrating races and social classes* does not help. But many compensatory education programs were started precisely to *avoid* integration; they were political ploys to satisfy minority parents without having to integrate. Consequently, compensatory education has often led to *more* segregation under the pretense of helping ghetto children.

It is only fair to note, however, that many compensatory education plans have been judged failures on very slim evidence and over very short time spans. Compensation programs cannot be expected to overcome decades of neglect and discrimination overnight. In addition, many proponents of compensatory education claim that the harsh judgments

A Head Start class. Head Start is a federal compensatory education program designed to overcome disadvantaged backgrounds.

of failure are grossly unfair because so much money has been spent unwisely and wasted on administrative overhead and misallocation of funds that the children are shortchanged. Moreover, several investigations showed that many school districts were actually using compensatory funds designated for low-income children to supplement the already high budgets of middle-class schools. In fact, it is highly probable that the majority of federal compensatory education money *never reached the low income students it was supposed to serve.* Small wonder that it did not improve conditions.

Most of the proponents of compensatory education have not been merely trying to avoid integration. Many were sincere social reformers who felt that integration would be a long time coming and that it was therefore better to move into the ghetto with whatever help could be offered immediately. Current advocates of compensatory education are demanding that compensation and integration proceed simultaneously so that the combined benefit of both approaches can help the child. Of course, such strategies would require close supervision to see that funds actually reached the low-income students they are supposed to serve.

IMPROVEMENT STRATEGY THREE: COMMUNITY CONTROL OF SCHOOLS

Many social reformers have virtually given up on school integration because the social and political forces opposing it are so overwhelming. And over the last decade minority communities have become more militant. Many blacks feel that they have been deserted, that integration may never work, and that their children are being crushed by a school system that cannot teach them and squeezes out all their pride and dignity. Under the circumstances many minority parents are convinced that their only recourse is to take over the schools that teach their children, reform the curriculum, and hire teachers who will be appreciative of the minority culture. This movement calls for community control of schools.

Intense local control has always been characteristic of white, middle-class schools, but has never worked in big cities where parents—especially in the ghettos—are powerless to influence the educational bureaucracy. But as parents have become more disillusioned about their children's education, they have become more determined to have an impact on the schools. As one ghetto parent put it, "Listen, we may not know how to educate our children either, but damn it, we can't do much worse than the school system is doing now—so give us our chance!"

Community control takes many forms, but in all cases the local community is demanding that the huge school bureaucracies be broken down into smaller units, that teachers who are sympathetic to the needs of minority children be hired, that the curriculum be reformed so it is relevant to the needs of minority children, and that the cultural heritage of the minority groups be treated with respect. An appreciation for minority cultures has become an integral part of the local community's attempt to win control over its schools.

What will be the long-range impact of the community-control movement? A number of cities—for example, Washington, New York, and Philadelphia—have embarked on fairly successful attempts to decentralize their school bureaucracies. Will such action help to improve educational opportunity for ghetto children? It is virtually impossible to answer this complex question with any assurance. Some people are very much afraid that the community control movement may hinder integration and thereby worsen ghetto education. And it is true that some minority militants have begun to join forces with white segregationists. In Mobile, Alabama, for example, community-control advocates joined with white antiintegrationists in 1970 to argue against integration and for community schools, with each race demanding control of its own schools. Many reformists were extremely discouraged by the development of this new style of segregation.

But many advocates of this movement believe that strong community control by ghetto parents is a first step in building self-respect among minority groups, in improving schools that have failed to educate ghetto children, in redirecting the curriculum that has downgraded the minority culture, and in vesting control over the child's destiny in a responsive body. As one militant aptly put it:

Look man, community control is our thing to get some control over our kids' lives. That doesn't mean we don't want integration, or that we want a separate culture. It just means that we need some time to build self-respect, and time to revamp this educational process. Then—and only then—will we have the guts to stand up and be counted as men. And then—and only then—can we ever think about true integration, integration as equals, as men, not as little ghetto dummies who don't know anything, little people who have the pity of the white man but not the respect of the white man.

ANALYZING SOCIAL AND ECONOMIC BARRIERS

Thus far in the chapter our social policy investigation has examined the critical problem of educational discrimination and amassed much data about its nature and cause. In addition compensatory education, integration, and community control of schools have been identified as three possible solutions to the problems. But there have always been a number of social barriers that stand in the way of change. To be effective we must therefore consider the social forces that will block the proposed changes and plan ways of getting over that resistance.

BARRIERS TO INTEGRATION

One of the most obvious barriers blocking any plan to integrate schools is white resistance. Although national polls consistently show that whites are becoming more favorable to integration, there is still enough resistance to block it in many cities. For example, in San Francisco as late as 1971 there were only 17 elementary schools out of 100 that met minimum state requirements on racial balance. A second major barrier to desegregation is that both black and white are moving out of the cities in such large numbers that there simply are not enough middle-class children to integrate effectively in cities such as Washington, D. C., Baltimore, Maryland, Gary, Indiana, Cleveland, Ohio, Oakland, California, and Newark, New Jersey. Moreover, this population shift has had budget implications; as middle-class taxpayers move out and are replaced by lower-class residents, the tax base of the city is lowered and the expensive proposals for ending discrimination are even more difficult to finance. This population shift is one of the reasons cities are appealing to the federal government for additional help, whether it be in the form of money for compensatory education or general revenue sharing where the federal government gives unrestricted funds to local governments.

BARRIERS TO COMMUNITY CONTROL: THE CASE OF OCEAN HILL-BROWNSVILLE

Community control, too, is a reform strategy that faces many obstacles. The controversy over community control in the Ocean Hill-Brownsville section of New York City in 1968 led to a number of political battles. The City of New York has the largest school system in the world. There are over 1 million students and more than 60,000 teachers and supervisors in about 900 schools. Many students are from migrant families—some immigrants from foreign nations (even today about 20 percent of the residents were *born* outside the United States), but even more from the rural South and the hinterlands of the Midwest. The city is a mixture of foreign-born, blacks, Puerto Ricans, whites, Jews, and countless other ethnic groups, and unemployment is always high among the minority groups of New York. On the eve of the Ocean Hill-Brownsville controversy the nation had an unemployment rate of about 4 percent, but the black population of New York City had an unemployment rate of about 30 percent. Moreover, over 35 percent of the total population of the city was living below the poverty level.

The New York City schools are ineffective by almost anyone's standards. Although the city spends about $1000 per pupil each year (well above the national average), the children are in such miserable school settings and come from such disadvantaged homes that one in every three children is more than a year behind national reading and math averages. And whereas about 30 percent of the students are Negro and 21 percent are Puerto Rican, over 90 percent of the teachers are white. Ninety percent of the teachers were educated in New York City, and their backgrounds and training separate them from their lower-class students.

On top of this system was a rigidly centralized bureaucracy headquartered at 110 Livingston Street in Manhattan, both literally and emotionally a long way from the ghettos where many of the children lived. At the time of the Ocean Hill crisis most of the power over the New York public schools was held by the central school board. There was a teacher examination system controlled by the board and a supervisor policy that allowed the central board to make all appointments. In addition, the United Federation of Teachers, one of the most powerful teacher unions in the nation, had strong interests in maintaining the *status quo*, which they had built up to their advantage over a long period of time.

Faced with this ineffective school system ghetto parents began in the mid-1960s to call for improvement. At first reformists worked for integration, but they quickly realized that, with the outflow of white, middle-class families to the suburbs, integration was impossible. Thus the emphasis shifted from integration to "community control." Very simply, community control involves breaking down the school bureaucracy into small units that will be more responsive to the unique needs of the individual community. It was hoped that the small units would better understand the needs of the students.

A number of factors combined to make an experiment in community control possible. First, parents from the ghetto organized a series of boycotts in 1966, especially against the white administrators of the new experimental Intermediate School 201. The goal of the boycott was to replace principals and teachers who were deemed anti-Negro with more sympathetic black people. Second, the Ford Foundation made a grant of $139,000 to plan three experimental school districts that would have strong community involvement—Ocean Hill-Brownsville in Brooklyn, Two Bridges in lower Manhattan, and I.S. 201 in Harlem. Third, during the 1967 budget battles with the State Legislature, Mayor John Lindsay was promised additional state aid if he could work out a decentralized system for the New York City schools. Because he was encouraged by this additional money and because he was convinced that decentralization could be effective for improving the public school system, Lindsay became one of the leading advocates of school decentralization. Finally, McGeorge Bundy of the Ford Foundation was asked by the state legislature to draw up a plan for decentralizing the entire city school system. In September 1967 the Bundy Commission recommended dividing the city into 30 to 60 independent school districts, each to be governed by an elected local school board with the power to hire and fire teachers and principals, to set curriculum policy, to select textbooks, and to manage the budget. These suggestions, if enacted, would have broken the power of the central school board and given much control to the local communities.

These pressures mounted to the point that the City Board of Education, using the Ford Foundation grant, instituted the three experimental decentralized programs. Ocean Hill-Brownsville, which became the center of a political storm was described as

> *. . . an old and run-down section of Brooklyn that lies between the heavily Negro Brownsville section and the ghetto of Bedford-Stuyvesant. About 70 percent of its inhabitants are Negro and 25 percent Puerto Rican. More than half of all family heads earn less than $5000 annually. It is a black slum, suffering all the social ills of deprivation, disease, and despair, pockmarked by abandoned buildings and broken storefronts. (Levine, 1969, p. 31)*

From the beginning the Ocean Hill district was a battleground. Many people claimed that the city board was trying to set up a demonstration project that would undermine the state's more radical plan (formulated in the Bundy Report), and there was immediate controversy between the central school board and the local district. Unfortunately, the United Federation of Teachers (UFT) was largely left out of the original planning and from the start was uncooperative. It was believed that the hostile local board wanted to fire many of the teachers, and the decentralization therefore threatened job security and teachers' rights. But fi-

A teacher picket line at Ocean Hill-Brownsville confronts angry parents' group.

nally, after weeks and months of controversy over establishing the local board, school opened in 1967 with Rhody McCoy, a powerful black community leader, as the local district administrator.

The storm at Ocean Hill broke almost immediately. In the first year the district faced a collection of political fights: the central administration disputed the election of the local board; controversy arose over the definition of the local board's power; the supervisors' union objected to the hiring of four principals by the local board and a court suit was filed to stop the hiring; teachers staged a 12-day strike and resigned from the local boards.

Let us review briefly the groups involved and their interests.

1. The *local board* at Ocean Hill-Brownsville, directed by Rhody McCoy, was determined to prove that it had the power to run the district, regardless of what the central school board said or did.

2. *The United Federation of Teachers*, headed by Albert Shanker, was determined not to lose its painstakingly acquired power to the local board.

3. *Mayor John Lindsay*, the *Ford Foundation*, and the *State Board of Education* all favored decentralization and wanted Ocean Hill-Brownsville to serve as a successful model.

4. The *central Board of Education* was not in favor of decentralization, which would replace the central board with local boards. Later Mayor Lindsay did appoint a more favorable board, but in the early stages the central board blocked many proposals.

All this was only the beginning. In May 1968 the local board tried to transfer 19 teachers who were judged "unacceptable" out of the district without follow-

INSERT **13.II**

CHRONOLOGY OF EVENTS AT OCEAN HILL-BROWNSVILLE

September 9–November 18, 1968: Massive Teacher Strike
Local board charged white racism; teachers accused blacks of antisemitism. Schools completely shut down. Many teachers attacked physically. Many nonunion teachers tried to teach, charging that union was trying to destroy decentralization plans.

November 18: Compromise Reached
State appointed a three-man overseer board with Dr. Herbert Johnson as "trustee" to supersede local board. Local board lost much of its power.

November 19: Classes Resumed
Three principals favored by black community were removed by trustee Johnson. Violence broke out in the schools. Many arrests, some boycott of classes.

November 29: Black Boycott of Schools Began
Many blacks stayed away, and many schools closed. The violence continued. Federal court ruled that the local board was powerless, and remaining powers were suspended.

December 2: Dr. Johnson Resigned as Trustee

December 3: New Violence Rocked Schools in Ocean Hill Area
Teacher stabbed; many teachers attacked. Violence spread to Harlem.

December 11: New State Trustee Appointed. He fired Rhody McCoy

December 13: New Boycott by Parents, Students, Nonunion Teachers
Most schools closed. Continued violence.

December 16: Trustee Firman Resigned. New Trustee Wilbur Nordos Appointed
Nordos reinstated McCoy. Union head Shanker attacked Nordos as "weak, vacillating, and ill-informed."

January, 1969: Schools Gradually Returned to Normal

March 7, 1969: Local Board Reinstated

ing established procedures. The battle over this action began when school opened in the fall. The teachers' union under Albert Shanker organized a massive strike that paralyzed the entire New York public school system. In the turmoil that followed the local board at Ocean Hill was nearly destroyed, the union virtually declared war on the whole concept of decentralization, the black community rose up in violent attacks against the teachers, and racism was kindled as black leaders struggled with the predominantly Jewish teachers. Some of the dismal events of that fall and winter are included in the chronology of Insert 13.II.

In the aftermath of the violence at Ocean Hill the local board was completely undermined and much of the progress toward community control lost. The teacher's union had essentially won the fight against decentralization. Many mistakes had been made. The central Board of Education had been hostile to the whole idea and effectively undermined the local board. The UFT was concerned with its own "teacher rights" questions and neglected the needs of the local community. The local board leaders were probably overly hostile toward the teachers and made several blunders when they might have quietly eased out the teachers they wanted dismissed. The State Board had not provided enough leadership at the right time, and the Mayor's office often appeared to vacillate at critical points in the dispute.

All in all, Ocean Hill looks like a disaster in retrospect, but it did at least begin the idea of community control. The community control issue lost its first round at Ocean Hill, but the idea has been well planted and certainly many more experiments will be tried in the near future. However, if New York is any indication, there will be serious barriers to implementing the idea.

THE NEED FOR BASIC SOCIAL CHANGE

Both integration and community control, then, face serious resistance. In addition, some people feel that it is the entire political, economic, and social system that is blocking educational equality, and they therefore advocate *basic social change*. This more radical approach is based on the theory that the school system is so embedded in the society that the society itself must change if the schools are to be improved. The schools are part of the political system, so one way to influence them is to reshape the political networks to be more responsive to the needs of minority groups. The schools are also interconnected with the economic system, so one way to affect the schools is to alter the occupational structure of the society to ensure every group an adequate standard of living.

Children from broken homes often do poorly in school, and, since the father's economic success or failure affects family stability, and the present power structure often denies the minority father an adequate job, it is the underlying structure that must be changed. Another basic social change would be to desegregate residential communities so that neighborhood schools would be integrated schools.

Political powerlessness, economic discrimination, and residential segregation are a few of the barriers that social reformers are attacking to achieve equal education for all children. Because the barriers to any change are so great, these reforms will not occur at once. Progress has been made, but we must be realistic about the difficulties faced by anyone interested in social change.

CAN EDUCATION HELP TO EQUALIZE SOCIAL OPPORTUNITIES?

This chapter has examined the issue of educational opportunity and racial discrimination. The assumption is that equalizing those opportunities will help to reform the whole society. But is that a reasonable hope?

Some leading social scientists are now embroiled in controversies about whether more attention should be paid to other social inequalities and less paid to education. For the past six or seven decades it was an article of faith among social reformers that by improving education the society could also equalize job opportunities and help equalize incomes. Education, it was assumed, could assure "equality of opportunity" for everyone and then it was up to the individual to succeed in the occupational marketplace. Several generations of social reformers viewed education as the critical linkpin—if education could be improved, job opportunities would be equal for everybody. And the statistics that showed education's strong impact on income backed up these hopes.

However, since the early 1970s the hope that education could be a reform tool has been openly questioned. Christopher Jencks and his associates at Harvard published a major book in 1972 entitled *Inequality: A Reassessment of the Effect of Family And Schooling in America.* The authors argue that although equalizing education may be a good thing in itself, the society has placed too much faith in education's ability to help eliminate inequality in the larger society. After analyzing much data about the link between education and occupational success, Jencks and his associates conclude:

> *. . . if we are interested solely in equalizing opportunities for economic success, making schools more equal will not help very much. Differences between schools have very little effect on what happens to students after they graduate. (Jencks, 1972, p. 37)*

Jencks' conclusion is widely debated. Some critics (e.g., Levin, 1972) argue that the Harvard group analyzed their data very poorly and that in fact there is a strong relation between education and occupational success. Jencks and his associates almost surely overstated their case; there is too much evidence from too many sources to abandon the idea that increased education helps occupational advancement.

However, one of their basic arguments clearly stands; if we want to equalize opportunity, eliminate poverty, and eliminate occupational inequities, then we must not put all our faith in the schools to do that complicated task. Instead, it will require a serious attack on *all* the major institutions of society, especially the political and economic systems. This is a point we have made throughout this book, and a quote from Bane and Jencks will serve to end the book on the same note that it was started.

If we want an income distribution that is more equal, we can constrain employers, either by tax incentives or direct legislation, to reduce wage disparities between their best- and worst-paid workers. We can make taxes more progressive, and we can provide income supplements to those who do not make an adequate living from wages alone. We can also provide free public services for those who cannot afford to buy adequate services in the private sector. Pursued with vigor, such a strategy can make "poverty" (i.e., having a living standard less than half the national average) virtually impossible. Such a strategy would also make economic "success," in the sense of having, say, a living standard more than twice the national average, far less common than it now is. The net effect would be to make those with the most competence and luck subsidize those with the least competence and luck to a far greater extent than they do today. Unless we are prepared to do this, poverty and inequality will remain with us indefinitely.

***

In America, as elsewhere, the long-term drift over the past 200 years has been toward equality. In America, however, the contribution of public policy to this drift has been slight. As long as egalitarians assume that public policy cannot contribute to equality directly but must proceed by ingenious manipulations of marginal institutions like the schools, this pattern will continue. If we want to move beyond this tradition, we must establish political control over the economic institutions that shape our society. What we will need, in short, is what other countries call socialism. Anything less will end in the same disappointment as the reforms of the 1960s. *(Jencks, 1972, p. 43)*

SUMMARY

A *critical sociology* requires that we go beyond theoretical analysis and try to use our knowledge in *social policy* decisions, in the improvement of social conditions. In this chapter we have examined the five steps that sociologists take in attacking a social problem.

1. *Identifying the Problem.* There are enormous variations in the educational opportunities for different races, ethnic groups, and social classes in the United States.
2. *Gathering New Information about the Problem.* The Coleman Report was commissioned by Congress to gather new data about educational opportunity. The report showed that segregation was widespread and that minority children fell far below the majority in academic achievement.
3. *Analyzing the Data.* The next step was to discover why opportunities were so unequal for minority children. Coleman and his associates proposed that the two most important factors affecting a child's achievement were the social background of the child's

family and the social class and racial balance of the school. In addition, the child's sense of "fate control" had immense impact on his achievement. Surprisingly, the Coleman Report did *not* find that the quality of the school itself had as great an impact as these other factors. Whatever impact it did have was largely due to the quality of the teachers.

4. *Proposing Improvement Strategies.* The three major improvement strategies offered were integration (to improve the racial and social-class balance), compensatory education (to improve the quality of the schools), and community control of schools (to give parents a greater voice in the schools and hopefully to increase the child's sense of fate control).

5. *Analyzing the Social Barriers to Improvement.* A number of social barriers stand in the way of using these improvement strategies, including white and minority resistance to integration, population shifts that take middle-class children out of the cities, and changes in the tax base that prohibit expensive improvements. Effective change in the educational system must be coupled with changes in the political and economic system. However, given the difficulty of making all those changes at once, it seems important to attack the problem anywhere possible, and especially in the schools where the damage is being done. In addition, we must remember that the schools alone can never reform the whole society, and serious reform involves changes in the other social institutions, especially the political and economic systems.

REFERENCES

Cohen, Elizabeth G. *A New Approach to Applied Research: Race and Education* (Columbus, Ohio: Charles E. Merrill, 1970).

Coleman, James S. *Equality of Educational Opportunity* (Washington, D.C.: U.S. Government Printing Office, 1966).

Cronbach, Lee J., and Patricia Suppes, eds. *Research for Tomorrow's Schools: Disciplined Inquiry for Education* (New York: Macmillan, 1969).

Jencks, Christopher, et al. *Inequality* (New York: Basic Books, 1972).

Kozol, Jonathan. *Death at an Early Age.* (New York: Bantam Books, 1968).

Levine, Naomi. *Ocean Hill-Brownsville: Schools in Crisis: A Case History* (New York: Popular Library, 1969).

Malcolm X. *Autobiography of Malcolm X* (New York: Grove Press, 1966).

Mosteller, Frederich, and Daniel P. Moynihan. *On Equality of Educational Opportunity* (New York: Vintage Books, 1972).

Racial Isolation in the Schools: A Report of the U. S. Commission on Civil Rights, Vol. 1, (Washington, D.C.: U.S. Government Printing Office, 1966), pp. 4, 5.

Sewell, William H. "Inequality of Opportunity in Higher Education," *American Sociological Review*, October 1971.

ILLUSTRATION CREDITS

Chapter 1: George Roos, 6, 7; Culver Pictures, 11; The Bettmann Archive, 12 (left); Staatsbibliothek, Berlin, 12 (right); Culver Pictures, 13 (left); Brown University, 13 (right); Culver Pictures, 26 (top); Ken Heyman, 26 (bottom).

Chapter 2: Fujihira/Monkmeyer, 36 (top); Mimi Forsyth/Monkmeyer, 36 (bottom); Christa Armstrong/Rapho Guillumette, 37; Arthur Sirdofsky/Editorial Photocolor Archives, 60; Jerry Cooke, 62.

Chapter 3: These photographs used through special permission granted by the Optometric Extension Program Foundation, Inc., Duncan, Oklahoma, 83; Friedel/Black Star, 100 (top); Rene Burri/Magnum, 100 (bottom; Bonnie Freer, 101 (top); Bill Owen/Magnum, 101 (bottom); Bonnie Freer, 104; Abigail Heyman/Magnum, 105 (top); U.S. Forest Service, 105 (bottom); Burke Uzzle/Magnum, 106 (top); Harry Wilks, 106 (bottom); Freelance Photographers Guild, 110 (top); New York Public Library Picture Collection, 110 (bottom), 111.

Chapter 4: David Powers/Jeroboam, 122; Misha Erwitt/Magnum, 123; Brown Brothers, 136; Caio Garrubba/Rapho Guillumette, 138; Culver Pictures, 141 (top); Joe Munroe/Photo Researchers, 141 (bottom); Bruce Davidson/Magnum, 149.

Chapter 5: Kenneth Murray/Nancy Palmer, 161 (top); Ben Ross/Photo Researchers, 161 (bottom); Brown Brothers, 163.

Chapter 6: Francis Miller, copyright © Time, Inc., 197; George Ballis/Black Star, 202; Falk/Monkmeyer, 205; Wide World Photos, 209.

Chapter 7: Roger Malloch/Magnum, 228; Bruce Davidson/Magnum, 243; Paul Sequeira/Rapho Guillumette, 250.

Chapter 8: David Seymour/Magnum, 280; United Press International, 283; Howard Petrick/Nancy Palmer, 287.

Chapter 9: Max Thorpe/Black Star, 305; State Historical Society of Colorado, 309; Library of Congress, 314 (top); The Sophia Smith Collection, Smith College, 314 (bottom left); Library of Congress, 314 (bottom right); Brown Brothers, 315; The Sophia Smith Collection, Smith College, 318; United Press International, 332 (top); Brown Brothers, 332 (bottom).

Chapter 10: Charles Gatewood/Magnum, 339; Kenneth Murray/Nancy Palmer, 340; Ken Heyman, 341.

Chapter 11: Joan Sydlow/Nancy Palmer, 381; Environmental Protection Agency, 394; Staatsbibliothek, Berlin, 395; New York Public Library Picture Collection, 396; General Motors Corporation, 401.

Chapter 12: Culver Pictures, 417; Bruce Davidson/Magnum, 431 (top; United Press International, 431 (bottom); Jason Lauré/Rapho Guillumette, 441.

Chapter 13: Bern Keating/Black Star, 459; Frederick deVan/Nancy Palmer, 460 (top); Ken Heyman, 460 (bottom); Joan Shearer, copyright © Time, Inc., 467; Rita Freed/Nancy Palmer, 477; Ernest Baxter/Black Star, 482.

PERMISSIONS (continued from page iv)

p. 130 Lenore Weitzman, Deborah Eifler, Elizabeth Hakoda, and Catherine Ross, "Sex Role Socialization in Children's Picture Books," paper presented at the 1971 Annual Meeting of the ASA, portions of pp. 1, 2, and 5. By permission of the American Sociological Association.

p. 137 and 139 Excerpt from "The Changing Soviet Family," by Urie Bronfenbrenner, from *The Role and Status of Women in the Soviet Union,* p. 120, edited by Donald Brown, Teachers College Press.

p. 156 Excerpt from "Welfare is a Woman's Issue," by Johnnie Tillmon, p. 111. Copyright © 1972 by Ms. Magazine Corp. Reprinted by permission of Ms. Magazine.

p. 156 Excerpt from "Salaries in the Year of the Wage Freeze," by Milton Moskowitz, June 3, 1972 issue of the *San Francisco Chronicle,* p. 33. Used with permission.

p. 160 Excerpt from "Social Stratification," by Leonard Reissman in *Sociology: An Introduction,* edited by Neil J. Smelser. Copyright © 1973 by John Wiley & Sons, Inc. Reprinted by permission.

p. 165 Excerpt from *Toward A New Sociology,* by C. H. Anderson, 1971, p. 78. Reprinted by permission of the publishers (Homewood, Ill.: The Dorsey Press, Inc.)

p. 166 and 191 Excerpts from *Power and Privilege,* by Gerhard Lenski. Copyright © 1966 by McGraw-Hill, Inc. Used with permission of McGraw-Hill Book Company.

p. 177 Figure from "Occupational Prestige in the U.S. 1925–1963," by Robert W. Hodge, Paul M. Siegel, and Peter H. Rossi, pp. 324–325 from *Class, Status & Power,* edited by R. Bendix and S. M. Lipset. Copyright © 1966 by The Free Press, a Division of the Macmillan Company. Reprinted by permission of the MacMillan Company, Inc.

p. 186 Excerpt from pp. 165–166, "The climax came . . . I ducked out of the room." in *Black Boy* by Richard Wright. Copyright © 1937, 1942, 1944, 1945, by Richard Wright. By permission of Harper & Row, Publishers, Inc.

pp. 195, 196, and 198 Excerpts from "Black Progress and Liberal Rhetoric," by Richard M. Scammon and Ben Wattenberg, from *Commentary,* April 1973, p. 41.

p. 209 Figure from "Woman as a Minority Group," by Helen Hacker, p. 65 in *Social Forces,* Vol. 30, 1951. Reprinted by permission.

p. 213 Excerpt from an article by Tom Braden, *San Francisco Chronicle,* September 16, 1971, by permission of the author.

p. 224 Excerpt from *In the Midst of Plenty: The Poor in America,* by Ben Bagdikian, 1964. Reprinted by permission of the publisher, The Beacon Press.

p. 226 Excerpt from "Redefining Poverty and Redistributing Income," by Victor Fuchs, *The Public Interest,* No. 8, Summer 1967, p. 91. Reprinted by permission.

p. 230 Excerpt from "Family on Relief," by Philip Dougherty, April 5, 1964. Copyright © 1964 by The New York Times Company. Reprinted by permission.

p. 236 Excerpt from *Political Ideology:Why the American Common Man Believes What He Does,* by Robert E. Lane. Copyright © 1962 by The Free Press of Glencoe, a division of The Macmillan Company. Reprinted by permission.

p. 239 Excerpt from "Who Are the Urban Poor?", by Anthony Downs, 1970. Reprinted by permission of the Committee for Economic Development.

p. 232 Excerpt from *The Challenge of Facts and Other Essays,* by William G. Sumner, edited by Albert Keller, 1914. Reprinted by permission of Yale University Press.

p. 245 Excerpt from "Who's on Welfare," by Charles McCabe, May 17 and 18, 1972. Reprinted by permission of the *San Francisco Chronicle.*

pg. 249 and 255. Excerpts from *Regulating the Poor,* by Frances Fox Piven and Richard A. Cloward. Copyright © 1971 by Frances Fox Piven and Richard A. Cloward.

p. 267 Excerpt from *The Lonely Crowd,* by David Riesman, Nathan Glazer, and Reuel Denney. Doubleday & Company abridged edition, p. 257. Copyright © 1950, 1953 by Yale University Press.

p. 266 Excerpt from *Who Governs: Democracy and Power in an American City,* by Robert A. Dahl, Yale University Press, 1961.

p. 271 Excerpt from *Ronnie and Jesse,* by Lou Cannon, 1969, p. 44. By permission of the publisher, Doubleday & Company, Inc.

p. 274 Excerpt from *The Politics of Land,* by Robert C. Fellmeth. Copyright © 1971, 1973 by the Center for the Study of Responsive Law, Washington, D.C. Reprinted by permission of Grossman Publishers.

p. 276 Excerpt from *Power and Discontent,* William A. Gamson, 1970, pp. 3–4. By permission of The Dorsey Press, Homewood, Ill.

p. 310 and 312 Excerpt from "Toward a Theory of Revolution," by James C. Davies, *American Sociological Review,* Vol. 27, February 1962, by permission of the American Sociological Association.

p. 311 Excerpt from *Sexual Politics* by Kate Millett. Copyright ©1969, 1970 by Kate Millett. Used by permission of Doubleday & Company, Inc.

p. 338 Excerpts from *Inequality,* by Christopher Jencks, Basic Books, Inc., 1972, pp. 37 and 43.

p. 347 Excerpts from *The American Occupational Structure,* by P. M. Blau and O. D. Duncan. Copyright © 1967 by John Wiley & Sons, Inc., p. 157.

p. 353 Excerpt from *The Educational Decision-Makers* by Aaron V. Cicourel and John I. Kitsuse, copyright © 1963, by The Bobbs-Merrill Company, Inc., reprinted by permission of the publisher.

p. 354 Excerpt from *Coming of Age in America,* by Edgar Friedenberg. Copyright © 1965 by Edgar Friedenberg. Reprinted by permission of Random House, Inc.

Fig. 10.11 From "Parental Education and Children's Aspirations," by Sewell and Sham, *American Sociological Review, 33* (2), April 1968, p. 196. By permission of the American Sociological Association.

pp. 24, 370 and 406 Excerpts from *Future Shock,* by Alvin Toffler. Copyright © 1970 by Alvin Toffler. Reprinted by permission of Random House, Inc.

pp. 379 and 384 Excerpts from *Woman's Place,* by Cynthia F. Epstein, 1971, pp. 6, 88–89, 190–191. By permission of the University of California Press. (Including an excerpt quoted from Time Magazine, August 27, 1965. p. 40) Reprinted by permission from Time, The Weekly Newsmagazine; Copyright Time Inc.

p. 390 Excerpts from "Cultural Lag as Theory," by William Ogburn, from *Sociology and Social Research,* No. 41, 1957, pp. 171–172. Reprinted by permission of the editor.

p. 392 From *Cultural and Social Anthropology,* by Peter B. Hammond. Copyright © 1964 by Peter B. Hammond. By permission of Macmillan, Inc. Reprinted with permission from Anderson, *Toward A New Sociology* (Homewood, Ill.: The Dorsey Press, 1971) p. 221.

p. 400 Excerpt from *Radical Perspectives on Social Problems,* by Frank Lindenfeld, Macmillan Company, Inc., 1968, p. 216.

p. 414 and 432 Excerpts from *The Population Bomb* by Dr. Paul R. Ehrlich. Copyright © 1968 by Paul R. Ehrlich. Reprinted by permission of Ballantine Books, Inc. All rights reserved.

p. 416 Figure from *Population and Society,* by Charles B. Nam. Houghton Mifflin Company, 1968. Reprinted by permission of the publishers.

p. 450 Excerpt from *The Autobiography of Malcolm X.* Reprinted by permission of Grove Press, Inc. Copyright © 1964 by Alex Haley & Malcolm X. Copyright © 1965 by Alex Haley and Betty Shabazz.

p. 461 Figure from James S. Coleman "The Concept of Equality of Educational Opportunity", *Harvard Educational Review,* Vol. 38, Winter 1968, p. 20. Copyright © 1968 by the President and Fellows of Harvard College.

p. 468 Figure from Daniel P. Moyniham ("Sources of Resistance to the Coleman Report"), *Harvard Educational Review,* Vol. 38, Winter 1968, pp. 32 and 34. Copyright © 1968 by the President and Fellows of Harvard College.

p. 465 Excerpt from *Death at an Early Age,* by Johnathan Kozol, Houghton Mifflin Company, 1968, p. 114. Reprinted by permission of the publisher.

p. 481 Excerpt from *Schools in Crisis; A Case History,* by Naomi Levine, Popular Library, Inc., 1969, p. 31. Reprinted by permission of the author.

INDEX